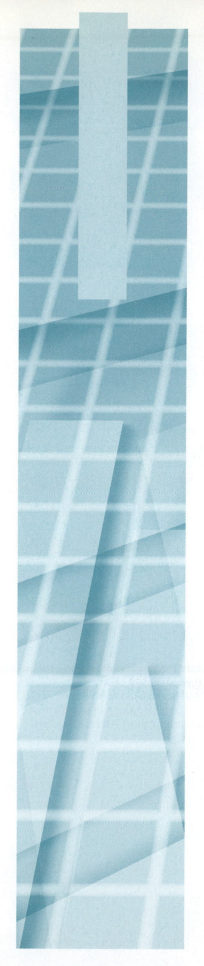

Procedures for the Automated Office

SIXTH EDITION

Sharon Burton

Nelda Shelton

PEARSON

Prentice
Hall

Upper Saddle River, New Jersey 07458

Library of Congress Cataloging-in-Publication Data
Burton, Sharon.
   Procedures for the automated office / Sharon Burton, Nelda Shelton.—6th ed.
      p. cm.
   Includes bibliographical references and index.
   ISBN 0-13-112149-9
   1. Office practice—Handbooks, manuals, etc. 2. Secretaries—Handbooks, manuals, etc.
I. Shelton, Nelda. II. Title.
HF5547.5.J45 2004
651.3—dc22   2004003770

Executive Editor: Elizabeth Sugg
Director of Production and Manufacturing: Bruce Johnson
Editorial Assistant: Cyrenne Bolt de Freitas
Marketing Manager: Leigh Ann Sims
Managing Editor—Production: Mary Carnis
Manufacturing Buyer: Ilene Sanford
Production Liaison: Denise Brown
Full-Service Production and Composition: Carlisle Publishers Services
Design Director: Cheryl Asherman
Senior Design Coordinator: Christopher Weigand
Cover Design: Kevin Kall
Director, Image Resource Center: Melinda Reo
Manager, Rights and Permissions: Zina Arabia
Interior Image Specialist: Beth Brenzel
Cover Image Specialist: Karen Sanatar
Image Permission Coordinator: Robert Farrell
Cover Printer: Lehigh Press
Printer/Binder: Banta/Harrisonburg

Pearson Prentice Hall™ is a trademark of Pearson Education, Inc.
Pearson® is a registered trademark of Pearson plc
Prentice Hall® is a registered trademark of Pearson Education, Inc.

Pearson Education LTD.
Pearson Education Singapore, Pte. Ltd.
Pearson Education Canada, Ltd.
Pearson Education—Japan

Pearson Education Australia PTY, Limited
Pearson Education North Asia Ltd.
Pearson Educatión de Mexico, S.A. de C.V.
Pearson Education Malaysia, Pte. Ltd.

PEARSON
Prentice
Hall

10 9 8 7 6 5 4 3 2
ISBN 0-13-112149-9

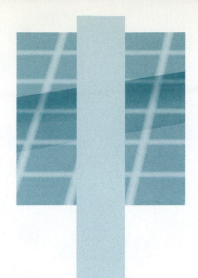

Contents

CHAPTER 5   Preparing Communications   119

PART THREE WORKING WITH THE OFFICE TEAM 239

CHAPTER 8 Handling Financial Procedures 241

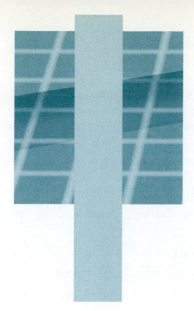

Preface

Welcome to the sixth edition of *Procedures for the Automated Office* by Sharon Burton and Nelda Shelton. This text/workbook has continued to be a leader in the office administration market because of its in-depth treatment of office procedures. This edition continues to offer students additional information and currency on topics of importance in the digital workplace. Because of its comprehensive yet concise coverage and cost, it has been especially appealing to students who want to develop their office skills in a short period of time. This text truly provides students with only one resource for efficient, economical instruction.

This latest edition of *Procedures for the Automated Office* includes these enhancements:

- Easy-to-read flow of text
- Quick Tips reinforce often overlooked simple procedures that increase productivity
- More than 40 business- and office-related terms added to this edition
- More than 25 new topics added to this edition
- Chapter tests added to this edition
- Each chapter includes Microsoft Office tips to increase skills on less common features
- More than 25 percent of all figures replaced with updated photographs
- Legal office procedures chapter added to this edition
- Medical office procedures chapter added to this edition
- Revised student CD with over 60 files in Microsoft Word and Excel documents so that students do not have to rekey text before responding to an activity

Success in today's competitive, diverse, and global business environment requires office professionals to be on the cutting edge of the latest office procedures. Even though job functions may vary from company to company, in most companies there are common office tasks that require basic office procedures.

NOTES TO THE TEACHER

This book is intended for use as a stand-alone textbook or in combination with other short projects and Internet applications in a one-quarter or one-semester course. The material presented provides an in-depth treatment of basic office procedures. After completing this course, students will be able to:

- Understand their role in the structure of business organizations
- Use interpersonal skills to develop effective working relationships and function as a member of the office team
- Manage their work, time, and resources effectively
- Understand the impact of office technology on office procedures
- Prepare written communications and distribute processed information
- Set up and maintain records
- Perform basic financial tasks
- Schedule appointments, set up meetings, and receive visitors
- Make travel arrangements
- Use the telephone effectively
- Prepare legal and medical documents
- Prepare for their employment search

Although the sixth edition represents a substantial revision, it retains the features that have been so widely accepted by students and their instructors. The following major features offer exciting, rich, and thorough end-of-chapter material to reinforce the chapter learning outcomes.

Each chapter contains step-by-step boxes. Throughout the text, valuable tips describe step-by-step directions on how to perform specific office tasks.

Each chapter ends with the following:

- **Quick Tips.**   Selected tips using Microsoft Office 2002 are presented to enhance use of these applications.
- **Overview.**   This section summarizes the chapter material, making this summary invaluable in reviewing and preparing for tests.
- **Key Terms.**   This list of key terms will aid students in mastering the chapter material. The terms are defined and are shown in boldfaced type.
- **For Your Discussion.**   This section summarizes the chapter material in the form of ten questions. Each question stimulates the students' thinking and provides an additional review of key concepts.
- **Basic Skills Workshops.**   These workshops provide a review of grammatical skills, business math, and reading in the form of exercises. The students are asked to review the rule in Appendix A and then complete the exercise at the end of the chapter applying the rule.
- **On-the-Job-Situations.**   Four situations present opportunities for applying critical thinking skills to solve realistic office-related problems.
- **Projects and Activities.**   This section allows students opportunities to research the latest trends in office procedures and concepts.

- **Surfing the Internet.** These activities offer opportunities for using Internet resources in real-world office-related situations.

- **Using MS Office.** These activities offer opportunities to use some of the less common features of Office 2002 applications.

- **Application Problems.** The applications allow students to practice procedures using forms and documents that are similar to those used in the office.

- **Your Action Plan.** In this section, students begin their way toward becoming a lifelong learner by encouraging career planning and goal setting.

- **Your Portfolio.** In this section, students have opportunities to take pride in their work by creating a portfolio to present to a prospective employer to more effectively demonstrate their office skills.

NOTES TO THE STUDENT

- The key terms in this book will aid you in mastering the chapter material. The key terms are defined and shown in boldfaced type within the chapter and are listed with their definitions at the end of the chapter. Pay close attention to the terms.

- Forms needed for the end-of-chapter applications are located in at the back of the text and are identified by their form number, which is referenced in the directions under the applications. Follow your instructor's directions in the use of these forms.

- Electronic files are provided for the Discussion Questions, Workshops, and On-the-Job Situations and are located on your student data disk. For some activities, you will be directed to use additional files stored on your data disk. Follow your instructor's directions in the use of these files.

- This sixth edition of *Procedures for the Automated Office* will prepare you to perform office skills in today's rapidly changing business environment, and help you take the necessary steps to plan your future career goals.

To successfully complete the steps given in the Using MS Office feature will depend on the version of MS Office installed. The steps provided were creating using MS Office 2002. If you have questions, check with your instructor.

COURSE SUPPLEMENTS AND RESOURCES

For additional classroom practice and online distance learning support, visit www.prenhall.com/business_studies and click on Companion Website.

Instructor's support, including classroom manuals and testing materials, can be found by visiting www.prenhall.com/business_studies and clicking on Instructor's Resources. This passcode protected site can be accessed through systems available from your local Pearson Prentice Hall representative.

ACKNOWLEDGMENTS

No author can produce a textbook without the contributions of many out-standing professionals. First, and foremost, we warmly thank Lucy Mae Jennings for her original work on the first two editions of *Procedures for the Automated Office*.

For her computer expertise, we thank Wanda Shelton, Computer Applications Support Specialist and Microsoft Certified—Master level, who developed the Quick Tips and Using MS Office features for each chapter.

We gratefully acknowledge the following reviewers whose excellent suggestions have been invaluable to revise the sixth edition of *Procedures for the Automated Office*.

Nancy Stacy, Lead Business Analyst, Origin Technology

Janice M. Brown, Concierge, Hewlett-Packard Company

Shelly M. Duke, Branch Manager, Kelly Services

Lisa Stone, Nortel-Business Prime

Cathy Gaona, Corporation Safety Secretary, Printback, Inc.

Monica Morales, Administrative Assistant, Brookhaven College

Kelly Murray, Supervisor, Administration & Budgets, Burlington Northern Santa Fe

Cathy Moore, Administrative Assistant, Ameriserve

Doris Youngman, Insurance Coordinator, Florida Sports and Orthopaedic Medicine, Palm Harbor, Florida

Sharon Burton and Nelda Shelton

Your Working Environment

1

chapter 1

Understanding the Changing and Challenging Office

OUTLINE

The Role of the Office Professional
Job Titles
The Virtual Office
Office Support Functions

Organizational Structure

Classifications of Authority
Line Organization
Line-and-Staff Organization
Participatory Management
The Organization Chart

International Employment

LEARNING OUTCOMES

When you have completed this chapter, you should be able to:

✔ Explain the role of the office professional.

✔ Describe current office trends.

✔ Explain the concept of organizational structure.

✔ Define and explain the classifications of authority.

✔ Explain international employment challenges.

The new millennium promises to be exciting, rewarding, and challenging. Technology is continually changing office procedures. Everything that can be automated is being automated and the faster the better. Today's office professionals must possess a broad array of skills to keep pace with change and must commit themselves to lifelong learning.

Throughout the remainder of this text, the word *manager* will be used to refer to persons at all levels of management, and *office professional* will be used to refer to support personnel.

Office professionals are finding themselves the center of a workforce that is fast-paced and is becoming more widely dispersed as companies engage in global activities. The office of the future will depend upon the support and expertise of office professionals who are information coordinators.

These **information coordinators** (ICs) are the support staff who act as central coordinators to facilitate communication among managers. They assist in carrying out important management functions, which include:

- Developing policies
- Making decisions
- Planning for future operations
- Planning and organizing new projects
- Staffing and directing new and ongoing operations
- Handling personnel problems
- Evaluating and controlling day-to-day operations

THE ROLE OF THE OFFICE PROFESSIONAL

Office professionals such as administrative assistants, executive assistants, office managers, and receptionists are needed in almost every type of organization. Their role is to assist managers at all levels of management. The office professionals of today have been described as the knowledge workers, because they constantly deal with both oral and written communications and are responsible for the flow of information.

Even though technical proficiency is also important to today's office professional, to be successful in the workplace, you must also possess strong people skills. These people skills will involve:

- Facilitating team projects
- Providing the human element needed to enhance electronic communication among employees and between the company and its customers
- Aiding in problem solving
- Demonstrating high ethical standards
- Being open-minded
- Demonstrating leadership, persuasiveness, and an interest in furthering your education

Here is a description of the current office trends that office professionals need to adapt to.

1. The flow of information in areas such as records, reprographics (copying and printing), computer services, word processing, and telecommunications is connected through technology, as is shown in Figure 1-1. As an information coordinator, you must be able to use the technological tools at your disposal to make you and your company more effective, efficient, and productive in a competitive market. Following are examples of ways you will use technology:
   - Sending and receiving faxes
   - Scheduling meetings
   - Merging data from a mainframe computer with information processed on a desktop computer
   - Composing and sending e-mail messages

■ Figure 1-1
The flow of information is linked through technology.

- Using computer application software, such as database management and spreadsheet, to process information
- Using an intelligent copier to send documents unattended
- Using electronic and multimedia technology such as that needed for teleconferences
- Using voice mail to prevent telephone tag
- Distributing documents electronically
- Querying an online database for current facts
- Using desktop publishing software to develop polished communications
- Researching information on the Internet
- Creating, maintaining, and editing Web sites
- Mastering and remaining current on office operations as they relate to an increasing globalization of the workplace

2. The level of skill and responsibility has changed. Office professionals are expected to handle people as deftly as they handle computers. In fact, many office professionals have what a decade ago were considered strictly managerial responsibilities. The gap between management and the office professional is closing. In the office of the future, keying letters and paper filing may be the least of what administrative assistants do.

3. Working hours have become very flexible. The concept of working 9 a.m. to 5 p.m. Monday to Friday is disappearing. With computer networking, many office professionals perform some of their responsibilities from their home computer. Flextime is a growing trend that saves both the employer and the office professional time and money; flextime is discussed in detail in Chapter 3. Self-discipline for these office professionals is an essential skill.

4. Companies have become more employee-friendly by adding wellness programs and quality management programs that require input and recommendations from the staff. Therefore, office professionals cannot simply bring problems to the attention of management. Instead they are required to make recommendations and offer solutions.

The future is bright and the opportunities are infinite. Office professionals should always be looking for new opportunities and responsibilities.

Job Titles

As office support roles become more diversified, job titles are also changing. Although some of today's office professionals are still called *office assistant, clerical assistant, clerk typist, secretary, senior secretary, executive secretary,* or *administrative secretary,* the newest titles are **assistant, administrative assistant (job title replacing office assistant or clerk typist), executive assistant, administrative support specialist (job title replacing office assistant or clerical assistant), coordinator (job title replacing office manager or executive secretary),** and **office manager (job title replacing executive or senior secretary).** Usually a job title that includes the word *administrative* denotes a higher level of responsibility than the word *assistant* does. *Assistant* is a generic term that is being used more and more to denote an employee who performs all types of basic office functions. *Executive assistant* denotes an office professional who works for one or more managers. The **receptionist** typically greets the public and answers phones. Office professionals who spend the majority of their time doing word processing and specializing in software applications are sometimes called **word processing specialists** and **software specialists.**

The Virtual Office

The Internet and a growing list of breakthrough telecommunication services have made today's world smaller and more accessible. An increasing number of managers are abandoning the problems and politics of corporate life in favor of working independently in their own **small office/home office (SOHO).** These home-based offices provide office-skills assistance to entrepreneurs. By doing so, the need for full professional assistance with a variety of support responsibilities is provided by **virtual assistants (VAs)** with just the click of the mouse. Virtual assistants assist entrepreneurs from their own SOHOs with the following tasks:

- Desktop publishing
- Internet research
- Event planning and reminder services
- Word processing
- Travel arrangements
- Technical writing and grant proposal writing
- Marketing support

Communications are generally by, but not limited to, e-mail, mail, fax, telephone, and file and diskette transfer. The VA works from a fully equipped home-based office. The business manager avoids insurance, payroll tax, and Occupational and Safety Health Administration (OSHA) issues that employees bring and pays only for "time on task" or by project. Because VAs save entrepreneurs money, are available beyond a nine-to-five schedule, work only when needed, and require no office space and no equipment, their popularity is growing.

Virtual assistant opportunities are growing so fast that VAs have founded their own International Virtual Assistants Association (IVAA). You may obtain more information about this organization from their IVAA Web site on the Internet at http://www.ivaa.org.

Office Support Functions

Typical office support functions range from routine to managerial functions. These functions fall into five categories—routine, technical, analytical, interpersonal, and managerial.

- **Routine functions:** require minimal *original* thinking; include essential skills, such as filing, photocopying, and keeping logs.
- **Technical functions:** require judgment and advanced office skills, such as a high level of keyboarding and proficiency with various software applications including spreadsheets, databases, and presentations.
- **Analytical functions:** require critical and creative thinking and decision-making skills, such as creating and analyzing reports, and making decisions regarding equipment purchases.
- **Interpersonal functions:** require judgment, analytical (decision-making), and people skills, such as coordinating a team project.
- **Managerial functions:** require planning (analytical), organizing (analytical), measuring (analytical), and motivating (interpersonal communication); examples include budgeting, staffing, evaluating personnel, and problem solving.

ORGANI-ZATIONAL STRUCTURE

Organizational structure emphasizes people-to-people relationships. Automated office concepts in organizational structure are centered on the flow of information and the communication needs for decision making, and they involve a systems approach to organizational structure. Regardless of the approach used, chains of command, authority, and responsibility must be established.

CLASSIFI-CATIONS OF AUTHORITY

When beginning your employment, it is important that you understand the classifications of authority within your organization. The distinction among managers in terms of importance is expressed as *levels of management*. Most organizations have three common divisions—top level, middle (intermediate) level, and supervisory (operating) level. These management levels are shown graphically in what is called an **organization chart.** The higher the level of management, the greater the responsibility and decision-making power the manager has. The lower the level of management, the more responsibility the

Start Off on the Right Foot

Face it! It costs a company a lot of money to find the right office professionals, train them, and keep them motivated enough to remain working with the same company. So, it's very important that the company start off on a positive note with new employees. Here's what many companies do on Day 1 to ensure a good start with their new office professionals.

✔ Let new office professionals see the big picture by discussing the company's mission and purpose.

✔ Take a skills inventory of all new employees so the company can place them in positions where they will be productive.

✔ Connect new employees to a work team that depends on their professional skills.

✔ Acquaint new office professionals with their new surroundings and new coworkers.

✔ Assign each office professional a volunteer mentor whom he or she can rely on to answer questions, give support, and receive encouragement.

✔ Make new office professionals feel welcome and like valued members of the staff.

It may sound simple enough, but it takes good management to make it a reality.

manager has for day-to-day functions. Top-level management usually consists of the president or chief executive officer (CEO) and vice president. Middle-level management typically is comprised of the division heads, sometimes called regional heads, or area heads. Supervisory-level management generally consists of the department heads or functional managers.

Line Organization

The oldest and simplest organizational structure is **line organization.** In line organization, authority flows vertically down within the organization. In this type of organization, *line authority* allows supervisors to control workers immediately below them. They are usually charged with the responsibility to give orders, hire, terminate, and take disciplinary action. See Figure 1-2 as an example of line organization.

Line organization is frequently referred to as **scalar** or military type of authority or chain of command. You will learn more about chain of command in the next section of this chapter. Authority is delegated from top management to middle management. The middle managers are in charge of specific activities, and they in turn delegate authority to supervisors who are in charge of workers carrying out their operational duties.

Line authority flows in a straight line from top management to the supervisory level. If there are several top executives, the authority flows from the president to the vice presidents to managers to supervisors.

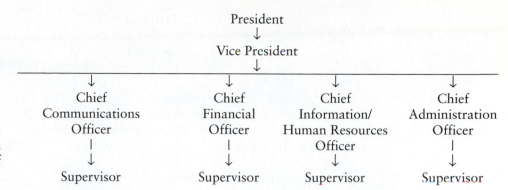

■ **Figure 1-2**
Line organization with
arrows showing flow of
authority.

The advantages and disadvantages of the line organization are as follows:

Advantages

■ The structure of the organization is easily understood.

■ Employees have direct accountability to their superiors.

■ There is a clear-cut place for each worker.

Disadvantages

■ Each supervisor has large areas of responsibility.

■ This type of organization is more structured, thus less flexible.

■ The flow of communication and information is often restricted.

■ The ability to transfer employees to where they are most needed is limited.

Line-and-Staff Organization

When a manager or supervisor is responsible for several areas, he or she must rely on others' expertise. In these cases, knowledge specialists called *staff managers* may be available to advise the line manager. In an organization where *line managers* use staff specialists to assist them, the organization structure is called a **line-and-staff organization.** Staff managers usually do not have authority—they supply information or expertise to specific line managers. **Line managers** have direct responsibility and final authority; staff managers work in an advisory, functional, or service capacity. **Staff managers** usually advise line managers and make recommendations. Line managers have the final say in accepting or rejecting the recommendations of staff managers. If the organization is a large one, probably more than one level of middle managers will be established. See Figure 1-3 as an example of line-and-staff organization.

Staff managers are influential in the decision-making process. In addition to assisting, advising, and recommending, a staff manager can be given line authority. To recognize the **chain of command,** in other words the line of authority in an organization, you need to understand how the authority has been established. You also need to recognize that a manager can have line authority, staff authority, or both. Studying the organization chart will not reveal what you need to know. Be observant; watch for the functions for which the staff manager makes recommendations but does not have the authority.

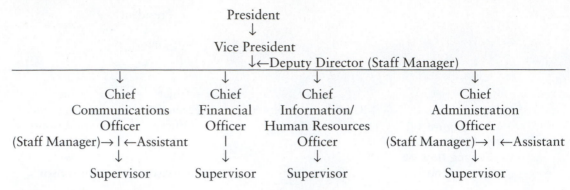

■ **Figure 1-3**
Line-and-staff organization with arrows showing line of authority.

The advantages and disadvantages of line-and-staff organization are as follows:

Advantages

■ Line personnel have freedom from performing specialized tasks.

■ Staff has flexibility to pursue unique projects.

■ Expertise is available to line personnel.

Disadvantages

■ Line employees do not have a clear understanding of the staff manager's duties.

■ Problems arise if staff managers with line duties contradict the line manager.

■ New goals can be pursued just because there is a staff manager available.

Participatory Management

A management technique used by many companies that can affect lines of authority is the concept of **participatory management.** Participatory management has been in existence for a long time. Simply put, in isolated situations, project teams are formed, bringing together employees with the talents needed to work on a specified project.

Organizations today, in an effort to increase productivity and to meet competition, are focusing more on participatory management. This management style is in contrast to the traditional line-and-staff management style. Employees are invited to work in smaller units within large organizations and are encouraged to communicate with different levels of management. Employees are asked for input about their areas of responsibility and frequently are brought together in conferences to discuss problems and offer solutions. Under participatory management, each employee reports to someone in the formal structure, but while on a team working on a specific project or problem, each team member has equal authority even if the team is made up of a deputy director, an office professional, an accountant, and a custodial employee.

You should be aware that opportunities to participate in quality circles, project teams, and other forms of participative decision making may exist

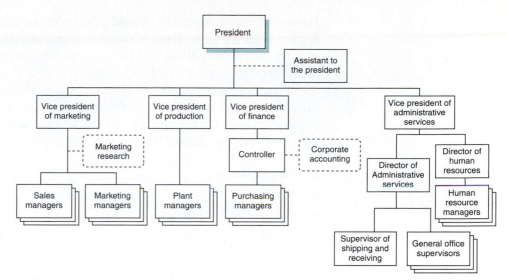

■ **Figure 1-4**
Line-and-staff organization chart.

where you are employed and that you should accept your responsibility in making valuable contributions. The quality management approach is discussed in Chapter 3.

The Organization Chart

As mentioned earlier, an organization chart is a graphic illustration of the formal structure of an organization. To understand an organization chart, look for lines of authority, the existing division of work (into what may be called divisions, departments, teams, units, or some other appropriate title), and the relationship of the work groups to each other. If an organizational manual exists, a description of the division of work and the positions shown on the organization chart will be given in the manual or will be located on the company's intranet system. The titles shown in an organization chart may be expressed as either functions or positions, but the form chosen should be used consistently throughout. Functions that occupy the same level of management should be shown on the same horizontal line, as illustrated by the Vice President of Marketing and the Vice President of Production in Figure 1-4. The solid straight lines indicate line authority. Broken lines indicate staff authority.

INTERNATIONAL EMPLOYMENT

More and more companies are moving their operations outside the United States to take advantage of a cheaper labor market. **International employment** offers employees the opportunity to work abroad. You might have noticed that many of the products you purchase are made outside the United States. Our government has also signed trade agreements with other countries that make it easier for us to do business with those countries. One example is our agreement with Mexico and Canada—the **North American Free Trade Agreement (NAFTA)**. This agreement has allowed companies to move to Mexico or Canada, resulting in goods flowing freely across U.S. borders.

With more and more companies establishing offices in countries outside the United States, the office professional is faced with new employment challenges. What if your company advertised a position in Mexico, Canada, Spain,

Japan, or South America? Would you be up to the challenge? Businesses are coping with massive changes that are occurring as a result of ever increasing market internationalization. One of these changes is offering its personnel opportunities to work abroad.

If you consider working abroad, you will see many similarities to employment in the United States, from skills required to job titles. For instance, some job titles are the same as in the United States; others are only slightly different, as you can see from the following list:

- Receptionist
- Secretary
- Administration assistant
- Medical secretary
- Team secretary
- PA (personal assistant) or PA to general manager
- Secretary/commercial assistant
- Medical transcriptionist

The following are examples of positions for which you might be qualified. They appear exactly as they are advertised. Notice the skills required and the wording of the ads.

Office Manager
LONDON, UK
An assistant to a busy property developer/entrepreneur with good organizational skills. The successful candidate will be proficient in Excel and Word, be numerate, have good telephone manners, plenty of initiative and self motivation. If you want a challenge and enjoy working alone contact . . .

Secretary
FRANCE
Truly international team seeks English mother tongue member. Working at a high level for this household name you will use plenty of initiative as well as your basic secretarial skills. As part of the team you will organise the travel and internal and external meetings of 5 vice-presidents and have the experience and confidence to work autonomously when necessary. Spoken French is important, other languages are useful. Word and PowerPoint are vital.

Secretary/Office Co-Ordinator
MT. COLAH
AUSTRALIA
Small firm of architects in Mt. Colah requires the services of an all rounder. Duties include reception, general office duties and bookkeeping including payroll. Experience with Word, Excel & MYOB essential. Minimum 2 years experience in a similar position and driver's license is necessary. Salary negotiable depending on experience. Please fax resume to . . .

---

quicktips

E-mail Etiquette

Do:

- Be polite
- Type a subject. Make it reflect your message.
- Remember that e-mail is not private. Treat it like you would a postcard.

Don't:

- Type in all caps. This is considered shouting and rude.
- Send e-mail when you are angry.
- Say anything you would be ashamed for your spouse, parents, or children to read.
- Assume the person receiving your e-mail is the only one who will read it; they may pass it on without asking your permission!

You will notice that whether you work in the United States or abroad, the role of the office professional and the assigned duties are basically the same. You will learn more about employment information in Chapters 15 and 16.

The free flow of people, capital, ideas, and products continues to increase between the United States and other countries, thus creating job opportunities that weren't there a few years ago.

Overview

✔ The role of the office professional involves facilitating team projects; providing the human element needed to enhance electronic communication among employees and between the company and its customers; aiding in problem solving; demonstrating high ethical standards; being open-minded; and demonstrating leadership, persuasiveness, and an interest in lifelong learning. The level of responsibility has changed and often involves managerial responsibility. Working hours have become flexible. Wellness programs are available as well as quality management programs that allow input from today's professional.

✔ Office support staff, such as administrative assistants, executive assistants, and receptionists, are needed in almost every type of organization. In the next decade they will find job opportunities exciting, rewarding, and challenging.

✔ Job titles vary. They range from *secretary*, to *assistant*, to *administrative assistant*, to *office manager*, to *receptionist*.

✔ The duties of the office professional will involve

- Sending and receiving faxes
- Scheduling meetings

- Merging data from a mainframe computer with information processed on a desktop computer
- Composing and sending e-mail messages
- Using computer application software, such as database management and spreadsheet, to process information
- Using an intelligent copier to send documents unattended
- Using electronic and multimedia technology such as that needed for teleconferences
- Using voice mail to prevent telephone tag
- Distributing documents electronically
- Querying an online database for current facts
- Using desktop publishing software to develop polished communications
- Researching information on the Internet
- Creating, maintaining, and editing Web sites
- Mastering and remaining current on office operations as they relate to an increasing globalization of the workplace

✔ Organizations can be structured following the line or line-and-staff organizational structure.

✔ Participatory management is becoming increasingly popular in business today. It also has an effect on the organizational structure.

✔ International employment opportunities are available to today's office professional. The job titles and duties are similar.

Key Terms

Administrative assistant. Newer job title replacing *office assistant* or *clerk typist*.

Administrative support specialist. Newer job title replacing *office assistant* or *clerical assistant*.

Analytical functions. Functions that require critical and creative thinking and decision-making skills, such as analyzing reports and making decisions regarding equipment purchases.

Assistant. A generic term that is being used more and more to denote an employee that performs all types of basic office functions.

Chain of command. The line of authority in any organization.

Coordinator. Newer job title replacing *office manager* or *executive secretary*.

Executive assistant. Newer job title replacing titles such as *office assistant*; denotes an office professional who works for one or more managers.

Information coordinators (ICs). The support staff who act as central coordinators to facilitate communication among managers.

International employment. The opportunity for employees to work abroad.

Interpersonal functions. Job functions that require judgment, analytical (decision-making), and people skills, such as coordinating a team project.

Line-and-staff organization. A formal organizational structure in which staff managers serve as specialists in their area and are available to assist and advise line managers throughout the organization.

Line managers. Managers who have direct responsibility and final authority.

Line organization. Line of authority (also called chain of command). Authority flows vertically down and allows supervisors to supervise workers immediately below them. The oldest and simplest type of organizational structure.

Managerial functions. Job functions that require planning (analytical), organizing (analytical), measuring (analytical), and motivating (interpersonal communication) skills; examples include budgeting, staffing, evaluating personnel, and solving problems.

North American Free Trade Agreement (NAFTA). This agreement allows companies to move to Mexico or Canada, resulting in goods flowing freely across U.S. borders.

Office manager. New job title replacing *executive secretary* or *senior secretary*.

Organization chart. A graphic illustration of the formal structure of an organization.

Participatory management. A management style in which employees are invited to work in smaller units within large organizations and are encouraged to communicate with different levels of management for problem solving.

Receptionist. Job title of a person who supports management at all levels. A receptionist usually greets the public and answers phones.

Routine functions. Job functions that require minimal *original* thinking; include essential skills, such as filing, photocopying, and keeping logs.

Scalar. A military type of authority or chain of command.

Small office/home office (SOHO). Home-based offices that provide office-skills assistance to entrepreneurs.

Software specialists. Job title for one who specializes in using word processing and other software applications.

Staff managers. Managers who work in an advisory, functional, and service capacity to line managers.

Technical functions. Job functions that require judgment and advanced office skills, such as a high level of keyboarding and demonstrating proficiency with various software applications.

Virtual assistants (VAs). Job title for those who provide full professional assistance with a variety of support responsibilities in home offices, such as desktop publishing, Internet research, event planning and reminder services, word processing, travel arrangements, technical writing, grant proposal writing, and market support.

Word processing specialists. Job title for those whose work consists mainly of processing written information, such as keyboarding and demonstrating proficiency with various software applications.

Note: Follow your instructor's directions for all chapters regarding the use of the computer files or the textbook hard copies.

For Your Discussion

 Retrieve file C1-DQ.DOC from your student data disk.

Directions

Enter your response after each question.

1. How has the technology explosion created a greater need for office professionals to become knowledge workers?

2. What is the primary role of today's office professional?

3. How is technology used to perform office functions?

4. Describe the five basic office support functions. Include in your discussion examples of each function.

5. Discuss the advantages and disadvantages of a SOHO.

6. Explain the difference between line authority and staff authority and compare the advantages and disadvantages of each.

7. What is the purpose of an organization chart?

8. What is meant by participatory management and how does it affect the organizational structure?

9. Explain what is meant by "chain of command" in relation to classification of authority.

10. Discuss whether or not you would be interested in international employment opportunities. Explain why or why not.

PUNCTUATION WORKSHOP

Commas are used to set off words, phrases, and clauses in sentences. Complete the exercises below by applying punctuation rules for commas.

For Review

Appendix A: Rule 1: Commas Used with Conjunctions

Rule 2: Commas Used with Nonrestrictive Words, Phrases, and Clauses

 Retrieve file C1-WRKS.DOC from your student data disk.

Directions

Insert commas, if required, in the sentences below. Circle the sentence number or key a **C** at the end of the sentence if the sentence is punctuated correctly.

Rule 1: Commas Used with Conjunctions

1. We carefully entered the data in the computers but the accounting clerk decided to double check our work.

2. A person should always take the time necessary to do every job well yet should be aware of the need to be efficient.

3. New application software usually comes stored on a CD-ROM disk but you can also request it on floppy disks as well.

4. Absenteeism is a problem in many offices and management constantly strives to reduce it.

5. "Just Say No" to drugs is one of the very worthwhile programs against drug abuse yet each year drug use continues to devastate our youth.

Rule 2: Commas Used with Nonrestrictive Words, Phrases, and Clauses

1. One of the most important features of our computer a Pentium with a CD-ROM disk drive and a 3.5-inch floppy drive is its speed.

2. The manager who was recommended by the committee did not get the promotion.

3. The president is the one responsible of course for the final decision.

4. A delay in the morning mail whatever the reason may cause a delay at the bid-opening meeting.

5. John Curtis our production manager has been in that position for five years.

On the Job Situations

 Retrieve file C1-OJS.DOC from your student data disk.

Directions

Enter your response after each situation.

1. Your boss, Ms. Chen, has 35 employees reporting to her. When she receives a policy memorandum from top management, she rewrites portions of it, condensing much of the material, and asks you to keyboard and make copies of what she has written for distribution to the 35 employees. The employees frequently do not understand her summary as it is rewritten and often come to you for clarification. One coworker, Jim Elton, has demanded that you let him see the original memorandum. Should you show him the original memorandum or discuss the situation with Ms. Chen first? Why do you think that Ms. Chen always rewrites the communications from top management before distributing them?

2. One of your temporary assistants, Marty Williams, is upset. She accidentally saw on your desk a memorandum written by a staff member in the human resources department recommending that all temporary employees throughout the organization be laid off in three months. She asked you why no one had been advised about this recommendation. You explained you have not had time to process all the work that was stacking up on your desk and reminded her this was only a recommendation. You suggested that she talk with your manager, Henry Roberts, before reacting to the memorandum. Were you justified in suggesting to Marty that she talk with Mr. Roberts? Why or why not? Who do you think will make the final decision about Marty's employment?

3. You are considering creating a SOHO in your home and advertising your services via the Internet. What equipment would you need? What services would you provide? How would you structure your work time with family time? Discuss why someone might use a virtual assistant.

4. Your company has a manufacturing plant in Mexico City. You do not have to communicate with this plant to do your job, but, Mark, whose office is next to yours, is required to communicate daily with the office in Mexico City clarifying and resolving problems. Mark does not speak Spanish; therefore, all communication is in English. He constantly complains about the poor English skills the employees have in that office and how much time it takes him to resolve problems. You speak Spanish fluently. Should you offer to translate for Mark? What would be the advantages and disadvantages of your offering this service to Mark?

Projects and Activities

1. Visit a company in your area and find out how many levels of management it has.

   a. Obtain a copy of the company's organization chart and be prepared to present your findings to the class.

   b. If the company you selected does not have an organization chart, ask for a copy from a friend's or relative's company. Be prepared to discuss your findings with the class.

2. Read an article in a business periodical (such as the *Wall Street Journal, Business Week, U.S. News & World Report,* or *e-Business Advisor*) concerning one of the following topics:

   a. Office equipment

   b. Changes in organizational structure

   c. Virtual assistants

   d. International employment

   Prepare a short summary of the article. Include a source note. Photocopy or print a copy of the article and attach it to your summary.

3. Review the ads in local newspapers for various types of office positions that are available. Select three ads for comparison.

   a. Type a list of job requirements for each ad.

   b. Be prepared to share the comparisons with your class.

4. Analyze your office. (If you are not currently working in an office, interview someone who is.) Complete the following statements:

   a. The specific changes in our business that have caused changes in our office technology are . . .

   b. Specific changes in our business that I *feel* should have caused changes in our office technology are . . .

   c. Our future purchases in office technology, both software and hardware, will be . . .

   Key your written responses to each statement, to be discussed in class or turned in to your instructor. Add any additional information from your office analysis or the interview you believe is important.

Surfing the Internet

You have been asked by your instructor to give a presentation. You have always wanted to travel and see the world; therefore, you have decided to find out all you can about working abroad and make a presentation about that information.

1. Connect to the Internet and access a search engine, such as Excite, Lycos, LookSmart, or Google.

2. Enter the following key search words, including the quotation marks and the plus sign, to help narrow your search: "international + employment."

3. Locate an ad for a position in a foreign city and country where you might like to work. Locate information about the American Embassy, living overseas, danger abroad, language requirement, and any other interesting information you find. Summarize or print any information you could use in your presentation.

4. Outline the information to be included in your presentation.

5. Write a short summary of your presentation.

Using MS Office 2002

Create an Organization Chart

Directions

To successfully complete the following steps, you must have the Organization Chart feature installed on your computer. If you have questions about the availability of the feature, check with your instructor. Use Figure 1-2 and Microsoft Office to create an organization chart. The following steps were created using Microsoft Word 2002.

1. Open MS Word. Make sure a blank document screen displays.

2. Click on the Insert menu and select Picture.

3. Click on Organization Chart.

4. In the highlighted box centered at the top of the chart type President.

5. To add a fourth square, click on the square above (President) where you want the new square to appear. Click on Select, Level, Insert Shape, Subordinate. The fourth square will be added.

6. Type the information in the four squares under President. To enlarge the chart to accommodate the titles, click on the chart, then click on Layout, Scale Organization Chart; drag the handles to enlarge the chart.

7. To add each subordinate under the officers, click on each box where you want a new square to appear. Click on Select, Branch, Insert Shape, Subordinate.

8. If you need to remove a square, click on the square until you get the round handles then press Delete key.

9. Type in the remaining text.

10. Increase font size as needed.

APPLICATION PROBLEMS

Welcome to Supreme Appliances. You are employed in an entry-level position for Supreme Appliances, Inc.

Company Location

Supreme Appliances, Inc.
14 Shady Lane
Rochester, NY 14623

Company Mailing Address

Supreme Appliances, Inc.
P.O. Box 7290
Rochester, NY 14623-7290

During your three-month orientation, Amanda Quevedo, vice president of marketing, and her four assistant vice presidents will assign you different responsibilities. Mrs. Quevedo will supervise your work and evaluate your performance. Henry Pippen serves as president of Supreme Appliances, and his administrative assistant is Kirk Lawrence.

Before you begin your training, note the following information about Supreme Appliances. Supreme Appliances, Inc. sells both large and small appliances for the home. It also manufactures its own line of refrigerators, electric ranges, freezers, and dishwashers. The marketing department measures and analyzes market potential and assists in short- and long-range forecasting. The marketing department has four regional vice presidents, an advertising manager, and a market research manager.

Vice Presidents of the Marketing Department

J. R. Rush, assistant vice president of marketing, Eastern Region, Extension 6534

Thomas Strickland, assistant vice president of marketing, Southwestern Region, Extension 6535

Sid Levine, assistant vice president of marketing, Northwestern Region, Extension 6536

Karen Baxter, assistant vice president of marketing, Western Region, Extension 6537

Most of your communications are with the four regional sales offices and the two manufacturing plants.

Managers of Regional Sales Offices

Sales Office, Eastern Region, Boston, MA; Manager, Joanna Hansen, 85 Jefferson Street, Boston, MA 02116-5508

Sales Office, Southwestern Region, Dallas, TX; Manager, John Reddin, 1508 Commerce Street, Dallas, TX 75201-4904

Sales Office, Northwestern Region, Portland, OR; Manager, Mary Anderson, 803 N.W. Everett Street, Portland, OR 97209-3313

Sales Office, Western Region, Denver, CO; Manager, Kyle Rhodes, 1400 Lincoln Street, Denver, CO 80203-1523

Plant Managers of Manufacturing Plants

Southwestern Manufacturing Plant, Fort Worth, TX; Plant Manager, Raymond Jones, 2600 W. Vickery Boulevard, Fort Worth, TX 76102-7105

Western Manufacturing Plant, San Francisco, CA; Plant Manager, Eugene Harrison, 3509 Mission Street, San Francisco, CA 94110-5429

At your workstation you have the latest model computer on the market today. Your computer is connected online to the four regional sales offices and the two manufacturing plants. You send and receive information instantly from these six locations. All the input is saved on disks.

APPLICATION 1-A

Organization Chart

Supplies needed: Plain paper or MS Word; information about the marketing department for Supreme Appliances (see page 21).

Directions: The form shown in Figure 1-5 accompanies requests for documents to be created and revised. This form is typical of those used in organizations where one office professional works for several managers or where one assistant supports a manager who frequently travels.

Using this form at your workstation helps you to know the date work was requested, turnaround time, and any special instructions. Another advantage of this form is that it helps eliminate the number of times you are interrupted by someone to give you information or instructions.

Read the handwritten instructions on the request form shown in Figure 1-6, then follow the steps on page 20, Using MS Office, to create the organization chart for the marketing department.

REQUEST FORM

Today's Date: _____

From: _____

Turnaround Time: Normal ☐   Rush ☐

Special Instructions:

_____

_____

_____

_____

_____

_____

_____

■ **Figure 1-5**
Request form.

REQUEST FORM

Today's Date: _____9/29_____

From: _Mrs. Quevedo_

Turnaround Time: Normal ☑ Rush ☐

Special Instructions:

_____

Create an organization chart
of the Marketing Dept. Do
not include any personnel
names; include only job
titles. Use your computer word
processing software or a ruler
to create the boxes.

■ **Figure 1-6**
Completed request form.

APPLICATION 1–B

Skills Evaluation

Supplies needed: Form 1-A, Skills Evaluation Checklist, pencil, pocket calculator (optional). (Forms for application problems can be found at the back of this text.)

 Retrieve file C1-SKI.DOC from your student data disk.

Directions: Complete the self-evaluation following the steps given on the form.

Your Action Plan

To make the information you are learning more relevant, you will be developing your own Action Plan throughout the semester, chapter by chapter. Your plan will be unique to you—what you select as your goals. These goals will be the goals you plan to work toward to become a successful office professional in the business workforce. Goals should be:

- **Specific.** Each goal you set should state in exact words what you want to accomplish.
- **Measurable.** You should state exactly how you are going to measure your goal so that you can tell when you have reached it.

- **Attainable.** Goals must be attainable and realistic and yet should require you to grow and improve yourself.
- **Time-limited.** You should not direct your goal to some vague future time but select and set a reasonable time limit in which to accomplish it.

Here is an example of a goal that meets the above guidelines:

> "When I go to work today, I am going to locate a copy of our organization chart, determine if it is a line or a line-and-staff type chart by following the chapter information, and make a copy of it to give to my instructor. I will do this before I leave by 5 p.m., Friday, October 30, to give to my instructor on Monday, November 2."

Follow these steps:

1. Retrieve the file ACTION01.DOC from your data disk or see Form 1-B at the back of your text and study the completed Action Plan shown. The plan shows how you would complete the form now (Specific Goal and comments after each heading) and after the time limit for reaching your goal has expired (Results at end of time limit). You should make a note on your to-do list (discussed in Chapter 3) and calendar to remind you of the goal you have set and to see if you have reached it by the end of the time limit. You may follow this format for typing your Action Plan for each chapter. Print a copy of the plan for reference.

2. Following the guidelines outlined above, set one goal using the information you learned in Chapter 1.

3. Retrieve file ACTION02.DOC or use Form 1-C at the back of your text. When keying your information, if you need more space, drag and drop the horizontal lines down to create more space in the desired section. Follow your instructor's directions for formatting and assembling, and turning in Your Action Plan.

Your Portfolio

Finding the right job for you in today's competitive job market can sometimes be difficult. You have to do more than what is expected of you to make a lasting impression during an interview. During your study of office procedures, you will be creating sample documents that can present your skills to an interviewer much better than words. You will be creating your portfolio, chapter by chapter, so that you might show an interviewer the quality of work you are capable of producing.

What Is a Portfolio? A portfolio is a collection of samples of your best work arranged in an attractive binder or file folder—whatever you choose—that will show anyone the kind of work you are capable of doing. Remember the key word is *best*. You would *not* want to include any work that has errors, is unattractive, or is unclear to the reader.

What Is the Purpose of the Portfolio? It presents your abilities in a much stronger, more positive way than your describing the work you are capable of doing. Its purpose is to build confidence in your abilities in the interviewer's mind.

Follow these steps:

1. After all papers have been returned from Chapter 1, with the help of your instructor select your best papers from your answers to the For Your Discussion questions, your responses to the On-the-Job Situations, your Projects and Activities, your organization chart, your surfing the Internet search, your self-evaluation, or Your Action Plan. Make certain you select papers you feel represent the best of your work. Remember, in your portfolio you may make corrections and reprint after your instructor has returned papers to you, so that the papers reflect superior work.

2. If you include your responses to For Your Discussion or On-the-Job Situations, make certain the question or situation is keyed followed by your response.

3. Follow your instructor's directions about formatting, assembling, and turning in the portfolio.

Communicating Effectively

OUTLINE

What Is Human Relations?

Your Company and Its Place in Industry

Human Relations in the Workplace
Maintain a Positive Attitude
Be a Team Player
Learn to Work with Difficult People
Show Your Human Side
Keep Confidential Information Confidential
Deal with Change

Develop a Positive Professional Image

International Human Relations

LEARNING OUTCOMES

When you have completed this chapter, you should be able to:

✔ Discuss the desirable attitudes and traits that contribute positively to communicating with others.

✔ Describe your role in forming the image of the organization.

✔ Describe the human relations skills necessary to work in an international environment.

Business offices are connected to the global marketplace by the telephone, written and electronic communications, and telecommunication systems. Office professionals never know what situations they will encounter until they answer the telephone, open the postal mail, access their e-mail, listen to their voice mail, or greet clients or customers. Nevertheless, they are expected to respond in a manner that will create a positive customer service climate for their organizations.

To be an effective office professional, you must be aware at all times that each person you meet, whether customer or coworker, is forming an image of the organization, your manager, and you. You must rely on your business personality to communicate effectively in writing, orally, and nonverbally with everyone you come in contact with in your business activities.

WHAT IS HUMAN RELATIONS?

You cannot depend on knowledge, skills, and abilities alone for success in your job. Your performance as an effective office professional and your happiness on the job will be closely linked to your ability to communicate and to get along with people, and this in turn will depend on your understanding the importance of human relations.

Human relations is not just getting along with people. It is more than that. **Human relations** is:

- Building and maintaining relationships with many different people, such as coworkers of different cultural backgrounds.
- Knowing how to handle difficult situations when they arise.
- Understanding yourself and others (personality, behavior, and attitudes).

YOUR COMPANY AND ITS PLACE IN INDUSTRY

To project the image that you are a professional who knows what is going on in your company, you must first spend some time getting to know your company. Look beyond the job you are required to do and keep abreast of company happenings. You should know the answers to the following questions:

- Is my company a national or international company?
- Where are the various plants or offices located?
- Who are the top executives?
- What products does my company sell or manufacture or what services does it provide?
- Who are my company's competitors?
- How does my company rank in its industry?

Knowing your company allows you to leave the impression with others that you are knowledgeable and can be a source of information that can be relied upon. Much of this information is available in annual reports, files, or office manuals. Your experiences, and inquiries, however, will also increase your knowledge. You should constantly desire to know as much about your company as possible. Showing interest in learning about the company can enhance your advancement within the company.

HUMAN RELATIONS IN THE WORKPLACE

When you accept a position with a company, management expects you to do the best job you can and to get along with all people to the best of your ability. Remember that your contribution is essential to have a smooth-running, productive, and efficient office. In all instances, the role you play is a central one on the office team.

Maintain a Positive Attitude

Personality is what you are, the sum of all your mental, physical, and emotional experiences. Everyone's personality is affected by the experiences of daily living. Psychologists tell us that one's personality is formed early in life, yet at no time is one's personality completely fixed. Changes in personality take place gradually, but they do occur; therefore, personality development or improvement is possible.

Projecting a pleasant personality is easy when things go right. To be successful in business, you must be able to:

- Maintain composure when things go wrong
- Say "no" tactfully
- Soothe the feelings of an irate customer or coworker
- Be considerate and tolerant of someone who is inconsiderate of you
- Exhibit poise under extreme pressure

When you are in a situation that is tense, stop and think before you speak. Give yourself time to analyze the reaction of others to what you might say. This time can allow you to organize your thoughts and response, help you develop the desired attitude, and avoid reacting inappropriately.

You should seek to cultivate attitudes and traits that will contribute to your success. When you succeed in displaying an appropriate attitude or trait in a difficult situation, you will be able to apply that experience in coping with the next difficult situation.

Be a Team Player

In every organization, management expects each employee to be a productive worker whose efforts contribute to the goals and objectives of the organization. You and your manager should be working for common goals and functioning in harmony with others in the organization.

As you learn your job, find out what the organization's mission and objectives are. Be quick to discover your manager's scope of operation and how his or her objectives contribute to the overall mission of the organization.

If you will think in terms of what you can contribute rather than of what you can get, you will find it easier to do the right thing at the right time. You may perform much detailed work, but you need not feel subservient. On the contrary, you should feel that you are part of a team.

Teamwork ranks with communication and trust as components for a good relationship with your manager. Communication is highly important; keep your manager informed. Because your role is to assist, do everything possible to assist your manager in being successful. Here are some ways you can be a team player (see Figure 2-1):

- Take full responsibility for your part of the workload and for the problems that arise within the scope of the work.
- Study the problems, ask for help in deciding what to do if you need help, or make the necessary adjustment.
- Be a productive worker, improving your skills and knowledge and accepting additional responsibility as you gain experience on the job.
- Strive for excellence and be enthusiastic about your job.
- Make others feel important.
- Be courteous and show respect, but be yourself.
- Let your personality sparkle just enough for others to be glad that they had a chance to work with you.

■ **Figure 2-1**
Office professionals
working as a team.

Learn to Work with Difficult People

No matter how congenial you are, how much a team player you are, how nice and cooperative you are, you will encounter people who are difficult to work with. Difficult people tend to bring out the worst in us. Many know how to "push our buttons" to cause us to react emotionally, to cause us distress, or simply to create tension. Here is a plan to follow to help you deal with these difficult situations.

1. Do not react emotionally; stand back and take a look at the situation. If you do not have to respond immediately, take time to write down everything in as much detail as possible.
2. Analyze the behavior of the difficult person. Identify exactly what was said that caused you to feel threatened, upset, and so on. What do you believe motivated the person to make the statement or to create the situation?
3. Analyze your behavior—what you felt: anger, frustration, disappointment, and so forth.
4. Decide exactly what behavior—all or part—you believe you must acknowledge and react to and why.
5. Define all the ways you might respond.
6. Decide on a plan: What will you say—making sure you form the statements using "I" and not "You"—where will you say it, and when will you say it?
7. Imagine how the person might respond.

Show Your Human Side

A friendly smile and cheerful "Good morning" may be classified as ceremonial language, but they are highly desirable when they are coupled with sincerity and an optimistic approach to life. Take the initiative to speak

■ **Figure 2-2**
An office professional
interacting with a coworker.

first; call others by name. Make an effort to get acquainted with as many coworkers as possible.

Try to be the coworker you would want everyone else to be (see Figure 2-2). Here are some tips to reach that goal:

- Be pleasant, courteous, responsive, and understanding.
- Listen attentively when someone is talking with you.
- Be responsive to what is going on around you.
- Treat others as you wish to be treated.
- Avoid being condescending when giving instructions.
- Suggest rather than command; request rather than demand.
- Show consideration for others in all the things you do, both large and small.
- Be thoughtful; for instance, stop at the office professional's desk when you must go in to see his or her manager.
- When you must interrupt someone, time the interruption so that the person is at a stopping point when you ask for his or her attention.
- Respect the rights of others.
- Knowing what not to say is as important as knowing what to say. Do not discuss religion, money, morals, personalities, or politics.
- You gain the trust of others by never talking about anyone. Be especially careful not to make remarks about coworkers.
- Be polite enough not to pry into personal affairs; avoid asking personal questions.
- When you are conversing, take the time to say exactly what you intend to say, but be tactful.
- Think and then speak; otherwise, your statements may come out wrong and place you in an embarrassing position.

- Be cooperative and do more than is expected of you.
- Be generous, but not to the point of punishing yourself.

Remember that little things do count. You can create a pleasant, businesslike atmosphere for you and your manager by your rapport with the employees at all levels and with outsiders who come to your office or call on the telephone. Be consistent, not moody, as you show your human side. In addition to creating a pleasant atmosphere, your thoughtfulness will help you enjoy your relationships with others.

Keep Confidential Information Confidential

Whatever management system you work for, you will always have to practice discretion when it comes to confidential information.

Refrain from repeating your manager's opinions. In fact, most activities that take place in your office should be kept confidential. To gain the trust of your organization, your manager, and your coworkers, do not discuss, mention, or refer to company business outside the office.

When there is an upcoming company announcement and you are aware of it, keep it confidential. Company announcements should come from management.

Be careful not to give away confidential information to your friends and colleagues or to your company's competitors. Sometimes just one isolated fact obtained from you is all the information that a competitor needs. Confidential information is often given away without intent. For example, you may be very proud of where you work and the decisions that are made by management. As a result, you discuss this information with new acquaintances at a social event. When this happens, you never know where the information will be shared, with whom, and how it will be used.

When it comes to sharing company information, use good judgment and discretion at all times.

Deal with Change

People resist change because they want to continue to be in control of what is happening. They seem to have a natural inclination to do so. But changes do come in our lives, and they come sooner than we expect them. Changes are brought about rapidly today because:

- Office technology is being continually updated.
- Competition is now increased because companies are competing in a global marketplace.
- Businesses are **restructuring,** in other words, making changes to meet competition. They are doing this by combining or eliminating functions, and by **downsizing,** which means reducing staff by eliminating jobs and sometimes whole departments and divisions.

Regardless of where you work, you will experience change. Anticipate change and realize it is a constant. Expect to use new equipment and use new software, experience several new job assignments, and shift priorities during your career. Welcome change and view it positively.

Adapt to Your Manager and Your Job

✔ Each time you are assigned to a new manager, learn his or her priorities, preferences, and work habits.

✔ Adjust your schedule to that of your manager. After you are well acquainted with your manager, perhaps you can make helpful suggestions, provided you have thought an idea through carefully. But do not attempt to change your manager. Keep in mind that the only person you can change is yourself.

✔ Admire and respect your manager, and do what you can to build his or her morale.

✔ Refrain from expressing your manager's opinions. Everything that goes on in your office should be kept confidential.

✔ Refrain from giving your personal interpretation of a company policy. That is your manager's job.

✔ Be careful not to give away secrets inadvertently to your friends and coworkers, your manager's counterparts, or competitors.

✔ Be loyal. **Loyalty** (being devoted or true to one thing or person) is rated as one of the most desirable traits that an office professional can possess. It means that you support a person and his or her ideas and actions.

DEVELOP A POSITIVE PROFESSIONAL IMAGE

You can boost your own morale and develop a positive professional image by developing your personal skills, such as

■ **possessing integrity**

Integrity encompasses sound moral or ethical principles, fairness, honesty, sincerity, and the courage to stand up for these moral precepts. A person who has strength of character and integrity has one of the most, if not *the most*, important traits a person can possess.

■ **understanding diversity**

What is diversity? **Diversity** refers to the variety of experiences and perspectives that arise from differences in race, culture, religion, mental or physical abilities, heritage, age, gender, sexual orientation, and other characteristics. Respect, tolerance, and goodwill are the keystones to enjoying the rich diversity of our world. Offices today are diverse. As an office professional, you must be knowledgeable about diversity in the workplace and embrace it.

■ **promoting excellent customer service**

One of the most successful ways to develop a positive professional image is to offer excellent customer service. Customer service does not mean just offering excellent service to those customers outside your business; it also means that you see each person within your organization as a customer as well and treat him or her as such (see Figure 2-3).

■ **Figure 2-3**
A loyal and supportive relationship between manager and office professional is important.

■ **being a self-starter**

Take the initiative to begin a task for which you are responsible. Don't wait for your manager to ask you to do something—be observant and anticipate what you are expected to do without having to be told.

■ **being dependable**

You can help create a desirable atmosphere by having an excellent attendance record and by being prompt in arriving at work each morning and in returning on time to your workstation after breaks and lunch.

■ **displaying self-confidence and composure**

A person who is self-confident relies on the correctness of his or her own judgment and competence in spite of the discouragement and influence of others. A confident person maintains composure, which is a feeling of calmness and tranquility, and exhibits poise, which denotes ease and dignity of manner. Here are some ways to become confident:

1. Believe in yourself.
2. You cannot control the circumstances under which you work; they are beyond your control. You can remain in control of your reactions, however. Don't overreact to minor upsets.

3. The business world is demanding and fast-paced. To cope with it, proceed with assurance and keep your cool.

4. Be patient; be quick to distinguish between fact and fiction; withhold judgment until you obtain all the facts.

5. Accept criticism; in fact, welcome it. Use it as a tool to help improve your skills and knowledge.

6. Develop a sense of humor and use it at the right time. Laugh at yourself and laugh with others. Do not take yourself or your problems too seriously.

■ **learning and growing professionally**

Sir Walter Scott said, "Success or failure is caused more by mental attitude than by mental capacity." Approach life and your job with a positive attitude. Periodically take inventory of your needs and your accomplishments. Set new goals and keep reaching. Your rewards will be many, including physical vitality, an alert mind, and an optimistic attitude toward life. Learn about professional organizations such as the International Association of Administrative Professionals (IAAP), formerly Professional Secretaries International (PSI). Its Web site on the Internet is http://www.iaap-hq.org. IAAP is the world's largest association for administrative support staff, with nearly 700 chapters and 40,000 members and affiliates worldwide. As an office professional, you should be involved with organizations such as IAAP to keep informed about up-to-date research on office trends to enhance your skills and to help you become a more effective employee. IAAP charges annual dues, prints a publication titled *OfficePRO*, which is an outstanding resource, and provides many other benefits to today's office professional.

■ **displaying ethical behavior**

Every office professional must display ethical behavior to be viewed as a professional. What are ethics? **Ethics** are a system of deciding what is right, or more right, in a given situation. Ethics involve your values and what you believe to be the right way you should live your life; therefore, you behave in ways that display these values. You will learn more about ethics in Chapter 3.

Many questionable employee practices are common in the workplace. They are often associated with irresponsible work practice and the theft of time and resources (see Chapter 3, "Ethics in the Office").

Without rules, good ethical practice becomes ambiguous. Codes of ethical practice are an increasingly popular tool for reducing that ambiguity. A **code of ethics** is a formal document, developed by your organization, that states the organization's primary values and ethical rules of conduct. Codes of ethics can be effective depending on whether the organization supports them and how employees are treated when they break the code. In the end, as an employee you have the responsibility to do the right thing based upon your own judgment and personal principles.

INTERNATIONAL HUMAN RELATIONS

If you should be lucky enough to work in an office in a country outside the United States, you have several things to consider. Among the questions you might ask yourself are the following:

Acknowledge the Unique Spelling of a Supervisor or Coworker's Name:

- Spelling proper names with accent marks could possibly help build a better relationship with that person.
- In written correspondence—for example, on a "While You Were Out" note—use the accent mark; for instance, José González.
- When typing a document, use Microsoft Word symbols. (See the Using MS Office feature later in this chapter to learn how to type accented characters.)

- *What general traits are expected of an overseas worker?*

  You must be ready and willing to change; possess a sense of adventure; have a desire to be challenged; be open-minded; be patient; and above all be flexible.

- *What type of adaptation and coping skills must I possess?*

  You must be emotionally stable; be able to cope with stress; be prepared for culture shock; have a sense of humor; and be observant and willing to make adjustments when needed.

- *What intercultural communication skills must I possess?*

  You must have tolerance, sensitivity, good listening skills, good nonverbal skills, and possess a second language.

- *What traits and skills must I possess personally to be effective in an office?*

  You must be independent, self-reliant, resourceful, persistent, versatile, organized, loyal, and energetic. You must possess leadership skills, good verbal communication skills, and a commitment to working overseas.

Professional and technical expertise alone is not enough when working overseas. You must embrace the characteristics listed above to deal with problems of global survival. You could see many things you aren't used to, such as poverty, war, and ecological destruction. You must rely on your inner strength to continue to develop those human relations skills necessary to be successful when working in an international environment.

Overview

✔ Human relations is building and maintaining relationships with many different people, such as coworkers of different cultural backgrounds; knowing how to handle difficult situations when they arise; and understanding yourself and others (personality, behavior, and attitudes).

✔ To project the image that you are a professional who knows what is going on in your company, you must first spend time getting to know your company. Ask questions such as, Is my company national or international? Where are its offices located? Who are its top executives? What products are sold or manufactured or what services are provided? Who are its competitors? How does it rank in its industry?

✔ To project a positive attitude, you must be able to maintain composure when things go wrong, say "no" tactfully, soothe the feelings of an irate customer or coworker, be considerate and tolerant of someone who is inconsiderate of you, and exhibit poise under extreme pressure.

✔ Be a team player whose efforts contribute to the goals and objectives of the organization.

✔ Learn to work with difficult people by not reacting emotionally, analyze the behavior of the difficult person, analyze your behavior, decide exactly what behavior you must acknowledge, define the ways you might respond, decide on a plan, and imagine how the difficult person might respond.

✔ To show your human side, be pleasant, responsive, and understanding; listen attentively to others; be responsive to what is going on around you; treat others as you wish to be treated; avoid being condescending when giving instructions; suggest rather than command; show consideration for others; be thoughtful; time interruptions when that person is at a stopping point; respect the rights of others; know what not to say; don't talk about other people; be polite; take the time to say exactly what you intend to say but be tactful; think, then speak; be cooperative; and be generous.

✔ Keep confidential information confidential. When it comes to sharing company information, use good judgment and discretion at all times.

✔ Accept change readily and anticipate change and realize it is constant.

✔ Develop a positive professional image by displaying ethical behavior, possessing integrity, understanding diversity, promoting excellent customer service, being a self-starter, being dependable, being a team player, displaying self-confidence and composure, and learning and growing professionally.

✔ When deciding to work outside the United States ask yourself, What general traits are expected of an overseas worker? What type of adaptation and coping skills must I possess? What intercultural communication skills must I possess? What traits and skills must I possess personally to be effective in an office?

Key Terms

Code of ethics. A formal document, developed by your organization, that states the organization's primary values and ethical rules of conduct.

Diversity. The variety of experiences and perspectives that arise from differences in race, culture, religion, mental or physical abilities, heritage, age, gender, sexual orientation, and other characteristics.

Downsizing. Reducing staff by eliminating jobs and sometimes whole departments and divisions.

Ethics. A system of deciding what is right, or more right, in a given situation.

Human relations. Building and maintaining relationships with many different people, such as coworkers of different cultural backgrounds; knowing how to handle difficult situations when they arise; and understanding yourself and others (personality, behavior, and attitudes).

Loyalty. Being devoted or true to one thing or person.

Personality. What you are, the sum of all your mental, physical, and emotional experiences.

Restructuring. Making changes to meet competition.

For Your Discussion

 Retrieve file C2-DQ.DOC from your student data disk.

Directions

Enter your response after each question or statement.

1. Describe the office professional's role in forming interoffice relationships where he or she works.
2. Explain why it is important to learn how to work with difficult people.
3. Suggest several ways to show respect for a manager.
4. How can you show loyalty to your manager? To your company?
5. How is a positive professional image related to personality traits?
6. Explain what is meant by the statement "Remain in control of your reactions."
7. How does a person acquire strength of character?
8. How can you accept constructive criticism?
9. What would you do if your manager's business practices seemed unethical to you?
10. Explain what you think would be your greatest barrier to overcome if you chose to work overseas.

PUNCTUATION WORKSHOP

Commas are used to set off words and phrases in sentences. Complete the exercises below by applying punctuation rules for commas.

For Review

Appendix A: Rule 3: Commas Used with a Series
Rule 4: Commas Used Between Adjectives
Rule 5: Commas Used with Introductory and Parenthetic Phrases

 Retrieve file C2-WRKS.DOC from your student data disk.

Directions

Insert commas, if required, in the sentences below. Circle the sentence number or key a **C** at the end of the sentence if the sentence is punctuated correctly.

Rule 3: Commas Used with a Series

1. Please tell us when you plan to arrive at which hotel you will be staying and if you will need transportation to and from the meeting.

2. The faxes were from A. C. Produce Morgan Grocery and Henson Fish and Poultry.

3. He went to the meeting and made the presentation.

4. We received three packages from AirExpress Overnight Transport and Fast 'n Fair.

5. The copier was giving us trouble and was repaired quickly.

Rule 4: Commas Used Between Adjectives

1. The computer room must be a relatively cool dust-free room.

2. Ellen was an efficient effective employee.

3. Human resource managers want you to maintain a relaxed confident manner during an interview.

4. The filing system is an old outdated system.

5. The papers were handed out at the well-attended well-received conference.

Rule 5: Commas Used with Introductory and Parenthetic Phrases

1. When an employee reaches age 55 he or she is eligible for retirement benefits.

2. The date of the meeting is March 15 rather than April 15.

3. Unless we receive written permission from the company the text may not be used.

4. He received an answer by fax after he sent the information.

5. We attended the conference of course because we had purchased our tickets.

On the Job Situations

 Retrieve file C2-OJS.DOC from your student data disk.

Directions

Enter your response after each situation.

1. You are an administrative assistant in the purchasing department. Another administrative assistant, Joan Lopez, is getting married in three weeks. The purchasing department employs 12 office workers, two of whom are administrative assistants. According to a rumor, Joan is not coming back to work after the wedding, and two of the office workers want to apply for the position. They have come to you to find out if the rumor is true. You have not seen an official announcement about Joan's employment plans after she gets married. However, Joan did tell you that she does not plan to come back to work after the wedding. What should you say to your two coworkers?

2. You wanted to take your vacation during the last week in November, but you did not request it because Robert Lawson, who fills in for you when you are absent, had already requested vacation during the same week. Yesterday Robert canceled his vacation for November because his personal plans fell through. The vacation schedule is approved six months in advance, but you still would like to take vacation during the last week of November. Today is November 15. Your department is working on a huge project that must be completed by November 30. Someone would have to finish your part of the project and the staff is short. Are you justified in making this request now? Explain why you think you are or are not justified in making this request.

3. You work with Dillan. Dillan is difficult to work with because of his negative attitude toward everything—his personal life, his relationships, his job, and his supervisor. Dillan rarely makes a positive statement about anything or anyone. You are beginning to have negative feelings too. You like your work and your supervisor, and you can see there will be opportunities for advancement in this job. Analyze the situation. What can you do to overcome your negative feelings? Outline a specific plan for working with Dillan.

4. You handle the paperwork for travel reimbursements in the accounting department. The comptroller returned three travel reports that contained errors you made, commenting on how important it is for you to check each report more carefully to avoid errors. The comptroller also stated

that, after all, this is the accounting department and employees expect accurate and timely payment of their expenses. Analyze the situation. Identify the problem. What should your response to the comptroller have been immediately after she handed you the reports? Be specific in your reply.

Projects and Activities

1. Interview an assistant who works for more than one person—several managers or engineers, salespeople, everyone within a department, or everyone within a division. Ask questions about how the assistant organizes and handles the work. Create a list of questions in advance. (This could be a class project.) Develop your questions carefully. As you formulate your questions, be sure to inquire about priorities for completing work, standards of acceptability, telephone and filing responsibilities, use of services of others, problems encountered, and suggestions that might be helpful to you on the job. Do not limit your questions to the ideas given here. Report your findings to the class or to the instructor. Include the list of questions you used.

2. Think of someone whose personality you admire. Make a list of this person's personality traits that you like and then select the most outstanding traits and describe them in detail. Try to decide why these traits appeal to you. Do you think these traits would appeal to others? Write a memorandum to your instructor or share your ideas with the class.

3. Read three articles on criticism in such periodicals as *Psychology Today* or *OfficePRO* concerning the following topics:
   a. How to deal with criticism when you know it is justified
   b. How to deal with criticism when you know it is invalid
   c. How to control your emotions
   d. How to deal with unjust criticism

4. You have been selected to serve on the company Ethics Committee. The responsibility of the committee is to research other companies' code of ethics to use to help develop a code of ethics for your company. After the first committee meeting, the committee chairperson asked each member to bring to the next meeting an example of a company code of ethics. To have your example ready for the meeting tomorrow, you are to complete the following:
   a. Go online and research various companies such as Microsoft, General Electric, or Wal-Mart.
   b. Locate a code of ethics using search terms such as:
      "code + of + ethics"
      "standards + of + business + conduct"
   c. Summarize your findings in a short report.
   d. Include the location of the Web site and attach a copy of the code of ethics you found.

Surfing the Internet

You are to search the Internet to locate information on personality assessment for a presentation that you must make at your local Association of Administrative Professionals (IAAP) meeting next month.

1. Connect to the Internet and access a search tool, such as Excite, Yahoo!, or Lycos.
2. Enter the following key search phrase: "personal + assessment."
3. Refine your search if needed by using the following key search words: "personality + types."
4. Print any articles you believe will help you prepare your presentation.

Using the information you printed, create a presentation on personality assessment using presentation software such as Microsoft PowerPoint. Make certain you give credit to your sources. Attach the printed copies from the sources you used.

Using MS Office 2002

Use Accented Characters and AutoCorrect

Directions

Review the steps below to add accented characters to words.

1. With MS Word open to a current file, position your cursor where you need the accented character.
2. Click on the Insert menu and select Symbol.
3. On the Symbols tab, select (normal text) in the Font text box.
4. Using the scroll bar, scroll through the symbols until you find the accented character you need.
5. Click on the Insert button, and then click on the Close button.
6. The accented letter should be inserted into your document.

If you plan to use the accented word many times, you can save the name with the accent and omit having to repeat the above steps each time you want to use the word.

1. Select the name you just typed that contains the accented letter.
2. Click on the Edit menu and select Copy.
3. Click on the Tools menu and select AutoCorrect Options.
4. On the AutoCorrect tab, in the Replace text box type the name using plain text.
5. Press the Tab key to jump to the With text box.
6. Press the Ctrl + V keys to insert the "accented" name if it is not already there.

7. Click on the Add button, and then click on OK.

The next time you type *Jose,* for instance, it will automatically change to *José.*

Practice entering accent marks in the following names:

José (Spanish for Joseph)

Estéban (Spanish for Stephen)

Adélaïde (French for Adelaide)

'Aziz (Arabic for powerful or beloved)

Dàibhidh (Scottish for David)

Niño (Spanish for child)

APPLICATION PROBLEMS

APPLICATION 2-A

Employee Self-Assessment

Supplies needed: Memo from Mrs. Quevedo, (see below); Form 2-A, Diversity Self-Assessment. (Forms are at the back of the text.)

 Retrieve file C2-DIV.DOC from your student data disk.

Directions: Mrs. Quevedo gave you the following memo and asked you to complete the Diversity Self-Assessment form.

SUPREME APPLIANCES MEMORANDUM

TO: All Employees
FROM: Human Resource Department
SUBJECT: Diversity Self-Assessment
DATE: (Current)

To continue our ongoing Employee Training Program, we are offering you the opportunity to attend a workshop on "Diversity in the Workplace." The workshop will be held November 30 in Room 116 from 4 to 5 p.m. Please complete the following self-assessment and bring it with you to the workshop.

APPLICATION 2-B

Traits and Skills Inventory

Supplies needed: Request form from Mrs. Quevedo (shown below); Form 2-B, Self-Assessment Inventory. (Forms are at the back of the text.)

 Retrieve file C2-SEL.DOC from your student data disk.

Directions: Using the Self-Assessment Inventory, evaluate each statement and then enter an **S** (strong), an **A** (average), or an **I** (needs improvement) in the Assessment column.

REQUEST FORM

Today's Date: _____(Current)_____

From: _____Mrs. Quevedo_____

Turnaround Time: Normal ☑ Rush ☐

As a self-assessment tool, please complete this inventory. These particular traits and skills are emphasized as being critical for success in a technological environment. We will discuss them at our next meeting.

Your Action Plan

 Retrieve ACTION02.DOC file saved on your student data disk, or refer to Chapter 1, Form 1-B, if necessary.

Your Portfolio

With the help of your instructor, select the best papers representative of your work from Chapter 2. Follow your instructor's directions about formatting, assembling, and turning in the portfolio.

chapter 3

Managing Your Work, Time, and Resources

OUTLINE

Total Quality Management (TQM)
What Is TQM?
How Does TQM Work?

Effectiveness and Efficiency
What's the Difference?

Be the Boss of Your Own Time
Learn the Job
Assign Priorities
Adopt a Flexible Plan
Start the Day with a Difficult Task
Group Similar Tasks
Manage Details
Avoid Procrastination
Work at One Task at a Time
Cope with Interruptions
Get It Right the First Time
Build Relaxation into Your Schedule
Make a Daily Plan
Prepare in Advance
Manage a Large Project

Office Organization
Organize the Office Supplies
Organize the Workstation

Learn to Cope with Stress

Ethics in the Office

Environmental Office

How Is Time Understood by Different Cultures?

LEARNING OUTCOMES

When you have completed this chapter, you should be able to:

✔ Define the concept of Total Quality Management.

✔ Explain how Total Quality Management affects the work of an office professional.

✔ Explain the difference between working efficiently and working effectively.

✔ Describe at least ten guidelines to follow to establish your own work habits.

✔ Establish two follow-up organizers.

✔ State suggestions for organizing both the office supplies and the workstation.

✔ Suggest methods for practicing environmental consciousness in an office.

✔ Discuss the principles of ethical conduct in the workplace.

Organizing work and managing time are essential for measurable accomplishments day after day, year after year, throughout a lifetime, regardless of the goals a person endeavors to reach. A major aspect of organizing work is the process of dividing a block of work into manageable components or segments.

TOTAL QUALITY MANAGEMENT (TQM)

Through globalization, new markets have opened in the United States, Canada, and abroad. To stay competitive in this global marketplace, many businesses have adopted a sound and effective approach for achieving success. It is fundamental and practiced through four basic principles:

1. Customer focus.
2. Continuous improvement and learning.
3. Strategic planning and leadership.
4. Teamwork.

The approach is known as Total Quality, and it recognizes the customer (both internal and external) as the real judge of the quality of your company's products or services. Companies that adopt Total Quality not only plan for strategic business improvement but also encourage learning and new leadership ideas from their employees. As an office professional in a company that embraces this approach to business, you are likely to become a member of a problem-solving team, or a team working to improve a business process somewhere in the organization. Most certainly you will be empowered to make broader decisions within your discipline.

What Is TQM?

The *Quality* approach—making the customer the number one priority—does not, at first thought, seem to be significantly different from other customer-focused strategies. However, an all-out quality commitment requires companies to eliminate wasteful practices, redesign business methods, and adopt a focused approach to managing total quality.

Thus, **Total Quality Management (TQM)** can be defined as a management philosophy that stresses the delivery of a quality product or service through optimization of the people and processes that produce it. TQM is not a new concept. In the late 1940s, Dr. W. Edwards Deming, an internationally renowned statistician and consultant, took his revolutionary management philosophy to Japan, where it became pivotal to that nation's successful economic recovery after World War II. Inspired by Japan's initial success, businesses worldwide have adopted quality management techniques in order to survive in the new marketplace. According to Dr. Deming, "The consumer is the most important part of the production line. Quality should be aimed at the needs of the consumer; present and future."

This statement forms the main principle of all Quality initiatives. In simple economic terms, we are all either producers or consumers, or both. Relating to the main principle is not difficult, but implementing it will be one of the challenges you face as an office professional.

How Does TQM Work?

There is no single TQM formula that works for every organization; fundamentally, however, TQM makes all employees responsible for strengthening the competitive position of their company by improving its products and services. The optimization of labor, materials, and time is seen as the key to the success of the Total Quality approach. Anything less simply drives up the expense to the customer; inevitably, this results in loss of market share, profits, jobs, and ultimately the business itself.

The organization's suppliers of products also need to be aware of the Quality approach. It should no longer be acceptable to deal with suppliers that are unreliable or produce poor quality products. Depending on your responsibilities, you may wish to review your list of suppliers and develop an alliance with only one supplier for the benefit of cost, reliability, and quality.

In the office, TQM means that each employee is involved with office teamwork and focused on customer satisfaction. Employees at every level are encouraged to find new and innovative ways of doing their jobs more effectively and to be flexible enough to assist others. You may be empowered— that is, given more autonomy and broader responsibilities—with the goal of simplifying office operations. You will be given responsibility for making decisions that affect your own effectiveness and performance.

You will be judged on your team contribution and on your innovation: If the filing system does not correspond to the operation—change it! If your colleague is having difficulty completing a project—help out! If a customer has a complaint—resolve it!

As an example, the office professional may be invited to become part of a team that reviews the problem of products that aren't being delivered to the customer on time. The team of employees would be directly involved in the delivery process under review. Every member of the team has equal responsibility and an equal voice in identifying all the steps and problems involved in the delivery cycle. The problem must be clearly understood and stated in written form. All the issues that team members consider important are recorded. Team members then prioritize the stated problems. The problem that is deemed the most significant is the first one the team resolves.

To resolve, the first-priority problem is thoroughly examined. Each step of the current procedure is analyzed for its effectiveness and necessity. The process of examining the entire procedure will inspire improvements. Additionally, each member will feel that he or she has contributed to a solution for improving customer satisfaction.

This team problem-solving approach is typical of the process improvement activity that organizations are conducting as part of their Quality approach. Let's review a sequence of events that might occur as a cross-functional team is formed to address a late delivery problem:

1. A team of employees who are directly involved in the order and delivery process is formed. This team may include the office professional—department or division assistant.
2. A team leader is selected to chair the meeting.
3. A designated recorder will document all input.
4. A facilitator may be involved to organize the team members' input.
5. The general problem is clearly defined during the first team meeting.
6. Each team member has an equal opportunity to state what he or she believes to be the contributing factors to the general problem. This step, which allows the employees the freedom of open suggestion without criticism, is known as **brainstorming**. In this case, examples of contributing factors to the general problem may be:
   a. The person who places the orders is often away from work.
   b. When the orders are placed, the suppliers do not have ready stock; they must get stock from foreign markets.
   c. When suppliers deliver stock, it is sometimes in damaged condition, and, therefore, must be reordered.
7. The team members now decide on what they believe to be the most important specific problems (contributing factors). In this case, the most significant factor may be that the stock is often received in poor condition and must be reordered.
8. Next, each team member helps outline the exact steps that take place in the process. In the case of goods arriving in damaged condition, it may be discovered that the foreign suppliers are not packing the goods carefully enough.
9. As the process is completely examined, team members provide input about possible changes until an improved process is developed. In this case, employees might suggest that proper packaging and careful handling of goods would expedite the delivery of the product to the customer.
10. The team will now make a delivery process improvement recommendation to management.

It should be noted that there are no set rules for Total Quality Management; its application is broad and varied. But underlying TQM are the four principles outlined in the beginning of this section—customer focus, continuous improvement and learning, strategic planning and leadership, and teamwork.

EFFECTIVENESS AND EFFICIENCY

For the office professional, being effective and being efficient are equally important. However, these two qualities are often confused with each other. Although interrelated, these terms have very different meanings.

What's the Difference?

Effectiveness means producing a definite or desired result. For example, an effective professional completes the right task correctly. **Efficiency** means producing the desired result with a minimum of effort, expense, and waste. Whereas it is possible to be effective without being efficient, the cost of inefficiency is usually too great for profit-making organizations; they must couple efficiency with effectiveness.

Office professionals are hired to perform a variety of tasks, being responsible to one or to a group of managers. Yet they continually must do three things to organize their work so that they can perform efficiently:

- Divide large projects into manageable segments of work.
- Group related isolated tasks to reduce the time consumed in changing from one unrelated task to another.
- Match the work to the time frame in which it must be performed by classifying it as work that must be done today, work that must be done this week, or work that has no specific deadline.

Organizational skills are a requirement for success in today's workplace. Office professionals work with a constant and rapid flow of information. To contribute to the processing of information, professionals must be able to organize their work and manage their time. They also must be able to evaluate their effectiveness and efficiency and to look for ways to increase their contributions to the organization.

The need for effective time management techniques becomes clear when professionals answer the following questions:

1. Do I never seem to get everything done that I had hoped to accomplish?
2. Is my desk cluttered with papers that I am constantly reshuffling but never dealing with?
3. Do I often work overtime at the office? Do I often take work home to complete?
4. Am I continually being interrupted by telephone calls, visitors, others who monopolize my time, and coworkers who want to socialize?
5. By failing to set priorities, do I spend most of my time on trivial details without enough time remaining to work on the important jobs?

Office professionals who answer "yes" to all or most of these questions probably spend the bulk of their time on tasks that produce only minimal benefits.

Time management involves:

- Developing work habits that result in maximum efficiency.
- Acquiring knowledge and skills to extend performance beyond present capabilities.
- Controlling attitudes and emotions that have a tendency to steal time.
- Developing an effective reminder method for following through on each task at the appropriate time.

BE THE BOSS OF YOUR OWN TIME

There is no single "right way" for managing time on the job. The rules are often job specific and change from organization to organization. Exactly what constitutes successful time management is difficult to define without reference to specific examples from the workplace. There is no doubt that effective employees establish recognizable work *patterns*, but no two employees necessarily follow the *same* pattern. Nevertheless, the ideas presented in this chapter can be used as a guide to establish your own work habits and time management techniques. It is important to remember, though, that this is only a guide. You will have to work hard and think about how best to adapt these rules and suggestions to your own situation.

For example, balancing family responsibilities and work responsibilities is a significant challenge to many office professionals. Organizations are developing employee-friendly policies and support systems that provide flexible work schedules and permit more work-at-home and telecommuting options.

In a type of schedule redesign known as **flextime**, employees work a set number of hours each day but vary the starting and ending times. Flextime allows management to relax some of the traditional "time clock" control of employees' time. Similarly, working from home and telecommuting present an extraordinary opportunity to be the boss of your own time.

Learn the Job

The organization expresses its objectives—the tasks to be accomplished—in terms of long-range, intermediate, and short-range goals. Management focuses its attention on achieving organizational objectives by accomplishing those goals. In any given week, your manager will devote time to both dealing with the work at hand and also addressing longer range goals. As you join this dynamic environment, be as flexible, adaptable, and tolerant as you can in order to provide real value-added assistance.

In a new job, you will have to understand how your manager works. Organize your day's work so that it dovetails with that of your manager; do not expect your manager to adjust to your work schedule. At first you should:

1. Concentrate on learning.
2. Be cautious about taking initiative until you understand what is expected of you.

Before you can organize work, you must know what the position or job entails. In most cases, someone will explain your new position and duties to you. This might be the office assistant you are replacing, an administrative assistant in your department, a mentor, an office manager, or your manager. During this orientation, you should:

1. Listen.
2. Take notes.
3. Ask questions that will increase your understanding of what is being explained. Be alert to what are considered priority items.
4. Learn your manager's preferences.
5. Write down the names of people you meet, note their department, and learn quickly what they do.

Every day make an effort to learn more about your job and exactly how your manager prefers the work to be done. Learn the job not just for the current week and the next but also for three months to a year in advance. Become familiar with the information in your office. For instance:

1. Carefully study all the instructions left for you by the previous office professional.
2. Check on the different kinds of stationery and forms in your desk or supply cabinet and determine when each is to be used.
3. Read instruction sheets that have been prepared for certain tasks you are to perform.
4. Find out what is in the active files.
5. Study the organization of electronic folders either in the word processing directory or in the electronic mail system.
6. Refer to the organization directory to learn the names of the executives and other employees and their titles.

When you report to work, the former employee may not be there to train you. You may not find a procedures or desk manual describing your duties or tasks. In this situation, your manager may be able to direct you. However, if your manager cannot help you with the procedures, you will have to rely heavily on your resourcefulness and judgment in finding answers. Keep in mind that you cannot perform at maximum value to the organization until you fully understand the scope and responsibilities of your job.

Assign Priorities

Setting priorities will be the most difficult part of organizing your work and assigning your time.

Although you are guided by general policies about priorities, you will need to make judgments concerning performing the work in the most beneficial way for your manager and for the organization. Performing the work in the order in which it will be submitted to you will not always be feasible because some tasks will have more pressing deadlines than others. An example of a low-priority item is a memorandum written only as a matter of record. It can be keyboarded and filed at any time.

It helps to prioritize work into three categories:

1. Must be done immediately (identified as "A" or "1")
2. Must be done today (identified as "B" or "2")
3. Must be done as soon as time allows (identified as "C" or "3")

As time passes, tasks that are in category 3 will move to categories 2 and 1. If you are unsure how to determine priorities, ask yourself the following questions about each task:

1. Is this task or project a priority of my immediate supervisor or manager?
2. Is this work needed immediately? Is this a daily task or a long-range task?
3. How much time is required to complete this task?

4. Are others involved in the completion of this task?
5. Is there a specific deadline for this task?

You can learn the order of priorities in at least four ways:

1. Ask questions of those involved in the process.
2. Study documentation, such as the office manual.
3. Listen to your manager's requests to determine a "pattern."
4. Keep a record of how work flows in and out of the office.

For example, know when routine reports are due and how much in advance to request work from other departments, learn mail pickup and transportation schedules, and be aware of the most convenient times to reach executives by telephone.

The demands of managers and others for whom you work will be the overriding factor in how you divide your time. When you are working for two executives, one may have more work for you and the other very little. When you work for a group, it may be made up of salespeople who are out of the office much of the time. Each one may have very little work for you, but each one will expect you to do it on the day he or she returns to the office. Under this arrangement, prepare a schedule a week in advance showing who will be in the office on which days of the week. This information may not be easy to obtain, but it will be helpful when it comes to answering the telephone and anticipating your own workload.

Eventually you will learn how much time you need to devote to performing each person's work. For your own use, keep a record of how you spend your time. Prepare a time distribution chart, as shown in Figure 3-1. The **time distribution chart** is designed to show the distribution of work and time for several workers performing related office tasks; however, with minor changes it can be used to show the distribution of time and duties performed by one worker for several others. To complete the chart, follow these steps:

1. At the top of the columns, write the names of those for whom you perform work.
2. Enter the time used and a brief description of the task performed in the columns below the names.
3. After keeping the charts for several weeks, total the time used on behalf of each person and compute percentages.

Your analysis will give you some estimate of how much work to expect from each person, and it will reflect what you are doing that could be channeled elsewhere. When you have so much work to be done that some of it must be reassigned, your charts will be especially helpful to you and your manager in deciding which duties or activities can be handled by someone else.

Most office professionals who work for groups comprising employees of different ranks give highest priority to the work of the top-ranked person in the group, second priority to the next in rank, and so on. This arrangement may ensure a good relationship with your manager, but it may also create problems, particularly if some of the employees at the lower ranks feel that they can never get their work done on time or at all. Eventually they will complain. Avoid this situation by learning how to assess the urgency of the work

Susan Clark												April 16, 20— —
				TIME DISTRIBUTION CHART								
MAJOR ACTIVITIES	James	Hrs.	Chung	Hrs.	Rodriquez	Hrs.	Parker	Hrs.	Ramos	Hrs.	For Group	Hrs.	TOTAL
Incoming Mail											Open and distribute	1-1/2	1-1/2
Telephone	Handle calls	1-1/2			Handle calls	1/2							2
Transcribing	Letters	1/2	Report	1/2			Letters	1/4	Memos	1/4			1-1/2
Appointments	By telephone	1/2					Telephone and in person	1/2					1
Payroll											Time sheets, distribute checks	1/2	1/2
Misc.											Replenish supplies	1/2	1/2
TOTAL		2-1/2		1/2		1/2		3/4		1/4		2-1/2	7

■ **Figure 3-1**
Time distribution chart.

of the senior managers in the group. You will discover that some of their work can wait. Make your own judgment without discussing it with anyone and proceed with completing the tasks. However, when your work is backed up to the extent that it must be discussed formally, the most senior manager has the responsibility of assessing the total workload and determining the need for extra help.

Some employees, in an effort to gain priority for their requests, will label all requests "Rush." In each case you will have to judge what is a rush item and what is not. When you sense that these employees are under a lot of pressure, you might occasionally prevent a disruption by giving priority to their work; however, this practice must not become the norm. By giving priority to managers who mark all items "Rush," you are encouraging this behavior at the expense of other managers' work. Those managers who decrease stress in the office by practicing effective time management should not be penalized. You will have to deal with this issue in a diplomatic way. The best advice is to collect facts before you approach the problem. For example:

■ How many rush items are you receiving?

■ Which managers are giving you the rush items?

■ What are the rush items?

■ On what dates are you being given the rush items?

■ When are the deadlines?

The time distribution chart will assist with collection of this information.

You can maintain more control over your work schedule by relying on your own judgment about the order in which work should be done, instead of trying to follow rigid rules. Your judgment must be good, and you will need to be as concerned about your rapport with the members of the group as you are about the quality of the work you perform.

Some office professionals aspire to work for only one manager. Advantages and disadvantages to such a situation include the following:

Advantages of Working with Only One Manager Versus Several Managers

1. You are often viewed as having more status within the company.
2. You do not have to adjust to conflicting management styles.
3. Your manager has a clearer idea of your time constraints. Where several managers share the same office professional, the managers often are not aware of pressures being placed on you by their colleagues.

Disadvantages of Working with Only One Manager Versus Several Managers

1. Your responsibilities may be more routine. When an office professional works for more than one manager, the worker often receives a greater variety of projects to complete. Remember—the more experience you receive, the more marketable you become.
2. An office professional working for only one manager gains business contacts from only that source. If you work for a number of managers, your chances of networking are improved; this, of course, could improve your future employment opportunities.
3. Working for only one manager may not allow you to practice your organizational skills to the same degree that working for multiple managers would.

The preference is a personal one. Both positions may require equal challenges. If the challenges do not present themselves, find them!

Adopt a Flexible Plan

Management consultants recommend planning work and then following the plan. This is good advice; however, there may be disadvantages of planning. Consider these issues:

- Planning may create rigidity.
- Plans are difficult to create in a dynamic environment.
- Plans tend to focus on what works today and not how to deal with the issues of tomorrow.

In the end, you must plan for the ideal distribution of your time, but your plan must be flexible. Use your plan as an overall guide, but do not become discouraged when you cannot follow it closely. Your reputation of being flexible, adaptable, and tolerant with your plan will serve you well for the rest of your career.

One of your major responsibilities is to save your manager time. To accomplish this,

- Perform as much of your manager's work as you can.
- Decrease interruptions or at least schedule them.
- Collect and verify facts and assemble materials that he or she will need to perform the task.

To enable your manager to perform with maximum efficiency, tackle the most pressing or important job first and keep adjusting your plan so that you can meet the corresponding deadlines.

You must recognize that your work schedule is not truly your own. Your work schedule is governed not only by your manager's objectives and deadlines but also by the inherent schedule of the organization's information. For example:

- You may plan to devote the morning hours to starting a lengthy assignment only to discover that your manager wants you to process a new expense summary, in order to meet a scheduled payroll run.
- A telephone call from the corporate home office requesting critical information may take precedence over everything else.
- The deadline for sending the department's weekly and monthly revenue report is based on a routine and defined schedule.
- Whenever an interrelated department with which you work changes its schedule, you may have to adjust your schedule to accommodate that department.

Start the Day with a Difficult Task

Begin your day in an unhurried way so that you will not need the first thirty minutes at the office to "pull yourself together." If you commute and frequently worry about your bus or transportation being late, try to improve your day by taking an earlier bus (or train or subway). If you drive, allow an extra five or ten minutes to get a head start on the morning traffic rush. Arrive early, go over your plans for the day (which you prepared the day before), and then tackle a task that requires concentration and effort on your part. Tackle either a task that is difficult or one that you dislike. It will seem easier when you are more energetic and your mind is clear.

Make the first hour one of accomplishment, not one in which you simply get ready to work. Perhaps your first tasks will be to listen to the voice mail, take down messages and direct them to the person who is to receive them, and read your electronic mail. As soon as you finish these regular duties, start a challenging task. Of course, there will be times when you use the first hour to complete unfinished work from the day before.

Some workers claim that they can perform best early in the day; others, in the afternoon; and still others claim that they concentrate best very late in the day. In fact, psychologists have confirmed that every person has his or her own preferred work cycle. If you consider yourself an afternoon performer, use your afternoon hours for your most creative and challenging work, but force yourself to make the first hour a brisk one. Workers who waste time getting started are putting themselves under unnecessary pressure to accomplish their work in what remains of the day. At any rate, do not use the beginning of the day to perform those easy tasks that can provide relaxation at intervals during the day.

Group Similar Tasks

You can save time and energy by not shifting from one task to another. For example, replenish your supplies once a week or less often. Avoid making a trip to the supply area every day. If supplies are delivered to you, fill out one requisition for all the supplies that you will need for several weeks.

Different work requires different degrees of concentration and, in turn, requires a different pace. Therefore, in order to control your pace, group together the tasks that require the same degree of concentration. Letters to grant appointments and to make routine requests are favorable in tone, usually short, and easy to write. Group these letters and compose them rapidly; then use a slower pace to compose a letter requiring a long explanation.

In addition, group tasks to increase effectiveness. For instance, making a telephone call should not be a routine task to be sandwiched between other work in an offhand way. A telephone call conveys an impression of the organization to the receiver. By grouping your telephone calls, you can give them your complete attention and project your personality in a thoughtful, businesslike manner.

Manage Details

Keep an ongoing list of the tasks you have grouped and add miscellaneous items by completing a daily **to-do list**. This list must be updated daily, preferably at the end of the day. To keep your to-do list current, use Microsoft Word, WordPad, NotePad, or one of the integrated software programs, such as Microsoft Outlook or Lotus Organizer. If you prefer, write your to-do list in a notebook or on a form.

Form 3-D, at the end of the book shows a sample format for a to-do list. Numbering priorities according to the 1, 2, and 3 categories mentioned earlier will help you to constantly update and reassess your list.

You, like every other office professional, will be faced with the problem of keeping up with myriad details. In fact, you will be forced to devise methods for managing them. Not only must you record these details immediately but you also must put them in a form that will enable you to locate and use them later.

To capture details, use notebooks or forms. Use a separate notebook or form to record telephone dialogue or voice mail messages and subsequent action or conversations. Use another notebook or to-do list form to record reminders to yourself of action you must take, as mentioned earlier (see Figure 3-2).

The computer may also manage details and reminders. Forms and simple templates are readily available in most word processing applications enabling office professionals to store the recorded detail in electronic format. The advantage of electronic format is that the detail is easily changed or modified, and that its distribution to other staff is simple.

To decrease the time you spend recording certain kinds of information, design a form in which you key and duplicate the constant information and

GANTT CHART

Name of project: Keying analysis   Name of team leader: Ilka Stiles

ESSENTIAL TASKS		\n CRITICAL DATES													
		May 01	May 03	May 05	May 07	May 09	May 11	May 13	May 15	May 17	May 19	May 21	May 23	May 25	
1. Design a questionnaire to examine the keying equipment used in offices.	S	▓													
	A														
2. Make appointments with admin. assistants to collect answers for questionnaires.	S		▓	▓											
	A														
3. Prepare and mail confirmation letters with attached questionnaires to admin. assistants.	S				▓										
	A														
4. Interview admin. assistants to collect info. and questionnaires.	S							▓	▓						
	A														
5. Send each admin. assistant a thank-you letter for his/her contribution.	S								▓						
	A														
6. Collate, calculate, and analyze the results of the questionnaires.	S								▓	▓					
	A														
7. Prepare graphs to indicate results of information collected on questionnaires.	S										▓				
	A														
8. Compose and edit report to describe the finding of the data.	S											▓	▓		
	A														
9. Key, assemble, and bind report.	S												▓		
	A														
10. Submit report to general manager.	S													▓	
	A														
	S														
	A														

S = Scheduled time   A = Actual time

■ Figure 3-2
Gantt chart.

leave space to write in the variable information. Forms bring related information together in one place and prompt the user to record all the essential facts. The Daily Mail Record and other mail records that you will learn about in Chapter 6 are examples of forms you can create.

Recording facts as soon as they become available to you is an important aspect of capturing details. You will discover that the practice of "do it now" is in conflict with the concept of grouping tasks to save time and energy; nevertheless, you need to capture details at the precise moment they arise in order to keep up with them.

Actually, the means you devise for keeping up with details can vary from task to task according to the work involved and your personal preferences. That being said, recognize in all your work:

■ The importance of having some method for capturing details.

■ The need to be consistent in following your method.

You can use check marks, initials, codes, and symbols to indicate the status of each detail that you want to capture. For instance,

■ The date stamp you place on a piece of incoming mail will tell you that you have already seen it.

■ The check mark by the enclosure notation on the file copy of a letter will remind you that you did include the enclosure.

■ The electronic date and time stamp attached to a computer file will indicate when the file was last updated.

In addition, if you are consistent in using each type of notation to convey its respective meaning, the absence of an appropriate notation will alert you to give attention to that particular item.

When you encounter a new task, spend a little time deciding how you are going to keep up with the details and then be consistent in doing so.

Details arranged in the chronological order in which they were originally recorded usually are not in their most usable form. Details must be arranged so that they can be located quickly. The organization can range from indexing on cards to computer information search tools.

Organizing the details you need to keep—such as the names of new contacts, telephone numbers, changes of address, and schedule changes—can be done with great efficiency with a computer because you need to record it only once. Not everything you write down needs to be transferred; this is especially true of reminders of things to do or other temporary items. Cross out the reminders as you complete the tasks, but go over your list carefully and transfer the reminders of tasks yet to be done to your to-do list for the following day. You may also want to transcribe detailed instructions that you have in your notebook and place them in your office manual.

Some office professionals are giving up traditional personal organizer notebooks, in favor of a palm-sized personal digital assistant, such as a Palm Pilot. The personal digital assistants (PDAs) retain the essential phone book, calendar, memo pad, and to-do lists. The wireless models enable you to read the airline schedules without having to plug into a telephone. In addition, you can send and receive electronic mail. Having a computer backup of your calendar, action list, and names and telephone numbers is a lifesaver. If you lose or misplace your traditional personal organizer notebook, you've lost it all.

Avoid Procrastination

Procrastination is an unproductive behavior pattern that causes you to delay working on your most important assignments and to focus on tasks that aren't priorities. We all procrastinate to some degree at certain times; but to some people it is a habit. To break the habit of procrastination, you must first gain an understanding of your behavior and then work to overcome it. You can gain a better understanding of this behavior by:

1. Admitting that you are procrastinating.
2. Asking yourself what types of projects cause you to procrastinate. Some office workers might see a major project as a horrendous task, whereas others might find daily routine tasks too much to face.
3. Asking yourself why you avoid these projects or tasks. Are you bored with the routine or afraid of the challenge? Are you avoiding interaction with certain office workers or authority figures? Do you fear failing at greater responsibility?

After answering these questions, you will be better prepared to overcome this unproductive behavior. The following tips will help you avoid procrastination and become more productive.

1. Ask yourself what is the worst thing that can happen while you perform this task. Once you think it through, you will find that the risk created

by the project is not that great; in fact, the benefits of completing the project will far outweigh the difficulties.

2. If the project is large, divide it into smaller sections. Several small tasks always appear to be easier to accomplish than one large task. For more suggestions, refer to the "Manage a Large Project" section presented later in this chapter.

3. Reward yourself often. Allow yourself a break or a more pleasant task once you have completed a portion of the work. Small and frequent rewards work better for procrastinators than one large reward after completion of a very strenuous task.

4. Ask yourself what is the downside of not completing the task on time—or worse, not completing the task at all. Does not doing the project mean the loss of your job, a demotion, or the loss of respect from your peers and managers?

5. If you are a perfectionist, you may be avoiding a simple task because of your working style. Remember that not all work must be flawless. Working *smarter,* instead of *harder,* means recognizing the difference between work that must be perfect and work that can contain minor flaws, and acting on it.

Work at One Task at a Time

Schedule your work so that you can keep at one task until you finish it or until you come to a logical stopping place, such as a new subheading. If a stopping place does not exist, try to work at one task for two hours or, at the very least, one hour. Jumping from one task to another is confusing. Furthermore, reviewing work to figure out where to begin and recalling what has and has not been done results in wasted time and energy. You will be rewarded threefold when you stay with a task until it is completed.

- You will be motivated by the satisfaction of having finished the task.
- You will save time you otherwise would lose locating where you left off.
- You will decrease the risk of forgetting to perform a part of the task.

As you work, thoughts about other tasks will flash across your mind. Write down each usable thought on your to-do list and continue to concentrate on the work at hand. Learn how to handle interruptions and shift back quickly to the immediate task; coping with interruptions is discussed in the next section of this chapter.

Form the habit of working at an uncluttered desk. On the immediate work area of your desk, place only the materials you need for the task on which you are working. Because you can give attention to only one main task at a time, put the other work aside, carefully organized and labeled. Stacking work on top of work in a disorganized way leads to confusion; it is how papers get lost and nerves become frayed. The time you spend organizing work in progress will not be wasted. When you put aside everything except the task on which you are working, you will feel more relaxed and be able to focus upon it.

You will be double rewarded when you stay with a task until it is complete:

- You will feel satisfaction having finished the task.
- You will experience the emotion of accomplishment.

Cope with Interruptions

Every challenging office job that demands a variety of duties will be punctuated by interruptions. The following ways will help you avoid some interruptions:

1. Practice avoidance by organizing your work area so that it is less accessible to coworkers who wish to socialize during work hours. Try moving extra chairs away from your desk, or moving or angling your desk so that it cannot easily be seen by passers-by.

2. Interruptions are often caused by noise. You can avoid this type of interruption by having noisy equipment relocated away from your desk.

3. When you are working on a project that requires your full attention, ask another worker to handle your telephone calls; explain the urgency of your task to coworkers and then move to a location away from your desk.

Your success in coping with interruptions will depend on your attitude toward them and your ability to handle them. You know that interruptions will occur—the telephone will ring, a caller will walk in, a coworker will ask you a question, your manager will need assistance. What you do not know is the precise moment when the interruption will occur.

Recognize that interruptions are part of the job, and allow time for them in your planning. Keep a record of the number of telephone calls you receive in a typical day, the number of callers you receive, and the number of times you assist your manager and coworkers. Estimate the time consumed by these interruptions and determine how much time you have left for other tasks. Do not create your own frustrations by planning to accomplish more than you can get done.

Do not resent interruptions. Keep calm; do not allow yourself to become upset. You will feel less frustrated if you know how much time you will need to perform each of your normal tasks. For example, keep a record of how long it takes to key a 2-page letter, to compose a 1-page memo, to develop a 12-page formal report, and to process the daily mail. This is useful information for future planning and scheduling. If you discover that you are running out of time to meet a deadline, decide for yourself which work can be postponed. Use your time for the priority items.

Give adequate time to handling each interruption. Do not appear to be rushed. Be courteous, but do not waste time because of an interruption. To reduce the time used for each interruption, proceed in the following ways:

1. Mark your place as soon as you are interrupted—a light, erasable check mark in the margin with a soft-lead pencil will suffice.

2. Once you are interrupted, handle the interruption immediately if it can be dealt with in only a few minutes. If a coworker asks for information, look it up and supply the information while the coworker is at your desk. In response to a telephone call you can handle, follow through on the caller's request, even looking up information if you can do so without keeping the caller waiting a noticeable length of time. However, if the interruption requires prolonged attention, you may have to postpone action on it. Realize, however, that each time you must postpone following through on a request, you are creating a new item for your to-do list.

3. Quickly resume work where you left off at the time of the interruption. Do not encourage coworkers to linger in your office. Be courteous, but do not continue a telephone conversation beyond the time actually necessary to handle the call.

4. Avoid interrupting yourself because of lack of planning.

5. Keep a pencil in your hand, or keep your hands on the keyboard. These actions inform the visitor that you are eager to continue your work.

6. Do not get involved in office gossip. Small talk creates big interruptions.

7. When a coworker drops into your office for a visit, stay standing. Often a person feels invited to sit if you are sitting. If the coworker sits down and you feel the need to sit, do so on the edge of your desk. This does not invite the coworker to become too comfortable.

8. When possible, hold meetings in another person's office. This allows you to leave as soon as the business is complete. Meeting with visitors in reception areas or conference rooms helps to keep the meeting short because these areas often do not provide the privacy of an office.

Get It Right the First Time

To produce acceptable work on the first try, plan each task before you begin, focus on the exactness of the details as you perform, and then check each finished task for correctness and completeness before you release it.

Remember that waste results when work that could have been completed correctly on the first try must be redone.

Before you start performing a task, make sure you understand the instructions; then review the facts, visualize the work in its finished form, and make a plan.

The speed with which business information flows, especially with the advent of computer networks, has placed a premium on accuracy. An error that has been released is difficult to retrieve. Problems created by errors that are released into the channels of information are not only time consuming to cor-

When You Must Interrupt Others, Be Considerate

- Wait until the other person is at a break in his or her work.
- Direct your questions to the correct person, and do not interrupt others unnecessarily.
- Do not ask others to answer questions to which you can find the answers by looking them up.
- Accumulate the questions you must ask your manager; then ask several at one time to cut down on interrupting her or him.
- Write a concise memo or electronic message enumerating your questions. This is an excellent way to avoid a direct interruption and to obtain a quick response.

How to Check Your Work

1. Edit the copy for meaning. At the same time, watch for typographical, spelling, and punctuation errors. Do this while the copy is still on the screen so that making corrections will be easy.

2. Go over the copy a second time, scanning it for figures such as dates and amounts of money. Then check their accuracy.

3. Use a calculator to check a long list of keyed figures that have been totaled.

4. When a long series appears in a paragraph, count the items and compare the number with the list in the original. Also count the items included in a tabulation.

5. When you are copying from keyed material that you must follow line by line for proofreading, use a rule to keep your place if you do not have a copyholder with a line finder.

6. Always proofread the two-letter state abbreviations and the postal codes in addresses. One wrong stroke at the keyboard, if not caught, can mean a delayed letter or important contract.

rect but can also result in losses to the organization. So check your work carefully. Refer to the guidelines shown in the box that should be observed for checking printed work.

Build Relaxation into Your Schedule

Most organizations provide a lunch hour and short morning and afternoon breaks during a regular workday. With these exceptions, employees are expected to perform efficiently through the day.

To maintain your best performance throughout the day and the week, experiment with alternating difficult and easy tasks to establish the best combination for conserving your energy. Observe which tasks consume a great deal of energy and which ones seem to require little energy. Rotate tasks that require more concentration and effort with tasks that require less thought and energy. Whether a task is difficult or easy for you to perform will depend on your ability, your experience in performing the given task, and your attitude toward it.

Performing an undesirable task requires an extra expenditure of energy. Repetitive tasks are often disliked because of their repetitious nature rather than for the work itself. Fortunately, the computer and its various peripherals have introduced new and interesting methods of accomplishing routine tasks.

Once you discover which tasks are easy for you, save them to perform between difficult tasks. Use them to provide relaxation as you work. Start your day with a difficult task and work at a vigorous pace. Keep at one task for at least two hours or until you reach a stopping place. Throughout the day, alternate difficult tasks with easy ones. When possible, also alternate sitting with standing tasks. When you cannot change the task, change your pace. After lunch and after your morning and afternoon breaks, tackle difficult tasks.

When you are estimating the time needed for performing a long, complicated task, allow for a decrease in production as you continue working. You cannot expect to perform at your maximum rate for six or seven hours. Your productivity will be highest when you can keep fatigue to a minimum. Discover and maintain a pace that will make it possible for you to do your best work.

Because of the pressure of work, you may forgo your morning or afternoon break and shorten your lunch hour. You will stick to the difficult task and postpone other work. You may be asked to work overtime, and others in the office may be asked to assist you. You may feel that you have no control over your work schedule. When you face these situations, evaluate your working plan.

Make a Daily Plan

Many management consultants agree that if you use the last ten to twenty minutes of your day to get organized, you will notice there is far less clutter after a week or so. This activity can help you wind down at the end of a hectic day and ease your transition from work to home.

At the end of the day, review the work you must do the following day. Estimate the time each of your tasks will take and fit them one by one into time slots. Go through the same steps daily, and then leave your office with the satisfaction of knowing that your work is well organized for the following day. To prepare a systematic daily plan, you could proceed as follows:

1. Verify that everything you have entered into the computer during the day that should be saved has been backed up.

2. If you use an electronic calendar or desk calendar pads, make sure that the appointment entries in your manager's calendar and yours are identical.

3. Go over your to-do list. If something on the list must be carried out the following day, enter it in your daily calendar. As you are planning your work, you will think of tasks that must be done sometime later. Put notes about these on your to-do list.

4. Locate the reports, correspondence, and other items to which you know your manager will need to refer during meetings, conferences, or before he or she places a telephone call, writes a report, or carries out other responsibilities. Flag these with colored stickers so that you can retrieve them quickly the following day. Likewise, locate the information you will need in order to precede with your own work. Also make computer printouts of information you and your manager will need.

5. Complete your paper filing and lock the files. As a part of your filing routine, transfer copies of completed work and the related data from your work-in-progress folder to the file. All papers should be stored in cabinets, for protection from fire or perusal.

6. Clear your desk, putting everything in place.

The next morning, review the entries in your daily appointment calendar. By using the system described above, you will be well prepared to start your work immediately. You will enjoy the satisfaction of having a plan for your tasks and priorities.

How to Balance Your Workload

1. Establish the duration of peak workload, how often it will occur, and what you can do about it, if anything.

2. Determine what preparation you can make in advance to lessen the peak workload. To avoid crises and to prepare for the "peaks and valleys," set your own personal deadlines a few hours or days before others set deadlines for you.

3. If there is no let-up in the work, either you are not approaching your job in an efficient way or you need assistance. Discuss the situation with your manager and be prepared to offer viable solutions.

Prepare in Advance

With the exception of routine duties, office work requires planning. The amount of planning time needed depends on how complicated the job is, the length of it, and whether or not the person doing the work has ever performed similar tasks.

Executives in successful organizations plan three to five years in advance. Managers at all levels plan at least one year in advance. Observe how your manager and others in your organization think ahead, and then apply some of their techniques to your own assignments. The time you spend thinking through what needs to be done will save you minutes and hours of redoing work.

Take time to study a job until you can visualize it to its completion regardless of how complicated or lengthy it is. People who work aimlessly seldom reach the goals toward which they should have been working. If necessary, ask yourself and others what the expected outcome of the specific assignment is. Do not hesitate to ask about the purpose of an assignment. When an assignment is new to you, you may find it difficult, if not impossible, to visualize it to its completion. If necessary, ask your manager to guide you.

Don't let thoughts of complicated tasks and deadlines interfere with getting today's work completed. Do one job at a time. Schedule "thinking" time in the same way you schedule time for word processing. Start by writing down your thoughts at random. Organize them later. As you study the job, estimate the time needed to complete each part of it. Start with the completion date and work backward to the current date.

The most critical parts of an assignment are the ones that require other people—either to supply information or to actually perform certain tasks. Begin your preparation with the segments of the work that involve others.

Assume that you are compiling data for a report. Make a checklist of your needs. For instance, will you need special information or materials, such as the most recent figures from the accounting department, a comparative analysis from the data center, or pictures to be taken by the audiovisual department, charts that must be reduced in size by the printing department, or the public relations department's approval for the illustrations to be included in the report? Make each of these requests as soon as you are certain of your needs.

As you prepare an assignment in advance, plan it so carefully that you can put it aside and not think about it until you are ready to start it. This is important because thinking about an endless stream of work has a negative effect on performance. Label a folder for the assignment and put everything pertaining to it in that folder. Budget your time. Allow some time for delays. Keep careful notes on what you have and have not done. Once you actually start performing the assignment, make a daily check of the work completed against the projected time schedule.

Figure 3-2 illustrates a Gantt chart. This chart is an excellent tool for comparing your planned work schedule against the actual time that is required to complete a task.

Manage a Large Project

When you start a large project, you will need to allocate some time each day for planning and controlling. The following suggestions should help you manage a large project.

1. Determine what the desired goal is. Know exactly what you are to accomplish. Being unsure about the goal is a real time waster.
2. Write down the target date.
3. Divide the project into manageable segments and then, as far as it is possible to do so, work with one segment at a time.
4. Set completion dates for each segment; as you progress, check the dates to ensure that you are on schedule.
5. Check out all the supplies you will need; have a few extras on hand of those that are quickly used.
6. Locate the equipment you will need to complete the project.
7. Delegate some of your regular duties to make time for working on the project.
8. If you will need the services of others, either within or outside the organization, contact them at the planning stage of the project to find out about scheduling. Determine what you will have to do to meet their schedules.
9. Determine what data you will need, how to obtain it, and when.
10. As soon as you begin the project, make copious notes in a large bound notebook.
11. Divide the notebook into segments, matching the segments of the project.
12. As you plan for each segment or part of a segment, list everything that must be done. Keep adding to your list at random.
13. As you complete each item, mark a line through it. Circle in a different color the items still to be done. Do this very carefully because the most helpful part of your notes will be the notations about unfinished items.
14. When you have completed an entire segment, write "Completed" at the top of the corresponding page in your notebook.
15. When you make a change, be sure to make it everywhere the change occurs.

16. Separate the in-progress segments so that you can add to them or reorganize them with ease.

17. Carefully recheck all the circled items to be sure that nothing has been left undone.

Creating a detailed project plan and keeping it up-to-date for most nontrivial projects can be a very time-consuming process if completed manually. Today, thanks to the use of the computer, there are solutions that enable everyone to benefit from using project management methods. There are easy-to-use project management programs such as Microsoft Project that anyone can master in a few hours.

OFFICE ORGANIZATION

By organizing office supplies and the workstation, an office professional can save a great deal of time, as well as save the company money. Following are suggestions for getting the office supplies and workstation organized.

Organize the Office Supplies

1. Label the shelves where supplies are kept. This way other workers who use the supplies will know where to look without interrupting you. This procedure also helps you keep track of supplies on hand.

2. Make sure that one person is responsible for controlling inventory and ordering supplies. This is a task that you or a senior office professional will often delegate.

3. Develop your own requisition form, if necessary. Keep these forms in the supply area. Staff will be expected to complete the form if they notice a product is running low. Be sure the form has room for a full description. Encourage the staff to fill in as much information as possible (descriptions, quantities, colors, sizes, and so on). This will simplify your work when it comes to completing the requisition for ordering.

4. Compose a list of all items you use on a regular basis. Include the item unit numbers, unit prices, descriptions, colors available, and so on. Post this list in the supply area along with a stack of the requisition forms you have developed. This is necessary if you expect staff members to partially complete the requisition forms.

5. Discourage staff members from placing verbal orders with you. This type of interruption can be very time consuming: you must stop your work, listen to the request, write down the information, check the supplies, and perhaps get back to the staff members for further clarification. Insist that all orders be completed on requisition forms.

6. When staff members have rush orders, request that they fill in a requisition, mark it "Rush," and bring it to your desk.

7. Take inventory on a regular basis. Taking inventory once or twice a month on a designated day works well for most offices.

8. Before placing an order, compare prices between the office supply catalogs and advertisements sent to you. Be sure you know your company's

procedures for placing orders. If designated procedures are to be followed, do so with accuracy as you will save time and money by getting the order right the first time.

9. Do not overorder supplies, unless you are ordering supplies in standard-sized packages. Too many supplies will cause confusion. Because space is often at a premium, excess supplies tend to create a storage problem. As well, some supplies have a shelf life: if not used before a certain date, they become less useful.

10. When you place an order, be prepared with all the required information. Having requisition forms returned or needing to make a follow-up telephone call to clarify an order will delay delivery.

Organize the Workstation

A cluttered desk gives clients, coworkers, and managers the impression that you are disorganized. A cluttered desk is not necessarily a sign that you are busy; in fact, a cluttered desk simply adds to your workload. It is essential that you purge any extraneous materials and then organize the materials you intend to keep.

Place Work Within Easy Reach. An unorganized desk area accounts for one of the greatest time wasters in the office. Normal and maximum working areas at a desk have been established through time and motion studies. Materials and supplies should be positioned within the normal working area if the worker is to attain maximum efficiency. You can determine the normal working area of the desk for either the right or left hand by swinging the extended hand and forearm across the desk.

Before you begin a task at a desk or a table, place the supplies, tools, and equipment you will need in the normal working area. Use the space in your desk to store supplies, stationery, and work-in-progress. Materials should pass across the top of your desk but should not be stored on it. Keep a minimum number of items on top of your desk.

File all your work-in-progress in one drawer unless your manager is working on a project that generates so much paperwork that the materials have to be subdivided into several folders. Allocate separate space in a vertical file drawer for a project of this magnitude. Never put a single folder of pending material in an unusual place—relocation of this material can lead to confusion and wasted time.

In case you might be absent, let your manager know where you keep important project folders and other work in progress. If the work-in-progress is highly confidential, you may have to store it in file cabinets with special locks at night.

If you have a drawer that is not deep enough to hold file folders in a vertical position, keep it empty. Use it as temporary storage when you want to clear your desk to store the papers on which you are currently working—for instance, while you sort the mail or go to lunch.

Do not use sections of your desk for permanent storage. File completed items immediately after completing a task so that you will not be searching in two places to locate one item. Furthermore, you will need the desk space to store the data for the new project or assignment.

Purge Unnecessary Items. One of the first steps to take in organizing your desk is to eliminate all that you don't need. Each time you pick up a document from your desk and wonder where to file it, ask yourself whether there's a law that says you must keep it. If not, consider the recycling box or the garbage bin.

If any of the following applies to a document, you have just cause to purge yourself of paper:

1. Another coworker has filed it where you can access it if needed.
2. The document is duplication. Once you get organized, one copy is all you need of any document.
3. The document is out-of-date. Newer information is usually better information. You can always get current information from the Internet, or from the reference section of the library.
4. Chances are you will never find the time to read the information. If the information is "nice to know" rather than essential, rid yourself of it until you are organized.

You will find that you work much more efficiently after you have organized your desk.

Organize Necessary Items. Ridding your workstation of excess paper is only the first step in getting organized. The importance of a highly organized workstation cannot be emphasized enough.

One of the most frustrating time wasters is searching for information that has been filed incorrectly or has simply disappeared. Of course, employing the correct Association of Records Managers and Administrators (ARMA) filing rules is imperative; these rules are discussed in Chapter 7. However, there is much more to organizing your workstation. When your workstation is organized, you save valuable time.

The following suggestions will help you get started:

1. Consider how and where you want incoming work to be placed. Place all the new mail and paperwork that arrive during the day in the IN box. Once you have processed everything, invariably there are papers and pieces of mail that need to go out; place these in the OUT box. IN and OUT boxes should be clearly labeled and should be either wood or wire because these boxes are the roomiest.
2. If your workstation is currently in a cluttered condition, plan several uninterrupted hours you can use to attack the problem.
3. Once you have organized the workstation, take a mental snapshot of it and vow that you will never leave it disorganized at the end of the day. Start the day with a clear mind and a clear desk. Many offices now practice a clean desk policy, which stipulates that each evening employees must leave their desks in either a totally clear or very tidy condition.
4. If your office does not have a paper shredder, approach your manager about purchasing one. Employees are often reluctant to discard confidential material, so they let it accumulate in what eventually becomes a very thick folder tucked into a corner of the desk. Compact shredders can be placed on top of wastebaskets.

5. A basket placed in your workstation to hold work that is pending often becomes a storage bin. If you do not intend to work on a document immediately, file it in its appropriately labeled folder. Then place the folder in the file cabinet and make a comment in your calendar on the day this document must be dealt with. This way the phrase "out of sight—out of mind" will not apply.

6. Use one calendar for all your appointments. Referring to several calendars—personal and business—is a waste of time and will result in disorganization.

7. Wherever you store information—drawers, cabinets, folders, baskets, and so on—affix a label that describes the type of information that should be stored in this location. While you are getting organized you will have stacks of paper. Organize them by placing a temporary label on the top of the pile. Not only will the labels assist you in locating information but they will also assist others in your absence.

8. Attempt to follow this rule: *Never handle a piece of paper more than once.* At times this rule may be unrealistic, but it will force you to make a decision rather than procrastinate, then rehandle and reread a document.

9. Never use the surface of your desk as storage space. Your desk is a work area; you need all of it available to remain organized while you conduct your work.

10. Keep your computer reference information current. If names, addresses, and telephone numbers are indexed on your computer system, consider it a priority to update the system as often as possible. You cannot enjoy the efficiency of using a computer system unless it provides correct information.

11. Create a reference for frequently called telephone or fax numbers. Place this reference list nearby or code the numbers into the memory of the telephone or fax machine.

12. Place reference books at an arm's length from your work area. These references should include a dictionary, a thesaurus, an office reference manual, office manual, telephone directories, and the like. When you need these books, you need them *now*; you should never have to look for any of them.

13. Do you really know what is in your desk and cabinets? Schedule fifteen to thirty minutes every month to purge your current bookshelves, desk drawers, and cabinets. You must keep current with the contents of your workstation. Keep the wastebasket and recycling box handy; you should constantly purge your workstation of unwanted materials.

14. If there is a bulletin board in your workstation, be sure the information is current and well organized. If the bulletin board is not easy to use, it is just occupying space and adding to the office clutter. A bulletin board is sometimes an invitation to clutter; if not in use, you may consider removing the bulletin board.

15. After you take a telephone message, place the message in a designated location, off your desk. In this way, you have dismissed the task immediately. You are then free to continue with your other tasks, and your desk is less cluttered.

16. Use colored paper to coordinate your tasks. This will assist you in locating categories of information. Colored paper draws attention. For ex-

ample, you will be able to quickly spot blue telephone messages or green memos in a pile of white documents. Not only will the colored paper help you get organized but it will also draw the attention of others to requests for action or information that you place on their desks. Try using fluorescent-colored paper when you want your paper interoffice requests to get immediate attention.

17. Your workstation will require drawer space for office supplies. Store only a limited supply at your desk; store larger amounts away from your workstation in a supply area or cabinet. The small supplies you keep at your desk such as a stapler, tape, pens, clips, and the like can be stored with drawer organizers. Letterhead, envelopes, forms, and other major paper supplies should be placed in drawer trays, not left out in visible stacks.

18. Your personal items need a place too, but do not crowd your desk surface with family photos. Leave the desk surface as clear as possible and place the photos on top of your credenza or filing cabinet. Keep personal items to a minimum. The workstation is professional space, not personal space.

Use Follow-Up Organizers. Follow-up organizers aid office professionals in remembering details and meeting deadlines. In addition to the daily appointment calendar, which you will study in Chapter 9, and the to-do list, office professionals must have a foolproof method of following up on work that will be pending for a week, a month, or longer. The tickler file, which provides reminders according to dates, is the most widely used. A pending file can be used for actual documents-in-progress to be processed by specific dates.

Tickler File. Folders can be used to organize a tickler file, depending on the work to be followed up. A **tickler file** is a paper time-management system that can be used for reminders of (1) work to be done at a specified time, and (2) incoming information that is anticipated at a specified time. A tickler file set, available at office suppliers, consists of twelve folders with the names of the months printed on the tabs and thirty-one folders with 1 through 31 printed on the tabs to indicate the days of the month. To set up a tickler folder file, place the folders for days of the month, followed by the guides for the months as shown in Figure 3-3.

Do not put original correspondence in the follow-up folders. Make a copy of the original or prepare a memo referring to it for the tickler file; note the location of the original paper on the memo. When you put memos in the folder, use either $8\frac{1}{2} \times 11$-inch sheets of paper or staple small notes to a large sheet. All your notations for the tickler file do not have to be printed. If you recorded the information in longhand as instructions were given or a request was made, you may file these notes as a reminder.

Place a reminder in the file for the date you must begin a task, not the date you must complete it. Follow the same plan concerning reminders for your manager. For instance, if you estimate that it will take you three days to type a periodic report due on Friday, June 30, file the reminder for it after the June 27 guide.

A tickler file cannot jog your memory unless you use it. Each morning, without fail, remove the reminders for the day from the tickler file. Place that folder at the end of the numbered folders. As a result, the current folder will always be at the front of the file.

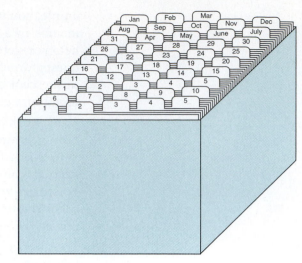

■ **Figure 3-3**
Tickler folder file.

The reminders will fall into three categories:

1. Those that have already been taken care of
2. Reminders of work you must carry out that day
3. Items that must be postponed.

Discard any copies or notes pertaining to items completed. Return to the file an item that is still pending. For instance, if you received an acknowledgment saying that a catalog you requested will be sent as soon as the new catalog is reprinted, probably within two weeks, put the reminder back in the file at a date approximately two weeks later.

Near the end of each week as you are planning your work for the following week, review the reminders in the tickler file for the entire week. Estimate the time you will need to complete each task. Remember to coordinate the items to be completed in your tickler file with your action list.

On the first day of each month, arrange any reminders for the current month by dates. For example, on the first day of April remove the papers in the April folder and sort and file them by date into the numbered files. Place the folder labeled *April* behind the March folder. As you transfer the items from the month file to the daily files, turn folders representing dates for Saturdays and Sundays backward, and then you will be less likely to inadvertently file a reminder in a folder with a weekend date.

You can accomplish the same thing as a tickler file by adding notes to your calendar. However, if you have bits of notes posted to your computer monitor or on the wall in your work area, you can eliminate these notes by placing them in the tickler folders.

Pending File. A **pending file** supports your regular calendars and holds the actual documents to be completed by specific dates. You should check the pending file regularly to be sure nothing has been overlooked. A pending file is a booklet, made of sturdy card stock, and has dividers labeled 1 through 31.

LEARN TO COPE WITH STRESS

Jobs can be stressful, yet some people seem to thrive on stress whereas others crumble under the strain. The difference is that those who cope with stress best have control of their jobs and themselves. They are meeting deadlines, but they are setting their own deadlines to the extent that it is possible to do so and working at their own pace. Furthermore, they have a positive attitude toward their work.

A person who has a lot of responsibility outside his or her job often suffers from stress because he or she is trying to do too much—accepting responsibility for family and home, volunteering for community work, going to school, and so on.

To cope with stress, analyze what is happening to you. Frequently, it is not the situation that causes stress but how you react to it and what you do about it. Also, the longer the duration of the problem the more likely it is to produce stress.

A certain amount of stress helps us to be alert, efficient, and creative, but it is important to learn to cope with stress before it becomes too great.

How to Cope with Stress

✔ Recognize that anger and frustration are energy wasters. Handle conflicts calmly, as they occur, rather than letting things build up.

✔ Organize your work and your time for the entire day. Prioritize your duties. Do not plan more than it is possible to do in a day.

✔ Analyze an overload of work and discuss it with your supervisor. Offer solutions. You will relieve stress when you face a situation rather than allow yourself to be overwhelmed by it.

✔ Do not be overly critical of your work and yourself; do not expect too much of others. Strive for excellence—not perfection—but at times be pleased with an acceptable performance.

✔ Slow down! Work at a comfortable pace that will enable you to keep mistakes to a minimum, to relate well with others, and to avoid backtracking and revising.

✔ Avoid taking on too much. Learn to say "no," but say it tactfully.

✔ Talk out your stressful problems. Find someone in whom you can confide—someone away from the company, someone who is an effective listener.

✔ Eat nourishing food regularly and in moderate amounts.

✔ Program relaxation into your schedule. During a break on the job, be quiet and practice relaxing techniques. Allow yourself a quiet hour at home. Schedule some time for a hobby.

✔ Get regular exercise of the right kind for you.

✔ Escape to a movie, to your favorite TV program to spend time with others, or do something for someone in need. Escaping from your daily problems will give you fresh energy to cope with them.

ETHICS IN THE OFFICE

Ethical concepts have a far-reaching effect on contemporary business offices. The ethical office is, of course, an extension of the ethical organization: an organization that acts with integrity and lives up to its responsibilities and obligations. It encourages employees to assume their responsibilities by authorizing and entrusting people to complete their job or task ethically and to the best of their ability.

It's with this level of trust that our ethical responsibilities need to be reviewed. If you find yourself considering any of the following, recognize that your organization's policies and trust are likely to be compromised.

With Regard to Work

- Practicing **plagiarism**, using the words or ideas of someone else as your own without permission or reference to the original source
- Harassing coworkers
- "Padding" your resume
- Making false claims of illness
- Spreading untrue information
- Overstating expense claims or required resources
- Endangering others with unreasonable conduct or deception
- Providing negative public statements about the organization

With Regard to Time

- Going home early—always
- Taking extended lunch breaks
- Taking frequent smoking breaks
- Getting to work late—consistently
- Gossiping (for too long) in the office
- Taking personal telephone calls—consistently
- Talking too long on personal telephone calls

With Regard to Resources

- Exaggerating expense claims
- Exaggerating accomplishments
- Playing games on your computer
- Conducting personal research on the Internet
- Exaggerating time devoted to a task or project
- Taking paper, paper clips, binders, stamps, and other supplies from the office

Consider your corporation's code of ethics as well as your own standards. Ask yourself if you would feel comfortable if the results of your decision or action were to be published on the front page of a national newspaper or discussed on local television tomorrow. You'll know the difference between right and wrong!

ENVIRONMENTAL OFFICE

If your office has not yet committed itself to becoming environmentally conscious, you should initiate this change. Here are some suggestions:

1. When you must discard paper, ask yourself if the paper can be recycled. Special paper baskets, boxes, trays, and bins for the collection of recyclable paper should be set around the office in convenient locations.

2. Fax cover sheets are often a waste of paper; they almost always end up in the wastebasket. Temporary adhesive fax-transmittal labels will often suffice. These small adhesive notes can be adhered to the first page of the fax and are adequate when a lot of cover information is not necessary. The adhesive notes can be purchased in office supply stores.

3. Ask the office staff to contribute additional ideas about resource management that might pertain to your office. Continue to explore options.

HOW IS TIME UNDERSTOOD BY DIFFERENT CULTURES?

The essence of time management is organizing and sequencing tasks—a notion that seems unusual to other cultures. Suppose you were a simultaneous-task worker (from the home office in Venezuela), and a new employee from Canada, who has a sequential-task orientation, came by your cubicle for her 2 p.m. appointment. She arrived on time and as you began to help her you also handled a telephone call, answered a coworker's question, and sent a fax to someone else. Do you think the new employee would think that you were efficient or perhaps a little disorganized?

Everyone has his or her personal style and preference for getting work done; that is, within a sequential-task culture, people know at the start of the day what they will do during segments of the day: morning, lunch, afternoon, and evening. When unexpected tasks arise, others that had been scheduled are rescheduled. These people are interested in performing their tasks or activities.

In contrast, although the simultaneous-task worker knows in general what the tasks in a given day will be—the day has a fluidity that allows for more and less important tasks that take more or less time—and the worker assumes many tasks will be handled simultaneously. Simultaneity is extremely useful when people and the relationships between people are valued highly; you can spend all the time you want or need with a person when at the same time you are giving some attention to other (valued) persons. In other words, these people are interested in achieving their results through relationships.

From your point of view, you feel you are efficient because in effect you are accomplishing several other tasks besides dealing with the visitor. From your visitor's point of view, however, he or she feels the unfocused activity is not nearly as efficient as it could be. In other words, the visitor believes that if you were to work exclusively with her during the appointed time, the time spent would have been much more efficient.

Learn to understand other cultures' personal styles and preferences for getting work done by discussing these issues with people who are members of the culture you want to understand.

Lack of Communication or Misunderstood Instructions Can Cause a Waste of Time

- ■ If you receive e-mail instructing you to do something:
  - ■ Print the message and keep it as a reference while you work.
- ■ If you are verbally given information:
  - ■ As soon as you can, return to your office and read through your notes.
  - ■ Send e-mail to the requesting person and list what you understood the task to entail.
    - ■ If there is a problem, it is resolved quickly before you waste a lot of time.

Overview

✔ Total Quality is a management approach that recognizes the customer (both internal and external) as the judge of the quality of your company's products or services. It's an all-out commitment requiring companies to eliminate wasteful practices, redesign business methods, and adopt a focused approach to managing quality. Total Quality Management is practiced through four basic principles:

1. Customer focus
2. Continuous improvement and learning
3. Strategic planning and leadership
4. Teamwork.

✔ Effectiveness and efficiency, although interrelated, are distinct concepts. Effectiveness means producing a definite or desired result, whereas efficiency means producing the desired result with a minimum of effort, expense, and waste.

✔ Time management involves

1. Developing work habits that result in maximum efficiency
2. Acquiring knowledge and skills to extend performance beyond present capabilities
3. Controlling attitudes and emotions that have a tendency to steal time
4. Developing an effective reminder method for following through on each task at the appropriate time.

✔ Effective work habits include

1. Learn the job
2. Assign priorities
3. Adopt a flexible plan
4. Start the day with a difficult task

5. Group similar tasks
6. Avoid procrastination
7. Work at one task at a time
8. Cope with interruptions
9. Get it right the first time
10. Build relaxation into your schedule
11. Make a daily plan
12. Prepare in advance
13. Manage a large project

✔ Organize your office supplies; it will save time as well as money. Be sure that someone is responsible for controlling inventory and ordering supplies. If you are responsible for ordering supplies, discourage staff members from placing verbal orders with you. This interruption can be time consuming; help others to follow through with ordering supplies by completing requisition forms.

✔ Organize your workstation; an unorganized desk area accounts for one of the greatest time wasters in the office. Designate necessary items to be placed on top of your desk and location for projects-in-progress.

✔ Assume responsibilities for ethics in the office. Recognize that your organization's policies and trust are likely to be compromised with regard to work, time, and resources.

✔ Become part of an environmentally conscious office. If a recycle program hasn't been created, designate locations for collection of recyclable paper; use adhesive fax-transmittal labels; and explore options to contribute ideas about resource management with the office staff.

Key Terms

Brainstorming. Allows employees the freedom of open suggestion without criticism.

Effectiveness. Produce a definite or desired result.

Efficiency. Produce the desired result with a minimum of effort, expense, and waste.

Flextime. A type of schedule designed for employees to work a set number of hours each day but vary the starting and ending times.

Pending file. Used for actual documents-in-progress to be processed by specific dates.

Plagiarism. Use of words and ideas of someone else as your own without permission or reference to the original source.

Procrastination. An unproductive behavior pattern that causes you to delay working on your most important assignments and to focus on tasks that aren't priorities.

Tickler file. Can be used for reminders of (1) work to be done at a specified time, and (2) incoming information that is anticipated at a specified time.

Time distribution chart. A chart showing the distribution of time and duties performed by one worker.

Time management. Organizing and sequencing tasks so that they are accomplished in an efficient manner.

To-do list. A summary of priority items to be accomplished during a day.

Total Quality Management (TQM). A management philosophy that stresses the delivery of a quality product or service through optimization of the people and processes that produce it internally and externally.

For Your Discussion

 Retrieve file C3-DQ.DOC from your student data disk.

Directions

Enter your response after each question.

1. How will TQM change the way the office professional works?

2. Distinguish between effectiveness and efficiency; include examples in your discussion.

3. What effect will a manager's work preferences have on the way the office professional's work is organized?

4. Why should an office professional who works for several managers ask them to resolve assignment conflicts among themselves?

5. Suggest at least ten guidelines an office professional can follow to establish his or her work habits.

6. Describe how to organize yourself at the end of the day.

7. Describe the importance of planning and organizing large projects.

8. Distinguish between a tickler file and a pending file; include examples in your discussion.

9. Explain why a situation that seems stressful to one person is not stressful to another.

10. Identify at least five ethical concepts regarding work, time, and resources.

CAPITALIZATION WORKSHOP

Letters are capitalized for two basic reasons: (1) to show the beginning of a sentence; (2) to show that a proper noun or adjective is more important than a common noun. Complete the exercises below by applying capitalization rules.

For Review

Appendix A: Rule 6: Personal Titles

Rule 7: Organizations, Institutions, and Education

 Retrieve file C3-WRKS.DOC from your student data disk.

Directions

Write C to the left of the sentence if the capitalization is correct. If the sentence is incorrect, use a proofreader's mark to make the necessary corrections. Example: A (to show capitalization).

Rule 6: Personal Titles

1. The advisory committee to president Martin quickly approved the sale of the property.

2. Our main reason for setting the appointment at 8 a.m. was so Gregg Evers, our comptroller, could attend.

3. Danielle Sterns, president of Sterns & Sterns, is a very respected attorney.

4. Our Mayor, Ruth Steinback, spoke at the Executive Assistants Annual Conference.

5. Please send a copy of the proposal to Jonathan Hatfield, president, Hatfield and Associates.

Rule 7: Organizations, Institutions, and Education

1. San Francisco hopes to host the republican national convention in the future.

2. Our American Records Management Association meeting was held last month at the Dunston hotel.

3. The senior class officers presented a skit in english.

4. Mr. Gordon, our managing editor, encouraged all employees to seek their bachelor or master's degree.

5. The local police department provided security at the Democratic national convention.

On the Job Situations

 Retrieve file C3-OJS.DOC from your student data disk.

Directions

Enter your response after each situation.

1. You have a new job and have been working for three weeks. Each afternoon before leaving work, you carefully plan your work for the next day. You are having difficulty keeping up with your plan because the telephone rings continually. You are becoming frustrated because you must answer so many telephone calls.

   ■ What problems can you identify in this situation?

   ■ What stress-reducing techniques can you use?

   ■ What are some solutions to resolve situation?

2. When you started working for Mr. Diaz, he suggested that paper filing was a low-priority item and that you should let filing go until you do not have other work to do. You have followed his suggestion for four weeks, and the papers in your filing baskets are about to reach the ceiling. You never seem to find the time to file. The situation is compounded when Mr. Diaz calls for a document, and you must go through the unfiled stacks to find what he wants. What can you do to solve this situation?

3. You work for five managers, and today one of the managers, Jean Forrester, has sent three reports to you for final completion with a special request to finish by this afternoon at 5:30 p.m. However, the other three managers have also given work to you and expect you to complete the assignments right away. You have had some difficulty in completing one of the assignments, you have missed lunch, and now you are becoming frustrated due to the pressure of completing all the work.

   ■ What problems can you identify in this situation?

   ■ What stress-reducing techniques can you use?

   ■ What can you do to resolve this situation?

4. Mickel Rasmussen is a new member on your team. You have noticed that his desk is messy; he cannot find certain telephone directories, supplies, and reference materials. He is constantly asking others for information that he has but doesn't want to locate. Mickel has materials stacked in piles on his desk and on the floor around his desk. He has had trouble determining priorities and has not produced his work in a timely fashion. You realize that Mickel's work is being haphazardly performed. Your manager has come to you to discuss Mickel's inefficient performance.

   ■ Identify the problems in this situation.

   ■ Suggest ways that Mickel could improve his efficiency.

   ■ In your approach to Mickel, consider what you want to achieve and what you want to avoid.

Projects and Activities

1. How many unfinished projects do you have? Are you burdened with the thought that "everything is started and nothing is finished"? Make a list of your unfinished projects and tasks. Select the one you can finish in the least amount of time and complete it. Select another task that you can complete in a few minutes and then complete it. Notice how you lighten your load by finishing tasks. Use what you have discovered to remind yourself to finish tasks as soon as possible, leaving your mind free to tackle new assignments. Write a memorandum to your instructor about what you have learned.

2. Are you using bits and pieces of time? To find out, keep a record. Begin by keeping a to-do list. Refer to Form 3-D at back of the text. Jot down at random everything you think of that you must do other than the major tasks. Leave space to the right of each item on your to-do list. As you complete each task, write down the date, the number of minutes used, and when. For example, was it between classes? While you were waiting for your ride? At lunchtime? At the end of one week, determine how much extra time you gained by using bits and pieces of time. Multiply your answer by 52 to estimate the time you could gain in one year. Write a brief summary; report your results to the class or your instructor.

3. Keep a time distribution chart for two weeks similar to the one in Figure 3-1. Write down what you are doing; what the task involves or refers to; and other people involved if the task is a meeting or appointment. Also assign a priority to the task: 1 for urgent or demanding tasks, 2 for middle-range basic tasks, and 3 for low-priority tasks. Then note whether the activity was planned (P) or involved an interruption (I). At the end of two weeks, analyze your chart for the following:

   a. **Telephone calls.** Add up the calls made or received during the two-week period. How many qualified as legitimate; how many were unwelcome interruptions?

   b. **Drop-in visitors.** Add drop-ins; what percentage of the day do these get-togethers consume? How many were legitimate; how many qualified as unwelcome?

   c. **Paperwork, projects, writing, planning.** How many of these activities qualified as number 1 priority? As 2s, 3s? Averaging more than three or four number 1 priorities per day means ineffective planning or inaccurate rating.

   d. **Other activities.** Consider all remaining entries. Again, ask yourself if the remaining tasks are legitimate or unwelcome, unnecessary, or "firefighting."

   After your analysis, respond to the following questions:

   a. Am I complicating tasks, putting more time into them than necessary?

   b. Am I using efficient techniques whenever possible?

   c. Am I taking on inappropriate work? Doing too much for others? Failing to delegate, if possible?

4. **a.** Divide into teams and visit an office supply store and look at work and time organizers. Next, compare these organizers with available time organizer software (for example, paper desk calendars vs. electronic calendars). Summarize your findings of the manual versus electronic work and time organizers. Be prepared to share your summary with the class teams.

   b. Set up a tickler file system and use it for the quarter or semester. Show your system to your instructor. Once a month, share your progress with your instructor in using the system. At the end of the term, report the results to your instructor. Outline the benefits of using this follow-up system. In the report, include any difficulties you had either in using or maintaining the system.

Surfing the Internet

A. You have been asked to search the Internet to locate various software programs that will improve office productivity. Two of the managers that you support are particularly interested in locating the names of software related to financial calendars and law calendars. Complete the following procedure.

1. Connect to the Internet and access a search engine such as Yahoo! or Lycos.

2. Enter the following key search words to locate information about productivity software: *productivity management software or productivity improvement management (PIM)*.

3. Summarize your findings, listing at least three site addresses. If possible, print a copy of your findings.

4. Enter the following key search words to locate information about financial calendars: *computers, software, calendar, financial*. Summarize your findings, listing at least three site addresses. If possible, print a copy of your findings.

5. Complete the search for the law calendars. Record at least three findings, listing the site addresses. If possible, print a copy of your findings.

6. Complete the search for the recreational sports calendar. Record one finding, listing the site address. If possible, print a copy of your finding. Summarize your findings in a memo to be turned in to your instructor.

B. You are to search the Internet to locate information on stress management for a presentation you must give at your local student organization next month.

1. Connect to the Internet and access a search engine such as Yahoo!, Lycos, or Net Search.

2. Enter the following key search words: *stress management tips*.

3. Print any articles or information you believe will help you prepare your presentation.

4. Write a memo to your instructor outlining tips or techniques to reduce stress. Be certain to include the Internet site addresses.

C. You have been asked to locate information about total quality management for your next brown bag lunch session. Complete the following steps:

1. Connect to the Internet and access a search engine.

2. Enter the following key search words to locate the information: *total quality management* or *TQM*.

3. In a memo to your instructor, briefly describe the elements of Total Quality Management; include examples to support the elements. Be sure to include the Web site addresses.

Using MS Office 2002

Define Your Tasks

1. Open Microsoft Outlook and make sure a blank document screen displays.

2. Click on the Tasks icon (either from the Outlook Shortcuts bar or the Folder List).

3. Click on the New icon on the Standard toolbar.

4. Fill in the information for each field.

   a. If you have received a task assignment via an e-mail message, simply drag that message to the Task folder. This will insert the subject and body information automatically into a new task.

   b. You can edit any field information for more clarity.

5. Save the task.

6. View your tasks each day to see what tasks you have pending and the deadline for each.

   a. Click on the View menu and point to Current View.

   b. Click on Detailed List.

      1. Each task is displayed on separate rows with field headings.

      2. Double-click on any task that you want to view and/or edit.

      3. It's up to you to keep the Status field up-to-date, change the deadline date, add additional information in the body part, and so on.

      4. Save and close.

      5. If you mark it complete, a line will be drawn across the row.

Get in the habit of using the Tasks feature of Microsoft Outlook; Post-it notes can be misplaced or lost easily.

APPLICATION PROBLEMS

APPLICATION 3-A

Setting Priorities

Supplies needed: Form 3-A, Daily Plan Chart (forms are at the back of this text). Retrieve file C3-DA.DOC from your student data disk.

Directions: Complete Form 3-A by indicating the work to be done and assigning priorities to the items.

It is 9 a.m. on Monday, June 2, and you have enough work to keep you busy for one week. Mrs. Quevedo is leaving on a business trip at noon today. At 7 a.m., before you arrived, Mrs. Quevedo dictated three letters, and at 8 a.m. she discussed work with you to be done in her absence. Here are the notes you took during your conference with her.

1. Send copies of the combined sales report for the week of May 19 to the four regional managers.

2. Call J. R. Rush, Assistant Vice President of Marketing, Eastern Region, locate the extension number, and ask him to see David Walters, an out-of-town supplier, who had an appointment with Mrs. Quevedo for Wednesday, June 4, at 10 a.m.

3. Transcribe the letter to Allen Fitzgerald. Mrs. Quevedo emphasized that it must be mailed today. The letters to Nancy Evans and Robert Berger may be mailed tomorrow.

4. Make a daily digest of the important incoming mail. Hold all mail for Mrs. Quevedo to answer. Contact her if something is urgent.

5. Write a letter to Nancy Cromwell, Dallas, providing an appropriate address, telling her that Mrs. Quevedo will accept her invitation to speak at the National Sales Conference in Dallas on November 28 at 2:30 p.m.

6. Keyboard the last two pages of the speech that Mrs. Quevedo gave at the chamber of commerce and send a copy of the speech to Art Winfield. He needs a copy by Friday afternoon. Provide a local address for Art.

7. Call Mr. Levine, Assistant Vice President of Marketing, Northwestern Region, confirm the extension number (6537), to remind him that Mrs. Quevedo will be out of town for the week and that she is confirming his agreement to represent her at the Executive Committee meeting, held every Wednesday at 10 a.m.

8. Make copies of an article on time management and distribute the copies to the four assistant vice presidents of marketing.

9. Call Lakeside Restaurant at (953) 555–0871 to set up a luncheon meeting for Monday, June 9, at 12:30 p.m. for twelve members of the planning committee for the November Sales Seminar.

10. Call American Airlines at (953) 555–5200 to cancel Mrs. Quevedo's reservation to New York City on Wednesday, June 4.

Here are additional items from the assistant vice president:

1. A six-page report prepared by Mr. Strickland to be proofed and formatted in final form by Wednesday afternoon.

2. An electronic mail (e-mail) note from Mr. Rush asking you to obtain the sales figures for the four regions for the week of May 26. He wrote, "Please create presentation slides showing the sales figures by region so that I may refer to them in a staff meeting at 10 a.m. on Tuesday."

3. An e-mail from Mr. Levine asking that you add the figures he has circled in red on the computer printout to the report he sent earlier to you. He wrote, "I need this information by 2 p.m. today (Monday)."

4. A revised twelve-page report prepared by Miss Baxter. She needs to receive the final report on Friday to review it before she presents it to Mrs. Quevedo on Monday, June 9. You have previously keyboarded this document and have saved it on your computer.

APPLICATION 3-B

Evaluation Form

Supplies needed: Form 3-B, Evaluation Form.

 Retrieve file C3-EV.DOC from your student data disk.

Directions: Complete Form 3-B.

APPLICATION 3-C

Stress Assessment Questionnaire

Supplies needed: Form 3-C, Stress Assessment Questionnaire.

 Retrieve C3-STR.DOC from your student data disk.

SUPREME APPLIANCES MEMORANDUM

TO: All Employees
FROM: Human Resources Department
SUBJECT: Consideration for an Employee Assistance Program
DATE: (Current)

We are requesting that you complete this form on a voluntary basis for the purpose of determining the need for an employee assistance program.

Understanding that many of you have been subjected to internal stresses with our recent company restructuring, we ask that you be candid with your responses because we do not *require* you to identify your responses with a signature. The results of this survey will be compiled and published for your review once an independent consulting firm has analyzed the results.

Thank you for your assistance.

Mrs. Quevedo gave you the memo shown above and asked you to complete Form 3-C.

Your Action Plan

Complete your Action Plan; if necessary, review the guidelines in Chapter 1. Set one goal using the information you learned in Chapter 3.

Your Portfolio

With the help of your instructor, select the best work representative of your work from Chapter 3. Follow your instructor's directions for formatting, assembling, and turning in the portfolio.

Processing Information

85

chapter 4

Using Technology and Understanding the Office Professional's Role

OUTLINE

Types of Computers

Basic Components of Computers
Input Devices
Central Processing Unit
External and Internal Storage
Output Devices

Operating System Software

Application Software
Microsoft Office
Web Application Software
Desktop Publishing

Computers in the Office
Gathering Accurate and Complete Input
Using Integrated Office Information Systems
Networking Computers

Security Issues

The Internet

Ergonomics
Office Layout
Décor
Furniture

Increasing Your Productivity

International Computer Links

LEARNING OUTCOMES

When you have completed this chapter, you should be able to:

✔ Describe today's business computers.

✔ Discuss the basic components of a computer.

✔ Distinguish between disk operating system software and an application software program.

✔ Describe the types of application software used in most offices.

✔ Discuss the basic components of an integrated office information system and the importance of accurate and complete input.

✔ Describe the various networking systems.

✔ Explain the dangers of computer viruses and computer crime and how each can be prevented.

✔ Explain what the Internet is and what it provides for the office professional.

✔ Explain the importance of ergonomics in the automated office.

✔ Describe the ways the office professional can increase his or her productivity after entering the job market.

✔ Describe the kinds of problems a world traveler might encounter when attempting to link to his or her home office.

Office technology is truly amazing. Today's information-age office employs a full-time office professional who is highly computer literate. The office has a computer system with automated office management programs that handle many functions. Examples of these functions include accounting functions such as billing, accounts receivable, monthly statements, and payroll. Correspondence is typed using a word processing program and printed on a laser-quality printer. After-hours calls to the office are routed to a voice mail system that can even activate a pocket pager in emergencies. Faxes are sent from a computer or fax machine that is on a dedicated phone line. The office also has a sophisticated voice mail system that has distribution groups and preprogrammed "messaging" for emergency paging. Information is routinely communicated to and from other computers through electronic transmission.

Technology has caused businesses to operate differently today than ten years ago—before faxes, cell phones, and Internet connections made business transactions around the world as quick and easy as those across town. With technology now evolving at a rate tenfold as fast as in the past decade—from teleconferencing to workspaces in cyberspace—today's office must have the flexibility to support the business tools that enable a company to compete in the fast-paced global business environment.

TYPES OF COMPUTERS

The computers used in business are identified by several factors, including size (capacity and speed) and cost. The biggest, fastest, and most expensive of all the computers is the supercomputer. Supercomputers are not designed for increasing proficiency and processing for individual users. **Supercomputers** are designed to solve very difficult problems, such as weather forecasting, creating designs showing nuclear reactions, or for military purposes, such as managing and operating missile defense systems. Their costs run into the millions of dollars.

The largest computers commonly found in today's offices are **mainframe computers**. They are very powerful, fast, and expensive. The mainframe computer is a computer with the capacity to process and distribute information quickly and efficiently to multiple users.

■ Figure 4-1
A Gateway 400 microcomputer with floppy drive, ZIP drive, CD-ROM drive, and other peripherals. (Courtesy of Gateway.)

Minicomputers are smaller and less expensive than mainframe computers; however, they perform many of the same functions, except on a smaller scale. For instance, they support various departments that have related business functions, such as manufacturing, sales, and accounting. This chapter discusses the **microcomputer**, also referred to as the **personal computer (PC)** or **desktop computer** (see Figure 4-1). Although PCs are by far the most common desktop computer in business today, other desktop models such as the Macintosh (also called Mac) are still popular in many offices; especially those where graphics play an important role. The popularity of the PC has proven that its power and capabilities are more than adequate to perform specific business applications.

Laptop computers, also called **notebook computers**, are small portable computers often weighing only a few pounds. They are scaled-down PCs. Laptops are used by everyone from business men and women who send and receive data, e-mail, or files to and from the office while they are away, to those who use them for personal pleasure to play games. The business traveler often uses a laptop computer to sign on or log on to the office network from anyplace there is a telephone connection or wireless capability. PCs have become so necessary that many colleges are now making it a requirement that all students registering have a PC.

The computer is getting smaller. **Personal digital assistants (PDAs)** are the smallest of all the personal computers. PDAs are often called **palmtops**. They can be the size of your checkbook, but can be as powerful as a notebook or desktop PC. PDAs are usually used for special applications, such as storing addresses and telephone numbers, keeping calendars, connecting to the Internet, sending and receiving e-mails, or using word processing or creating spreadsheets. When communication is important, many PDAs can be connected to other computers to send and receive data. Data is inputted through the use of an electronic pen or a tiny built-in keyboard. You will learn more about palmtops in Chapter 9.

To meet the competitive demands of businesses today, most large and small businesses find PCs a must. Mainframes and minicomputers are used in centralized areas, but the PC is distributed throughout the organization and often found on every desk.

BASIC COMPONENTS OF COMPUTERS

For all tasks that the computer is given, certain basic functions must be performed. These functions are:

1. **Input.** The means of getting data and instructions into the computer.
2. **Processing.** The central processing unit completes the instructions entered to produce the desired results.
3. **Storage.** The place for internal and external storage of information.
4. **Output.** The means of getting data out of the computer.

Input Devices

Input devices are used to enter data into the computer. The various kinds of input devices are the keyboard, mouse, monitors, voice processing, writing tablets, scanners, bar code readers, and optical character readers. Of all these devices, the most frequently used in the office are the **keyboard** and the **mouse.** Wireless keyboards and mice are available that use infrared lights much like the remote for your television.

Touch-sensitive monitors, which you might have seen used at restaurants to enter items ordered, are also used frequently in conjunction with the keyboard. Users use their fingers or an **electronic pen** to press or touch the monitor to enter data.

Voice processing, which gives speech commands to the computer, offers home and small office users powerful features to maximize productivity. Voice processing is gaining popularity as the solution to transcription. Legal proceedings, medical case histories, and the like are dictated into a microphone and immediately appear on the computer screen.

Dragon NaturallySpeaking is a popular voice-processing software. After completing about five minutes of training, you can begin talking to your computer and watch your words instantly appear in virtually any Windows-based application, including Microsoft Word, Microsoft Excel, Outlook Express, Internet Explorer, and Corel WordPerfect. *Dragon NaturallySpeaking* will allow you to launch programs, create documents, and manage your desktop—all by voice input. You can even dictate into your pocket PC or handheld digital recorder, and then automatically transcribe your dictated speech when you sync with your PC. The software contains a vocabulary of over 250,000 standard and business terms.

Another choice of input device the user has is a writing tablet. A **writing tablet** is a padlike unit on which you can actually draw or write using a wired or wireless stylus (see Figure 4-2). The pad reads the movement of the stylus, thus controlling the cursor. Some tablets come with a stylus that allows the user to apply more or less pressure on the pad to create a wider or narrower line or image. A stylus also is available with a "digital eraser" and buttons that act like the right and left mouse buttons. Users who need to create graphics or drawings find writing tablets especially useful.

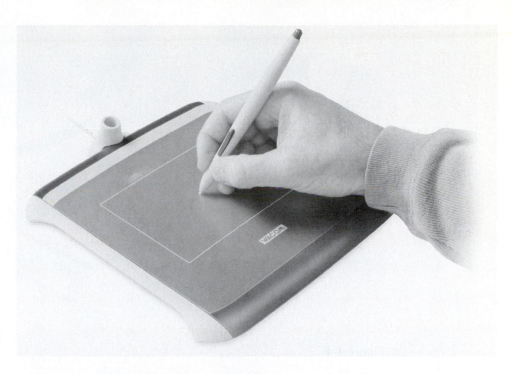

■ **Figure 4-2**
Writing tablet.

■ **Figure 4-3**
Optical character reader
(OCR), or scanner.

Scanners are another common input device (see Figures 4-3 and 4-4). Scanners read information from hard copy. The two types of scanners that will input information to a PC are (1) bar code readers, and (2) optical character readers.

■ **Figure 4-4**
The Ricoh 15450 DE desktop
scanner. (Courtesy of Rich.)

Bar code readers are widely used by businesses. Grocery stores use scanners to read bar codes. The scanner at the checkout counter is connected to a computer that houses a large database that contains the product name and current price, among other information. In medical offices bar codes are used on patients' file folders instead of keying labels. The bar code handheld scanner records information about the patient that is quickly downloaded into the computer to update patient records.

An **optical character reader,** usually called **optical character recognition (OCR),** is commonly used to scan typewritten material and convert the text to electronic signals that can be received and understood by word processing software. OCR scanners can transfer all types of material into the computer, such as pictures, forms, and graphics, as well as text (see Figures 4-3 and 4-4).

Central Processing Unit

The **central processing unit (CPU),** commonly referred to as the "brains" of the computer, is a **microprocessor chip.** The silicon chip, smaller than a dime and containing 2,250 transistors, was introduced in 1971 and has made the PC possible. As computer technology improves, CPUs are continually increasing in processing speeds. Intel makes one of the most popular chips.

The CPU is an electronic device. It has no power on its own. Data to be processed by the computer are converted into **binary code** electronic impulses. Various combinations of two digits, "0" and "1," indicating "off and on," represent all letters, numbers, and symbols in the binary code. One character in binary code is called a **byte.** A **megabyte** is approximately one million bytes. A **gigabyte,** equivalent to approximately one billion bytes. These are common measures of storage capacity that can be purchased.

The function that temporarily remembers where data are and the instructions indicating what to do with the data is called **memory**. Memory usually is located inside the computer with the CPU. The computer's memory is divided into **read-only memory (ROM)** and **random-access memory (RAM)**.

The manufacturer places read-only memory on the memory chips. It holds the instructions the computer needs when it is first turned on. ROM is permanently recorded memory. The user cannot change it, and turning off the computer will not destroy it.

Random-access memory temporarily holds the program or application and data currently being used. It is the working space in the computer. For example, if you create a word processing document with a keyboard, the document will be entered in RAM. Data in RAM must be saved, or they will be lost.

External and Internal Storage

The capacity of the computer's memory is not large enough to store all data internally. Therefore, computer data that should be kept permanently or for a period of time should be stored on floppy disks, hard disks, or compact discs (CDs). Diskette, optical, cartridge-based, and tape storage are available as removable storage.

Floppy disks, ZIP disks, and hard disks are the most common types of storage. **Floppy disks** are the 3.5-inch external disks used to store data. A **ZIP drive** allows documents to be stored on **ZIP disks**, which have a much larger storage capacity than a 3.5-inch disk. **Hard disk** is a storage area usually installed inside the case or tower with the CPU, but external hard drives can also be added to a computer. Storage capacity varies depending on the type of drive your computer has.

Compact disc (usually known by its abbreviation—**CD**), is used for storing large amounts of digital information. Today several types of CDs are used, for instance, CD-R (compact disc-recordable), CD-RW (compact disc-rewriteable), and DVD-RW (digital video disc-rewriteable or digital versatile disc-rewriteable). CD-Rs can be read using a standard compact disc drive, but CD-RWs and DVD-RWs require a special digital video disc drive. Manufacturers have created a new *MultiRead* CD-ROM/DVD disc drive that includes a *CD burner* (a slang term meaning to *write* data to a CD-ROM) that will read each type of CD. The CD burner requires special software that enables you to download information, such as music, from the Internet, and burn the music to a CD-R or make copies of any CD.

The **compact disc–read-only memory (CD-ROM)** disc drive has played an important role in the development of PC storage. A CD-ROM disc drive is used to access information stored on CDs. Without it you will have a hard time getting software for your computer. The reason is that almost all software comes in the form of CD-ROM discs. Each CD disc can hold more storage per disc than the floppy. The floppy holds 1.44 megabytes (MB) per disk, whereas the CD-ROM disc holds 650 MB per disc.

A single CD-ROM has the storage capacity of about 700 floppy disks, enough memory to store about 300,000 pages of text. Remember the CD-ROM is *read-only* memory and cannot be written to and from like a floppy disk.

The **compact disc-recordable (CD-R)** has emerged as the best choice of media for amounts of data required to digitally record music, video, and presentations. More and more writable CD drives (CD burners) have become standard equipment on new PCs. CDs store data in digital format in the form of 0s and 1s that are bumps and flat areas on the reflective surface of the CD. The bumps are interpreted by the CD player as a 0 and the flat areas as a 1. A laser is used to pass over the bumps and flat areas to read and interpret the information. CD burning software is used to actually burn or record the information. CD-Rs can be written to only one time and cannot be reused. To obtain a higher quality of sound for music, special music CD-Rs are available. CD-Rs are considered by some to be the best storage choice for archival purposes because the data cannot be accidentally modified or tampered with.

It took a few years, but the **compact disc-rewriteable (CD-RW)** has become the dominant rewriteable compact disc format. It is a rewriteable version of CD-ROM. Most CD-RW drives can write once to CD-R discs as well. CD-RW discs cannot be read by older CD-ROM drives built prior to 1997. CD-RWs are more expensive than CD-Rs. The advantage of the CD-RW format is that it enables you to write onto it unlimited times. Its main disadvantage is cost. The software will allow you to write files to the disc then gives you the option to add more files later. If you plan to add more files later, you must answer yes to this option.

Digital versatile discs (DVDs) are used to store high-capacity multimedia all on a single disc. Discs are available that have huge storage capacity, for instance 4.7 gigabytes (GB). CD disc drives combine DVD + RW + CD-RW for versatility. A DVD can hold a full-length film up to 133 minutes of high quality video and audio.

The following table summarizes the information about the various types of CD storage available to you.

Drive Type	"Read" & "Write" Capability
CD (CD player)	Reads audio CD only
CD-ROM (Compact Disk–Read-Only-Memory)	Reads audio CD, CD-ROM, CD-R
CD-ROM multiread (Compact Disk–Read-Only-Memory, Multiread)	CD-ROM, CD-R, CD-RW
CD-R (Compact Disk-Recordable)	Reads CD-ROM and CD-R, some read CD-RW (Writes once on CD-R disks)
CD-RW (Compact disc-Rewriteable)	Reads CD-ROM, CD-R and CD-RW (Writes and rewrites on CD-RW disks)
DVD-RAM (Digital Versatile disc–Random-Access-Memory)	Reads all CD formats. Reads DVD ROM. Reads and writes DVD disks.

Cartridge-based storage is commonly used in PC backup systems. The explosive growth of computer disk storage, networks, and database applications has increased the demand for backup data storage devices to meet these needs.

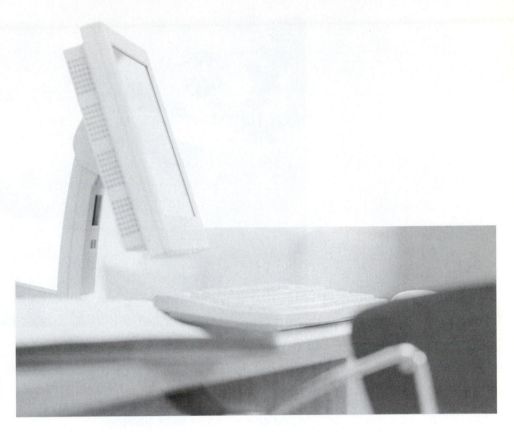

■ **Figure 4-5**
Microcomputer with a flat-panel monitor.

The tape cartridge drives are slower than other removable storage devices; however, one advantage is that you can back up most hard drives on only one tape.

Output Devices

Output devices are used to get information out of a computer, and include video display terminals (monitors), printers, and modems. There will be no output unless the computer is instructed to display it, print it, or send it.

Monitors. Data that have been entered can be displayed instantly on the **monitor**. The data can be viewed, changed, and rearranged without being printed. Many affordable desktop systems include a 17-inch monitor, high-end systems often include 19-inch monitors, and 21-inch monitors are desirable for intense graphics use. Flat-panel monitors have gained popularity because of their excellent displays and minimal space requirements (see Figure 4-5). Some of their advantages are:

■   They can connect to a PC or Mac without having to change the graphics card.

■   They occupy one-fourth of the desk space of the cathode ray tube (CRT) monitors they replace.

■   They are lighter weight, thus easier to move.

■   They offer a better picture than most CRT monitors.

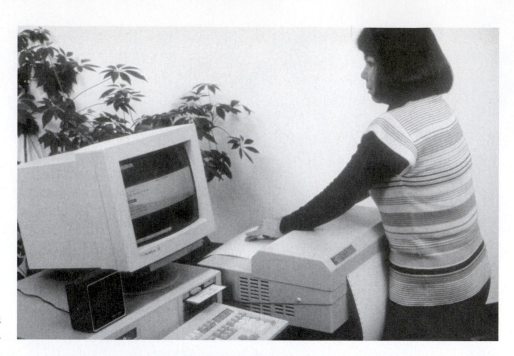

■ **Figure 4-6**
An office assistant using a
laser printer.

Printers. Inkjet and laser printers are the most commonly used printers in homes and businesses. **Inkjet printers** are inexpensive for both color and black printing, have lower operating costs, and offer high quality and speed when compared to laser printers.

Laser printers offer high-quality printing and speed, but they are more expensive than inkjet printers. One of their main advantages is their convenience (see Figure 4-6).

To avoid problems associated with running cables to connect printers over longer distances, newer printers have an added feature—an infrared light that makes them wireless. Printers are also available that perform multiple functions—faxing, color and black and white printing, scanning—all in one piece of equipment.

Printers that print in color are available at moderately low prices. These printers enhance documents with color, print color transparencies to enhance presentations, and even print stationery, business cards, and all types of greeting cards.

Modems. A **modem** (*m*odulator-*dem*odulator) is a device that connects a computer to a telephone line in order to transmit data by telephone to a remote computer. Modems are internally or externally installed with computers. Although data can be transmitted from computer to computer using a modem, the connection to the Internet has expanded the use of the modem. The most common use is for sending and receiving e-mail messages. You will learn more about e-mail in Chapter 6.

With a modem, if you are online, you are also using your phone line and blocking calls. Devices are available that will allow you to use your computer and be alerted to incoming calls as well.

Cable and **digital subscriber lines** (DSL) allow you to go online without tying up your phone line. A cable modem lets data flow between your PC and the Internet by using something found in most homes and offices—cable

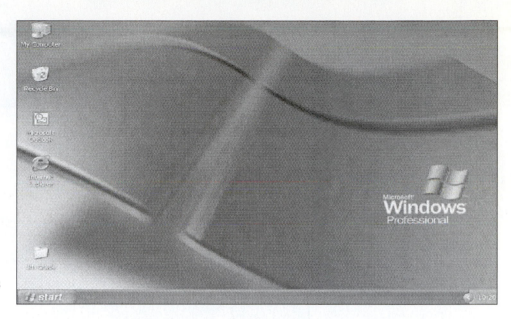

■ **Figure 4-7**
Opening screen for Windows 2000.

wiring. DSL is a feature simply added to your existing phone line. The function of the DSL splitter is to handle the voice calls and route the data separately to your computer. The major disadvantage of DSL services is that they aren't accessible nationwide, and they are usually more expensive than a dial-up service.

OPERATING SYSTEMS SOFTWARE

Everybody who uses a computer uses an operating system; therefore, it is an important part of your computer system. The **operating system** (OS), also called system software, gives instructions to the computer. The most commonly used computer operating system is Microsoft Windows (see Figure 4-7). Windows NT (WinNT) is primarily a business-oriented OS designed with the stability and security to serve companies with computer networks. The current operating system from Microsoft is Windows XP; however, Microsoft is working on a new version of Windows operating system code named "Longhorn." Other operating systems are UNIX and Linux.

An operating system contains a number of commands needed to operate the computer system. The operating system must be loaded into the computer's memory before the application software is loaded because the operating system must tell the computer to run the application software program. Each application program must be compatible with the operating system of the computer being used. There are variations from system to system.

APPLICATION SOFTWARE

Software programs include operating system and application software. An **application software** program is a set of instructions written for a specific task, such as word processing. These instructions tell the computer what to do and when to perform various operations.

Examples of application software are word processing (see Figure 4-8), spreadsheet (see Figure 4-9), database (see Figure 4-10), communication,

■ **Figure 4-8**
Microsoft Word XP
Windows 2000 new
document screen.

■ **Figure 4-9**
Microsoft Excel XP for
Windows 2000.

graphical presentation (see Figure 4-11), and specialized applications, such as programs written specifically for Web development, real estate, insurance, construction, and financial organizations.

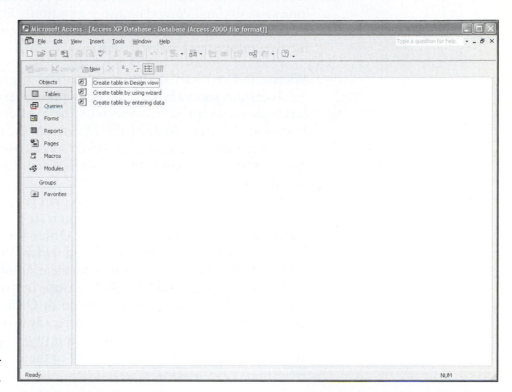

■ **Figure 4-10**
Microsoft Access XP for
Windows 2000.

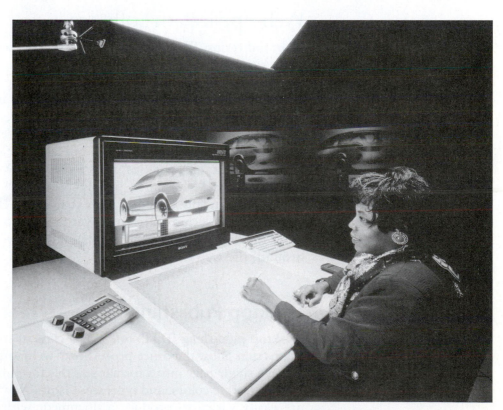

■ **Figure 4-11**
Office worker using a
graphics software program.

Microsoft Office

The most commonly used application software is Microsoft Office, which includes Word (word processing), Excel (spreadsheet), Access (database), Outlook (e-mail), and PowerPoint (presentation). The success of this integrated software package is the common thread of commands that runs throughout the five applications making each easy to learn.

Microsoft Certification. Microsoft offers a program whereby users can reach certain software skill levels by taking tests and receiving **Microsoft certification** as an Office Specialist or a Microsoft Office Specialist for Microsoft Project. To earn the Microsoft Office Specialist certification, you must pass a performance-based exam over one or more of the Microsoft Office desktop applications—Word, Excel, PowerPoint, Outlook, and Access.

Microsoft Project is for users who plan projects with multiple tasks, customize graphs and reports, and communicate project information and status. To receive certification as a Microsoft Office Specialist for Microsoft Project, you must pass a performance-based exam that focuses on the use of Microsoft Project as a project management "tool."

These exams provide a valid measure of your ability and expertise by evaluating your overall comprehension of Office or Microsoft Project. The Microsoft Office Specialist Program typically offers certification exams at the "Core" and "Expert" skill levels. Visit http://www.mous.net for more information about the cost and availability of these certification exams.

Web Application Software

In broad terms, **Web application software** is software designed to create a Web site that delivers dynamic information, such as Amazon.com or eBay.com. The person that maintains and updates the Web site is often called a **Webmaster.** Web applications can be used to handle **e-Commerce** (buying and selling online), inventory tracking, online auctions, or anything that uses a large amount of information. A **Web site** is made up of several Web pages that are connected to one another using links. **Links** reference the files that are part of the web site. Web site software, such as Dreamweaver MX created by Macromedia™, creates each Web page in code automatically called **hypertext markup language (HTML).** Web design software such as Dreamweaver is used to create each Web page then enter the links that connect the pages to allow the user to "**surf**" (navigate around) the web site.

Desktop Publishing

Desktop publishing (DTP) refers to a class of sophisticated application programs that allow the office professional to manipulate text, data, and graphics on a single page into a format suitable for publishing. Type sizes (10-, 12-, 14-pitch, etc.), colors, and typefaces (Times New Roman, Courier, Ariel, etc.) are easily varied to produce a document with a professional appearance.

Many office professionals are using DTP simply to enhance the professional look of any document. Others are producing documents so professional looking they appear to have been typeset by print shops. Once the office professional masters the art of desktop publishing, these specialized skills may be applied to nearly every document that crosses his or her desk. A scanner or document reader can enhance a publication by permitting the user to include original text or graphics produced on other equipment, such as newspapers or photographs.

Documents such as reports, memorandums, forms, procedures manuals, newsletters, annual reports, and advertisements are significantly enhanced by the use of desktop publishing; therefore, attract more attention than those produced by more conventional means. The office professional is now able to create brochures, flyers, newsletters, and business cards in-house, without the expense and time delays that use to be unavoidable when private printing contractors were used.

Other forms of DTP may include drawing, charting (such as organizational charts, flowcharts, and productivity charts), and designing (such as **computer-aided design [CAD]** applications). These applications are usually employed for specific purposes; also, they may require special system components, such as a plotter or larger display screen. You should research carefully both hardware and software before implementing a DTP application.

COMPUTERS IN THE OFFICE

The office professional will never be expected to write computer programs. Programmers will perform these tasks. But office professionals must be able to use the computer with confidence, ease, and efficiency, and be proficient in all the pertinent software applications, such as the ones previously mentioned.

Office professionals and others will ascertain that the input for computer operations is accurate and complete. In addition, they will not always find the record for which they are searching in the form of a sheet of paper in a file cabinet. It may exist in external computer storage only, and the professional will have to know the procedure for obtaining the information sought.

Many offices are moving toward a paperless or near-paperless office. One example is the health care industry. Many medical offices are making great efforts to computerize medical records. Claims are submitted electronically, all patient information is inputted directly into the computer, transcription systems are used that allow reports to be faxed electronically to physicians' offices, X-ray data is downloaded to the radiologist's office from the hospitals it serves, and so on. All X-rays are scanned and stored digitally. Hard copies of X-rays are shredded after being archived.

The use of the computer for decision making has also increased. Managers and executives are using computers to do budgeting, scheduling, and general planning. The computer is a powerful tool for increasing productivity. Managers rely on the computer for planning production schedules, monitoring and controlling manufacturing processes, and analyzing sales reports. The office professional who has learned to analyze and interpret data will be an invaluable asset to the manager or executive.

Gathering Accurate and Complete Input

Computers receive data to be processed and instructions for processing the data, but computers do only what they are instructed to do. For data to flow smoothly from the computer to the recipient, the input must be accurate and complete. PCs increase the speed of the flow of information and the demand for accurate input.

When incorrect data are fed into a computer, errors are processed and distributed so rapidly that the results usually are far reaching. A customer's order will not be shipped, an employee's check will not be written, or some delay will occur in completing a business transaction. Your role is to prevent problems, but when they do occur, solve them. If the customer or client or employee who is the victim of a computer error calls you, be attentive and understanding. Give assurance that the problem will be corrected. Apologize. Be positive. Tell them what you *can* do for them, not what you *cannot* do. Tell your manager about the problem and how you solved it.

Do everything you can to decrease errors in your documents. Keep a record of:

- The frequency of errors
- The types of errors that occur
- The originator of the error.
  Analyze the problem to determine:
- How to decrease the frequency of errors
- How to eliminate errors altogether
- How the process can be improved.

Your role as an employee and as an office professional includes both preventing problems and attempting to resolve those that do occur.

Using Integrated Office Information Systems

Very sophisticated electronic offices have integrated the technologies available to create integrated office information systems. Systems such as Microsoft Office are able to integrate the basic software applications—word processing, spreadsheet, database, and presentations—with telecommunications, scanning, image processing, reprographics, electronic mail, electronic files, and voice-processing technology. Some or all of these technologies may be available on an integrated system.

Telecommunications allow office professionals to transmit and receive information to and from different geographic locations through computers, telephone systems, and satellites. This may be done through an Internet connection or a direct network that links different company operations.

When telecommunications technology is used to link different company operations, workers have direct access to information needed to carry out their jobs. This technology can provide increased efficiency and productivity. For example, with an online inventory control system, information on inventory balances can be made available to salespersons in branch offices.

They are able to enter orders directly into the centralized system, and the inventory balance is automatically updated.

Image processing technology allows the office professional to reproduce visual and graphic data at the workstation. For instance, one might use word processing and spreadsheet software to create information for a report and then create charts and slides for a presentation.

In an integrated office information system, office professionals also can send and receive **electronic mail (e-mail)**. Electronic mail can be printed, stored electronically, or deleted after it has been received. You will learn more about electronic mail in Chapter 6.

Some integrated systems have direct linkage to scanning technology, described earlier, and to **reprographics** equipment, which is the equipment that performs copying functions. With reprographics technology an office professional can give instructions to a computerized system for copying a final document from his or her workstation without having to send out or go to another location for duplicating services. Chapter 5 discusses reprographics in more detail.

In integrated systems, office professionals will keep their own **electronic files**, stored on floppy disks or hard disks, at their workstations. In addition, they might have access to centralized electronic files of information that may be stored on mainframe computers in another location. Data can be accessed and transferred directly from one location to another. Security measures are designed so that information is not disseminated in a haphazard fashion.

Voice processing is used extensively in integrated systems. As mentioned earlier, this technology allows voice input and output. The most common use of this technology is voice mail and messaging systems that can be used to answer telephones, as well as take and store messages.

Networking Computers

Many organizations use **local area networks (LANs)** for connecting their internal computers. LANs are designed not only to provide a means of communication between users of computers but also to facilitate the sharing of common documents, hardware, and software.

LANs typically connect computers that are in the same area. The computers may be connected by fiber optic or coaxial cable (to permit higher transmission speeds) or by simple telephone cable or as a windows system. For enhanced capabilities, LANs can be connected to other networks, such as a **metropolitan area network (MAN)**, which as the name implies, provides networking facilities within a town or city. In much the same way, a **wide area network (WAN)** provides networking facilities over a yet wider area (perhaps an entire country, or even the entire world.)

Through the use of networks, an office professional can now

- Communicate with other employees through electronic mail (e-mail)
- Send draft copies of documents to individuals for validation or correction before committing them to final form
- Sequentially and electronically route a document for approval
- Co-author or co-edit large documents
- Conduct virtual and Net meetings

SECURITY ISSUES

A **computer virus** is a program that attaches itself to a file, reproduces itself, and spreads from one file to another from one computer to another. Viruses can be harmless or damaging. Damaging viruses can erase files, show irritating messages that pop up on your screen at various times, or disrupt computer operations.

Common categories of viruses are Trojan horse, time bomb, and logic bomb. **Trojan horse** is a computer program that actually does something to your software or data (such as format your hard drive and destroy your data) while appearing to perform a common function (such as executing a program). A **time bomb** virus stays in your computer system until a certain time (such as on Michelangelo's birthday), and then it is triggered by the computer's system clock to destroy data on that date. A **logic bomb** virus is a program that is triggered by the appearance or disappearance of certain data, such as when an employee is terminated and that termination is entered into the employer's database file. The trigger might be to format the hard drive when that data appears.

To combat computer viruses, several antivirus software programs are available. **Antivirus software** is software that detects and removes viruses brought into your computer system by data files. Anyone who connects to the Internet should protect their computer and its programs and data with an antivirus software program. Two of the most popular programs are McAfee Anti-Virus and Norton AntiVirus software. Both of these software makers provide updates that can be downloaded from the Internet so that users can be assured of protection against the latest viruses detected.

Computer crime is a growing problem for businesses today. **Computer crime** is illegal use of the computer to invade privacy, spread viruses, steal data, abuse e-mail, or pirate software—all over the computer. As the Internet grows, it attracts more people to work and play, and more online predators to prey on them. Myriad problems have arisen from invasion of privacy, spread of viruses, theft, e-mail abuse, software piracy, and more. It is estimated that computer crime costs individuals and businesses billions of dollars each year.

To deal with the problem of computer crime, the state and the U.S. government have enacted laws designed to prosecute persons who use computers for criminal or terrorists' purposes.

As thousands over the Internet exchange ideas and comments, it is difficult to know who has the ownership of ideas. Remember, as you use your computer either as an individual or as a member of your organization, the programs, documents, images, or sounds may be owned by someone else. When in doubt, make certain you give the individual or company credit for ownership or for creating it; better yet, obtain written permission for its use.

THE INTERNET

In its simplest form, the **Internet** is a global network of computer-based information available to anyone with a computer, a modem, and a subscription to an Internet Service Provider (ISP). The Internet is really a network of networks with international telecommunications facilities connecting them. By using a computer with a modem or DSL line, the user may connect to the Internet network. The user then has access to a vast amount of information and services. You will learn more about the Internet in Chapter 12.

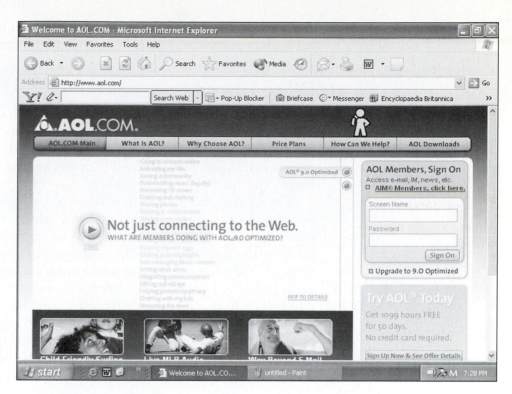

■ Figure 4-12
An online information
screen.

Users with Internet connections have access to **online information services** (see Figure 4-12), such as America Online (AOL) and Prodigy, and receive free e-mail and access to other services such as airline reservations, weather reports, news updates, and financial service information. Other **Internet service providers (ISPs)** such as Flash Net, Yahoo!, SWBell, and many others provide connections to the Internet and, with software called **browsers** (such as Netscape, Internet Explorer, AOL), provide many of the same services. These connection services charge monthly fees that range from $10 to $20 and more.

ERGONOMICS

With most Americans spending 70 percent of their waking hours at work, the office environment should be as safe, healthy, comfortable, and productive as possible. Then why don't we feel more at home in the workplace? The answer is that we have traditionally been expected to conform to the workplace. However, workers have not conformed as was expected by management. One reason has been that as computer technology advanced and more office workers began using computers, problems of user comfort arose. Since the introduction of personal computers in the 1980s, an entire market of products has evolved that supports computer workstations. Office furniture and computer accessories designed for comfort, including office supplies like halogen task lights, mouse pads, ergonomic keyboards, monitor arms, ergonomic chairs, wrist rests, and adjustable seating and reception desks, are all available.

With such emphasis being given to the development of computer products and the work environment, the field of ergonomics evolved. **Ergonomics** is the science of fitting the workplace to meet the physical and psychological needs of the employee. Everything that affects the worker must be taken into consideration—office layout, décor, furniture, lighting, workspace, air quality, heating and cooling, acoustics, and equipment placement.

Office Layout

You should position your computer, monitor, keyboard, and mouse pad to avoid stress or strain on your body (see Figure 4-13). This placement is crucial to your good health. What seems to be only a minor problem can become a major one when allowed to go unchecked for months and sometimes years.

Computer screen glare or a copyholder that does not adjust presents additional problems. Complaints arise about eyestrain, backaches, and headaches. The greatest complaint of office professionals has been about screen glare. Long hours at the computer can also lead to repetitive motion illnesses, the most common of which is **carpal tunnel syndrome**, a wrist ailment typically caused by incorrect alignment of hand and wrist. A wrist pad placed in front of the keyboard to rest hands when not keyboarding and a wrist pad attached to the mouse pad to rest the wrist when using the mouse helps to alleviate this problem. Workers also have to cope with "computer squeal," a high-frequency, barely detectable squeal that some computer terminals emit. This problem can cause anxiety, headaches, and nausea.

Décor

Colors that blend tastefully should be used throughout each office area. The color scheme should be harmonious, yet contrasting colors should be used to break the monotony of look-alike stations. The colors in your work environment can affect health and productivity as much as a supportive chair. Psychologists know that color can affect a person's mood, efficiency, and

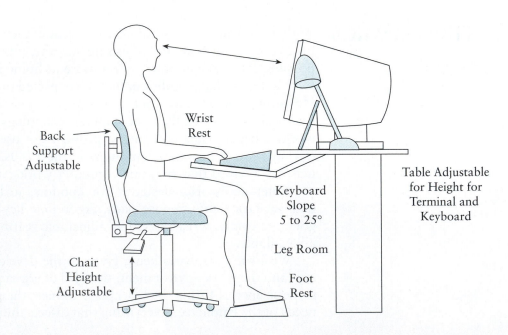

■ Figure 4-13
Correct posture at the keyboard.

perception of time, temperature, and noise. Most office planners agree that cool tones are best for tasks requiring high levels of concentration; large areas of yellow, bright green, bright red, and dark brown can have negative effects on workers.

Furniture

Office furniture manufacturers have designed modular furniture to carry out the office landscape concept. Modular furniture consists of separate components that can be fitted together in various arrangements to meet the needs of the user. If the worker's duties change, creating a need for a change in working surface, the modular furniture can easily be rearranged.

The chair is one of the most important pieces of furniture in the office. A poorly designed or maladjusted chair can be a major contributor to poor circulation and stress on the spine, back, and neck. When selecting a chair, consider the following:

- **Does the size of the seat fit your shape?** The seat should be slightly wider than your hips and thighs.
- **Is the chair height adjustable?** Most modern chairs can be pneumatically adjusted. You sit on the chair and a pneumatic lever located under the seat allows you to adjust the seat up or down.
- **Does the chair support your lower back?** The chair back should be adjustable up and down and forward and back to adjust to your size.
- **Can you adjust the seat to tilt downward and upward?** This adjustment allows you to adjust the seat to ensure good circulation in your legs and feet.
- **Does the chair have a five-pedestal base?** If you are moving from desk to desk in your workstation, for your safety you should have a chair with a five-pedestal base. This type of base helps to keep the chair from turning over as you move.

When equipment is set up correctly, the keyboard should be placed at a comfortable height that allows the arms and wrists to move without strain. The monitor should be placed behind the keyboard, positioned so that the worker can look slightly down at the screen. Improper positioning of the monitor can increase glare and affect the worker's posture and productivity. Office professionals that require bifocal glasses often complain of neck problems that are caused by the angle they must hold their head to see the screen. If you wear bifocals, you should wear reading glasses to correct this problem or make certain you can look down to view the monitor. Figure 4-13 shows correct positioning of the equipment and the user.

Work surfaces and chairs should be adjustable. Disk drives should be within easy reach of the worker. In summary, make certain you

1. Give support to your lower lumbar region of your back to avoid fatigue and stress on the spine.
2. Use wrist pads to reduce the risk of carpal tunnel syndrome.

3. Tilt the seat forward to decrease muscle strain and back pressure and improve blood circulation.

4. Use a copyholder to minimize head and eye movement and avoid neck strain.

5. Elevate your feet to take the strain off the legs and back.

6. Tilt the monitor so you are looking down into the monitor rather than up.

7. Purchase a monitor screen glare cover.

Creating a good ergonomic working arrangement is important to protecting your health. Every situation is different, and if you can't seem to get your arrangement to feel right or you are confused about how to arrange your workstation so that it is ergonomically correct, you should seek professional advice.

INCREASING YOUR PRODUCTIVITY

When you enter the job market, you should possess skills in keyboarding, word processing, spreadsheet, database, and presentations. Many opportunities to learn on the job will be available to you. Be receptive to the challenge.

First, refine the skills you already possess and accept change readily. Computers and software are being improved at a rapid pace. When the computer you currently are using is replaced or upgraded, study your new computer's manuals to become thoroughly familiar with the new features it offers. Be aware that improved software will make your job easier.

Learn other computer applications. Have a plan for professional growth on the job. Take advantage of in-house training sessions, study manuals, read technical magazines, attend night classes. Continually search for ways that the computer will help you perform your job. The computer is a tool that allows today's office professional to broaden the scope of his or her job.

INTERNATIONAL COMPUTER LINKS

As the world becomes smaller, with more and more businesses offering their employees opportunities to work abroad, often a link must be maintained with the home office. This link is usually via a laptop and a modem. What kind of problems might a world traveler encounter when attempting to link with his or her home office?

- Telephone connections are not available in most overseas hotel rooms. A connection may or may not be made through the business office of the hotel. Often the number of phone lines out of the country is inadequate to meet the demand; therefore, it may take time to get a line.

- Electrical plug-ins are usually not compatible with those in the United States. The traveler usually takes kits that offer a variety of adapters that allow hair dryers, computers, and other equipment to connect to electrical lines within the hotel room.

- Local service providers may not be able to provide consistent service. Check with the hotel's business services department to determine if Internet connections are available. Ask about any special equipment or plug-ins needed.

quicktips

Keep your computer clean:
- Don't eat or drink over your keyboard. Crumbs and liquid can damage the unit.
- Don't stack items on top of your monitor! This will prevent the air vents from working properly.
- Never place magnetic items on your CPU. Magnets can erase data.

Store printer paper properly:
- Store paper flat in a clean, dry area.
- Read your printer manual for types of suitable paper allowed.

Overview

- ✔ Office technology is truly amazing. Computers range from supercomputers, mainframe computers, and minicomputers, to desktop PCs, laptops, and personal digital assistants. Each of these computers has basic components: input devices, a central processing unit, external and internal storage capacity, output devices, and some type of operating system software.

- ✔ Basic input devices include the keyboard, mouse, monitors, voice processing, writing tablets, scanners, bar code readers, and optical character readers.

- ✔ Touch-sensitive monitors are used in conjunction with the keyboard.

- ✔ Voice processing software such as *Dragon NaturallySpeaking* is becoming popular. After five minutes of training you can begin talking to your computer and watch your words instantly appear in virtually any Windows-based application, including Word, Excel, Outlook Express, Internet Explorer, and Corel WordPerfect.

- ✔ The central processing unit (CPU) is an electronic device that has no power of its own. Data to be processed by the computer are converted into binary code electronic impulses. The CPU has read-only memory (ROM) and random-access memory (RAM).

- ✔ External and internal storage consists of floppy disks, ZIP disks, hard disks, CD-ROM, CD-rewriteable (CD-RW), recordable CD (CD-R), DVD (digital versatile disk) and cartridge-based storage.

- ✔ Output devices include inkjet and laser printers, modems, cable, and digital subscriber line (DSL).

- ✔ Operating system software gives instructions to the computer. Microsoft Windows is the most common operating system software used.

✔ Software programs are a set of instructions written for a specific task such as word processing.

✔ Web application software is software designed to create a Web site that delivers dynamic information, such as Amazon.com. The person that maintains and updates the Web site is called a Webmaster. A Web site is made up of several Web pages that contain links to one another.

✔ Desktop publishing refers to a class of sophisticated application programs that allow the office professional to manipulate text, data, and graphics on a single page into a format suitable for publishing.

✔ Using computers in the office demands that information gathered is accurate and complete. Your role is to prevent problems, but when they do occur, solve them.

✔ Integrated office information systems such as Microsoft Office are able to provide integrated software. This software such as word processing, spreadsheet, database, and presentation can integrate them with telecommunications, scanning, image processing, reprographics, electronic mail, electronic files, and voice-processing technology.

✔ Computers may be networked as local area networks (LANs) that connect internal computers in an organization, wide area networks (WANs) that connect wider areas such as a country, or metropolitan area networks (MANs) that connect a town or city.

✔ The Internet is a global network of computer-based information available to anyone with a computer, a modem, and an Internet Service Provider (ISP). The Internet is a network of networks.

✔ To assure business of a return on its investment, application software and hardware devices are designed to increase worker proficiency. Today the PC is used for word processing, financial, and communication functions, with e-mail being the application most often used.

✔ With the increased use of the Internet and of transferring data, there is an increase in computer viruses and computer crime. Myriad problems have arisen from invasion of privacy, spread of viruses, theft, e-mail abuse, software piracy, and more. It is estimated that computer crime alone costs individuals and businesses billions of dollars each year. Antivirus software helps alleviate this problem.

✔ Because office professionals are spending more and more time at their computer, the issue of comfort in the work environment has recently received more attention. With such emphasis being given to this area, the principles of ergonomic design have been increasingly applied. Businesses today must be concerned with fitting the workplace to meet the physical and psychological needs of the employee. This means planning the office layout, décor, furniture, and equipment to fit each employee's needs and to protect each employee's health.

✔ Should you have the opportunity to work abroad, you may be called upon to link to your home office. You should be aware of the kind of problems you might encounter when attempting to link with your office.

Key Terms

Antivirus software. Software that detects and removes viruses brought into your computer system by data files.

Application software. Instructions that are written specifically for a specific task such as word processing.

Bar code readers. Scanners that read coded information such as for products and price.

Binary code. Electronic impulses, "0" and "1," that represents all letters, numbers, and symbols in the computer.

Browsers. Software programs such as Netscape, Internet Explorer, or AOL that allow you to move around the Internet.

Byte. One character.

Cable. Used to connect to the Internet without tying up your phone line.

Carpal tunnel syndrome. A wrist ailment typically caused by incorrect alignment of hand and wrist.

Cartridge-based storage. Cartridges used to store information, such as when backing up information and programs on your computer.

Central processing unit (CPU). The "brains" of the computer; the microprocessor chip that tells the computer what to do.

Compact disc (CD). Usually known by its abbreviation—CD is used to store large amounts of digital information on time.

Compact disc–read-only memory (CD-ROM). A disk drive used to access information stored on compact disks.

Compact disc-recordable (CD-R). Compact discs used to digitally record music, video, and presentations.

Compact disc-rewriteable (CD-RW). A compact disk that can be written thousands of times and used as a storage device.

Computer-aided design (CAD). An application software used to create designs.

Computer crime. Illegal use of the computer to invade privacy, spread viruses, steal data, abuse e-mail, and pirate software.

Computer virus. A program written to intentionally do damage to computer programs, files, or disk drives.

Desktop computer. A personal computer or a Macintosh computer that is used on one's desktop.

Desktop publishing (DTP). A class of sophisticated application programs that allow the office professional to manipulate text, data, and graphics on a single page into a format suitable for publishing.

Digital subscriber line (DSL). A line that allows hookup to the Internet without tying up your phone line.

Digital versatile discs (DVDs). Used to store high-capacity multimedia all on a single disc.

e-Commerce. Electronic commerce—selling products and services online.

Electronic files. Files stored on hard drives or floppy disks.

Electronic mail (e-mail). Documents and messages transmitted over telephone lines or through cables on a network that links computer equipment.

Electronic pen. A pen used to input data by touching a computer screen.

Ergonomics. The science of fitting the workplace to meet the physical and psychological needs of the employee.

Floppy disks. 3.5-inch computer disks used to store data.

Gigabyte. Storage capacity equivalent to approximately one billion bytes.

Hard disk. Storage area found inside the computer.

Hypertext markup language (HTML). A language that enters codes to create Web pages.

Image processing. The process of reproducing visual and graphic data into a computer.

Inkjet printers. Inexpensive printers for both color and black printing. They have lower operating costs, and offer high quality and speed.

Input devices. Devices used to input data into a computer, such as the keyboard and mouse.

Internet. A network of worldwide computers.

Internet Service Providers (ISPs). Businesses such as Flashnet, Yahoo!, and many others that provide computer connections to the Internet.

Keyboard. One of the most common input devices used to enter data into the computer.

Laptop computers. Also called notebooks, they are small portable computers often weighing only a few pounds.

Laser printers. High-quality printers offering speed and convenience.

Links. Connections that reference files that are part of the Web site.

Local area networks (LANs). Connect computers within an organization that are designed not only to provide a means of communication between users of computers but also to facilitate the sharing of common documents, hardware, and software.

Logic bomb. A computer virus program that is triggered by the appearance or disappearance of certain data.

Mainframe computers. The largest computers commonly found in today's offices. Smaller than a supercomputer, but larger than a minicomputer.

Megabyte. Equivalent to approximately one million bytes.

Memory. In a computer, the function that temporarily remembers where data are and the instructions indicating what to do with the data.

Metropolitan area network (MAN). A network of computers that connects branches of a business located in outlying cities or towns.

Microcomputer. Also referred to as a PC or a Mac or a desktop computer.

Microprocessor chip. The chip that tells the computer what to do; the CPU or "brains" of the computer.

Microsoft certification. Microsoft offers a program whereby users can reach certain software skill levels by taking tests and receiving certification as a Microsoft Office Specialist.

Minicomputer. A computer smaller and less expensive than mainframe computers, yet it performs many of the same functions but on a smaller scale.

Modem. A *mo*dulator-*dem*odulator; a device that connects a computer to a telephone line in order to transmit data by telephone to a remote computer.

Monitor. An output device where data are instantly displayed. The data can be viewed, changed, and rearranged without being printed. Usually resembles a television screen.

Mouse. A desktop communication device that allows you to input or manipulate data in the computer.

Notebook computers. Small laptop computers often weighing only a few pounds.

Online information services. Companies that provide users with e-mail service, access to airline reservations, weather reports, news updates, financial services, and other information.

Operating system (OS). Also called system software, the OS gives instructions to the computer.

Optical character reader. Also called optical character recognition (OCR). Scans typewritten or graphic material and converts it to electronic signals that can be received and understood by the computer.

Optical character recognition (OCR). The process of using an optical character reader.

Output devices. Devices used to get data out of a computer, such as video display terminals (monitors), printers, and modems.

Palmtops. Small computers, often the size of a checkbook; also called PDAs.

Personal computer (PC). The most common desktop-sized personal computer used in most offices.

Personal digit assistants (PDAs). Also called palmtops. Small computers that can be the size of a checkbook, but less powerful than notebook or desktop PCs.

Random-access memory (RAM). Memory that temporarily holds the computer program and data currently being used. It is the working space of the computer.

Read-only memory (ROM). Memory that is permanently stored in the computer by the manufacturer.

Reprographics. The process of using equipment that performs copying functions.

Scanners. Input devices that read information from hard copy and input it into the computer.

Software programs. Application or operating system software.

Supercomputer. The biggest, fastest, most expensive computers used to solve difficult problems such as weather forecasting and managing and operating missile defense systems.

Surf. Navigate around the Internet.

Telecommunications. Allow users to transmit and receive information to and from different geographic locations through computers, telephone systems, and satellites.

Time bomb. A computer virus program that stays in your computer system until a certain time or date, at which point it is triggered by the computer's clock or calendar to destroy data.

Touch-sensitive monitors. Monitors that allow the user to input data by touching the screen.

Trojan horse. A computer virus program that does damage to your computer or data while appearing to perform a common computer function.

Voice processing. A process by which the user can input data by speaking into a microphone connected to the computer.

Web application software. Software used to create Web sites; an example would be Dreamweaver MX Web design software.

Webmaster. The person that maintains and updates a Web site.

Web site. Web pages that are connected to one another using links.

Wide area network (WAN). A system of connected computers that cover a wide area such as the country or even the world.

Writing tablet. A padlike unit on which you can draw or write using a wired or wireless stylus.

ZIP disk. A disk used to store data. Its storage capacity is much greater than a floppy disk.

ZIP drive. A disk drive used to store data on a ZIP disk.

For Your Discussion

 Retrieve file C4-DQ.DOC from your student data disk.

Directions

Enter your responses after each question.

1. Describe the basic computer and its components.
2. Name six input devices used to input data into computers.
3. Distinguish between read-only memory (ROM) and random-access memory (RAM). Include the definition of each.
4. Name three types of storage media.
5. Name three types of computer viruses and explain how each works.
6. Distinguish between operating system software and application software.
7. What is the difference between hardware and software?
8. Why has the computer placed such a premium on accuracy?
9. Define the term *ergonomics* and discuss the factors that contribute to an ergonomically designed office.
10. Identify the problems you may face when transferring data from your laptop computer abroad to your home office. Include what you would do prior to leaving the United States to prepare for such problems.

CAPITALIZATION WORKSHOP

Letters are capitalized for two basic reasons: (1) to show the beginning of a sentence; (2) to show that a proper noun or adjective is more important than a common noun.

For Review

Appendix A: Rule 8: Enumerations
                   Rule 9: Nouns and Adjectives

 Retrieve file C4-WRKS.DOC from your data disk.

Directions

Write C at the end of the sentence if the capitalization is correct. Otherwise, make the necessary corrections.

Rule 8: Enumerations

1. The Board of Trustees decided on three issues: (1) the board will grant an across-the-board increase in salary for all employees. (2) all insurance premiums will be paid by the company as of January 1. (3) after five years of employment, each employee will receive four weeks of paid vacation.

2. Some important issues facing your company are
    1. layoffs
    2. high cost of insurance premiums
    3. worker morale

3. The publication listed the two most important concerns employers are faced with as (1) absenteeism and (2) accidents on the job.

4. Each employee in our department is required to know
    1. word
    2. lotus 1–2–3
    3. basic writing rules
    4. keyboarding: 50 wpm

5. He asked (1) would she be available to begin work immediately, (2) would she accept the salary offered, and (3) would she supervise the office if asked.

Rule 9: Nouns and Adjectives

1. The last act of the legislature was to pass public law 590, which increased the taxes on consumer goods.

2. Security nearest our office is precinct 12 of the Dallas police department.

3. The employees' credit union put on a comedy play called "Fast Money" in which the audience was given $1 each in act III.

4. The regulation in section F identified the steps we were to follow to investigate the problem.

5. She was grade 12, and he was grade 9.

On the Job Situations

 Retrieve file C4-OJS.DOC from your student data disk.

Directions

Enter your response after each situation.

1. You are administrative assistant to the general sales manager in an organization that has four sales regions. You are responsible for seeing that the appliances requested by the regions are shipped promptly from the manufacturing plants. You operate a computer that is on a network with the offices of the sales regions and the manufacturing plants. Recently the regions have been receiving the correct number of appliances ordered but the colors have not been the ones that were requested. You analyze the data that you have used for the last month. What should you look for in your analysis? What recommendations could you make to improve your accuracy?

2. You are teaching an assistant to input data. This week the assistant has entered the data for all the orders. Every Friday the mainframe computer prints a summary of all the orders for the week. This Friday the computer did not print the summary of your orders for the week. What do you do now to obtain a summary? What else should you do?

3. Your organization stores data on microfilm. One of your managers has asked you to verify data in a report that is being prepared. The data you need have been stored in the centralized computer database system. You do not know how to retrieve the data you need. What should you do?

4. Randy, your coworker, has become a close friend of yours. At lunch one day, Randy remarked that he had taken the software disks home to install a copy of Microsoft Office on his home computer. He said he felt justified because he took so much of his work home to work on it in the evenings. Analyze the situation. Did Randy commit a computer crime? Was he justified in what he did? Write a detailed explanation of how you would handle the situation as a friend.

Projects and Activities

1. Review the components of an integrated office system presented in this chapter. Determine to what extent there is an integrated system in your company. If you are not currently working in an office, ask a friend or relative. Note your findings and be prepared to report them to the class.

2. Inquire about the student record system at your school. Is a computer used to maintain the entire system or a part of it? If so, what data entry is used for students' schedules? For grades? How are data stored? Who has access to students' records? Organize your findings and be prepared to report your findings to the class.

3. Set up an interview with someone in an office or a school lab that has an integrated information system. Determine how many individual computer workstations there are. How many workstations share resources, such as printers and scanners? How many share the central processing unit (CPU)? Organize your findings and be prepared to report your findings to the class.

4. Choose a category of application software and make a list of three commercial software programs available in it. Include in your findings the latest versions, features, and prices for each. Consult current magazines, the Internet, or visit computer stores for information. Organize your findings and be prepared to report your findings to the class.

Surfing the Internet

You are on the ergonomics committee for the new office building your company is planning to build. Your company wants to make certain its new offices are ergonomically correct. Your committee's function is to obtain information that identifies an ergonomically correct office design. As a committee member, your assignment is to research the Internet to gain information to report to the committee.

1. Connect to the Internet and access a search engine such as Yahoo!, Lycos, or Excite.
2. Enter the following key search words: *health, articles, ergonomics.*
3. Browse through the listings, then summarize or print any information you could use in your report to the committee.
4. Enter a new search or refine your search by entering the following words: *office design, ergonomics.*
5. Repeat step 3.

Using the information you found, write a report on the importance of designing ergonomically correct offices. Include any recommendations about design that would help your company meet this goal. Attach to the back of your report a printed copy of each of the sources you used.

Using MS Office 2002

Zooming Your Screen's Data

Directions

 If your mouse has a "roll button" on top, practice the following steps.

1. While looking at the text or data on your screen in Word, Excel, or PowerPoint, you can easily zoom in or out without having to go through the Menu bar. Open Microsoft Word and type your entire name.
2. Press and hold the Ctrl key located on your keyboard.
3. Roll the mouse roll button "forward" to increase the size of the data.
4. Roll the mouse roll button "backward" to decrease the size of the data.
5. This feature is used only for viewing and has no effect on the data when it is printed.

APPLICATION PROBLEMS

APPLICATION 4-A

Preparing a Final Draft—Word Processing

Supplies needed: Form 4-A, Draft of Supervision (use the forms at the back of the text).

 Retrieve file AP4A.DOC from your data disk.

Directions: Miss Baxter is assisting with a seminar on supervision for beginning supervisors. She is preparing some handouts for the attendees. Form 4-A is a draft of the handout. Make all the handwritten changes shown in draft in Form 4-A; proofread, spell check, and print one copy.

APPLICATION 4-B

Spreadsheet

Supplies needed: Spreadsheet software.

Directions:

1. Key the spreadsheet shown in Figure 4-9 using a spreadsheet software program. Be sure to enter the formulas to total each quarter vertically and the sales items horizontally.
2. Print one copy of the completed spreadsheet.
3. Display all formulas and print one copy showing the formulas.

Your Action Plan

Complete your Action Plan; if necessary, review the guidelines in Chapter 1. Set one goal using the information you learned in Chapter 4.

Your Portfolio

With the help of your instructor, select the best papers representative of your work from Chapter 4. Follow your instructor's directions about formatting, assembling, and turning in the portfolio.

chapter 5

Preparing Communications

LEARNING OUTCOMES

When you have completed this chapter, you should be able to:

✔ Create effective verbal communications.

✔ Recognize meanings of nonverbal communications.

✔ Practice effective listening techniques.

✔ Prepare to write effective business messages.

✔ Create routine business communications.

✔ Use various communication formats correctly.

✔ Prepare routine communications for distribution.

✔ Use proofreading techniques to create final documents.

✔ Distinguish among different types of copiers.

✔ Be aware of the need for applying ethics to all writing.

✔ Address envelopes with international addresses.

Effective communication is the responsibility of every person in the organization. Technology has brought about a greater emphasis on increasing productivity. This greater emphasis involves not only increased electronic communication skills but also personal communication skills. As an office professional you will be expected to have excellent verbal, nonverbal, and written communication skills in both the electronic and personal realm.

VERBAL COMMUNICATION

Much of the communication in the office is verbal. The most effective verbal communication takes place in a comfortable atmosphere and on a one-to-one basis.

When communicating verbally with another person follow these guidelines:

- Listen and watch for verbal and nonverbal feedback. Many factors affect how someone reacts to what you are saying. Among them is past experience—what happened to that person in a similar situation.

- Choose your words carefully when the topic you are discussing is sensitive or controversial. You may wish to withhold your opinion entirely if you know your view will offend the listener, put the listener on the defensive, or force the listener to disagree with you.

- Encourage the other person to talk; communication should be a two-way street. Communication will be open and honest if the person trusts you; it will be restricted if the person does not.

- Give the other person your undivided attention. Performing another task while you are talking is distracting and rude.

- Avoid talking incessantly. Pause often, to give your listener an opportunity to respond.

- Summarize the important points in logical order and give the listener a chance to ask questions at the end of a conversation. Communication does not take place until the listener truly understands what you are saying.

NONVERBAL COMMUNICATION

Most people are skilled at communicating a message without speaking even one word. Our facial expressions, our body gestures, and the way we dress often express our feelings and opinions better than our spoken words. Make certain the receiver doesn't misinterpret what is often seen as subtle nonverbal cues. It is imperative that your actions convey a clear meaning—that is, the meaning you intend. Verbal communication can be completely discredited by the nonverbal kind. The following factors can be studied to interpret nonverbal meanings:

- **Image.** It is no surprise that the way we dress sends a message to customers and colleagues. Conservative dress conveys the message that you are a professional and want to be taken seriously. Make sure you are dressed presentably even on "casual Fridays" that many companies allow.

■ **Personal space.** Everyone has expectations about personal space. *Personal space* refers to the distance at which one person feels comfortable talking to another. People who stand too close are viewed as aggressive or perhaps overfriendly; people who stand too far away may be seen as aloof. Always be considerate and do not violate another's personal space.

■ **Eye contact.** In American culture, a person shows confidence and interest when looking directly into someone else's eyes when speaking with him or her. Eyes are one of the most important nonverbal language tools—we use our eyes to read the other person's body language and, in turn, our eyes give off our nonverbal messages. In other cultures, direct eye contact can make a person feel uncomfortable or even threatened; in such situations avoid prolonged direct eye contact.

■ **Posture.** The way you stand, sit, and walk tell others a story. But it may not be the story you intend to tell, so be cautious about how your posture is perceived.

■ **Facial expressions.** The face is capable of many expressions that reflect our attitudes and our emotions. In fact, the face speaks a universal language. When it expresses happiness, fear, anger, or sadness, other cultures share these same expressions. Others interpret your meanings from your facial expressions. Be aware of the impact this powerful nonverbal tool can have.

Because nonverbal language is far more powerful than verbal communication, it is imperative that we pay attention to the messages our body language sends.

LISTENING

Few people listen as attentively as they are capable of listening, and those who do have trained themselves to listen. Recognize that good listening skills can be learned and adopt a plan for improving your listening skills.

To improve your listening skills, do the following:

■ Concentrate on what is being said and on grasping the meaning of what is said. Avoid saying you understand when you do not.

■ Become aware of your listening barriers, such as allowing your mind to wander, planning on what you are going to say next, or lacking open-mindedness to what is being said.

■ Repeat information to ensure complete understanding between you and the other person.

■ Take notes and confirm that what you understand is what was meant.

WRITING EFFECTIVE BUSINESS MESSAGES

Excellent writing skills are one of the most important skills you can possess. The business letter is one of the main vehicles for transmitting messages between the business and its customers or clients. You will, therefore, need to develop techniques that enable you to write, just as you would develop your other office skills. A common technique among office professionals is to use the keyboard to prepare drafts of documents they originate.

The Writing Process

Letters, reports, and sometimes memorandums are the types of documents the office professional writes. The writing process applies to each of these written communications. However, the office professional will most often be required to write letters; therefore, our discussion here will emphasize writing letters. Letters fall into three categories: (1) those written as an assistant to the manager, (2) those written for the manager's signature, and (3) those written as a correspondent for the organization. Most office professionals today write letters in one or more of these categories. Writing letters is an executive's or manager's responsibility that he or she can delegate to others; consequently, an office professional composes only those letters that the manager asks him or her to write.

Writing business letters is a significant endeavor. Think of the business letter as your organization's representative, going out alone to do a job. Keep in mind that communication does not take place until the reader comprehends and responds to the message. Realize that the effectiveness of each letter you write depends on how well you have written the letter to accomplish its task. As you compose a letter, ask yourself this question: Will the letter get the results I am seeking? Although you may learn many guidelines for writing letters, recognize the significance of giving more thought to anticipated reaction and results than to rigid procedures for writing letters.

The person who writes outstanding business letters works at it continually, weighing each word, anticipating reader reaction, and carefully organizing the contents to accomplish its purpose.

An effective business letter:

- Centers around a single purpose
- Is written from the reader's viewpoint
- Conveys a meaningful message through completeness, correctness, coherence, conciseness, and clearness
- Reflects a positive, sincere, and appropriate tone
- Is expressed in an interesting style through the use of natural, vivid, and varied language

Know Your Purpose. The purpose of a letter may be to inform, to create understanding and acceptance of an idea, to stimulate thought, or to get action.

Isolate the main purpose of the letter you are writing and develop your message around it. Make other points secondary to the main purpose; give the secondary points a subordinate position. Use one letter to do the job when you possibly can, but do not overwork your letter. Sometimes you will need a series of letters to accomplish one purpose. Unrelated topics that require answers should be presented in separate letters.

Focus on the Reader. Keep the reader in mind at all times. Make an effort to write all the sentences in a letter from the reader's point of view. Years ago when this writing technique was developed, it was called the **you-attitude.** The you-attitude techniques do not mean to use the words "you" or "your" in every sentence. It does mean to show consideration for the reader—to explain what benefit the reader will enjoy, to put the reader's needs first, to emphasize the reader's interests, and to use words that are meaningful to the reader.

Actually try to put yourself in the reader's place. Get to know the reader through the letters in your letter files and try to visualize the reader in the reader's type of business. Be aware that self-interest is an important drive in motivating readers to accept ideas or to carry out suggested actions. Reflect the same interest in a reader's needs in a letter that you would if you were talking with him or her in your office or over the telephone. Here is an example of writing from the reader's point of view:

Your point of view	Reader's point of view
We will ship all future	You will receive all future
orders by express mail.	orders by express mail.

Convey a Meaningful Message. To determine that your message will be meaningful to the reader, check it for completeness, correctness, coherence, conciseness, and clearness. These requirements are sometimes called the Cs of letter writing.

Completeness. When you are responding to a letter, you must answer all the questions that the reader asked or include a discussion concerning all the topics mentioned in the reader's letter. Often you can use bullets to list the items or number the items to make each point clear for the reader. When you are making a request, ask all the questions to which you need answers. Always anticipate the background information that you must supply the reader so that the full meaning of your message will be grasped. Also, anticipate the questions that the reader will have when reading your letter; inject the response to those anticipated questions.

Correctness. Correctness denotes accuracy in every detail: accurate facts and figures in the content, perfect spelling of every word, flawless grammar and punctuation in every sentence, an absence of keyboarding errors, and the entire letter's being centered on the page so that it is pleasing to the eye. Inaccurate information will confuse the reader and delay the response and, furthermore, could irritate the reader. Therefore, try to eliminate the confusion and additional communication generated by inaccurate, incomplete, or vague information.

Coherence. Coherence refers to the arrangement of words and ideas in logical order. Words and ideas must be arranged so that they fit together naturally within each sentence, within each main paragraph, and in the remaining paragraphs that hold an entire communication together. In fact, a coherent communication is woven together so carefully that the reader is always sure of the relationship of the words and ideas.

Conciseness. To write concise messages, use all the necessary words, but not more. Send the reader a complete message, but avoid obscuring the thought with needless words. To distinguish between completeness and a profusion of words, watch for irrelevant details, obvious information, and unnecessary repetition of words and ideas. Eliminate them.

To be concise does not mean to be brief. When you concentrate solely on brevity, you run the risk of writing a message that is incomplete or curt or both. Instead, write the full message and stop.

Wordiness also results from the inclusion of expressions, often called trite expressions, that convey no meaning. Here are some examples of wordiness:

Wordy	Concise
A check in the amount of	A check for
Made the announcement that	Announced
For the purpose of providing	To provide
At the present time	Now

Wordiness is an obstacle to concise writing because long phrases are used in place of one or a few meaningful words.

Clearness. Clearness in writing cannot be isolated entirely from correctness, completeness, coherence, and conciseness, but clearness does involve an added dimension: choice of words. Words have different meanings to different people. Nevertheless, as much as possible you must choose words that will have the same meaning to the reader, as they do to you.

To write a message that can be understood is not enough. You must write a message that cannot be misunderstood. Use familiar words, explain technical words, and avoid colloquialisms, slang, and coined phrases. Words are symbols; they are tools of thought. Your purpose is to choose a word that will penetrate the reader's mind and create the image you want the reader to associate with the word. To do this, you need a vocabulary large enough to enable you to select a word that conveys the precise shade of meaning you want to express. You must understand both the denotation and connotation of the words you use. **Denotation** is the explicit dictionary meaning of the word. The suggested idea or overtone that a word acquires through association, in addition to its explicit meaning, is called **connotation**. Avoid any word with a connotation that would be distasteful to the reader.

Reflect an Appropriate Tone. Your attitude toward the reader will have a noticeable effect on the tone of the letter. Even though your attitude is not described in the letter, it has a way of creeping in. Therefore, to set the appropriate tone, examine your feelings toward the reader. Show consideration for the reader and reflect a sincere attitude.

The tone of each letter must be appropriate for the given situation. Whenever it is appropriate, write informally and radiate a warm, friendly tone. Be courteous and tactful. Do not write sentences or include words that later you would regret having said.

One way to achieve tact in business letters is to replace negative words and phrases with words and phrases that are positive in tone. Watch for negative words; do not let them creep into your writing. Compare the tone in the phrases illustrated below. The italicized words in the left column are negative in tone. They have been omitted from the phrases in the right column.

Negative	Positive
1. We are *disappointed* at your *failure* to include your report.	1. We had hoped to receive your report
2. If you would *take the trouble*	2. Please send (commit, let, do)

How to Make Your Writing Interesting

When a reader receives a letter that is well written and interesting, it holds his or her attention. Often the reader has received so many pieces of communication, your letter is competing for attention. One way to get and keep that attention is to make the writing interesting. Follow these guidelines to help you create an interesting style of writing through using natural, vivid, and varied language.

✔ Use active verbs, except when you want the statement to be impersonal.

✔ Make the subject of the sentence a person or a thing.

✔ Use specific, meaningful words. Use general or abstract words only when a concept has not yet been reduced to specific terms.

✔ Use familiar words and phrases in place of the unfamiliar.

✔ Use a phrase or a clause to describe rather than an adjective or an adverb.

✔ Use short words instead of long words.

3. You are probably *ignorant* of the fact that

4. It is *not possible* for us

5. We *must* ask that you send us

3. Perhaps you did not know

4. We can

5. Please send us

TYPES OF WRITTEN COMMUN- ICATION

To carry out your daily work, you may find yourself writing messages concerning appointments, requests, orders, routine replies, acknowledgments, transmittals, delays, follow-ups, and other business situations. For letters that you sign, use the title "Assistant to" followed by your manager's name.

Writing Letters for Your Manager's Signature

In some instances you will be asked to write letters for your manager's signature. Writing letters for a manager's signature requires a special skill. It is not an easy assignment because the letter must sound as though the person signing the letter actually wrote it. The reader should not be able to detect that an assistant wrote the letter.

The letter that is the easiest to write for another person's signature is the letter report presenting a series of facts. The personality of the writer is not so apparent in factual reports. If the message is lengthy, the assistant could write an informal report to be accompanied by a cover letter actually written by the manager.

When you are asked to write letters for your manager's signature, study your manager's letters to become thoroughly familiar with his or her vocabulary and style. Use phrases that your manager uses, use the same salutation and complimentary close, and organize the letters in the same way your manager does. Actually use paragraphs, making appropriate changes, from letters your manager has written previously if similar paragraphs are available. When it is feasible, prepare a draft of the letter and ask your manager to review it and make changes before you keyboard the letter in final form. Remain anonymous. Do not reveal that you are writing letters for your manager's signature.

Routine Letters

Following are some of the types of routine letters you may have to write either for your signature or for your manager's signature.

Appointments. Appointments are requested, granted, confirmed, changed, canceled, and sometimes refused as part of regular business procedure. An appointment can be handled entirely by letter, by telephone, by e-mail, or by a combination of telephone and e-mail. You will learn more about e-mail in Chapter 6. This chapter covers the specifics of what should be included when writing an e-mail message about appointments.

E-mails concerning appointments should follow the same guidelines used when appointments are arranged by telephone: (1) refer to the purpose of the appointment; (2) clearly set forth the date, day, time, and place; and (3) request a confirmation of the appointment when it is applicable.

When you are postponing or canceling an appointment for an indefinite period, always express regret and suggest some provision for a future appointment. When you are postponing the appointment, suggest another specific date and ask for a confirmation.

Routine Requests, Inquiries, and Orders. When writing routine requests and inquiries, anticipate that the reply to your message will be favorable. State the request or inquiry directly, include only essential information, and create a pleasant tone. These messages will be short. If the message seems curt because it is too brief, add a sentence or two to improve the tone. For example:

> Will you please send me a copy of your booklet, "21 Ideas: Tested Methods to Improve Packing, Shipping and Mail Room Operations." We are continually searching for methods to improve our mailing operations and are looking forward to receiving this booklet.

Routine Replies. When a reply is favorable, state it in the opening sentence. The message of a favorable reply carries a favorable tone; therefore, even a brief message is effective. In a disappointing reply, add a sentence or a paragraph to cushion or soften the message. When declining a request, give at least one reason before you state the refusal.

Acknowledgments. Most acknowledgments either state or imply that another communication will follow. Frequently, the office professional has the responsibility of writing acknowledgments when the manager is away from the office for an extended period. Refer to Chapter 6 for further discussion of answering mail in the manager's absence.

Acknowledge messages promptly, preferably the same day they are received. Be cautious about giving away business secrets; make statements about your manager's absence in general terms. Avoid making promises or commitments your manager cannot keep or would prefer not to keep.

Make copies of the messages you refer to others and of the messages you forward to your manager.

What you say in an acknowledgment depends on what you are doing about the message. You can acknowledge the message without answering it, supply the answer yourself, and say that you are referring the message to someone else for reply, or let the reader know that you are forwarding the message to your manager for reply.

Other uses of acknowledgments are to let the sender know that important business papers have arrived and to confirm an order when the recipient is not expecting immediate shipment.

Cover Letters. A cover letter may be brief, merely stating that an item is being transmitted, and whom it is from. Here is an example of a short cover letter:

> Here is your copy of the report "Ten Years Ahead." Mr. Whitehall asked me to send each member of the Goals Committee a copy of the completed report.

Follow-Up Letters. Write a follow-up letter when you have not received something promised or due or when you have not received a reply to a letter after a certain period. Keep a careful record of missing enclosures and other items promised and write follow-up letters to obtain them. See Chapter 6 for additional suggestions concerning missing enclosures. Write follow-up letters also as reminders.

Be specific about what is being requested. If you are referring to an unanswered letter, send a duplicate of it. Avoid making the reader feel at fault.

Appreciation Letters. Numerous situations arise in business for expressing appreciation. Do not neglect writing thank-you letters. Be prompt in sending a thank-you letter, for the letter loses its effectiveness if it is delayed.

To let the reader know that the letter was written especially for the reader, be specific. For example:

> Thank you for sending your proposal for needed changes in the contract with dealers.

Letter Formats

With the efficiency of e-mail messages, fewer formal letters are being prepared. Further, unless the letter is very formal, contemporary letters usually adopt a basic style. The most popular and recognized formats are the full-block and modified-block letter styles. However, there are many acceptable letter styles. When you are new to the office position, begin by following the letter style already used in the office. Once you have established your credibility, you may want to introduce one of the following styles.

Full-Block Letter Style. Figure 5-1 illustrates a *full-block letter style*. Note that

- Every line from the date to the reference initials begins at the left margin.
- Paragraphs are single-spaced and not indented.

MA MILLENNIUM APPLIANCES, INC.
1611 Rutherford Blvd. Mission, KS 66202
(Tel) 1-800-873-9090 (Fax) 316-795-3982

September 5, 200X

Mr. Samuel Jenkins
Director of Architecture and Design
Grayson Contemporary Housing
1000 Mountain View Street
Pineville, LA 71360

Dear Sam:

We were very pleased to read about your recent promotion to Director of Architecture and Design for Grayson Contemporary Housing. No doubt, you will add to the already dynamic team that Pineville has been building for the past three years.

Call me once you get settled into your new position. We should have lunch together and discuss a potential business partnership where Millennium Appliances, Inc. can supply you with top-of-the-line home appliances at a wholesale price. Millennium's quality appliances would work well with the very attractive contemporary designs you are putting in your new housing. I am enclosing our latest brochure showing our new kitchen appliances.

Again, congratulations on your promotion and good luck with your new challenges. I look forward to hearing from you.

Sincerely,

Ms. Charlene Azam
Assistant Vice President of Marketing
Western Region

lr

Enclosure

■ **Figure 5-1**
Full-block letter style with mixed punctuation.

- A double space separates paragraphs.
- Four blank lines are left after the complimentary close to leave room for a signature.

Figure 5-1 also shows an example of **mixed punctuation** (a colon is used after the salutation and a comma is used after the complimentary close).

Modified-Block Letter Style. Figure 5-2 illustrates a modified-block letter. Note that the format is the same as the full-block style with the following exceptions:

- The date, complimentary close, and signature lines begin at the center of the page and are keyed to the right of center (not centered).
- Although not shown in Figure 5-2, the paragraphs are sometimes indented. However, the preference is to block them at the left.

MA MILLENNIUM APPLIANCES, INC.
Rutherford Blvd., Mission, KS 66202
(Tel) 1-800-873-9090 (Fax) 316-795-3982

September 5, 200X

Mr. Samuel Jenkins
Director of Architecture and Design
Grayson Contemporary Housing
1000 Mountain View Street
Pineville, LA 71360

Dear Sam

We were very pleased to read about your recent promotion to Director of Architecture and Design for Grayson Contemporary Housing. No doubt, you will add to the already dynamic team that Pineville has been building for the past three years.

Call me once you get settled into your new position. We should have lunch together and discuss a potential business partnership where Millennium Appliances, Inc. can supply you with top-of-the-line home appliances at a wholesale price. Millennium's quality appliances would work well with the very attractive contemporary designs you are putting in your new housing. I am enclosing our latest brochure showing our new kitchen appliances.

Again, congratulations on your promotion and good luck with your new challenges. I look forward to hearing from you.

Sincerely

Ms. Charlene Azam
Assistant Vice President of Marketing
Western Region

lr

Enclosure

■ **Figure 5-2**
Modified-block letter style with open punctuation.

Figure 5-2 also shows **open punctuation.** This punctuation style uses no punctuation after the salutation or after the complimentary close.

E-Mail Memorandums

Memorandums as we once knew them are becoming a thing of the past. They have been replaced by another form of memorandum—e-mail. E-mail memorandums are the most common form of communication within an organization. They transmit, confirm, request, inform, persuade, and report. E-mail is used to

■ provide in writing a written record of information.
■ identify the person who wrote the memo and when it was written.
■ make certain the right people get information.

Because companies commonly have network systems where all computers are linked or have Internet capability, e-mail memos are the main line of communication of an organization. You will learn more about e-mail in Chapter 6. The writing principles discussed above for letters also apply to writing memorandums.

- Use the "you" approach.
- Use positive language.
- Know your purpose.
- Be coherent, concise, correct, complete, and clear.
- Make your writing interesting.

Standard Memorandums

You will, however, be called upon occasionally to write a memorandum, also called a memo, rather than send the information as an e-mail message. You should continually strive to improve your writing skills whether writing letters or memos. Keep a reference manual handy for resolving questions about grammar, punctuation, capitalization, and number usage. When asked to write a memo, use the following guidelines:

- ✔ Use a standard format (most software programs have memo templates from which to choose).
- ✔ Write informally.
- ✔ Keep the memo to one page.
- ✔ Make sure the memo covers only one topic.
- ✔ Use lists whenever possible to itemize for easier reading.

PREPARING DOCUMENTS FOR DISTRIBUTION

An effective business document is a package of information containing essential facts, knowledge of business procedures and policies, and a specific message. All of these ingredients are carefully woven together and sent to a specific destination.

Once the task of creating a final draft is completed, several steps must be taken to ensure that the information package is accurate and complete. This section discusses the procedures necessary to complete the preparation process: proofreading, submitting letters for signature, assembling enclosures, making copies, and addressing envelopes.

Proofreading

All communication must be proofread and, if necessary, corrected. An office worker's mistakes easily could cost an organization goodwill, not to mention time and money. It is essential that all documents are correct in grammar, punctuation, content, format, and style. You can use proofreader's symbols when editing hard copy. Refer to the proofreading symbols on the back cover of this text. Remember that people will judge the competence of your organization, your manager, and you by the quality of work they receive.

You can proofread using your word processing software's spell checker. Most word processing software will automatically check grammar and style.

Proofreading at the Computer

1. Always consider your first version as a rough draft.
2. Be sure to turn on widow/orphan protection when using word processing, so that a single line will not be left stranded at the top or bottom of a page.
3. Print a hard copy to double-check for spacing errors.
4. Do a thorough job of editing before you begin making your corrections.
5. Check cross-references to other pages to make certain the information to which you are referring is still on those pages after editing.
6. After you finish making your editing corrections, proofread each change carefully.
7. Do a spell/grammar check again of the corrected version.

How to Double-Check Outgoing Documents

1. **Check facts and figures.** Verify specific information, such as dates (verify dates with days of the week), time, amounts of money (verify both figure and written amounts), columns of data, proper names, and locations.
2. **Check format.** Make sure the date line, enumerations (verify correct numbering, especially where corrections have been made), centering (check spacing before and after centered lines), salutation and closing lines, signature line, and enclosures have the correct placement and spacing.
3. **Check format.** Make sure information is complete (verify substitutions, and omissions). Proofread for meaning.
4. **Check mechanics.** Grammar, punctuation, spelling, capitalization, and number usage must be perfect.

Remember, however, that word processing software cannot detect every possible error, such as *then* for *than*, and should not replace your own proofreading and checking of a document.

Submitting Letters for Signature

To save time and to decrease interruptions, group the letters and submit them for signature. Submit as many letters as you can complete, allowing time for your manager or others to sign them and for you to insert them in the envelopes before mail pickup. The most appropriate time or the number of times each day to submit letters will depend on the mail pickup schedule in your organization and what is convenient for your manager. Written communication

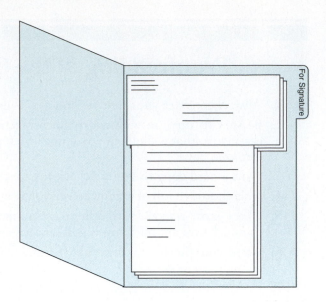

■ **Figure 5-3**
FOR SIGNATURE folder.

is most manageable when nothing is in the FOR SIGNATURE folder (see Figure 5-3) but the material to be sent. Place the addressed envelope over each letter and its accompanying enclosures to separate each item from the others in the stack. If a copy of a letter is to be mailed, place the matching envelope over it and put it in the stack immediately after the original.

When the same letter is sent to two or more persons, all these letters must be signed and should be arranged in the FOR SIGNATURE folder in the same order in which the addresses appear on the letter.

Some managers will want to see the letters being answered. If your manager does want to see the letters, submit them in a second folder, arranged in the identical order of the items to be signed.

Some office professionals have the responsibility of writing letters for their manager's signature as mentioned earlier. Submit separately any letters that you or someone else has written for your manager's signature. Your manager may want to read the letter before signing it. Before you put a letter in an envelope:

1. Glance at the signature to know that it has been signed.
2. Verify the enclosures and at the same time make a check mark on the file copy by the enclosure notation to indicate that the enclosures were sent.
3. Ascertain that the addressee on the envelope and on the letter is the same.
4. If your manager has written a note on a letter, photocopy it for the file.

Staple the file copy to the front of the letter being answered, and put these items in the to-be-filed location. When a letter your manager initiates is two or more pages long, staple the pages of the file copy before placing it in the to-be-filed location.

Sometimes all parts of a letter are not answered at one time. You should keep track of this. Never file a letter that is only partially answered. Mark the part that is unanswered and give it back to your manager. If your manager asks you to sign a letter for him or her, write the signature and place your initials below it.

Assembling Enclosures

An enclosure notation is typed on a letter to provide a checklist both at the time the letter is being sent and at the time it is received. Therefore, choose the type of notation that will be most helpful to you. Here are some tips to follow.

- You have the responsibility, whenever an enclosure is mentioned, of obtaining or preparing it and attaching it to the document. When you submit documents for signature, you should include all the enclosures with them. If you do submit a document for signature without its enclosure, attach a note to inform your manager and serve as a reminder to yourself to include it.

- Remember that copies being mailed also require enclosures. You can make the copies after the documents are signed. The recipient of the copy may need the enclosures that accompany the original document, plus additional ones, in order to be brought up-to-date on the transaction.

- If the item to be enclosed is on your desk, put the enclosure with the document. Make a list of the enclosures needed on your to-do list and collect all the enclosures at one time. Check off the enclosures as you obtain them. On this same list, jot down reminders of all the tasks you must complete later pertaining to the processed documents. For instance, you may need to register a letter and request a return receipt or to ask another department to package material for mailing separately.

- Keep a record of the persons receiving the copies and the date of distribution. You can write this information on the original near the top of the page.

- Letter-sized enclosures are placed behind the document and folded simultaneously; small enclosures are placed in the fold of the document. Enclosures that have been prefolded mechanically should be placed in the fold of the document.

- To hold small enclosures temporarily in place—until you are ready to insert the document and the enclosures in the envelope—put them in the envelope or fasten them to the document with a paper clip. Paper clips do make imprints and will sometimes catch and tear. To prevent this, fold a small sheet of paper over the assembled items before you fasten them with the paper clip. Do not put a paper clip in an envelope to be mailed.

- Do not staple enclosures to the document. Today, mail must go through four or five high-speed machines at the post office. When you use a staple, you run the risk of having the document torn up in a machine and of damaging several other pieces of mail.

- When typing an e-mail message and sending an attachment, make certain the receiver will be able to open and read the attachment. Remember that higher versions of word processing software can read lower versions, but lower versions cannot always read higher versions, and not all word processing software can convert files from other software. When using a PC, you can send files as text files (files saved with a *.txt* extension) and any software program can read them. When using a Mac, text files aren't readable without a special translating system. You will learn more about e-mail and sending attachments in Chapter 6.

■   When you must mail large items, you are responsible for preparing the labels, even if the items will be wrapped and sent by someone in another department. When you forward an item to another department for handling, it probably will be processed immediately. However, it is your responsibility to see that the item is mailed. If follow-up is necessary, place a note to do so in your tickler file (Refer to Chapter 3 for tickler file).

Making Copies

Make one file copy of all letters. The method that you use will be determined by the organization for which you work and will vary from item to item, depending on how the copy will be used.

Some organizations maintain a reading file, arranged in chronological order, of all outgoing letters. If your organization maintains such a reading file, make an extra copy of all outgoing documents for this chronological file.

Also, a predetermined number of copies will be required for certain items. Frequently these are forms already assembled in sets of different-colored sheets of paper with notations for distribution. When you are given additional information concerning who is to receive copies of standard forms, record the information in your office manual.

When copies are to be mailed to others in addition to the addressee, list the names of the recipients as part of the copy notation. A colon following the copy notation is optional. You may use *cc* to indicate carbon copy, *pc* to indicate photocopy, or simply *c* for any kind of copy.

To guide you in sending all the copies that are to be mailed, check off the names. On the first copy, check the first name; on the second copy, the second name; on the third copy, the third name; and so on.

Remember to make a copy for your tickler file of items that you must follow up on. Never put the file copy in your tickler file.

Addressing Envelopes

The information in the inside address on an external letter and the address on the envelope should be identical; the form could differ. The U. S. Postal Service requires that all envelopes be addressed in all-capital letters and that no punctuation appear in the entire address as shown in the following example.

MR HAROLD MARTIN
1515 REGAL ROW
DALLAS TX 75225

The inside address is usually typed with uppercase and lowercase letters. If window envelopes are used, the scanners used by the U. S. Postal Service can sort the all-caps, no-punctuation style more rapidly. Also, if your equipment will store the address to be automatically printed on the envelope and you want the address on the envelope to be in all-caps style, you can accomplish this by using all caps for the inside address. Address the envelope and place it face up over the top of the letter.

If your organization uses window envelopes for external letters, key the inside address at a position on the letters that will ensure that all the lines of

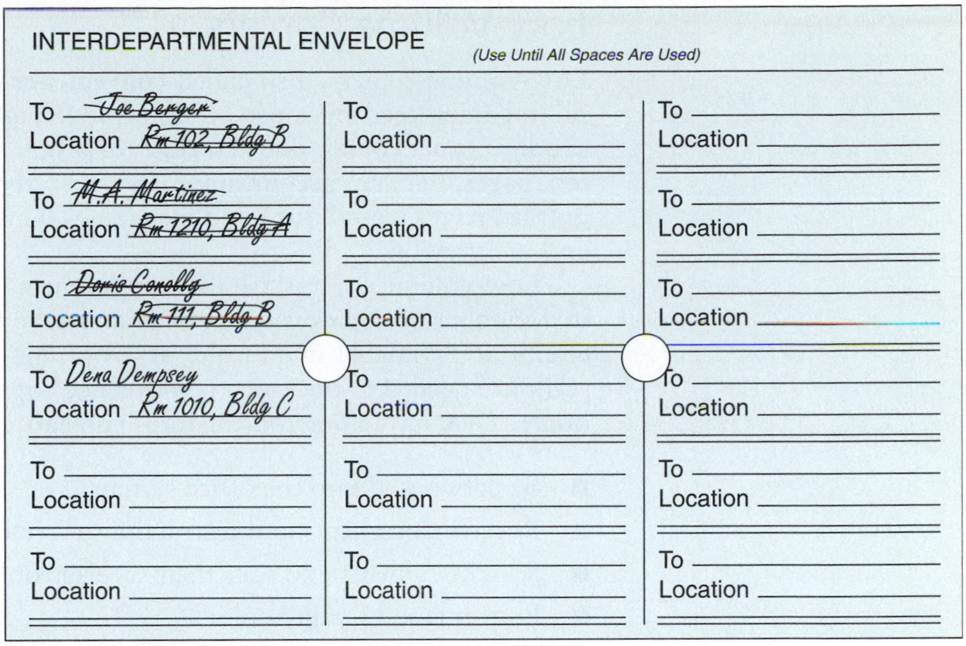

INTERDEPARTMENTAL ENVELOPE (Use Until All Spaces Are Used)

To ~~Joe Berger~~ Location ~~Rm 102, Bldg B~~	To Location	To Location
To ~~M.A. Martinez~~ Location ~~Rm 1210, Bldg A~~	To Location	To Location
To ~~Doris Conolly~~ Location ~~Rm 111, Bldg B~~	To Location	To Location
To Dena Dempsey Location Rm 1010, Bldg C	To Location	To Location
To Location	To Location	To Location
To Location	To Location	To Location

■ **Figure 5-4** A reusable interoffice envelope.

the address are clearly discernible through the window. Fold the letter so that it cannot shift in the envelope, obscuring part of the address. According to the U. S. Postal Service, there should be at least one-fourth inch between the address and the left, right, and bottom edges of the window when the insert moves to its full limits in the envelope. If the address contains more than five lines, do not use a window envelope because the entire address will not show.

For interoffice communications at your location and for packet mail, use a reusable interoffice envelope. An example is shown in Figure 5-4. Be sure that the name of the last addressee is crossed out. Write the name of the addressee and an address that is complete enough for the communication to be delivered without delay. Seal an interoffice envelope if the enclosure is confidential. Some organizations do not use interoffice envelopes except for confidential information. When envelopes are not provided for nonconfidential interoffice mail, staple a routing slip with the appropriate information on it near the top left edge of the communication. Do not fold the communication.

WHAT ARE REPROGRAPHICS?

Some years ago the first desktop publishing software program hit the market and changed the publishing world forever. Since then the pace of the imaging world has done nothing but speed up. Hundreds of applications are available to use to make an image or construct a page. These advances have allowed the office professional to create high-quality, time saving, inexpensive, digital files on the computer that rival the most sophisticated reprographics shops.

However, when large mailings or lengthy documents must be distributed, you will need to use large-volume reprographics equipment. All reproduction processes are called **reprographics.** Copiers are classified as low-, mid-, and high-volume machines.

Low-Volume Copiers

Low-volume copiers, also called **convenience copiers,** are the very popular photocopier used by most office professionals. These copiers quickly reproduce exact copies, one at a time, of original materials, such as typewritten pages, letters, accounting papers, statistical reports, tables, charts, graphs, pages from books and magazines, newspaper articles, illustrations, and pictures.

Low-volume copiers are used in decentralized areas because of the limited number of copies usually made and save the user travel time. The machines are available in console, desktop, and portable models. No special skills are needed to operate a convenience copier. Limited instruction is adequate. They have numerous features and can

- Be networked into the office system
- Receive documents and instructions directly from computers
- Scan documents and save them as electronic files
- Print in good-quality color
- Reduce and enlarge documents
- Accommodate a variety of paper sizes
- Automatically feed documents
- Print up to approximately 65 copies per minute

Mid-Volume Copiers

These machines have all the features of the low-volume copiers, along with some additional features. **Mid-volume copiers** are desktop models and are used in both decentralized and centralized areas of the office environment depending on the office's copy needs. Most mid-volume copiers can

- Operate through touch control screens
- Accommodate more paper sizes and weights
- Store multiple instructions
- Perform **duplexing**—copying on both sides of the paper
- Print in high-quality color
- Sort and stack multiple copies
- Staple and hole-punch documents
- Bind documents into book-style covers
- Center an image on the paper
- Print up to approximately 145 copies per minute

High-Volume Copiers

High-volume copiers are floor console models. They are located in centralized reproduction departments or are available in several dispersed locations within large organizations. Because of their many features they may often require extensive training. Figure 5-5 shows a high-volume copier.

■ **Figure 5-5**
A high-volume copier.

Some high-volume copiers can create images according to programmed instructions and are called **intelligent copiers.** They contain microprocessors that enable the copier to produce copies from instructions transmitted by computers and prerecorded magnetic media, as well as by remote equipment by means of telephone wires.

In addition to all the tasks that low- and mid-volume copiers can do, high-volume copiers can

- Produce documents in book format with adjusted headers, footers, margins, and page numbers
- Hold large supplies of paper
- Sort at faster speeds
- Insert tabs and coversheets where programmed to do so
- Print in color with even better quality
- Produce up to approximately 200 copies per minute

Which Copier Do I Use?

In a number of situations, office professionals must select the appropriate copier. Knowledge of reprographics helps the office professional to make an efficient decision. The decision depends on a number of considerations. Here are a few factors to consider:

1. How many copies are needed?
2. How quickly are the copies needed?
3. How professional should the final copy be?
4. Is the original document usable as is?

Considerations Regarding Reprographics

It is important to consider areas of reprographics that can raise copying costs. Consider the following scenario:

> Juan, assistant to the regional sales manager, was asked to study the department's rising copying costs. After investigating the procedures and copying habits of the department staff for three weeks, Juan reported the following problems to his manager:
>
> 1. Additional copies were made—more than needed.
> 2. Individuals were copying documents that the in-house reprographics center should have handled.
> 3. Individuals were making copies for personal use.

Organizations have different options available to them. One popular method of controlling the use of a copier is to provide the appropriate people with individual copy cards or keys. When the card or key is used, the copier registers the number of copies made. This method discourages people from making too many copies and making personal copies. Often the copy cards can be purchased in advance, thus allowing the department to prepay for copying privileges.

Another important consideration is that of copying materials that infringe on the U. S. copyright law. The term **copyright** is used to identify the legal right of authors (and artists) to protect their work against unauthorized reproduction. Materials that are protected contain a notice of copyright. In many organizations in areas where copying is done, a notice of the copyright law is posted at the copier to ensure that employees are aware of their responsibilities.

A third consideration is that of setting guidelines, if necessary, for your office work group to follow when determining the most efficient copier use. It may be necessary for you to establish a range of number of originals to be copied and the type of copier to use in your department. For example, if fewer than 50 originals are to be copied, use a convenience copier; if more than 50 originals are to be copied, use the in-house reprographics center. If 500 or more copies are needed, consider using a high-volume copier. This may sometimes mean contracting with an outside printing company. Here are some tips to make the copying process efficient and economical.

1. Copy when you have several items.
2. Determine the best times to use the copier. Avoid high-traffic times.
3. Keep track of the monitoring device assigned to you for copying purposes.
4. Plan ahead for large copying needs.

ETHICS IN WRITING

Many businesses today have a written code of ethics that encompasses everything from ethics in business practices to ethics in receiving and writing e-mail. Use the following guidelines when writing for you or your manager's signature.

■ Make certain the information included in your writing is correct. Document your writing with source information where necessary or make a note on your file copy of the source you used. If you are asked later where you obtained your information, you will have a ready reference.

■ Keep all confidential information away from prying eyes. Place sensitive information in a folder when you are not working on it rather than just in your in-basket or on your desk where others might read it.

■ Don't participate in e-mail chain letters or sending and receiving jokes or other humorous material. Given the length of some messages and the extent of participation, system administrators and security personnel are justified in their concern. Participation in these activities can negatively impact both the system and performance and workforce productivity.

■ Make certain the information you write is your own. Taking credit for another's ideas or thoughts is called **plagiarism.** Always give credit where credit is due when you use others' work.

■ Never violate copyright laws. Make certain you have permission to use any material that is copyrighted before you copy it.

INTERNATIONAL ADDRESSES

When keying international addresses on envelopes, type the name of the country on a separate line in all-capital letters. Do not abbreviate the name of the country. Study the following example.

```
HANS HAAR
TIETGENSKOLEN
ODENSE BUSINESS COLLEGE
NONNEBAKKEN 9
500 ODENSE C
DENMARK
```

If you are writing from outside the United States to someone in the United States, type *UNITED STATES OF AMERICA* as the last line of the address.

quicktips

Don't Depend on Your Computer's Spell Checker to Catch Grammar Errors!

■ When you are talking, words that sound alike aren't a problem.
  ■ If you say "I like *you're* office," would that person know you should have used the adjective *your*? No, he or she wouldn't.
■ When you are sending written correspondence, words that sound alike but have different meanings are a problem. Double-check your information:
  ■ If you write "*There* ideas are always the best," would the recipient know you used an *adjective* when you should have used the *pronoun their*? Probably so, and would wonder if you were sloppy in other areas of your business.

Overview

✔ Verbal communication guidelines include:

■ Listen and watch for verbal and nonverbal feedback.

■ Choose your words carefully when the topic is sensitive or controversial.

■ Encourage the other person to talk—communication should be a two-way street.

■ Give the other person your undivided attention.

■ Avoid talking incessantly.

■ Summarize the important points and give the listener a chance to ask questions.

✔ Factors that can be used to interpret nonverbal communications are image, personal space, eye contact, posture, and facial expressions.

✔ Improve your listening skills by:

■ Concentrating on what is being said and on grasping the meaning of what is being said

■ Becoming aware of your listening barriers

■ Repeating information to ensure understanding

■ Taking notes and confirming that what you understand is what was meant.

✔ An effective business letter:

1. Centers around a single purpose

2. Is written from the reader's point of view

3. Conveys a meaningful message through completeness, correctness, coherence, conciseness, and clearness

4. Reflects a positive, sincere, and appropriate tone

5. Is expressed in an interesting style through the use of natural, vivid, and varied language.

✔ The requirements of good writing sometimes called the Cs of letter writing are completeness, correctness, coherence, conciseness, and clearness.

✔ The various types of written communication are letters and memos written about appointments, requests, orders, routine replies, acknowledgments, transmittals, delays, follow-ups, and other routine business situations.

✔ The two most popular contemporary letter formats are full-block letter style and modified-block letter style.

✔ E-mail memorandums are used to:

1. Provide in writing a written record of information

2. Identify the person who wrote the memo and when it was written

3. Make certain the right people get information.

✔ Guidelines for writing standard memos include:

1. Use a standardized format.

2. Write informally.

3. Keep the memo to one page.

4. Make sure the memo covers only one topic.

5. Use lists whenever possible for easier reading.

✔ Do not rely completely on your spell checker to catch all errors. Read each document once for content and again for mechanics, such as grammar and punctuation. When proofreading at the computer:

1. Always consider your first version as a rough draft.

2. Be sure to turn on widow/orphan protection when using word processing so that single lines are not left stranded at the top or bottom of a page.

3. Print a hard copy to double-check for spacing errors.

4. Do a thorough job of editing before you begin making your corrections.

5. Check cross-references to other pages to make certain the information to which you are referring is still on those pages after editing.

6. After you finish making your editing corrections, proofread each change carefully.

7. Do a spell/grammar check again of corrected version.

✔ Letters and memos are most manageable when nothing is in the FOR SIGNATURE folder except the material to be sent out. Place the addressed envelope over each letter and its accompanying enclosures to separate each item from the others in the stack. Place copies to be mailed behind the original of the letter with matching envelope.

✔ An enclosure notation is typed on a document to provide a checklist both at the time the letter is being sent and at the time it is received.

✔ Make one file copy of all documents.

✔ The U. S. Postal Service requires that all envelopes be addressed in all-capital letters and that no punctuation appears in the entire address.

✔ Reprographics are all reproduction processes.

✔ Copiers are classified as low-volume copiers (also called convenience copiers), mid-volume copiers, and high-volume copiers.

✔ When making copies, here are some factors to consider:

1. How many copies are needed?

2. How quickly are the copies needed?

3. How professional should the final copy be?

4. Is the original usable as is?

✔ Copying tips include:

1. Copy when you have several items.

2. Determine the best times to use the copier. Avoid high-traffic times.

3. Keep track of the monitoring device assigned to you for copying purposes.

4. Plan ahead for large copying needs.

✔ An office professional should follow these guidelines of ethics in all writing:

■ Make certain the information you write is correct and documented if necessary.

- Keep all confidential information away from prying eyes.
- Don't participate in e-mail chain letters or jokes or other humorous material.
- Never violate copyright laws. Always have permission before you copy a document.

✔ When typing international addresses on envelopes, type the name of the country on a separate last line in all-capital letters.

Key Terms

Connotation. The suggested idea or overtone that a word acquires through association, in addition to its explicit meaning.

Convenience copiers. Low-volume copiers used in decentralized areas.

Copyright. Identifies the legal right of authors or artists to protect their work against unauthorized reproduction.

Denotation. The explicit dictionary meaning of a word.

Duplexing. Copying on both sides of the paper.

High-volume copiers. Floor console models that can produce up to approximately 200 copies per minute.

Intelligent copiers. High-volume copiers that can create images according to programmed instructions.

Low-volume copiers. Copiers that can produce approximately 65 copies per minute. Also called convenience copiers.

Mid-volume copiers. Copiers that produce approximately 145 copies per minute.

Mixed punctuation. This punctuation style requires a colon after the salutation and a comma after the complimentary close.

Open punctuation. This punctuation style requires no punctuation after the salutation or complimentary close.

Plagiarism. Taking credit for another's ideas or thoughts.

Reprographics. Any of the various reproduction processes.

You-attitude. A letter-writing technique in which the writer shows consideration for the reader by putting the reader's needs first, emphasizing the reader's interest, and using words the reader can understand.

For Your Discussion

 Retrieve file C5.DQ.DOC from your student data disk.

Directions

Enter your response after each question.

1. What precautions should be taken to protect confidential information while it is being processed?

2. When letters are to be signed, how should they be arranged in the FOR SIGNATURE folder?

3. What are three purposes for memos?

4. Name three items you should check before you place a letter in an envelope.

5. Explain what is meant by the "you-attitude" in writing letters.

6. Name the five Cs in writing an effective message.

7. Describe the different types of routine letters that office professionals originate and sign.

8. Assume that you have been given the assignment to write a letter for your manager's signature. What can you do to make your composition sound as though the manager wrote the letter?

9. Distinguish among the different types of copiers.

10. Discuss at least three important considerations relating to reprographics.

CAPITALIZATION WORKSHOP

Letters are capitalized for two basic reasons: (1) to show the beginning of a sentence; (2) to show that a proper noun or adjective is more important than a common noun. Complete the exercises below by applying capitalization rules.

For Review

Appendix A: Rule 10: Money

                  Rule 11: Geographical Terms

                  Rule 12: Government and Political Terms

 Retrieve file C5-WRKS.DOC from your data disk.

Directions

Write C at the end of the sentence if the capitalization is correct; otherwise, make the necessary corrections.

Rule 10: Money

1. A check in the amount of one thousand forty-two dollars ($1,042.00) was mailed to you today.

2. The company profits were over $50,000.

3. The estate ran the company and paid dividends of five hundred sixty dollars ($560.00) to each stockholder.

4. When the auditor finished the report, he found that over $600.00 was missing.

5. The fee for use of said property is to be three hundred fifty dollars ($350.00) a month and is to be paid by June 15. (Legal document)

Rule 11: Geographical Terms

1. Our headquarters is on the west coast.

2. The south central part of the United States is sometime called the bible belt.

3. The Higgins building is located six blocks North on Fifth and Elm Streets.

4. Our company moved to Western Colorado because of the economic growth in that area.

5. The regional office located on the Florida coast is planning an expansion.

Rule 12: Government and Political Terms

1. Our federal reserve system is the central banking system of the United States.

2. Our national parks provide tremendous entertainment to millions of people.

3. The Water District has approved new regulations for the next fiscal year.

4. Statewide reforms are being carried out throughout Washington State.

5. The board of health has been reviewing the fruit and vegetable quarantines.

On the Job Situations

 Retrieve file C5-OJS.DOC from your student data disk.

Directions

Enter your response after each situation.

1. You sent a confirmation e-mail of an informal meeting called by your manager. In the e-mail message, you referred to reports that your manager asked the participants to review before the meeting. You sent the message without attaching the reports. What do you do now?

2. You requested that reproduction services make 500 copies of a speech your manager will make at a national convention next week. The speech is eight pages long. The copies will be distributed at that convention. By mistake, you attached a draft of the speech to the reproduction requisition instead of the clean copy you had prepared. Even though *DRAFT* was typed on each page, the duplicating operator did not catch your mistake. He ran 500 copies of the pages you submitted and assembled them. Several of the pages had minor editing changes, but the last three pages had numerous deletions and additions in longhand. You were not aware that you had sent the wrong revision of the speech until the 500 copies were delivered to you. What do you anticipate happens next? What will you do?

3. You have observed a new employee, Jan, whom you supervise, using the copier for personal use. It is against company policy to do so. You know she has been told not to use the copier for personal use because the company policy is discussed during new employee orientation meetings. Analyze the situation. How would you handle this situation?

4. The office manager's assistant reviews all the writing you do, which is mostly letters and reports. Your documents are constantly changed to suit the assistant's personal writing style; many changes are simply another way of saying the same thing. You think these changes are not errors on your part but preferences on the assistant's part. Because you have to do so much editing, you are often not able to complete all your work. Also, the assistant seems to enjoy pointing out your errors, and he is really getting under your skin. What should you do? Identify three ways to handle the situation—assuming each time that the previous attempt to do something didn't work.

Projects and Activities

1. Visit a local reprographics equipment manufacturer, research the Internet, or look in an office equipment magazine to find the name and address of one. Write a letter to the manufacturer requesting informational brochures on their latest equipment.

2. Interview an assistant who is responsible for copying or a person who works in a copy center and ask what considerations are given in determining which type of copier is used for their copying purposes.

3. In a group, create a checklist for writing letters. Include such tasks as checking grammar and punctuation as well as format. Be prepared to share your final product with the class.

4. Research the library or the Internet for books and articles on nonverbal communication and make a list of the various nonverbal expressions and their meanings. Be prepared to share your findings with the class.

Surfing the Internet

You have been in charge of the copying needs for your company. Your manager suggested you check into the International Reprographic Association and the services it provides. He said perhaps there would be enough money to pay your dues. You are to research the association on the Internet.

1. Connect to the Internet and enter the following url: http:// www.irga.com.

2. Locate information about the International Reprographic Association—what services it provides, how you join, cost of dues, whether it sends newsletters, magazines, and so on.

3. Write a memo to your instructor concerning the information you found.

4. Locate information about copyright laws. Print the first page listing the main topics. Turn in the list to your instructor.

Using MS Office 2002

Format with Bullets

 In Microsoft Word, use bullets to emphasize parts of your document to draw attention to important issues. Use the first five Key Terms on page 142 to practice this exercise.

1. Open Microsoft Word and make sure a blank document screen displays.

2. If the Bullets Icon is not at the top of your screen, click on the View menu, point to Toolbars, and then select Formatting. The Bullets icon will appear on the Formatting toolbar toward the top of the screen.

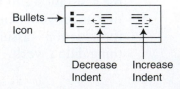

3. If desired, you can type the listed items first, pressing Enter after each item. Another method is to click on the Bullet icon prior to typing the list and a bullet will appear before each item.

   a. Type each item and press Enter for a new line, and a new bullet will automatically appear.

   b. When finished with the list, simply press Enter twice and the unwanted bullet will disappear.

Use whichever method suits your needs—you don't have to retype to display bullets! Type the key words again without the bullets.

4. To add bullets to your list, drag the mouse over all the listed items to highlight them.

5. Click on the Bullets icon on the Formatting toolbar.

6. Your list will automatically be displayed with preceding bullets.

7. While the items are still *highlighted* you can

   a. Decrease or increase the indent by clicking on the Decrease Indent or Increase Indent Icons located on the Formatting toolbar.

   b. Change the bullet style by

      1. Right-clicking on the highlighted list.

      2. Clicking on Bullets and Numbering on the shortcut list that displays.

      3. On the Bulleted tab, viewing the various styles available to you.

      4. Clicking on the style you want and then clicking on OK.

APPLICATION PROBLEMS

APPLICATION 5–A

Keying an Instruction Sheet from Longhand

Supplies needed: Longhand notes on Form 5-A, Making Blind-Copy Notations (located at the back of the text.); plain paper.

Directions: The transcriptionist in the word processing center requested clarification about typing blind-copy notations. Mrs. Quevedo asked you to prepare the instructions. You are to keyboard the handwritten instruction sheet shown on Form 5-A. Ask Mrs. Quevedo to approve your copy before you submit it to the supervisor of the word processing center. Save the file as AP5-A.

APPLICATION 5–B

Inserting Proofreader's Marks

Supplies needed: Form 5-B, memorandum about seminar.

 Retrieve file AP5B.DOC from your student data disk.

Directions: Using the proofreading symbols on the inside back cover of this text, mark the memorandum on Form 5-B ready for processing. Check your copy to be sure that you have marked all the corrections needed. Make all your marked corrections in file AP5-B.DOC; print one copy.

APPLICATION 5-C

Presenting Letters for Signature

Supplies needed: Form 5-C-1, Letter Copy; letterhead for Supreme Appliances, Inc. (Forms 5-C-2, 5-C-3, 5-C-4); two No. 10 envelopes.

 Retrieve files FORMS5C2.DOC, FORMS5C3.DOC, and FORMS5C4.DOC from your student data disk.

Directions: You may use the letterhead Forms 5-C-2, 5-C-3, and 5-C-4, you may make copies of the forms, you may scan the forms into your word processing software, or you may use plain paper. Put the letterhead forms in your printer tray when you get ready to print. Follow your instructor's directions.

Type the two letters and one memo shown on Form 5-C-1, using a correct letter and memo format. Make one copy of each letter or memo. Address an envelope for each letter to be mailed. Arrange the letters and envelopes in a folder for Mrs. Quevedo's signature. Because Mrs. Quevedo frequently makes notations on file copies, include the file copies in a folder.

APPLICATION 5-D

Reprographics

Supplies needed: Copier.

 Retrieve file AP5-A.DOC from your student data disk and print one copy of it; then follow these steps:

1. Using a copier, reduce each page of the file to 90 percent.
2. Set the copier to copy, duplex, collate, and staple three copies of the file.

Your Action Plan

Complete your Action Plan; if necessary, review the guidelines in Chapter 1. Set one goal using the information you learned in Chapter 5.

Your Portfolio

With the help of your instructor, select the best papers representative of your work from Chapter 5. Follow your instructor's directions about formatting, assembling, and turning in the portfolio.

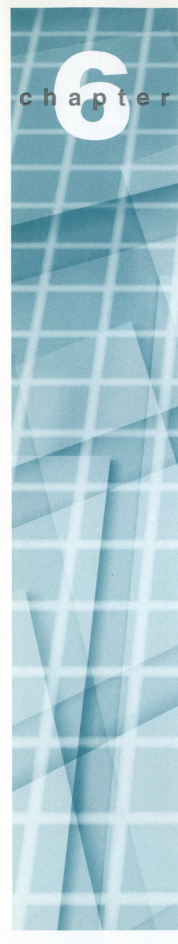

chapter

6

Processing Mail

LEARNING OUTCOMES

When you have completed this chapter, you should be able to:

✔ Follow electronic mail etiquette.

✔ Handle incoming mail.

✔ Handle outgoing mail.

✔ Distinguish among domestic and international mail classifications and mail services.

One of the most exciting developments in office communication has been the rise of electronic mail (e-mail). Organizations use e-mail among their own departments and to send messages to distant branch offices or to other companies. Just as office professionals are responsible for handling the telephone traffic, they are also likely to be first choice when it comes to sorting through the e-mail traffic awaiting their managers' reply. Both managers and office professionals often become overwhelmed by the volume of messages they must sort through daily. Making this task easier for your supervisor often becomes the responsibility of the office professional.

Although electronic mail, courier services, and other mail alternatives have been introduced to the business world, traditional mail services remain the primary means of moving information from one location to another. Whether you are an executive assistant in a large organization or an accounting assistant in a small office, mail will arrive at your desk daily.

Each piece of mail represents a contact with a customer outside your organization or another employee within your organization. The promptness with which you and your manager answer and deliver outgoing mail is an important factor in building goodwill and increasing profits for your organization. It is in your and the company's best interest to choose the most efficient means of delivery. Although far from comprehensive, this chapter introduces alternatives and suggestions for working with selective technology-based mail services, as well as the traditional incoming and outgoing mail.

HANDLING MAIL

Electronic Mail

Telecommunications involves the transmission of information from one location to another by electronic devices. The information is transmitted in a variety of formats, such as voice, data, image, and text. Electronic mail (e-mail) systems are popular because of the high speed with which information can be sent within or outside an organization. A second big advantage is that information can be distributed to a specific location and stored in electronic form until the recipient is ready to receive it. This section introduces you to electronic mail transmissions.

Today, e-mail is rapidly replacing telephone calls and business letters—for good reason. E-mail eliminates frustrating phone tag, saves on expensive overnight delivery charges, and makes it easy for customers to place orders and receive immediate support. Plus, your e-mail partner has a printed record of the message—an advantage over a telephone call.

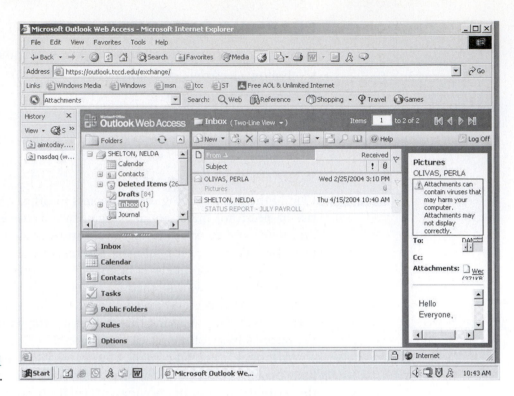

■ **Figure 6-1**
An electronic mailbox.

For sending memos and other documents, e-mail is faster and, in most cases, more reliable than traditional mail services; it's even more convenient than the same-day delivery services offered by express mail carriers. In some companies, e-mail has reduced the amount of intracompany regular mail service by at least 20 percent.

Electronic mail (e-mail) can be defined as the transmission of messages by computer from one person to another. It entails using the computer, the modem, and communications software. Each e-mail user has a mailbox that must be entered with a special code or password. The user checks routinely for incoming messages. Figure 6-1 shows an example of an electronic mailbox. When the user accesses the mailbox, the message will appear on the computer screen. If necessary, the user can save or print the message.

E-mail does have its drawbacks. Messages can also be lost or delayed if there are problems with the host computer that handles the e-mail service. Another growing problem is junk e-mail, called spam. With more businesses going online, e-mail is another outlet for direct-mail solicitation. Despite these drawbacks, it is reported that between thirty and fifty million people use e-mail. Because e-mail is fast, efficient, and convenient, it has become one of the primary forms of business communication.

E-mail can be an effective, convenient way to communicate with your manager, your team members, and customers—but only if you manage your mail efficiently. Without careful management, e-mail can bring frustration and confusion to even the most organized employees. Here are a few tips to help you get the real benefits of this service:

1. Check your messages frequently throughout the day. E-mail messages are like pieces of paper on your desk. The messages must be treated with the

same importance as you give to traditional incoming mail. You might want to check your messages first thing in the morning, at noon, and again late in the afternoon. If you schedule regular times throughout the day to check e-mail, you'll be able to better manage your correspondence.

2. Respond to messages immediately. Get in the habit of answering messages when you check your e-mail. Answering the messages promptly lets everyone know you are on top of things and can be relied on for prompt response. If you need more time to gather information before responding, let the receiver know you received the message and are working on gathering the requested information.

3. Delete messages regularly. Doing so will save you from having to read through old ones. If there are messages you want to keep, you can save them to electronic folders or to a diskette. If you save messages to a diskette, attachments cannot be viewed. Attachments must be saved separately.

It is a fact that e-mail is increasingly replacing standard letters, memos, and faxes as a form of fast, easy, inexpensive, and effective communication. However, many people have not yet learned the basic e-mail etiquette for sending concise and courteous electronic messages.

Here are a few basic e-mail etiquette, or "netiquette," rules to follow:

1. Never send anything through e-mail that you don't want made public. E-mail messages travel to many readers—some of whom you may never meet. Remember that coworkers, managers, and others may have opportunities to read your e-mail. There's no way of knowing who will eventually read your messages, so make sure that whatever you enter on the computer screen cannot return to haunt you later.

2. Address the receiver by name in the opening sentence. E-mail etiquette dictates that you simply include the receiver's name in the first sentence. For example, "Marilyn, thank you for your quick response."

3. Always reread messages before sending them. Use your spell checker. Even if the receiver knows that you were rushed in sending the message, misspelled words show carelessness and make an unfavorable impression. Double-check all facts and figures. Sending out incorrect information can cause delays in signing contracts, loss of sales, and so on.

4. Keep your message as concise as possible. Unless you are passing along information that has been specifically requested by your receiver, try to keep your message to a maximum of two screens. With the increase in use of electronic mail, office professionals may receive up to thirty messages daily. Just as clear and concise writing is important in business writing, it is equally important in writing electronic messages. Most people do not have the time or inclination to read lengthy postings.

5. Use capital letters sparingly. In the e-mail world, a message or phrase written in all caps is called "shouting." Not only is shouting impolite, but messages written in uppercase are difficult to read. Use capital letters only for emphasis. Some users recommend that if you want to emphasize certain words or phrases, enclose them in quotation marks, such as "confidential."

6. Most e-mail applications will automatically display the original messages in "replies" and "forwarded" messages. When replying to another person and the original message isn't displayed, quote excerpts of the original message. This eliminates the need for you to summarize what the other person has written. Furthermore, you will remind the receiver of his or her original request and save the person time from pulling up the original message for review. Your browser can be set to repeat the sender's message each time you reply.

7. Always get a writer's permission before forwarding or posting an e-mail message. When someone sends you a message, the person may assume that the message will be kept confidential. If you forward the message without the writer's permission, you may cause problems for that writer. If the writer knew the message was to be forwarded, he or she may have written the message in a different style, made a telephone call, or not written the message at all. In reality, many people don't obtain the writer's permission before forwarding or posting it in another location. Be careful of what you write. It most likely will be passed on without your consent or knowledge.

8. When posting a message to a group, make sure that your message is pertinent to all members of the group. People dislike having to take the time to weed out messages that are not appropriate or important to their specific work-related activities.

E-mail messages have three components: a heading, a body, and a signature. Here are a few guidelines to follow when formatting your e-mail:

Heading. When people review or scan their messages, they often look at the subject line to determine the message's topic. For example, you scan your messages to see if the messages are informational, urgent, or require action. For best results:

■ Keep each e-mail message to one topic. Information on multiple topics confuses the reader and makes paper and electronic filing more difficult.

■ Be concise in writing the subject line. For example, if you are sending a message about a revision to your vacation policy or procedure, "Update of Vacation Policy" is more specific than "Vacation Policy."

■ Label subject headings. For example, it is helpful to the reader if the message is marked as "FYI" or "Urgent" or "Action Needed." Your browser can be set to flag messages that are important.

■ Send yourself a copy or blind copy of important messages to save in your files.

Body. The body of your message should follow basic guidelines of effective business writing. Here are a few tips:

■ Explain what you want in the first several sentences. In traditional business writing, you learn to lead up to the point, especially if you are delivering a negative message. For best results in writing e-mail messages, tell your reader in the first sentences who you are and what you want.

■ Remember to focus on one topic. For best results, keep your message as brief as possible.

Signature. Here are a few guidelines for closing your message.

- Avoid traditional closings such as "Sincerely" or "Sincerely yours." Most electronic programs allow the user to add signature footers designed to include your name, company, department, address, and telephone and fax numbers, and these should be used instead. These footers are automatically attached to all messages you send.

- **Emoticons** are visual expressions equivalent to your attitudes or emotions, such as a smile or a frown. Although most people will not use them in business e-mails, you will undoubtedly see them. Here are a few commonly used emoticons.

:-) happy   :-(sad   :-( ) shouting

Electronic Bulletin Board

Much like their corkboard predecessors, **electronic bulletin boards** are public message centers that appear on computer networks. A **bulletin board system (BBS)** is a host computer that can be reached by computer modem for the purpose of sharing or exchanging messages or other files. Whereas e-mail is intended for addressed recipients, electronic bulletin board messages are intended for anyone and everyone with access to the network. Electronic bulletin boards are also an integral part of such commercial networks as Prodigy, America Online (AOL), and Delphi Forums.

Facsimile

The **facsimile,** commonly known as the **fax machine,** is a device that will copy and transmit, over telephone lines, graphical (charts, photographs, drawings, longhand messages) or textual (typed or forms) documents to a corresponding remote fax machine. The document will be reproduced on paper at the destination fax or computer. See Figure 6-2.

Faxing may be the quickest way to get a document across the city, country, or even the world. The rates are more expensive than using the U.S. Postal service but less expensive than most courier services, depending on the size of the document. The speed of fax transmission varies with the size of the page, the density of the image to be faxed and, of course, the levels of technology of the fax machine sending and receiving documents. However, the sender can be sure that regardless of the distance, the document will reach its destination within seconds of being sent.

Fax transmission uses telephone lines to send documents—in fact, sending a fax is as easy as making a telephone call. Fax machines operate automatically, allowing you to send documents without first notifying the recipient. The general procedure is very simple:

1. Place the document to be transmitted in the sending fax unit. Check the instructions to know whether the document must be placed face up or down.
2. Dial the fax number of the receiver. For transmission outside the local area code, check to see if you need to dial a long-distance access code.

■ **Figure 6-2**
Ricoh 1400L stand-alone
fax machine.
(Courtesy of Ricoh.)

3. Once the connection is made, press the send button.

Most offices purchase both a **stand-alone fax machine,** which is a self-contained unit, and computer software because it gives them the versatility to send and receive documents using either technology. Some small offices are purchasing a combined unit, which functions as a fax machine as well as a scanner, copier, and printer as shown in Figure 6-3.

To send a fax from your computer, you need special fax software that comes with a variety of features. Some software programs allow you to send a "broadcast" fax to many other computers; other fax programs allow you to receive incoming faxes in the screen background so that you can continue working on the computer while the fax is being sent. Remember, a fax sent via a modem is only a *picture* of the document—not the document itself—so it cannot be edited.

In an office where fax machines are connected to a network, polling may be required. **Polling** allows one fax machine to test others on the network for information. Users can store their messages on the fax network. The person waiting to receive the messages instructs his or her fax station to poll the other machines for faxes with the correct poll code. When the correct code is found, the message is transferred to the polling fax machine. A head office wishing to pick up orders or check inventory from its stores, for example, may require the polling feature.

Establishing clear, simple guidelines for using the fax can reduce unnecessary transmissions and save both time and money. Follow these tips to help establish your guidelines.

1. Determine if the message should be faxed or distributed using another method.

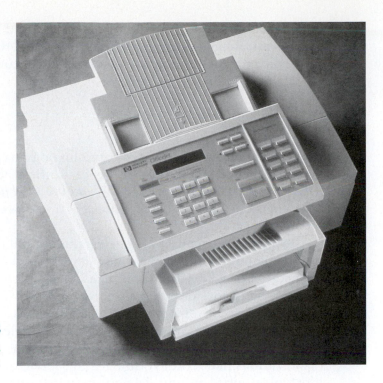

■ **Figure 6-3**
A combination fax, copier,
and scanner.

Fax Transmission
<Organization>
<Address>
<City, State Zip>
<Telephone>
Fax: <Fax>

To: [Name of Recipient]   **Date:**   July 9, 200X

Fax #:   [Fax Number]   **Pages:**   [Pages (including cover sheet),

From: <Name>   including this cover sheet.]

Subject: [Regarding]

COMMENTS:

■ **Figure 6-4**
An example of a fax
transmittal memo.

2. If a document is delivered by fax, type an appropriate notation on the line below the reference initials or on the line below the enclosure notation, if used. A notation such as "By fax" is appropriate.

3. Decide which type of cover sheet will be used. WordPerfect and Microsoft Word offer fax transmittal forms, such as the one shown in Figure 6-4.

4. Determine guidelines regarding confidentiality. Confidentiality is perhaps the highest concern facing businesses using fax machines. Consider arranging for only authorized staff members to transmit and receive confidential fax transmissions.

5. Determine how you will report misdirected messages. Nothing is more frustrating than to have sent a message and then find out that it was misdirected and that no one made an effort to let the sender know about the error.

Telegrams

The telegram is the oldest type of technology-based mail. Samuel Morse invented the telegraph and sent his first official telegraph message in 1844. As he tapped out the message *"What hath God wrought!"* it is unlikely that he envisioned the rise and demise of this once revolutionary method of communication

Except for e-mail and fax, telegrams are still the quickest textual method of communication. They are now mostly used for celebratory greetings or emergencies, where the recipient has no access to e-mail or fax machine. You may wish to consider telegram services for delivering critical information to company executives working in remote regions.

However, the advent of high-speed telecommunications and the Internet has largely superseded the traditional telegram. Some private organizations maintain hybrid telegram services, which incorporate e-mail, or voice initiation and delivery by voice or an express delivery service. Two such companies are Western Union and Telegram Gateway. Western Union's telegram service is restricted to delivery in the United States, whereas Telegram Gateway guarantees overnight delivery to any part of the world.

Voice Mail

Because of its name, voice mail must be mentioned in this chapter. In its simplest form, **voice mail** allows callers to access or record voice information from a list of prerecorded options. However, voice mail technology is really much more than stated here. To better understand this technology, refer to Chapter 12, Telecommunications in the Office.

HANDLING INCOMING MAIL

Traditional incoming mail is very different than it was even a few years ago. With the priority of the Internet and electronic mail, as well as voice mail, the office professional is seeing, reading, and controlling less traditional mail now than ever before. Even so, every office still receives paper mail, and handling the mail is still a high priority for an office professional. When the mail is handled accurately and expeditiously, other office employees are able to respond more efficiently to the needs addressed in the mail items.

As an office professional, you may or may not have direct contact with the post office—this will depend on whether your organization has a central mailing department. Nonetheless, as an information worker, you should become knowledgeable about handling incoming mail in your office.

You must keep up with every piece of mail that arrives, and you must be able to distinguish between important and less important mail. As you will be handling mail daily, establish a plan for handling it and then follow your plan consistently. As soon as the mail arrives, stop what you are doing, unless it is a rush job, and handle the mail. The information provided in this section on incoming mail is comprehensive. For an office professional to perform all these steps would be too time consuming. Although it is not expected that every office will handle mail with this degree of care, the office professional is certain to perform at least some of the steps listed below.

1. Sorting mail
2. Opening mail
3. Inspecting contents
4. Registering special mail
5. Date-time stamping mail
6. Reading and annotating mail
7. Presenting mail to manager
8. Handling packages, publications, and advertising by mail
9. Distributing mail
10. Answering mail in the manager's absence

Some large organizations still have their central mailing departments, although with the decreased volume of paper mail, one encounters fewer of these. Such departments are responsible for receiving all of the organization's mail and for routing it to the correct departments or individuals. Usually, the mailing department provides at least one pickup and delivery to each department every day. At one time, central mailing departments opened, date-time stamped, and distributed the mail. They rarely do so now; instead, recipients open their own mail, or the office professional performs this task for the managers or for the entire department.

When the mail is delivered to one location, someone must sort the mail and deliver it to the appropriate workstations. If this task should be assigned to you, sort and make the deliveries at once so that the other office support professionals may start processing their own mail.

Sorting Mail

When mail comes to your desk unopened, begin sorting it into the following groups:

1. Mail sent with urgency (express, special delivery, certified, and courier)
2. Letters, including bills and statements
3. Interoffice mail
4. Personal mail
5. Newspapers and periodicals
6. Booklets, catalogs, and other advertising materials
7. Packages

The office professional may have to sign for couriered mail and other insured, registered, or expedited pieces of mail before they can be received.

Keep the priority mail separate from the rest of the mail, open it as soon as it arrives, and then put it on the addressee's desk in a way that calls attention to it. Priority mail refers to couriered mail that is delivered via an expedited service.

In the stack of mail to be opened immediately, assemble letters and interoffice memoranda. All interoffice mail is important. Each item either requires a reply or provides your manager with information he or she needs.

You must decide whether mail addressed to an employee who is no longer with the organization is personal or business related. If the mail is personal, clearly write the forwarding address on the envelope and put it in the outgoing mail. On the other hand, if mail is addressed by title to someone no longer with the organization, you can assume that it is a business letter. When you distribute the mail, deliver it unopened to the person who has the title or is responsible for the work implied by the title. If this person is your manager, put the document with the mail to be opened. Letters, including bills and statements, can be forwarded without additional postage.

As you sort, put aside all circulars, booklets, advertisements, newspapers, and periodicals until you have opened and processed the more urgent mail.

Opening Mail

Before you begin opening the mail, assemble the supplies you will need: opener, date stamp, stapler, paper clips, tickler file, to-do list, and pencils (for notations).

Should you open an envelope by mistake, seal it with transparent tape, write "Opened by mistake" and your initials, and distribute or forward the envelope to the addressee.

You can establish "Personal and Confidential" mail procedures with your manager when you first start working. Some high-level executive assistants open personal and confidential mail for their managers. Either way, don't assume—ask.

Inspecting the Contents

Here are some tips for removing and inspecting the contents.

- Keep the envelopes until you are certain that all the enclosures and addresses are accounted for.
- Inspect each document for the address and signature of the sender, the date, and enclosures. When a document is not dated, write the postmark date on the document and staple the envelope to the back of the letter. Also, if you notice a major discrepancy between the date on the document and the date of arrival, staple the envelope to the document.
- Check the enclosures received against the enclosure notations. If enclosures are missing, make a note in the margin of the document. Follow up by requesting the missing enclosure. Make a note on your to-do list at once.
- Staple an enclosure that is the same size as a letter or larger to the back of it. Use paper clips to temporarily fasten an item that a staple would damage; for example, a check or a legal document.

MAIL REGISTER			
Date/Time Received	Sender's Name	Recipient's Name	Description/ Type
6/3	Abbot Industries	W. Steele	Fed Express
6/4	Nelson & Nelson	B. Caldwell	Insured pkg.

■ **Figure 6-5**
Mail register.

Registering Special Mail

A **mail register** provides a record of special mail, including insured and registered mail and packages. If you are not provided with a mail register, you can easily design your own form. The form should include:

■ Date and time received
■ Sender's name
■ Recipient's name
■ Description of type of mail

In some offices, the receptionist maintains the mail register. A mail register may be kept in a loose-leaf notebook or in a computer file. Figure 6-5 shows an example of the kind of mail register you can create.

Date-Time Stamping Mail

The time of arrival of certain correspondence has legal significance. For example, the date a payment is received can be a factor in allowing a cash discount, or a specific time of day can be set for opening bids. When correspondence is received too late for the recipient to comply with a request, the date received is protection for the addressee.

Organizations do not prejudge which correspondence should be date-time stamped. With the exception of a few documents that should not be marred in any way, organizations stamp all incoming mail either with the date or with both the date and the hour of arrival. The date-time stamp should have the name of the person's office as well as a date and time indicator. As mentioned, there will be situations when it is important to know the exact date that something was received, so do not skip this step.

Stamp the date received on each piece of correspondence in the white space at the upper left, right, or top edge. The same pieces of correspondence may come to your desk several times while they are being processed. If you date-time stamp all the mail as you read it, you will know as soon as you see that stamp that you have already seen and read a particular piece of correspondence. Consistently stamp booklets, catalogs, and periodicals on either the front or the back cover.

Reading and Annotating Mail

You can save a lot of time for your manager and yourself by marking and grouping correspondence according to the next step to be taken for each piece. You do this by reading the correspondence in search of the important facts, underlining key words and dates, and writing marginal notes. In some cases, you will not know what the next step should be; in other cases your manager will not agree with your notations. Even so, by using good judgment you can organize the correspondence so that your manager can spend his or her time on the correspondence or documents that truly need attention.

Some managers prefer that nothing be underlined or written in the margins of incoming letters. For this reason, get approval before you underline and annotate.

Read the correspondence rapidly, concentrating on the content and using a systematic method of making notes on which you can rely for following through. Develop a questioning attitude—one that will ensure you pick out significant facts and decide what the next step should be. For instance, keep your eyes open for letters that

1. Contain the date of an appointment that must be entered in the appointment calendars
2. Mention that a report is being mailed separately
3. Confirm a telephone conversation
4. Request a decision that cannot be made until additional information is obtained

Use a pencil to underline and make marginal notes. Underline sparingly; otherwise, your attempt to emphasize will lose its effectiveness. Underline keyboard and figures that reveal who, what, when, and where.

Provide your manager with additional information in the margins. This is called **annotating.** Use small handwriting and make your notations brief.

Jot down what you would remind your manager of if you were talking to him or her about it. For example, if the letter is a reminder to send a booklet that was requested earlier and it has been mailed, write "Mailed" and the date of mailing. If an item referred to in a letter arrived separately, write "Received." See Figure 6-6 for an example of an annotated letter.

Annotating is preferable to verbally reminding your manager. The use of marginal notes eliminates interruptions; as well, your manager is able to refer to those notes as he or she answers the correspondence. Remember to ask your manager about preferences in annotating. Marginal notes can confuse readers, and underlining can irritate the readers to whom a letter is circulated.

As you read correspondence, pay close attention to the items that require following up. Make the entries in the proper places in your reminder system. Your follow-up plan needs to be foolproof; do not rely on your memory. Enter the date of a meeting or the time of an appointment in both your manager's appointment calendar and your own.

MA MILLENNIUM APPLIANCES, INC.
3431 Bloor Street, Toronto, ON M8X IG4
(Tel) 416-795-2893 (Fax) 416-795-3982

06 September 20 - -

Mr. Kyle Rhodes
Manager, Sales Office
Millennium Appliances, Inc.
3152 - 45th Avenue
Vancouver, BC V6N 3M1

Dear Mr. Rhodes

NOVEMBER SALES SEMINAR

One of the speakers for the November Sales Seminar is in the hospital. Therefore, he will be unable to present a program for the Sales Seminar.

The members of the Executive Committee of the November Sales Seminar suggested that you would make an excellent speaker for the Seminar. You would receive an honorarium to cover any expenses you may incur. Your presentation would last approximately lone hour and be shared with an audience of approximately 50 sales professionals. If you agree to speak at the Sales Seminar, we will make arrangements for your accommodation at the Hilton Hotel where the Seminar will be located.

The dates for the Seminar are Tuesday, November 11 and Wednesday, November 12. We would ask that you present your topic twice, once on each day.

May we suggest that your topic relate to the successful methods of team building. I am enclosing a list of topics which will be used by other speakers at the Seminar.

Your acceptance of this invitation would be greatly appreciated.

Sincerely,

W. Wilson

W. Wilson
Chairperson, Sales Seminar
lr
Enclosure

■ **Figure 6-6**
Annotated letter.

Locate any additional related materials and attach them to the back of the respective incoming correspondence or documents. However, do not delay getting the mail to your manager. You can obtain previous correspondence, locate information, and verify figures while your manager is reading the mail.

Keep a record of any special items, such as checks and important forms, forwarded to another person.

Presenting Mail

When placing mail on your manager's desk or in-box, follow these simple rules:

1. Remember that the mail is a priority; act on it as quickly as possible.
2. Place the most urgent items on top and the least urgent items on the bottom. When items are couriered or faxed, they may be urgent; however,

you will need to determine this by reading the content. The longer you have worked for a particular organization or manager, the better your judgment will be in separating urgent mail from routine mail.

3. Mail should be placed in such a way that it is not visible to people visiting your manager's office in his or her absence. Often, you can protect the confidentiality of the mail by placing it in a large envelope or a folder.

Handling Packages, Publications, and Advertising by Mail

Packages should receive priority over newspapers, periodicals, and advertising materials. Expedited parcels should receive the same priority as letters. In some cases you will be watching for the arrival of packages. When handling packages, follow these procedures:

- Packages that have letters attached or that are marked "Letter Enclosed" should be processed with the important mail. However, do not open a package or separate a letter from it until you have time to check the contents carefully against the packing slip or invoice. Always avoid opening a package with the intention of checking the contents later.

- Your manager will want to know that certain items have arrived but will be interested in seeing new items, not routine ones. For instance, if a shipment of a recently revised form arrives, your manager will want to know if what has been received is what was specified. Place one of the forms on your manager's desk. Store regular supplies in their proper places without your manager seeing them.

Follow these simple procedures when handling publications.

- Unwrap newspapers and try to flatten them. On the front cover of newspapers and periodicals, affix circulation lists. A **circulation list** is a type of routing slip. See Figure 6-7.

- If the manager wishes to see the newspapers and periodicals before they are circulated to the rest of the staff, key his or her name at the top of each list. Otherwise, names are commonly arranged in alphabetical order or according to the staff hierarchy.

- As people pass the newspaper or periodical to the next person on the list, they should draw a line through their name on the circulation list.

When handling advertising materials, follow these procedures:

- Do not throw away advertising materials until your manager has had a chance to glance at them. Managers want to know about new products in their fields; perusing advertising materials is one way to become aware of what is new. If your manager tells you to screen advertising materials, be sure you clearly understand which items he or she has no interest in.

- After your manager has seen the advertising materials, booklets, catalogs, and so on, you will have to decide what to do with them. For instance,

  - Which ones should you keep?

```
                    ROUTING SLIP

                                    DATE _____

From:          Paul V. Compton

Periodical:    Internet World

Please read, initial, and pass this around.

                        Office No.

Denton, H. V.       672 _____

Barlow, C.          605 _____

Winton, R. M.       616 _____

Peebles, L. M.      682 _____

Donnell, W.         561 _____

FILE:  Return to Paul V. Compton
```

■ **Figure 6-7**
Routing slip or
circulation list.

■ Which ones should you route to someone who has an interest in a particular subject?

■ Which ones should you discard?

Ask your manager to initial anything that might be looked at again.

■ Do not clutter your correspondence files with advertising materials. Throw away most ads. For those you save, set up a separate file that you can go through quickly and update periodically. Advertising materials are usually not dated. However, if you date-stamp them, you can separate the old from the new by looking at the Date Received stamp. Replace old catalogs with new ones. If you keep many catalogs, work out a satisfactory filing system for them. Pamphlet and magazine files are available from manufacturers of filing supplies and are an attractive and organized way to file your catalogs, booklets, and magazines.

Distributing Mail

A manager distributes mail to others to:

1. Obtain information so that he or she can reply
2. Ask someone else to reply directly
3. Keep others informed.

Important mail can be delayed and can even get "lost" on someone's desk. Nevertheless, top management expects mail to be answered. Your manager is still responsible for the reply to a letter even when the actual writing of it has been delegated to someone else.

As a general rule, your manager will make notations on letters or send memoranda asking others to provide information or to reply directly. Some managers attach "Action Requested" or routing slips as they read the mail so that they don't have to handle the same pieces of correspondence again. However, an office professional can handle much of this responsibility. When given the responsibility for making requests, realize that a considerate tone will play a significant part in getting someone to comply. In contrast, a demanding tone will detract from your efforts and sometimes will result in the letter getting lost.

For informal requests for action, use an Action Requested slip similar to the one shown in Figure 6-8. For example, attach an Action Requested slip to a letter that has been misdirected to your manager and obviously should be handled in another department. Write the recipient's name, and check "Please handle."

Sometimes a letter requires two types of action, one of which your manager can handle and another that someone in another department must handle. When this situation arises, let the other person know precisely which part of the letter he or she is to answer. In the margin of the letter, indicate the part on which your manager will follow through.

Decide whether the person who is to reply will require earlier correspondence. If you think he or she will need it, attach it to the letter being distributed.

DATE ________

TO ______________________________

_____ For your information; do not return.

_____ Let's discuss.

_____ Note and file.

_____ Please note and return to me.

_____ Please handle.

_____ RUSH — Immediate action necessary.

_____ Please answer.

_____ Your comments, please.

_____ Other

COMMENTS:

FROM ______________________________

■ **Figure 6-8**
Action Requested slip.

To obtain information, you will be communicating with people in numerous departments throughout the organization. Make an effort to get acquainted with them, at least by telephone. When you must obtain information from a service department, for example, you should be aware of the work schedule followed by that department. Find out how much time must elapse between the time you request information and the time the material will be ready. Often you will be pressed by a time line, and you must communicate this. You may have to request special service in order to meet your time line.

When you ask someone who is not following a predetermined schedule to assemble facts for you, request that the information be ready by a designated time. Suggest a realistic due date. Often, work that can be done when it is convenient to do it gets relegated to the bottom of the stack. Here are some procedures to follow when circulating materials:

- Attach a circulation list or routing slip to mail that is to be distributed to more than one person. A **routing slip** is a small sheet of paper on which are listed the names of the people to whom an item is to be distributed. Each recipient should initial and date the slip after he or she has seen the material, and then forward it to the next person on the list.

- When mail is often circulated to the same people, the names can be preprinted. On a preprinted slip, you can change the order in which material is to be circulated by writing numbers in front of the names on the list (see Figure 6-7). Be sure to include "Return to" near the bottom of a routing slip.

- When you distribute a letter, memo, or report to inform others, you will have to decide whether to attach to the original a routing slip listing the names of the recipients, make a copy and attach a routing slip, or make a copy for each person on the list. When deciding, consider the important factors, such as the number of pages, whether each person on the list must be informed at the same time, your immediate need for the original, and the risk that the original will be lost while it is being circulated. Also consider paper wastage when you ask yourself how many copies are actually necessary.

- Your records should show what information has been disseminated. When a circulated item is returned to you, staple the routing slip to the document. This makes a permanent record of who saw the item and the date he or she saw it. When you do not use a circulation list or routing slip and must make separate copies for each individual, write on your file copy the names of the people to whom you sent the item.

Answering Mail in the Manager's Absence

What happens to the mail when your manager is away from the office depends on his or her preferences and length of absence, and on the time and attention your manager can give—or chooses to give—to what is going on at the office while he or she is away.

While your manager is away from the office, he or she will usually either call or e-mail. With electronic capabilities of telephones, hotels, and airlines, managers can quickly access their e-mail and keep up with their own messages.

If your manager is away from the office for only a day or two, his or her preference probably will be for you to put aside all the mail you cannot answer. However, never put aside correspondence that must be handled immediately. If there is no one in the office who is authorized to reply to an urgent message, you may choose to call or e-mail your manager.

Send letters that require immediate action to the person designated to answer them; make copies of the letters and write the name of the person receiving each one on the letter itself. Put the copies in a folder for your manager marked "Correspondence to Be Read."

Answer the letters that you can answer. Acknowledge the e-mails not being answered immediately, indicating that your manager will return to the office on a specific date and that the sender can expect a reply soon after he or she returns. Note and reply to the e-mail address on the incoming e-mail. This form of response is expedient and can provide a concise record of your actions. Most browsers can be set to send an automatic reply to all e-mail messages received when the person is away from the office for several days.

Organize in folders all the business mail that accumulates during your manager's absence. Place the folders, along with your summary of the mail, on your manager's desk in the order listed below. Keep personal mail in a separate folder and put it on your manager's desk in a separate place. The folders might be labeled as follows:

- "Correspondence for Signature"—for letters you prepared for his or her signature, and any other documents ready for signatures.
- "Correspondence Requiring Attention"—for all correspondence, including any e-mails left unanswered, your manager must answer.
- "Correspondence to Be Read"—for copies of letters you and others have answered, and copies of your replies.
- "Reports and Informational Memos"—for all informational items.
- "Advertisements"—for advertising brochures and other literature for your manager's perusal.

HANDLING OUTGOING MAIL

Outgoing mail is handled by mailroom personnel in large organizations or by office professionals in smaller organizations. Regardless of who processes the outgoing mail, as an office professional, you should be familiar with basic procedures, such as special mail services and international mail. The more familiar you are with these procedures, the more efficiently you can process the outgoing mail without delays or additional costs incurred in mailing items.

The following steps will help you in preparing items to be mailed:

1. Review all documents for signatures and enclosures.
2. Verify the correspondence address with the envelope address.
3. Determine the most accurate way of mailing an item.
4. Presort mail for speedier handling by the post office. Separate mail into categories, such as local, out-of-town, and metered.

Outgoing mail is divided into two classes: domestic and international. **Domestic mail** is transmitted within, among, and between the United States and its territories and possessions; Army–Air Force post offices (APO) and Navy post offices (FPO); and to the United Nations, New York City. To learn more about domestic mail, contact your local post office and request the U.S. **Domestic Mail Manual (DMM)** or access the United States Postal Service (USPS) Web site at http://uspc.com.

Mail sent within the United States and its possessions should always be addressed using approved two-letter postal abbreviations for state and possession names and the five-digit **ZIP Code** (for Zone Improvement Plan, a number that identifies postal delivery areas) or ZIP + 4 Code for the area.

ZIP + 4 Code

The expanded ZIP Code, called the **ZIP + 4 Code,** is composed of the original five-digit code plus a four-digit add-on. Use of the four-digit add-on number is voluntary for most mail. However, this add-on number helps the USPS direct mail efficiently and accurately. Even if you prefer not to use the four-digit add-on number, using the correct five-digit ZIP Code helps prevent delays.

The ZIP + 4 identifies a geographic segment within the five-digit delivery area such as a city block, an office building, an individual high-volume receiver of mail, or any other unit that would aid efficient mail sorting and delivery. Using ZIP + 4 reduces the number of handlings and significantly decreases the potential for human error and the possibility of nondelivery. You can purchase a publication listing ZIP + 4 at your local post office.

The following list shows the standard state abbreviations.

State	Abbrev.	State	Abbrev.
A		**I**	
Alabama	AL	Idaho	ID
Alaska	AK	Illinois	IL
Arizona	AZ	Indiana	IN
Arkansas	AR	Iowa	IA
American Samoa	AS	**K**	
C		Kansas	KS
California	CA	Kentucky	KY
Colorado	CO	**L**	
Connecticut	CT	Louisiana	LA
D		**M**	
Delaware	DE	Maine	ME
District of Columbia	DC	Maryland	MD
F		Massachusetts	MA
Florida	FL	Michigan	MI
G		Minnesota	MN
Georgia	GA	Mississippi	MS
Guam	GU	Missouri	MO
H		Montana	MT
Hawaii	HI		

continued

State	Abbrev.	State	Abbrev.
N		**S**	
Nebraska	NE	South Carolina	SC
Nevada	NV	South Dakota	SD
New Hampshire	NH	**T**	
New Jersey	NJ	Tennessee	TN
New Mexico	NM	Texas	TX
New York	NY	Trust Territory	TT
North Carolina	NC	**U**	
North Dakota	ND	Utah	UT
No. Mariana Islands	CM	**V**	
O		Vermont	VT
Ohio	OH	Virginia	VA
Oklahoma	OK	Virgin Islands	VI
Oregon	OR	**W**	
P		Washington	WA
Pennsylvania	PA	West Virginia	WV
Puerto Rico	PR	Wisconsin	WI
R		Wyoming	WY
Rhode Island	RI		

Classes of Domestic Mail

The basic classifications of domestic mail are first class, priority, express, parcel post, bound printed matter, and special standard mail (book rate). The one you choose depends on (1) what you are mailing and (2) how rapidly you would like the mail delivered. Because the rates and weights are subject to change, access the Internet, contact your local post office, or call the USPS 800 number to obtain current information for the following classes of domestic mail.

First-Class Mail. **First-class mail** includes all personal correspondence, all bills and statements of accounts, all matter sealed or otherwise closed against inspection, and matter wholly or partly in writing or typewriting. Any mailable items may be sent as first-class mail. Each piece must weigh 13 ounces or less. Pieces over 13 ounces can be sent as priority mail.

Priority Mail. **Priority mail** offers two-day service to most domestic destinations. Items must weigh 70 pounds or less and measure 108 inches or less in combined length and girth. Priority mail envelopes, labels, and boxes are available at no additional charge at post offices. Pickup service is available but at a charge. Priority mail flat-rate envelope service is available for matter sent in a flat-rate envelope.

Express Mail. **Express mail** is the fastest service, with next-day delivery by noon to most destinations. Express mail is delivered 365 days a year—no extra charge for Saturday, Sunday, or holiday delivery. All packages must use an express mail label. Items must weigh 70 pounds or less and measure 108 inches or less in combined length and girth. Features include merchandise and document reconstruction, tracking and tracing, delivery to post office boxes and rural addresses, domestic rates for APO and FPO addresses, money-back guarantee, **collect on delivery, (COD)** return receipt service, and waiver of signature.

Insurance is provided at no additional cost up to $500. Pickup service is available for a fee. Express mail flat-rate envelope service is also provided for matter sent in a flat-rate envelope provided by the USPS.

Parcel Post. Parcel post is used for mailing certain items—books, circulars, catalogs, other printed matter, and merchandise weighing 1 pound or more but not more than 70 pounds. Parcel post packages must measure 130 inches or less in combined length and girth. Each piece should be marked "Parcel Post" or "PP" in the postage area. Rates are based on the weight of the piece and the zone (distance from origin to destination ZIP Code).

Bound Printed Matter. Bound printed matter must weigh at least 1 pound but not more than 15 pounds. Rates are based on the weight of the piece and the zone. Packages must measure 108 inches or less in combined length and girth. Each piece should be marked "Bound Printed Matter" in the postage area. For special mailing conditions, contact your local post office.

Special Standard Mail (Book Rate). The special standard mail (book rate) classification is generally used for books (at least eight pages), film (16 millimeters or narrower), printed music, printed test materials, sound recordings, play scripts, printed educational charts, loose-leaf pages and binders consisting of medical information, and computer-readable media. Packages must measure 108 inches or less in combined length and girth. Mark each package "Special Standard Mail" in the postage area.

Supplemental Services

As an office professional preparing outgoing mail, you should know what special services are available from the U.S. Postal Service and when to apply them.

Certificate of Mailing Receipt. A Certificate of Mailing receipt provides evidence of mailing. The receipt must be purchased at the time of mailing; no record is kept by the post office. A fee is charged in addition to the postage.

Certified Mail. The certified mail service provides the sender with a mailing receipt. A record is kept at the post office of delivery. A return receipt can also be purchased for an additional fee. This service is available only with first-class and priority mail. A fee is charged for certified mail plus the postage.

Collect on Delivery (COD). This service allows the mailer to collect the price of goods and/or postage on merchandise ordered by addressee when it is delivered. COD services can be used for merchandise sent by first-class, express, priority, and standard mail. The service may be combined with registered mail. This service is not available for international mail or for mail addressed to APO and FPO addresses. The fees charged include insurance—the maximum amount is $600.

Insured Mail. The **insured mail** service provides coverage against loss or damage. Coverage is up to $5,000 for standard mail as well as standard mail matter mailed at priority or first-class mail rates. The amount of insurance coverage for loss will be the actual value, less depreciation. No claim payments are made for sentimental losses or for any expenses incurred as a result of the loss.

Postal Money Orders. You should never send cash through the mail. **Postal money orders** are a safe way to send money. The special color blend, Benjamin Franklin watermark, metal security thread, and double imprinting of the dollar amount are incorporated security features. You can buy domestic and international money orders at all post offices in amounts up to $700.

You can purchase multiple money orders at one time in the same or different amounts. There is a $10,000 daily purchase limit, and customers who purchase more than $3,000 in money orders in a single day are required by federal law to complete Form 8105-A, Funds Transactions/Transfer Report.

If your money order is lost or stolen, you must present your customer receipt to apply for a replacement. For a small fee, you can obtain a copy of a paid money order up to two years after the date that it is paid. You can obtain a money order from providers, such as local grocery stores.

Registered Mail. **Registered mail** service provides maximum protection and security for valuables and is available only for items paid at priority and first-class mail rates. Registered mail may be combined with COD, restricted delivery, or return receipt. Postal insurance is provided for articles with a declared value up to a maximum of $25,000. Only items with no declared value may use registered service without insurance.

Return Receipt. The **return receipt** provides a mailer with evidence of delivery. It also supplies the recipient's actual delivery address if it is different from the address used by the sender. A return receipt may be requested before or after delivery. The service is available only for express, certified, or COD mail, mail insured for more than $50, and registered mail. A fee is applied in addition to the postage as well as the fee paid if the receipt is requested at the time of mailing or requested after mailing.

Return Receipt for Merchandise. The **return receipt for merchandise** provides the sender with a mailing receipt and a return receipt. A delivery record, for an additional fee, is kept by the post office of address, but no record is kept at the office of mailing.

Restricted Delivery. **Restricted delivery** service permits a mailer to direct delivery only to the addressee or addressee's authorized agent. The addressee must be an individual specified by name. The service is available only for certified or, COD, mail insured for more than $50, or registered mail. In addition to the postage, a fee is charged.

Special Situations

The mail does not always go through without problems. Can all classes of mail be forwarded? What happens to undelivered mail? Is it possible to recall a piece of mail or to refuse mail? As an office professional, you will encounter these questions, and you will have to decide what to do when there is a change in procedure.

Changing an Address. When the organization for which you work changes its address, someone within the organization must notify the local post office of the change. If doing this is your responsibility, follow these steps:

1. Access the Internet and locate the U.S. Postal Service Web site.
2. Search the information for "change of address."
3. Once the Official Change of Address Form is displayed, you can complete it directly on your computer screen. Be sure to print it for your files.
4. You will then need to sign the form and either give it to your mail carrier to mail or mail it to your local post office.

Additionally, you can use the entered information to print Address Change Notification Letters and mail them to business associates to let them know of your move.

Recalling Mail. If you make an error in mailing that is serious enough to warrant recalling a piece of mail, you may be able to do so if you act quickly. Call the post office branch in your mailing zone if the document is for local delivery; call the central post office if the document is for out-of-town delivery. Request that the document be held. For identification, type an address identical to the address on the envelope being recalled. Go to the post office, complete a Sender's Application for Withdrawal of Mail, and present it and the duplicate address to the postal clerk or representative.

Returning Undelivered Mail. Keep mailing lists up-to-date and address envelopes and labels with absolute accuracy to avoid the cost and delay involved when mail is returned. A returned letter must be placed in a fresh envelope, correctly addressed with new postage.

If the addressee has moved or simply refuses to accept mail, if there is insufficient postage or an incorrect or incomplete address, or if for other reasons the mail cannot be delivered, the post office will return the item to the sender.

Dangerous Goods

Articles or substances that could be dangerous to postal workers and postal equipment, or that could damage other mail, are prohibited from being mailed both domestically and to points outside the United States. It is an offense to use the domestic service to deliver:

- Explosives
- Flammable solids and flammable liquids
- Radioactive materials
- Gases, oxidizers, and organic peroxides
- Corrosives
- Toxic and infectious substances
- Miscellaneous dangerous goods, such as asbestos, air bags, and dry ice

A list of restricted items is available for international mail as well. If you are in doubt about any item you wish to mail, call your local post office.

Domestic Mail Addressing Tips

The USPS uses computerized systems that can scan a wide range of addressing styles; this includes both handwritten and keyed addresses. To increase the speed and efficiency of mail handling, the USPS has designed a consistent format for users. It requests that we use this optimum format whenever possible, but recognizes some other formats as acceptable for computerized scanning. To review addressing envelopes, see "Addressing Envelopes" in Chapter 5.

Properly addressed mail saves time and avoids errors in delivery. This is especially important for mail addressed in some languages other than English.

To ensure that your mail is addressed correctly, follow these addressing tips.

1. Type the complete address.
2. Always use a return address.
3. Always use complete address information, such as the suffixes AVE, BLVD, and ST. Always include locators such as the apartment or suite number.
4. Always use correct directionals, such as N, W, and SW.
5. Don't let an incorrect ZIP Code delay delivery of your mail. Local post offices and the USPS Web site (http://www.usps.com) offer ZIP Code information.
6. Use the four-digit add-on, ZIP + 4, in your addressing. Hyphenate the ZIP + 4.
7. Always use the two-letter state abbreviations listed previously.
8. Place endorsements for special services, such as priority, first-class, or insured mail, above the destination address and below and to the right of the return address.

Metered Mail

Many organizations use in-house postage meters. Metered mail need not be canceled or postmarked when it reaches the post office; however, it must be turned in at a postal outlet counter and not simply dropped into a mailbox. Metered mail is sent directly for sorting because it does not need canceling by the USPS. **Canceling mail** refers to the process of printing bars over the stamps, as well as printing the date and time where mail processing has occurred. This process prevents a person from reusing the postage; more importantly, it also allows the receiver to track the actual time, date, and place where processing occurred.

Because properly prepared metered mail can go directly to the sorting machine in the postal center, it may be dispatched slightly sooner than mail that must be canceled. However, the real advantage to the user is the convenience of not using stamps, not waiting in line at the post office, and being able to apply whatever amount of postage is needed.

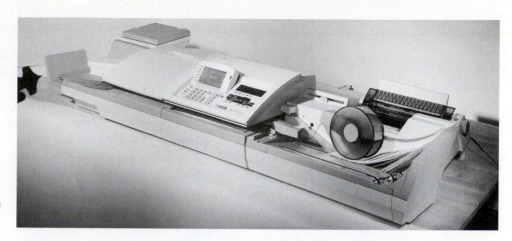

■ **Figure 6-9**
Automated postage meter.

Postage meter machines vary in size from lightweight desk models to fully automatic models that feed, seal, and stack envelopes in addition to printing the postage, the postmark, and the date of mailing (see Figure 6-9). The machine itself is purchased, but the meter is leased from the manufacturer (one of several authorized by the USPS) and is licensed without charge by the post office. If you have questions about postage meters, contact a postage meter company, such as Pitney Bowes or Mail Technology, Inc., or contact the USPS.

The user of a basic postage meter must take the meter to the post office and pay for a specified amount of postage. The postal agent then sets the meter dials for this amount. Each time an envelope is imprinted with an amount of postage, the unused balance on the meter is decreased by that amount. When the unused balance runs low, the meter must be taken to the post office to be reset. Here are some simple procedures to follow when using a postage meter.

1. Check the manual dials or electronic readout to make sure that the correct postage will be printed on the mail.

2. Check the meter date to be certain that it is the correct date of mailing, not the previous day's date.

3. In order to work efficiently, group your mail and stamp all mail requiring the same denomination in one batch.

4. Set aside pieces of mail requiring irregular amounts of postage until the rest of the mail is stamped.

5. After you have processed all the mail, reset the machine so that the next user will not waste postage because the meter was set for the wrong amount.

6. Bundle metered mail with addresses facing one direction, and group the pieces by the class of mail.

Try to avoid making mistakes when stamping mail, but if you do make a mistake, you can request credit from the leasing agent. When complete and legible meter stamps cannot be used because of misprints, spoiled envelopes or cards, and the like, the agent will credit the postage. You should note that in order to receive a credit, you must supply the complete envelope as proof, not just the meter impression.

Other Delivery Services

Other delivery services are available through private companies, such as Emery Air Freight Corporation, United Parcel Service (UPS), Federal Express Corporation, (FedEx) and Purolator Courier Corporation. These companies provide pickup services as well as dropoff locations. They offer online services that allow you to electronically complete the necessary forms and to track a shipment through to its destination. UPS offers an online courier service that allows you to integrate with Microsoft Word and Excel so that you can send your document without leaving the computer application software.

Western Union provides a **Mailgram,** an electronic message service that provides next-day postal service delivery for messages sent to any address in the United States. The messages are transmitted for delivery with the next business day's mail. Mailgram service is also available for Canadian addresses. You can send Mailgram messages by calling Western Union and dictating your message to the operator. For more information, call Western Union Telegraph Company. In Hawaii, call your local post office for information on how to send a message. In Alaska, call Alascom, Inc., for Mailgram service.

To select the best provider, compare the services, rates, and regulations of these companies as well as those of the U.S. Postal Service.

Messenger or courier services can save you money and ensure immediate delivery within the city. They are useful if you have a constant flow of local deliveries and pickups. You can arrange to have pickups and deliveries made at a set time of the day, or you can ask the service to be on call for your varying needs. Check your telephone directory for local messenger services.

In addition, private companies such as Eagle Mail and Pak Mail provide packing and shipping to anywhere in the world. Additional services include mail boxes, mailing label preparation, and meter mail. They will also insure your mail, accept COD, sell money orders, and send and receive faxes. Many of these companies are dropoff locations for UPS and FedEx.

Mail Software Programs

Ensuring that your mailing operations are working in the most optimal manner is crucial for maximizing efficiency and cost savings. It's also critical for managing the impact from any postal regulation changes made by the USPS. Maximizing the efficiency of your organization's mailing operations involves optimizing every component of the mail preparation process: address standardization, presorting, identifying customer moves, and updating the information in your customer files.

Any organization wants its mailing to reach its destination as quickly as possible at the best possible price. However, three major problems can surface in an organization's mail operations: too much returned mail, unreliable delivery, and excessive mailing costs. To solve these problems, organizations have turned to mailing software. The advantages of using a mail software program include the following:

- Reads files in different formats, such as Access and dBase
- Validates addresses
- Standardizes addresses to U.S. Postal Service requirements

- Produces postal reports and forms to track costs
- Produces bar-coded labels to qualify for automation postage discounts
- Presorts mail according to classes of mail and prints labels in presorted order
- Saves time and money

Information on the Internet

A wealth of information is available at your fingertips when you visit the U.S. Postal Service Web site on the Internet at http://www.usps.com. You can look up ZIP + 4 codes, track your express mail, get information on the latest postal rates, and find answers to frequently asked questions. If you are interested in stamps and stamp collecting, you will find information on stamps and stamp releases and can view images of the recent stamp issues.

If you keep exploring, you can find postal news releases and learn about the history of the Postal Service. The Inspection Service has included information on consumer fraud and other crimes as well as information about the history of the Inspection Service. The Web site is continually changing; visit often for new postal information. You also have an opportunity via the Web to make inquiries and request additional information.

Additional mail delivery sites are available for Federal Express (http://www.fedex.com), United Parcel Service, (http://www.ups.com), and Purolator Courier (http://www.purolator.com).

INTERNATIONAL MAIL

International Mail is mail that is distributed beyond the United States and its territories or possessions. The *International Mail Manual (IMM)* sets forth the policies, regulations, and procedures governing international mail services provided to the public by the USPS. The *IMM* is distributed to all postal facilities and is available to the public on a subscription basis only from the Superintendent of Documents, Government Printing Office. You can also access the *IMM* via the Internet at http://www.uspsglobal.com.

Special International Services

The traditional international mail service has been the "letter-post," consisting of three primary classes of services: letters and cards ("LC" service from the French term *lettres et cartes*), printed papers, and small packets. Printed papers such as regular printed matter, books and sheet music, and small packets are collectively referred to as "AO" service (for the French term *autres objets*—"other articles"). The term *printed papers* refers to items reproduced in several identical copies; *small packets* refers to postal items weighing up to 4.4 pounds that are not printed and are not in the nature of current and personal correspondence.

In response to private competition and changing business practices, the Postal Service has since introduced specialized outbound services for business mailers. The major new international services include the following:

- International Surface Air Lift (ISAL) is a bulk mailing service for international shipment of publications, advertising mail, catalogs, directories, books, other printed matter, and small packets.

- International Airmail Priority (IPA) is a service for bulk letter mail.
- International Customized Mail (ICM) is a negotiated contract service for large and potentially large mailers.
- International Express Mail Service provides both Global Package Link (GPL), a bulk express and priority service, and Global Priority Mail (GPM), an expedited airmail service providing fast, reliable, and economical delivery of all items mailable as letters.

If you are a last-minute international mailer, do not despair. The average Global Priority Mail delivery is four days to many countries for items up to 4 pounds. The average International Express Mail Service delivery is one or two days to most major cities.

Certified and COD services are not available for international mail, but most other special services, money orders, insurance, recorded delivery, registered mail, return receipt, special delivery, and special handling are provided with certain restrictions.

International Postage

It is essential to have some foolproof way of ensuring that correct postage is put on international airmail. Nothing is more frustrating to your manager to learn that an urgent package went by sea because the postage was insufficient. You, as the office professional supporting your manager, should see that the mailroom has current postage information for all countries that you deal with. Make sure that the information is clearly posted, so that even the casual user, like your manager, can calculate the correct postage if he or she should need to over the weekend when no office support staff are available.

International Addressing Tips

Here are a few tips for addressing international mail:

- Put foreign postal codes, if known, in front of the city or town name and on the same line.
- Place the city or town name and the province or state name on the next line after the street address information.
- Write the name of the foreign country in capital letters on the last line of the address. For example:

MR THOMAS CLARKE
117 RUSSELL DRIVE
LONDON WIP 6HQ
ENGLAND

MS CORINNA IGLESIAS
APARTDO 3068
46807 PUERTO VALLARTA JALISCO
MEXICO

INTERNATIONAL HOLIDAYS

People who conduct international business know how important holiday information can be when mailing or faxing important documents. Did you know that over 70 percent of holidays celebrated each year change from year to year? Some countries have such diverse ethnic populations that they observe religious holidays for over ten major religions. So how does this knowledge affect the way you and your manager conduct your business communications?

A surprisingly common reason for getting no answer from an international number is that you are faxing a document on a country's national or local holiday. Conducting business may be difficult if people take extra days off from work in order to take advantage of the long holiday. Before you try to mail or fax an important document or package to a country outside the United States, check out that country's schedule of holidays. For a current list, connect to the Internet and access a search tool such as Yahoo!, Lycos, or InfoSeek, and search under the key words *international holidays*.

Overview

✔ Electronic mail (e-mail) is the most popular and cost-efffective mail system found in business. It is a computerized mail service that enables users to transmit messages and documents over networks from one computer to another.

✔ Electronic bulletin boards are public message centers that appear on computer networks and are intended for anyone and everyone with access to the network.

✔ The facsimile, commonly known as the fax machine, is one of the most essential pieces of office equipment and can electronically send copies of original documents from one location to another.

✔ Except for e-mail and fax, telegrams, the oldest type of technology-based mail, are still the quickest textual way of communication. They now are mostly used for celebratory greetings or emergencies, where the recipient has no access to e-mail or fax machine.

quicktips

Tips for Sending Attachments with Your E-mail Message:

■ Mention in a line above the attached file what type of file it is and the application it was created in.
  ■ Example: "The attached document was created in MS Excel 2002."
  ■ This information helps the recipient know if he or she has the software that will open the file without losing any formatting and so on.
■ Don't attach too many documents in the same e-mail message.
  ■ Large files can overwhelm the network.
  ■ State the number of documents you are attaching.

✔ In its simplest form, voice mail allows callers to access or record voice information from a list of prerecorded options. To better understand this technology, refer to Chapter 12, Telecommunications in the Office.

✔ The steps, in sequence, for handling incoming mail are

1. Sorting mail
2. Opening mail
3. Inspecting the contents
4. Registering special mail
5. Date-time stamping mail
6. Reading and annotating mail
7. Presenting mail to manager
8. Handling packages, publications, and advertising by mail
9. Distributing mail
10. Answering mail in the manager's absence

The more familiar you are with processing outgoing mail, the more efficiently you can process the mail without delays or additional costs incurred in mailing items.

The following steps will help you in preparing items to be handled:

1. Review all documents for signatures and enclosures.
2. Verify the correspondence address with the envelope address.
3. Determine the most accurate way of mailing an item.
4. Presort mail for speedier handling by the post office.

✔ For information about domestic mail, the *Domestic Mail Manual (DMM)* sets forth the policies, regulations, and procedures governing domestic mail services provided to the public by the USPS.

✔ Classes of domestic mail are first class, priority, express, parcel post, bound printed matter, and special standard mail (book rate).

✔ Supplemental services include certificate of mailing receipt, certified mail, collect on delivery (COD), insured, postal money orders, registered mail, return receipt, return receipt for merchandise, and restricted delivery.

✔ The mail does not always go through without problems. You should be familiar with the procedures you will need to use when recalling mail or changing an address.

✔ Articles or substances that could be dangerous to postal workers and postal equipment, or that could damage other mail, are prohibited from being mailed both domestically and to points outside the United States. These items include explosives; flammable solids and flammable liquids; radioactive materials; gases, oxdizers, and organic peroxides; corrosives; toxins and infectious substances; and miscellaneous dangerous goods such as asbestos, air bags, and dry ice.

✔ To ensure that your mail is addressed correctly, follow these tips:

1. Type the complete address.
2. Always use a return address.

3. Always use complete address information, such as the suffixes AVE, BLVD, and ST. Always include locators such as the apartment or suite number.

4. Always use correct directionals, such as N, W, and SW.

5. Don't let an incorrect ZIP Code delay delivery of your mail. Local post offices and the USPS Web site (http://www.usps.com) offer ZIP Code information.

6. Use the four-digit add-on, ZIP + 4, in your addressing. Hyphenate the ZIP + 4.

7. Always use the two-letter state abbreviations listed in the section on ZIP + 4.

8. Place endorsements for special services, such as priority, first-class, or insured mail, above the destination address and below and to the right of the return address.

✔ Many organizations use in-house postage meters. Because properly prepared metered mail can go directly to the sorting machine in the postal center, it may be dispatched slightly sooner than mail that must be canceled. When using a postage meter, keep the following tips in mind:

1. Check the manual dials or electronic readout to make sure that the correct postage will be printed on the mail.

2. Check the meter date to be certain that it is the correct date of mailing, not the previous day's date.

3. In order to work efficiently, group your mail and stamp all mail requiring the same denomination in one batch.

4. Set aside pieces of mail requiring irregular amounts of postage until the rest of the mail is stamped.

5. After you have processed all the mail, reset the machine so that the next user will not waste postage because the meter was set for the wrong amount.

6. Bundle metered mail with addresses facing one direction, and group the pieces by the class of mail.

✔ Other than using e-mail, faxes, and the USPS, you should become familiar with private delivery services, such as Emery Air Freight, United Parcel Service (UPS), and Federal Express (FedEx). Check out these services via the Internet or refer to the yellow pages for current information.

✔ Mail software programs provide the following advantages:

- Reads files in different formats, such as Access and dBase
- Validates addresses
- Standardizes addresses to USPS requirements
- Produces postal reports and forms to track costs
- Produces bar-coded labels to qualify for automation postage discounts
- Presorts mail according to classes of mail and prints labels in presorted order
- Saves time and money

✔ For information about international mail, the *International Mail Manual (IMM)* sets forth the policies, regulations, and procedures governing international mail services provided to the public by the USPS.

✔ With the increase in international shipments, you should be able to distinguish among the categories of mail:

1. International Surface Air Lift (ISAL) is a bulk mailing service for international shipment of publications, advertising mail, catalogs, directories, books, other printed matter, and small packets.

2. International Airmail Priority (IPA) is a service for bulk letter mail.

3. International Customized Mail (ICM) is a negotiated contract service for large and potentially large mailers.

4. International Express Mail Service includes both Global Package Link (GPL), a bulk express and priority service, and Global Priority Mail (GPM), an expedited airmail service providing fast, reliable, and economical delivery of all items mailable as letters.

Key Terms

Annotating. The practice of making notes in the margin.

Bound printed matter. A U.S. Postal Service classification. Package must weigh at least 1 pound but not more than 15 pounds. Rates are based on the weight of the piece and the zone. Packages must measure 108 inches or less in combined length and girth.

Bulletin board system (BBS). A host computer that can be reached by computer modem for the purpose of sharing or exchanging messages or other files.

Canceling mail. A process of printing bars over the stamps, as well as printing the date and time where mail processing has occurred.

Certificate of Mailing receipt. Provides evidence of mailing. The receipt must be purchased at the time of mailing; no record is kept by the post office. A fee is charged in addition to the postage.

Certified mail. Provides the sender with a mailing receipt. A record is kept at the post office of delivery.

Circulation list. A type of a routing slip.

Collect on delivery (COD). Allows the mailer to collect the price of goods and/or postage on merchandise ordered by addressee when it is delivered.

Domestic mail. Mail that is distributed within, among, and between the United States and its territories and possessions; Army–Air Force and Navy post offices; and to the United Nations, New York City.

Domestic Mail Manual (DMM). Sets forth the policies, regulations, and procedures governing domestic mail services provided to the public by the U.S. Postal Service.

Electronic bulletin boards. Public message centers that appear on computer networks, available to anyone with access to the network.

Electronic mail (e-mail). The transmission of messages by computer from one person to another; it uses the computer, the modem, and communications software.

Emoticons. Visual expressions used in e-mail messages equivalent to your attitudes and emotions, such as a smile or frown.

Express mail. A U.S. Postal Service Classification. The USPS's fastest service, with next-day delivery by noon to most destinations. Express mail is delivered 365 days a year—no extra charge for Saturday, Sunday, or holiday delivery.

Facsimile or fax machine. A device that will copy and transmit, over telephone lines, graphical (charts, photographs, drawings, longhand messages) or textual documents to a corresponding remote fax machine.

First-class mail. A U.S. Postal Service classification. Includes all personal correspondence, all bills and statements of accounts, all matter sealed or otherwise closed against inspection, and matter wholly or partly in writing or typewriting.

Insured mail. Provides coverage against loss or damage. The amount of insurance coverage for loss will be the actual value, less depreciation.

International mail. Mail that is distributed beyond the United States and its territories, or possessions.

International Mail Manual (IMM) Sets forth the policies, regulations, and procedures governing international mail services provided to the public by the U.S. Postal Service.

Mailgram. An electronic message, transmitted by Western Union, that provides next-day postal service delivery for messages sent to any address in the United States.

Mail register. Provides a record of special incoming mail for quick review.

Parcel Post. A U.S. Postal Service classification. Used for mailing certain items—books, circulars, catalogs, other printed matter, and merchandise weighing at least 1 pound but not more than 70 pounds.

Polling. Allows one fax machine to test others on the network for information.

Postal money orders. A safe way to send money through the mail; can be used in place of a personal check.

Priority mail. A U.S. Postal Service classification. Offers two-day service to most domestic destinations. Items must weigh 70 pounds or less and measure 108 inches or less in combined length and girth.

Registered mail. A U.S. Postal Service classification. Provides maximum protection and security for valuables and is available only for items paid at priority and first-class mail rates.

Restricted delivery. Permits a mailer to direct delivery only to the addressee or addressee's authorized agent.

Return receipt. Provides a mailer with evidence of delivery. It also supplies the recipient's actual delivery address if it is different from the address used by the sender.

Return receipt for merchandise. Provides the sender with a mailing receipt and a return receipt. A delivery record, for an additional fee, is kept by the post office of address, but no record is kept at the office of mailing.

Routing slip. A form that is used to route or circulate correspondence, documents, and magazines to other team members or staff within a department. Also called circulation list.

Special standard mail (book rate). A U.S. Postal Service classification. Used for books, film, printed music, printed test materials, sound recordings, play scripts, printed educational charts, loose-leaf pages and binders consisting of medical information, and computer-readable media.

Stand-alone fax machine. A self-contained unit that uses scanning and printing technology.

Voice mail. A telephone network-based message routing, storing, and retrieval system.

ZIP Code. Stands for Zone Improvement Plan, a five-digit number that identifies postal delivery areas in the United States.

ZIP + 4 Code. An expanded ZIP Code, composed of the original five-digit code plus a four-digit add-on. The expanded code identifies a geographic segment within the five-digit delivery area such as a city block, an office building, an individual high-volume receiver of mail, or any other unit that would aid efficient mail sorting and delivery.

For Your Discussion

 Retrieve file C6-DQ.DOC from your student data disk.

Directions

Enter your response after each question.

1. What makes handling the mail such a critical task for the office professional?
2. What types of incoming electronic mail could make demands on an office professional's time?
3. When should you send an e-mail versus a fax?
4. Describe at least five guidelines to follow when faxing materials.
5. List the steps, in sequence, for processing incoming mail.
6. How should you sort the mail? Why do you think sorting is necessary?
7. What are the recommended ways for placing mail on the manager's desk?
8. Suggest ways to group mail that has arrived in your manager's absence before presenting it to him or her.
9. Distinguish between Certificate of Mailing and certified mail.
10. Distinguish among the classes of international mail.

NUMBER USAGE WORKSHOP

To make a document look professional, numbers should be used in a consistent manner. Do not spell out numbers in one section of a document and use figures in another section. As a general rule, spell out numbers ten and under; use figures for numbers over ten.

For Review

Appendix A: Rule 13: Numbers One Through Ten

Rule 14: Dates

Rule 15: Percentages

 Retrieve file C6-WRKS.DOC from your student data disk.

Directions

Write *C* at the end of the sentence if the number usage is correct. Otherwise, make the necessary corrections.

Rule 13: Numbers One To Ten

1. Tomorrow we will hire three accounting clerks, eleven packers, and seven drivers.
2. The new employee is on a six months' training program.
3. Nearly 300 people have been laid off from their jobs in the plant.
4. Over two hundred people will attend the conference next month.
5. Their new address is 7098-A 5th Avenue, Dallas, TX 75234.

Rule 14: Dates

1. The computer user groups will meet on April 10th.
2. The engineers will meet for their monthly meeting on the fifteenth.
3. The staff meeting will be on 7 September.
4. The invoice is due on the first of each month.
5. Please see that all e-mail notices are sent by March 15.

Rule 15: Percentages

1. We want an increase of five percent in sales next month.
2. At least 25% of the participants agreed to the changes in the program for the next meeting.
3. We have received only 7.8% interest on our investment.
4. The new product requires at least 12 percent of the market share.
5. The computer prices have dropped by 10%.

On the Job Situations

 Retrieve file C6-OJS.DOC from your student data disk.

Directions

Enter your response after each situation.

1. James told you that his manager was furious when he admitted that he had been throwing away over half of the advertising material at the time it arrived, never giving his manager an opportunity to see it. His manager discovered this through conversations with different callers who asked about the mailed advertisements. James seems confused about what to do with booklets, advertising material, and other standard mail, and has asked for your advice. Knowing that his manager wants to see all the mail, what guidelines can you suggest?

2. As the office assistant to a management consulting firm, you have the responsibility for controlling certain cost areas, one of which is the mail operation. For the past three months you have noticed an increase in mail costs. After you reviewed the mail-related expenses, you discovered the following: an increase in express and priority mail to meet deadlines; letters returned with incorrect and insufficient addresses; and several items sent using incorrect mail classifications. Explain how you would approach this situation to reduce mailing costs in these areas.

3. As an office professional to your new office manager, you would like to suggest that she let you review and preview her mail each day before you distribute it to her. Knowing that your previous manager never delegated this task, how can you propose this suggestion, giving sound reasons for it, and indicating how it would assist her by saving her time?

4. You support six managers. Every day each manager receives at least twenty pieces of mail in addition to the following: *The Wall Street Journal,* two or three newsletters, two or three trade journals, and advertisements. Three of the managers want you to log in their important mail, and the other three managers need all the help you can give them. They are not well organized in handling their paperwork, much less handling the incoming mail in an efficient way. What actions can you take to avoid mixing up their mail?

Projects and Activities

1. If you are using e-mail in your organization, complete the following (if not, interview someone who is using e-mail):

   a. How often are e-mail messages checked?

   b. What are at least two etiquette tips that this user believes could be used in this organization?

   c. What e-mail system is being used? Microsoft Outlook? GroupWise? ProCom?

2. Obtain a schedule of current rates and fees for the following:
   a. Certified mail
   b. Return receipt requested at the time of mailing
   c. Return receipt requested after an item has been mailed
   d. Special handling of an item weighing over 10 pounds
   e. Special delivery of first-class mail weighing less than 2 pounds
   f. Money order for $200
   g. Insurance for a package valued at $60
   h. Registration for an item with a declared value of $300
   i. Mailing a 16-pound parcel within your own local postal zone

3. Obtain a copy of an organization's policies and procedures for e-mail etiquette or netiquette. Compose a memo to your instructor summarizing your findings and attach the copy to the memo.

4. Interview an office professional who can answer the following questions:
   a. How is the mail delivered in your office? Do you pick up the mail from a centralized mailroom in your company? Is the mail distributed by mail personnel?
   b. How often is the mail delivered to your work area?
   c. How often is the mail picked up from your work area?
   d. How many people do you handle mail for in your work area?
   e. Describe the steps you use to handle the incoming mail for the people you support.
   f. Describe the steps you follow to handle the outgoing mail.

Organize the responses into a report memo and be prepared to share the report with the class.

Surfing the Internet

The operations manager has asked you to locate information about postal services. Rather than calling or visiting the post office, you want to search the Internet.

1. Connect to the Internet and access a search tool such as Yahoo!, Lycos, and InfoSeek.

2. Enter the following key search words: *United States Postal Service*, or go directly to the Web site http://www.usps.com.

3. Select the Business section. Search the following three areas: international, business publications, and postage rates.
   a. Summarize the most important information from the international section. Print the page if possible and attach it to your summary.
   b. Enter the following key search words: *postal software* or *mailing list software*.
   c. Summarize at least three different software products. Print each page if possible and attach each to the appropriate summary.

    d. Enter the following address: http://www.uspsglobal.com. List at least three services or products that are displayed.

    e. Summarize your findings in a report memo to be turned in to your instructor.

4. While on the Internet, go to the Web site of United Parcel Service (UPS) at http://www.ups.com.

    a. Review the products and services. Locate information about tracking a package.

    b. Write a brief memo to your instructor summarizing your findings. If you can print the information, attach a copy to the memo.

Using MS Office 2002

Create an E-Mail Template

 Situation: You frequently send the same information to the same group of people, with limited *added* or *changed* information.

Solution: Create the basic message with the recipients' names in it and save it as a template. Each time you need to send this message, you can quickly open the template and add your information.

Creating the Template

1. Open Microsoft Outlook and click on the New Mail Message button on the Standard toolbar.
2. Enter the recipients' names in the To text box, separated by commas.
3. Type the subject in the Subject text box.
4. Type the
   - leading paragraph(s)
   - closing paragraph
   - signature information
5. Click on File and select Save As.
6. By default your message's subject is the file name. You have the option to change the name.
7. Change the Save As type field to: Outlook Template (*.oft).
   This causes the *file location* to change; accept this.
   This will place a *.dot* extension on the file name.
8. Click on Save to save the message as a template.
9. You are returned to your e-mail message. Assume at this time you do not want to send it out because you are just creating a template.
10. Close the message without saving it. Your original message is already saved as a template.

Using the Template:

1. Click on the File menu, point to New, and then select Choose Form.
2. The Choose Form dialog box opens.

3. Click on the down-pointing arrow next to the Look In text box.

4. Select *User Templates in File System*.

5. All Outlook templates created by you display on the screen.

6. Click on the template you need and then click on the Open button.

7. The message is opened with the standard information you need.

8. Place the cursor above the closing information in the body section and type the updated information.

9. Proof your message and click on Send.

APPLICATION PROBLEMS

APPLICATION 6–A

Processing Incoming Mail

Supplies needed: Forms 6-A-1 through 6-A-7; plain bond paper.

 Retrieve files C6-NOTE.DOC, C6-DA.DOC, C6-TODO.DOC, and C6-ROUTE.DOC from your student data disk.

Directions: Mrs. Quevedo is out of the office during the week of July 14. You are processing the mail on Monday morning, July 14.

1. Read Form 6-A-1, Notes on Incoming Mail for Monday, July 14.

2. Mrs. Quevedo always wants mail from a regional office routed to the respective assistant vice president for the region. However, Mrs. Quevedo expects you to open the letters and to keep a record of the mail forwarded to the assistant vice presidents. Complete Form 6-A-2.

3. You route magazines and advertising letters from other organizations to the assistant vice presidents. Complete Forms 6-A-4 through 6-A-7, Routing Forms (if needed), to attach to the magazines and advertising letters.

4. Complete Form 6-A-3, To-Do List; add reminders to yourself and notes about items that you should follow up on.

5. Place the other letters, memorandums, and important items in a folder for Mrs. Quevedo. For your instructor, make a list of the items you will place in a folder for Mrs. Quevedo. Label the list "Items for A. Quevedo's Folder."

APPLICATION 6–B

Classes of Mail

Supplies needed: Form 6-B, List of Outgoing Mail.

 Retrieve file C6-LIST.DOC from your student data disk.

Directions: To reinforce your knowledge of classes of mail, indicate the class of mail for each item listed. Complete Form 6-B, List of Outgoing Mail.

APPLICATION 6-C

Mail Operations–Field Trip

Supplies needed: Form 6-C, Mail Operations—Field Trip Activity; plain bond paper.

 Retrieve file C6-MAIL.DOC from your student data disk.

Directions: Based on your instructor's directions, either individually complete Form 6-B or complete it with your team members. To receive maximum points, be sure to answer each question. Be prepared to share it with other class members. Submit your final report to your instructor for evaluation.

Your Action Plan

Complete your Action Plan; if necessary, refer to the guidelines outlined in Chapter 1. Set one goal using the information you learned in Chapter 6.

Your Portfolio

With the help of your instructor, select the best activity representative of your work from Chapter 6. Follow your instructor's directions about formatting, assembling, and submitting the portfolio.

chapter 7

Records Management

OUTLINE

Rules for Filing According to Address
Variations in Alphabetic Filing Rules

What About the Future?

LEARNING OUTCOMES

When you have completed this chapter, you should be able to:

✔ Describe the main file classification systems.

✔ Describe the steps for preparing visible and electronic documents to be stored.

✔ Describe visible and electronic filing supplies and equipment needed.

✔ Describe storing information for visible and electronic documents.

✔ Describe the guidelines for records retention and transfer.

✔ Describe alphabetic filing procedures.

✔ Apply basic alphabetic filing rules.

Processing documents creates a never-ending cycle in the work of an office. As an office professional, you will be involved in most phases of the cycle. Documents are created, reproduced, mailed, and answered. Internal mail, such as memos, reports, and forms, is created, reproduced, and distributed, and in some cases reproduced again. This cycle of activity leads to the next steps:

■ Discard unnecessary documents.

■ Store copies of outgoing mail; all memos, reports, and other internal mail; and incoming mail once it has been acted on so that each piece of paper or electronic file is easily located when it is needed.

You have very likely discovered, through the processing of your own school papers, that if you allow your documents to accumulate haphazardly, you find yourself wasting precious time frantically sorting stacks of paper in a last-minute effort to prepare for your final exams. The same thing may be true in handling your personal business records. Similar panic, of course, can happen in an office when a letter, report, or form is needed in a hurry and cannot be found.

Today's offices generate so many papers each day that twenty desktops could never hold them all, except in a very small business. As a matter of fact, finding room for the ever-expanding quantity of papers is a great concern in today's offices.

Much has been written about the paperless office, but today, for most organizations, the prospect of a paperless office is only a dream. Modern technology makes it so easy to produce and reproduce documents. Sales of paper, professionally designed filing systems, and filing supplies and equipment provide evidence that paper documents are still the dominant medium for most of our records. Many offices also have specialized paper documents, such as large engineering drawings or maps, microfilm/microfiche, and photographs, that have inherent filing problems. The creation and retention of electronic documents result in another set of problems specific to this medium.

Part of today's paperwork problem is that the federal government, as well as state and municipal governments, demands so much data from each business. Apart from the growing need for businesses to supply government agencies with data and to maintain enormous quantities of records to meet the government's varying regulations, business records have become increasingly more complex with the information explosion of our world.

One way businesses have reacted to the need to cope with so much paper has been for them to apply a "systems" approach to their paperwork problems. Many large businesses find it productive to designate one employee to supervise the management of documents for the entire organization. The **records manager** supervises all the company's files. He or she also determines how the files will be maintained and who will maintain them, how long each document is to be kept in the file, and when a file is to be removed to an inactive area or made ready for more permanent storage or destruction.

This chapter discusses what an office professional needs to know about maintaining files in a typical office or work area. It specifically covers basic procedures for filing and retrieving records, file retention, as well as filing supplies and equipment.

RECORDS MANAGEMENT

Records management is the systematic management of the creation, maintenance, retention, destruction, protection, and preservation of records. A **record** is any type of recorded information that is stored for quick retrieval and for preservation. Types of records include paper and image. Paper records are stored in file folders. **Image records** are documents, such as letters, charts, and photographs, that have been converted to either microfilm/microfiche or digitized electronic data that can be stored and retrieved immediately. Image processing offers extremely high capacity, durability, and security. Companies that have high volumes of documents and high activity in the files prefer image processing.

As long as paper is still our main record type, office personnel must process and maintain each piece of paper while it is in use or until it is stored in some other form. Records management involves a number of steps, including:

1. Designing a system of storing records
2. Developing procedures for identifying the types of records to be filed
3. Determining how long records should be stored
4. Developing the arrangement of records in a sequence so they can be retrieved quickly
5. Protecting records from loss or damage

Location of Files

File locations are usually set up in one of two ways: centralized or decentralized. When setting up a filing system, the records manager should consider which system to use.

In a **centralized filing system,** files are placed in one location that is convenient for a group of people who must work with the same information. Records are more accessible if centrally located, and duplication of equipment and files is eliminated. In a centralized system, establish a procedure for employees to "check out" files, so that they can be located at all times. A disadvantage to this system is that a file may be in use when another employee needs it. An advantage to the system is that security is enhanced because only a select group of employees are authorized to use the files.

In a **decentralized filing system,** individuals or very small groups of employees maintain files at their workstations. An example would be a small department where several assistants maintain correspondence and project files at their workstations. You can create a centralized file where shared information, such as reference materials, reports, and catalogs, is kept. The main advantages of a decentralized system are accessibility and confidentiality. When individuals maintain their own files, they can usually control the movement of those files and keep the files locked when not in use, so that others cannot access them. The main disadvantages of this system are that more copying is required to allow others access to materials, and, if the filing task is not done on a regular basis, the information requested may not be readily available.

In considering location, answer the following:

- Who needs to have access to the records in the files?
- What kind of information is stored in the files?
- How frequently will the files need to be accessed?
- What procedures are needed to protect the files from loss, damage, theft, and unauthorized use?

File Classification Systems

File classification systems are based on standard rules that determine how files will be arranged. The major systems are *alphabetic, numeric, geographic*, and *subject*. These systems are often used in combination with each other.

The filing system used should be based on the kind of information being stored and how it will be retrieved for future use. For instance, a sales department might want to set up customer files by region (geographic), by name (alphabetic), and by account number (numeric). One advantage of electronic filing systems is that software programs are designed so that records can be sorted and retrieved by simply keying a few commands. With paper records, cross-referencing systems are used to locate files from one system to another.

Alphabetic. The alphabetic system is one of the most commonly used systems. An **alphabetic filing system** uses the alphabet to sequence personal, business, and government names. Figure 7-1 shows an alphabetic system for a small office. The alphabetic system has the following advantages:

- Alphabetic filing is direct because you can go directly to the file and locate an item without having to first refer to an index. An **index** is a listing of the filed items.
- Everyone knows the alphabet.
- All other systems are directly or indirectly combined with the alphabetic system.

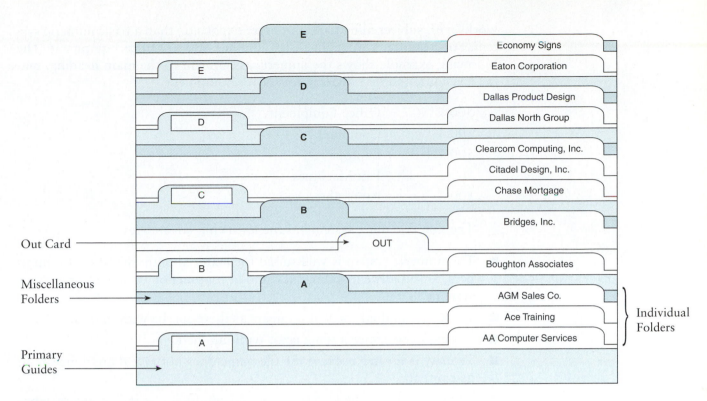

Figure 7-1
An alphabetic system for a small office.

Some of the disadvantages include:

- Because material is filed alphabetically according to correspondent or name, each individual using the system files material according to the alphabetic scheme he or she believes appropriate. If everyone doesn't strictly follow a uniform set of rules for alphabetizing records, individuals could file records in many possible locations, making retrieval inefficient.

- Expansion may create problems when the expansion takes place in a section of the file where there is no space to insert additional folders.

- Confidentiality of the files cannot be guaranteed because the file folder labels can be seen by anyone retrieving a file.

Numeric. In the **numeric filing system** (one of the two most common filing systems), material is filed in some logical numerical order. Examples of users include insurance companies that keep records according to policy numbers, medical offices that assign a number to each patient, and legal firms that assign a case number to each client. A numeric filing system requires a separate alphabetic listing of names in case an assigned number has been lost or forgotten.

Numbers are assigned in two ways: terminal-digit filing and decimal-numeric filing. **Terminal-digit filing** divides numbers into groups of digits that point to the location of the records. For example, the first group of digits identifies the sequence of the folder behind the filing guide, the next group of digits indicates the guide number in the drawer, and the last group identifies the drawer number. This system is advantageous because it reduces "misfile." **Decimal-numeric filing,** also known as the *Dewey decimal system,* works with subject filing to permit more expansion than a basic numeric system. For instance, you might assign number 500 to Office Equipment. The following example shows the numeric assignment to the main heading, major divisions, and first division for Office Equipment.

500	Office Equipment
500.1	Computers
500.1.1	Laptops
500.2	Fax Machines
500.3	Paper Shredders

The numeric filing system has the following advantages:

- The numeric system is well suited for material with identification numbers, for rapidly expanding files, and in conjunction with data-processing systems.
- There are no duplicates of numbers as there can be with names.
- It is easier to notice a filing error with numbers.
- Security is greater because the file name does not reveal anything about its contents.
- Numeric filing is the fastest to use and results in the fewest errors. Coupled with shelf filing equipment and color-coding, numeric filing systems simplify document processing.
- It is easy to expand the system.

Disadvantages include the following:

- You must use an index, listing the name of the person, organization, or subject to which the number is assigned. For this reason, a numeric system is called **indirect filing.**
- You must use an **accession register** or book to show the next number available for assignment.

Geographic. The **geographic filing system** is commonly used by sales and marketing personnel and others who are concerned with the location of companies and individuals. Using this system, you file material alphabetically in some logical pattern, such as by city, by state, or by region or territory. An example of a geographic filing arrangement is shown in Figure 7-2.

The geographical filing system has the following advantages:

- It allows for direct filing if the location is known.
- It provides easy access because groups of records are filed together.

Some disadvantages include:

- An index is required if the location is not known.
- Sorting the records by city, state, or region increases the possibility of error.

Subject. The **subject filing system** allows you to file material alphabetically according to main subject because the subjects are considered to be more im-

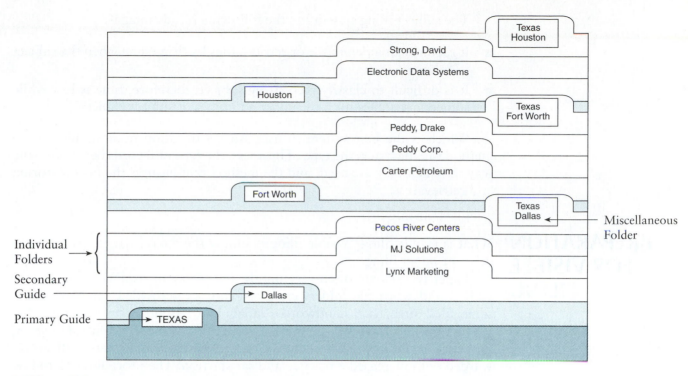

■ **Figure 7-2**
Geographic filing arrangement.

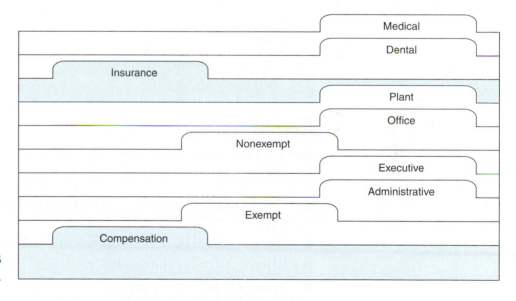

■ **Figure 7-3**
A subject file.

portant than the individual or business name. Companies that deal with products, supplies, advertising, and so forth use subject systems. Subject files are popular with travel agencies for filing brochures by destination, such as San Francisco, Las Vegas, and Seattle. An example of a subject file is shown in Figure 7-3.

Some of the advantages of the subject filing system are:

■ Easy access because subject filing relates to groups of records.

■ Subdivisions easily expand the system.

The subject filing system has the following disadvantages:

- It requires an index to file or retrieve files by firm name when the subject is unknown.
- It is difficult to classify records by subject; therefore, time is lost while someone searches for a file under a number of subject choices.

Which is the best system to use? An organization must decide on the method that best suits the type of business, the type of records being filed, the way in which they are used, and the method that ensures the fastest storing and retrieval.

PREPARATION FOR VISIBLE FILING

What is *visible* filing? **Visible filing** is simply the most current term used to describe *paper* filing.

Paper records are often very untidy and disorganized. We have all seen stuffed and worn file folders crammed into overcrowded cabinets. These same files often have handwritten labels and redundant information. No wonder the task least enjoyed by many office professionals is filing. However, an office professional who follows procedures suggested here will be rewarded with increased efficiency and satisfaction. The procedures to follow before placing a paper inside a file folder are:

1. Reviewing
2. Indexing
3. Coding
4. Cross-referencing
5. Sorting

Reviewing

Review each document before you determine how to file it. Follow these guidelines:

- Check papers that are stapled together and decide if they should be filed together.
- Staple together related papers where one document refers to the other.
- Remove all paper clips and extra staples.
- Remove small slips of paper that are no longer needed; for instance, a slip marked "Please file."
- Keep the routing slip with the appropriate documents. You may need to determine later to whom the document was circulated.
- Determine if documents are duplicates and should be deleted/destroyed, or filed.

Indexing

Indexing is thinking about how you will file each paper. It is the mental process of determining the key word or number under which a paper will be filed. Careful indexing is the most important part of the process of filing papers. The key word can be a name, a subject, or a geographic location. For example, if you wanted to file a document where the name is *Mr. Benjamin Ross*, you would determine that the most important word for filing is *Ross*.

When you are filing correspondence by name, scan the correspondence to decide which name to use. Anticipate the name your manager will use when he or she calls for that particular document. Note the following:

1. Incoming letters are often called for by the name of the organization appearing in the letterhead, so index them by the name of the organization in the letterhead.

2. Outgoing letters are often called for by the name of the organization appearing in the inside address, so index them by the name of the organization in the inside address.

To learn how to index for the variety of names you will encounter, follow the standardized indexing rules presented later in this chapter under "Alphabetic Filing Rules."

Coding

After you decide how a paper should be filed, mark the indexing caption on it. This process is called **coding.** To code by name, underline the name with a colored pencil.

In the following three examples, the key words have been bolded and the number of indexing units has been identified. The order in which to consider the units for filing is shown with a number following the unit. The first unit or the most important word in the sequence has been underlined.

- Mr. **Benjamin** (2nd) <u>**Ross**</u> (1st) = 2 indexing units
- <u>**National**</u> (1st) **Geographic** (2nd) **Photography** (3rd) = 3 indexing units
- <u>**Hawthorne**</u> (1st) **Publishers** (2nd) Inc. = 2 indexing units

The code on the paper should be complete enough that you can return the paper to the same folder each time it has been removed. As you study the indexing rules, you will learn how to determine the order of units within a name.

Cross-Referencing

When a document is apt to be called for by two different names at different times, you should be able to locate it by looking under either name. To make this possible, file the document according to the **caption** (the name arranged in index order) by which it is most likely to be requested. Also, file a reference to it by the second name. Handling this task is referred to as **cross-referencing.**

To make a cross-reference for a card file, use a card of the same size as the cards in the file; you may use a different color. Notice in Figure 7-4 the two cards prepared for McDonald Hunter Inc. The information printed below *SEE* on the cross-reference card is the caption on the original card.

To prepare references for correspondence, use preprinted letter-sized cross-reference sheets. Make a large *X* on the actual correspondence in the margin near the name used as a cross-reference; underline the name.

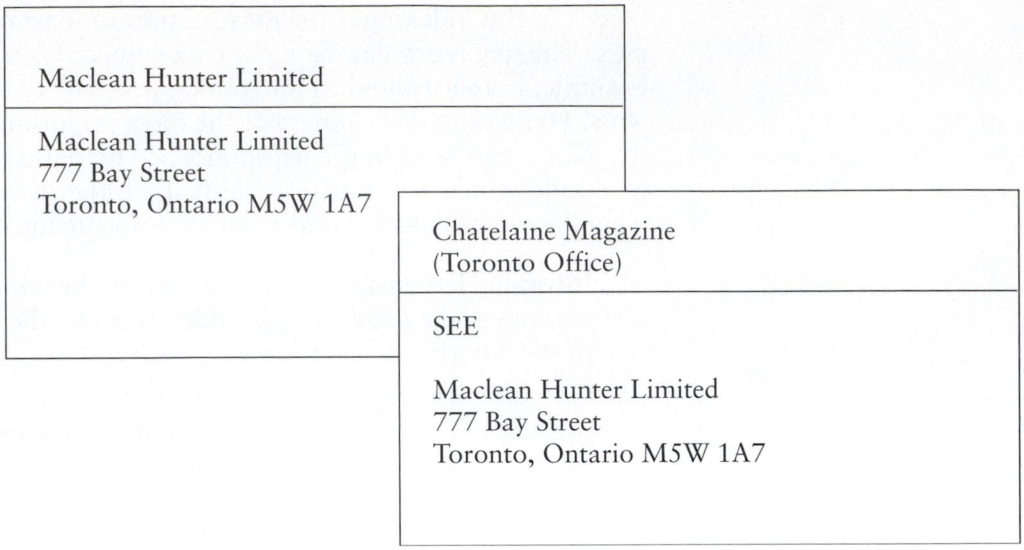

Maclean Hunter Limited

Maclean Hunter Limited
777 Bay Street
Toronto, Ontario M5W 1A7

Chatelaine Magazine
(Toronto Office)

SEE

Maclean Hunter Limited
777 Bay Street
Toronto, Ontario M5W 1A7

■ **Figure 7-4**
Original card; cross-reference card.

Make two copies of the cross-reference sheet:

1. One copy will be filed in the cross-reference folder. It should be the only piece of paper filed in the folder, because the purpose of the cross-reference sheet is to send you to the correct file. If you have an effective card file system that clearly identifies cross-references, you may eliminate the need for the cross-reference folder and the cross-reference sheet.

2. The second copy will be filed in the actual folder where you want all the correspondence to be placed. This cross-reference sheet will serve as a reminder to you that a cross-reference folder exists. If you are missing information, you will need to check the cross-reference folder to see whether someone has inadvertently filed documents in the cross-reference folder.

Avoid preparing unnecessary cross-references, but if you are in doubt, make one. There are various situations in which cross-referencing is necessary. Consider the following:

1. Correspondence pertaining to individuals may be filed by subject (for example, Temporary Employees) instead of by name.

2. It may be difficult to determine the individual's surname. Consider the name *Kent Ross*. Is the surname *Ross* or is it *Kent*? If the surname is *Ross*, the correct file will read *Ross, Kent* and the cross-reference file label will read *Kent, Ross*. Inside the folder, the cross-reference sheets will read:

   SEE Ross, Kent

3. A married woman may be known by
   a. Her maiden name. For example, in the name *Ms. Heather Ross*, the name is indexed as *Ross, Heather (Ms.)*.
   b. Her married name. For example, in the name *Mrs. Heather Whyte*, the name is indexed as *Whyte, Heather (Mrs.)*.

c. Her husband's name. For example, in the name *Mrs. Robert Whyte*, the name would be indexed as *Whyte, Robert (Mrs.)*.

A cross-reference will be necessary for two of the three cases. Most commonly, correspondence would be filed under either *Ross, Heather (Ms.)* or *Whyte, Heather (Mrs.)*. Only one of these files should contain documents; the other two must serve as cross-references.

4. Subdivisions of a parent company are filed under the name used on their letterhead; they are not filed under the parent company name. To avoid confusion, file correctly under the name of the subdivision, but prepare a cross-reference for the name of the parent company. For example, a subdivision business called *Office Supply Town* with a parent company called *Office Supply Enterprises* would have the correspondence filed as *Office Supply Town*; but a cross-reference sheet would be placed in the *Office Supply Enterprises* folder to send the records manager to the *Office Supply Town* folder.

5. Some organizations are referred to by their acronym because they are better known that way—for example, IAAP (International Association of Administrative Professionals). It is acceptable to file the correspondence under either name; however, it is best to check the organization's letterhead or business card to see how the organization refers to itself. Whether you file by the full name or by the popular abbreviation, *consistency must prevail*. A cross-reference will be necessary to keep all the correspondence in the same file.

6. A business name may include several surnames. For *Johnson, Baines, and Strafford*, file the original by *Johnson* and cross-reference *Baines and Strafford*.

7. A company may change its name. File by the new name, and record the date of the change. Retain the old name in the files as a cross-reference only.

8. Names of foreign companies and government agencies are often written in both English and the respective foreign language. For a government agency, file the original paper by the English name, and place a cross-reference sheet in the folder with the foreign spelling.

9. For a foreign company, file the original by the name as it is written, and the cross-reference sheet in the folder under the English translation.

10. When confusion exists concerning a filing rule, alleviate the confusion by making a cross-reference. A cross-reference will send the reader to the correct name of the business.

11. When a department is renamed because of restructuring within the organization, internal correspondence filed by subject is often affected. File the correspondence by the new name; however, retain the old name in the files as a cross-reference.

Sorting

Using the code marks (see "Coding") as a guide, prearrange the documents in the same order in which they will be filed. This preliminary arrangement is called **sorting**. By sorting the documents carefully, you will eliminate unnecessary shifting back and forth, from drawer to drawer or from shelf to shelf, as you file the documents. As a result, you will be working efficiently and saving time.

Portable vertical sorting trays and/or booklets with dividers and guides are available in a variety of sizes. Use a sorting tray or booklet to hold the documents until you file them. If you accumulate a stack of documents in the to-be-filed basket each day and do not have sorting equipment, request it. In the meantime, use an efficient method of sorting manually.

Sitting at your desk or at a table, first divide the documents into manageable groups. For example, if you are sorting by name, first stack the documents in groups A–E, F–J, K–P, Q–T, and U–Z. Next arrange the papers in the first group in A, B, C, D, and E stacks, and then assemble the documents in each stack in alphabetical order. Sort the remaining groups in the same way. Remember, where two pieces of correspondence share the same name, the most recent document is placed on top.

Where there is a very large amount of paper filing to handle, automated sorting systems are available. By means of a computerized control panel, the slots required are brought in front of the operator, eliminating unnecessary steps and stretching.

TECHNIQUES FOR PUTTING AWAY PAPERS

Filing is the actual placing of papers in folders. Allow at least thirty minutes a day in your schedule for this activity.

Many office professionals rate filing as their most disliked duty. When unfiled papers stack up, a simple task becomes a burden. You will spend much more time locating a document when it is in an unarranged stack than when it is properly filed. Note also that you run the risk of losing papers when they are disorganized. It is crucial to keep up with your filing on a daily basis.

In any new office job, you will be placing and locating materials in the files that were maintained by your predecessor. If, as part of your orientation to the job, he or she explains the filing system to you, listen carefully, ask questions, and take notes. If the organization has a central indexing system, learn it as rapidly as you can. Study it and memorize the rules and procedures that relate directly to your files. Do not try to reorganize the files in your office until you are familiar with what they contain. Allow yourself several months to learn the system. In the meantime, become thoroughly familiar with the contents of the files. Write down your suggestions for improving the filing system.

The following are very important practices for putting away papers. If your office is not currently doing these, implement them as quickly as possible.

- Always file the most recent correspondence at the front of the file (on top).
- When a file folder is held horizontally, the tops of the documents inside the folder should all be on the left side.

Charge-Out Methods

Charge-out methods, a system for tracking files that are removed from a designated location, do not apply to electronic filing. In fact, one of the advantages of electronic systems is that when you retrieve a document from the filing system, you just take an electronic copy. This means, of course, that there is never any reason to return the document to the folder because the original never left the folder.

Paper filing is a very different story. Materials are kept in active files for use; therefore, effective charge-out methods must be followed in order to keep track of materials that have been borrowed from the files and are to be returned.

Charge-out procedures can be electronically controlled. This reduces the time spent searching for files.

Manual charge-out systems are very popular. A manual system uses special cards, folders, and pressboard guides with the word *OUT* printed on the tabs to substitute for papers and folders taken from the files. When only a few sheets of paper are removed from the files, an *OUT* card is used; when the entire folder is removed, either an *OUT* folder or an *OUT* guide is substituted. Paper filing systems use two types of charge-out guides:

- Guides with printed lines for writing a description of the materials removed, the name of the person who has taken the file or the materials, and the date issued.
- Guides with a slot or a pocket to hold a card. The charge-out information is written on the card.

In both cases, the guides are placed into the filing system to take the place of the materials or files that have been removed. The *OUT* card or guide remains in the file until the charged-out material is returned. Both types are reusable.

In large companies where files are maintained electronically, bar coding may be used. **Bar coding** requires software, a label printer, and a scanning device. This electronic tracking method scans a label and the user and location codes. Bar coding virtually eliminates lost files. In sophisticated systems each document or disk can be bar coded for easy retrieval.

The method you use for keeping up with materials removed from the files you maintain will depend on what works best in your organization.

Organization of Electronic Files

Because most businesses depend heavily on electronic methods as well as paper filing methods, it is essential that the office professional has an effective and efficient means of filing and locating documents on both the office network and on removable disks.

In some ways, the electronic system works much like the paper system. Put simply, in the paper system we have cabinets that contain folders that contain files that contain documents. In an electronic system, we have directories that contain folders that contain files that contain documents. A **directory** is a section of the network that is allotted to certain people for their files. Having your own directory is like having your own filing cabinet.

When using the office network, certain directories will be allotted for your use. In these directories, you can create folders for your own use. Other directories will be available for you to access and read but not to alter, whereas still other directories will be completely off-limits for your use. This is comparable to confidential paper files.

A removable disk will either be a CD-ROM, ZIP, or floppy disk. Removable disks will either be used as the primary means of electronic storage, or they will be used as backup for the documents stored on the office network.

Be sure to label the outside of your removable disks stating what directories they contain. Some offices assign different disks for each member of the staff or different disks for different topics such as expense accounts, budgets, or correspondence for each month.

When labeling your directories either on the network or on removable disks, be sure to use descriptive words so that you can return to the directory, folder, or file at a later date. As well, it is essential to be consistent with your labeling. If you identify your letters as "Correspondence—March" on one folder, don't label the next directory as "Corr—April." Consistency in labeling is an important key to locating information efficiently.

SUPPLIES ONLINE

Products for both visible and electronic filing should make your systems more organized, efficient, and effective. Companies have provided numerous products, styles, sizes, and shapes to make a filing system work well for the organization. Many products are available at the local stationery store; however, to get the greatest variety in products, shop online through the Internet.

Online shopping for your supplies has a number of advantages, including:

- The catalog will be dynamic; that is, the pictures, descriptions, and prices displayed will be up-to-date. With a conventional paper catalog, the information is often out-of-date before it's printed.
- The delivery is fast because the online companies use courier services to get the package to your office. Because of the competition among the online supply stores, the customer service tends to be very good.
- Online products usually cost less than those in a conventional store because they do not have the same expenses—fewer employees, no magazine printing costs, no rent for store space, and so on.

Examples of online shopping sites that offer the latest products in both visible and electronic filing supplies are:

- http://www.officedepot.com
- http://www.ebay.com
- http://www.officeworld.com

The following is a brief discussion of some basic items that will help you manage your records. Once you have the basics, you will need to enhance and improve on what you have.

Supplies for Visible Filing

Every filing system can be expanded. To add to the files, use supplies to match what is already in use. The style of supplies needed is dependent upon the style of cabinet in your office (vertical or lateral—defined in the section titled

■ **Figure 7-5**
Open-shelf filing.

"Storing Information") as well as existing supplies. Among the supplies needed for filing documents are guides, folders, and labels.

Guides. Dividers in conventional filing drawers or compartments are called **guides.** They serve as signposts, separating the filing space into labeled sections. Guides also support the folders in an upright position.

Guides have a **tab** projecting from the edge. Tabs are available in a variety of sizes and colors. Whereas you can purchase blank tabs in order to customize your system, you can also purchase tabs that list the days of the week, the names of months, or numbers.

Guides for open-shelf filing differ from guides for vertical file drawers. Figure 7-5 shows an open-shelf filing. Note that the tabs on the guides are along the side and not on the top, as they would be on vertical files.

Folders. **Folders** are the containers for holding the correspondence and other paper. Because folders tend to take a lot of abuse, they are constructed of a heavy paper or plastic. They can be purchased in a variety of colors, sizes, and weights. The tab on the folder also comes in a variety of positions and sizes. Figure 7-6 shows some of the possible tab cuts.

All folders should have creases at the bottom. The creases are called **scores.** When the folder begins to fill with correspondence, the score allows you to fit more documents in the folder without damaging the papers.

Expandable folders are available for oversized files. The folders shown in Figure 7-7 have a gusset instead of a score; **gussets** allow a folder to expand more than a conventional folder.

Hanging or suspending folders are popular for active files. Figure 7-8 shows a hanging folder with labels. **Hanging folders** are suspended by extensions at their top edges across a metal frame within the file drawer, which means they don't rest on the bottom of the cabinet. Materials filed in hanging folders are easily accessible because the folders open wide and slide smoothly on the hanger rail. Attachable tabs are inserted into slots at the top of the folders and are used in place of conventional guides with tabs.

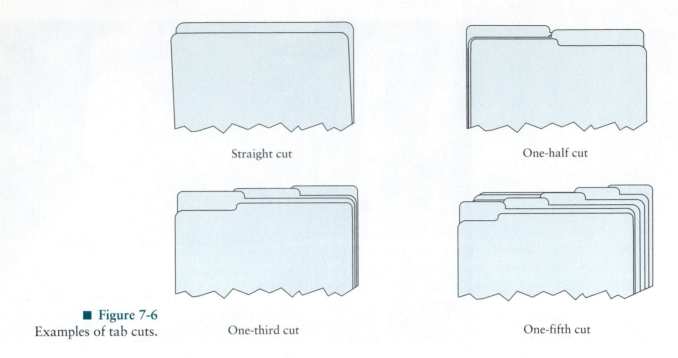

Straight cut   One-half cut

One-third cut   One-fifth cut

■ **Figure 7-6**
Examples of tab cuts.

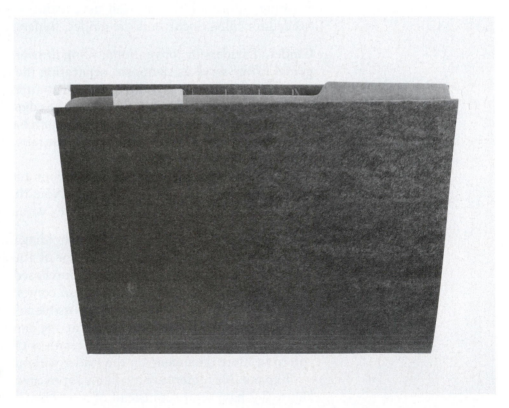

■ **Figure 7-7**
A folder with a gusset.

Labels. Labels help us find our way through the file cabinet and are used to identify the folder or file drawer. Each folder and each guide needs a label. Labels come in a variety of sizes, shapes, and colors so you can customize your filing system to meet the needs of your organization. Colors should not be used at random. Use colors to represent a topic or the status of a file.

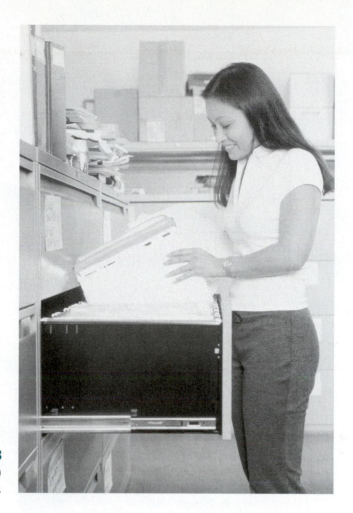

■ Figure 7-8
Hanging (or suspension)
folder.

Labels can be purchased either on a continuous strip or on flat sheets, which work well with a printer. They are self-adhesive and pressure sensitive.

If the labels can be read from both sides, such as with open files, be sure that both sides of your label bear accurate and attractive information.

Key the names on your labels in the indexed order. Capitalize the first letter of each word. Words keyed in all-capital letters are sometimes difficult to read. If your labels consist of only one or two words and you use an easy-to-read font, full capitalization will work well. Above all, remember to be consistent with labeling throughout your system.

The captions on the labels of your files should resemble an aligned list of names as shown in Figure 7-9.

Label drawers or sections of files with either open or close notations. A **closed notation** indicates the entire span of the contents. A typical example of a closed notation would be

CORRESPONDENCE A–H

A typical example of an open notation would be:

CORRESPONDENCE.

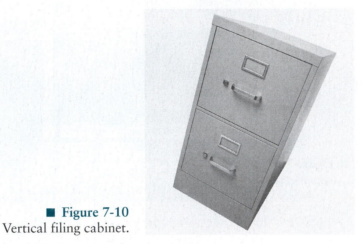

■ **Figure 7-9**
Captions on labels.

■ **Figure 7-10**
Vertical filing cabinet.

Supplies for Electronic Filing

One of the advantages of electronic filing is that very few supplies are needed. Depending on the requirements of your office, you will need a supply of CD-ROM, ZIP, or floppy disks. Each of these disks has a different storage capacity. Refer to Chapter 4 for a discussion on these supplies.

All disks require adhesive labels of varying sizes. The label should reflect the contents of the information stored on the disk.

STORING INFORMATION

Storing is the process of placing the record into the file folder or on microfilm, or saving the electronic file on a computer hard drive. Paper correspondence is usually filed in drawers. Information printed on cards is filed in a variety of ways—in drawers, in trays, on wheels, in panels—to make it easily accessible to the operator. Some filing units are automated, so that the operator can bring the files or cards within easy reach by pressing a button.

Storing Visible Documents

Paper correspondence is usually filed vertically, standing upright and supported by guides and folders in file drawers. The two types of popular filing cabinets for paper are the vertical filing cabinet shown in Figure 7-10, and

■ Figure 7-11
Lateral filing cabinet.

the lateral filing cabinet shown in Figure 7-11. The type you choose will depend on your office space, budget, and your personal preference.

Lateral files save space because 25 to 50 percent less aisle space is needed in which to pull out the lateral file drawer than is needed to pull out a vertical file drawer.

Cabinets may be used as single units or may be grouped to serve as area dividers. They can be adapted to store almost any kind of records; for example, letters, legal documents, cards, and so forth. Check the cabinets available at the Web sites listed in the "Supplies Online," section earlier in this chapter.

One type of lateral file is open-shelf, used to save floor space, filing and retrieval time, and initial installation costs. For open-shelf filing, the tabs project from the side of the folder. For an illustration of open-shelf filing, refer to Figure 7-5.

Lateral files are equipped to handle either regular or hanging folders. The folders may be arranged either side by side or from front to back. The tabs are at the top of guides, and the folders are arranged in closed drawers.

A popular device, designed to hold files upright inside the filing drawer, is the wire organizer. See Figure 7-12. With the **wire organizer**, folders may be placed directly into the file drawer without any hanging folders being used. Folders remain upright, and space is saved. Time is also saved because duplicate labels for the hanging folders are not needed.

Storing Disks

Although CD-ROM disks may be the most desirable storage, they are still not the most commonly used storing device. Floppy and ZIP disks are sensitive to heat, magnetism, dust, and other problems. Because of their sensitivities and because we store so much data on a single disk, the loss of data on one disk can be a disaster to an office.

To provide the utmost protection to your disks, avoid the following:

- Leaving disks exposed to heat.
- Eating or drinking while handling the disks.
- Placing a disk under a heavy object.

■ **Figure 7-12**
Wire organizer.

■ Using magnetized objects near disks. This could include telephones with recording devices, air conditioners, radios, televisions, vacuum cleaners, and so on.

Correct storage and backup are some of the keys to protecting your electronic data. Disks should be stored in sturdy plastic cases, such as the one illustrated in Figure 7-13. Some of these cases have antistatic components to protect the disks from dirt, dust, lint, and static electricity.

The plastic storage case should have a key lock to control unauthorized access. Because these cases are portable, they should be stored overnight in a locked filing cabinet.

Manufacturers produce a variety of cases to suit your filing requirements. Check the Internet Web sites provided in the "Supplies Online" section of this chapter to review options.

All *critical* information needs to be backed up for safety. The backup copy may be kept on another disk or on the computer system. Whatever you decide, store the original and the copy away from each other so that the same accident will not destroy both copies.

Storing in Electronic Databases

Most business professionals keep their own list of contacts. They develop an electronic database from all the business cards they collect from clients, cus-

■ **Figure 7-13**
Storage disk case.

tomers, agents, competitors, and so on. Executives will either maintain their own database or ask for help from the office professional.

The database should consist of the client's name, title, company, geographical address, e-mail address, telephone, and fax numbers. Office professionals often collect all client information into one database and make it accessible to all employees.

Computer records lend themselves perfectly to storing and sorting lists of just about anything, including records on employees, projects, product inventory, and lists of paper files and description of their contents. A variety of computer software is available for creating databases.

The following terms will help you become more familiar with databases.

- A name or number, such as a family name, postal code, e-mail address, or telephone number, is called a **field.**

- The complete information about one person or one item is called a record. An example of a record would be all the information about a customer. The record would include the customer's name, employee number, date of hire, and so forth.

- A collection of records is called a **file.** An example of a file would be all the records of employees in the finance department.

- A **database** is a set of logically related files. An example would be all the department files for a company.

Electronic databases are essential to the efficiency of a professional office. Accessing information through a database saves a lot of time. Remember that having the ability to locate information gives you a professional advantage over people who don't have these skills. Take every opportunity to learn how to use the electronic databases in the office.

RECORDS RETENTION AND TRANSFER

When the file cabinets or the computer's disks become full of files, what do you do? Should you destroy the files? Should you transfer them to another location? These decisions cannot be made at random. Records retention and transfer is strictly governed by policy of both your organization and the government.

Some records must be kept permanently; many records are kept from three to twenty years; others are useful for only a short period and are kept for a year or less; some records are disposed of without being stored. Records that are kept for a year or longer are usually transferred from the active files to a storage area. The records manager prepares a **retention schedule,** which indicates the length of time a record must be kept, if microfilming is required, and when the final disposition of records should occur. An office professional should not dispose of any records or papers from the files without written authorization.

Retention

The following factors determine how long records must be preserved:

1. The nature of an organization's business operations
2. State statute of limitations
3. Regulations of the federal government

Each state has its own statute of limitations, specifying the time after which a record cannot be used as evidence in the courts. Among the records affected by state statutes of limitations are written contracts, open accounts, injury claims, and accident reports.

Determining which records to keep and for how long is a critical function. An office professional should not dispose of any records or papers from the files without clear knowledge of retention legislation.

Categories of Records

Information and records are the lifeblood of any business or organization. With increases in the volume of information and in the cost of storing and retrieving information, it is extremely important that records be categorized as to their importance and usefulness to the organization. In other words, some records are important and require special attention, whereas others may be read and discarded.

Determining the categories of records helps an office professional know whether a record is to be kept, where it is to be stored, how it will be stored, and how long it is to be retained. For example, advertisements, requests, and inquiries have little or no future use to an organization and should not be kept. Stop and think about the time it takes you to file this type of material, the supplies and equipment needed, and the expensive space that it uses.

Categorizing records as to their current and future usefulness and legal implications is necessary to save your organization money in terms of employee time, supplies and equipment, and expensive company space. Decisions about types of records are based on a number of factors, including the knowledge that someone must have about the operation of the organization and about the state and federal laws relating to business functions. Categories of records include vital, important, useful, and nonessential.

Vital records include records that are essential to the operation of the organization, or to the continuation or resumption of operations; the re-creation of the legal or financial status of the organization; or the fulfillment of its obligations to stockholders and employees in the event of a disaster. Vital records may include such records as those pertaining to property, patents, copyrights, insurance, tax, and accounts receivable. Vital records should be identified and stored in a separate location for safekeeping. Vital records may include tape backup of essential computer databases and files.

Important records, such as customer and personnel records, are meaningful to the business operation but must be limited as to the length of time they are retained.

Useful records are documents, such as correspondence and reports that are needed to conduct the daily business operations. Important and useful records are maintained in fire-resistant file cabinets and are kept on-site.

Nonessential records are not needed beyond their current use and should be discarded after their use because they cost money in space, equipment, and employee time. Examples of nonessential records are requests, acknowledgments, notices of meetings, and duplicate copies of correspondence.

If there is no retention schedule developed for your organization or your department, you can establish some guidelines to follow. Here are some areas you can consider:

- **Retain two years,** files such as inventory records
- **Retain three years,** files such as petty cash vouchers
- **Retain eight years,** files such as expense reports and expired contracts and leases
- **Retain indefinitely,** files such as correspondence on legal and tax matters and annual reports

Before putting any guidelines into practice, get legal advice about time limitation statutes in your state. In order for retention guidelines to meet established acceptable standards, the guidelines and their implementation must be a standard part of the way the office conducts its business.

Transfer of Records

The most accessible file space should be used for active files; this means that the less active papers must be moved from time to time to free up the most accessible space for the current files. Organizations use two methods of transfer: perpetual and periodic. Paper storage consumes much more space than disks. However, the concept of perpetual and periodic transfer is applied to both visible and electronic documents. Paper files may be transferred to a back room, whereas electronic storage is archived or moved to a more permanent form of storage such as CD-ROM.

Perpetual Transfer Method. **Perpetual transfer method** is continually transferring files to inactive storage as a project or case is completed. It is highly applicable for records in construction companies, attorneys' offices, and any organization that handles projects or cases. All the records for one project or case are transferred at the time it is completed.

Periodic Transfer Method. The **periodic transfer method** provides for transferring files to inactive storage at predetermined intervals such as six months, one year, or eighteen months. The inactive files are transferred to the storage center, leaving more space to house the active documents.

ALPHABETIC FILING PROCEDURES

Organizations do not follow identical filing rules, but, with few exceptions, the names usually are indexed according to the rules presented and explained in the next section of this chapter.

The supplies you need to set up the simplest system in strict sequential order for filing correspondence in regular folders are:

- Primary guides—at least one for each letter of the alphabet
- Individual name folders
- Miscellaneous folders
- Special guides
- Color coding (optional)

Primary Guides

Primary guides divide a file into alphabetic sections. A guide is placed at the beginning of each section. Guides direct the eye to the section of the file in which the folder being sought is located.

Guides are not needed with hanging folders, as the folders are supported from a metal frame and the guide tabs are attached directly to the folders. When guides are used, the correspondence is filed in either individual or miscellaneous folders placed behind the guides.

Individual Name Folders

When you accumulate at least five papers for one correspondent, or when you determine from the current letter or memo that much communication will take place between the correspondent and your manager, prepare an individual folder with the name typed in indexed order in the caption.

Arrange individual folders in order immediately following the appropriate primary guide, as shown in Figure 7-14. File correspondence within individual folders in chronological order, so that the correspondence bearing the most recent date is placed at the front of the folder.

Miscellaneous Folders

For every primary guide in your file there should be a miscellaneous folder with a caption corresponding to the caption on the primary guide. **Miscellaneous folders** belong *behind* individual folders and contain the papers to and from all correspondents for whom you do not have individual name folders.

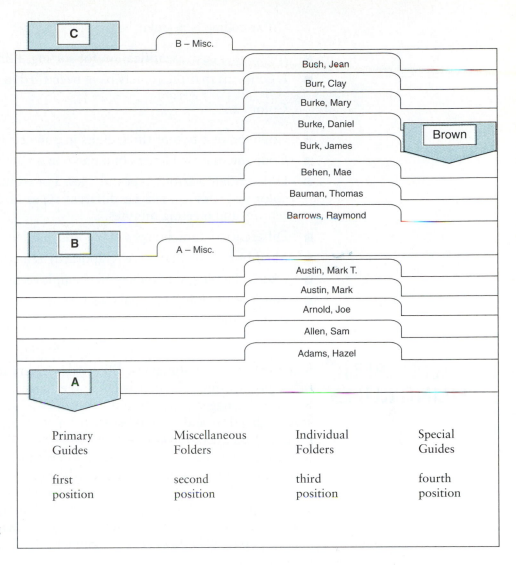

Primary Guides — first position

Miscellaneous Folders — second position

Individual Folders — third position

Special Guides — fourth position

■ **Figure 7-14**
Individual folders following primary guide.

Within a miscellaneous folder, arrange the papers in alphabetical order by name. When you have two or more papers for one correspondent, arrange them in chronological order, so that the one with the most recent date will be in front of the others. Staple related papers together to increase the ease of locating them.

Special Guides

Special guides direct the eye to individual folders that are used frequently. Special guides are also used for subdivisions of the alphabet, or to mark the section of a file containing individual folders for several correspondents with the same surname, such as Smith.

Color-Coding

Color-coding can be applied to any filing system—alphabetic, numeric, geographic, subject, or chronological.

Color-coding is popular because:

- It provides easy identification for sorting, filing, and finding
- It confirms that the folders have been filed in the right places

Color can:

- Code the first two or three digits in numeric filing systems.
- Code the first two letters of a name in an alphabetic filing system.
- Differentiate various types of files. For example, you can use different color diskettes to back up different types of documents, such as weekly reports and meeting minutes.
- Differentiate similar types of records that belong to various departments.
- Identify records that were temporarily removed from files.
- Check the filing methods of new employees.
- Simplify the filing of media such as micrographics, diskettes, and computer printouts.

ALPHABETIC FILING RULES

Standardization of alphabetic filing rules is very important because it allows office procedures to be consistent and efficient. In 1960, the Association of Records Managers and Administrators (ARMA) recognized the need for standardization and so published the first rules for alphabetic filing. Although the association still refers to itself as ARMA, it has expanded its role to include training, publications, and development of ethics and standardization of the most sophisticated records management systems. The full name for ARMA is now the Association for Information Management Professionals. However, because the name ARMA is so highly respected and recognized, it's likely that the ARMA acronym will continue to be used for years to come. The best way to contact ARMA is through its Web site at http://www.arma.org.

The alphabetic filing rules presented in this section are based on standardized rules suggested by ARMA.

Order of Filing Units

Before you begin any filing process it is important that you understand the following three terms:

Unit. Each part of a name that is used to determine the filing order is called a **unit**. For example, the name *B. R. Grove* has three units: *B., R., Grove*. The business name *The Wacky Wig Boutique* has four units: *The, Wacky, Wig, Boutique*.

Indexing. Names are not always filed the same way they are written. In preparation for alphabetic filing, the format and order of a name is often altered. This process of arranging units of a name in order for filing purposes is referred to as indexing, as defined earlier. An example of indexing is where *B. R. Grove* has his name indexed as *Grove B. R.* Indexing always precedes alphabetizing.

Alphabetizing. Placing names in an A-to-Z sequence is considered **alphabetizing.** This process is necessary to maintain an alphabetic filing system. For example, placing the name *Adamson* before the name *Bolton* is alphabetizing.

This process appears relatively simple; however, because the English language is made up of words from other languages, word derivatives, prefixes, suffixes, compound words, and other combinations, the filing process may become complicated and inconsistent unless rules are applied.

Before working with the rules, remember four basic principles.

1. **Alphabetize by comparing names unit by unit and letter by letter.** When first units are identical, move on to compare the second units; when second units are identical, compare third units, and so on. For example, in comparing the following indexed names, you would need to make the distinction in the third unit because the first and second units are identical.

Unit 1	Unit 2	Unit 3
Black	Jeff	Peter
Black	Jeff	Robert

2. **Nothing comes before something.** Thus, in comparing the following indexed names you would file *Ross William* first because the first two units are identical and *Ross William* does not have a third unit. Nothing is filed before something (*Robert*).

Unit 1	Unit 2	Unit 3
Ross	William	
Ross	William	Robert

Another example of this principle would be:

Unit 1	Unit 2	Unit 3
Chatham	Bus	Depot
Chatham	Business	College

In this case, Bus would come before Business under the principle that nothing comes before something.

3. **All punctuation marks should be ignored when indexing.** Examples of punctuation marks found in names include periods, quotation marks, apostrophes, hyphens, dashes, and accent marks. Where words have been separated by a hyphen or dash, consider them together as one indexing unit.

4. **When the name of a person or business is known in more than one format, file it in the way that is most common.** Then prepare a cross-reference. Refer to the discussion on cross-referencing in this chapter for further details on this process.

The following are simplified filing rules that have been organized into four categories: names of individuals; business and organization names; government names; and addresses.

Rules for Filing Names of Individuals

Rule 1: Names of Individuals

Names of individuals are transposed. The surname is the first filing unit, followed by the first name or initial, and then the middle name or initial. Because nothing comes before something, initials (such as *M*) are filed before a name (such as *Martha*) that begins with the same letter.

As Written	Unit 1	Unit 2	Unit 3
M. Appleton	Appleton	M	
M. A. Appleton	Appleton	M	A
Martha Appleton	Appleton	Martha	
Martha A. Appleton	Appleton	Martha	A
Martha Ann Appleton	Appleton	Martha	Ann
Hung Luk Kim	Kim	Hung	Luk

Rule 2: Abbreviations in Names of Individuals

Abbreviated and shortened personal names are indexed as they are written, and are cross-referenced, if necessary, as if they were written in full.

As Written	Unit 1	Unit 2	Cross-Reference
Bob Browning	Browning	Bob	Browning, Robert
Geo. Little	Little	Geo	Little, George
Bill Watson	Watson	Bill	Watson, William

Rule 3: Prefixes in Names of Individuals

Names of individuals with prefixed surnames, such as *De, Des, Du, La, Les, Mac Mc, O', Saint, San, St., Van, Vonder, Vander,* and the like, are filed with the surname as one unit regardless of whether the surname is written as one word or two. Ignore apostrophes and spaces that follow the prefix.

As Written	Unit 1	Unit 2	Unit 3
Agnes Lasalle	Lasalle	Agnes	
Paul R. La Salle	La Salle	Paul	R
Adam Vandermallie	Vandermallie	Adam	
Sue Vander Mallie	Vander Mallie	Sue	

Note: When many names begin with a particular prefix, the current trend is to treat that prefix as a separate group and to file the prefix group preceding the basic listing; for example, *Mac* and *Mc* could be filed before the other *M* names.

Rule 4: Hyphens in Names of Individuals

Hyphenated names, whether surnames or first or middle names, are treated as one filing unit. The hyphen is ignored during filing, and the two words are placed together as one unit.

As Written	Unit 1	Unit 2	Unit 3
Bertha S. Daleraven	Daleraven	Bertha	S
Irene Dale-Scott	DaleScott	Irene	
Helen Ann Dixon-Jones	DixonJones	Helen	Ann
Sara Laura-Lee Wilkes	Wilkes	Sara	LauraLee
Sara Lauralie Wilkes	Wilkes	Sara	Lauralie

Rule 5: Titles, Designations, and Degrees in Personal Names

When titles, designations, or degrees are written before or after a name, they are used as indexing units at the end of the name. Punctuation is disregarded as written.

As Written	Unit 1	Unit 2	Unit 3	Unit 4
Ronald McDerrit, II	McDerrit	Ronald	II	
Professor June Ship	Ship	June	Professor	
Robert E. Smith, M.D.	Smith	Robert	E	MD

Rules for Filing Names of Businesses and Organizations

Rule 6: Names of Businesses and Organizations

Names of businesses and organizations are indexed in a similar fashion to the names of individuals. However, names of businesses and organizations should be indexed in the order they are written by the business or organization. Therefore, a surname is not necessarily the first unit. If you are unsure of the correct wording or format, refer to the company's letterhead or business card, or make a telephone call to the organization's receptionist.

When the name begins with *The*, place that word at the end as the last indexing unit.

When names of businesses and organizations are identical, indexing order is determined by the address. If the names of cities are identical, indexing order depends on names of states, followed by street names and building numbers. When street names are written as digits (13th Street), the street names are considered in ascending order and filed before alphabetic street names. Street names with compass directions are indexed as written.

As Written	Unit 1	Unit 2	Unit 3	Unit 4	Unit 5
Central Trust Company	Central	Trust	Company		
Columbia Pizza	Columbia	Pizza	2128 13th Street		
Columbia Pizza	Columbia	Pizza	138 15th Street		
General Insurance Amarillo, TX	General	Insurance	Company	Amarillo	TX
General Insurance Company Rochester, MN	General	Insurance	Company	Rochester	MN

Rule 7: Punctuation in Names of Businesses and Organizations

Treat punctuation that appears in business and organization names the same way you would for personal names. Ignore all punctuation marks. Where a hyphen separates two words, disregard the hyphen and index the two words as one unit.

Rule 8: Numbers in Names of Businesses and Organizations

Names using either Arabic numerals *(3, 26)* or Roman numerals *(IV, V)* are filed in numeric order before the alphabetic characters. The complete numeral is considered as one unit and is not spelled out. Of course, if the company writes out the number in words, such as *One Hour Cleaners,* the number is spelled out and filed alphabetically after the numerals are filed.

Where a number is hyphenated, such as in *7–11 Convenience Store,* only the number before the hyphen is considered; the number that follows the hyphen is ignored.

When a digit contains a suffix *(st, d, th),* ignore the suffix and index only the number itself. In order words, *1st* is indexed as 1, *2d* is indexed as 2, and so on.

When a number is spelled out and hyphenated—for example, *Seventy-Seven Sunset Shop*—the hyphen is ignored and the two numbers become one unit *(Seventy-Seven).*

As Written	Unit 1	Unit 2	Unit 3	Unit 4
4 J's Barber Shoppe	4	Js	Barber	Shoppe
12 Corners Sweet Shop	12	Corners	Sweet	Shop
101 Parking Lot	101	Parking	Lot	
Forty-Two Hundred Club	Forty-two	Hundred	Club	
Roberta's 4216 Main Salon	Robertas	4216	Main	Salon
Twelve Corners Service Center	Twelve	Corners	Service	Center

Rule 9: Symbols in Names of Businesses and Organizations

Symbols should be indexed the way they are pronounced. Examples of such symbols include:

As Written	Unit 1	Unit 2	Unit 3	Unit 4
One $ Store	One	Dollar	Store	
Rickman & Hope Intl.	Rickman	And	Hope	Intl
The 100% Team	100	Percent	Team	The

Rule 10: Abbreviations in Names of Businesses and Organizations

When abbreviations are used in business names, they should be filed as they are written. They are spelled out only when the organization writes them that way. Remember, initials in a person's name are separate units. To determine whether initials should be separate units, check to see if they have been separated by spaces or periods. If they have been, write them as separate units.

As Written	Unit 1	Unit 2	Unit 3	Unit 4
ARK Transport	ARK	Transport		
C.A.N. Company	CAN	Company		
Carvel Insurance Co.	Carvel	Insurance	Co	
L V N Technology	L	V	N	Technology

Rules for Filing Names of Governments

Rule 11: Government Names

11a. Federal Government. Federal government agencies are indexed by the name of the government unit *(United States Government)* followed by the most distinctive name of the office, bureau, or service as written.

As Written	Units 1–3	Unit 4	Unit 5	Unit 6
Broadcast Bureau	United States Government	Broadcast	Bureau	
Social Security Administration	United States Government	Social	Security	Administration
Internal Revenue Service	United States Government	Internal	Revenue	Service

11b. State and Local Governments. Index state, county, town, and city governments by their distinctive names. Add the words *state of, county of,* and so on for clarity and consider them as filing units. Index the words *State, Department, County,* and *Bureau* after the distinctive name; disregard *of.*

As Written	Unit 1	Unit 2	Unit 3	Unit 4	Unit 5	Unit 6
Monroe Community Hospital	Monroe	Community	Hospital			
Monroe County Department of Public Words	Monroe	County	Public	Works	Department of	
New York State Department of Health	New	York	State	Health	Department of	
New York State Human Rights Division	New	York	State	Human	Rights	Division
Rochester Animal Control Center	Rochester	Animal	Control	Center		
Rochester Recreation Bureau	Rochester	Recreation	Bureau			

Rules for Filing According to Address

Rule 12: Names and Addresses

At times, two or more names will be identical. In such cases, use the geographical address to determine the filing order. Consider the following elements in this order:

- Country
- State
- City/municipality
- Street name
- Street number
- Compass point (N, S, E, W)
- Building number

Be sure to spell out in full all elements of the address.

Variations in Alphabetic Filing Rules

Because conflicts in alphabetic indexing have existed for many years and continue to exist, you need to be aware of the conflicts as well as the standardized rules. When you report for a new work assignment, you will have to retrieve papers that have been filed by someone else. Furthermore, the organization for which you work may have its own rules for indexing and alphabetizing. If so, learn them and apply them so that the files you maintain will be consistent with the other files in the organization.

The variations in filing rules presented here are based on an analysis of published filing rules. Watch for the following variations in indexing and alphabetizing names of individuals.

Alphabetic Filing Rule Variations for Names of Individuals

1. The hyphenated surname of an individual might be treated as separate units rather than as one filing unit.
2. Names beginning with *Mac* and *Mc* might be filed under names beginning with *M*.
3. A nickname used in the signature might be filed under the true given name, such as *Lawrence* instead of the nickname *Larry*.
4. Numeric seniority designations, such as *II* and *III*, might be filed as spelled out rather than in numeric sequence; also *Sr.* is filed before *Jr.*
5. The name of a married woman might be filed under her husband's name instead of her own name.

There are many variations in the alphabetic filing rules for business establishments, institutions, and other group names. Watch for the following variations:

Alphabetic Filing Rule Variations for Names of Businesses, Institutions, and Groups

1. Each part of a hyphenated business name made up of surnames might be indexed as a separate filing unit, instead of the hyphenated name being treated as one filing unit.
2. Each part of a coined business name might be indexed as a separate filing unit, instead of the entire coined word being considered as one filing unit.
3. Geographic names beginning with prefixes might be filed as two separate units rather than one.
4. Words involving more than one compass point (northeast, northwest, southeast, and southwest, and their variations) might be treated as two words instead of being indexed as written in the company name.
5. Geographic names that are spelled as either one or two English words—such as *Mountain View* and *Mountainview*—might be filed inconsistently, with the result that papers pertaining to one business establishment are filed in two different places.
6. Names beginning with numbers expressed in figures, as opposed to written out, might be filed in regular alphabetical sequence with all the numbers spelled out in full rather than filed in strict numeric sequence preceding the entire alphabetic file.
7. The *s* following an apostrophe might be disregarded, so that the word is indexed without the *s*.

WHAT ABOUT THE FUTURE?

Information management is changing and evolving. Requirements for International Organization for Standardization (ISO) certification are an example of the changing needs of documentation. Technology is changing and evolving. More compact ways to store and retrieve documents are becoming possible with newer optical disk and image technology.

The increasing use of scanners to store documents on CD-ROMs or optical disks is one of these newer technologies. Microfilm and microfiche are still acceptable storage media for certain applications. Now that there are more options available, care must be given to selecting the best option for your office environment. The newer technology applications have as a disadvantage the need to consider the cost of migrating or moving scanned or stored document images to newer software or hardware as the technology evolves. For example, many offices no longer have 5.25-inch floppy disk drives on the desktop computers. Consider the following scenario:

> All those files in your organization are eating up more and more room. And the warehouse for old files is a mess! You even find yourself hoping that no one will ever ask you to locate anything that has been put into boxes and moved there. And that's the real problem—finding that one piece of paper that's urgently needed, among hundreds of thousands of others. You've considered redoing the whole system, but the staff and equipment available simply don't allow you to do that.
>
> So the problem is getting bigger and bigger every day. You've even had bad dreams about being buried under a mountain of paper and squeezed between file cabinets that come closer and closer together. "So," you ask, "what can I do about it?"

This is where the professional records manager, a records management consulting firm, or a micrographics service enters the picture. These professionals are trained, experienced people who can help analyze your records management needs and design systems, procedures, and retention schedules. They can also evaluate different technology applications, such as

- Whether to scan and store images on optical disk or CD-ROM
- Whether to microfilm documents
- How to safeguard your vital records
- How you can benefit from color-coding and bar coding
- How to best store unusual documents such as large engineering drawings, maps, and photographs
- How to improve daily office procedures to become more productive

If you need microfilming done, they will do it for you. With microfilm you can store the contents of 54 file drawers in a space about the size of a shoebox. Microfilming reduces your files to less than 2 percent of the space they now occupy in paper form.

You may think that if your records are on microfilm it will be difficult to find them. Not at all. Microfilm can be loaded into cartridges, and you can use equipment that automatically locates a specific image. But microfilm doesn't have to stay on rolls. It can be loaded into clear microfiche jackets

File Your Computer Documents by Year:

■ Create and name a folder for each of your software application data files (e.g., Word Data FY 2004, Excel Data FY 2004, Access Data FY 2004, etc.).

■ Make subfolders within each of those to allow a more defined organization.

■ When searching for files on your computer, you can quickly determine which folder year you need.

that are titled with the name of your file. One 4 × 6-inch microfiche jacket can hold the equivalent of sixty sheets of paper and can be duplicated for distribution to other locations. What about paper copies? No problem. Paper copies can easily be made from microfilm. Which organizations are already using microfilming? Organizations in a wide range of fields, including banking, construction, education, health care, hotel management, insurance, manufacturing, retail, telecommunications, transportation, and utilities.

You can see that **microfilming** permits the retention of large volumes of current records in minimum space as well as the retention of long-term information at minimum expense. The advantages of using microfilm are:

1. Savings in storage space
2. Records protection
3. Ease and reduced cost of mailing
4. Efficiency of retrieval

The entire field of microfilming and related processes is called **micrographics.** The micrographics field provides various career opportunities that you may want to consider.

Overview

✔ The major file classification systems are alphabetic, numeric, geographic, and subject.

✔ The visible (paper) filing steps are reviewing, indexing, coding, cross-referencing, and sorting.

✔ Filing electronic documents requires directories.

✔ Visible filing supplies include guides, folders, and labels.

✔ Electronic filing supplies include CD-ROM, ZIP, or floppy disks, depending on the needs of your office.

✔ Visible documents are stored in vertical or lateral filing cabinets.

✔ Electronic documents must be backed up and stored safely, whether on CD-ROM, ZIP, or floppy disks.

✔ Office professionals store client information in databases, including client name, title, company, geographical address, e-mail address, and telephone and fax numbers.

✔ Electronic databases increase office efficiency by storing easily accessed information related to employee records, projects, product inventory, and so on.

✔ A retention schedule lists the records of a department and indicates the length of time a record must be kept, if microfilming is required, and when the final disposition of the record should occur.

✔ The three major factors that determine how long records must be preserved are (1) the nature of an organization's business operations, (2) state statutes of limitations, and (3) regulations of the federal government.

✔ Categories of records are vital records, important records, useful records, and nonessential records.

✔ Two record transfer methods are perpetual and periodic.

✔ To arrange guides and folders effectively, most organizations use primary guides, individual folders, miscellaneous folders, and special guides.

✔ Color-coding is popular because it provides easy identification for presorting, filing, and finding. It also confirms that the folders have been filed in the appropriate places.

✔ The field of microfilming and related processes is called micrographics. Microfilming permits the retention of large volumes of current records in minimum space as well as the retention of long-term information at minimum expense.

✔ To improve the consistency with which filing procedures are used, you must follow standard guides to file management.

Key Terms

Accession register. A book that shows the next number available for a record.

Alphabetic filing system. A filing system that uses the alphabet to sequence personal, business, and government names.

Alphabetizing. The arrangement of a group of names in A-to-Z sequence.

Bar coding. Allows files to be maintained electronically and requires software, a label printer, and a scanning device.

Caption. The key word under which a document is filed. This can be a name, a subject, or a geographic location.

Centralized filing system. A system in which files are placed in one location that is convenient for a group of people who must work with the same information.

Charge-out methods. Systems that are established to keep track of materials that have been borrowed from the files and are to be returned.

Closed notation. Indicates the entire span of the contents of either a file drawer or a section of files.

Coding. Marking the indexing caption on the document.

Cross-referencing. A system that allows you to locate a record or document by two different names.

Database. A set of logically related files.

Decentralized filing system. A system in which individuals or very small groups of employees maintain files at their workstations.

Decimal-numeric filing. Also known as the *Dewey decimal system;* works with subject filing to permit more expansion than a basic numeric system.

Directory. A section of the network that is allotted to certain people for their files.

Field. A name or number, postal code, e-mail address, or telephone number.

File. A collection of records.

Filing. Actual placing of papers in folders.

Folders. Containers for holding correspondence and other paper.

Geographic filing system. A filing system in which material is filed alphabetically in some logical pattern, such as by city, by state, or by region or territory.

Guides. The dividers in conventional filing drawers. They serve as signposts, separating the filing space into labeled sections; they also support the folders in an upright position.

Gussets. Allow a folder to expand more than a conventional folder.

Hanging folders. Folders that are suspended by extensions of their top edges across a metal frame within the file drawer.

Image records. Documents, such as letters, charts, and photographs, that have been converted to either microfilm/microfiche or digitized electronic data that can be stored and retrieved immediately.

Important records. Documents, such as customer and personnel records, that are meaningful to the business operation but must be limited as to the length of time they are retained.

Index. A listing of the filed items.

Indexing. The process of determining the key word or number under which a record will be filed.

Indirect filing. A filing system in which you use an index, listing the name of the person, organization, or subject to which the number is assigned.

Labels. Used to identify the folder or file drawer.

Microfilming. Permits the retention of large volumes of current records in minimum space as well as the retention of long-term information at minimum expense.

Micrographics. The field of microfilming and related processes.

Miscellaneous folders. A folder that holds documents for which you do not have individual folders. There should be one miscellaneous folder for every primary guide, and it should be placed behind the individual folders.

Nonessential records. Documents that are not needed beyond their current use and that should be discarded after their use.

Numeric filing system. A filing system in which material is filed in some logical numerical order.

Periodic transfer method. A system in which files are transferred to inactive storage at stated intervals such as six months, one year, or eighteen months.

Perpetual transfer method. A system in which files are continually transferred to inactive storage as a project or case is completed.

Primary guides. These divide a file into main sections and are placed at the beginning of each section.

Record. Any type of recorded information that is stored for quick retrieval and for preservation.

Records management. The systematic management of the creation, maintenance, retention, destruction, protection, and preservation of records.

Records manager. Supervises all the company's files. He or she also determines how the files will be maintained and who will maintain them, how long each document is to be kept in the file, and when a file is to be removed to an inactive area or made ready for more permanent storage or destruction.

Retention schedule. Indicates the length of time a record must be kept, if microfilming is required, and when the final disposition of records should occur.

Scores. The creases at the bottom of a folder.

Sorting. The process of prearranging the records in the same order in which they will be filed.

Special guides. These direct the eye to individual folders that are used frequently.

Storing. The process of placing the record into the file folder or on microfilm, or saving the electronic file on a computer hard disk.

Subject filing system. A filing system in which material is filed alphabetically according to main topics.

Tab. The portion of the guide projecting from its edge.

Terminal-digit filing. Divides numbers into groups of digits that point to the location of records.

Unit. Each part of a name that is considered in alphabetic filing.

Useful records. Documents, such as correspondence and reports, that are needed to conduct the daily business of the operation.

Visible filing. The most current word used to describe *paper* filing.

Vital records. Documents, such as records pertaining to property, patents, copyrights, and insurance that are essential to the operation of the organization, or to the continuation or resumption of operations; the re-creation of the legal or financial status of the organization; or to the fulfillment of its obligations to stockholders and employees in the event of a disaster.

Wire organizer. A popular storage device designed to hold files upright inside the filing drawer; folders may be placed directly into the file drawer without any hanging folders being used.

For Your Discussion

 Retrieve file C7-DQ.DOC from your student data disk.

Directions

Enter your response after each question.

1. List the steps involved in records management.
2. Compare a centralized filing system with a decentralized filing system. Include in your response the advantages and disadvantages of each.
3. Describe the main file classification systems.
4. List the steps necessary to get documents ready to be filed.
5. Name five or six situations in which cross-references would be needed for locating materials from the files.
6. Suggest an informal way of keeping up with materials you take out of the files for your manager for a few hours during the day.
7. Distinguish between vertical and lateral filing. Which method is more advantageous?
8. Distinguish among the categories of records.
9. State three factors that determine how long records must be preserved.
10. What are the advantages of using a color-coded system for files?

NUMBER USAGE WORKSHOP

To make a document look professional, numbers should be used in a consistent manner. Do not spell out numbers in one section of a document and use figures in another section. As a general rule, spell out numbers ten and under; use figures for numbers over ten.

For Review

Appendix A: Rule 16: Time

Rule 17: Serial and Similar Numbers

 Retrieve file C7-WRKS.DOC from your student data disk.

Directions

Write C to the left of the sentence if the number usage is correct. Otherwise, make the necessary corrections.

Rule 16: Time

1. The meeting was scheduled for 3:00 p.m., and the refreshments arrived at 3:15 p.m.

2. I will make my presentation at 4 p.m.

3. Our pre-meeting party will begin at 6 o'clock and dinner will be served at 7:00 p.m.

4. Their appointments were scheduled 15 minutes apart as shown here.
   4:15 p.m.
   4:30 p.m.
   4:45 p.m.
   5:00 p.m.

5. The three executives will arrive at 7 o'clock.

Rule 17: Serial and Similar Numbers

1. The blouses, style 4513, were found in the box marked as skirts.

2. The calculator, serial no. 2–145–9087, was reported missing on June 14.

3. The printer is marked as Model II-XL-A and the Serial No. is 666–545–798.

4. They needed caps in serial no. 15–8977–12, not in 15–8077–12.

5. They paid Invoice no. 43219 in ten days and received the 2 percent discount.

On the Job Situations

 Retrieve file C7-OJS.DOC from your student data disk.

Directions

Enter your response after each situation.

1. You are convinced that the office assistant who previously worked in your office made up his own filing rules. You have been working for three weeks and have extreme difficulty finding anything that your predecessor filed. Your manager has told you to reorganize the files and to set up your own system. You are eager to set up a better filing system, but this is the peak season for your department. It will be at least two more months before you have time to reorganize the files. What can you do in the meantime?

2. You have set up an electronic filing system for your office, complete with directories and folders. At numerous staff meetings you have asked the managers in your organization to please file their completed proposals into the correct folders that you have set up. However, whenever you have to search for a proposal, you rarely find it in the correct folder or even in the correct directory. What ideas do you have for solving this problem?

3. The four managers for whom you work have been doing their own filing. However, today you were told that you are to maintain the correspondence files for all four of them. Their files will be moved to your area. You are to maintain separate files for each manager. What can you do to make it easier to get the materials in the right file each time?

4. Your company centralizes files for economy and efficiency. Your manager, however, tends to resist releasing materials to the central location, preferring to build up his and your in-office files. The records supervisor has called you several times to remind you to return materials to the central filing area. What can you do to help resolve this conflict?

Projects and Activities

1. Use the yellow pages to find the name of a business that is listed two ways. How would you cross-reference it? Using the illustration given in this chapter, prepare two filing cards. On one 3 × 5-inch card, key the name as you would file it. On the other card prepare the cross-reference.

2. Visit an office either at your school or at a local business that uses an alphabetic filing system. Inquire about
   a. types of folders used
   b. types of labels used
   c. how the tabs are prepared

    d. the use of cross-references

    e. charge-out methods

    f. sorting trays

    g. how the materials are coded before they are filed

    h. in what types of cabinets or shelves the materials are housed

    i. retention and transfer methods

3. Visit three Web sites that sell filing supplies and equipment online. Select five items that you would need to set up a filing system. Compare the products and the prices among the three Web sites. Be sure to state the Web site address and name. Use an electronic spreadsheet to display your information.

4. Visit your school library or a large organization, such as a hospital or insurance company. Ask to see how information is processed using microfilm. Ask to see how microforms are stored and used.

Surfing the Internet

Your office manager, Charlotte, has just concluded a meeting with the office staff regarding misplaced records. All of you are concerned because the misplaced folders are a source of irritation and are also costly because your company must pay for employees' time while they search for the records. Charlotte has asked you to help her to locate information about records management.

1. Connect to the Internet and access a search tool such as Yahoo!, Lycos, or NetSearch.

2. Locate information on records management software by using search key words.

3. Summarize in memo form the information found on records management software.

4. Enter the address for the Association for Information Management Professionals and locate information about the organization: http://www.arma.org.

5. Locate the code of professional responsibility. Summarize the code for your manager.

6. Locate information on the *Glossary of Records Management Terms—A Guideline.* Identify this publication by ISBN number and current price.

7. Summarize your information in memo form to submit to your instructor.

Using MS Office 2002 "File"

E-Mail Messages Within Outlook's Inbox

 Creating a New Folder

1. Open Microsoft Outlook and click on the View menu. Select Folder List.

2. A column displays Outlook folders in a "tree" format.

3. Right-click on the Inbox folder.

4. Click on New Folder.

5. Type a name for the new folder and press Enter.

Moving Messages to the New Folder

1. With the e-mail message closed and visible in the Inbox, position the mouse pointer over the message.

2. Hold down the left mouse button and drag the message to the new folder.

3. Release the left mouse button.

4. The message is now "filed."

Viewing or Not Viewing Subfolders

1. If you see a minus (−) symbol next to the Inbox:

   ■ It means the Inbox subfolders are visible.

2. If you see a plus (+) symbol next to the Inbox:

   ■ It means the Inbox subfolders are *not* visible.

   ■ The + and − symbols work like a toggle switch; click on the symbol to change.

APPLICATION PROBLEMS

APPLICATION 7-A

Indexing and Filing Names

Supplies needed: Thirty-five 3 × 5-inch cards; set of alphabetic guides, A to Z; Form 7-A, Answer Sheet for 7-A.

 Retrieve file ANSWER-1.DOC from your student data disk.

Directions: You have many names, addresses, and telephone numbers stored on cards. Because the cards are worn, you have decided to make new cards. The names, addresses, and telephone numbers are computer stored. You have requested a new computer printout of address labels for all your cards. Key the names in indexing order at the top of each card. In the upper right corner of each card, key the corresponding number for each name. (You will need the number to record and check your answers.) The first day that you worked on this project, you keyed thirty-five cards.

After you have keyed cards 1–35, separate the cards into five groups, arrange the cards in alphabetical order, and file them in correct sequence. Complete Answer Sheet for 7-A by writing the card numbers in the squares above the letter. For example, card number (1) would be written in the square above "L" on the answer sheet. Be sure to list the card numbers in alphabetical sequence above the letter. Submit your answer sheet to your instructor. Before proceeding to Application 7-B, check with your instructor to see that you are ready.

Do *not* remove the thirty-five cards from your file. In Applications 7-B and 7-C, you will add more cards to your file.

Here are the names for cards 1–35:

(1) James R. Larsen

(2) Bob O'Donald

(3) Helen Vandermallie

(4) Martha Odell-Ryan

(5) Sister Edward

(6) Georgia Ann Harris

(7) Mrs. Georgia Harris

(8) Father Jenkins

(9) Ty Chen

(10) Martha Odellman

(11) Allen's Swap Shop

(12) J. T. Larson

(13) Herbert Vander Mallie

(14) George Haris

(15) Mary Allen's Beauty Shop

(16) Marshall Field & Company

(17) Georgia Harris

(18) Allens' Print Shop

(19) Trans-Continent Truckers

(20) George Harris

(21) James Larson

(22) Hubert Vander Mallie

(23) George E. Harris

(24) South Carolina Industries

(25) North East Fuel Supply

(26) AAA Batteries

(27) WHAM Radio

(28) Higgins Cleaners

(29) 24 Hour Grocery

(30) New Jersey Office Supply

(31) Over–30 Club

(32) Prince Arthur's Hair Styling

(33) Human Rights Division, Illinois

(34) First Baptist Church

(35) Hotel Isabella

APPLICATION 7-B

Indexing and Filing Names

Supplies needed: Thirty-five 3 × 5-inch cards; the card file prepared in Application 7-A; Form 7-B, Answer Sheet for 7-B.

Retrieve file ANSWER-2.DOC from your student data disk.

Directions: The next time you work on your filing project, you key 35 additional names in indexing order on cards. (Be sure to key the corresponding number on each card so that you can record and check your answers.)

Here are the names:

(36) James Danforth, Jr.

(37) Burns Travel Agency

(38) Caddo County Water Department

(39) Norton R. Henson

(40) Sister Marie

(41) The Lone Ranger

(42) The Jefferson Party House

(43) El Rancho Inn

(44) Cecil Young-Jones

(45) RCT Manufacturers

(46) Administrative Management

(47) Hotel Baker

(48) Tri-State Enterprises

(49) Miss Robert's Charm School

(50) The Daily Oklahoman

(51) Bob Guerin

(52) William T. Au

(53) Thomas Kaplan, M. D.

(54) Irene McGregor

(55) Arthur P. Van der Linden

(56) College of Notre Dame

(57) John Wilkins Supply Corp.

(58) Southwestern Distributors

(59) Internal Revenue Service (Department of the Treasury)

(60) Four Corners Answering Service

(61) The University of Oklahoma

(62) Montgomery & Co.

(63) South East Pipeline

(64) Webbers' Home for the Aged

(65) People's Republic of China

(66) New Orleans Printing Co.

(67) Marine Midland Bank–Rochester

(68) Miss Laura's Candy Shop

(69) Strong Memorial Hospital

(70) Surv-Ur-Self Pastries, Inc.

After you key the names on the cards, separate the cards into five groups, arrange the cards in alphabetical order, and file them with the 35 cards you filed in Application 7-A. Complete Answer Sheet for 7-B and submit your answers to your instructor.

Next, prepare for Finding Test No. 1. If you had a card filed incorrectly, find out why. Before you take Finding Test No. 1, be sure that all 70 cards are arranged in correct alphabetical order. Ask your instructor for Finding Test No. 1.

When you have completed Finding Test No. 1, you are ready for Application 7-C. Leave the 70 cards in your file in order.

APPLICATION 7-C

Indexing and Filing Names

Supplies needed: Forty-four 3 × 5-inch cards; the card file prepared in Applications 7-A and 7-B; Form 7-C, Answer Sheet for 7-C.

 Retrieve file ANSWER-3.DOC from your student data disk.

Directions: Key forty names in indexing order to complete your list of names. Here are the names:

(71) Jason Wayne Suppliers

(72) General Insurance Company, Rochester, New York

(73) Prince Charles

(74) Federal Communications Commission

(75) Hank Christian

(76) East Avenue Baptist Church

(77) KRLD Radio

(78) Maudeen E. Livingston

(79) Jim Waldrop

(80) Social Security Administration (Department of Health and Human Services)

(81) The Royal Inn

(82) Human Rights Division of New York

(83) Ellen Jan Elgin

(84) Robert Edward Kramer, D.V.M.

(85) Robert E. Kramer

(86) United Hauling, Ltd.

(87) Prince James Portraiture

(88) Harold Roberson

(89) General Insurance Company Rochester, Minnesota

(90) First National Bank Chicago, Illinois, Oaks Branch

(91) Harold O. Roberson

(92) M C Tree Service (formerly Collier Tree Service)

(93) Mrs. Maudeen Livingston

(94) George Zimmer Corporation

(95) The Johns Hopkins University

(96) Rain or Shine Boot Shoppe

(97) M. T. Torres

(98) Marion Burnett

(99) Harold Robertson

(100) John R. de Work

(101) Del Monte Properties

(102) Mason-Dixon Consultants

(103) Robert Edwin Kramer, M.D.

(104) Ciudad Acuna Television Repair

(105) Pierre Chez

(106) North Carolina Pipeline

(107) Frank T. Forthright

(108) Bill Carter Petroleum Corporation

(109) General Insurance Company Amarillo, Texas

(110) First National Bank Chicago, Illinois, Aspin Branch

You anticipate that you may have difficulty finding cards 71, 75, 79, and 92 because they could be called for by different names. Therefore, make cross-reference cards for them. In the upper right corner of each cross-reference card, key **71X**, **75X**, **79X**, and **92X** respectively.

After you have keyed all the names on the cards, including the cross-reference cards, separate the cards into five groups. Arrange the cards in alphabetical order, and file them with the 70 cards you filed in Applications 7-A and 7-B. Complete Answer Sheet for 7-C and submit your answers to your instructor.

Next, prepare for Finding Test No. 2. If you had a card filed incorrectly, find out why. Before you take Finding Test No. 2, be sure that all the cards are arranged in correct alphabetical order. Ask your instructor for Finding Test 2.

Your Action Plan

Complete your Action Plan; if necessary, refer to the guidelines outlined in Chapter 1. Set one goal using the information you learned in Chapter 7.

Your Portfolio

With the help of your instructor, select the best work representative of your work from Chapter 7. Follow your instructor's directions for formatting, assembling, and turning in the portfolio.

part three

Working with the Office Team

CHAPTER 8
Handling Financial Procedures

CHAPTER 9
Providing Customer Service, Scheduling Appointments, and Receiving Visitors

CHAPTER 10
Making Travel Arrangements

CHAPTER 11
Planning Meetings and Conferences

CHAPTER 12
Using Telecommunications in the Office

chapter 8

Handling Financial Procedures

OUTLINE

Banking Procedures
Nonelectronic Funds Transfer
Electronic Funds Transfer
Bank Checks
Bank Statement Reconciling

Accounting Procedures
Petty Cash Fund
Payroll
Financial Statements
Budgeting
Office Supplies Inventory
Accounting Department

International Currency Exchange

LEARNING OUTCOMES

When you have completed this chapter, you should be able to:

✔ Identify and understand the use of a cashier's check, bank draft, bank money order, and traveler's check.

✔ Identify the various ways funds are transferred electronically.

✔ Prepare checks, make stop-payment notification, and endorse checks.

✔ Reconcile a bank statement.

✔ Calculate and keep an accurate petty cash fund.

✔ Calculate a weekly payroll on a payroll register.

✔ Understand and identify the parts of an income statement and balance sheet.

✔ Understand the budgeting process.

✔ Keep an inventory of supplies and order supplies as needed.

✔ Understand the functions of the accounting department and its staff.

✔ Demonstrate how to change U. S. dollars to foreign money using current currency exchange rates.

Larger companies have staff that is hired specifically to handle the financial functions of the company. These functions include budgeting, accounting, making payments, billing, banking, and other operations, depending on the type of business and the size of the company.

In small companies or professional offices, such as a medical or dental practice, office professionals may handle certain financial tasks in addition to the usual office duties. As an office professional, you need to become familiar with some of the basic banking transactions and recordkeeping tasks that you may need to perform if you go to work for a small company.

BANKING PROCEDURES

Nonelectronic Funds Transfer

A depositor establishes a checking account at a bank as a convenient means to transfer funds. The instrument most used for transferring funds is the ordinary **check,** which is defined as a written order of a depositor upon a commercial bank to pay to the order of a designated party or to a bearer a specified sum of money on demand.

The parties to a check are the **drawer,** the person who draws the check on his or her account, the **drawee,** the bank upon which the check is drawn, and the **payee,** the person to whom payment is to be made.

If you are to sign checks for your manager, the organization where you work, or both, you will be asked to complete a signature card, placing your authorized signature on file with the bank.

In addition to the ordinary check, the following are used to transfer funds: cashier's check, bank draft, bank money order, and traveler's check.

Cashier's Check. A **cashier's check,** also called a treasurer's check or official check, is written by an authorized officer of the bank on its own funds that guarantees payment to the payee by the drawer's bank. A depositor may obtain an official check by writing the bank a check on his or her own funds for the amount plus a fee.

In order for the official check to stand as proof of payment, the officer of the bank gives a copy of the check to the person making the payment. The name of the purchaser is on the official check.

Bank Draft. A **bank draft** is a check drawn by a bank on its own funds (or credit) in another bank located either in the same city or another city. The draft is made payable to a third party, which, upon endorsing it, may cash the bank draft at the bank on which it is drawn.

A bank draft can be used to transfer money to another person or organization in another geographical location within the United States or abroad. A bank draft payable in foreign currency may also be purchased.

In order for an office professional to obtain a bank draft, he or she should present to the bank his or her manager's or organization's check made payable to the bank for the desired amount plus the fee. In exchange, the office professional will receive a bank draft made payable to the person or organization specified.

Bank Money Order. A **bank money order** similar to the postal money order may be obtained from a bank. Money orders are often used in place of personal checks.

A bank money order requires the endorsement of the payee to transfer the funds. It may be cashed at any bank. The fee for obtaining a bank money order is nominal. The amount for which a single money order may be written is limited, but the number of money orders that may be issued to the same person to be sent to one payee is not restricted.

Traveler's Check. Traveler's checks are used in place of cash. The advantage of traveler's checks is that when they are lost or stolen, the owner usually can obtain a refund immediately by contacting a representative office of the company whose checks were purchased. Traveler's checks may be purchased at banks or from other sources, such as credit unions.

One source is American Express. American Express traveler's checks can be purchased at a bank, as well as at American Express offices throughout the world. American Express traveler's checks are sold in denominations of $20, $50, $100, $500, and $1,000 (U.S.). They may also be purchased in foreign currencies. The cost is usually 1 percent of face value. There is no time limit on their validity. A traveler who plans an extended stay in a foreign country may find it economically advantageous to purchase some traveler's checks in the currency of that particular country.

The purchaser must obtain traveler's checks in person because the purchaser must sign each one in the presence of the agent from whom the checks are purchased. American Express also has a two-party check. Only one person must sign for the checks. A 2 percent fee is charged for two-party checks. The purchaser's signature on each check is his or her identification and protection. The purchaser can cash a traveler's check at a hotel, bank, other places of business, or an American Express office. In order to cash a traveler's check, the purchaser must sign the check in the presence of the person accepting it.

Traveler's checks are numbered serially. When you purchase traveler's checks for your manager, you should prepare a list of the serial numbers of the checks in duplicate, one for your files and the other for your manager to carry, preferably in a place separate from the traveler's checks.

When traveler's checks are lost or stolen, the owner should contact the nearest representative office of the bank or company from which they were purchased. The company will need to know the serial numbers of the missing checks and the total amount of the checks.

Electronic Funds Transfer

Electronic funds transfer (EFT) is an electronic delivery system for financial transactions. With the use of computers, financial institutions can perform numerous banking transactions without the use of checks. Advantages are that there are no lost or stolen checks and that payments are made quickly and on time.

The major EFT services are automated teller machines, automated clearinghouses (centers for electronic funds transfer between financial institutions, and individuals), payment by telephone, and point-of-sales transfers.

Examples of services rendered by automated clearinghouses are social security payments, dividends and annuities paid by large companies, and payroll.

Automated Teller Machines. **Automated teller machines (ATMs)**, located at banks, in shopping malls, in supermarkets, and many other places, enable customers to obtain cash and make deposits. When a customer activates an automated teller machine with an EFT card and enters a personal identification number or a secret password, the computer is ready to answer an inquiry about the customer's account, supply balance data, or dispense cash.

Debit Card. Another way funds are electronically transferred is by using a debit card. **Debit cards** are used in the place of checks. Debit cards are obtained through the bank by completing a credit application for a debit card through companies such as VISA or MasterCard. Once the application is approved, the bank issues the debit card, which can be used either as a debit card or a credit card. When using a debit card, a secret password must be entered and then the money is taken directly from the individual's or company's checking account. The only drawback is if the card is lost, it can still be used as a credit card.

Direct Payroll Deposit. **Direct payroll deposit** enables an organization to pay its employees without writing checks. Instead, the organization furnishes the bank with a magnetic tape with a description of all payroll disbursements to be made to the employees. The bank credits the account of each of the employees with his or her net pay and withdraws the amount from the account of the employer making payment. The employee receives a statement often produced by a third party from his or her employer. The statement shows the gross payment, the type and amount of deductions, and the net payment. Another example of automatic deposits might be federal payments, such as social security checks.

Automatic Deposits. Funds can be automatically deposited as well. The company making the **automatic deposit** must be given the account's American Banking Association (ABA) electronic routing number and the account number in which the money is to be deposited. This routing number and bank account number is usually printed on the bottom of all checks.

Automatic Debits. **Automatic debits** are preauthorized automated transfer of funds for an individual or company from one account to another within the same financial institution. For example, a customer can transfer funds from a checking account to a savings account, from a savings account to a checking account, and from a checking account to a loan payment.

To have funds electronically drafted from a checking account, such as payment of utilities, you must complete a form authorizing the draft and provide the utility company with a canceled check or blank deposit slip and your account number. The company drafting your account usually requires a signature authorizing the draft as well. EFT services represent an important change in the banking industry. Banks are encouraging their customers to use EFT services, and their use is increasing.

Web Banking. Most banks offer business banking, investing, and insurance facilities to their customers on the Internet. **Web banking** provides easy management of banking transactions online wherever you have access to the Internet. Primary functions of such services enable business customers to make electronic transfers between accounts and get real-time information on balances and transactions. Accounts may be viewed and manipulated "on screen" just as you might with more traditional methods of banking.

Establishment of a Web banking account is achieved by first visiting the company's bank to provide a company profile and, perhaps, to acquire software that is loaded to your PC, or computer network. This software will allow you to make the connection with the company's bank and its accounts.

In some cases, downloading the software may provide the connection. In either case, Web banking should be established with the assistance of a commercial banking expert at your company's bank.

Access to your Web banking services will depend upon your bank, your company's unique identification, and password. A unique password can be established for each authorized user of the business account. Commercial banking services are comprehensive but varied in design.

Telephone Transfers. Some companies allow payments to be made by phone. **Telephone transfers** can be made by calling the company to whom you wish to make payment, writing a check, giving them the check number and amount, and the company will draft the amount from your checking account and the bank will honor the check. Not all companies provide this service. The advantage is payment does not have to be made until the exact due date and late charges can be avoided.

Bank Checks

Businesses use various ways to prepare checks. Checks may be prepared with a check-writing machine, a computer and a printer, or a pen. Some businesses use check-writing machines as a safety measure against possible alteration of checks. Others make use of commercially available software for check writing such as Intuit's Quicken or Simply Accounting.

Stop-Payment Notification. At the request of the drawer, a bank will place **stop-payment notification** on a check for a fee at any time until it has cleared the bank upon which it is drawn. Stopping payment is a safety measure that should be taken when a check has been lost or stolen; it may also be taken when a check is written for an incorrect amount, when certain conditions of an agreement have not been met, or for other reasons.

Check Endorsement. Banks require **check endorsement** (signing) by the payee when a check is presented for cash or deposit. The payee signs on the reverse side of the check—preferably at the left end. A bank will accept for deposit checks that have been endorsed by a representative of the payee. The endorsement may be made with a rubber stamp, or it may be handwritten in ink.

Endorsements are of three types: blank, restrictive, and full. See Figure 8-1.

Blank Endorsement. A **blank endorsement** consists of only the signature of the payee. A check endorsed using a blank endorsement is payable to the bearer; therefore, the holder should use a blank endorsement only when he or she is at the bank depositing or cashing the check in case the check is lost or stolen.

Restrictive Endorsement. A **restrictive endorsement** limits the use of a check to the purpose stated in the endorsement. Words such as "For deposit only" or "Pay to the order of" are written before the organization's name or the depositor's signature. As a result, further endorsement of the check is restricted. A restrictive endorsement should be used when deposits are sent to the bank by mail.

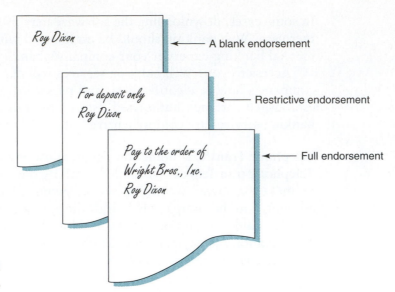

■ **Figure 8-1**
Endorsements.

Full Endorsement. A **full endorsement,** also called a two-party check, transfers a check to a specified person or organization. "Pay to the order of" followed by the name of the person or organization to which the check is being transferred is written on the check preceding the signature of the endorser.

Bank Statement Reconciling

Each month the bank issues a current bank statement to the depositor. A comparison of the final bank balance on the bank statement with the checkbook balance is called **bank reconciliation.** To balance with the statement's figure, checks listed on the bank's statement are checked off in the check register. Some banks return checks that have been paid by the bank with the bank statement each month; other banks return photo copies of each check; and still other banks provide copies of checks upon request. See Figure 8-2, which shows an example of a bank statement. The **canceled checks** are the ones that have been paid by the bank. The statement shows the previous month's balance, deposits made, checks paid, bank charges, and the ending balance.

Reconcile the bank statement with the checkbook balance as soon as you receive the bank statement. Compare the final balance on the statement with the balance in the checkbook and then account for the difference. Usually the two balances do not agree for the following reasons:

- Checks have been written that have not been presented to the bank for payment
- Deposits may have been made since the statement was sent
- Automatic credits (deposits) and debits (withdrawals) have been made by the bank
- Errors in recording checks or deposits may have been made

Most bank statements have bank reconciliation forms printed on the back of each page of the bank statement for the user's convenience.

BANK STATEMENT
GILBERT BANK OF ROCHESTER

NAME:	November Sales Seminar C/O Amanda Quevedo 14 Shady Lane Rochester, NY 14623	BRANCH: Rochester Main	

ACCOUNT NO. 3570-810-73-1000	TRANSIT NO. 00011-112000	BEGINNING BALANCE October 25, 20--	$8,380.25

CODE	DESCRIPTION	DEBIT	CREDIT	DAY/MO	BALANCE
				10/25	8,380.25
DD	Direct deposit		300.00	10/26	8,680.25
DD	Direct deposit		1,500.00	10/26	10,180.25
DD	Direct deposit		3,000.00	10/29	13,180.25
CK	Check #2009	1,224.00		10/31	11,956.25
CK	Check #2010	510.00		11/03	11,446.25
CK	Check #2015	450.00		11/05	10,996.25
DD	Direct deposit		2,250.00	11/09	13,246.25
CK	Check #2016	1,700.00		11/15	11,546.25
CK	Check #2017	2,000.00		11/18	9,546.25
SC	Service charge	20.00		11/23	9,526.25
CK	Check #2018	2,723.85		4/23	6,802.40
No. of Checks: 6	No. of Credits: 4	Total Debits: $8,627.85	Total Credits: $7,050.00	November 25, 200X	Ending Balance: $6,802.40

■ **Figure 8-2**
Bank statement.

To reconcile the bank statement with the checkbook:

a. From the bank statement, record in your checkbook register all automatic transactions from your statement that you have not previously entered, including:

■ + any interest earned

■ + automatic deposits

■ − service charges

■ − automatic payments

■ − ATM withdrawals and charges

■ − telephone transfers and charges

b. Enter in your checkbook register a check mark for all canceled checks and deposits received by the bank that are listed on the bank statement.

c. Total all **outstanding checks** (checks not paid by the bank) from your check register.

d. Total all deposits shown in your check register that are not shown on the bank statement.

e. Adjust your statement balance.

- Enter your checking account closing balance shown on the front of your statement.
- Add any deposits not yet shown on the statement.
- Subtract the total outstanding checks.

f. The adjusted bank statement balance from your reconciliation should agree with your adjusted checkbook balance.

If the adjusted bank statement balance and the adjusted checkbook balance do not agree, follow these steps:

1. Find the difference between the two.
2. Check the bank reconciliation to make certain you have made no errors.
3. Look for omissions of checks or deposits.
4. Check for a math error in the check stubs.

Always file your canceled checks. The retention period for checks and the method of disposing of them will be determined by your company's policy. The person in your organization who is responsible for records retention will provide you with information about destroying checks. Records retention was discussed in Chapter 7.

ACCOUNTING PROCEDURES

Most organizations maintain computerized accounting records. Accounting is a separate business function, performed by accountants, but recordkeeping occurs wherever a record originates. Consequently, office workers maintain and assist with various financial records. Some office professionals, especially those who work for owners of businesses, help the owners with personal business records.

You may also be responsible for a petty cash fund. In addition, you may be asked to keep a record of office supplies on hand or to assist with payroll records.

Petty Cash Fund

When the amount of office expenditure is small and payment should be made immediately, it may be more convenient to make the payment by cash rather than by check. To provide cash to pay for incidental items, such as messenger service, postage due on a package, a collect telegram, or emergency purchases of office supplies, organizations establish a **petty cash fund.** The fund can range from $10 to $100 or more, depending on the cash needs for a certain period, usually a month. Even though the petty cash is used to make miscellaneous payments, the petty cash must be accounted for.

```
AMOUNT $ __2.36__              NO. __22__

              RECEIVED OF PETTY CASH

                              March 16  200X _____
   FOR __Cleaning Supplies_____
   CHARGE TO __Misc._____

   _____

   APPROVED BY              RECEIVED BY

   __JHW_____          __Jack Morse_____

✦ FORM DI-3685
```

■ **Figure 8-3**
Petty cash voucher.

Generally the office professional is responsible for handling the petty cash fund. To keep track of petty cash, observe the following standard procedures:

1. Keep the cash and the completed vouchers in a box or an envelope and put them in a safe place. They should be in a locked desk drawer or file or in an office safe. Balance the petty cash record at least once a week. If the cash and vouchers are left unlocked, balance the record at the end of each day.

2. Prepare a petty cash voucher for each expenditure you make. An example is shown in Figure 8-3. The **petty cash voucher,** which is a receipt, should show the amount paid, the voucher number, the date, to whom the payment was made (received by), the purpose of the payment, the expense category to which the payment will be charged, and the signature or initials of the person authorizing payment. Some organizations also require the signature or initials of the person receiving payment.

3. Keep an accurate petty cash record, using either a petty cash book or a distribution sheet or envelope (see Figure 8-4). For each payment from the petty cash funds, enter the date, the amount, the voucher number, and an explanation of the petty cash record. The total of the expenditures plus the cash on hand should equal the original amount of the petty cash fund.

   Some petty cash books provide columns for distribution of payments by expense categories; others do not. The columns and the appropriate headings for the petty cash record can be printed on a sheet of paper or a manila envelope. Accounting departments frequently supply manila envelopes imprinted with the columns and headings for the petty cash record, including columns for the distribution of payments. Posting the expenditures in the columns provided for each predetermined expense category simplifies preparing the summary of expenditures when you need to replenish the petty cash fund.

4. Replenish the petty cash fund soon enough to keep an adequate supply of cash on hand. In some organizations, petty cash is replenished at a predetermined time, for instance, when only one-fourth of the cash is on hand. In others, replenishing the petty cash fund is left to the judgment of the person who is responsible for maintaining the fund.

| FROM May 3 _____ 200X__ TO June 12 _____ 200X__ CASHIER AUDITED BY | | **PETTY CASH ENVELOPE** PETTY CASH ENVELOPES PROVIDE A COMPLETE RECORD OF ALL PETTY CASH DISBURSEMENTS. ALL PAYMENTS SHOULD BE SUPPORTED BY A BILL OR VOUCHER SIGNED BY RECIPIENT. EACH VOUCHER SHOULD BE LISTED BELOW AND DISTRIBUTED IN THE COLUMNS HEADED ACCORDING TO YOUR GENERAL LEDGER ACCOUNT NUMBERS OR TITLES. | REIMBURSED BY CHECK NO. 6872 REFERENCE JOURNAL FOLIO | | | | | | | |

DATE 200X	VOUCHER NUMBER	PAID TO	DISTRIBUTION									TOTAL
			Supp	Postage	Misc	Del	Tele					
		Petty Cash Fund: $50.00										
5 3	161	Office Supplies	4 08									4 08
5 3	162	Telegram					3 16					3 16
5 3	163	Stamps		3 90								3 90
5 3	164	Reg. Package		3 84								3 84
5 3	165	Cleaning Supplies			2 87							2 87
5 3	166	Carfare				2 50						2 50
5 3	167	Office Supplies	3 64									3 64
5 3	168	Reg. Package		2 79								2 79
5 3	169	Messenger				2 75						2 75
5 3	170	Office Supplies	4 96									4 96
5 3	171	Delivery				3 75						3 75
	TOTAL		12 68	10 53	2 87	9 00	3 16					38 24

■ **Figure 8-4**
Petty cash envelope.

5. To replenish the petty cash fund, balance the petty cash record, formally request a check for the amount needed to bring the fund amount back to its beginning balance, and prepare the petty cash report.

6. Submit the records called for by the accounting department. When the accounting department supplies a petty cash distribution envelope, the usual procedure is to submit the envelope with the supporting vouchers enclosed. Before you release an envelope, copy the record for your files. If you keep a petty cash book, submit a petty cash report similar to the one shown in Figure 8-5. Attach the petty cash vouchers.

7. Cash the check. Enter the beginning amount and the date on the first line of the "paid to" column of the petty cash record each time you replenish the petty cash record.

Payroll

One of the common accounting procedures an office professional might be required to do is payroll, especially if he or she works for a small company. As with petty cash, a record must be kept that summarizes the payroll for a particular period. This record is called a payroll register. The **payroll register**

INTEROFFICE MEMORANDUM

TO: M. Seifert, General Accounting Office   DATE: June 13, 200X

FROM: R. C. Delano

SUBJECT: Petty Cash Report

The following report is a summary of petty cash paid out from

May 3 until June 12, 200X.

<u>Petty Cash Report</u>

June 13, 200X

Opening Balance		$50.00
Expenditures		
Supplies	$12.68	
Postage	10.53	
Delivery	9.00	
Telegrams	3.16	
Miscellaneous	<u>2.87</u>	<u>38.24</u>
Closing Balance		<u>$11.76</u>

Please issue a check for $38.24 to replenish the petty cash fund

to the original amount of $50. Eleven petty cash vouchers are

attached.

mk

attachments

■ **Figure 8-5**
Petty cash report.

summarizes for each employee the status of wages earned, payroll deductions, and final take-home pay. The summary can be done manually or by computer using a payroll software program, but no matter which method is used, all employers are required by law to create and keep a payroll record for each payroll period. Payroll records usually are prepared weekly, semimonthly, or monthly.

Figure 8-6 shows a typical payroll register. Notice that the register shows columns for **employee data** (name, marital status, withholding allowances, hourly rate), **regular hours** worked (first forty hours worked in the payroll period), and the number of **overtime hours** worked (any hours worked over forty hours). Next, **total earnings** (total regular earnings plus overtime earnings) are calculated.

The deductions begin with the Federal Insurance Contributions Act (FICA)—two taxes required for all employees: social security—the **Old Age,**

Steps to Replenish Petty Cash

Refer to Figure 8-4 as you read these steps.

1. Count the cash on hand. In the example, you should have $11.76, which is the difference between the amount in the petty cash fund, $50.00, and the amount paid out, $38.24.

2. Total each Distribution column and the Total column of the petty cash envelope.

3. Subtract the total amount paid out ($38.24 in this example) from the amount of petty cash (example is $50.00). The difference should agree with the cash count left in the envelope ($11.76 in the example).

4. Total the amount of all the vouchers to see that they agree with the Total column ($38.24 in the example).

5. Add the totals across the bottom under the Distribution columns to see that the sum is equal to the amount shown in the Total column.

6. Write a check or request the amount paid (Total column $38.24) to bring the petty cash fund back to its original amount ($50.00 in the example).

Survivors, and Disability Insurance (OASDI), as of January 2004, is deducted at the rate of 6.2 percent of the first $87,900 earned. Federal **health insurance (HI),** commonly called **Medicare,** has no wage base. All wages earned each year, as of January 2004, are subject to the 1.45 percent set by law. Both of these rates are subject to change by legislation. The rate is combined for social security and Medicare, and is 7.65 percent. **Deductions** are amounts deducted from gross pay, such as group medical insurance, dental insurance, union dues, savings bonds, and charitable contributions, as well as federal income tax and social security.

Follow these steps to complete a payroll register:

1. Enter each employee's name, marital status (single, married, or head-of-household), number of withholding allowances (the number of exemption allowances claimed on his or her W-4 form), the hourly rate (amount earned per hour), the number of regular hours worked, and the number of overtime hours worked.

2. Calculate regular earnings by multiplying the hourly rate by the regular hours worked.

3. Calculate overtime earnings by multiplying the hourly rate by the overtime hours worked by 1.5 (time-and-one-half).

4. Add regular earnings and overtime earnings to obtain total earnings.

5. Multiply total earnings by 6.2 percent to calculate OASDI.

6. Multiply total earnings by 1.45 percent to calculate HI.

7. The amount of **federal income tax** (money withheld from a paycheck and paid to the federal government as a tax on wages earned) withheld is obtained by looking at *Circular E, Employer's Tax Guide* federal income tax table booklet. The booklet gives instructions, and tables for

WEEKLY PAYROLL REGISTER

For week ending: June _____ July 31, 200X

Name	Marital Status	Withholding Allowance	Hourly Rate	Reg Hrs	Overtime Hrs	Regular Earnings	Overtime Earnings	Gross Earnings	OASDI	HI	Federal Income Tax	Group Med Ins	Group Dental Ins	Total Deductions	Net Pay
Barton, V. L.	M	3	12.00	40	10	480.00	180.00	660.00	40.92	9.57	36.00	22.00	13.00	121.49	538.51
Carr, S. A.	M	1	12.00	40	9	480.00	162.00	642.00	39.80	9.31	51.00	38.00	8.00	146.11	495.39
Dean, B. B.	M	1	10.00	40	12	400.00	180.00	580.00	35.96	8.41	42.00	41.00	11.00	138.37	441.53
Ellis, R. J.	M	1	11.90	40	8	476.00	142.80	618.80	38.37	8.97	46.00	22.00	5.00	120.34	498.46
Franklin, D. O.	M	3	13.50	40	5	540.00	101.25	641.25	39.76	9.30	33.00	12.00	8.00	102.06	539.19
Gonzalez, P. I.	M	2	12.00	40	13	480.00	234.00	714.00	44.27	10.35	53.00	41.00	10.00	158.62	555.38
Han, T. A.	M	2	12.50	40	11	500.00	206.25	706.25	43.79	10.24	51.00	38.00	11.00	154.03	552.22
Johnson, J. R.	M	0	10.85	40	15	434.00	244.13	678.13	42.04	9.83	64.00	22.00	8.00	145.87	532.26
Kelly, J. S.	M	0	11.00	40	12	440.00	198.00	638.00	39.56	9.25	58.00	38.00	13.00	157.81	480.19
Leamon, D. D.	M	4	13.10	40	10	524.00	196.50	720.50	44.67	10.45	36.00	38.00	10.00	139.12	581.38
Totals						$4,754.00	$1,844.93	$6,598.93	$409.14	$95.68	$470.00	$312.00	$97.00	$1,383.82	$5,215.11

Notes: Calculated using Excel XP for Windows 2000.

All tax information taken from 2004 tax tables.

Figure 8-6

Completed payroll register.

■ **Figure 8-6**
Payroll register.

weekly, biweekly, semimonthly, and monthly payrolls, each showing amounts to be withheld for single, married, or head-of-household deductions for federal income tax. The amounts shown here reflect 2004 figures.

8. Enter any other deductions. Examples are group medical insurance, dental insurance, union dues, purchase of savings bonds, contributions to charitable organizations such as United Way, and savings or payments sent to credit unions, to name a few.

9. Total all deductions.

10. Subtract total deductions from total earnings to calculate **net pay** (total earnings minus deductions).

Financial Statements

Most office professionals will not be required to have an extensive knowledge of accounting procedures, but you should be familiar with two major financial statements. These are the income statement and the balance sheet.

An owner or manager of a business must determine the condition of the business he or she owns or manages. Financial reports such as an income statement or a balance sheet, when compared with prior years or with industry averages, can tell the owner or manager whether the business is healthy. Reading or interpreting financial statements can tell the owner or manager if a problem exists, to what degree the problem has advanced, and can also pinpoint certain strengths or weaknesses about the problem. As an office professional, you should understand the purpose of the income statement and the balance sheet and recognize what accounting information goes on each.

Income Statement. An **income statement** is often also referred to as a profit and loss (P & L) statement or operating statement. The income statement shows the results of the operation of a company in terms of money earned (revenue) and expenses incurred. Figure 8-7 shows an income statement.

The income statement covers the results of the operation of a company for a certain period. In Figure 8-7 you will notice the period is for one year. The first part of the income statement summarizes the total amount of sales (revenue) that was made and the cost of the merchandise that was sold. The difference between the two is called **gross profit on sales.** The gross profit is not the profit the owner can take for personal use because the company has incurred many **expenses** (the cost of operation) that will reduce that revenue to a truer picture of what the company made. The income reported after expenses is also not the final income figure. Income tax must be accounted for (estimated and deducted) to arrive at the final income figure for the company.

Balance Sheet The balance sheet summarizes the balances of the **assets** (what the business owns), **liabilities** (what the business owes), and the **owner's equity** (what the business is worth). The **balance sheet** reports what a company is worth on any one given day—usually reported at the end of the month or year. It shows the company's complete financial condition. As an office professional, you should understand its various sections. Figure 8-8 shows a completed balance sheet.

The balance sheet is divided into three parts—assets, liabilities, and owner's equity. The assets are what the company owns and are shown as ei-

Rayborn Air Conditioning & Heating Service
Income Statement
For Year Ended December 31, 200X

Revenue		
Sales		$135,000
Cost of goods sold		
Merchandise inventory, January 1	$46,000	
Purchases	19,050	
Merchandise available for sale	$65,050	
Less inventory, December 31	13,000	
Cost of goods sold		52,050
Gross profit on sales		$187,050
Operating expenses		
Wages expense	$25,000	
Depreciation, office equipment	9,000	
Depreciation, trucks	15,000	
Repair expense	4,000	
Advertising expense	1,200	
Oil and gas expense	3,500	
Truck insurance expense	2,900	
Total operating expenses		60,600
Net income before estimated income tax		$126,450
Estimated income tax		34,935
Net income after income tax		$ 91,515

■ **Figure 8-7**
Income statement.

ther current assets or long-term assets. **Current assets** are those assets that can be sold or turned into cash quickly or can be consumed in a short period. **Plant and equipment,** often referred to as **fixed assets,** are those assets with a long life that will be used over many years in the operation of the company such as land and buildings. **Liabilities** are the debts that the company owes. **Current liabilities** are short-term debts—usually debts that can be paid in one year. **Long-term liabilities** are debts due for long periods of time—usually more than one year. Owner's equity is the capital the owner has invested in the company.

Even though you will probably not create income statements and balance sheets, depending on the size of the company where you work, you may be asked to work with them in some manner. Being familiar with these financial statements will tell you more about your company and its stability.

Budgeting

Budgeting is the process of planning future business operations and defining those plans in a formal report. The report expressed in financial terms is called a **budget.** Budgets may be developed for short periods, such as a month,

Rayborn Air Conditioning & Heating Service
Balance Sheet
For Year Ended December 31, 200X

Assets

Current assets			
Cash		$86,000	
Accounts receivable	$32,000		
Less allowance for bad debts	2,000	30,000	
Merchandise inventory		35,000	
Supplies		5,000	
Prepaid insurance		2,500	
Total current assets			$158,500
Plant and equipment			
Office equipment	$20,000		
Less accumulated depreciation	10,000	$10,000	
Shop equipment	$36,000		
Less accumulated depreciation	8,000	28,000	
Land		56,000	
Total equipment and plant			94,000
Total assets			$252,500

Liabilities

Current liabilities			
Accounts payable	$45,000		
Estimated income tax payable	18,000		
Salaries/wages payable	22,000		
Interest payable	45,000		
Total current liabilities		$130,000	
Long-term liabilities			
Mortgage payable	$55,000		
Notes payable	28,000		
Total long-term liabilities		83,000	
Total liabilities			$213,000

Owner's Equity

Ralph Rayborn, owner's equity			39,500
Total liabilities and owner's equity			$252,500

■ **Figure 8-8**
Balance sheet.

or long periods, such as a year. Annual budgets are often divided into shorter periods to better evaluate a company's ability to stay within the prescribed budget. Budgetary control is very important to the successful operation of a business, and as an employee you will be asked to participate in the budget process in some way. You might be asked to serve on the budget committee that is asked to review and revise various estimates of income and expenses by other employees. Usually budgeting procedures begin at the department level and move upward, with each area of responsibility combining figures submitted from below them and passing them upward in the company. The ultimate result is the master budget. The **master budget** consists of various budgets that collectively express the future activities of the company.

Anytime you or your department wants new equipment, additional personnel, or anything that comes down to costing the company money, you must justify how that spending will benefit the company in some way. It might mean increased productivity or even financial savings if approved. Unless you can paint a clear picture that shows these benefits, however, you are not likely to have your requests approved. When it comes to setting budget figures, everyone is asking for money. The request that most clearly shows justification usually gets approved if the money is available.

What if your office really needs an additional part-time person to get all the work done? How would you go about justifying money being spent from next year's budget when you have been asked to cut your budget by 5 percent? You would begin by determining how cost effective that part-time person will be. Study the following scenario:

One Full-Time Office Professional

Salary and benefits	$34,000
Office supplies used	2,500
Telephone line	500
Depreciation expense	2,700
Total annual cost	$39,700

$39,000 divided by 2,080 hours (52 weeks 40 hours per week = 2,080 hours) worked per year = $19 per hour cost (rounded)

Amount of hours worked overtime last year =
824 × $28.50 rate = $23,484

One Part-Time Office Professional (from Manpower or Kelly Services, for example)

Salary (no benefits) 1,040 hours @ $14/hour	$14,560
Office supplies (1/2 of full time)	1,250
Telephone (shared with another)	0
Depreciation expense (1/2 of full time)	1,350
Total annual cost	$17,160
Savings ($23,484 − 17,160)	$ 6,324

Management could quickly see that by employing a part-time office professional, $6,324 could be saved.

Office Supplies Inventory

Office professionals should replenish their office supplies during the time of day or week when they are least busy. Yet they need to plan so that they are not searching for supplies when they are pressed for time to complete a rush job. Sometimes an office professional is responsible for stocking office supplies for an entire floor or a department. To manage this, you need a record of supplies on hand.

An easy way to determine supplies needed is to keep an inventory of each item. You can do this on your computer, using a spreadsheet program or on a 4×6-inch card to create a **perpetual inventory record.** When you check supplies out of the main supply department or order them directly, enter the amount of each item received and then add the amount to the figure in the balance column. When you take supplies from the supply cabinet or shelf, enter the amount in the checked-out column and then subtract the amount to show the new balance. Encourage others who check out supplies to follow the same procedure.

By looking at the perpetual inventory record, you can decide (1) whether or not the item you need is on hand in sufficient quantity and (2) when it is time to check out or order additional supplies.

In most companies a request for supplies would begin with a purchase requisition that indicates the supplies needed and the amount to be ordered. Combining all requests for supplies from all departments is cost effective. The purchase requisition is used to generate a purchase order, which is sent to the supplier. The supplier fills the order and sends your company an invoice. A bill of lading, listing the goods shipped to you, will accompany the shipment. When the supplies are delivered, the goods received are checked against the purchase order. If all information is correct, authorization to pay the invoice is made.

Often when several supply orders are made, the invoices will be held until a statement is sent at the end of the month. You may pay all or a portion of the amount due depending on the business arrangement with the company. Figure 8-9 shows the forms cycle. In large companies, a computer generates these forms. Using your computer, you would call up the purchase order file and enter the request for office supplies. This information could be printed and sent by e-mail to the purchasing department that would process the order.

Electronic procurement of supplies is improving the way businesses buy from and partner with suppliers. Instead of wading through purchase orders and purchase requisitions that may take days or weeks to process, some employees go right to their computers and use a Web-based procurement system to summon a virtual shopping cart and order items they need right away over the Internet. These Web-based systems have actually changed employees into strategic buyers by granting them control over a subset of preapproved and budgeted items. They do not have to ask permission to order something. Based on the amount of purchasing power the company grants them, they can order at will and be alerted if their purchase isn't allowed or

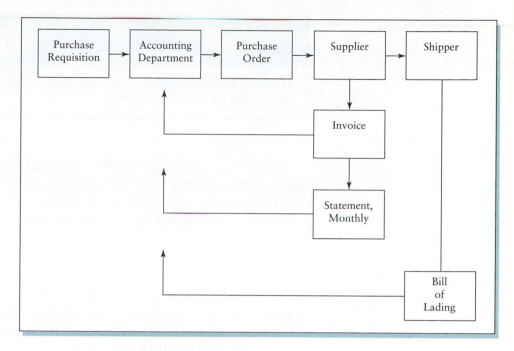

■ **Figure 8-9**
Forms cycle.

if they've reached their spending limit. The only constraint is that they must use approved vendors.

Accounting Department

The office professional must be familiar with the accounting department. Your company may have a cost center in the accounting department that handles cost control for the company. You must learn the following:

■ The budget account titles and numbers the manager is responsible for

■ Which accounts are used most often

■ How the accounts may be used

■ The correct procedures to follow when placing orders or spending money

■ How to charge certain expenses and what expenses are allowable

■ Your department code to be used

Often a company hires an outside certified public accountant (CPA) to handle the more complicated aspects of accounting for the company. You may find that you must provide current accounting information for the CPA. For instance, if you kept the budget information on a spreadsheet, you might be asked to save a copy on disk and send the file to the CPA as an attachment to an e-mail message. If you are using accounting software, such as QuickBooks, to make your entries during the month, you might be asked to make a backup copy of that software which includes your entries for the period and send it to the CPA as an attachment to an e-mail message. The CPA would open the software and make the necessary reports from your information, then alert you when you may continue making entries into your software.

quicktips

While in Excel or Access, if you want to repeat the data from the cell directly above just press Ctrl+'.

Every office professional will be involved in some way with the accounting function in a company. Therefore, as a professional you should know the overall accounting cycle and how it works within the company to efficiently handle the responsibility assigned to your manager.

INTERNATIONAL CURRENCY EXCHANGE

An office professional might find it necessary to provide his or her manager with the current **currency exchange rate** available when the manager travels abroad. You might also have to exchange money in the United States before the manager leaves or exchange money back into U.S. dollars after the manager returns from a trip abroad.

You can research the current exchange rate for any country's currency in many ways. For instance, you can quickly search on the Internet, call your local bank, check the newspaper or if your airport has international flights, usually there is a company at the airport that exchanges currency. Exchange rates are quoted per $1 U.S. Once you know the rate, you can multiply the rate times the number of dollars you want exchanged.

When exchanging foreign currency for U.S. dollars, most banks exchange only currency and not coins. When your manager arrives at his or her foreign destination, exchanging currency is often one of the first things to be done. Even if it is a small amount, he or she might need money for transportation to the hotel, tip money, or money on which to eat. To avoid having to do this while traveling, you might be asked to obtain the foreign currency prior to the manager's trip.

To help you prepare for your manager's departure, make a checklist of those items the manager needs to take—passport, visa, currency, traveler's checks, birth certificate, letter of credit and other business papers, airline tickets, hotel reservations, and confirmation numbers, to name a few. You will learn more about these topics in Chapter 10.

Your job as an office professional is to assist your manager with the many details involved with international travel. The manager should not have to deal with these details. The more efficient you are in anticipating every possible need, the smoother his or her travel will be.

Overview

✔ The instrument most used for transferring funds is a check. The parties to a check are the drawer (the person who draws the check on his or her account), the drawee (the bank on which the check is drawn), and the payee (the person to whom payment is written).

✔ The various ways funds might be transferred are cashier's check, bank draft, bank money order, traveler's check, and electronic funds transfer (EFT).

✔ The most common types of electronic funds transfer are automated teller machines, debit cards, direct payroll deposit, automatic deposits, automatic debits, Web banking, and telephone transfers.

✔ Office professionals may be responsible for bank check writing, stop-payment notification, check endorsement, and bank statement reconciliation.

✔ A petty cash fund is used to pay cash for incidental items in an office, such as a messenger service, express mailing packages, and postage due on a package, just to name a few.

✔ The payroll register summarizes for each employee the status of wages earned, payroll deductions, and final take-home pay.

✔ An income statement, often referred to as a profit and loss (P & L) statement or operating statement, shows the results of the operation of a company in terms of money earned (revenue) and expenses incurred.

✔ The balance sheet summarizes the balance of the assets, liabilities, and owner's equity on any given day.

✔ Budgeting is the process of planning future business operations and defining those plans in a formal report called a budget. Care must be taken to clearly justify reasons for making requests that will cost the company money.

✔ An easy way to determine supplies needed is to keep an inventory of each item. Supplies should be replenished when you are least busy.

✔ An office professional might find it necessary to provide his or her manager with the current currency exchange rates available when the manager often travels abroad. Exchange rates can be determined by researching the Internet, calling your local bank, checking the newspaper, or calling a currency exchange company at the airport.

Key Terms

Assets. What is owned.

Automated deposit. Funds that can be automatically deposited using an American Bankers Association (ABA) electronic routing number and the account number in which the money is to be deposited.

Automated teller machines (ATMs). Machines located in banks, shopping malls, or supermarkets that enable bank customers to obtain cash and make deposits.

Automatic debits. Preauthorized automated transfer of funds for an individual or company from one account to another within the same financial institution.

Balance sheet. Summarizes the balances of assets, liabilities, and owner's equity and reports what the business is worth on any given day.

Bank draft. A check drawn by the bank on its own funds.

Bank money order. Similar to a postal money order but obtained from a bank.

Bank reconciliation. A comparison of the final balance on a bank statement with the checkbook balance, then accounting for any difference.

Blank endorsement. The signature of the payee on the back of a check.

Budget. The budgeting process expressed in financial terms.

Budgeting. The process of planning future business operations and defining those plans in a formal financial report.

Canceled checks. Checks paid by the bank.

Cashier's check. A check, also called a treasurer's check or official check, written by an authorized officer of the bank on its own fund that guarantees payment to the payee by the drawer's bank.

Check. A written order of a depositor upon a commercial bank to pay to the order of a designated party or to a bearer a specified sum of money on demand.

Check endorsement. A check presented for cash or deposit must be signed (endorsed) by the payee on the reverse side of the check—preferably at the left end.

Circular E, Employer's Tax Guide. Federal income tax table booklet.

Currency exchange rate. The ratio at which $1 U.S. may be traded for a foreign currency.

Current assets. Those assets that can be sold or turned into cash quickly or can be consumed in a short period.

Current liabilities. Short-term debts usually paid in one year.

Debit cards. Take the place of a check; money is deducted immediately from one's checking account.

Deductions. Amounts deducted from gross pay, such as group medical insurance, dental insurance, union dues, savings bonds, and charitable contributions.

Direct payroll deposit. Payroll money automatically deposited to an account.

Drawee. The bank upon which a check is drawn.

Drawer. The person who draws the check on his or her account.

Electronic funds transfer (EFT). Electronic delivery system for financial transactions.

Employee data. The name, marital status, withholding allowances, and hourly rate information for each employee for payroll purposes.

Expenses. The cost of operation of a company.

Federal income tax. Money withheld from a paycheck and paid to the federal government as a tax on wages earned.

Fixed assets. Those assets with a long life that will be used over many years in the operation of the company.

Full endorsement. Also called a two-party check; transfers the check to a specified person or organization by the endorsement.

Gross profit on sales. The difference between revenue and the cost of the merchandise sold.

Health insurance (HI). Commonly called Medicare; one of the two taxes required for all employees by the federal government.

Income statement. Also called a profit and loss (P & L) statement or an operating statement, this is a financial record showing the results of the operation of a company in terms of money earned and expenses incurred.

Liabilities. What is owed.

Long-term liabilities. Debts due for long periods.

Master budget. Consists of various budgets that collectively express the future activities of the business.

Medicare. Federal health insurance.

Net pay. Total earnings minus deductions.

Old Age, Survivors, and Disability Insurance, (OASDI). Commonly called social security; one of the two taxes required for all employees by the federal government.

Outstanding checks. Checks written but not paid by the bank.

Overtime hours. Any hours worked over the first forty hours in a payroll period.

Owner's equity. What a business is worth.

Payee. Person to whom payment is to be made.

Payroll register. A record that summarizes, for each employee, the status of wages earned, payroll deductions, and final take-home pay.

Perpetual inventory record. A record used to keep track of office supplies inventory.

Petty cash fund. A fund used to provide cash for the purchase of incidental office items and services.

Petty cash voucher. A receipt for each expenditure from the petty cash fund.

Plant and equipment. Those assets, also called fixed assets, with a long life that will be used over many years in the operation of the company such as buildings and land.

Regular hours. The first forty hours worked in a payroll period.

Restrictive endorsement. Limits the use of a check to the purpose stated in the endorsement, such as "Pay to the order of."

Stop-payment notification. A notice to stop payment on a check for a fee at any time until the check has cleared the bank upon which it is drawn.

Telephone transfers. Payments made by telephone.

Total earnings. Regular earnings plus overtime earnings.

Traveler's checks. Checks used in place of cash.

Web banking. A service that provides easy management of banking transactions online wherever a person has access to the Internet.

For Your Discussion

 Retrieve file C8-DQ.DOC from your student data disk.

Directions

Enter your response after each question.

1. Name the various check endorsements and explain how each is used.

2. Summarize the steps for completing a petty cash record.

3. What is EFT and what are some of the ways it is used?

4. When you replenish the petty cash fund, how do you determine the amount of money to request?

5. Summarize the steps for completing a payroll register.

6. Summarize the steps for reconciling a bank statement.

7. What is included on an income statement and how does it help management?

8. What is included on a balance sheet and how does it help management?

9. What is the function of a budget committee?

10. Summarize the procedures for efficiently keeping up with office supplies.

BUSINESS MATH WORKSHOP

Handling financial tasks requires the use of business math skills. Even though you will likely use a calculator or a computerized spreadsheet, your basic math skills will be needed to ensure that your work is error-free. In order to use a spreadsheet, you will need to know how to work with formulas.

More than likely you have already been introduced to the term *formula*. A formula is an equation in which all the terms are represented by letters. The concept relating to formulas is an important one because many questions or issues in business and in other areas involve the use of formulas. For instance, what if you needed to know the answer to the following basic business questions?

a. What is 13 percent of 92.20? (finding the part, sometimes called percentage)
b. 11.34 is what percent of 75.40? (finding the rate)
c. 9.75 is 12 percent of what amount? (finding the base)

Each question can be answered based on knowing the part, rate, or base formula. These formulas are the most commonly used formulas in business. Applying the part formula, you can calculate commissions, percent of increase or decrease, discounts, and sales tax.

Review the part formulas in Appendix A to answer the question: What is 13 percent of 92.20?

For Review

Appendix A: Business Math

 Retrieve file C8-WRKS.DOC from your data disk.

Directions

Sometimes office workers have difficulty determining the solution to a business application involving the part formula because they cannot identify the part. Before you determine the part, rate, and base, complete this exercise by identifying each part. Use a ? for the part unknown. Do not calculate the answers.

Exercise 1

1. 31 is what percent of 125?
   Part _____
   Rate _____
   Base _____

2. 15 is 70 percent of what number?
   Part _____
   Rate _____
   Base _____

3. What is 1.43 percent of 450?

Part _____

Rate _____

Base _____

4. 23 is 50 percent of what number?

Part _____

Rate _____

Base _____

5. 25 is what percent of 235?

Part _____

Rate _____

Base _____

6. What is 2.9 percent of 330?

Part _____

Rate _____

Base _____

Exercise 2

Find the part in each of the following problems. Carry your answers to two decimal places.

1. 20 percent of 340 is _____

2. 1.37 percent of 120 is _____

3. 3 percent of 969 is _____

4. 13.2 percent of 260 is _____

5. 33 percent of 139.98 is _____

On the Job Situations

 Retrieve file C8-OJS.DOC from your student data disk.

Directions

Enter your response after each situation.

1. Your boss is out of town and calls to tell you that his briefcase was stolen from his hotel room this afternoon. He had locked his remaining traveler's checks in the briefcase. He is frantic and doesn't know what to do. Analyze the situation and outline a plan of action for him, assuming you have followed all the correct procedures concerning traveler's checks.

2. You are new on the job. Because you keep the petty cash fund, Leah, a coworker, has come to you and asked to borrow $10 until tomorrow.

Other employees have told you that the manager does not care if they borrow from petty cash. No one has asked you until today. Analyze the situation and explain what you would do and why.

3. You supervise the payroll department. Several department heads have recently been late in turning in time cards, and your employees have been complaining that they are rushed and believe that being rushed has caused them to make the careless errors in employees' paychecks that have been reported. It is budget time, and you know your manager wants the department heads to get their budget recommendations in—they are under pressure to finish. Explain how you will handle the situation.

4. You have been responsible for handling the petty cash fund in your department. The money and petty cash receipts are kept in a drawer that is locked, and both you and your manager have keys to the drawer. When you attempt to balance your receipts and cash remaining in the drawer, you realize that $50 is missing from the fund. After an employee borrowed from the fund on Monday, you balanced the fund; it is now Thursday. Analyze the situation and explain what you would do and why.

Projects and Activities

1. Interview an office professional and ask him or her about the methods used for setting up a budget each year. Identify the process in a step-by-step approach—what does he or she do first, second, third, and so on. Summarize your findings, including the steps.

2. Call two local banks, credit unions, or other financial institutions and obtain information about certified checks, official checks, bank drafts, money orders, traveler's checks, ATM charges, and whether or not you can electronically pay your utilities if you have a computer and modem and what the charge is, if any. Write a comparison of what you found at the two banking institutions.

3. If you have a job, ask if someone is in charge of the petty cash fund at your workplace. Interview that person and write a report on the procedures followed. If you do not work, ask someone you know who works to find out at his or her job, or call local companies and ask to set up an interview. Explain that you are completing a class project.

4. Locate exchange rates for six countries. Create a table showing the country, the current exchange rate, and the amount of foreign currency you would be able to obtain for $75 U.S.

Surfing the Internet

You may have heard on the news about people being robbed at ATM machines and the importance of being safe when withdrawing money. The American Bankers Association offers some consumer tips for ATM safety on the Internet. Follow these procedures to locate the tips:

1. Connect to the Internet.

2. Enter the following: http://www.aba.com.

3. Locate Consumer Connection at the left of the screen. Click on ATMs under Banking Services, and read the ATM Safety Tips article. Print a copy and summarize the information in a report. Include what you think are the three most important tips.

4. Locate information about the Federal Reserve System, and how it acts as a clearinghouse for checks, by searching the key words *federal reserve bank system.*

5. Browse and read about the Federal Reserve System. Print any information you need.

6. Summarize the information and write a report about the Federal Reserve System. Explain how the Federal Reserve System affects you as an employee, consumer, and citizen.

Using MS Office 2002

Create a Travel Log

 Situation: You need a way to keep up with personal car mileage for local meetings and errands.

Solution: An Excel worksheet with column information that automatically calculates the rate allowed times the mileage traveled.

1. Open Microsoft Excel. From a new worksheet, type the information shown in the following table into the cells indicated.

	A	B	C	D	E	F
1	Date	Name	Purpose	Roundtrip mileage	Rate	Total
2	04/13/02	Jeff Stoner	Met with Jen Long at Curtis Electric	10	0.35	
3	04/30/02	Jeff Stoner	Picked up Sue Carey at airport	30	0.35	
4	05/04/02	Steve Adams	Picked up supplies from Office Depot	18	0.35	
5						
6						

Tip: To create the heading for column D, type **Roundtrip Mileage** and then position the cursor between the two words. Hold down the Alt key and press Enter.

2. Click in cell F2.

3. Key the equals sign (=) or press the equals sign on the Formula bar.

4. Point to cell D2, key an asterisk (*), and then point to E2 and press Enter. This formula will multiply D2 by E2.

5. Copy the formula down column F. Make F2 the active cell, click on the Edit menu, then click on Copy or press the Copy button on the standard toolbar. Select the range F2 : F4 and press Enter. The formula will be copied down the column.

6. Format cells F2 : F4 as currency:

   a. Select cells F2 : F4.

   b. Click on the Format menu and select Cells.

    c. Click on the Number tab and select *Currency* from the drop-down list.

    d. Accept 2 decimal places and the $ symbol.

    e. Click on OK.

    f. Press the Esc key to remove the flashing border.

7. Print according to your instructor's directions.

APPLICATION PROBLEMS

APPLICATION 8–A

Handling Petty Cash

Supplies needed: Form 8-A-1, Petty Cash Envelope; Forms 8-A-2 through 8-A-13, Petty Cash Vouchers.

 Retrieve file AP8-A-1.DOC from your data disk.

Directions: Mary Higgins, who had been handling petty cash transactions for the marketing division, was transferred to another division, and you were asked to handle petty cash.

    You started with the beginning balance of $100.00 in the petty cash envelope. In the "Received" column, write $100.00.

    You paid out cash for the following items. Complete each of the voucher forms (Forms 8-A-2 through 8-A-10) for each of the following transactions.

December 1	Paid Meyers Stationery $3.69 for special drawing pen. (Supplies)
December 3	Paid U. S. Postmaster $29.00 for mailing box priority mail. (Postage)
December 3	Paid U. S. Postmaster $6.85 for postage and insurance on a package. (Postage)
December 4	Paid City Taxi $8.50 to deliver a package to Airlift Shipping office. (Miscellaneous)
December 5	Paid Williams Drugstore $5.25 for two magazines for the reception area. (Supplies)
December 8	Paid B. J. Florist $15.50 for a plant for the reception area. (Miscellaneous)
December 8	Paid Williams Drugstore $6.80 for fertilizer tablets for plants at the office. (Miscellaneous)
December 9	Paid Western Union $15.95 for a telephone-delivered telegram. (Miscellaneous)
December 9	Paid Meyers Stationery $4.25 for box of No. 10 plain envelopes. (Supplies)

    Your ending balance in the fund is $4.21. On the petty cash envelope record the totals for the Paid Out and the Distribution of Payments columns. Carry the balance forward to the Received column but label it as "balance." Type a petty cash report in a memo format and ask for enough money to bring the petty cash fund to $100.00. Attach the petty cash vouchers to the report. You are authorized to sign the vouchers.

APPLICATION 8-B

Bank Reconciliation

Supplies Needed: Copy of Figure 8-2, Bank Statement; Form 8-B-1, Bank Reconciliation Form.

 Retrieve file AP8-B-1.DOC from your data disk.

Directions: On November 26 you received the bank statement for the November Sales Seminar account for Supreme Appliances shown in Figure 8-2, page 247. On November 23 you received a check from Al's Print Shop for $170.00 as a 10 percent discount for paying promptly. You mailed this check to the bank, but it is not shown on the bank statement. You have checked off all the canceled checks and the following checks are outstanding and have not been paid by the bank:

No. 2111	$386.50
No. 2115	$ 52.40
No. 2120	$110.80
No. 2121	$ 12.15

A service charge of $20.00 has been charged to your account.

Ending balance in the checkbook was $6,430.55. Reconcile the bank statement shown in Figure 8-2 using Form 8-B-1. Key the bank reconciliation.

APPLICATION 8-C

Payroll

Supplies needed: Form 8-C-1, Weekly Payroll Register; or spreadsheet software.

 Retrieve file AP8C1.XLS from your data disk.

Directions: You are filling in for John Lehew, the company payroll clerk, who is on vacation. Follow the steps given in the chapter to complete the payroll below.

1. Retrieve the file AP8C1.XLS from your student data disk.
2. Use a spreadsheet file to complete the payroll register. If you do not have access to spreadsheet software, complete by hand the payroll register shown on Form 8-C-1.
3. Print one copy of the completed payroll if you are using a spreadsheet.

Your Action Plan

Complete Your Action Plan; if necessary, review the guidelines in Chapter 1. Set one goal using the information in Chapter 8.

Your Portfolio

With the help of your instructor, select the best papers representative of your work from Chapter 8. Follow your instructor's directions about formatting, assembling, and turning in the portfolio.

Providing Customer Service, Scheduling Appointments, and Receiving Visitors

OUTLINE

Providing Excellent Customer Service

Making Appointments
Keeping an Appointment Schedule
Making Appointments by Telephone or E-Mail
Using the Electronic Calendar
Using Web-Based Calendars
Using Paper Desk Calendars
Making Entries in Desk Calendars
Canceling Appointments
Preparing a List of Appointments

Receiving Visitors
Greeting Visitors
Attending to the Visitor Who Has an Appointment
Attending to Staff Visitors
Terminating Conferences
Interrupting a Meeting
Attending to Unscheduled Visitors
Refusing Appointments

Handling Difficult Customers
Dealing with Unwanted Callers

Hosting International Visitors

LEARNING OUTCOMES

When you have completed this chapter, you should be able to:
- ✔ Apply good customer service techniques.
- ✔ Schedule and confirm appointments for one or more managers.
- ✔ Use appropriate scheduling aids.
- ✔ Greet and direct visitors.
- ✔ Manage difficult customers.
- ✔ Host international visitors.

Every time you meet another person, whether a visitor or coworker, you are affecting that person's image of your company, department, or office. You should work toward ensuring that each person you deal with believes that you sincerely want to help him or her. The impression you leave will make each person want to come back again.

In this chapter you will learn how to create a positive company image by providing excellent customer service, using scheduling aids, making appointments, and receiving visitors.

PROVIDING EXCELLENT CUSTOMER SERVICE

Organizations have customer service departments that devote full time to creating and maintaining a favorable image of the organization. However, public relations do not begin and end with a customer service department. Every employee who deals with people from inside or outside the organization is engaged in customer service, a vital aspect of office work.

As an office professional, whenever you talk with people over the telephone and in person, you represent the organization. To people who deal only with you, *you are* the organization. The first impression and the lasting impression that you make with your voice, your appearance, and your self-expression must be favorable. Your personality, as well, must be pleasing to others. You create the atmosphere in which your manager must discharge his or her responsibilities by the way you respond to people within and outside your organization. Remember the saying, "You only have one opportunity to make a first impression."

Here are some customer service tips to help you excel in serving your customers:

- Take pride in your work—especially in how you serve every customer both internally and externally.
- When a person appears, immediately acknowledge him or her with a nod, even if you are on the phone.
- Maintain good eye contact at all times. Never act distracted or impatient.
- Identify yourself by name and title. Say: "I'm Kim Ahan, Mr. Gray's assistant. How may I help you?"
- If a customer has to wait for any reason, always explain why.
- Tell the customer what you can do, not what you can't do.
- Always do what you say you'll do in a timely manner.
- Always return all calls and e-mails.
- Always invite the customer back by saying: "Please come back to see us again *(and mean it!)*."
- Remember, if you ask the customer if he or she was satisfied, be prepared if the answer is "No, I wasn't."

You should go that extra mile to make a visitor feel special. Making a visitor feel special—that you are concerned only with giving him or her your undivided attention—at that moment creates the image of a company that offers outstanding customer service. In today's competitive business world, excellent customer service is noticed and can make your company rise above competitors, which often can increase your company's image as well as profits.

MAKING APPOINTMENTS

Who makes appointments for managers? The answer is both managers and their assistants. The freedom that an office professional is given in making appointments depends on the office professional's ability to schedule the manager's time exactly as he or she wants it scheduled. From the first day on the job, you will have two distinct responsibilities concerning your manager's appointments: to keep track of all appointments so that one is not overlooked, and to keep both your manager's appointment calendar and yours up-to-the-minute to avoid conflicts in scheduling.

Keeping an Appointment Schedule

You and your manager will need to keep to an appointment schedule. Begin by learning (1) your manager's preferences for scheduling appointments, (2) which appointments should be given priority, and (3) how much time appointments should take.

Your best guides for scheduling appointments will be your knowledge of your manager's work habits and your awareness of who his or her business associates and friends are. You will learn this by observing how your manager uses time and works with associates and by being aware of your manager's plans. Remember what your manager tells you about how he or she works best. His or her work habits may vary with the peaks and valleys of the job. Someone once said that the busier one is, the more work one manages to get done. Your manager may be a person who speeds up when the workload is heavy, scheduling just as many appointments, but allowing less time for each caller than during a normal workweek.

Couple your knowledge of how your manager plans work with the previous overall suggestions and use them as guides in setting up appointments.

Making Appointments by Telephone or E-Mail

When someone requests an appointment by telephone or e-mail, establish immediately whether your manager is the person the caller should see. You will be able to decide this as soon as the caller tells you the reason for requesting an appointment.

If your manager has to approve all appointments, tell the caller that you must confirm the appointment and that you will let the caller know if the appointment has been set as soon as you can check with the manager. Be sure to follow through on what you say you will do. Check with your manager and then call the person or send an e-mail message confirming the appointment.

Office professionals that work for executives, doctors, and dentists usually finalize an appointment during the initial telephone conversation. You may be charged with responsibility for making your manager's appointments, and when you are, you can eliminate almost all follow-up telephone calls. Give the caller a definite appointment. If you have any doubt about your manager confirming it, say, "I will call you back immediately if there should be a conflict that I do not know about." This method is the opposite of following through on all appointments to confirm them.

Make sure that both you and the person seeking the appointment understand the correct time, date, and location. While you are talking on the telephone, repeat the date, day, and time and write them down or enter them into

How to Set Up Appointments

✔ Leave Monday mornings free to start on plans for the week and to handle the mail that has accumulated during the weekend.

✔ Schedule no appointments for your manager on his or her first day back after being out of the office for several days.

✔ Avoid crowding your manager's schedule with appointments the day before he or she leaves on a trip. Preparation for the trip has priority.

✔ Schedule appointments so that they will not overlap.

✔ Be aware of top-priority conferences and allow plenty of time for them.

✔ Avoid scheduling a top-priority conference immediately after one of equal significance.

✔ Avoid scheduling an appointment for your manager in another location immediately after a conference that is likely to run overtime.

✔ Schedule unstructured time frames of ten to fifteen minutes between appointments, giving your manager a chance to make telephone calls, sign letters, think about the next conference, or just take a break.

✔ Schedule appointments with others with whom your manager has a close working relationship late in the afternoon. These appointments are easy to shift when your manager is not keeping to the schedule.

✔ At the time someone is requesting an appointment by telephone, suggest specific times, preferably giving the person a chance to select a time from at least two choices.

✔ Predetermine regularly scheduled times for answering the mail and taking care of other daily activities and consistently reserve the time slots for these activities.

✔ Learn which conferences can be limited to fifteen minutes or less.

✔ When you are arranging an appointment for a short period, let the person know the length of the appointment. If you are setting up the appointment for 2 p.m., say tactfully, "from 2 until 2:15."

✔ When you arrange for an unexpected visitor to see your manager, let the visitor know that the next appointment is within ten minutes if it truly is.

✔ Arrange appointments in another part of the city so that your manager, if he or she chooses, can go directly from home to an early-morning appointment or not return to the office after a late-afternoon appointment.

your calendar immediately to reduce the chance of a mistake. Ask callers if they need directions to your location. Unless you already have it, be sure to get the telephone number and e-mail address of each person who makes an appointment. You will need it to confirm the appointment, or you may need it to change the time of a definite appointment.

Using the Electronic Calendar

The traditional calendar has been turned into something that will stagger the imagination, all because of the personal computer. If your organization has a fully integrated electronic network, you will be able to use an **electronic calendar** (see Figure 9-1) that is on your computer or network to schedule all of your manager's appointments. Office automation systems are available that enable the user to switch from one function to another with a simple keystroke (Alt + Tab in Microsoft Office) or movement of the mouse. You can exit an application, such as word processing, to enter appointments, rearrange the schedule to make substitutions, or cancel appointments and then quickly return to the application.

Automated calendaring systems allow you to have an accurate, up-to-the-minute schedule. You can also enter items in the tickler file, add reminders, and note any items that need to be acted on at a definite time of the day. The page on the screen looks the same as the page in a desk calendar. You can select a meeting time by comparing your manager's schedule with that of others on the network, who make their calendars available.

You need to keep only one computerized calendar because either you or your manager can access the calendar at any time. At the end of the day, you can print or type your manager's schedule for the next business day and place it on his or her desk.

Certain major software programs combine several functions with the calendar. An example is Microsoft Outlook. It takes managing your schedule and information a step further than just a calendar. Outlook allows you to juggle everything from electronic mail and calendars to contacts and task

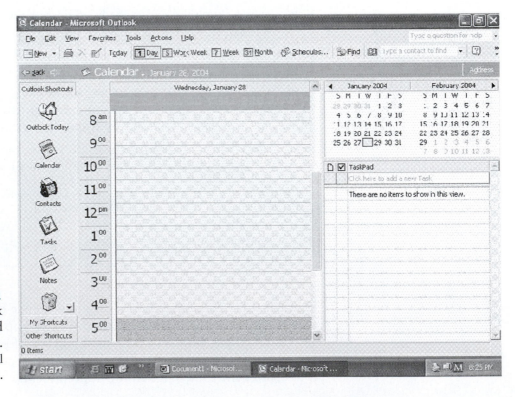

■ **Figure 9-1**
Microsoft Outlook electronic calendar displayed on a computer screen.

lists. You can "connect, communicate, and collaborate," says Microsoft. Here are some of the things Microsoft Outlook enables you to do:

- Publish calendars as Web pages
- Schedule group meetings
- Send and receive e-mail messages
- Manage client information—tracking their locations and scheduling meetings
- Manage multiple e-mail accounts

Using Web-Based Calendars

Web-based calendars are calendars available for use free on the Internet (see Figure 9-2). The Internet is taking electronic calendars a step further as well. The best part is they are free. These calendars are scaled-down versions of the all-in-one scheduling, e-mail, and address-book software that you find on your desktop computer. In the long run, Web calendars will be more useful for the following reasons:

- They store information online; therefore, accessibility is a major advantage.
- They are communal, plugged in, and wired to the world.
- They are available in various languages.
- They are integrated with e-mail, address books, instant messaging, and areas where community groups can publish material (see http://www.calendar.yahoo.com).

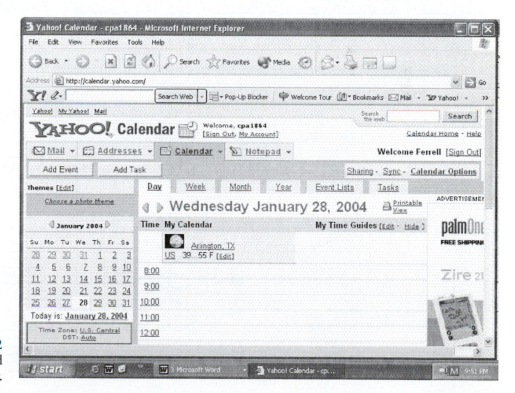

■ **Figure 9-2**
Yahoo! free Web-based calendar.

■ Three levels of permission may be offered. Events can be made totally private, totally visible to everyone from anywhere on the Web, or a hybrid in which other people can see which time slots are booked but not for what purpose (see http://www.calendar.yahoo.com).

The Web-based calendars are becoming important tools in the struggle to attract loyal audiences to commercial sites.

Using Paper Desk Calendars

Many organizations that use computers do not perform all their business activities on the computer. The computer's capacity may be limited, and word processing, database management, and accounting functions may be given priority. Your manager may have the responsibility of keeping his or her own calendar and may prefer not to take the time to enter information in computerized software because of the number of entries and changes required. As a result, you may need to use desk calendars to keep appointments.

Choose appointment calendars and yearbooks that meet both your manager's needs and yours. A wide selection is available, and they are made in a variety of sizes with a choice of a page for each month, a page for each week, or a page for each day. Figure 9-3 shows a monthly calendar.

Executive Appointment Books and Calendars. Managers who make commitments months in advance like a full month displayed on one page with small in-

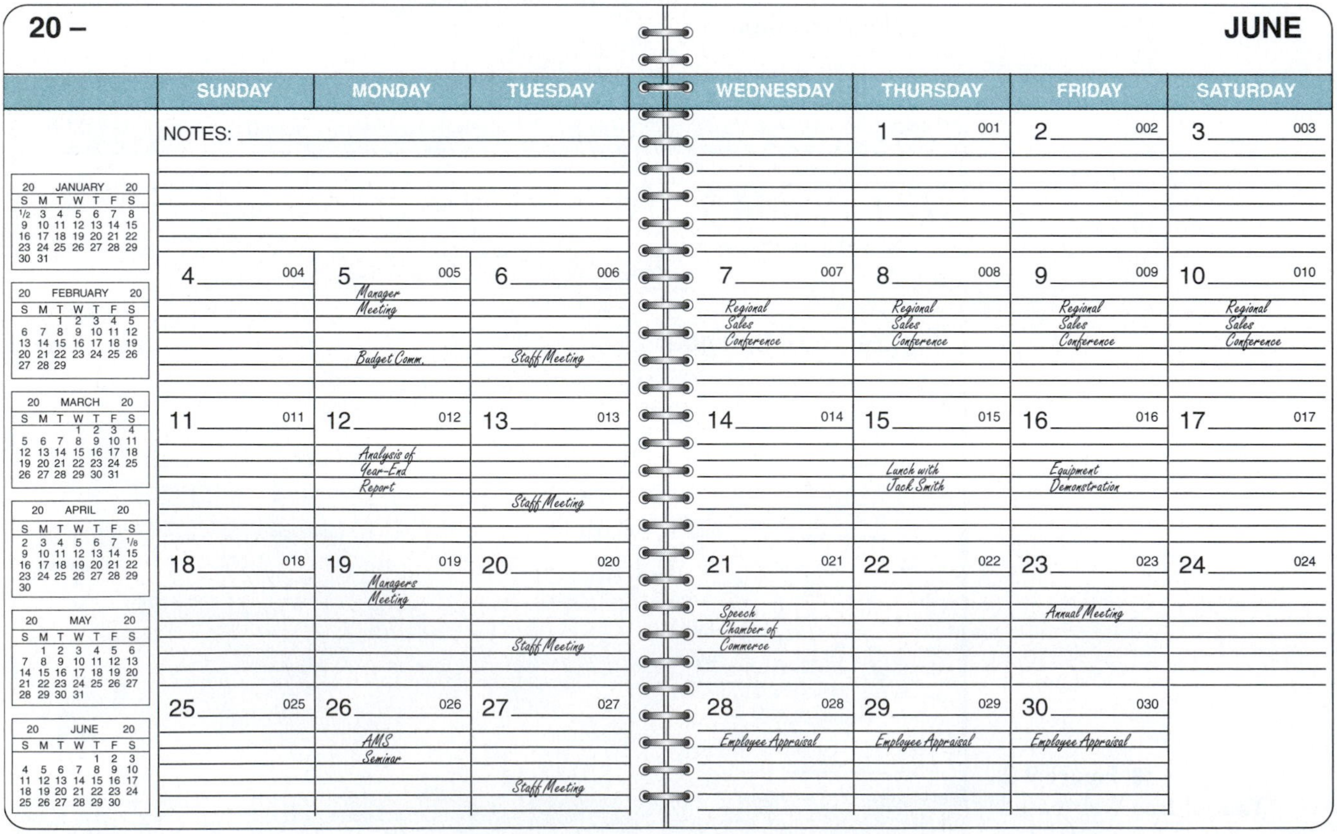

■ **Figure 9-3**
Monthly calendar.

sert calendars of the preceding and the following months. The monthly calendar enables them to review engagements without flipping through several pages. Managers who make several appointments in one day need a daily appointment calendar. Many managers prefer pocket calendars or small **electronic organizers** that include a calendar, scheduler, and address area for immediate access.

The Office Professional's Daily Appointment Calendar. If you are not using an electronic calendar, on your desk you need a preprinted calendar divided into fifteen- or thirty-minute segments of each day, with the time printed in the left column. See Figure 9-4.

Enter in your calendar all your manager's appointments, everything you must remind your manager of that must be taken care of within a given time slot, and a list of all the activities that must be followed through by your manager at the end of the day. Also enter in your calendar, but not your manager's, reminders of the items you must take care of at a specified time. In addition, prepare a to-do list to remind you of other tasks that you must perform at some time during the day.

DATE		Monday, December 9, 20--
8	00 / 15 / 30 / 45	
9	00 / 15 / 30 / 45	Call for hotel reservation / R. C. Thompson, ABC Corp.
10	00 / 15 / 30 / 45	Manager's
11	00 / 15 / 30 / 45	Explain procedure / Ruth Raines, Adv.
12	00 / 15 / 30 / 45	
1	00 / 15 / 30 / 45	Interview Applicant— / Jane Albright
2	00 / 15 / 30 / 45	Assemble forms / Len Smith, Forms Design
3	00 / 15 / 30 / 45	Interview Applicant— / Louise Petruzza
4	00 / 15 / 30 / 45	Complete Proposal / Meet Jane Hunter — Airport
5	00 / 15 / 30 / 45	
6	00 / 15 / 30 / 45	AMA Meeting

■ **Figure 9-4**
Daily appointment calendar.

Making Entries in Desk Calendars

All appointments made by telephone, by e-mail, by letter, and in person—including those your manager makes—should be entered in both the manager's and your appointment calendars. Regularly scheduled meetings should also be entered in the appointment calendars.

Be consistent and prompt in recording all appointments and commitments in your manager's calendar. To do this, adopt a systematic plan for making the entries and then do not deviate from your plan.

Make tentative entries in pencil and firm commitments in ink. As soon as the appointment is confirmed, write it in ink in both calendars. Write small enough to put complete information in the space provided in the calendar. Draw a diagonal line through each entry once the conference is held or the task is completed; then you will readily know that any item not crossed out is yet to be completed.

Record an appointment confirmed by an incoming letter at the time you are processing the incoming mail or checking e-mail; record an appointment confirmed in an outgoing letter as an immediate follow-up to keyboarding the letter or e-mail message. When you grant an appointment by letter, obviously you would check with your manager before you write the letter.

You may need to request information about appointments that your manager makes, especially those that your manager makes while away from the office. Do this at least once a day. If your manager spends a few minutes each morning discussing the work for the day, ask your manager then or suggest that he or she jot down the information and hand it to you soon after the appointment is made.

Once each day, preferably at the end of the day, check your manager's daily calendar with yours to make sure that all recorded appointments are identical in both calendars.

At the end of each day, review the items for that day in search of an item that has not been crossed out. In fact, never turn the page of your calendar until you have searched for incomplete items. Transfer any item that still needs attention to the page for the following business day.

When you are uncertain whether or not your manager returned a telephone call or followed through on a promise he or she made, type a separate note concerning each item you think might be incomplete at the time you are clearing your calendar. As you check these with your manager, you can throw away the unnecessary notes and give your manager the others as reminders to follow through on them.

Once each week, either on Friday afternoon or on Monday morning, check your follow-up file for the entire week. Make notations, if you have not already done so, in both appointment calendars concerning work that must be completed by a specified time within the week.

Canceling Appointments

When someone calls to cancel an appointment, offer to schedule another one. Be sure to free both appointment calendars, if you keep two calendars, of the canceled appointment.

When you must cancel an appointment for your manager, let the person whose appointment is being canceled know at once. Get in touch with the person by telephone or e-mail.

Use the following guidelines for canceling an appointment:

- Express regret on your manager's behalf.
- Mention that the appointment must be changed.
- State a reason in general terms.
- Offer to schedule another appointment.

Think twice about how you are going to state the reason. You can say that your manager was called out of town, if he or she was, but as a general rule do not say where or why. By doing so you could reveal confidential information. Avoid dwelling on what your manager cannot do. Quickly shift your conversation to a positive comment, such as, "She is expected back in the office on Monday. Shall I set up another appointment for you early next week?"

Preparing a List of Appointments

Some managers prefer to have a separate list of appointments for each day, such as the one shown in Figure 9-5. If so, near the end of each day, prepare your manager's list of appointments for the next business day in a form that he or she prefers. Keep a duplicate copy on your desk. If you are using a computer to keep the appointment calendar, a printout may be sufficient.

APPOINTMENTS FOR MONDAY, MAY 25, 20--	
TIME	APPOINTMENT
0800	Meet with Dini Corbett to discuss ACCC promotions. Remember to take the F. P. Manufacturing folder.
0930	Interview Linda Nimchuck (applicant for Office Manager).
1100	Meet with Total Management Committee - Room 520. Connie Walters should be contacted prior to meeting for info. on the conference.
1200	Lunch with Sandy Wolfe at the Pasta Place.
1400	Pick up Edward Kaye at the Greater Rochester International Airport.
1600	Meet with Edward Kaye, Heather Thomas, Ben Ross and Amelia Taylor in the boardroom located on the first floor. Copies of the plan for new equipment purchase are attached. Don't forget to take info. on tax concessions.
1800	Speak at IAAP meeting, Rose Room, Ramada Inn. A copy of the program and your speech are attached. Good luck!

■ **Figure 9-5**
List of appointments.

When you keyboard the list, arrange it so that it is easy to read. Use an appropriate heading. For example, if you are keyboarding lists for more than one person, include the person's name in the heading. For each appointment, indicate the time, the name of the caller, his or her affiliation, and the purpose of the visit. Also, include reminders, such as a dinner meeting or a commitment to meet someone at the airport. When an appointment is someplace other than your manager's office, indicate clearly where it will be.

RECEIVING VISITORS

Receiving office visitors is an important part of office work, requiring the office professional to be gracious and diplomatic at all times and courteous to all visitors. In your contact with visitors, put forth a special effort to represent your manager and your organization favorably. Your duties are threefold:

1. To carry out your manager's wishes
2. To make friends for your manager and the organization
3. To help visitors, within the policy limitations of the organization, to accomplish their purposes for coming to your office

In some organizations the office professional serves as the receptionist and is the first person the visitor meets. Large organizations usually have a reception area in the lobby near the main entrance to the building, and all visitors check in with the receptionist. Sometimes there are receptionists on more than one floor. A visitor tells the receptionist with whom he or she has an appointment, and then the receptionist calls the manager's assistant.

Whether an organization does or does not have a receptionist, the office professional usually receives the visitor before the visitor is admitted to the manager's office. Therefore, regard receiving visitors as a regular part of your job. As you plan your work, allow time for receiving visitors.

Among the visitors who come to see your manager will be visitors from outside the organization. Many will have appointments and some will not. Some may be employees who report directly to your manager; others may be managers and supervisors within the organization—including your manager's superiors—friends, and members of your manager's family.

Find out your manager's policy for seeing visitors. What you need to know most of all is whom your manager will not see and to whom, if anyone, you should direct these visitors. Organizations do strive to make friends of all visitors. Therefore, the policy could be to arrange for visitors, with few exceptions, to see someone within the organization for a few minutes at least.

An office professional can easily make the mistake of being too protective of the manager's time, turning away visitors whom the manager should see. As a result, the office professional could destroy favorable relationships that already exist or that could develop between the manager and others. Guard against being overly protective of your manager's time. When you are uncertain, either make an appointment for the visitor or ask if your manager will see the visitor.

Be especially courteous to visitors you must turn away. How to arrange an appointment for a visitor with someone else in the organization and how to refuse appointments are discussed later in this chapter.

Greeting Visitors

Visitors are influenced by their first impressions of the office and the office professional. A favorable first impression, along with your courteous efforts to make visitors feel welcome, will create a receptive climate in which your manager can develop and maintain a good rapport with others. The visitor's first impression should be that of an efficient assistant working in a well-organized office.

One of your duties will be to keep your office in order. A busy office does not have to be cluttered. To maintain a well-organized office:

1. designate and use specific locations for supplies, files, and work-in-progress
2. remember that completion of each task includes "putting away"
3. follow through by clearing your desk of materials you are not using

If you continually put away items you are not using so that nothing accumulates, the few items you have on your desk will enhance the appearance of your office.

Immediate Attention. Your job is to make all visitors, whether they have appointments or not, feel at ease. When a visitor comes directly to your office, you should greet the visitor the minute he or she arrives. As the visitor approaches your desk, look at the visitor directly, smile graciously, and speak immediately. Nobody likes to be ignored, even for a few seconds. To continue keyboarding until you reach the end of the line or paragraph or to continue reading copy is extremely rude. To continue chatting with another employee is inexcusable. If you are talking on the telephone, the visitor probably will hesitate before approaching your desk. Immediately nod and smile so that the visitor will know that you are aware of his or her presence.

Manage to put your materials out of sight of glancing eyes without shuffling papers in the visitor's presence. By keeping the materials on which you are working in a folder, you can unobtrusively close a folder as a visitor nears your desk.

Greet an office visitor by saying, "Good morning" or "Good afternoon." Use the visitor's name if you know it. If you are expecting a visitor whom you do not know, but you are sure who he or she is, use the visitor's name. The greeting goes something like: "Good morning, Mr. Slattery, I'm Chris Rogers, Mr. Wilmont's assistant. Mr. Wilmont is expecting you." When you receive visitors for several managers, do not guess who they are. Wait for visitors to introduce themselves; they will.

The atmosphere within many organizations is informal, and employees call their managers by their first names when visitors are not present. However, you should always call your manager by his or her last name when you are speaking of your manager and when you are addressing your manager in the presence of others.

Advance Preparation. Your manager may need materials from the files—correspondence and records—to refer to during conferences. Anticipate what materials will be needed and locate them the day before, even though you do not remove them from the files until the next morning. Find out if your manager wants to review the material in advance of the meeting (see Figure 9-6).

■ **Figure 9-6**
An assistant works with the manager to determine preparation needed for scheduled meetings.

If not, take the materials your manager will use during a conference to his or her office just before the conference.

You may have to compile data or collect information from other departments. Get an early start on these tasks so that you will have the information ready when it is needed. In fact, present information you compile enough in advance for your manager to review it adequately prior to discussing it with someone else.

Your manager will often need special materials for meetings. Anticipate the needed items and have them ready. They will be varied; for example, they could be notes taken during a previous committee meeting; printed brochures to be distributed at a department meeting; slides or overhead transparencies and a projector used to supplement a talk your manager is giving as an after-dinner speaker; a list of the names, addresses, and affiliations of new members of a professional group; a copy of shipping procedures and proposed revisions to discuss with your manager's superior; or whatever is related to the purpose of the meeting.

Attending to the Visitor Who Has an Appointment

Make the visitor feel comfortable. Indicate where to leave his or her coat and escort the visitor to your manager's office. Pronounce both the visitor's name and your manager's name distinctly when you introduce them. The business relationship, not the social rule of introducing the man to the woman, or the younger to the older person, is the guide for making introductions in business. A visitor who has a name that is difficult to pronounce will not mind if you ask him or her to pronounce it for you. Mention the visitor's affiliation or the purpose of the visit. Say, "Mr. Wilmont, this is Mrs. Harris of R. C. Products." Stand to one side, not between your manager and the visitor, as you make the introduction. If your manager knows the caller, you can be less formal. As soon as your manager is available, you can invite the caller to go in or you can open the door, if it is closed, and say, "Mr. Wilmont, Mrs. Harris." If appropriate, you may offer the visitor a beverage or ask your manager if anything is needed before you leave.

Invite visitors who must wait to have a seat. Keep current magazines, the morning paper, and other interesting reading material nearby so callers who must wait for any length of time can read. You are not expected to entertain the visitor by carrying on a conversation while he or she is waiting. You can continue with your work.

A visitor who arrives early expects to wait until the time for the appointment. However, when your manager is free, tell him or her immediately that the visitor has arrived and ask if he or she is ready to see the visitor. Eventually you will learn your manager's preference about seeing visitors ahead of the appointed time. It will depend on who the visitor is, the purpose of the visit, and tasks that your manager must complete between appointments.

A visitor who has an appointment should not be kept waiting. The visitor's time is valuable, too, and asking the visitor to wait is inconsiderate. Nevertheless, a manager who has numerous appointments in one day may have difficulty keeping to an appointment schedule and, when the manager does have difficulty, visitors will have to wait. Having visitors wait occurs even though the manager and the office professional are making a real effort to usher visitors in and out in the time allotted. When a delay occurs, assure the visitor that the wait will not be long. When you say "Mr. Wilmont should be available in a few minutes," you can sound reassuring. Use this statement only when you anticipate that the ongoing conference is almost over.

The real test of how well you receive office visitors lies in what you say and what you do when the wait will be long. First of all, do not let your actions reveal that the day is hectic. When emergencies occur or the day is not going smoothly, regardless of the reason, slow down, put some of your own work on tomorrow's list, and approach visitors in a very relaxed manner. Give the visitor the impression that your only duty at the moment is to meet his or her needs. Your relaxed manner will be contagious.

Be cautious about how you state the reasons for a delay. You can apologize and say that all appointments are running behind schedule, but do not explain why. Avoid statements referring to important business, problems, or inefficiency. The visitor is thinking about what is happening to his or her time and wants to know how long the wait will be. If the wait will be very long, tell the visitor approximately how long. The visitor may decide to make an appointment for later in the same day or for another day.

Do not forget about a visitor. Reassure the visitor. If you can judge that a conference is ending, turn to the visitor and indicate that it is. If a visitor whose appointment is delayed cannot wait any longer and tells you that he or she must leave, offer to make another appointment and volunteer that your manager will call. Write yourself a note to follow up, for this visitor has been inconvenienced and deserves special attention.

Attending to Staff Visitors

A difficult aspect of every manager's job is maintaining two-way communication with the employees who report directly to him or her. In spite of a manager's effort to establish an easy flow of two-way communication, breakdowns occur and misunderstandings arise, frequently resulting in personnel problems that should have been avoided. Therefore, many managers announce that they have an "open-door" policy for seeing members of their staff.

Arrange for employees who report to your manager to meet in your manager's office or in a conference room designated by your manager. When your manager's supervisor requests a conference with your manager, the implied message is that your manager will go to the supervisor's office unless a specific statement is made to the contrary concerning the place of the meeting.

Terminating Conferences

Arrange with your manager how you are to assist in terminating conferences. Be sure to follow your manager's preference.

On those days when your manager's appointment schedule is crowded, watch the time and tactfully interrupt a conference, following predetermined guidelines. One appointment that runs overtime on a busy day can throw all the other appointments off schedule, inconveniencing many people and giving the impression of inefficient planning. Find out if your manager wishes you to aid in getting rid of visitors who overstay their time.

When a visitor arrives promptly for an appointment and someone is in your manager's office, but you know that your manager wants you to interrupt, you can proceed in one of the following ways:

1. Take the visitor's business card or name written or typed on a slip of paper with the notation that the visitor has arrived and hand it to your manager.

2. Enter your manager's office and say, "Excuse me. Your three o'clock appointment is here. May I tell her how soon you can see her?"

3. Call your manager on the interoffice telephone, especially if you think that he or she does not want to be interrupted. Suggest a time for the conference to end, enabling your manager to answer "Yes" or "No" without comment.

If you must remind your manager of an appointment outside his or her own office and, in addition, you are using the reminder as a means of terminating a conference, do not reveal where your manager's next conference is or with whom. Your interruption either in person or by telephone may be all that is needed to prompt the visitor to leave. If not, it will be adequate to enable your manager to terminate the conversation.

What are you going to do when your manager does not have another appointment but the visitor stays and stays, taking up your manager's time unnecessarily? This situation presents a different problem, but it really should not. Most managers are skilled at terminating office visits. They thank the person for coming, stand, and tactfully make statements that let the visitor know the conference is over. At times, however, managers rely on their office professionals to rescue them from persistent visitors.

Be sure that you understand what your manager expects you to do when he or she is having difficulty getting rid of a visitor. In what manner does your manager want to be interrupted? Some assistants pretend that the manager has another appointment. You could type a note reminding your manager of work to be done, walk into your manager's office, deliver the note, and say nothing. Another effective tactic is to call on the interoffice telephone, giving your manager an opportunity to say "We are finishing now" or "Yes, in just a few minutes" or a similar comment that would prompt the visitor to leave. If your manager prefers to continue the conference, he or she could reply in such a way that you would know the conference will last awhile longer.

Interrupting a Meeting

Until you know, anticipate that your manager does not want to be interrupted while someone is in his or her office. Most managers discourage interruptions while they are conferring with someone. Nevertheless, the interruptions a manager will tolerate are governed by their judgment and personality.

You must arrive at a definite understanding with your manager concerning what conditions are important enough to justify interrupting during a conference. At times, your manager may instruct you to interrupt to take a telephone call. At other times, he or she may indicate that there should be no interruptions at all. When you are left to your own judgment and do not know what to do, do not interrupt. An intrusion detracts from the tone of a conference as well as the train of thought. Whether or not you interrupt your manager when an unexpected visitor comes to the office will depend on who the person is and the purpose of the visit.

Clearly establish the method that your manager prefers you to follow when you must deliver an urgent message. The following method is frequently used: The assistant types the message, quietly enters the manager's office, delivers the message or places it face down on the desk, and leaves unless an immediate answer is necessary.

To keep telephone interruptions to a minimum, offer to take the message or to assist the caller yourself. If you cannot help the caller, ask the person to leave his or her number so that your manager can return the call. Having to answer a telephone call when someone is in your manager's office places your manager in an awkward position. Your manager needs privacy for a telephone conversation and, furthermore, does not want to appear discourteous to the visitor by taking up the visitor's time with a telephone call.

When you receive an urgent telephone call for your manager while someone is in the office, write the name of the person calling and the purpose of the call, deliver the note to your manager, and wait for instructions. Your manager will either give you a message or take the call.

When you receive a telephone call for a visitor, let the visitor know. As you enter the office or conference room, apologize for the interruption. Address the visitor, tell the visitor who is calling, and ask if the visitor would like to take the call in your office. When several visitors are in the room, type the message, walk in and hand it to the person addressed, and wait for the reply. Instead of taking the call, the visitor may tell you that he or she will return the call. Give the message to the person calling, ask for the number, and type it on a telephone message blank for the visitor.

Attending to Unscheduled Visitors

Be just as pleasant and friendly toward the unexpected visitor as you are toward the visitor who has an appointment. Never judge a visitor by appearance, for appearance is not indicative of the importance of the person to your manager or to the organization.

As soon as you greet the visitor, the visitor probably will tell you his or her name and the purpose of the visit. Listen carefully and decide what to do. The visitor could be in your office for any one of a long list of reasons. The visitor could be a member of your manager's family, a friend, an important executive, or an aggressive salesperson.

When the visitor is a member of the family, a friend, or an executive, invite the visitor to be seated. If there is someone in your manager's office, you could say "Someone is in his office, but I will let him know you are here." Either write a note to take to your manager or call him or her on the telephone. Members of the family may prefer that you not interrupt your manager and suggest that they wait, but an executive usually does not show up unless he or she has something to say immediately. Do not keep an important executive waiting.

After you establish that a visitor is a friend, offer to let your manager know that the friend is waiting. Sometimes salespeople who should not take up your manager's time use this approach. Consequently, keep a conversation going long enough to be sure that you should tell your manager about the visitor. When you are uncertain, do not risk turning away someone your manager would want to see.

Someone may come to your office and decide not to wait when he or she discovers that it would be inconvenient to see your manager. Always offer to help the person yourself. When you know that your manager would like to talk with this person, ask if the person would like your manager to call him or her. If the person indicates that he or she would, write the information on a telephone message blank. Add a note saying that the person came to the office. Even when you do not suggest that your manager will call, let him or her know who came to the office. Your manager can take the initiative to call.

When a salesperson drops in unexpectedly, find out the purpose of the visit to determine if (1) the salesperson should see someone else, (2) you should offer to make an appointment for the salesperson with your manager, or (3) you should tell the salesperson your manager is not seeking the product or service.

If the salesperson has been calling on your manager, but your manager is no longer involved in purchasing the product or service that the salesperson represents, tell the salesperson whom to see. Next, call this person, give the salesperson's name and business affiliation, explain that the salesperson is in your office, and ask the person with whom you are talking if he or she will see the salesperson. Write down the name of the person, the person's title, floor, and office number, and hand the note to the salesperson. Be courteous enough to explain to the salesperson how to reach that person's office.

When your manager is too busy to see a salesperson or observes strict guidelines for seeing salespeople, offer to make an appointment. Say you are sorry, but be sure to end the conversation on a positive note. For instance, say "We will expect you at two o'clock on Thursday. Mr. Wilmont will be glad to see you then."

When you know that your manager is not seeking the product or service that the salesperson represents, graciously tell the salesperson so. Obviously, the salesperson wants an opportunity to convince your manager of the need for the product or service. Invite the salesperson to leave a business card and literature about the product or service. Tell the salesperson that you will give it to your manager and offer to contact the salesperson if your manager is interested in learning more about the product. Suggest that the salesperson write your manager a letter.

Remember that your job is to make friends for the organization as well as run an efficient office. Give a reason, at least in general terms, before you say "No." Visitors who are turned away should feel that they have been received courteously and can hope that they will be successful in seeing your manager at some time in the future.

Occasionally you will encounter visitors who will not state the purpose of their visit. When you ask, the visitor will say that it is personal or confidential. Here are some hints to use to screen visitors:

- **Establish clear guidelines with your manager.** If your manager often has visitors who simply drop by without an appointment, have your manager explain how aggressive he or she wants you to be. Establish guidelines for when you should allow the visitor access to your manager.

- **Ask direct questions.** Most visitors who have legitimate reasons for seeing your manager will be willing to state the reason. The visitor who is evasive or refuses to give the reason is often concealing the fact that he or she is trying to sell something.

- **Offer to help the visitor.** If the visitor refuses to explain the purpose of the visit, try "I am Mr. Hagerman's assistant. If you explain the nature of your visit, perhaps I can help you." If you are sincere and are willing to help, visitors are more likely to tell you the purpose of the visit.

- **Politely stick to your guns.** Keep stating "I will be glad to help you if you tell me the nature of your visit"—even though the visitor may try to distract you with information.

- **Have the visitor write a note to the manager.** Another approach when you are in doubt about whether your manager might like to see the visitor is to offer a notepad and an envelope and suggest that the person write your manager a note. Then take the note to your manager. Try to do this between visitors rather than interrupting while someone is in your manager's office. Wait for your manager's instructions about what to do.

What can you do when a visitor is overly aggressive or even rude? Be gracious; do not engage in an argument with the person. Speak normally, but convincingly. Receptionists are given the names of managers to call when they encounter a difficult situation that they cannot handle. The manager who is called shows up immediately at the receptionist's desk. If you anticipate that a difficult visitor will come back again, mention it to your manager and arrange how you are going to handle the situation.

Refusing Appointments

Managers have much work to do in addition to conferring with callers and talking on the telephone. Some managers plan blocks of time when they hope to work without interruption. At other times, a manager is forced by the pressure of a deadline to devote full time to a task that must be completed.

On those days or half-days when your manager is not seeing anyone, you do not have to pretend that he or she is not in the office or in conference. "In conference" has been used as an excuse so much that it is regarded as a joke. Furthermore, do not say your manager is solidly booked with appointments except when it is true. Your manager may change plans and confer with a visitor. If your manager does this, the visitor will discover that your manager is not solidly booked.

Simply state that your manager cannot crowd anything more into today's schedule and then center the discussion on future arrangements. Handle telephone requests and unexpected office visits in the same way. Say when your manager will have time to see the visitor. Ask questions such as "Shall I ask my manager to call you?" or "Would you like to make an appointment?" What you suggest would vary according to the importance of the request.

HANDLING DIFFICULT CUSTOMERS

What can you do when a caller is aggressive or rude? Every office professional experiences difficult customers or clients. Although this situation is undesirable, by learning how to handle these situations you will be providing benefits to the company, the customer, and yourself.

Dealing with Unwanted Callers

How do you deal with a caller who is obnoxious or one who makes you feel threatened? Many office buildings have security twenty-four hours a day. If this is the case in your organization, you would call security to have the individual removed. Dealing with unwanted callers is something you need to discuss with your office team. Your colleagues may be able to provide names of people who have an abusive history with your office and are, therefore, not welcome in the office. Your company may have an organizational policy for handling unwanted callers. If so, follow it. If no policy exists, your office team should draft a policy and submit it to management for approval. Every organization wants to provide excellent customer service, but customer abuse toward employees should never be tolerated.

Tips for Success. The following are tips for turning an undesirable situation into one that is satisfactory to both parties:

1. **Use common courtesies.** Immediately learn the customer's name and use it along with the appropriate courtesy title (*Mrs.*, *Mr.*, *Ms.*, *Dr.*, or some other). Be sure your tone of voice and body language always convey a positive and sincere message.

2. **Listen to the customer.** Listen to the spoken words, but also listen to the unspoken—that is, to the tone of voice and the body language. Often there is more information in what customers *don't* say than what they do say. Listen quietly and carefully as the customer explains the source of distress. Take notes if necessary and ask questions to ensure clarity.

3. **Apologize if it is appropriate to do so.** If your company has not performed to the highest of standards, a full apology is in order. Remember to use your tone of voice and your body language to reinforce the sincerity of your message.

   Remember, however, that customers are not always right, especially in situations where they have been dishonest or unethical. Where the company is not at fault, an apology might be phrased this way: "We apologize for any inconvenience our company may have caused. However, [company name] has done everything possible to provide you with a quality product [or service]."

4. **Show empathy and understanding.** Demonstrate that you have listened carefully and that you understand the customer's reason for distress. Paraphrasing the customer's story may be helpful.

5. **Promise follow-up.** Commit to assisting the person yourself or to have someone else take action. Tell the customer exactly what your action plan will be and when he or she can expect to hear from you.

6. **Follow through.** Carry out the action plan just as you promised you would. Be certain to keep the customer informed of your progress.

If you follow these basic rules, a more satisfactory situation should result.

HOSTING INTERNATIONAL VISITORS

If your manager travels to meet international clients, it's very possible that those clients will also visit your office. The work of handling international clients requires a completely new set of knowledge and skills.

Tips for Success. Being able to build positive relationships with international clients is highly desirable and worth achieving. The best advice is to be flexible, adaptable, and tolerant (FAT). Remember, their experiences and customs are different than yours. This is your chance to learn and grow. Here are some tips for your success:

1. **Do your homework!** The comfort of your guests should be your top priority. This means researching their culture and company and incorporating as much of their custom into the visit as possible. Have enough information that you can show an interest and ask intelligent questions.

2. **Learn a few words and phrases in the visitor's language.** Examples might be *hello, how are you, please, thank you, goodbye, it was a pleasure to meet you.* Even a few words and phrases will demonstrate to the client that you are interested in the client and the country. A good suggestion is to write the word *welcome,* in the visitor's language, at the top of the meeting agenda.

3. **Locate the client's nearest consulate's office.** As a courtesy to your international clients, have handy the nearest consulate's location, phone number, and ambassador's name for reference should you need them.

4. **Keep an open mind.** Do not judge behavior on your own standards. Attitudes, values, manners, greetings, and gestures, to name only a few, are likely to be foreign to you and at times what you might consider bad manners and in poor taste. They are not! They are simply the product of a different culture.

5. **Listen carefully.** Your international client may speak in broken English. Do not correct his or her pronunciation. Just remember that a person's English may be a lot better than your Arabic, Japanese, German, or whatever is their mother tongue.

6. **Research the attitude about time.** Different cultures treat time differently. In North America time is a priority, and we expect people to follow schedules very closely, to be on time for meetings, to complete projects before the deadline, and to show up when and where they say they will. Time does not have the same priority in all cultures. Some have a much more relaxed view of time. In fact, some cultures do not work in the afternoon and prefer to have only morning and evening meetings. This makes it difficult for us to schedule meetings, complete projects, and close deals. Keep this in mind when scheduling meetings and be as flexible as possible.

7. **Learn the preferred eating habits of the country.** Although many international travelers are open to experimenting with new foods, many are not. For example, some cultures do not eat pork. In this case, it would be a gross error to arrange a meal where pork was on the menu. Be certain that coffee and lunch breaks include food and beverages that the international clients will enjoy.

8. **Determine if gender plays a stronger role in the client's culture than our own.** In certain cultures, women do not hold high-level positions where decisions are made. In this case, conversation is often directed from the international client to the male members at meetings. The gender issue is important for a company to know before deciding whom to send to negotiate in the boardroom or even whom to send abroad as the best company representative.

9. **Identify the proper greetings.** Greeting clients in the United States is done with a firm handshake, whereas in many other cultures, bowing and kissing are the norms and yet in others men and women do not touch. Although women and men in these cultures do not shake hands, members of the same gender may deliver a very warm and physical greeting.

10. **Body language is often misinterpreted.** A friendly hand gesture in one country can be obscene in the next and actually illegal in another. Pay attention to how others use gestures (movements of the hands, arms, legs, or head) to say what they mean.

11. **Slow down so you can warm up.** Unlike in the United States, many cultures do not do business until they have established a relationship with you. This may mean many cups of tea and a lot of social conversation before business topics are ever broached.

12. **Learn to pronounce names correctly.** If needed, find out how to pronounce the visitor's name correctly. In some cultures, such as Chinese and Korean, the family's surname is placed first and then the given name. You will make a lasting impression on your visitor if you use his or her name correctly. Learn the titles of respect that go with others' names and when it is appropriate to use them.

13. **Determine if space when talking is different from our culture.** People may feel differently about space or distance in communication than you do. When receiving visitors from outside your culture, pay attention to what is considered an appropriate distance between you and the visitor when talking. With some visitors, standing too far away

quicktips

Appointment Reminders:

- When adding appointments and meetings to your electronic calendar, activate the reminder option, if available.
  - Most software products have various timeframes you can choose from.
  - Your computer will beep you at the predefined reminder date and time.

may be interpreted as your being unconcerned, too formal, or too distant. On the other hand, if you stand too close to a visitor, it may be interpreted as your being too casual or too informal. Learn how to use space or distance to your advantage so as not to offend any of your visitors.

The bottom line is that you want your international visitors to have a pleasant, positive visit to the United States. With more and more U.S. companies establishing branches outside the United States and trading with more global companies, you are very likely to need to develop your skills in this area.

Overview

✔ In today's competitive business world, excellent customer service is noticed and can make your company rise above competitors, which can often increase your company's image as well as profits.

Follow these tips:
- Take pride in your work.
- Acknowledge each person as they appear.
- Maintain good eye contact at all times.
- Identify yourself by name and title.
- If a customer must wait, always explain why.
- Tell the customer what you can do, not what you can't do.
- Always do what you say you'll do.
- Always return all calls and e-mails in a timely manner.
- Always invite the customer back and mean it.
- If you ask the customer if he or she was pleased, be prepared with an answer if the answer is "No."

✔ Both you and your manager will need to keep to an appointment schedule. Begin by learning:
1. Your manager's preferences for scheduling appointments
2. Which appointments should be given priority
3. How much time appointments should take

✔ You should know how to set up appointments for your manager:

1. Leave Monday mornings free to plan and handle weekend mail.
2. Schedule no appointments on the first day back from out of the office.
3. Avoid crowding the calendar the day before a trip.
4. Schedule appointments so there is no overlap.
5. Be aware of top-priority conferences and allow plenty of time for them.
6. Avoid scheduling two top-priority conferences back-to-back.
7. Avoid scheduling an appointment in another location after one that will run late.
8. Allow ten to fifteen minutes of free time between appointments.
9. Schedule appointments with others with whom your manager has a close working relationship late in the afternoon.
10. For phone appointments, suggest at least two specific times from which to choose.
11. Predetermine times for answering mail and handling routine daily activities.
12. Learn which conferences can be limited to fifteen minutes or less.
13. When arranging a short appointment, set it up by stating the beginning and ending time.
14. When you arrange for an unexpected visitor to see your manager, the visitor should be advised of the time of the manager's next appointment, if that time is soon.
15. Arrange outside appointments so that the manager can go to the other site directly from home in the morning or from the site to home after a late-afternoon appointment.

✔ More and more office professionals are using electronic calendars rather than desk calendars, such as Microsoft Outlook calendar.

✔ Web-based calendars are available for use free on the Internet (see http://www.calendar.yahoo.com).

✔ A manager may prefer using a paper desk calendar. Be sure your calendar matches your manager's. Be consistent and prompt in recording all appointments and commitments in both calendars. Put tentative commitments in pencil and firm commitments in ink.

✔ When canceling appointments:

1. Express regret on your manager's behalf.
2. Mention that the appointment must be changed.
3. State a reason in general terms.
4. Offer to schedule another appointment.

✔ If your manager prefers, prepare a list of appointments at the end of the day for the next business day.

✔ When receiving visitors, you should follow your manager's wishes, make friends for your manager and the organization, and help callers accomplish their purposes.

✔ When greeting visitors, make certain you have an organized desk. Make them feel at ease and give them your immediate attention.

✔ Anticipate what materials will be needed and locate them the day before even though you do not remove them from the files until the next morning.

✔ A visitor who has an appointment should never be kept waiting.

✔ Arrange for staff visitors to meet in your manager's office or in a conference room designated by the manager.

✔ When terminating a conference, prearrange with your manager how it should be handled.

✔ Clearly establish the method that your manager prefers you to follow when you must deliver an urgent message that will interrupt a conference.

✔ When a salesperson drops in unexpectedly, find out the purpose of his or her visit to determine the following:

1. If the salesperson should need to see someone else, call this person, give the salesperson's name and business affiliation, explain that the salesperson is in your office, and ask the person with whom you are talking if he or she will see the salesperson. Write the name of the person, the person's title, floor, and office number, and give directions to the person's office.

2. If you should offer to make an appointment for the salesperson with your manager, say you are sorry but be sure to end the conversation on a positive note.

3. If you should tell the salesperson your manager is not seeking the product or service, graciously tell the salesperson so. Ask him or her to leave a business card and literature about the product or service and offer to contact the person if your manager is interested in learning more about the product.

✔ Some hints to follow when screening visitors are:

■ Establish clear guidelines with your manager.

■ Ask direct questions.

■ Offer to help the visitor.

■ Politely stick to your guns stating "I will be glad to help you if you tell me the nature of your visit."

■ Have the visitor write a note to the manager when you think the reason for the visit might prompt the manager to want to see the person.

✔ When you must refuse appointments, simply state that your manager cannot crowd anything more into today's schedule and then center the discussion on future arrangements.

✔ Here are the tips for handling difficult customers:

■ Use common courtesies such as stating their name and title.

■ Listen to the customer and take notes if necessary.

■ Apologize if it is appropriate to do so.

■ Show empathy and understanding.

■ Promise to follow up.

■ Follow through.

✔ When working with people outside your culture, be concerned about the following:

- Do your homework and know enough about the person's culture to ask intelligent questions.
- Learn a few words and phrases in the visitor's language such as *hello, how are you, please, thank you, goodbye,* and *it was a pleasure to meet you.*
- Locate the client's nearest consulate's office for reference if needed.
- Keep an open mind about behavior, attitudes, values, manners, greetings, and gestures, to name a few.
- Listen carefully when the visitor's English is poor. Do not correct his or her speech.
- Research the culture's attitude about time.
- Learn the preferred eating habits of the country.
- Determine if gender plays a stronger role in the client's culture than in our own.
- Identify the proper greetings.
- Pay attention to body language and its meanings.
- Slow down so you can warm up—meaning social activity may come long before business.
- Learn to pronounce names correctly.
- Determine if space is important when talking to visitors from other cultures.

Key Terms

Electronic calendar. A calendar that is on your computer or network.

Electronic organizers. Pocket calendars that include a calendar, scheduler, and address area for immediate access.

Web-based calendars. Electronic calendars made available for free on the Internet.

For Your Discussion

 Retrieve file C9-DQ.DOC from your student data file.

Directions

Enter your response after each question.

1. Suggest how you can tactfully let a person know that his or her appointment is for a short segment of time.
2. To avoid conflicts in scheduling, what is the office professional's first step in granting an appointment when one is requested?

3. Describe how an electronic calendar can be used.

4. Why should you be cautious when you state the reason for canceling an appointment?

5. What are the office professional's main responsibilities concerning receiving office visitors?

6. Explain how to introduce a visitor to your manager.

7. Describe an office professional's role in making a visitor feel at ease when the visitor has an appointment but must wait.

8. What should you say if a visitor who has an appointment cannot wait and tells you that he or she must leave?

9. Suggest two ways to assist a manager in terminating a conference when he or she has another appointment soon.

10. Differentiate between the status of U.S. women in business and the status of women in other cultures. Why is this important to understand in business?

READING WORKSHOP

In today's technology-based office, reading skills are essential. Two components of reading office materials, comprehending and verifying information, are vital to your job success. An office worker's careless habits and errors easily could cost an organization time, money, and goodwill. Therefore, it is essential that you demonstrate your reading skill while handling appointments and other office functions.

For Review

Appendix A: Reading

 Retrieve file C9-WRKS.DOC from your data disk.

Directions

Karl works for two managers in the sales department. He maintains one appointment calendar for the two managers. In addition, he helps each manager by keyboarding a list of appointments for the day and placing the list on each manager's desk the evening before the next day's appointments.

1. Examine and read the calendar page and each list of appointments prepared by Karl (Figure 9-7).

2. Compare the calendar page (Figure 9-7) in your text with each list of Scheduled Appointments prepared by Karl (Figure 9-8) in your text.

3. Verify that the information on the Scheduled Appointments page (Figure 9-8) is correct.

4. In the blanks provided in Figure 9-8 or in the retrieved file, verify if the time, location, contact person, and company name are correct by writing a *C* if the information is correct or an *I* if the information is incorrect.

5. Ask yourself the following questions:

    a. What must I do to compare and verify the information?

    b. Are the details correct?

    c. When I verify information and find that I made errors, what must I do the next time to decrease the possibility of these kinds of errors being repeated?

Special Reminder

Error detection "after the fact" is always costly in time, effort, and supplies. In addition, undetected errors may lead to loss of customers or clients and your manager's confidence in your ability to get information out in an accurate and timely manner.

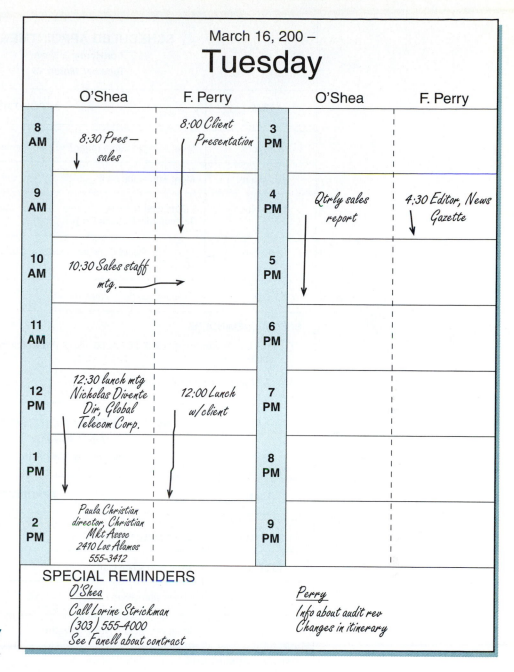

	O'Shea	F. Perry		O'Shea	F. Perry
8 AM	8:30 Pres— sales	8:00 Client Presentation	3 PM		
9 AM			4 PM	Qtrly sales report	4:30 Editor, News Gazette
10 AM	10:30 Sales staff mtg.		5 PM		
11 AM			6 PM		
12 PM	12:30 lunch mtg Nicholas Divente Dir, Global Telecom Corp.	12:00 Lunch w/client	7 PM		
1 PM			8 PM		
2 PM	Paula Christian director, Christian Mkt Assoc 2410 Los Alamos 555-3412		9 PM		

March 16, 200 –
Tuesday

SPECIAL REMINDERS
O'Shea
Call Lorine Strickman
(303) 555-4000
See Fanell about contract

Perry
Info about audit rev
Changes in itinerary

■ **Figure 9-7**
Calendar page.

On the Job Situations

 Retrieve file C9-OJS.DOC from your student data disk.

1. You work for eight managers. You make appointments for all of them and record their appointments in separate appointment books. Today as you were checking your calendar, you discovered that Mr. Yates had requested an appointment with Mrs. Roberts at 10:30 a.m. on Wednesday. You had entered the appointment in Mr. Robbins's appointment calendar by mistake. Mrs. Roberts has another appointment at 10:30 a.m. on

SCHEDULED APPOINTMENTS		C/I
For Henry O'Shea **Tuesday, March 15**		1. _____

TIME	APPOINTMENT	
8:30 a.m.	Meet with president regarding sales projections	2. _____
10:30 a.m.	Meet with sales staff	3. _____
12:30 Noon	Lunch with Nicholas Divente, Director, Global Telecommunications Corp.	4. _____
2:00 p.m.	Meet with Paula Christian, Director, Christian Marketing Associates	5. _____
4:00–5:00 p.m.	Prepare quarterly sales report	6. _____

SPECIAL REMINDERS

1. Call Lorine Strickman, (303) 767-4000, about presentation during sales conference — 7. _____

2. Contact Farrell about contract — 8. _____

SCHEDULED APPOINTMENTS		
For F. Perry **Wednesday, March 16**		9. _____

TIME	APPOINTMENT	
8:00 a.m.	Client presentation	10. _____
10:30 a.m.	Meet with sales staff	11. _____
12:30 Noon	Lunch with client	12. _____
4:30 p.m.	Meet with editor, <u>News Gazette</u>	13. _____

SPECIAL REMINDERS

1. Gather information regarding audit review — 14. _____

2. Let me know the changes in your travel itinerary — 15. _____

■ **Figure 9-8**
Appointments list.

Wednesday, and she will not be in the office on Wednesday afternoon. What should you do?

2. Recently Mrs. Garson has made three appointments with your manager, Mr. Stoney. Each time she has canceled the appointment the day before—once because she was ill, another time because of bad weather, and the last time because she was too busy to keep the appointment. The last time she canceled the appointment, Mr. Stoney said emphatically, "Do not grant her another appointment!" This morning Mrs. Garson called

requesting another appointment. You told her that Mr. Stoney could not work in another appointment this week and that he would be out of town next week. Mrs. Garson is furious and insists on talking with Mr. Stoney. What should you do? What will you say to Mrs. Garson?

3. Your manager, Mr. Harper, had a serious heart attack in his office late Tuesday afternoon. Today you are canceling his appointments for Wednesday, Thursday, and Friday of this week. You are explaining that the appointments will be rescheduled with someone else. What can you ask to find out about the urgency of each appointment? How much information can you give about Mr. Harper's illness? What can you say?

4. What would you do in each case if each of the following visitors did not have an appointment: (a) your manager's superior, (b) your manager's spouse, (c) your manager's former college roommate who is from out of town, (d) a salesperson with whom your manager wants to keep in touch but cannot see on the day that the salesperson calls, (e) a salesperson representing a product that your manager does not need and would have no occasion to purchase.

Projects and Activities

1. If you are currently working or have ever worked in an office, describe the manner in which office visitors are received in the organization. If you have no work experience, interview a friend that is working in an office. Answer the following questions:

    ■ Does the organization have a receptionist?

    ■ Are the visitors escorted or directed to the offices of the persons with whom they have appointments?

    ■ Are the salespeople's visits restricted? If so, how?

    ■ What is the visitor's first contact with the assistant?

    Write your responses and share your ideas with the class.

2. Go to an office supply store or look at a supply catalog and note the variety of desk appointment calendars available. Write down the name and cost of the one you would select for your own use as an office professional and for your manager. Beside the name of the one that you select, jot down the features that appeal to you. Share what you learned with the class.

3. Go to a computer store and look at the variety of software programs for keeping calendars. Write down the names, costs, features, and hardware requirements.

4. Interview an assistant for the following information about scheduling appointments:

    ■ Guidelines in setting up appointments

    ■ Ways in which calendars are coordinated between the office professional and manager(s)

    ■ Calendar aids

■ Preferences or procedures for handling visitors—procedures for greeting visitors, refusing appointments, and terminating visits

Write the interviewee's responses in report form and be prepared to share your findings.

Surfing the Internet

You are the office manager for a large manufacturing company. At a weekly staff meeting several of the supervisors indicated that they believed their employees would gain much from some type of training about cultural diversity because their workforce at the manufacturing plant is becoming more and more culturally diverse. The supervisors believe harmony among the workers will continue if the company offers training that would help them know more about other cultures and how everyone is affected when the workplace is culturally diverse. Your job is to locate companies that provide such training.

1. Connect to the Internet and access a search tool such as Yahoo! or Lycos.
   ■ Enter the following key search words: *business, cultural diversity.*
   ■ Identify three companies that offer training and print any explanations of their services.
   ■ In a memo to the supervisors, summarize the information you located and ask for their input.
2. Because you and your manager both have a new and more powerful computer, your manager has asked you to locate information about electronic calendars to be installed on both your computers. Refine your search and key the following search words: *business, software, electronic calendars.*
3. Locate three calendar software programs available for today's office. Identify the features of each program and summarize the information in a memo to your manager.

Using MS Office 2002

Set Appointment Reminders

 Directions
Use MS Outlook to set an appointment reminder.

1. Open Microsoft Outlook and click on Outlook Today in the Outlook Shortcuts.
2. From the Menu bar click on File, point to New, and then click on Appointment.
3. Enter your class name as the subject.
4. Enter the room or building number your class is in as the location.
5. Fill in the Start Time and End Time text boxes with dates and times of your choice.

6. Click in the Reminder check box to activate it.

7. Click on the arrow pointing down to select the specific time you want your computer to remind you of your appointment. For example, 15 minutes before your class ends.

8. Save and close your appointment reminder.

9. At the time you specified in step 7 for the reminder, your computer will beep and a dialog box will appear on your screen. (Note: Your computer must be on for you to receive the notice of the upcoming appointment.)

10. Click on Snooze if you want to be reminded again. (You can set the time you want the second reminder to appear if desired.)

11. Click on Dismiss to cancel any further reminders.

12. To delete an entry, click on it, then click on File from the menu, then click on Delete.

APPLICATION PROBLEMS

APPLICATION 9–A

Scheduling Appointments

Supplies needed: Form 9-A-1, Appointment Calendar, Amanda Quevedo; Form 9-A-2, Appointment Calendar (Student Name); plain paper.

 Retrieve file CH9-FORM.DOC from your student data disk.

Directions: Mrs. Quevedo has been scheduling her own appointments. She uses a monthly calendar and crowds the appointments into the spaces. During a discussion with Mrs. Quevedo on Friday, she asked you to schedule her appointments from now on.

You decided to use daily appointment calendars—one for Mrs. Quevedo and one for yourself. Mrs. Quevedo has no appointments scheduled for Monday and only one for Tuesday. She has the following appointments for Wednesday, August 6, entered in her monthly calendar:

9:00	Agnes Smith, Sales Representative for Small Home Appliances, Inc.
10:00	Pete Rollins, Sales Representative for Home Gadgets, Inc.
11:00	James Hansen, Manager of the Eastern Region of Modern Appliances, Inc., and J. R. Rush, Assistant Vice President of Marketing, Eastern Region
12:00	Lunch with Mr. Hansen and Mr. Rush
3:00	Karen Baxter, Assistant Vice President of Marketing, Western Region, to review marketing plans for fall

You are to transfer these appointments to Mrs. Quevedo's daily calendar or yours. On Tuesday, August 5, you receive the following telephone calls concerning appointments. Make these changes on Mrs. Quevedo's or your calendar as well.

1. From Thomas Strickland, Assistant Vice President of Marketing, South-western Region, saying that he must attend a funeral out of town on Wednesday. He has an appointment on Wednesday at 3:00 p.m. with O. C. Connors, President of Mapledale Homes, Inc. He asks if Mrs. Quevedo can see Mr. Conners at 3:00 p.m.

    Here is your response: "Mrs. Quevedo has an appointment with Ms. Baxter at 3:00 p.m. I'll see if I can move Ms. Baxter's appointment to 2:00 p.m. I'll call you and let you know."

    Later you call Mr. Strickland and confirm that Mrs. Quevedo will see Mr. Conners at 3:00 p.m.

2. From Pete Rollins's assistant, saying that Mr. Rollins had an automobile accident, is hospitalized, and obviously cannot keep his appointment.

3. From Ray Rogers, co-chair of the Eastern Region Sales Seminar, asking for an appointment on Wednesday to review plans for the November seminar. You suggest 10:00 a.m. and Mr. Rogers accepts.

4. From the Human Resources Department, asking Mrs. Quevedo to see a job applicant. You try to postpone this appointment, but the Human Resources Department insists that Mrs. Quevedo will want to meet this applicant while she is in the building on Wednesday. You schedule an appointment for Bill Boger at 4:00 p.m.

Before leaving the office on Tuesday, you keyboard Mrs. Quevedo's appointment schedule for Wednesday, August 6.

Wednesday at 10:05 a.m. Jason Rhodes, a college friend from out of town, comes to the office for a brief visit with Mrs. Quevedo. You say you will schedule him between appointments for a few minutes at 10:45 a.m.

On her way to lunch, Mrs. Quevedo asks you to remind her before she leaves at the end of the day to call the Lakeside Restaurant to tell the manager how many will be in her dinner party Wednesday evening. Be sure to enter this in the reminder section of your calendar and include the phone number—(953) 555–1892.

APPLICATION 9-B

Receiving Visitors

Supplies needed: Computer; student data disk.

Directions: Waymon Williams, the office professional who has been receiving visitors in the marketing department, is being promoted to an administrative assistant in another department. He is leaving in one week. Mrs. Quevedo has asked you to write procedures for receiving visitors in the marketing department. The procedures are to be included in an office procedures manual. From your experience in assisting Mrs. Quevedo, you have received the following visitors: manufacturers' reps, advertising reps, customers, and field sales reps.

1. Using the information from this chapter as well as suggestions from other sources, outline the procedures for receiving visitors in the marketing department in report form.

2. Address the topics of performing customer service, greeting visitors, receiving visitors who do and do not have appointments, terminating conferences, screening visitors, handling difficult customers, attending to staff visitors, interrupting managers, canceling appointments, and refusing appointments.
3. Proofread the document.

Your Action Plan

Complete Your Action Plan; if necessary, review the guidelines in Chapter 1. Set one goal using the information in Chapter 9.

Your Portfolio

With the help of your instructor, select the best papers representative of your work from Chapter 9. Follow your instructor's directions about formatting, assembling, and turning in the portfolio.

Making Travel Arrangements

OUTLINE

LEARNING OUTCOMES

When you have completed this chapter, you should be able to:

✔ Identify types of services and information resources needed to make domestic and international travel arrangements.

✔ Prepare for a business trip.

✔ Make travel and hotel reservations.

✔ Make special arrangements for international travel.

✔ Develop an overall trip plan that includes details to be handled before a trip, during a trip, and at the conclusion of a trip.

✔ Discuss the differences between priorities of time in different cultures.

Anyone who works as an assistant will eventually encounter making travel arrangements. If you work for a manager who travels, you should

■ Become thoroughly familiar with the organization's travel policies

- Know what travel accommodations are available and how to schedule them to meet the manager's preferences
- Keep the office running smoothly while the manager is away

PLANNING THE TRIP

Before you proceed to make travel arrangements, ask questions about the policies and procedures followed within the organization. For example:

- Who is responsible for making travel arrangements?
- Do designated office professionals handle the travel arrangements for all the managers of the organization?
- If the services of a travel agency are used, which agency?
- Are the managers to fly business class or economy class?
- What is the policy concerning the use of private cars and car rental services?
- Does the organization have a preference for a particular airline?
- If so, what are the policies for using it?
- How are payments for reservations handled?
- What is the procedure for getting a cash advance for a traveler?
- How is the manager reimbursed for additional travel expenses?

As soon as you have answers to a few of these questions, you will know whether to turn over the arrangements to someone else or to make them yourself. Regardless of who makes the arrangements, try to request all reservations far enough in advance to ensure that you obtain the travel arrangements and accommodations desired.

Internet Travel Services

The Internet offers an abundance of information that will help the office professional plan business trips. By searching the Web site of a travel service company, the office professional may access information about

- the company's background
- customs and immigration
- tourism
- flight schedules
- latest pricing
- telephone numbers
- travel tips
- e-mail, fax, and postal mailing addresses

When reservations are made through the Internet, the subscriber pays for the tickets with a credit card number, and the ticket voucher is either faxed to the subscriber or the tickets are picked up at a local travel agent's office or the airport.

A number of airlines no longer print a paper ticket. Instead, the traveler makes the reservations, pays over the telephone or Internet with a credit card number, shows identification at the airline counter prior to departure, and is simply given the boarding pass.

Travel Agencies

You will definitely appreciate the services of a travel agent when you make arrangements for international travel; you will find that working through a travel agent is the easiest and best way to make arrangements for domestic travel as well.

Travel agents receive their commissions from the airlines, hotels, and other organizations whose services they sell. A travel agency will not charge your organization for services.

The local travel agencies are listed in the classified section of the telephone directory. If you are concerned about finding a reputable agency, call the Better Business Bureau to inquire about local travel agencies.

Most travel agents are approved by the International Air Transport Association (IATA). IATA is a conglomerate of international airlines. It allows travel agencies that meet its stringent requirements to use its insignia. An agency seeking IATA's approval must have a solid reputation, as well as the financial backing to ensure its own stability.

Travel agencies use the Internet to maintain up-to-the-minute information on all airline schedules and hotel accommodations. Because of their experience and business connections, travel agents can obtain information quicker and find availability and better prices than most people who do their own bookings.

The travel agent represents *all* the transportation lines, hotels, and motels, not just certain ones. You, of course, must provide the travel agent with all the details needed. When planning a trip, try to deal with only one person at the agency, and rely on that person to prepare the complete package.

The travel agent will make out the itinerary, secure tickets, make hotel reservations, arrange for car rental, and perform other services related to the trip.

For international travel, travel agents perform many other services. They provide some information on visas and how you can obtain one, provide information about how much luggage is allowed, furnish guidebooks for the countries being visited, inform you of currency restrictions, and tell you about regulations for bringing foreign purchases through U.S. customs.

Travel agents do not give advice on immunizations, however. That advice should be obtained through your local health authority.

Trip Information Needed

As soon as your manager mentions a trip, start compiling information. Before you contact a travel agent or a carrier, compile the details concerning:

1. The destination
2. Intermediate stops, either going or returning or both
3. Date of departure and date of return
4. Date and time of the first business appointment and the time needed between arrival and the appointment

5. Preferred time of day for travel
6. Method of travel—air, car, rail
7. Type of service—business class, economy class
8. Preferred seat selection—aisle? window? front or back of the plane?
9. Hotel preference or the desired location of the hotel within the city
10. Need for transportation at the destination or at intermediate stops
11. Whether or not connecting shuttle service is needed
12. If car rental is involved, the make and/or size of car preferred

For use in planning future trips, maintain a folder labeled "Trip Preferences." When your manager returns from a trip, you should add comments about the transportation and hotel accommodations on a copy of the agenda for the trip. In this folder, keep the manager's comments and all other information that will help you recall preferences when you are planning another trip to the same city or part of the country. If you plan trips for more than one manager, maintain a Trip Preferences folder for each one. Figure 10-1 is an example of a trip-planning checklist.

ARRANGING THE TRAVEL

Making transportation arrangements for international travel is similar to making arrangements for domestic travel. When planning travel, you should consider the effect of a long trip through different time zones. Refer to Chapters 9 and 12 for a discussion of time zones around the world. **Jet lag** is a condition that is characterized by various physical and psychological effects, such as fatigue and irritability, following a long flight through several time zones. When planning an overseas trip, allow an adequate rest period following arrival in the country to be visited and following the return home.

To make travel arrangements with ease, you should know about air travel services and other types of transportation, including how to arrange for car rental services; how to make hotel reservations; how to obtain passports and visas; and what is involved in meeting immunization requirements. You will learn more about passports and visas later in this chapter.

Air Travel

Because many managers are required to fly to meetings in different cities, you need to be well informed about air travel services.

Sources of Air Travel Information. You can obtain air travel information about a specific trip by telephoning a local travel agent or airline. However, all this information is easily accessible on the Internet.

If you are involved in making extensive air-travel arrangements, consult the North American and international editions of the *Official Airline Guide (OAG)*. The *OAG* contains information on airline travel, from flight itineraries and special fares to baggage allowance. The *OAG Electronic Edition Service (EES)*, available for a fee on the Internet, is an online travel service allowing travelers to compare fares, check seat availability, and book flights from their computers on a twenty-four-hour basis. In addition, it provides information about hotel accommodations, restaurants, weather forecasts, and

---

Manager's Name _____

PREPARING FOR THE BUSINESS TRIP

Handling preparations:

_____ 1. Get transportation information from your travel agency, company travel department, or other sources
_____ 2. Submit time and route schedule
_____ 3. Make transportation reservations
_____ 4. Confirm that airline tickets have been sent or will be available at the ticket counter before departure
_____ 5. Check travel documents for accuracy (airline/train)
_____ 6. Prepare the travel itinerary and appointment schedule
_____ 7. Route copies of itinerary/appointment schedule to appropriate people
_____ 8. Assemble business information, file folders, and supplies to be taken on the trip
_____ 9. Make financial arrangements for the trip
_____ 10. Give hotel confirmations and transportation tickets to your manager

Transportation:

_____ 1. Destination(s)
_____ 2. Desired departure time
_____ 3. Desired arrival and departure times for stopovers
_____ 4. Airline decisions
_____ 5. Time schedules
_____ 6. Plane/train accommodations (class, seat assignments, meal specifics, etc.)
_____ 7. Car-rental arrangements (preferences of rental agencies, vehicle preference, dates and times, method of payment, whether drop-off in another city is desired)
_____ 8. Shuttle/limo arrangements at destination
_____ 9. Baggage identification tags and requirements (if international)

Hotel:

_____ 1. Desired arrival and departure times
_____ 2. Special accommodations (meeting/conference room)
_____ 3. Shuttle/limo arrangements to and from hotel (from airport)
_____ 4. Fax numbers at hotels

Business documents:

_____ 1. Summary of file folders taken (or copies made of information)
_____ 2. Passport
_____ 3. Visa
_____ 4. Immunization
_____ 5. Itinerary

■ **Figure 10-1**
A checklist for making travel arrangements.

---

access to the comprehensive variety of travel-related facts. You can locate this service by accessing the Internet and searching under *OAG.*

Types of Flights. The most desirable flights are those on which the traveler is least likely to be delayed or inconvenienced. Therefore, when making arrangements, consider the flights available in this order:

1. **A nonstop flight,** which is uninterrupted from point of departure to destination

2. A **direct flight,** on which regardless of the number of stops en route, the passenger remains on the same plane from departure to destination
3. A connecting flight with another flight of the same airline
4. A connecting flight with another flight of another airline

When a passenger changes aircraft without changing airlines, the gate for the connecting flight may be near the deplaning gate. The distance between boarding gates of two different airlines at a major airport may be great, and walking or being shuttled from one gate to another is time consuming. If the first flight is delayed, the passenger may not have enough time to meet the connecting flight.

Because delays cannot be predicted, use wise judgment when making reservations; if the traveler must make a connection, allow adequate time between the flights. Remember that many airports have more than one terminal and that many cities have two airports. A connection between two different airports in the same city can often take two hours, or even longer. Think of the activities involved: deplaning, picking up baggage, getting transportation to the second airport, and locating and boarding the next flight.

Commuter flights are short direct flights between two neighboring cities. These neighboring cities need to be close enough that significant numbers of travelers use the service as a convenience. Many business travelers rely on commuter flights to meet with clients or colleagues in neighboring cities and even to go to work each day. These flights leave frequently—often every hour. Although reservations are recommended, they are often not required because of the frequent schedules.

Classes of Service. The services passengers receive aboard the plane—especially where they sit and the food and beverages served—are purchased by **class of service.** The basic classes of service are business class and economy class. The priority services for business class traveling include expeditious check-in and boarding as well as additional comfort and service during the flight.

Some organizations require their executives to fly **business class** because it is considered more prestigious. It provides wider seats with more legroom and working room—an important consideration on long flights. Other organizations, for obvious financial reasons, require their executives to fly economy class. The **economy class,** in most cases, has less space between seats and limited meal service, and is the most common way to fly.

Flight Reservations. You can make a flight reservation yourself through the Internet or by simply telephoning the airline reservations office. Offices may be located in shopping malls and hotels. You can pay for your tickets by providing a credit card number, and then receive them through the mail or at the airport reservations desk.

Many airlines are preparing **electronic tickets (e-tickets).** The system now works like this:

- Book the reservation over the telephone or Internet.
- Use a credit card or charge account to pay for the tickets.
- Receive a faxed or e-mailed itinerary and confirmation from the airline carrier.

■ Just prior to departure, proceed to the airline ticket counter, state the flight number for which you have a reservation, show your identification, and receive your boarding pass.

It's that simple!

Before you contact the airline reservations office, collect all the trip information you need for making a flight reservation. The reservations agent will be using a computer system that stores all the reservations. The agent will establish whether the space you want is available. If it is, make the reservation during the initial contact. When the traveler does not know the return date, purchase an **open ticket.** As soon as the traveler knows the return date, call the agent and make the return reservation.

If space is not available on the flight you want, proceed with an alternative plan. Inquire about earlier and later flights with the same airline and with other airlines. If you can't select an alternative flight, ask that the manager's name be placed on a waiting list in case there is a cancelation on the flight desired.

Reconfirmation of airline reservations is required on international flights. The traveler should reconfirm reservations for each part (also called *leg*) of the trip.

Advantages to Making Online Reservations. Booking the airline reservations online can be very efficient for the office assistant. The assistant can access the availability of flights in minutes. Alternative schedules can be printed and then compared and selected by the traveler. Keep in mind that executive travel and flight plans change frequently and rapidly.

Time can be saved when the office professional makes the reservations and does not have to go through a travel agent every time a change must be made.

Many executives like to make their own reservations. In this case, the assistant should train the executives on how to access flight information to book flights online. This way the traveler can quickly change plans without getting the assistant involved. It's easy and interesting to do.

Timetables. No two airline timetables are identical, and airline timetables are different from rail timetables. Yet timetables are easy to read when you know what to look for. All carriers publish electronic and paper timetables and update them often. The timetable in Figure 10-2 illustrates most of these points.

Reading the Twenty-Four-Hour Clock. For air travel, the times shown are based on the twenty-four-hour clock. This is to eliminate confusion between a.m. and p.m. Under this system, time begins at one minute past midnight (0001) and continues through the next twenty-four hours to midnight (2400). Refer to Figure 10-3.

Ground Transportation. Airports are often located twenty or more miles from cities; for that reason, one or more types of ground transportation— airport limousine, taxi, bus, and car rental—are available at all airports.

The distance and direction of the airport, the travel time needed, the types of ground transportation available, and approximate costs are listed in the *Official Airline Guide* for all destination cities. The transportation services are coded as follows: limousine (L), taxi (T), car rental (R), and air taxi (A).

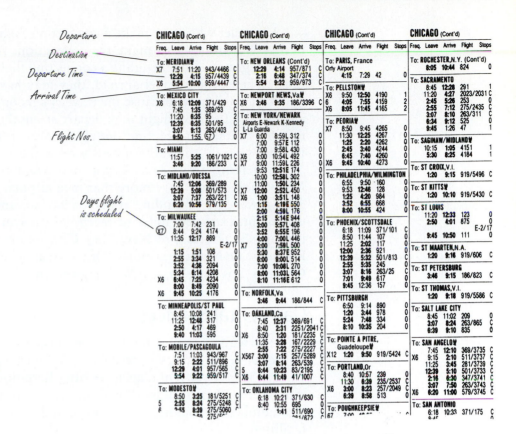

Departure

Destination

Departure Time

Arrival Time

Flight Nos.

Days flight is scheduled

■ **Figure 10-2**
American Airlines timetable.
Courtesy American Airlines.

■ **Figure 10-3**
Time conversion for the twenty-four-hour clock.

1:00 a.m. = 0100	1:00 p.m. = 1300
2:00 a.m. = 0200	2:00 p.m. = 1400
3:00 a.m. = 0300	3:00 p.m. = 1500
4:00 a.m. = 0400	4:00 p.m. = 1600
5:00 a.m. = 0500	5:00 p.m. = 1700
6:00 a.m. = 0600	6:00 p.m. = 1800
7:00 a.m. = 0700	7:00 p.m. = 1900
8:00 a.m. = 0800	8:00 p.m. = 2000
9:00 a.m. = 0900	9:00 p.m. = 2100
10:00 a.m. = 1000	10:00 p.m. = 2200
11:00 a.m. = 1100	11:00 p.m. = 2300
12:00 p.m. = 1200	12:00 p.m. = 2400

To determine what arrangements to make for ground transportation, ask the airline reservations agent or your travel agent.

Limousines and shuttle bus services operate on a regular basis between the airport and downtown hotels. They leave the designated hotels in time to get the passengers to the airport for departing flights, and they meet incoming flights.

Air taxi is a helicopter service that is available at some airports. Helicopters operate between two airports of a destination city, between an airport and downtown heliports, and between destination airport and an airport not served by jet aircraft. Compared to the cost of other types of transportation, air taxi service is expensive, but it saves time.

A traveler who must make a connecting flight at an airport may need air taxi service in order to make the connection. As stated previously, on domestic flights, avoid scheduling a connecting flight that involves a second airport. When people travel abroad, they may have to make a connection involving two airports because the traveler's incoming flight may arrive at one airport and the next flight may depart at another. Before making a reservation for air taxi service, find out about airport limousine or bus shuttle service between the central terminals serving the airports involved.

In making arrangements, you may want to consider another airport. Many major cities have more than one airport. You may find that you can get a lower fare by landing at one of the "alternative" airports and perhaps driving an extra few miles to reach your destination. For example, if your manager is traveling to New York City, he or she can land at LaGuardia, Kennedy, or Newark airports. Other areas where this is an option include Chicago, Los Angeles, and Washington, DC.

Car Rental Services

The best way to arrange for a car rental is either to telephone the local office of the car rental agency or to contact the agency online.

The largest car rental agencies offer both domestic and international car rental services, publish worldwide directories of their services, provide a toll-free number for making reservations, and have a Web site with reservation facilities.

When you are making arrangements for car rental, specify the following:

- The city, date, and time
- The size of car desired
- The location where the car is to be picked up
- The name of the person who will pick up the car
- The location where the car is to be left
- The length of time the car will be used
- The method of payment for the charges

A car can be picked up at the rental agency right at the airport rental agency near the airport when the passenger arrives. All the traveler has to do upon arrival is to go the airport car rental office, state that there is a reservation, present a driver's license, and complete arrangements for payment of charges.

Charges incurred are payable at the completion of the rental, but the arrangements for payment must be made in advance. Major credit cards are accepted. Cash may or may not be accepted. At the time you are making the reservation, be prepared to give the account number and the expiration date of the credit card to be used for payment. Your company may have arrangements with car rental agencies entitling you to a discount.

Hotel Reservations

Many hotels provide a toll-free number for making reservations. You can obtain the toll-free number by calling directory assistance at 1-800-555-1212.

If you are not familiar with the hotels in the destination city, contact a local travel agent. Most international accommodation information changes so rapidly that agents consult online computer information, which is updated frequently. Many of the larger hotels and resorts have their own Web sites so it's very possible to access this information and make your own reservations. Most of these Web sites provide online booking services and toll-free telephone numbers.

Here are some ways to save your organization money.

- Search the Internet for Web sites that specialize in offering "best" rates. For example, http://www.hotel.com and http://www.expedia.com are sites specializing in travel and hotel rates. You may want to search for similar sites as well to compare prices and in the event that these sites no longer exist.

- Book the right kind of room. Some hotel chains offer the option of rooms for business travelers. These rooms cost slightly more per night but can save money in the long run because they don't charge phone access fees. At seventy-five cents a call, phone access charges can add up quickly when your manager is calling customers, getting messages from the office, accessing the Internet, and so on. When making hotel reservations, be aware of the additional charges for these rooms, your manager's preferences, and your company's policies about rates.

- Check out concierge levels. Some hotels provide concierge-level rooms that include breakfast, newspapers, and an afternoon snack and drink buffet. Although these rooms carry a higher price tag, their cost is often less than your manager may spend on purchasing meals, periodicals, and cocktails.

- Avoid large hotel chains. Most major cities have cost-effective alternatives to the major hotel chains, such as independent hotels, short-stay efficiency apartments, or other money-saving alternatives. Again, be certain to ask your manager about his or her preference when it comes to reserving hotels. Ask your travel agent to investigate these options or call a chamber of commerce in your city of destination to obtain these details yourself.

Always ask for a confirmation of a hotel reservation. When the operator gives you a confirmation number or an electronic confirmation note, be sure to attach it to the itinerary so that the traveler will have it if there is any question about the reservation. Hotels require a deposit when you request that a room be held for late arrival. This is called a **guaranteed reservation.** Make the request and arrange for the deposit if there is the slightest chance that your manager might arrive late. Major credit cards are accepted by hotels to reserve the room for late arrival. Late arrival is usually after 6 p.m. Confirming with a credit card simplifies the process of making a deposit for a room reservation. Be aware: if the reservation isn't used, someone should cancel the reservation, as the credit card holder will be responsible for charges.

Passports

A **passport** is a travel document, given to a citizen by their own government, granting permission to leave the country and to travel in certain specified foreign countries. A passport serves as proof of citizenship and identity in a foreign country. It asks other countries to allow the bearer free passage within their borders. It entitles the bearer to the protection of his or her own country and that of the countries visited.

A U.S. citizen who goes abroad must carry a passport. Exceptions include short-term travel between the United States and Mexico, Canada, and some countries in the Caribbean, where a U.S. birth certificate or other proof of U.S. citizenship may be accepted. Inquire at your travel agent or local passport office regarding whether or not a passport is required.

To apply for a passport, a person must complete an application form. The application usually is made locally, but the issuance of passports is under the jurisdiction of the department of state. The addresses of passport acceptance facilities in your area are available on the Internet at http://travel.state.gov. The application form gives complete details for applying for a passport. A passport is valid for ten years.

Visas

Many countries require foreign travelers to hold a visa. A **visa** is a stamped permit to travel within a given country for a specified length of time. The visa is usually stamped or attached inside the passport. However, some countries provide loose visa documents so the visa can be removed when traveling to uncooperative countries.

Well in advance of the departure date, a traveler should check passport and visa requirements with the consulates of the countries to be visited. The traveler should obtain the necessary visas before going abroad.

Visa requirements are subject to change, and they can change rapidly. Travelers should apply directly to the embassy or nearest consulate of each country that he or she plans to visit, or consult a travel agent. Passport agencies cannot help you obtain visas. Most foreign consular representatives are located in principal U.S. cities, particularly New York, Chicago, New Orleans, San Francisco, Houston, Dallas, and Washington, DC. The addresses of foreign consular offices in the United States may be obtained by consulting the *Official Congressional Directory,* available in many public libraries, or city telephone directories.

After obtaining a passport, the traveler must send it to each consulate involved to obtain visas. The time and level of patience it takes to process a visa after it reaches a consular office can vary from one day to three weeks. Allow ample time and use prepaid courier services whenever possible. Some travel agents are experienced in obtaining visas, but you don't need to rely on travel agents because the process is usually straightforward.

Immunization Requirements

The International Health Regulations adopted by the World Health Organization (WHO) stipulate that vaccinations may be required as a condition of entry to any country. The WHO sends communications to local health departments advising them of required and recommended immunization for travelers.

For travel to many countries, an International Certificate of Vaccination is not required. If you need one, you can obtain it from the local health department, a travel agent, or the local passport office. The form must be stamped by the office where the vaccinations are administered.

Security

All travelers, both national and international, should be aware of security issues. As an office professional who makes travel arrangements and who helps the executive prepare for the trip, here are some factors to consider:

- Travel to and through some countries can put Americans at risk. When booking flights, choose flights that are reputable and ones that avoid countries that are unfriendly to Westerners.

- When booking hotels, consider the location. Be certain that you book reputable hotels in safe locations within the cities.

- Security at airports is very heavy. Executives who travel should expect to have their notebook computers, digital pocket organizers, pagers, cell telephones, and briefcases thoroughly examined before they board a flight.

- Be sure that the batteries in the notebook computers and pocket organizers are charged. With increased airport security, people carrying electronic devices may be asked to start these machines to prove they are truly business tools and not explosive devices.

- Many airports insist on jackets and shoes being removed as travelers pass through security.

- Travelers should expect to answer questions about why they are traveling to certain countries. Is it for business? If so, what business?

- Travelers should carry their passports and their immunization cards (for some countries) on their person because government officials can request these documents at any time.

- When executives are taking gifts to clients, they should not be wrapped prior to boarding the flight. Airport security can insist that you unwrap all parcels for inspection.

- Travelers should expect to be searched by security officers if any level of metal registers as the traveler passes through the metal detection gate.

FOLLOWING THROUGH

Whereas office professionals can rely on a travel agent when planning a trip, they are directly responsible for checking the completeness and the accuracy of the final arrangements.

Prior to the Trip

Just before your manager leaves on a business trip, your main duties will include checking the tickets, getting money for the trip, preparing the schedule, assembling materials for the trip, perhaps arranging to have new business cards made, and getting instructions about special responsibilities you will have in your manager's absence. Be sure that you understand your specific duties in completing this task. Assumptions can lead to costly and potentially embarrassing situations.

Checking the Tickets. Obtain the tickets in enough time to check them carefully. First compare the information on the tickets with what your manager requested; then thoroughly check each item on the tickets with the itinerary. The information on the tickets and the travel portion of the itinerary should be identical.

Getting Money for the Trip. Credit cards, such as American Express, Visa, and MasterCard, make it possible to travel without carrying large sums of money. Most people rely on credit cards while traveling.

However, everyone who travels needs some cash. Many organizations provide a cash advance to employees who travel. If this is the policy in your organization, complete the required form, and obtain the cash. Figure 10-4

TRAVEL FUND ADVANCE

Please forward completed forms to: Accounting Department
Millennium Appliances
3431 Bloor Street
Toronto, ON   M8X 1G4

Tel (416) 795-2893   Fax (416) 795-3982

Name of Employee Requesting Advance: *Iain Brown*

Date of Request: *25 March, 20xx*

Employee Number: *784244*

Destination: *Vancouver, B.C.*

Reason for Travel: *Meetings with sales staff & clients*

Departure Date: *5 April, 20xx*   Return Date: *7 April, 20xx*

Date Advance Required: *3 April, 20xx*

Amount Requested:

Accommodation	(Refer to Policy 430)	$ *370.00*
Meals	(Refer to Policy 431)	$ *120.00*
Transportation	(Refer to Policy 432)	$ *100.00*
TOTAL REQUESTED		$ *695.00*

Preferred Method of Payment/Distribution √ Company Cheque ____ Traveller's Cheque

Balance Outstanding (Includes this request) $ *0*

L. Phillips   *G.M.I. Marketing*   *26 March, 20xx*
Authorization   Date of Authorization
(as per Schedule of Authorities)

Approval Limits

$3000   -Manager
$10 000   -Director
$10 000+   -President

■ **Figure 10-4**
A travel fund advance.

shows a travel fund advance form. Although forms vary, it is important on all forms to fill all appropriate blanks with accurate information. This will help avoid delays in receiving the travel advance.

Whether you are obtaining cash from a bank or from the company cashier, get some small bills to be used for tips.

Occasionally managers prefer to carry **traveler's checks** in addition to cash. However, this is unlikely for business trips. Most business travelers take limited cash and often carry their company credit cards. Cash is readily available to the traveler through automatic teller machines found in most international hotels and near banks.

Understanding Per Diems. One of the first things you will need to understand is the per diem rate. **Per diem** is a Latin term meaning "per day." It means an amount of money determined by the company that it will pay per day to its traveler for expenses. There is usually a meal per diem and sometimes an accommodation per diem.

Become familiar with your organization's policies, as they vary between companies. Some companies allow travelers to claim more than the per diem if receipts can be provided, whereas other companies expect their traveler to cover his or her own expenses beyond the per diems allowed. Be sure to check your company's per diem rates and policies before you make travel arrangements.

Preparing the Itinerary. Usually, an **itinerary** is a combined travel and appointment schedule. However, the travel itinerary and the schedule of confirmed appointments can also be prepared as two separate lists. An itinerary shows when, where, and how the traveler will go. It should include the

- Day
- Date
- Local time of departure and arrival
- Name of airport
- Flight number
- Place of departure and arrival
- Car rental information
- Name of hotel for each overnight stay on the trip.

The itinerary should also include details about confirmed appointments. Examples of such details might be:

- The names and titles of the people the traveler will see.
- Personal notes about people the traveler may see. These comments are intended to aid conversation and familiarity. They may include reminders about family members, recent achievements, or personal interests.
- The dates and times of the appointments.
- The purpose of the appointments.
- Software and/or documents required for the appointments.

These details are illustrated in the itinerary in Figure 10-5.

As soon as the travel and hotel accommodations and the appointments have been confirmed, you can prepare the final itinerary. Make a step-by-step

ITINERARY FOR JASON PARKER

Oklahoma City - Tulsa - Dallas

May 3–6, 200-

MONDAY, MAY 3

6:55 a.m.	Leave Rochester Airport on AA Flight 476 to Chicago. AA Flight 406 from Chicago to Oklahoma City.
11:22 a.m.	Arrive in Oklahoma City. (Jack Lewis will meet you at the airport. Lunch with Mr. Lewis.)
	Reservation at Sheraton Hotel. (Confirmation in AA ticket envelope.)
3 p.m.	Appointment with M. J. Young, OC Branch Office.

TUESDAY, MAY 4

10:15 a.m.	Appointment with Ray Berger, Tulsa Office. (Rental car is with Avis.)
1 p.m.	Lunch with R. Berger and J. Caswell.
3 p.m.	Conference with Sales Group, Tulsa Office.
5:15 p.m.	Return to Oklahoma City.

WEDNESDAY, MAY 5

9:25 a.m.	Leave OC airport for Dallas on AA Flight 104.
10:09 a.m.	Arrive Dallas/Forth Worth airport. (Reservation at Americana Inn of the Six Flags.)
11:30 a.m.	Appointment with A. J. Masterson, Manager, Dallas Branch.
1 p.m.	Lunch with A. J. Masterson, Ray Packard, and Larry Jones. (Executive Dining Room.)
3 p.m.	Appointment with Janet Bradlow, Room 216, School of Business, Southern Methodist University.
6:30 p.m.	A. J. Masterson will pick you up at the Americana to join him and Mrs. Masterson for dinner.

THURSDAY, MAY 6

11:25 a.m.	Leave Dallas/Fort Worth airport on AA Flight 261; AA Flight 185 from Chicago to Rochester.
4:11 p.m.	Arrive in Rochester.

Parker Associates
14325 Washington Blvd.
Rochester, NY

■ **Figure 10-5**
An example of an itinerary.

plan that is so complete that the manager will know where to go, when, and what materials will be needed by referring to the itinerary.

Preparing an itinerary can be time consuming because you must obtain the information from several different sources. Arrange the papers relating to hotels and appointments in chronological order. Give the itinerary an appropriate heading. Use the days and dates as the major divisions, and list the entries under each division in order according to time. Check the final itinerary more than once to make sure it is 100 percent correct.

You should prepare the itinerary in the style your manager prefers. However, if the travel agent has already prepared a detailed itinerary, instead of rekeying it to add the appointments, prepare a separate schedule of appointments.

Just prior to departure, when all the details have been finalized, make at least four copies of the final itinerary, with one copy for

- the traveler
- the traveler's superior
- the traveler to give family members
- you

File your copy as a permanent record of the trip. If a major change in the manager's itinerary becomes necessary, inform everyone who has a copy.

Assembling Materials for the Trip. As you make arrangements for the trip, you should compile a complete list of items your manager will need on the trip. After you have assembled the items that will be needed, your last-minute responsibilities will include numbering them in the order in which they will be used and checking them off your list as you stack them to go into his or her briefcase.

Many people travel with a notebook computer. If a notebook computer is one of the items the manager will be taking, make sure he or she takes a fully charged spare power-pack, removable diskettes or CDs, and current data for en route work.

Place the papers for each appointment in separate envelopes or folders. Number each one in consecutive order to match the order of the appointments. If you use folders, fasten the materials to the folders.

Make two copies of the list you have compiled of items your manager must take. Staple the list inside Folder #1, or attach it to Envelope #1. Keep one copy for yourself.

Getting Special Instructions. Take notes as your manager gives instructions about what to do in his or her absence. Find out about:

- Mail that should be forwarded and location to send the mail
- Materials to be sent to meetings the manager cannot attend
- Any special responsibilities you must handle in the manager's absence

Determine if an automatic return e-mail message should be set up for your manager. For example, Microsoft Outlook and other electronic mail systems provide features to "auto-forward" e-mail (all or specified) to someone else or to activate the "Out of Office," which notifies the sender with a predefined message.

Be sure you understand how to follow through on important correspondence and telephone calls.

Printing Business Cards. Here's a suggestion that may improve foreign business relations. If your manager is traveling to a foreign country, before the business trip have new business cards printed. One side should contain the usual information in English; the reverse side should be printed in the foreign language. Foreign business contacts will view this as a courteous gesture.

During Your Manager's Absence

Work while your manager is away at the same pace as you normally would.

Most managers will use the Internet to access their e-mail while they are away from the office. If this service is not available to them, they will probably want their e-mail forwarded to them so they can keep up with information and work while they are away. Most managers will also telephone the office regularly. Be ready to report on significant events and important mail and telephone calls. In your notebook, make a summary of what you should discuss. If the manager keeps in touch with the office through e-mail, you can provide this information on a daily basis and get the manager's feedback immediately.

If possible, plan your schedule so you can spend the first day the manager is back in the office following through on work generated by the trip.

When the manager is away, you will have added responsibilities and may need to allow extra time to handle them. For example, you will want to read the manager's e-mail, postal mail, and faxes to determine if any of the information is urgent and needs to be handled by the acting manager or by you. Save some time for communicating with the person who has been designated to act in the manager's role. Offer your assistance if you can perform certain responsibilities.

Try to keep the manager's calendar free of appointments for the first day following the trip. Before the manager returns, key a summary of appointments you have made. Indicate the date, the persons your manager will meet with, and the purpose of each appointment. If the manager uses an electronic calendar, there should be no need to key a list of appointments because the software gives a clear picture of appointments and a summary can be printed.

After Your Manager Returns

Your activities on your manager's first day back in the office after a trip will center on briefing the manager on what happened during the trip, following up with correspondence, assembling receipts for his or her expense report, and filing materials your manager brings back.

Report the most significant happenings first. Put on your manager's desk:

- The digest of the mail and the correspondence that arrived in your manager's absence, arranged in folders as explained in Chapter 6
- The summary of appointments
- A summary of telephone calls that were directed to you and were not left on his or her voice mail
- A list of who came to the office to see him or her

Early in the day, call attention to anything that requires immediate action.

Review your list of the materials your manager took on the trip that must be returned to the files. Locate these materials and file them. Also, file materials your manager acquired during the trip. Copies of materials from the files

TRAVEL EXPENSE VOUCHER

NAME: *Iain Brown* PIN: *784244*

TITLE: *Sales Manager* DATE: *April 10, 200X*

CONTROL #: _____

Date	Location	Work Order	Transport*	Hotel	Other	Entertain	Meals	Total	Explain Other, Entertain & Meals
April 5	Chicago		55.00	185.00		70.00	— / 19.00	329.00	Taxi airport — hotel / Lunch with Edwards & Ross
April 6	Chicago			185.00		125.00	11.00 / —	321.00	Lunch with Bollen / Dinner with Wolfe
April 7	Chicago		55.00				11.00 / —	66.00	Taxi hotel — airport
April 7	St. Paul				45.00		— / —	45.00	Airport parking / 3 days at $15.00
EXPENSE TOTAL			110.00	370.00	45.00	195.00	41.00	761.00	
LESS: CASH ADVANCES								695.00	
BALANCE CLAIMED OR RETURNED								66.00	

LEGEND

*   Include vehicle from Side 2 (if applicable)

**   Enter on Side 2

***   Distribute on Side 2

CERTIFICATION OF EXPENSES AUDIT

I certify that I have incurred these expenses.

APPROVAL OF EXPENSES

K. Winters

Payment Approved by

V. P. Sales

I. Brown _____   *April 10, 200X* _____   _____   _____

Employee's Signature Date Checked by Date

Title

April 16, 200X

Date

■ **Figure 10-6**
A sample travel expense voucher.

that your manager took on the trip can be disposed of. First, however, check carefully for notes that may have been made on them.

Travel Expense Voucher. The manager may want you to prepare a **travel expense voucher,** which is to be completed once your manager returns from a trip. The form is completed showing the "reportable" expenses based on the receipts obtained during the trip. If you are not sure about your company's policy with regard to expense claims, be certain to consult a policy manual so that your work on the voucher is accurate. Completeness and accuracy are the two necessary ingredients for ensuring a quick return of funds owing to the traveler.

Refer to Figure 10-6 for a sample travel expense voucher. Note that all expenses must have the approval of a senior employee. Although these forms vary from company to company, most require at least the following information:

■ The date the expense was incurred.

■ The location where the expense was incurred.

■ The cost of transportation.

■ The cost of the hotel where the traveler stayed.

- The cost and explanation of other business expenses that relate to the trip (including telephone calls, laundry services, or a necessary business item that was purchased).

- The cost of company-related entertaining.

- The cost of meals.

- The amount of any travel fund advance that may have been received prior to the trip. This amount is deducted from the amount the employee will now receive from the company.

It is common practice for organizations to arrange and pay in advance for air transportation. For convenience, these arrangements are made through the organization's associate travel agent. In such cases the cost of air transportation will not appear on the traveler's travel expense voucher.

Remember that most claimed expenses must be verified by receipts, and must not exceed costs specified by company policy.

These expense forms may be completed by your manager, you, or any level of employee. If the travel expense voucher form is stored on your computer, you can key the information. If not, it is acceptable to submit these documents in handwritten form.

INTERNATIONAL TRAVEL TIPS

Customs vary widely from one country to another, and understanding and observing these cultural variables is critical to a traveler's success. Taking the time to learn something about the culture of a country before doing business there shows respect and is usually deeply appreciated, not to mention rewarding for the company. The following tips for success are offered to help U.S. businesspeople better understand other cultures so they can develop successful, long-term business relationships.

For instance, if you were traveling to France to conduct your business, would the breakfast hour be a preferred time to meet for business? The answer is no: Americans like to schedule meetings at the breakfast hour, but French businesspeople prefer to eat their breakfast and read their papers in peace. Did you know that the number seven is considered bad luck in Kenya, good luck in Czechoslovakia, and has magical connotations in Benin? Did you know red is a positive color in Denmark but represents witchcraft and death in many African countries?

Tips for Success

The key to success in the traveler's business dealings and personal relationships in a foreign country is thorough preparation in learning about the country and a sincere desire to fit in with the new culture. Other tips for success include the following:

- **Do your homework!** This means researching a country's culture and company and incorporating as much of its custom into the visit as possible. Have enough information so that you can show an interest and ask intelligent questions.

- **Keep an open mind.** Do not judge behavior on your own standards. Attitudes, values, manners, greetings, and gestures are likely to be foreign

Microsoft Outlook and Trip Planning Information

■ Did you know that you could open one of your contact cards and click on the map icon from the Standard toolbar to automatically display a map of the address?

to you and at times what you might consider as bad manners and in poor taste. They are not! They are simply the product of a different culture.

■ **Listen carefully.** Your international clients may speak in broken English. Just remember that their English is a lot better than your Arabic, or Japanese, or whatever is their mother tongue.

■ **Different cultures treat time differently.** In the United States, time is a priority and we expect people to follow schedules very closely, to be on time for meetings, to complete projects before the deadline, and to show up when and where they say they will. Time does not have the same priority in all cultures. Some have a much more relaxed view of time. In fact, some cultures do not work in the afternoon and prefer to have only morning and evening meetings. This makes it difficult to schedule meetings, complete projects, and close deals. Keep this in mind when scheduling meetings and be as flexible as possible.

■ **Body language is often misinterpreted.** A friendly hand gesture in one country can be obscene in the next and actually illegal in another.

■ **Slow down so you can warm up.** Unlike Americans, people from many other cultures do not do business until they have established a relationship with you and your company representatives. This may mean many cups of coffee or tea and a lot of social conversation before business topics are ever approached.

You will learn more about international travel tips in Chapter 11.

Overview

✔ Learn your company's policies and procedures for travel, including the procedure for making your manager's travel arrangements through your company's travel department or a travel agent.

✔ Establish a Trip Preferences folder; compile the details about the destination, date of departure, and date of return; date and time of the first appointment and the time needed between arrival and the appointment; preferred time of travel; type of airline service; hotel preferences; and rental cars.

✔ Be able to use references either on the Internet or in print, such as the *Electronic Edition Service* of the *Official Airline Guide*.

✔ Consider the types of flights and classes of air services when making travel arrangements.

✔ Arrange for ground transportation, car rental, and hotel reservations.

✔ International travel requires the appropriate documents, such as passports and visas, and the proper immunizations.

✔ Be alert to security issues pertaining to both national and international travel.

✔ Following through on final arrangements includes gathering information needed prior to the trip, obtaining travel funds, preparing the itinerary, assembling materials for the trip, and obtaining special instructions to be carried out during your manager's absence.

✔ During your manager's absence, prepare logs or summaries of appointments, mail received, and important telephone calls.

✔ After your manager's return, brief your manager on what happened during his or her absence, collect receipts to complete an expense report, and draft follow-up correspondence.

✔ Working with international clients requires a completely new set of knowledge and skills. When you work with international clients, be flexible, adaptable, and tolerant.

Key Terms

Business class. Considered to be more prestigious and provides wider seats with more legroom and working room—an important consideration on long flights.

Class of service. The basis on which a traveler pays for an airline flight. The class specifies type of seating, food and beverages served, and degree of service.

Commuter flights. Short direct flights between two neighboring cities.

Direct flight. A flight on which the passenger remains on the same plane from departure to destination, regardless of the number of stops en route.

Economy class. In most cases, has less space between seats and limited meal service and is the most common way to fly.

Electronic tickets (E-tickets). Unlike the old-fashioned airline ticket issued by an agent, the travel information is sent as an e-mail to customers.

Guaranteed reservation. A reservation held with a credit card or deposit that holds the reservation in case of late arrival.

Itinerary. A combination of travel and appointment schedules. It shows when, where, and how the traveler will go. Details about confirmed appointments are also included.

Jet lag. A condition characterized by various physical and psychological effects, such as fatigue and irritability, following a long flight through several time zones.

Nonstop flight. A flight on which the passenger travels from point of departure to destination without making intermediate stops.

Official Airline Guide (OAG). The leading reference containing information on airline travel, from flight itineraries and special fares to baggage allowance.

Open ticket. Purchased when traveler does not know the return date.

Passport. A travel document, given to a citizen by his or her own government, granting permission to leave the country and to travel in a foreign country and to return to his or her own country.

Per diem. A Latin term meaning "per day."

Traveler's checks. Checks that allow travelers to carry money in a form other than cash.

Travel expense voucher. A form to be completed upon the return of a trip. The form is completed showing the "reportable" expenses based on the receipts obtained during the trip.

Visa. An endorsement or stamp placed in a passport by a foreign government that permits the traveler to visit that country for a specified purpose and a limited time.

For Your Discussion

 Retrieve file C10-DQ.DOC from your student data disk.

Directions

Enter your response after each question.

1. Organizations have definite policies and procedures concerning travel. Name some areas in which you would expect policies to be clearly stated.

2. What information relating to a trip should an office professional compile before contacting a travel department, travel agent, or airline?

3. What is the official source of information on airlines?

4. Using the twenty-four-hour clock, write 6 a.m., 2 p.m., and 9 p.m.

5. Describe the services provided in the *OAG*.

6. Explain the difference between a passport and visa. Who issues passports and visas?

7. What main duties should an office professional perform just prior to the manager's leaving on a business trip?

8. What information should be included in an itinerary?

9. Explain how an office professional's time can be used efficiently during the manager's absence.

10. What are the main duties pertaining to the trip after the manager's return?

READING WORKSHOP

In today's technology-based office, reading skills are essential. Two components of reading office materials, comprehending and verifying information, are vital to your job success. An office professional's careless habits and errors easily could cost an organization time, money, and goodwill. Therefore, it is essential that you demonstrate your reading skill while handling appointments and other office functions.

For Review

Appendix A: Reading

 Retrieve file C10-WRKS.DOC from your student data disk.

Directions:

When you have completed an expense report, an important task remains: reading the documents for accuracy and completeness. To complete this task accurately, it is vital that you verify information transferred from one form to another.

1. Examine and read the expense worksheet (Form 10-B) kept by Sheryl Robinson during her recent business trip.

2. Compare and verify the information on the worksheet filled in by Sheryl and the completed expense report (Form 10-C).

3. In the numbered blanks provided on Form 10-C, indicate if the information on the final form is correct by writing a *C*, or an *I* if the information is incorrect, by the appropriate number.

4. Ask yourself the following questions when preparing the final expense report:
   a. What must I do to compare and verify the information?
   b. Is the transferred information correct (according to the worksheet)?
   c. Are the figures that were transferred in the appropriate column?
   d. Did the figures get transferred accurately?
   e. Are the calculations correct?
   f. Do I have all the necessary receipts to submit with the completed form?
   g. Did I get my manager's signature on the completed form?

On the Job Situations

 Retrieve file C10-OJS.DOC from your student data disk.

Directions

Enter your response after each situation.

1. Your manager is planning a business trip to Istanbul, Turkey, and she has a passport but says she doesn't need a visa. You are responsible for assisting her with the travel plans. What should you do about the visa in this situation? If she does need a visa, what will you say to your manager?

2. When Ms. Orlando, your manager, arrived in New York City, she could not find her luggage. Her notes for the talk that she is to give at the conference are in her suitcase. You have a copy of the notes. Ms. Orlando calls you at home on Saturday morning and asks you to go to the office, find the notes, and call her. She says the notes are brief, and you could read them to her over the telephone. How do you react to this request? What suggestions would you make about packing notes for future talks?

3. You work for three executives. Two of them are planning to attend a management conference in San Francisco, and you made travel reservations for them. Now the third executive has decided to attend the conference and has asked you to make travel arrangements for the same time that the other two executives are traveling. You call the airline. A seat is not available at that time. What should you do while you are talking with the reservations clerk?

4. This was the first time you made travel arrangements for your manager, and your manager had the following problems on his trip. How would you prevent these problems from reoccurring on the next trip?

   a. The hotel room was guaranteed for arrival, and a nonsmoking room was not requested. Because of a large convention being held at the hotel, your manager could not get a nonsmoking room when he arrived.

   b. Although you told your manager that a car had been rented, the rental agency did not have a reservation. Your manager could not rent his preferred car size.

   c. A schedule of appointments was not included in the travel file given to your manager.

Projects and Activities

1. Final a local airline schedule on the Internet. Select a departure city and a destination city. List the schedules of service available between these two cities.

2. For the following locations (New Delhi, India; Beijing, China; Manila, Philippines), obtain the latest information and prepare a report on one of the following topics:

    a. passport requirements and where passports may be obtained locally

    b. visa regulations and where they can be obtained

    c. immunization requirements

    d. ground transportation to and from the local airport

    e. city transportation

3. Interview an office professional who makes travel arrangements. Ask the following questions:

    a. Is a checklist used to complete the travel function?

    b. Is there a department within this organization to handle the travel arrangements?

    c. What are your specific responsibilities for making travel arrangements?

    d. Is international travel involved? If so, what specific information or steps must be completed for the traveler?

    e. Does the traveler call in while away from the office? If so, what items are discussed with him or her?

    f. What kinds of activities are completed during the traveler's absence?

    g. What procedures are followed to complete the travel function when the traveler returns?

    h. What advice can the office professional give to help when handling the travel function?

    Summarize your findings in memo form. Be prepared to share your findings with the class.

4. Your manager is traveling to Cairo, Egypt, for the first time and will be away from the office for three weeks. She is leaving for Cairo in one month. This is the first opportunity you have had to make international travel arrangements, and you want to ensure that all details are complete and accurate. Your manager has asked you to gather all the details and review them with her at the end of the week. Make a trip folder to present to your manager. In sequence, identify what you would do to plan this trip.

Surfing the Internet

1. Your manager travels extensively and has asked you to find out the cost of subscribing to the electronic version of *OAG*.

    a. Connect to the Internet and access a search tool such as Yahoo!, Lycos, or NetSearch.

    b. Locate cost information on the electronic version of *OAG* by keying in the following search words: *travel, official airline guide*.

    c. Summarize the information in memo form to turn in to your instructor.

2. Your manager has asked you to reserve a flight on Southwest Airlines for departure (prior to 10 a.m.) on Monday two weeks away and return on Thursday (after 2 p.m.) of the same week.

   a. Connect to the Internet; enter the following site: http://www. southwest.com.

   b. Enter the information and print out a copy of your findings.

   c. Submit your findings to your instructor.

3. Locate current local times anywhere in the world.

   a. Connect to the Internet, enter the following site: http://www. worldtimeserver.com.

   b. Enter at least three major cities in the world and determine current local times.

   c. Submit your findings to your instructor.

Using MS Office 2002

Categorize Contacts for Travel Information

Setting Up Contact Cards

1. Open Microsoft Outlook. Click on Contacts in the Folder List.
2. Click on the New Contacts icon on the Standard toolbar.
3. Create a contact card for each company or person you work with in preparing for travel.
4. While still creating the contact cards, click on the Categories button at the bottom of the screen.
5. Select from the many predefined categories or add a new one, i.e., Travel Agents. Add similar contacts to the same category.
6. Click on OK.
7. Click on Save and Close on the Standard toolbar.

Viewing Contact Cards by Categories

1. In Microsoft Outlook, click on Contacts in the Folder List.
2. Click on View on the Menu bar.
3. Point to Current View.
4. Select By Category.
5. The data is displayed in rows and columns, similar to an Excel worksheet.
6. Click on the *plus* (+) sign to display all contact cards for a category.
7. Double-click to open a contact card to see more data.
8. Click on the *minus* (−) sign to hide the contact card listings for a category.

APPLICATION PROBLEMS

APPLICATION 10–A

Preparing an Itinerary

Supplies needed: Form 10-A, Notes on Mrs. Quevedo's Trip to the Southwestern Region; plain paper.

 Retrieve file C10-NOTES.DOC from your student data disk.

Mrs. Quevedo will make a business trip to the Southwestern Region during the week of September 1 through 5. She will visit the regional sales office in Dallas and the manufacturing plant in Fort Worth. She will speak to the Sales Management Club at the University of Houston. From the notes provided in Form 10-A, prepare Mrs. Quevedo's itinerary.

APPLICATION 10–B

Making an Airline Reservation

Supplies needed: Plain paper or card.

Mrs. Quevedo asked you to make an airline reservation for her from Rochester, New York, to Dallas on Tuesday, October 10. You know that Mrs. Quevedo prefers to travel in the morning and that she prefers nonstop and direct flights.

You call the airlines. A nonstop flight is not available. You make a reservation for her with American Airlines on Flight 716. The flight leaves Rochester at 10:03 a.m., arrives in Chicago at 10:50 a.m., leaves Chicago at 11:27 a.m., and arrives at the Dallas/Fort Worth International Airport at 1:49 p.m. She will be on the same plane for the entire trip. She has requested an electronic ticket (e-ticket).

Compose a memo to Mrs. Quevedo giving her complete information about the airline reservation.

APPLICATION 10–C

Planning an International Business Trip

Supplies needed: Plain paper.

1. You are to plan an international business trip for Mrs. Quevedo. She is making a presentation in Mexico City and Guadalajara one month from today. Mrs. Quevedo needs reservations at the Marriott Hotel in both cities for one week each. She has asked you to determine specific information about these two cities. Your findings must include the following:

   a. Travel times

   b. Time zone changes

  c. Travel documents needed

  d. Medical requirements

  e. Airlines to use

  f. Approximate cost for transportation and lodging

  g. Nearest American Embassy location

  h. International country and city telephone codes

  i. Average weather temperatures

  j. Holidays during her stay

2. To assist her in understanding the hosts' cultural and business practices, Mrs. Quevedo asked you to research the following:

  a. Greetings: handling of introductions; using appropriate titles; exchange of business cards; any other important points

  b. Gift-giving for the hosts

  c. The hosts' work-hour practices

  d. The hosts' attitudes toward time in general

  e. Nonverbal communication patterns as they relate to the hosts

  f. The country's currency exchange

  g. Letter-writing styles

3. Summarize your findings in memo form.

4. Be prepared to present your findings to the class.

Your Action Plan

Complete Your Action Plan; if necessary, review the guidelines in Chapter 1. Set one goal using the information in Chapter 10.

Your Portfolio

With the help of your instructor, select the best papers representative of your work from Chapter 10. Follow your instructor's directions about formatting, assembling, and submitting the portfolio.

chapter 11

Planning Meetings and Conferences

OUTLINE

LEARNING OUTCOMES

When you have completed this chapter, you should be able to:

✔ Follow procedures to prepare for a business meeting.
✔ Prepare a checklist of activities to be done before, during, and after the meeting.

✔ Identify the structure and procedures used in team meetings.

✔ Identify the most common forms of virtual meetings.

✔ Identify the additional responsibilities required to plan an international meeting.

Informal meetings can vary from a meeting in your manager's office to small committee meetings or staff meetings in a conference room. Formal meetings may consist of meetings for board of directors or large meetings for a professional society. Depending on the formality, you may be responsible for any or all of the following:

- Arranging the date and time
- Reserving the meeting room
- Sending notices
- Preparing the agenda
- Planning for supplies, equipment, and software
- Planning food and refreshments
- Assembling materials
- Attending the meeting
- Handling telephone interruptions
- Recording the meeting
- Following up after the meeting
- Preparing and correcting minutes

An office professional is responsible for arranging meetings—either making the arrangements or seeing that they have been made. The office professional may also have responsibilities in connection with meetings conducted by teleconferencing.

Suppose you are headed into a meeting that you have been responsible for planning and someone hands you a note saying that the caterer will be late delivering the refreshments for the next break time. Suppose that the projector's bulb burns out and everyone looks to you for the extra bulb because you had the responsibility for handling media. Regardless of how well you have planned the arrangements for a meeting, difficult situations (and embarrassing ones) can and do occur. Judgments are made about your organizational skills based on how you handle meeting arrangements. These judgments reflect conscious evaluations of your abilities, skills, and potential for advancement within a company. In fact, how you handle yourself, how well you plan the arrangements, and how you work with others sends a message about what your abilities are.

The task of planning meetings gives you one of the very best opportunities to make your manager look good and to secure your relationship as a team member. The guidelines presented in this chapter will help ensure that you are successful in organizing and coordinating meetings.

BEFORE THE MEETING

There are numerous meeting arrangements to make and different options available to help you get organized. Before you begin, be certain that you fully understand your responsibilities for making the meeting or conference arrangements. Begin by clarifying your responsibilities toward planning meetings to help prevent any misunderstandings later.

Scheduling and Organizing

To be successful in planning informal or formal meetings, make a list of the items to be dealt with before the meeting.

The following items should be completed in ample time:

1. Reserve the meeting room.

2. Make and confirm hotel accommodations and transportation available to and from the meeting, if necessary, for any out-of-town participants or provide participants with several hotel and car rental options for them to make their own reservations.

3. Get a written confirmation or a confirmation number of all reservations.

4. Determine how the meeting will be announced. You may not be responsible for this task if a meeting or conference is to be held in a location other than your company. For a meeting held on the company's premises, this task is usually the office professional's responsibility. You will also need to keep track of responses to the announcement and follow up with reminders.

5. Determine audiovisual or any other special equipment needs. If this meeting is a formal conference where speakers or presenters are involved, ask for a written request for their audiovisual needs.

6. Order audiovisual equipment.

A sample checklist for an in-house meeting is shown in Figure 11-1. The checklist includes items to complete (1) before a meeting, (2) on the meeting day, and (3) after the meeting. This list can be kept on your computer, or you may want to work from a hard copy. Either way, plan in advance and check and double-check your list.

How you handle the tasks before a meeting depends on a number of things. If you and others in your company have access to a computer, then you can accomplish a number of pre-meeting tasks efficiently. For instance, arranging an in-house meeting is easy when the following conditions exist: (1) the managers in your organization use the computer to keep their calendars; (2) both scheduled time and free time can be accessed; (3) the calendars are not classified as private and, therefore, are available to others; (4) the managers use electronic mailboxes; and (5) the conference rooms are scheduled using the computer.

When you have access to the computer:

1. Check the availability of the facilities.

2. Review the calendars of those who are to attend the meeting.

3. Find a time when all the participants are free.

4. Schedule the meeting and send the information about the meeting to the electronic mailboxes of the participants.

5. Send reminders via the e-mail system.

MEETING CHECKLIST

BEFORE THE MEETING		
General	**Target Date**	**Completion Date**
Secure names/addresses		
Reserve meeting room(s)		
Make calendar notations		
Prepare meeting notice		
Prepare agenda		
Send notice/agenda		
Prepare list of materials, supplies, equipment needed		
Order refreshments (or meal)		
Prepare meeting evaluation forms		
Prepare handouts		
Make hotel reservation(s)		
Confirm meeting room(s)		
Meeting Room(s)		
Location of electrical outlets		
Extension cords		
Audiovisual equipment		
Audiovisual supplies		
Name tags/name cards		
Seating arrangements		
Arrange for water pitcher/glasses		
Arrange for pads/pens		
THE MEETING DAY		
Final check on meeting room(s)		
Final check on food		
Final check on equipment		
AFTER THE MEETING		
Prepare/distribute notes/minutes		
Prepare follow-up correspondence		
Summarize evaluation forms		

■ **Figure 11-1**
Meeting checklist.

If you and others do not have access to a computer for planning tasks, then you must make meeting arrangements using traditional methods. Using the telephone to find a room for an in-house meeting and a time when it is convenient for all the participants to meet can become a time-consuming task, so plan ahead when you are using this method.

At the time your manager asks you to schedule an in-house meeting or to find out when the other managers are available, he or she should give you at least first and second choices of meeting times and tell you the purpose of the meeting. Enter the meeting for both time choices in your manager's appointment calendar. Contact the other participants and request the meeting for your manager's first choice. Also, inquire whether each person could be available at the second time selected. By doing this, you already will have the information if some of the participants have a conflict and the meeting has to be scheduled for the time of the second choice. Scheduling a meeting of three or four people can become complicated, involving many telephone calls or e-mail messages, because executives and professionals make numerous appointments within one week and, in addition, some of them travel. Consequently, let the participants or their assistants know that you will respond immediately if you cannot arrange the meeting as tentatively scheduled. As soon as you schedule the meeting, enter the time as a firm commitment in your manager's calendar and yours; clear the calendar of the extra or alternate meeting time.

If you have any difficulty setting up a meeting time with other managers at your company's facilities because of telephone tag, consider using a schedule form similar to the one shown in Figure 11-2. Certain times that were not available for meetings have been blocked out on this form. The form is routed or electronically distributed and participants are asked to select a specific meeting time indicating their first and second choices. When this form is returned to you, you should get an idea of when the participants are available.

Another use of this form is to fill in the time participants are requesting as they call in or send their response by e-mail. If your manager has given you

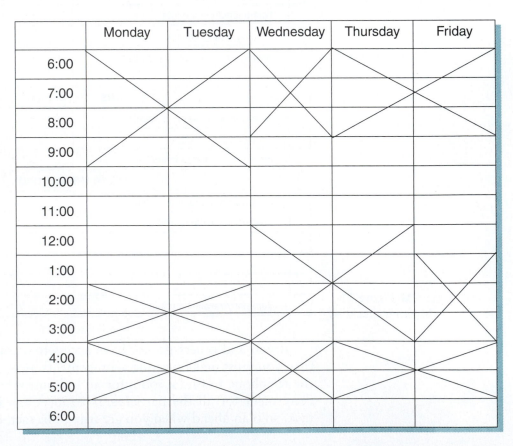

■ Figure 11-2
A form for scheduling meetings.

his or her first and second choices, then block out all other times and fill in only the responses from the participants.

Reserving a Meeting Room

The type of meeting or conference room needed will depend on the size of the group and the necessary equipment. For instance, a specially equipped room is needed for a video teleconference. You can determine the size of the room needed by checking the participant list. If minutes were kept for a formal meeting or conference held in the past, then you can check the previous minutes to get an estimate of attendance. Also, confer with your manager about facilities needed. For an off-site meeting, your manager may ask you to reserve a conference room at a hotel near the airport from which most participants will be arriving and leaving. You should confirm the approximate number of participants so that the hotel's meeting facilitator can reserve an appropriate-sized room. Hotels provide information online about their services. Some of the services provided by major hotels are:

- Equipment rental
- Meeting services that coordinate audiovisual services for associations, conventions, and corporate meetings coast to coast
- Banquet and meeting rooms
- Room setup and equipment specifications
- On-site supervision and labor coordination
- Exhibitor services—a department dedicated to the special requirements of exhibitors
- Business centers that provide services such as facsimile transmission, photocopies, computer workstations with Internet connections and office equipment rental, off-site printing and binding, color copies, and office supplies for purchase

If you must schedule a luncheon or dinner meeting at a hotel or a restaurant, call the banquet manager or the sales/catering manager. Inquire if there are costs in addition to the cost of the meal plus gratuity. You may have to guarantee a minimum number of attendees to avoid additional costs. On the other hand, if you are asking a hotel or a restaurant for a meeting room only, establish what the cost of the room will be before you work out other details.

Frequently room reservations at locations other than your company's facilities are made much in advance of a meeting date. Therefore, at the time you make the reservation, enter a notation in your calendar reminding you when to prepare and send out notices. You can enter the reminders at one time for a full year if you are to prepare and send notices for a group whose meetings are regularly scheduled a year in advance. Do be alert to any changes in meeting dates and indicate them in your reminder system. You need a reminder also to check the room reservation several days before the meeting (or if appropriate, several weeks).

As you make arrangements for meeting facilities, keep in mind the effect of the room and its furnishings. The atmosphere of the room will contribute significantly to an effective meeting. If the participants are distracted because they are physically uncomfortable, it will detract from the success of the

■ **Figure 11-3**
A conference room at the headquarters of a major corporation.

meeting. See Figure 11-3 for an example of an attractive, comfortable meeting room.

Here are some questions to ask when arranging for a room:

1. Do the room and its furnishings contribute to an effective meeting?

2. Does the arrangement of the room meet the purpose of the meeting? For example, if the purpose of the meeting was to resolve problem-solving situations, then a U-shaped or semicircular furniture arrangement would be most appropriate. On the other hand, if the participants are to review recommendations, then a circular or rectangular arrangement works best.

3. Is the room large enough to comfortably accommodate the participants and any planned audiovisual aids?

4. Is the room free from distractions and interruptions such as telephones and loud noises?

5. Is there adequate lighting, heating, and ventilation?

6. Does the room accommodate serving refreshments or a meal?

Sending Notices

The type of notice, timing, and details to be included are decisions you will make, depending on the type of meeting and how far in advance your planning occurs. For some routine meetings you might be able to create a form announcement. More formal meetings require drafting a notice for the specific occasion. Business professionals are busy people so it is important to announce meetings as soon as possible. Most participants have heavy schedules and prefer plenty of advance notice.

As soon as you have established a date, time, and venue, send out the notices by e-mail. When composing notices, always specify:

- The purpose of the meeting
- Time
- Date
- Location
- Deadline for accepting agenda items
- Action to take if member will attend
- Action to take if member cannot attend

Participants for a meeting are usually asked to submit topics for the agenda. Requests for items should be made early enough to prepare a final agenda based on the replies received. Clearly state the deadline for the latest time you will accept agenda items.

Time and Type. Determine the best time to send the notices. Consider also that often notices sent too early are ineffective because they can be forgotten. The amount of lead time for sending notices varies according to the formality of the meetings. For example, suppose it is now 10:00 a.m. and your manager asks you to set up a small informal meeting this afternoon at 2:30 p.m. with five other managers. Obviously, you do not have much lead time to send notices to the participants. What are your options? You may notify everyone using the e-mail system or telephone. Another way of notifying participants of an in-house meeting is by sending an interoffice memorandum. However, in this particular scenario, you probably will not have enough time to get the memo keyboarded, copied, and routed for the participants to read and respond to you with confirmation. In today's electronic world, e-mail is often solely used for all messages—replacing the routed memo entirely.

Some announcements for formal meetings and conferences may be sent to participants as far as one to three months in advance. These announcements may be in the form of specially designed brochures with registration forms, formal letterhead invitations, or printed forms.

For some types of meetings or conferences, enclose an addressed return card with the notice to make it easy for the recipients to reply. If you are not using e-mail to send the notice, add to the file copy the date the notice was mailed.

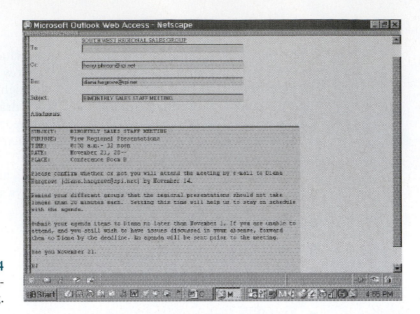

■ **Figure 11-4**
Notice of an informal in-house meeting.

Details in Notice. Use who, what, when, how long, where, and why as guides for composing notices. Be explicit about when: state the day, date, and hour. Include anything else in the notice that is essential. For instance, if you have a preliminary agenda, enclose it. If the participants need to bring along materials, mention this in the notice. Figure 11-4 is an example of a meeting notice.

Preparing the Agenda

Whether your manager is conducting an informal meeting or acting as chairperson of a more formal meeting or conference, he or she needs to follow a prepared agenda that has been provided to participants. An **agenda**, also called an *order of business*, is a list of topics to be covered during a meeting or conference, arranged in the order in which the topics will be discussed (see Figure 11-5). Preparing the agenda usually means that you, as an office professional, keyboard, copy, and distribute the agenda. Should your manager ask participants to submit topics for the agenda, the request should be made enough in advance to allow time for receiving the replies before preparing the final agenda.

If you are responsible for preparing the agenda, key it and send it out as an e-mail attachment. Even for a very informal meeting, an agenda should be distributed to all the members. Send the agenda early enough that each member receives it several days before the meeting. They will need time to prepare for the meeting. The more prepared people are, the more productive the meeting.

Choosing a Meeting Format

When the group has not already established the order of business, you can use the following two samples as guidelines.

AGENDA

MEETING NO. 4

QUALITY CONFERENCE COMMITTEE

DATE:	Wednesday, June 10, 20--
TIME:	2:00 p.m.
PLACE:	Conference Room 3
CHAIRPERSON:	Jeffrey Keaton
RECORDER:	Gina Darroch
COMMITTEE MEMBERS:	Jodi Alford, Satvinder Bhardwaj, Gina Darroch, Gordon McLeod, Chris Dennison, Jeffrey Keaton, Allan Kohut, Kenneth Skoye, Benjamin Ross, Brian Van Bij, Donna Welch, Marian Weston, Edward Woods.

TIME	TOPICS	MEMBER	DECISIONS AND FOLLOW-UP
2:00-2:10	Adoption of Minutes (Meeting No. 3)		
2:10-2:20	Facilities Report	B. Van Bij	
2:20-2:30	Registration Report	A. Kohut	
2:30-2:40	Awards Report	C. Dennison	
2:40-2:50	Communications Report	G. McLeod	
2:50-3:00	Budget Report	S. Bhardwaj	
3:00-3:10	Public Relations Report	B. Ross	
3:10-3:20	Publications Report	M. Weston	
3:20-3:30	Other Business		
3:30-3:40	Announcements		
3:40-3:45	Adjournment		

■ **Figure 11-5**
Agenda for an informal in-house meeting.

Formal meeting

1. Call to order by presiding officer
2. Roll call—either oral or checked by the secretary
3. Approval, amendment, or correction of minutes of previous meeting
4. Reading of correspondence

How to Prepare an Agenda

- Include the names of all participants.
- Include the date, time, and place.
- Include the topics of issues.
- Your manager may want to indicate the level of action to be taken by the participants for each topic or issue: discuss, decide, or recommend.
- Your manager may want to include time limits for each topic or issue.

5. Reports (in this order):
   - Officers
   - Standing committees
   - Special committees
6. Unfinished business from previous meetings
7. New business
8. Appointment of committee
9. Nomination and election of officers—once a year
10. Announcements, including the date of the next meeting
11. Adjournment

Informal Meeting

1. Check-ins or warm-ups (optional get acquainted activities)
2. Review goals of agenda or purpose of meeting
3. Review roles of members (optional)
4. Review ground rules (optional)
5. Discuss issues listed on agenda
6. Review follow-up actions that members have committed to
7. Closure
8. Determine date and time for next meeting if necessary

Assembling Materials

As soon as a meeting date has been set, start assembling the necessary materials. Just prior to the meeting, arrange them in a folder in the order in which your manager will refer to them. In addition to the agenda, materials that may be needed include:

- Extra copies of the agenda
- An up-to-date participant list
- Minutes of the previous meeting

- A list of standing and special committees
- A list of action items not yet completed by members
- Letters, memorandums, and reports related to the agenda items
- Copies of material your manager has prepared for distribution
- Materials available from others directly related to the topics or issues to be considered

You will be aware that certain supportive materials might be called for during the meeting. Assemble them, but if the meeting is in your manager's office, keep them on your desk. If you attend the meeting, take the folder of supportive materials with you; however, do not put these papers in with the other materials your manager will take to the meeting. Having to shuffle extra papers not only would disrupt your manager's thoughts but also would distract the group.

If the meeting is out of town, put the supportive materials in folders, carefully labeled so your manager can quickly find the papers. As a precaution, never put your file copies with materials to be carried around. Make copies and leave the originals in the files.

Ordering Refreshments, Meals, and Beverages

If your manager asks you to order refreshments and meals for participants, be sure to confirm the number of participants with the catering staff. Keep in mind the following guidelines for ordering:

1. For a morning meeting, coffee, tea, and juice can be served; also, water should be available. For light refreshments, consider fruit and pastries or bagels.
2. For a luncheon meeting, consider a salad or light entree.
3. For an afternoon meeting, coffee, tea, juice, and soft drinks can be served; in addition, cookies and fruit may be served.
4. For a dinner meeting at a location other than your company's facilities, consult with the catering staff for appropriate serving suggestions for the participants.

Handling Last-Minute Details

Someone once said, "We don't plan to fail, we just fail to plan." So, plan—and be prepared to make changes. Remain flexible. Prior to the meeting or conference, conduct a last-minute check of all details. At this point, a checklist serves as a very valuable tool in the planning process. A sample checklist was provided at the beginning of this chapter, but here is a quick checklist for you to use:

1. **Room Facilities**
   _____ Room arrangement check
   _____ Room temperature check
   _____ Meeting materials at each participant's place
   _____ Notepads/pencils (pens)

_____ Promotional items such as lapel pins, key tags, or pens with company logo

_____ Telephone message pad and pen next to meeting room phone

_____ Water/glasses

2. **Audiovisual Equipment**

_____ Notebook computer for presentations hook-up or for notetaking

_____ Flip chart paper, tripod, and colored markers

_____ Overhead projector and pens (extra bulbs)

_____ Microphone

_____ Laser pointer

_____ Projection screen

3. **Refreshments**

_____ Head count confirmed

_____ Special arrangements for table setup

_____ Food and beverages ordered

_____ Delivery time confirmed

4. **Meeting Materials**

_____ Extra copies of agenda

_____ Name tags or tents or name boards (if appropriate) and marker to write names

_____ Additional materials to be distributed

5. **Miscellaneous**

_____ Miscellaneous supplies (scissors, masking tape)

_____ System to take or deliver messages

DURING THE MEETING

Whether or not you are required to attend meetings with your manager will depend on the type of organization you work for and your manager's preferences. In some instances you may be asked to participate in the meeting, but frequently the office professional's role is to record the meeting proceedings. If you are asked to attend a meeting, arrange for someone to answer your telephone. Do not encourage interruptions, except for the most urgent calls.

Taking Notes

Before you take notes of any meeting, clarify the extent to which you are to take notes. For instance, in an informal meeting, you are not expected to record the entire conversation **verbatim** (word for word).

Notetaking usually is necessary near the end of a conversation when the participants are summarizing. When you think you have recorded all the essential information, you may read it to the participants, thus checking your notes and perhaps reminding them of something to add. After the meeting, your manager may use the notes to prepare a recommendation, such as a change in procedure or a request for new equipment. A popular way of taking notes today is to use a portable or laptop computer. Regardless of the method, after the meeting you can prepare a draft of your notes that will be meaningful to your manager.

Recording Minutes

As an assistant, you may be assigned the task of recording minutes and transcribing them. **Minutes** are notes recorded for a more formal meeting, such as for a meeting of officers of a corporation. Minutes serve as a record that an official meeting was held, discussions took place, and decisions were made during the meeting. There are different methods used for recording minutes, including using a tape recorder and a notepad.

Using a Notebook Computer. Most meetings do not require a verbatim transcript. In this case, the best practice is to key notes onto a notebook computer during the meeting. Your job of transcribing your notes into minutes will be mostly complete when you leave the meeting. All that will be required is some reformatting and editing. Refer to Figure 11-6 where a notebook computer is being used during a meeting.

During the meeting, your computer can be used for more than recording notes. It may operate independently but may also be connected online to the office network. The online connection allows access to information that may be needed to make informed decisions during the meeting.

Using a Tape Recorder. A tape recorder is used to obtain a verbatim record of a meeting for the purpose of (1) preparing a verbatim transcript, (2) assisting the secretary in writing the minutes, and (3) securing a record of discussions on controversial topics.

When you are recording a meeting on tape, you need to be alert to what is not being recorded and take essential notes. For instance, when a chairperson recognizes a speaker, the chairperson does not always call the speaker's name. Likewise, a chairperson does not always restate a motion as it is being voted on. When members are following distributed materials, reading as the

■ **Figure 11-6**
Notebook computer used during a meeting.

discussion ensues, the section to which the speaker is referring is not always clearly designated on the tape. Consequently, use notes to supplement the recording.

Record the time, date, and place of the meeting; attendance; reference to corrections and additions to the minutes; who is speaking—introducing reports and making motions; paragraph and page references to distributed materials being discussed; the exact statement of each motion if the chairperson does not state it; who volunteers for follow-up work; time of adjournment; and anything else that will be helpful to you in preparing the minutes. If you indicate in your notebook each time a motion is made, you can organize the minutes quickly as you listen to the tape.

Determine the policy for keeping tapes. Keep each tape until the minutes have been approved or for a much longer period when the topics are controversial or can become controversial. Some groups keep the minutes tapes permanently. Keep a tape until you have approval to erase it.

Put the tapes in their storage containers. Store the tapes being preserved where no one could inadvertently obtain one for recording, for a tape is simultaneously erased as a recording is made. Cassettes have a safety feature, two easy-to-remove knockout tabs at the rear of the cassette, to prevent accidental erasure of a recorded tape. Remove them to prevent the record push button from functioning if the tape is placed in a recorder. If you wish to make the cassette recordable again after removing the knockout tab, place a piece of adhesive tape over the holes.

Using a Notebook. When you take notes to provide a permanent record for a group, your task is similar in meetings conducted formally to those held informally. You are not expected to prepare a verbatim transcript. Only motions and a few other items must be recorded verbatim. Your job is to record the essential information that will serve as a basis for writing the minutes. Minutes provide a record of all the action taken during the meeting, not a detailed review of what was said; consequently, record all action and everything else that seems important.

Tips for Successful Notetaking

1. Prior to the meeting, study the minutes of similar meetings to become familiar with the form used.
2. Prior to the meeting, create a template with as much information as possible. During the meeting, have the template on the screen of your notebook computer where you can add information as the meeting progresses.
3. Sit near the chairperson so that you can assist each other.
4. Ask the chairperson to see that you get a copy of all materials read or discussed. These materials are part of the record and should be attached to the minutes. Do not wait until the end of the meeting to collect them.
5. Arrange a signal, such as slightly raising your hand, with the chairperson to let him or her know that you need assistance in getting statements that must be transcribed verbatim.

6. Before the meeting begins, record the name of the group and the date, time, and place of the meeting. Also record the names of those attending and those absent.

7. Using a list of participants that you prepared in advance, place a check mark in the appropriate column to indicate attendance and absence.

8. Write the exact words of anyone who asks that his or her view be made part of the record.

9. Be alert during the informal discussion about the details of a topic. Record each detail as it is discussed. After a detail is agreed on, and this usually is not by vote, write a word such as "Agreed" or "Yes" by it. Each of these items must be followed up. For information not needed, but that should be kept until you transcribe, you can use the "strikethrough formatting" command. If using Microsoft Word, to use the strikethrough formatting command

   ■ Select the text not needed

   ■ Click on Format on the Menu bar.

   ■ Click Font, making sure the Font tab displays.

   ■ Select Strikethrough by placing a check mark in the Effects box.

   ■ Check on OK.

   This will place a diagonal line across suggestions made but not accepted if you have entered them in your notes.

10. Indicate in your notes the name of each person making a motion.

11. Be sure to take detailed notes on any obligations your manager assumes during the meeting.

12. While a committee is being appointed, write the name of the committee, the full names of the members, and who accepted the position of chairperson.

13. When officers are elected, record the names of all the officers, incumbent as well as new, and their respective offices.

14. Make notes on the place, date, and time of the next meeting.

15. Write down the time of adjournment.

16. As soon as the meeting adjourns, verify any points about which you have doubt. You may need to ask about a person's title, the full name of a product or place, the correctness of technical terms with which you are not familiar, or any small details you need in order to prepare complete minutes.

MEETING FOLLOW-UP

There are numerous details to be taken care of immediately after a meeting has been held. Prepare a to-do list of all the actions you need to take. Here are some items that might be included:

1. Check the room for orderliness. Pick up extra copies of agendas, proposals, and reports left in the room. Also check the room for any articles left by the participants and clear away any leftover food and beverages or call the appropriate service department.

2. Make any necessary follow-up entries in the appointment calendars.

3. Send materials through e-mail to people who were absent.

4. Prepare a list to remind your manager of his or her obligations resulting from the meeting.

5. Put a copy of everything—agenda, reports, and so on—in a folder to use as reference at a later date. Be sure to include in your folder any summaries resulting from taking notes during the meeting.

6. Handle any requests that may have resulted from the meeting.

7. See that the audiovisual equipment is returned.

8. Enter the time of the next meeting in the calendars.

9. Make edits to the minutes of the previous meeting.

10. Complete the minutes.

11. Book the room and equipment for the next meeting.

To ensure that there is clear understanding of what was agreed upon, and to provide a complete record of transactions, the chairperson should write a memo to all members involved in follow-up actions. The chairperson should also send letters of congratulations to newly elected officers—even if these members were present at the meeting.

Preparing Notes

If you took notes, follow these general guidelines to produce the draft:

1. Produce the draft while the discussions are still fresh in your mind.

2. If an agenda was used, follow the sequence of topics or issues shown.

3. Prepare a concise summary in paragraph form without centered or side headings. Include the date, place of meeting, and the names of the participants. Keyboard the notes in summary form as shown in Figure 11-7.

Preparing Minutes

If you took minutes, here are some guidelines to follow to produce the draft:

1. If the meeting has been recorded on tape, listen to the tape and take brief notes. Do not waste your time making a verbatim transcript of the tape. When a meeting has been run smoothly, you can listen to a portion of the tape, compose that part of the minutes, listen to the next portion, compose, and continue until you reach the end of the recording. When the proceedings are difficult to follow, listen to the entire recording, taking notes as you listen, and then repeat portions of the tape to verify information as you compose.

2. Write the minutes immediately following the meeting. When you work from your manager's notes, it is more than likely that you will have to ask questions to elicit additional facts.

3. Keyboard a rough draft of the minutes, either double- or triple-spaced, and submit them to your manager for approval before you prepare the minutes in final form.

4. Follow a standard arrangement for each group for which you write minutes but not necessarily an identical arrangement for all groups. Your purpose is twofold: (1) to include all the essential information as a record

MINUTES OF THE EXECUTIVE TEAM OF CONTINENTAL TECHNOLOGY INC.
Meeting No. 9 — July 8, 200X

The Executive Team of Continental Technology Inc. met in a regular session at 10:30 a.m., Wednesday, June 8, 200X, in Conference Room 3. The following members were

PRESENT:	Verna Chiasson	(Quality Advisor)
	Penny Handfield	(Guidance Team)
	Maurice Ingram	(Team Member)
	Daniel Lawrence	(Team member)
	Laura Milton	(Team Leader)
	Betty Noble	(Guidance Team)
	Paul Noel	(Team Member)
	Gregory Patrick	(Recorder)
	Dana Rahn	(Facilitator)
	Michelle Savard	(Team Member)
	Gayle Schmitt	(Team Member)
	Mike Sherman	(Team Member)
ABSENT:	Wendy Scarth	(Team Member)

Maurice Ingram moved to approve as read the minutes of meeting No. 8. This motion was seconded by Mike Sherman. The following topics were then discussed:

REDUCTION IN ADMINISTRATIVE COSTS:

The ideas presented at the June 10 meeting for cutting administrative costs were revised and the following decisions were made:

Travel. Effective August 1, 200X, all executives of Continental Technology will no longer travel executive class; economy fare only will be paid by the company, with the exception of executive class fares approved by the vice-president. Where Continental executives are taking major clients on business trips, the executive class will automatically be approved by the vice-president.

Sales Incentive Trips. The consensus was that the yearly sales incentive trips, given to sales executives reaching their quotas, should be shortened in length. The trips will be shortened from one week to four days. As well, these trips will no longer be to extremely distant points; they will now be to warm weather North American resorts. It was felt that this would reduce both the air fare and accommodation charges considerably. This will be effective May of next year.

EMPLOYEE EVALUATIONS:

Laura Milton circulated copies of a new Employee Performance Evaluation which has been designed to follow ISO 2000 principles. The Executive Team votes unanimously in favor of using the new form beginning September 1.

ANNOUNCEMENTS:

Catalog. A new product catalog will be available July 25. Copies can be obtained by calling Betty Noble.

New Team Member. Wendy Scarth joined the team as of July 1. However, she is currently taking a training course and absent from meeting No. 9. Wendy works in the Marketing Department and was previously employed by CanTech in Montreal.

Next Meeting. The 10th regular meeting will be held in Conference Room 3 at 10:30 a.m. on Thursday, August 15, 200X.

ADJOURNMENT:

The meeting was adjourned at 11:45 a.m.

July 10, 200X

Date

G. Patrick

Gregory Patrick, Secretary

■ **Figure 11-7**
Summary of meeting notes.

that will be meaningful to others in the future, and (2) to make it easy for the reader to locate a single item.

5. When a meeting has been conducted so informally that motions were not made and agreement was by consent instead of voting, include the essential facts about the purpose of the meeting, who attended, when, and where and then summarize the action.

TEAM MEETINGS

The team concept of meetings focuses on equal participation. Each participant's input is considered to be as significant as all other participants', from the maintenance employee to the chief executive officer of the company. The team concept is effective because each member is empowered to participate regardless of his or her organizational status.

Teams make decisions at their level of authority. If a decision must be made at a higher level of authority, the team forwards a recommendation to management. Because team meetings encourage all participants to express their views, conflict and team dynamic challenges may occur.

Preparing for a Team Meeting

A meeting that follows team techniques requires the same preparation as any other meeting—a convenient time is established, people are invited, and an agenda is prepared and delivered to participants prior to the meeting.

When team techniques are followed, careful attention is given to issues that arise even at the preliminary stages.

- Choosing an appropriate time is important.
- The people who form the team may be from all levels of the organization.
- All team members carry equal status.
- The prepared agenda may be very general because the actual topics to be discussed should be decided by the team.

Selecting Participants

Part of the team philosophy is to get input from people who are actually working within the process. In other words, the people who know the most about a topic should be at the meeting to discuss it and to make wise recommendations and decisions about it.

Each role in the team is equally important. The following briefly discusses the roles of team participants.

1. **Team Leader.** The team leader acts as a chairperson, directing the meeting, moving from one topic to the next, and keeping on schedule.
2. **Guidance Team.** The guidance team should consist of two or more people who are very familiar with the organization. These people usually come from management positions; this enables them to provide information that other members may be unaware of and that will be helpful when team decisions are made. They should be people who have the authority to make changes and the clout to put decisions into practice.

3. **Project Team Members.** All members who will take part in the decisions and vote on issues are considered project team members.

4. **Facilitator.** The team leader often carries both the roles of team leader and facilitator. The facilitator's responsibility is to make the meeting process flow with ease.

5. **Recorder.** The recorder's task is to prepare minutes. This task is often rotated among team members so that no one team member always has the additional responsibility of taking notes at each meeting.

Starting the Meeting

Here are some suggestions that will make the team meetings productive:

- **Maintain the Schedule.** The team leader starts early, and the meeting begins and ends as scheduled.

- **Warm up.** If the team members do not know each other, the team leader should start the meeting by having all people introduce themselves. This activity is considered to be the warm-up.

- **Check in.** Checking in is an opportunity for each team member to express his or her present state of mind to the whole team. An example is "I've just had a relaxing weekend; my energy has returned and I'm ready to participate."

- **Agree on the goals.** Once the check-in is complete, the team leader should review the agenda.

- **Review the roles of the team.** At the first meeting, the roles of the team leader, guidance team, facilitator, and project team member should be reviewed by the team leader.

- **Establish the house rules.** These are also referred to as the "ground rules." The team should suggest and agree on some general rules before the meeting progresses. Here are some examples:
  - Everyone will be given an equal opportunity to speak.
  - Any person wishing to speak must raise his or her hand.
  - Criticize only the issue, not the person with the issue.
  - Side conversations are not allowed.
  - Each person must focus on the speaker.
  - Expect unfinished business.
  - The meeting will begin and end on schedule.
  - Everyone will focus on the topic and will not interrupt the team's work for outside reasons.
  - No negative body language is allowed.

VIRTUAL MEETINGS

Because managers today have a greater span of control—sometimes locally, nationally, and even internationally, they are constantly seeking ways to spend less time traveling and more time conducting business. (**Span of control** is the number of people and functions that one manager can supervise.) Virtual meetings, also called **teleconferencing**, are a means of holding meetings over communications links connecting two or more locations. The most common types of virtual meetings are audioconferencing, videoconferencing, data conferencing, and virtual conferencing.

Audioconferencing

Placing conference calls by telephone when the participants are located in different geographic areas is called **audioconferencing**, also called teleconferencing. Using this method to hold conferences saves travel time and costs and at the same time maintains effective communications. This is the most widely used teleconferencing tool today; it can be used effectively when there is no need for video transmission. The calls are transmitted either with operator assistance or through the use of dial-up lines or leased lines. Dedicated lines are directly connected to your teleconference destination. This eliminates the need for an operator. For small groups, speakerphones are convenient.

Videoconferencing

Because more and more businesses are allowing employees to work at home, called **telecommuting**, a greater need has arisen for virtual teams that hold virtual meetings using videoconferencing. Teleconferencing that combines telephone and video is referred to as **videoconferencing**. In a videoconference two or more persons who are at different geographic locations can conduct business verbally and visually as if they were in the same room (see Figure 11-8). Satellite carriers offer full videoconferencing, which resembles two television sets or two PCs (called desktop videoconferencing) talking to each other. Videoconferencing TV-based videophones that use a camera and microphone integrated into the unit are available to simplify the process. Videoconferencing is expensive because it uses numerous pieces of equipment that include

■ **Figure 11-8**
A videoconference.

cameras, monitors, microphones, speakers, and PCs. When participating in a videoconference, remember the following:

■ The other participants can see you, so you must conduct yourself in the same way as in a face-to-face meeting.

■ There may be a difference in timing between the audio and the video, so what you hear may be slightly ahead of or behind what you see.

■ With both audio- and videoconferences that take place over significant distances, there will be a delay in receiving the message. Even a delay of a second can cause confusion as to who should speak next. Slow down. Wait for your message to be received on the other end and wait for the other person's voice to be received on your end.

Direct Broadcast Video

Direct broadcast video, also called **one-way video,** is video transmission from a single location combined with telephone response from each of the receiving locations. Direct broadcast video is especially helpful in making immediate announcements about new products available through the organization, or a corporatewide announcement by the president.

Computer Conferencing

When organizations conduct conferences through computer terminals where the terminals are connected to a network, it is called **computer conferencing.** This network may be across the room or across the world because telephone lines or cable may be used to carry the signals. Messages are simply keyed back and forth.

The use of computer conferencing can include audio and video as long as all parties have the right multimedia software, and cameras and microphones adapted to their computers.

Data Conferencing

Data conferencing takes place when two or more persons interact visually and verbally while at the same time displaying text or graphics as computer images, usually using a second monitor. As an example, NetMeeting, a software program by Microsoft, allows you to communicate using audio and video capabilities. You use a PC and the Internet to hold face-to-face conferences and meetings. Using NetMeeting software, you can use any Windows-based application and exchange graphics on an electronic whiteboard, transfer files, and use the text-based chat program, just to name a few of its features.

Virtual Conferencing

Virtual conferencing can be used for business purposes to provide specific discussion groups the opportunity to share ideas through the use of the Internet. This system acts like a newsgroup, a message board, chat room, or a bulletin board system, in that a space is provided on the Internet where users can post electronic messages to other users. The purpose of the system is to foster a community-type atmosphere that will allow people to exchange ideas and information. A feature that is called *virtual reality* can be used to allow the participants to download files that allow them to experience the feeling of "being there." For instance, you might download the file of a museum of fine art. You may elect to allow the computer to take you on a tour of the museum, making you feel as if you are viewing the room from the computer screen. As the camera moves from room to room, you feel as if you were actually turning left or right, and looking up, down, and around the room. You may also elect to take the tour manually by using the mouse or arrow keys on the keyboard to advance through the tour. These experiences allow you to provide input to the discussion group based on realistic experience that you have had.

In addition to becoming familiar with one or all of the types of virtual conferencing, you will have the following responsibilities when you make conference arrangements.

- Notifying the conference participants and arranging a convenient time when all of them are available.
- Reserving the teleconference facility.
- Requesting any special equipment needed by the participants.
- Preparing and assembling materials to be distributed.
- Requesting a person to serve as a technical backup in case the conference leader has difficulty with the equipment.
- Taking notes during the teleconference.
- Completing the teleconference follow-up activities, such as summarizing notes and evaluation forms.

INTERNATIONAL MEETINGS

As world communications becomes more and more commonplace, the office professional may find it necessary to help the manager prepare an international conference or to participate in one. You may be required to manage all aspects of the meeting, including:

- Advertising
- Scheduling
- Soliciting papers
- Making announcements
- Serving as liaison and providing protocol
- Supervising staff members
- Selecting and negotiating a major hotel, which would involve obtaining information about:
  - Conference rooms
  - Exhibit and display space
  - Banquets
  - Meals
  - Tours of areas of interest to attendees and spouses
  - Registration
  - Audiovisual equipment

- On-site typing and administrative support services
- Refreshments breaks
- Tracking and handling finances and payments, including exchange rates
- Making travel and lodging arrangements
- Making security arrangements
- Arranging for transportation
- Providing interpreters, if needed

You might be asked to find information about all of the above while maintaining the correct protocol, dealing with cultural differences, and dealing with a different language. Here are some hints:

- Become familiar with the country where the meeting is to be held. What are its religious beliefs, social customs, business philosophy, and family structure?
- Familiarize yourself with the customary formats of business documents used in that country.
- Learn the name of major political leaders, sports figures, and other celebrities from that country.

All of this information will help you know what *not* to do as well as what to do. If you think globally, you can give yourself the edge as you are planning or progressing through your career. Take every opportunity to familiarize yourself with significant communications and cultural barriers that need to be overcome with various cultures. One of your best sources is the United States government. You can get information from the Small Business Administration's office of International Trade (http://www.sba.gov), the U.S. Department of Commerce, or the U.S. Department of State (http://www.state.gov).

---

quicktips

Scheduling Meetings—Avoid Telephone Tag:

1. Schedule meetings via the e-mail.
2. Use the e-mail option to code your message when the recipient reads it.
   - If your e-mail provides this option, you will receive a message telling when each person opened the e-mail.
     - If your system doesn't provide this, make a statement in your e-mail for the recipient to reply upon receipt.
   - Illness or vacations may detain a person from reading e-mail, so:
     - After an appropriate time, call those who haven't read the e-mail message; communication is key.
       - Make sure the person is notified of the meeting through *verbal* communication.
       - Talk with the office assistant if you can't reach the person directly.

Overview

✔ When scheduling a meeting:

1. Reserve the meeting room.
2. Make and confirm hotel accommodations and car rentals, if necessary.
3. Obtain written confirmation or a confirmation number for all reservations.
4. Determine how the meeting will be announced.
5. Determine audiovisual or any other special equipment needs.
6. Order audiovisual equipment.

✔ When a computer is available:

1. Check the availability of the facilities.
2. Review the calendars of those who are to attend the meeting.
3. Find a time when all the participants are free.
4. Schedule the meeting and send e-mail notices to all participants.
5. Send reminders via the e-mail system.

✔ Questions to ask when arranging for a room:

1. Do the room and its furnishings contribute to an effective meeting?
2. Does the arrangement of the room meet the purpose of the meeting?
3. Is the room large enough to comfortably accommodate the participants and any planned audiovisual aids?
4. Is the room free from distractions and interruptions such as telephones and loud noises?
5. Is there adequate lighting, heating, and ventilation?
6. Does the room accommodate serving refreshments or a meal?

✔ When preparing an agenda:

1. Include the names of all participants.
2. Include the date, time, and place.
3. Include topics or issues.
4. Your manager may want to indicate the level of action to be taken by the participants for each topic or issue: discuss, decide, or recommend.
5. Your manager may want to include time limits for each topic or issue.

✔ Decide whether the meeting will have a formal or informal format.

✔ When assembling materials, you may want to include:

1. Extra copies of the agenda
2. An up-to-date participant list
3. Minutes of the previous meeting
4. A list of standing and special committies
5. A list of action items not yet completed by members
6. Letters, memorandums, and reports related to the agenda items
7. Copies of material your manager has prepared for distribution
8. Materials available from others directly related to the topics or issues to be considered

✔ Minutes are notes recorded for a more formal meeting, such as for the meeting of the officers of a corporation. You may take minutes by hand or on a notebook computer, or if the minutes must be verbatim (word-for-word), you will need a tape recorder.

✔ Following the meeting, numerous details may need to be taken care of:

1. Check the room for orderliness.
2. Make any necessary follow-up entries in the appointment calendars.
3. Send materials via e-mail to people who were absent.
4. Prepare a list to remind your manager of his or her obligations resulting from the meeting.
5. Put a copy of all meeting materials in a folder.
6. Handle any requests resulting from the meeting.
7. Return any borrowed audiovisual equipment.
8. Enter the time of the next meeting in the calendars.
9. Edit the minutes of the previous meeting.
10. Complete the minutes.
11. Book the room and equipment for the next meeting.

✔ To make team meetings productive:

1. The team leader starts early.
2. The meeting begins and ends as scheduled.
3. The members participate in a warm-up activity.
4. Each team member "checks in."
5. The team leader reviews the agenda.
6. The leader reviews the roles of the team members.
7. The team establishes house rules.

✔ The most common types of teleconferencing are audioconferencing, videoconferencing, direct broadcast video conferencing, computer conferencing, data conferencing, and virtual conferencing.

✔ As world communication becomes more and more commonplace, the office professional may find it necessary to help the manager prepare an international conference or participate in one. Here are some hints:

■ Become familiar with the country where the meeting is to be held. What are its religious beliefs, social customs, business philosophy, and family structure?

■ Familiarize yourself with the customary formats of business documents used in that country.

■ Learn the name of major political leaders, sports figures, and other celebrities from that country.

Key Terms

Agenda. Also called an *order of business;* a list of topics to be covered during the meeting or conference, arranged in the order in which the topics will be discussed.

Audioconferencing. Placing conference calls by telephone when the participants are located in different geographic areas.

Computer conferencing. Conducting conferences through computer terminals when the terminals are connected to a network.

Data conferencing. A system in which two or more persons interact visually and verbally while at the same time displaying text or graphics as computer images, usually using a second monitor.

Direct broadcast video. Also called *one-way video*; video transmission from a single location combined with a telephone from each of the receiving locations.

Minutes. Notes recorded that serve as a record of an official meeting.

One-way video. See *Direct broadcast video*.

Span of control. The number of people and functions that one manager can supervise.

Teleconferencing. The means by which meetings are held over communication links connecting two or more locations.

Telecommuting. A system where businesses allow employees to work at home.

Verbatim. Stated word-for-word as it is said.

Videoconferencing. A system in which two or more persons who are at different geographic locations can conduct business verbally and visually as if they were in the same room.

Virtual conferencing. A system that acts like a newsgroup, message board, chat room, or bulletin board system, in that a space is provided on the Internet where users can post electronic messages to other users.

For Your Discussion

 Retrieve file C11-DQ.DOC from your student data disk.

Directions

Enter your response after each question.

1. How can the computer be helpful in arranging meetings?
2. In arranging meetings, what preliminary activities are the office professional's responsibility?
3. On the meeting day, what activities can the office professional accept responsibility for?
4. Why are the room and furnishings important to the success of a meeting?
5. After the meeting, what activities can the office professional accept responsibility for?
6. In arranging an international meeting, what aspects of the meeting might the office professional be responsible for?
7. What information should you provide your manager immediately following a meeting that he or she has chaired?
8. Describe an efficient way of organizing notes for writing minutes when the transactions of the meeting were recorded on tape.
9. Explain the various types of virtual meetings available to today's business.
10. What responsibilities might an assistant have concerning a teleconference?

BUSINESS MATH WORKSHOP

Chapter 8 reviewed the concept of finding the rate in the part, rate, base formula. You learned to calculate the rate and to distinguish the parts in questions such as "How much is the commission rate on an item that sold for $3,200 of which I earned $600?"

You have learned that once you know which part of the formula to use, you can substitute the given values for two of the terms to find the third unknown term. In this chapter you will review the third part of the part, rate, base formula—the base. You will learn to calculate the base component in the following question:

23 percent of what number is $12,500 (finding the base)?

Let's turn the preceding question into the following business application:

A new car depreciates at 23 percent the first year. At the end of the first year it has depreciated $12,500. What did the owner pay for the car?

To obtain the answer, divide the part ($12,500) by the rate (23 percent). The answer is $54,348 (rounded), which is the base (what the owner paid for the car). Check your answer by finding the part (rate times base). Your answer should be the $12,500 (rounded).

For Review

Appendix A: Business Math

 Retrieve file C11-WRKS.DOC from your student data disk.

Directions

Find the base in each of the following problems. Carry answers to two decimal places.

1. 124 is 1.9 percent of what? _____

2. 12 percent of what is 2.7? _____

3. 0.6 percent of what is 48? _____

4. 36.8 is 13 percent of what? _____

5. 13.5 percent of what is 235? _____

Find the rate (percent) in each of the following problems. Round to the nearest tenth.

1. What percent of 35 is 12? _____

2. 76 is what percent of 312? _____

3. What percent of 732 is 27? _____

4. 2.95 is what percent of 562? _____

5. What percent of 100 is 25? _____

Find the part in the following problems. Carry your answers to two decimal places.

1. What is 0.7 percent of 49? _____

2. What is 20 percent of 156? _____

3. What is 2 percent of 100? _____

4. What is 39 percent of 195? _____

5. What is 200 percent of 367? _____

On the Job Situations

 Retrieve file C11-OJS.DOC from your student data disk.

Directions

Enter your response after each situation.

1. You receive a long-distance call for Mary Ann Cortelli, who is supposed to be attending a meeting chaired by your manager, Allen Bigby. The meeting is being held near your office. About seventy-five participants are in attendance. Ms. Cortelli preregistered for the meeting, but she has not picked up her registration badge or her luncheon ticket. You speculate that she is not at the meeting. The telephone call seems urgent. What should you do?

2. Your manager, Ms. Corona, is giving a talk at a national conference in another state at two o'clock tomorrow afternoon. As soon as she arrives at her destination, she calls you to say that she does not have the slides she needs to illustrate her talk. "Are they there?" she inquires, and sure enough, they are. You forgot to put them in her briefcase. She is certain that the hotel where she is speaking has a slide projector. She says, "Get the slides to me in time for the presentation." You reply, "I will send them by air." It is now 3:30 p.m. What will you do?

3. One of the assistants in another department has come to you for your advice. Her manager has not been distributing an agenda prior to meetings. On occasion when her manager has used an agenda, it does not include all of the items and no time limits have been indicated for each topic or issue. Participants in the meetings have been coming to the assistant and complaining. They have asked her to get the manager of the department to use an agenda more effectively. What should an agenda include? What would you say to her?

4. You have scheduled a two-day training session for 18 employees. The meeting is scheduled in three days and all arrangements have been made. You receive a call from the instructor explaining he has become very ill. What should you do? Outline in detail your actions.

Projects and Activities

1. Interview an assistant who has handled all the details for a formal or informal meeting. Summarize the assistant's responses to the following questions:

   a. What are the most critical steps taken when you first plan a meeting?

   b. What methods are used to notify people of an upcoming meeting?

   c. Are you responsible for taking notes or minutes in meetings? If so, can you share how you format the notes or minutes?

   d. What types of activities, if any, are you involved in during a meeting?

   e. What types of activities do you complete after a meeting?

   f. Are you involved in making arrangements for teleconferencing?

   g. What are the most common problems that arise when planning meetings or conferences?

2. Research magazines, newspapers, or the Internet for articles relating to electronic conferencing. Summarize the information and be prepared to report your findings to the class.

3. With the use of audio and video electronic technology, public and private educational institutions are using virtual meetings. Interview a school administrator who is responsible for virtual meetings in his or her institution. Report your findings on the method used for virtual meetings, how questions and answers are handled during the meeting, and the most common problems that arise when planning virtual meetings.

4. Call the sales or catering department of two hotels in your area. Request the following information:

   a. Approximate cost of a room to hold a meeting for 10, for 30, and for 100 people.

   b. A price list for refreshments.

   c. Do they rent audiovisual equipment? If so, what types, and what do they cost?

   d. How far ahead do you have to reserve the room?

   e. What are the rules, if any, concerning canceling room reservations?

   f. What other features do they offer companies for planning meetings at their hotels?

Summarize your findings in report form for your instructor.

Surfing the Internet

You are constantly involved with scheduling teleconferences for meetings and training. You heard there is an association especially for employees that use electronic conferencing in the workplace. You mention the association to your manager, and the manager wants to know more about it.

1. Connect to the Internet and access a search tool such as Yahoo!, Lycos, or NetSearch.

2. Enter the following url: http://www.imcca.org.

3. Locate information about the Interactive Multimedia & Collaborative Communications Alliance (IMCCA). Browse the IMCCA website and find and print the following information on each of these areas:

   a. History of IMCCA

   b. Mission statement

     c. Newsletter

     d. Membership information

     e. Benefits of membership

     f. Resources

4. Write a report to your manager providing the information requested.

Using MS Office 2002

Schedule a meeting

Directions

1. Open Microsoft Outlook and click on Calendar in the Outlook Shortcuts.
2. Click on New then Appointment. The Untitled Appointment dialog box will appear.
3. Type a subject, location, and comments in the message area:

   Type as your subject: Office Procedures Meeting

   Type as your location: Room 224

   Type as your comments: Discussion will be about using Outlook to set up meetings.
4. Click on the Scheduling tab.
5. Click on "Click here to add a name" and type the name of two of your classmates or friends.
6. Fill in the date and time text boxes under Start Time and End Time.
7. You can send the meeting notice from either the Appointment or Scheduling tab window. You can also decide if the recipient's attendance is required or optional.
8. Click on the Send icon.
9. When the recipients receive your message, they can click on the Accept, Tentative, or Decline buttons on the toolbar.
10. You will receive their "accept, decline, or tentative" reply and any comments they have for you.
11. If you need to edit or delete this message, simply open it to make changes or to delete. You will automatically be prompted to notify attendees.

APPLICATION PROBLEMS

APPLICATION 11–A

Sending Notice of Meeting

Supplies needed: Plain paper.

Mrs. Quevedo has called a meeting of the Executive Committee of the November Sales Seminar. She has asked you to send the notices. The meeting will be held in Mrs. Quevedo's office at Supreme Appliances, Inc., at 5:00 p.m. on Wednesday, September 10. The purpose of the meeting is to finalize plans for the November Sales Seminar. The Executive Committee members include the assistant vice presidents of each region and the sales managers from Boston and Texas. Create a meeting notice and reply card to send to the participants.

Mrs. Quevedo needs to know (1) if the person can attend the September 10 meeting, (2) if the person has a report to make, and (3) if the person thinks that an October meeting of the Executive Committee will be necessary. Phrase your questions carefully on the reply cards. (Be sure to indicate a place for the signature so that you will know from whom you received the reply.) Mrs. Quevedo will approve a draft of the notice before the names, titles, and addresses are filled in.

APPLICATION 11-B

Composing and Keyboarding Minutes

Supplies needed: Form 11-A, November Sales Meeting Notes; plain paper.

Directions: Mrs. Quevedo put her notes from the September 10 meeting of the Executive Committee of the November Sales Seminar in your in-basket. The following note was attached: "Please compose and key these minutes." Compose and keyboard Mrs. Quevedo's notes from Form 11-A.

APPLICATION 11-C

Hosting International Visitors

Supplies needed: Form 11-B, Meeting Checklist; plain paper.

 Retrieve file FIGURE 11-1.DOC from your student data disk.

Directions: Mrs. Quevedo has asked you to help her with hosting an international group. She wants to avoid any miscommunication that may interfere with the success of the meeting. Mrs. Quevedo has asked you to make arrangements for hosting seven visitors from Guadalajara, Mexico. You have the responsibility for this group of five men and two women from their arrival time at DFW Airport on Sunday to their departure time (one week from their arrival).

During the group's visit, you are to make arrangements for two meetings: the first to be held at 10:00 a.m. on Tuesday and the second to be held at noon (a luncheon meeting) on Wednesday. In addition to making arrangements for the two meetings, you have been asked to make arrangements for dinner on Thursday at 7:30 p.m. Complete Form 11-B for the meeting.

In addition, Mrs. Quevedo has asked you to gather the following information in report format about the visitors:

The Country

- In which state of Mexico is Guadalajara located?
- What are the main industries in Guadalajara?
- What are some historical aspects of Guadalajara?
- What are some political aspects of Guadalajara?
- Who are some sports figures from Guadalajara?

Nonverbal Communication

- Are there any nonverbal communication patterns that we use which may be interpreted as "offensive" in their country?
- Can you anticipate some possible miscommunication problems? If so, identify a few.
- Can you determine the appropriate speaking distance between persons from this culture?

Daily Business Life

- How should we greet these visitors?
- Determine if gift giving is appropriate for these visitors. If so, what kind of gift is appropriate?
- What kinds and colors of flowers are appropriate to use for our meetings?
- How are business meetings conducted in the visitors' country compared to our own?
- What business etiquette or manners must we know before these visitors arrive?

Food

- What rules govern dining at our luncheon here at the company and at a restaurant?
- What kinds of food do these visitors eat?

Prepare your findings in report form. Be prepared to share the information with your class.

Based on your findings from the cross-cultural study, plan the three events incorporating the following. Write a memo to Mrs. Quevedo outlining these three meetings.

1. Morning meeting: Be versed in introductions; plan the seating arrangement (your manager; yourself; Henry Pippen and his assistant, Kirk Lawrence; J. R. Rush; Thomas Strickland; Sid Levine; Karen Baxter; and the seven visitors who will be in attendance); refreshments; and the flower arrangement.

2. Luncheon meeting: Plan the seating arrangement (your manager; yourself; Henry Pippen and his assistant, Kirk Lawrence; J. R. Rush; and the seven visitors who will be in attendance). Select the caterer, the menu, and the flower arrangement.

3. Dinner: Make the restaurant reservations, confirm the final count, make arrangements for travel from the hotel to the restaurant, and plan the seating arrangement (the group will consist of the seven visitors, you, Mrs. Quevedo and her husband, and J. R. Rush and his wife).

Be prepared to share your information with the class.

Your Action Plan

Complete Your Action Plan; if necessary, review the guidelines in Chapter 1. Set one goal using the information in Chapter 11.

Your Portfolio

With the help of your instructor, select the best papers representative of your work from Chapter 11. Follow your instructor's directions about formatting, assembling, and turning in the portfolio.

Using Telecommunications in the Office

OUTLINE

Effective Use of the Telephone
Using Telephone Directories
Speaking Clearly
Placing a Local Call
Answering the Telephone
Handling Angry Callers
Using Automatic Answering Services
Placing Domestic Long-Distance Calls
Receiving Long-Distance Calls
Placing International Calls
Reviewing Long-Distance Call Logs

Telephone Equipment, Systems, and Services
Interconnect Equipment
Common Telephone Equipment
High-Tech Conferences
Telephone Message Systems
Telephone Systems
Telecommunication Services

Voice Recognition

The Internet
Uses for the Internet
Getting Connected

International Telephone Calls

LEARNING OUTCOMES

When you have completed this chapter, you should be able to:

✔ Use a telephone directory to locate information.

✔ Describe the procedures for answering, transferring, and screening office calls.

✔ Describe the procedures for placing and receiving long-distance calls.

✔ Determine the appropriate time to call offices in other time zones.

✔ Describe the procedures for placing international calls.

✔ Identify office telephone services and telephone systems.

✔ Describe effective voice mail.

✔ Describe the ways in which the Internet is used for communicating.

✔ Explain how to troubleshoot problems experienced when making international calls.

Today, the telephone is an essential office tool that every employee has, and it rings, and rings, and rings. Couple this volume of telephone calls with a virtual deluge of faxes and e-mail, and we begin to recognize our dependence on contemporary telecommunication services in the office.

Organizations today depend on telecommunication services to conduct business but, although these services are important, the value of using them depends largely on how effectively they are used. Office professionals agree that proper techniques of handling business telecommunication should be emphasized in office technology programs and in-service training sessions.

EFFECTIVE USE OF THE TELEPHONE

When you use the telephone to communicate with people outside the company, you are the voice of the organization. In each conversation, you are creating an impression of your organization—the caller does not know whether your office is "under construction or under control." Whatever the situation may be, the caller forms an opinion of the organization, its management and employees, and its products and services by the way you answer and handle a call.

Businesspeople must always be aware of their telephone skills. Suppose your company has just spent thousands of dollars to update its telephone system but ignores the manner in which its employees use the telephone. Think about the small company that cannot afford to promote its image in the mass media but must rely on the image created by its employees who answer the telephones and make calls to customers and clients. Think for a minute about the image you project on the telephone. Is your voice pleasant? Are you positive? Are you sincere in helping to resolve a situation? It is easy to understand why employees who become proficient in their telephone skills will increase their value to any organization. The skills you use depend on several factors: your attitude, voice, and knowledge.

Using Telephone Directories

A local telephone directory is available for every telephone. Directories for other geographic areas may be obtained, for a nominal fee, by contacting the telephone company that publishes the directory. Organizations provide their employees with a staff directory for calling other employees within the organization. Organization or staff directories are usually provided as a list that is available from the office computer. Alternatively, some offices provide hard-copy office directories. Both computer-based and hard-copy office directories can be easily updated as staff and telephone assignments change. It is most likely that the task of updating the office telephone directory will be assigned to the office professional.

Refer to the introductory pages of your organization's directory for policies concerning telephone use and procedures to follow when placing calls. In addition to local numbers, an organization's directory will include the telephone numbers of its branch offices, plants, distribution centers, and so on that are located outside the local area.

An office professional should become skilled at using the alphabetic and the classified sections of public telephone directories and should be thoroughly familiar with the telephone procedures described in the introductory section of the local directory. If you frequently call government offices, become familiar with their listings. Government offices are listed in the alphabetic directory according to political divisions—federal, state, county, and city offices, respectively. Government listings are sometimes found in a special colored section in some directories.

The alphabetic directory, which may be a separate volume or may be bound with the classified directory, contains the name, address, and telephone number of every subscriber in the local calling area (except for those with unlisted numbers). Names of individuals and organizations are listed in alphabetical order.

For the sake of speed, circle new numbers in the alphabetic directory as you look them up. If you do not complete a call on the first attempt, write the number in your telephone notebook so that you won't have to look it up again. If you anticipate that you will be using a number often, transfer the name and number to your telephone card file or computer telephone list. When you are given an unlisted number, be sure to record it in your telephone card file, for you will not be able to look up the number elsewhere. Indicate on your telephone record that the number is unlisted.

The classified directory, called the *yellow pages,* is arranged by subject for products and services. Listings under each subject are then arranged in alphabetical order. To use the yellow pages, think of all the possible ways the reference you are seeking may be listed, and search first for the most likely classification. Some yellow pages directories offer a *Special Guide* section or a *Quick Reference* section at the beginning of the book; these sections can save a lot of time.

An alternative to the traditional yellow pages is the *talking yellow pages,* a supplemental publication. This service is provided by the local telephone company and small businesses; its purpose is to help the general public locate business information. It is similar to voice mail in two ways:

1. It has business information stored in voice mailboxes.
2. The public accesses those voice mailboxes through numeric instructions.

A company may list its telephone number in a directory as an 800 number. Companies using 800 numbers are automatically billed for charges. If you do not know if a company has an 800 listing, dial 1-800-555-1212 and give the operator the name of the company. A directory of 800 numbers is also available for those who use such numbers frequently.

You can locate telephone information about a company by accessing the Internet. For example, you can locate 800 numbers by using key search words such as *1-800 telephone directory*. The search will provide a listing of different references that will help you locate a 1-800 telephone directory.

Many companies offer free access to yellow pages online directories. Search the Web using key search words such as *yellow pages directories*. In some cases, once you have the information, you will be able to select a map to help you locate a particular company.

To obtain a phone number, dial Information at 1-411. Be prepared to give the operator the name of the person (or business) you wish to reach. In some situations, you are charged for this service. To prevent another request for the same number, be sure to record it for safekeeping.

Speaking Clearly

To be successful in communicating with your customer, you must have proper speaking skills. If you do not speak clearly, the customer can become frustrated with the conversation and be left with an unprofessional image of your company.

Because we cannot rely on nonverbal expressions when speaking on the telephone, our tone and words must be especially clear in order to communicate effectively. Make your voice an asset at all times and under all circumstances. The better you sound, the better you and your company are perceived. The voice you project is determined by four factors, all of which can be controlled.

1. **Volume.** Speak as though you were talking to someone across the desk from you.

2. **Speed.** If you speak too quickly, you may run one word into the next. Speak distinctly at a rate that is neither too fast nor too slow. Speaking at the proper rate will enable you to appear confident and poised. Furthermore, the caller will not be able to understand you if you talk too rapidly, and may ask you to repeat information. Avoid speaking rapidly in greeting your caller. Because you have to repeat the introduction so often, you may have a tendency to habitually say the greeting rapidly.

3. **Inflection.** Vary the tone of your voice to bring out the meaning of what you say and add emphasis to what is said. Emphasizing a person's name can leave a positive impression.

4. **Enunciation.** Speak clearly and distinctly by moving your lips, tongue, and jaw freely. How often do you hear—and say—*wouldja, wanna,* or *gimme?*

A clear voice increases your effectiveness and projects courtesy, confidence, and enthusiasm. Through your voice, you can show that you are ready and willing to help.

Placing a Local Call

Before you place a call, assemble the materials you may need to refer to during the conversation. Write down the questions you want to ask and the comments you want to make. Be sure you have the correct number and name of the person with whom you wish to speak.

If the first person you reach is the receptionist, give the extension number of the person you are calling. If you do not know the extension number, give the receptionist the person's name and department. Receptionists will often say the person's extension number as they look it up; others will give you a number if you request it. Write down extension numbers and add them to your telephone card file.

Give the person ample time to answer. Let the telephone ring at least five or six times or for a minute. If the person who answers is not the one with whom you wish to speak, ask for the person and identify yourself: "May I speak to Miss Wetherby? I am Sonja Alvarez of Delta Manufacturing." When you do not need to speak to a particular person, make your request of the person who answers. Although some people prefer to add a "good morning" or "good afternoon" to their identification, others feel it is time consuming.

Your organizational skills are evident when you can handle telephone calls in the most efficient manner. Be mindful of the receiver of your call, who is probably busy and on "information overload" as well.

Answering the Telephone

Every time you answer the telephone, you are projecting the image of your organization. To the caller, you are the organization. You must depend on your voice to project a pleasant, businesslike attitude, and to give the caller full attention. Refer to Figure 12-1.

Answer Promptly. Answer the telephone on the second or third ring. An unanswered telephone conveys an image of inefficiency. However, do not lift the receiver and let the caller wait while you finish a conversation with someone in the office—this is discourteous.

To be clearly understood, ensure that the mouthpiece or microphone is close to your lips—no more than one inch away—and speak directly into it in a normal, conversational tone; use just enough volume for your voice to be pleasant to the listener.

Remember proper speaking skills, such as speaking distinctly and at a rate that is neither too fast nor too slow. By speaking at a moderate pace, you

■ **Figure 12-1**
An office professional answers the telephone promptly.

will come across as confident and poised. As mentioned previously, the caller will not be able to understand you if you talk too rapidly, but may become impatient if you talk too slowly.

Give Proper Identification. Let the caller know that the right office has been reached. If the incoming calls are answered by a receptionist, he or she will say, "Good morning (or Good afternoon), Delta Manufacturing." When the receptionist rings your telephone, you can say, "Sales Department, Sonja Alvarez speaking."

Your manager may tell you specifically how the telephone should be answered. If your manager does not tell you, ask. Never answer a business telephone with "Hello." "Hello" is considered to be too casual for the business office. It is courteous to let the caller know who you are. To identify yourself, use both your first and last names.

When telephone calls come directly to your office, first let the callers know they have reached the right organization; then add the identification for the particular telephone you are answering, and give your name. Example: "Delta Manufacturing, Sales Department, Sonja speaking."

When you answer the telephone for many managers, code each station on your keyset or switchboard, so you can give proper identification for each person whose telephone you are answering.

Be Courteous. Authorities do not agree on whether a greeting such as "Good morning" and "Good afternoon" should be used when answering the telephone. Nevertheless, a greeting is a courtesy. As well, many callers do not hear the name of the organization if it is the first word spoken when a telephone is answered.

Listen attentively. Listening is an essential element in effective telephone usage. If the caller interrupts you, permit the caller to talk. Do not, however, permit the caller to complete a long explanation if the caller has reached the wrong office. You should interrupt by saying, "Excuse me, I believe you should speak to someone in the _____ Department. The number for that department is _____ .Would you like me to transfer you?"

When you must leave the line to obtain information, explain why and how long it will take. Give the caller a choice: ask whether (1) the caller would prefer to wait or (2) the caller would rather be called back. If the caller chooses to wait, avoid a wait of more than two minutes. When you return to the caller who is holding, offer your thanks for waiting.

During telephone conversations, use "please," "thank you," and other courteous phrases. At appropriate times, use the caller's name.

If you discover that neither you nor your manager can help the caller, redirect the call to someone who can. Do not leave the caller stranded by saying that your department cannot handle the issue. Make a special effort to be helpful. Give the caller the name and number of the appropriate person to call. Let the caller know when you are looking for a number. If the call is from outside the organization, offer to transfer the call. A caller usually is favorably impressed when someone is helpful; your time will be well spent.

When the caller has dialed the wrong number, be especially courteous. Callers often reach a wrong number because they have looked at the wrong number on a list of frequently called numbers. The caller may be one of your current or future customers.

The person who initiates a telephone call should terminate it. However, you can bring the call to an end by thanking the person for calling, or suggesting that you will give the message to your manager, or whatever is appropriate. When you initiate the call, let the other person know that you are going to leave the line. Do not end abruptly. You may close with "Good-bye" or "Bye." "Bye-bye" is too familiar; therefore, do not use it.

Take Complete Messages. You have several options when taking telephone messages; you may use your computer system's e-mail message form for telephone messages or keep a small notebook, a pen, and a pad of telephone message forms (Figure 12-2) by the telephone. Spare yourself the embarrassment of asking a caller to wait while you look for a pen or pencil. Many people think that taking telephone messages is a simple task. It is simple enough, but handling this task inefficiently causes time to be wasted and may cause loss of customer goodwill and business.

There are six essential elements for writing a complete telephone message:

1. The date and time of call.
2. The complete name of the caller, spelled correctly. Remember that your manager does not know every Lawrence or José who calls.
3. The telephone number with area code. Some callers will say that your manager or the person for whom this call is intended has the number. You can simply explain that you would like to save your manager the time it would take to look up the number.

■ **Figure 12-2**
A completed telephone
message form.

Message For:		Urgent ☐
For *K. Macri*		
Date *2/24/04*	Time *2:15*	
Message From:		
Mr. *Fred Dahl*		
Of *Inkwell*		
Phone *845-555-9518*		
AREA CODE	NUMBER	EXTENSION
Called while you were out ☑		Please call ☑
Stopped to see you ☐		Will call you back ☐
Returned your call ☐		Wishes to see you ☐
Message		
Follow-up on estimate		
Signed _____		

4. The business affiliation of the caller.

5. All pertinent information to help the person for whom the call was intended know what to expect when returning the call.

6. Your initials. If you are the only person taking messages, initialing the form is not necessary. If there are several people taking messages, it is very helpful to the person receiving the messages to know who took the message should there be any questions regarding the call.

When you must record the name and the number so that your manager can return the call, write it on a telephone message form as the caller gives you the information. A typical message form is illustrated in Figure 12-2. All of the information on the message form is important; do not skip any part. Telephone message books are available from office supply stores. In some companies, message books are filed for three to six months. If there is no office policy for filing your message books, consider keeping your book for three months and then discarding it. During that time if you need proof of a message taken or a person's telephone number, you will have it by having kept your message book.

In some companies, office professionals use their computer to record telephone messages. They take messages by entering the information using the keyboard. When the person for whom the calls are intended returns to his or her workstation, the telephone messages can be retrieved via the computer. As offices provide workers with integrated information systems, recording messages via the computer will become more popular.

Explain Your Manager's Absence. Be careful how you explain your manager's absence from the office. Here are some tips to follow:

■ Simply say "He is away from his desk at the moment. May I ask him to call you?" or "He is not here at the moment. How may I help you?"

How to Take a Telephone Message

✔ Always restate the message to assure both yourself and the caller that you have recorded it accurately and in its entirety.

✔ Ask for correct spellings. Do not assume that your manager will know how to spell callers' names and organizations.

✔ Get the area code and the name of the city, if this is a long-distance call. The person receiving the message may not immediately recognize an area code as being in another time zone until it is too late to return the call that day. Larger cities have more than one area code. For example, the Dallas/Fort Worth metropolitan area has 214, 972, 817, and 469.

✔ Record the time of the call. The time of the call is important; for instance, if your manager talked with the caller at lunch, your manager needs to know if the call was made before or after lunch.

✔ Write clearly on the first attempt so that you will not waste time rewriting.

■ Avoid statements such as:

"He is in Denver."

"He's still at lunch."

"He is in the hospital."

"He hasn't come in yet."

"He is in conference."

The conference explanation has been overused and will be perceived as an excuse. When it is in fact true, you should state in a sincere way that Mr. Berstein is in a meeting, and suggest what time you expect him back in the office.

If your manager is out of town for a period, he or she may choose to access his or her own calls by dialing the telephone number and using a private code. However, if you are responsible for answering your manager's calls, you might say, "Mr. Berstein is not in the office this week. How may I help you?" or "Mr. Berstein is not in the office this week. Nelva Kirkpatrick is assisting while Mr. Berstein is away. May I transfer your call?" Wait for a response. Give the caller the extension should there be other questions while your manager is away from the office.

Transfer Calls Properly. Explain to the caller that you are going to transfer the call to someone else who will handle the call. You might say, "Mr. Jenkins in our accounting department will be able to help you rather than Miss Truong in our department. May I transfer your call to him?" Be sure that you transfer the call to the right person. Never transfer a call unless it is absolutely necessary to do so. Never say, "I will transfer you; if I should lose you, Mr. Brighton's number is 531-6088." Say, "For your reference, Mr. Brighton's number is 531-6088. I will transfer you now." Give the caller the name and the telephone number of the person to whom he or she is being transferred, so that the caller can place the call if he or she is disconnected as you transfer the call. Be sure you know how to transfer a call. The method varies, depending on the telephone system being used.

Before you transfer the call, invite the caller to call you back if you have not referred him or her to the right person. If the caller does call back, offer to locate the right person and refer the request to that person.

If your department cannot handle the request and you do not know who should handle it, tell the caller so. You might say, "I don't know the answer to your question, but I will make some inquiries. May I call you back in half an hour?" Another approach is to say, "I need to find out who has that information. May I call you back in half an hour?" Be sure to follow through on your promise. Doing this will create work for you, but it may result in increased business for your organization.

Callers often find themselves being transferred three or four times. Imagine how frustrating this must be for them each time they must repeat their story. In addition, three or four people will have been interrupted by calls they cannot handle. When these callers reach you, stop the runaround. Offer to locate someone who *can* help. Never transfer a call on the *speculation* that the person to whom you are transferring the call might be helpful.

Answer a Second Telephone. Many managers have two or more telephone lines into their offices. If two telephones ring at the same time, answer one and ask the caller if you may be excused to answer the other telephone. For example, "Law firm, this is Shandra. I have another call coming in. May I put you on hold?" Do not leave the line until the caller consents. Press the hold button and answer the second call. Then you might say: "Law firm. This is Shandra. I am on another line. May I put you on hold?" When you return to the line of the first caller, say, "Thank you for holding. How may I direct your call?" or "Thank you for holding. How may I help you?" What you need to do to answer multiple calls depends on whether the calls are local or long distance.

If the call is local, offer to call the second person back, after you have explained why, and return to the first caller. As soon as this conversation ends, dial the second caller.

When the second call is a long-distance call, do not offer to call back. Either ask someone else to take the call or explain to the long-distance caller that you interrupted a local call on another line in order to answer. Excuse yourself long enough to get back to the first caller to say, "I will be with you in a minute." Complete the long-distance call as quickly as possible. Try not to keep the first caller waiting more than a minute. When you get back to the first caller, apologize for the delay and thank the caller for waiting.

Use these same methods if you are talking on the telephone when the second telephone rings.

Office professionals who are handling multiple lines must learn how to handle calls very efficiently and keep the overall image as their goal. There may be frustrating times when handling multiple telephone lines, but it is critical to business and customer goodwill to keep a positive attitude during these times.

Know When to Answer. In most organizations, managers answer their own telephones when they are in the office. Alternatively, you may be expected to take all telephone calls and immediately put them through to your manager. Here are some tips to follow:

- Know exactly whose telephones you are responsible for answering and when.

- Determine how you are to interrupt your manager with a telephone message when he or she is in a meeting.

- Tell the caller that your manager is not available to answer a telephone call before you ask who is calling. If you ask who is calling before you let the caller know that your manager is not available, the caller may think that he or she personally is being screened out. Refer to Chapter 9 for a discussion of how to interrupt your manager when you think that a call is urgent enough to do so.

Distribute Messages Promptly. Delaying the delivery of telephone messages to the appropriate people can cause costly and perhaps embarrassing situations for your manager. If you are taking messages for your manager or covering someone else's phone, place the messages in a designated location in such a way that they will not be covered by papers and overlooked. Avoid entering your manager's work area to deliver messages when he or she is trying to work without interruptions. The plan that your manager uses for returning his or her calls will depend on the daily schedule, the pace of work, and his or her preferences.

If you receive calls from people who have previously called and left messages with your manager but their calls haven't been returned, simply say, "I will be sure that the message is delivered." That's all you can guarantee. Do not promise that you will "have" your manager return the calls. It is up to your manager to decide which calls are of high (or low) priority.

When your manager is unavailable, don't just take messages—take the initiative. Many telephone requests can be satisfied by you or by other employees.

If your manager is away and telephones the office to check on the office activities, never say that nothing is happening. By this comment you are admitting that you are unaware of office activity. You should always be able to provide a brief summary of activities and incoming telephone calls. Remember, the office professional is an information worker. Your job is to collect, use, and provide information.

Screen Calls. Some managers have such heavy demands on their time that their calls must be screened, and many of those calls must by handled by someone else. If you must screen calls, probe courteously for information. Either respond to the caller yourself or determine what the caller's request is and refer the call to someone who can help the caller.

When screening calls, you are attempting to find out who is calling and what is wanted. You might say, "May I tell Mr. Morton who is calling, please?" You should never ask a caller bluntly, "Who is calling?" or "Who is this?" To find out what the caller wants, you might say, "May I tell Mr. Morton what you are calling about, please?"

There are times when a caller does not give his or her name for one reason or another. Remember that when screening calls, you want to determine what the caller wants. Your manager is better prepared to help the caller if he or she knows what the nature of the call is. If you cannot obtain the name of the caller and the nature of business, you have several options: (1) ask your manager for his or her preference as to how to handle this type of call or (2) tell the caller that your manager is not available.

Screening calls (1) saves your manager time and (2) assists the caller. All calls should be handled by someone. The more knowledge you have about the organization, the easier your job of screening calls will be. Never tell a caller "I don't know" and leave the caller wondering what to do next. If you really don't know, it's your responsibility to find out or to ask for assistance from someone who does know.

Handling Angry Callers

When handling angry callers, it is important to know and remember that anger is a *secondary emotion*. This means that when the caller is angry, he or she is usually not mad at you—so don't take it personally. Some other emotion, called a *primary emotion,* always precedes anger, even though you may not be aware of it. Specifically, before the caller feels angry, he or she perceives a threat of a loss or an actual loss of something that is important.

People often cover up primary emotions in order to defend or protect themselves. The negative primary emotions (e.g., disappointment, confusion,

How to Project a Positive Image

✔ Relax. Maintain good posture and breathe deeply. Relaxing gives your voice a tone of confidence.

✔ Smile when you speak. Talk to the person as if he or she were in front of you. Your smile will come across in your voice to indicate your helpfulness and level of interest.

✔ Be courteous. Demonstrate respect with a liberal use of "thank you" and "please," listen attentively and say the caller's name frequently.

✔ Answer promptly. If you do not answer within three rings, you may create an unfavorable impression.

✔ Use a greeting. Identify your company (or department), say your name, and ask, "How may I help you?" Using a standard greeting presents a professional image of your organization.

✔ Enunciate clearly. Pronounce words clearly; be distinct in your pronunciation.

✔ Concentrate. Stop what you are doing (keyboarding or shuffling papers) and give the caller your undivided attention. Concentration helps when obtaining or giving information.

✔ Don't leave callers hanging. Return to the caller frequently if he or she has been put on hold. Thank the caller for holding. If you cannot get needed information, ask the caller if you may return the call.

pressure) do not feel good, so to relieve the discomfort, people use secondary emotions (like irritation, anger) to shift the focus from themselves to others, usually blaming or criticizing them.

As an office professional, you must respond in a professional manner regardless of the caller's behavior. No matter what happens, avoid the following:

■ Hastily and or unnecessarily transferring a complaint caller to an unsuspecting coworker

■ Totally ignoring a complaint caller while he or she "talks it out and calms down"

■ Telling an angry caller, "Calm down," or "Don't be upset"

■ Promising to call back and then either failing to do so or allowing three or four days to pass without returning the call

Here are some tips to use when handling an angry caller.

1. Deal with the feelings first.
   a. Show understanding.
   b. Provide feedback.
   c. Summarize the situation.

2. Deal with the situation.
   a. Find out what the caller wants.
   b. If it is not possible to do what the person wants, suggest alternatives.
   c. Share information.
   d. Agree on a solution.
   e. Follow up.

Using Automatic Answering Services

Many offices are equipped with sophisticated telephone systems to handle incoming calls and to monitor outgoing calls. Incoming calls are often intercepted by automatic answering services known as auto announcements, or Interactive Voice Response (IVR). **Auto announcements** are similar to answering machines but are activated only when all incoming lines are busy, or after hours when the caller is prompted to leave a message or to call back during business hours. **Interactive Voice Response (IVR)** services can be programmed to:

- Respond after a predefined number of rings
- Respond between specific times of day
- Play a variety of announcements
- Prompt the caller through a menu of options to acquire information or leave messages
- Repeat messages based on the length of time the caller has been on hold

Office professionals are often called on to help optimize their office's IVR system. When they are, they should involve their local service provider or IVR manufacturer in designing scripts and procedures that appropriately represent the company.

Placing Domestic Long-Distance Calls

Long-distance calls are any calls placed outside the local calling area. Canada and the United States are divided into more than one hundred telephone areas. Each of these areas is identified by a three-digit area code. See Figure 12-3 for the numbering plan. The area code must be used to place all long-distance calls, even within your own area code range. Many international locations do not use a three-digit code; for example, Mexico uses some two-digit area codes. In such cases, however, a country code is used to direct the call first to the country, then the region within the country.

Placing and receiving long-distance calls saves not only time but also money and energy. Long-distance calls may be placed either point-to-point or person-to-person.

Point-to-Point Calls. Make a **point-to-point call** if you can talk to anyone who answers, or if you anticipate that the person to whom you wish to talk will be near the telephone. Be aware that the charges for your call begin when the called telephone or switchboard is answered. However, the cost of making a point-to-point call is lower than that of a person-to-person call. No charge is made when the called telephone is not answered.

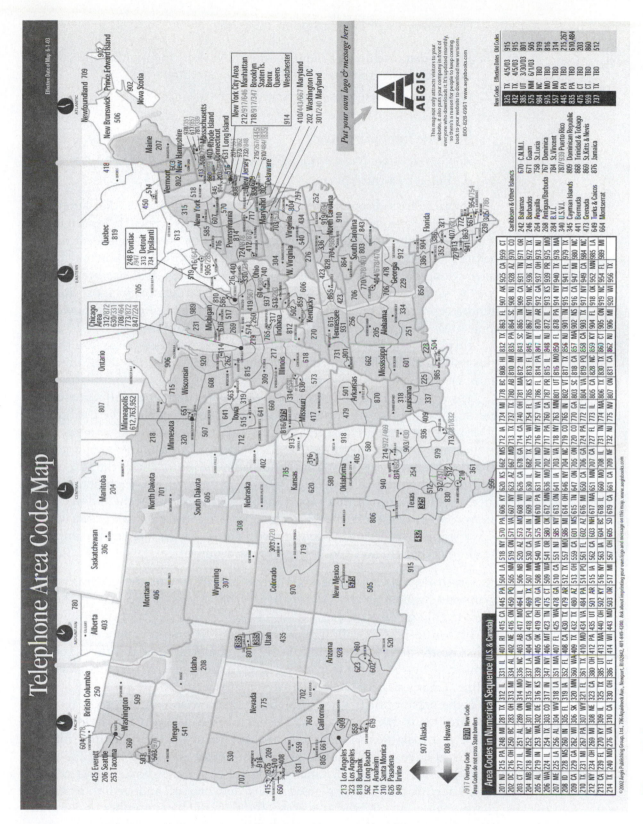

■ **Figure 12-3**

Area code map and time zones.
(Courtesy of Bell Atlantic.)

The two types of point-to-point calls are:

1. **Direct-distance dialing (DDD)**—the caller dials the number directly, and no special assistance is needed from the operator
2. Operator-assisted calls—necessary when calls are
   a. collect
   b. made from pay phones
   c. charged to a credit card
   d. billed to a third party

To place direct-distance dialing (DDD) point-to-point calls, dial a number—for example, 9—to get an outside line. Dial the access code "1," the area code of the geographic location you are calling, and the seven-digit local number. Before the number connects you to the person you are calling, you may have to enter a long-distance access code—for instance, 7856—that has been given to you by your company's information systems coordinator. In most areas the number from which you are calling will be recorded automatically; however, in some areas the operator will intercept to ask for your number.

To place point-to-point calls requiring operator assistance, use the **zero plus dialing** method. Simply dial "0," the area code, and the seven-digit local number. After you have dialed the complete number, a short automated process will start; next you have the choice of entering your calling card number or speaking to a live operator for special services. Give the operator the information essential for completing the call. For instance, to reverse charges to the number being called, say "collect" and give your name; to charge a call to a third number, give the area code and number to which the call is to be charged. When the call is placed from a pay telephone, the operator must check with a person at that third number before allowing the billing. This is necessary because there can be no trace of origin when a call is placed from a pay station. If there is no automated process for calling cards, simply say "calling card call" and give the calling card number.

Person-to-Person Calls. Rates for operator-assisted calls are generally higher than rates for comparable DDD calls. A table of rates is provided in the front of all telephone directories.

Person-to-person calls require assistance from the operator. For such calls, use the zero-plus method. Dial "0," the area code and the seven-digit number. When the operator answers, give the name of the person you are calling. Charges begin when that person answers.

If the person called is not available and you wish your call to be returned, indicate this to the operator. The operator will ask you for the number to which you wish the call to be returned, and then will say something like this: "Will you have Tom Hankins call Dallas, Texas, area code 972-123-4567."

For some time long-distance telephone companies have used a computerized operator. If you are placing a long-distance call and wish to reverse the charges, you dial "0," the area code, and then the local number. A computer-controlled voice will ask you which service you want and then ask you to state your name clearly. When the call is placed, the computer-controlled voice system announces your name and the fact that it is a person-to-person call. The receiver will accept or refuse the charges either by keying a response on the telephone pad or by responding to questions with a simple "yes" or "no." All of this takes place without the intervention of a human operator. At times this type of call can save you a charge in your long-distance phone bill because no charge is applied if the person being called cannot be reached.

Calling Card Calls. Telephone **calling cards** may or may not require the assistance of an operator. Many pay phones are now equipped with a magnetic strip reader to accommodate telephone calling cards. When you use this method of placing a call, operator assistance is not required and the charge is automatically billed to your personal or business account. The information stored on the card includes a coded account number.

Prepaid calling cards are the equivalent of a direct debit card. A magnetic stripe on the back of a prepaid card stores the original purchase value of the card and updates (debits) that amount each time a call is made. New pay telephone equipment can read and update a prepaid calling card as the call progresses.

Businesses are finding that calling cards and prepaid calling cards are both convenient and cost effective.

Directory Assistance. To obtain a number in order to make a long-distance call, dial "1," the area code of the geographic location you want, and 555-1212. You will reach the information operator, or the automated directory system for the area you are calling. First provide the name of the city or town you want and then the name of the person. Write down the number that is given to you and hang up. Now, dial "1," the area code, and the seven-digit number provided by the operator. This same procedure is used whether you are dialing inside or outside your own area code.

This service is called long-distance directory assistance. You are charged for this service whether you request a number inside or outside your area code. (Refer to the introductory pages of your telephone directory to determine how to request local directory assistance.)

You should note that of all the services offered by telephone companies today, those requiring the intervention of a live telephone operator are the most costly. The office professional is advised to become familiar with automated services and to avoid operator assistance wherever possible.

Conference Calling. A **conference call** is a call taking place when three or more telephone stations are connected across a network that supports the conversation. Conference calls can be initiated by:

1. a prearranged call through a telephone operator
2. using the special "conference" feature on most business telephone sets

When prearranging a conference call through a telephone operator, you must usually pay a nominal charge. Refer to your local or regional telephone company rate book for the current charge.

The operator will require essential information—cities, names, numbers, and the time of the conference. The operator will call each person involved to obtain acceptance of the time of the conference and will place the call to each participant at the time of the conference.

No special equipment is needed for conference calls. However, specially designed speaker/microphone conference sets, designed for boardroom use, may be used to enhance the clarity of the conference stations.

One special feature of most business telephone sets is the conference feature. Suppose your organization located in Texas has two branches located in New Mexico and Arizona. Your manager has asked you to arrange a telephone conference next week with the two branch managers. You can arrange the conference call yourself by dialing a number and asking the receiver of the call to hold while you conference another person into the call. You simply put the first caller on hold, press the conference button, and dial the second number. When the second caller is connected, you release the hold button to include the first person, who has been waiting on hold. A three-way conversation is now possible.

Time Zones in the United States. The United States is divided into five time zones: Atlantic, Eastern, Central, Mountain, and Pacific. From east to west, the time in each zone is one hour earlier than the time in the adjacent time zone. Review Figure 12-3 for both area codes and time zones. The time at the place where a long-distance call originates determines whether day, evening, or night rates apply. During certain months of the year when daylight saving time is in effect, the time in each zone will be one hour later.

When you are placing a long-distance call, know the time zone of the city you are calling. For instance, when it is 4:30 p.m. in Kansas City, you can anticipate that offices in New York City will be closed. When it is 5 p.m. in Kansas City, offices on the West Coast will still be open. Time zones around the world are explained in the following section and are illustrated in Figure 12-3.

Time Zones around the World. The world is divided into twenty-four time zones, which are based on degrees of longitude. The zones are one hour apart in time. Greenwich, England, is recognized as the prime meridian of longitude; in other words, standard time is calculated from Greenwich, England. The Greenwich zone is called the *zero zone* because the difference between standard time and Greenwich mean time is zero. Each of the zones in turn is designated by a number representing the number of hours by which the standard time of the zone differs from Greenwich mean time. The United States and its possessions are divided into eight standard time zones, established by Congress with the adoption of the Uniform Time Act of 1966. The time zones are Atlantic, Eastern, Central, Mountain, Pacific, Yukon, Alaska-Hawaii, and Bering. The time in these zones is earlier than Greenwich time by four, five, six, seven, eight, nine, ten, and eleven hours, respectively.

If you need to determine time in cities around the globe, obtain and use a time chart or access the Internet.

Receiving Long-Distance Calls

When answering a long-distance call that is point-to-point, quickly get someone on the line to handle the call, assist the caller yourself, or take a message. Remember that the caller must pay for the call because the telephone was answered.

Write the message in your telephone notebook and restate it to indicate your understanding of it. Prepare the telephone message immediately and place it on your manager's desk. If you assist the caller, key a summary of your assistance and give it to your manager.

When the long-distance call is person-to-person and your manager is not there, tell the operator when you expect your manager to return. If the operator asks your manager to return the call, carefully record the call-back information.

You can often help by telling the operator where your manager can be reached. You will have to make a judgment concerning your manager's reaction to taking the call in someone else's office.

Placing International Calls

Calls to Puerto Rico, the Virgin Islands, Bermuda, and other Caribbean Islands are regular long-distance calls. Each of these places has an assigned area code just like the codes in the United States. Thus, placing a direct-dialed long-distance call to Puerto Rico would require you to dial "1" + "809" (the area code for Puerto Rico) and the local number.

You can dial directly to most foreign countries as well. To place a direct-dialed call, dial "011" (the international long-distance access number); the code for the country being called; the city code if it is required; and the local number. To dial directly to Tokyo, Japan, for example, you would dial "011" + "81" + "3" + the local number. The international country and city codes are given in the front of the white pages of the local telephone directory. The time differences between each country and the city serviced by the telephone directory are also shown.

You may require operator assistance with your international call if you are making person-to-person call, a credit card call, or a third-party billing call, or are reversing the charges. In these cases, dial "01" + the country code + the routing code + the local number. Example: If dialing London, England, the procedure would be "01" + "44" + the local number. At this point the operator would intercept, asking you what special assistance you require.

Long-distance international telephone country codes are listed in most telephone directories, but are subject to change without notice. Here is a small sampling of country codes:

Code	Country	Code	Country
93	Afghanistan	376	Andorra
355	Albania	244	Angola
213	Algeria	54	Argentina
684	American Samoa	61	Australia

Reviewing Long-Distance Call Logs

In many offices, outgoing calls and other specially handled calls are recorded in a computer log. Computer logs will help management produce timely reports. If you receive a log for your area, carefully review it and report any discrepancies to your manager. Analyzing outgoing calls may help you and your work group reduce telephone costs.

TELEPHONE EQUIPMENT, SYSTEMS, AND SERVICES

Rapid changes have taken place in telephone equipment, systems, and services.

Interconnect Equipment

Interconnect equipment is the term used to refer to telephone equipment that organizations purchase or lease from suppliers other than from telephone companies.

The manufacturers of telephone interconnect equipment have placed new switchboards and other equipment with hundreds of features on the market. Most of the new features of the telephone systems are controlled at the central office. At the central office (which used to be known as the telephone exchange), most mechanical exchanges have been replaced by electronic digital switches. These digital switches are program-controlled and offer users a variety of services. These services are known as **call management services**. They include:

- displaying the caller's number on your telephone, called **caller identification (ID)**
- forwarding your call to another number when you are busy or away from your desk, called **call forwarding**
- having the telephone system monitor a busy number and inform you when that number becomes free

Other call management features can enhance your telephone effectiveness. For example:

- By touching a predefined button, the office assistant can speed-dial a number.
- By pressing a key, you may redial a previously dialed number.
- Most telephone systems provide electronic memory where names and numbers are stored.

With the electronic memory feature, frequently used numbers may be recorded and reused for dialing automatically and accurately.

Many more telephone features are gaining popularity as enhancements to productivity: bilingual displays and voice communication over the Internet. New developments include bilingual alphanumeric displays and the provision to check e-mail through the telephone set. Refer to Figure 12-4.

We make no attempt here to discuss all the new features that have been introduced by the interconnect industry; instead, we discuss the basic concepts of telephone equipment and systems. If you are using interconnect equipment, study the operator's manual to learn how to operate the special features.

■ **Figure 12-4**
Telephone with advanced
features including
digital displays.

Common Telephone Equipment

The following discussion provides basic information on common telephone equipment.

Touch-Tone Telephones. Most regular telephones are touch-tone activated. The touch-tone telephone provides both regular telephone service and tone transmission of data through a twelve-button keypad. Ten buttons represent the numbers 0 through 9 and the alphabet. The other two buttons, showing the # and the * symbols, generate unique tones that may be connected to special telephone company services. An example of such a service is *repeat dial,* which will redial the last number used.

The touch-tone telephone provides tone transmission of data, which can be received and converted by the central office. In this way, you communicate with the central office and access the call management services mentioned earlier in the section "Interconnect Equipment."

Key Telephones. Key telephones, or *keysets,* provide flexibility in making and receiving multiple calls simultaneously. Key telephones have multiple buttons, and the buttons on one phone set are the same as those on the other sets in an office. A number of calls from both inside and outside the office may be made or received simultaneously.

The basic key telephone is a regular telephone with push-button keys corresponding to the number of telephone lines terminating in the telephone. The push buttons flash on and off to indicate incoming calls on the lines. To answer a call, push the key that is flashing and lift the receiver. If a second call comes in while the first is in progress, suspend the conversation properly, push the hold button, then push the flashing key of the incoming call and

■ **Figure 12-5**
Key telephone set with
add-on module for
additional lines.
(Matsushita Electric
Corporation of America.
Reprinted with permission)

answer the call. To suspend this call and get back to the first call, push the hold button again, push the key of the first incoming call. When a push-button key glows steadily, it indicates that the line is in use. Figure 12-5 shows a key telephone with an add-on module that allows more telephone lines to be used.

Wireless Telephones. The wireless telephone service provides mobile communication. This telephone network uses radio waves rather than telephone wires to transmit messages. However, mobile telephone users may communicate with conventional telephone users because wireless systems interconnect with local and long-distance telephone networks. See Figure 12-6.

Whether for personal or business use, you will find that many people in your office will use a wireless telephone. Wireless telephone users can take advantage of most of the features offered to regular telephone users, including voice mail. With special portable modem and computer equipment, wireless telephones can be used as a remote Internet terminal.

For those office professionals and business executives who travel beyond North America, a new generation of wireless telephone may provide the reach and direct access required for calling back to the office. As technology improves, the wireless telephone will provide many advantages to offices and those who travel.

High-Tech Conferences

As mentioned in Chapter 11, many companies use telecommunications in the office to conduct virtual meetings, including teleconferences and videoconferences. These forms of meetings reduce travel costs and losses in productivity that result from time spent away from the office. Be sure to review the section on virtual meetings in Chapter 11.

Telephone Message Systems

Organizations often make arrangements for the telephone to be answered after regular business hours or when it is inconvenient for employees to answer

■ Figure 12-6
Wireless telephone in use.
(Courtesy of Rogers Cantel Inc.)

the telephone. Commonly used systems are automatic recording machines, answering services, and voice mail.

Automatic Recording Machines. With this system, a user can turn on a recorded message at the end of the business day. The message might tell callers when the office will be open and invite the callers to leave their number or a message. Sometimes, customers are encouraged to place orders at night by leaving their requests on the automatic recording machine.

Answering Service. A **telephone answering service** is a switchboard attended by an operator who answers subscribers' telephones at designated hours. The operator takes messages, records numbers to be called, and judges whether or not to reach the subscriber during after-business hours. For example, the telephones of many doctors are answered after regular hours by telephone answering services.

If you work for a manager whose telephone is answered when nobody is in the office, one of your early-morning tasks may be to listen to the automatic recording machine and transcribe the messages, or to call a telephone answering service for messages.

Voice Mail. **Voice mail** is a computer-based system that processes both incoming and outgoing telephone calls. Special computer chips and software convert the human voice into a digital recording that can be stored in the computer. The recording can then be retrieved at any time for playback.

Today, voice mail is a common method of messaging. Depending on the system, voice mail can help in the following ways:

1. Voice mail ensures that no telephone calls are missed.
2. Messages can be sent regardless of time zones or work schedules.
3. Office professionals can leave messages for anyone who has an access code. For example, if you are out of the office and want to leave details of a scheduled meeting, you can give those invited your access code and leave a descriptive voice mail message.
4. Voice mail allows messages to be recorded and saved in a mailbox. A voice mail system can also forward messages to another location or to other office members.
5. Voice mail messages can be sent to a number of people simultaneously.
6. Voice mail can also serve as an automated telephone operator by answering calls with a standard recording.

Voice mail also handles telephone messages quickly and efficiently and, if used correctly, may eliminate the annoying practice of **telephone tag** (telephoning back and forth by parties trying to reach each other without success). However, voice mail has some disadvantages.

- Callers forced to listen to long messages can find the system annoying.
- Voice mail also delivers the implicit message that the caller's time is less valuable than the recipient's.
- Some users do not access their mailboxes regularly.
- The recipient does not know when a message comes in unless the system has a signaling feature.

Because voice mail can be delivered as a public telephone network service, telephone companies provide many sophisticated voice mail features as a service. For example, voice mail can help employers deal with diversity in the workforce. The local telephone company can provide voice mail services in several different languages. A company's voice mail language of choice will provide workers and customers access to the company's voice mail without encountering a language barrier.

Although voice mail lacks the richness of direct communications, there are some fundamental practices that should be considered to improve voice mail interactions.

1. Consider stating and changing the date of your greeting message on a daily basis. Doing so provides the caller with information that you are, in fact, in touch with your voice mail system.
2. Record an appropriate announcement on your greeting message when leaving for vacation or other extended periods when you will not be checking your voice mail for incoming messages.
3. When leaving messages for others, state your name and phone number clearly and at a slow enough pace for transcription.
4. State your message clearly and succinctly.
5. Specify the action you wish to occur.

6. Indicate when you will be available to receive a return call.

7. Consider your tone of voice and impression that you are leaving with your message.

8. Avoid leaving lengthy messages.

The features and functions of voice mail systems are improving rapidly. It must be noted that unless used correctly, the voice mail system will annoy and frustrate callers, with the result that business suffers. It is essential that appropriate procedures be in place by any organization that uses voice mail. The following three practices will help minimize caller frustration:

1. Make it possible for the caller to speak to a representative of the company, in addition to being able to leave a message on the voice mail system.

2. Introduce organizational procedures for responding to voice mail in order to resolve the problem of messages not being collected or not being answered.

3. Ensure that all staff are fully trained to use the voice mail message system. When a system fails to meet its objectives, it is often because of inadequate staff training.

Just as technology is transforming office procedures, it is having a similar impact on telephone messaging. Voice mail and electronic meetings offer office professionals new tools for conducting more productive conversations and meetings.

Telephone Systems

Organizations that depend upon many telephone calls require the use of an office switchboard. These switchboards are known as Private Branch Exchange (PBX), Private Automatic Branch Exchange (PABX), Central Exchange (CENTREX), and the new Hybrid and Virtual Telephone Exchange systems. As an office assistant, you may never have to operate a large switchboard; even so, knowledge of how calls are handled within your organization will be valuable to you in placing calls rapidly and accurately.

Office Telephone Exchanges. **Private Branch Exchange (PBX)** provides exchange service for calls coming into and going out of the office. It also handles inside calls made between telephone extensions within the office. This type of exchange requires a full-time operator to handle incoming calls and to connect them with extensions within the office.

Private Automatic Branch Exchange (PABX) provides its users with the ability to dial another extension directly without having to engage the operator. With this system (see Figure 12-7), the telephone user can also dial inside and outside numbers without operator intervention. To dial an outside number, an extension user listens for the dial tone, dials "9," listens for the second dial tone, and dials the outside number. The PABX is capable of many computerized functions including the following:

1. Redialing busy lines automatically

2. Redialing the last number that was connected

Panasonic   Model VA-412

3. Storing up to thirty numbers

4. Informing a person that a call is waiting

5. Enabling an office professional to answer a telephone at someone else's desk by dialing a code, without leaving his or her desk

6. Call forwarding to a preselected phone

7. Allowing an office professional to place a call on hold, place a second call to retrieve information needed to complete the first call, and then return to the original caller

Central Exchange (CENTREX) provides direct dialing to an office extension without assistance from an operator. CENTREX is used by organizations that have many telephone extensions. The main feature of the CENTREX service is *Direct Inward Dialing (DID)*. Every telephone within a CENTREX system has the same three-digit prefix. To dial in-house, employees need only dial a two-, three-, or four-digit extension. You can save money on long-distance calls because your call to a CENTREX number is placed point-to-point.

Today, many different types of office telephone systems are available. The more expensive PBX, PABX, and CENTREX systems may be found in large offices; however, the emergence of new **Hybrid and Virtual Telephone Exchange systems** that use office PCs and the Internet are found in many smaller to mid-sized companies. These systems take advantage of existing equipment and the Internet to provide familiar voice services and local control at a fraction of the cost of traditional office telephone exchanges. It is conceivable that a new task for the office professional will be that of *office telephone exchange coordinator* as this new technology becomes more commonplace.

Telecommunication Services

In the United States, it is not uncommon to find a variety of telephone services provided to the office or home. The United States is both the leading developer of innovative telecommunications services and the largest consumer of those services. However, no matter how innovative a service may be, all telecommunication services can be categorized as voice, data, or wireless.

Voice Services. Probably the most common of services is *voice* (as it is known in the telecommunications industry). Sophisticated voice networks provide the telephone services we are most familiar with—and possibly take for granted. **Voice services** are characterized by telephone sets, a dial tone, and the international telephone network, which enables us to talk to other people around the world. Voice services may be as simple as a single, featureless desk telephone, or as complicated as a computerized switching system with every conceivable feature, designed to handle many calls.

Voice services are either *inbound* or *outbound*. **Inbound voice services** include calls made by someone calling into your home or office, at your company's expense. These services are commonly known as "toll-free services." They are only "free" to the caller; the subscribing company must cover the cost. **Outbound voice services** are originated and paid for by the caller. Each call made from your office or home is an example of an outbound voice call. Companies that wish to provide phone-in customer service, information, or a help line typically employ inbound, toll-free services.

The facsimile machine, otherwise known as the "fax," can also operate on telephone networks designed mainly for voice services.

Data Services. In addition to the familiar voice services, most offices will have some form of data service connection. Data services are those that are designed to provide a telecommunications network for information you transmit from and receive through your office computer system. Special telephone lines with data-handling equipment are used for public data networks. These networks may support a single point-to-point computer connection, or they may be the *backbone* of several networks connected together to form a wide area network (WAN) as you learned in Chapter 4.

Wireless Services. As the name implies, wireless services are those telecommunication services that are not dependent on *terrestrial* wires and cables for their main transmission network. Instead, radio waves are used to deliver the services. **Wireless services** include microwave systems, radio broadcast and reception, wireless telephone services, and direct-to-home television services. Emerging wireless technology has provided us with **personal communication systems (PCSs)** and with local area networks (LANs), as discussed in Chapter 4, that are connected without wires.

VOICE RECOGNITION

If you are weary of typing, concerned about repetitive stress injuries, or overwhelmed with transcribing tapes, you might want to consider **voice-recognition software**, which runs on PCs at full speaking speed.

Talking to a computer will soon be almost as commonplace as speaking into the intercom in a fast-food drive-through. Thanks to improvements in voice-recognition software, as well as greater computer processing power, vendors have developed systems that translate the spoken word into language a computer can understand more than 95 percent of the time. You will find yourself talking to a computer either at your desk or at the other end of a telephone line. Here is an example of the uses of voice-recognition technology: American Express and United Parcel Service have joined the group of adopters in deploying critical applications that rely on voice recognition. Meanwhile, on the computer desktop, more users will take advantage of newly affordable software that understands your natural language. Prices for some of these products have dropped below $100. Here is what you can expect voice recognition technology to do:

- Remind you of all your appointments. It remembers and reminds you up to a year in advance in your own voice.

- Get phone numbers for you instantly. You can instruct the computer to remember the phone numbers for several hundred people. Then, you just say the person's name, and the phone number is displayed and played back instantly.

- Review your schedule for any day. Say "Tuesday" or "January," and all of your appointments for that day are played back in your own voice.

Freed of the constraints imposed by the keyboard and the mouse interfaces, industrial, office, home, and large-screen entertainment, PC users can move outside the traditional "PC space" into a computing world controlled by voice.

THE INTERNET

The most popular means of communicating and researching information is the Internet, and the telephone plays a big part in Internet connection. The **Internet** (or **World Wide Web**) is a public global communications network that enables people to exchange information through a computer, as you learned in Chapter 4.

Uses for the Internet

What can you do with the Internet? Basically, there are five activities that people participate in on the Internet:

1. sending and receiving e-mail
2. transferring data files
3. joining newsgroups
4. performing remote computing
5. researching topics of interest.

Internet mail is the same as e-mail, which was discussed in Chapter 6. It is electronic text that can be addressed to another Internet user anywhere on the global network.

Data file transfers allow Internet users to access remote computers and retrieve programs or text. Many computers connected to the Internet can access public data files anonymously and copy them free of charge.

A **newsgroup** is a collection of users who exchange news and debate issues of interest. Many thousands of separate newsgroups are located on the Internet.

Remote computing can be done by those programmers and scientists who need the power of remote computers, or by those who need to tap into large information databases.

Collectively, these functions allow students and business professionals alike to research topics of interest, resources, such as books and periodicals.

Getting Connected

To join the Internet, you need a computer, a modem, and an ordinary voice-quality telephone line. With those, you will be able to establish an e-mail address, join newsgroups, and tap into endless information resources. Your local Internet service provider (ISP) will supply the software you need to use the connection.

INTERNATIONAL TELEPHONE CALLS

Telephones are easy to use, but some people tend to panic when an international call does not go through immediately. When something goes wrong, you may find yourself asking questions such as the following:

1. Why did a fax sound come on when I expected to hear a person answering the phone?
2. What do I do now that an unexpected person is answering the phone in a language that I don't understand?
3. Why did someone in Minnesota answer the phone when I was dialing Sydney, Australia?

When you are having difficulty making international calls, be sure to consider the following:

- Your own office phone system
- The correct format for dialing international numbers
- International holidays
- Time zone differences
- Language barriers

quicktips

Telephone Tip

When answering the phone:

- Don't use acronyms for your company's name—unless it's a very well known company, like AT&T or IBM.
  - Answering with "IS, this is Sue, may I help you"—may not be clear if the caller doesn't know *IS* stands for "Information Systems."

Overview

✔ Directories, such as the yellow pages, and the Internet are important telephone references.

✔ Speaking clearly requires the appropriate volume, speed, inflection, and enunciation.

✔ To save time when placing telephone calls, plan your call and gather any necessary materials; ask for the person and identify yourself immediately.

✔ Answering the telephone effectively requires the following: answering promptly, giving proper identification, being courteous, taking complete messages, effectively explaining your manager's absence, transferring calls properly, efficiently answering a second telephone, knowing when to answer, delivering messages promptly, screening calls, and handling difficult callers.

✔ When placing long-distance calls, the office professional must select the most efficient method of dialing, determine time zones, effectively place international calls, and arrange conference calls.

✔ Office professionals must understand how telephone equipment, systems, and services will affect the way they perform certain tasks.

✔ The office professional can use the Internet to send and receive e-mail, transfer data files, join newsgroups, perform remote computing, and research topics.

Key Terms

Auto announcements. Similar to answering machines but activated only when all incoming lines are busy, or after hours when the caller is prompted to leave a message or to call back during business hours.

Caller identification (ID). A telephone service provided that allows the caller's number to display on your telephone.

Calling cards. Equipped with a magnetic strip reader to accommodate placing a call. The charge is automatically billed to your personal or business account.

Call forwarding. A telephone service provided that allows the telephone system to forward a call to another number when you are busy or away from your desk.

Call management services. Services offered from use of interconnect equipment include displaying caller's number on your telephone and forwarding your call to another number when you are busy or away from your desk.

Central Exchange (CENTREX). Provides direct in-house dialing to an office extension without assistance from an operator. CENTREX is used by organizations that have many telephone extensions.

Conference call. A call between three or more parties in different geographical locations.

Data file transfers. Allow Internet users to access remote computers and retrieve programs or text.

Direct-distance dialing (DDD). A method of making long-distance calls that allows the caller to dial the number directly with no special assistance from an operator.

Hybrid and Virtual Telephone Exchange systems. These systems use office PCs and the Internet to provide familiar voice services and local control at a fraction of the cost of traditional office telephone exchanges.

Inbound voice services. Calls made by someone calling into your home or office, at your company's expense. These services are commonly known as "toll-free services."

Interactive Voice Response (IVR). Services that can be programmed to respond to different situations, such as a predefined number of rings and between specific times of day, and play a variety of announcements.

Interconnect equipment. Refers to telephone equipment that organizations purchase or lease from suppliers other than from telephone companies; equipment is digitally controlled from a central office and offers users a variety of services.

Internet. Also referred to as the *World Wide Web*, or *the Web*; a public global communications network that enables people to exchange information through a computer.

Internet mail. Electronic text that can be addressed to another Internet user anywhere on the global network; same as e-mail.

Key telephones. Provide flexibility in making and receiving multiple calls simultaneously by using multiple buttons.

Long-distance calls. Any calls placed outside the local calling area.

Newsgroup. A collection of users who exchange news and debate issues of interest.

Outbound voice services. Originated and paid for by the caller.

Personal communication systems (PCSs). Wireless technology as part of the local area networks (LANs) that are connected without wires.

Person-to-person calls. Telephone calls in which you call a specific individual by dialing "0," the area code, and the telephone number, and having the operator assist you.

Point-to-point call. Call made to any individual who answers, or if you anticipate the person to whom you wish to talk will be near the telephone.

Prepaid calling cards. The equivalent of a direct debit card; the card has a magnetic strip on the back of the card that stores the original purchase value of the card and updates that amount each time a call is made.

Private Automatic Branch Exchange (PABX). The service provides its users with the ability to dial another extension directly without having to engage the operator. The telephone user can also dial inside and outside numbers without operator intervention.

Private Branch Exchange (PBX). A switchboard that provides service for outside calls coming into and going out of the office and for inside calls between telephones within the office. Today's PBXs are desktop computerized consoles and require a phone attendant to answer incoming calls and forward them by pressing a button on the console.

Remote computing. Done by those programmers and scientists who need the power of remote computers, or by those who need to tap into large information databases.

Telephone answering service. A switchboard attended by an operator who answers subscribers' telephones at designated hours.

Telephone tag. Telephoning back and forth by parties trying to reach each other without success.

Voice mail. A telephone answering system that stores messages digitally.

Voice-recognition software. Allows a computer to translate the spoken word into language a computer can understand more than 95 percent of the time.

Voice services. Sophisticated voice networks provide telephone sets, a dial tone, and the international telephone network, which enables people to talk to others around the world.

Wireless services. Include microwave systems, radio broadcast and reception, wireless telephone services, and direct-to-home television services.

World Wide Web. See *Internet*.

Zero plus dialing. Operator assisted call activated by dialing "0," the area code, and the seven-digit local number.

For Your Discussion

 Retrieve file C12-DQ.DOC from your student data disk.

Directions

Enter your response after each question.

1. What information is essential for adequately identifying yourself when you are placing a telephone call?
2. When you must take a message, why is it essential to restate the message?
3. Describe how to handle a transferred call when the caller has been transferred several times.
4. Describe what to do when two telephones ring at the same time and you are the only one in the office.
5. Which two questions are you attempting to answer when screening calls?
6. What must a caller who has reached the wrong long-distance number do in order not to be charged for the call?
7. Describe how to place a direct-dial international call.
8. What are three advantages and three disadvantages of using voice mail?
9. Distinguish between PBX and CENTREX.
10. Describe how you will benefit from using voice-recognition technology.

BUSINESS MATH WORKSHOP

Previously you reviewed the percentage formula and solved problems such as, what is 13 percent of 92.20? You learned that the "what" is the part, 13 percent is the rate, and 92.20 is the base. You worked problems determining the "what" or the part. In this chapter you will review the rate formula; that is, you will determine the rate in questions such as, $600 is what percent of $3,200?

Suppose you made $600 on an item, which you sold for $3,200. What is the commission rate? Once you determine the rate, you can determine if this is an acceptable commission rate. You may need to increase the selling price or find another source from which to purchase this item at a reduced cost. This particular formula is, rate (percent) equals the part divided by base (the whole).

For Review

Appendix A: Business Math

 Retrieve C12-WRKS.DOC from your student data disk.

Directions

Find the rate in each of the following problems and enter it in the blank.

1. 39 is what percent of 302? _____
2. What percent of 60 is 185? _____
3. 0.6 is what percent of 65? _____
4. 6 is what percent of 136? _____
5. What percent of 1,350 is 45? _____
6. 52 is what percent of 87? _____
7. What percent of 80 is 30? _____
8. 15 is what percent of 215? _____
9. 233 is what percent of 654? _____
10. What percent of 60 is 52? _____

On the Job Situations

 Retrieve file C12-OJS.DOC from your student data disk.

Directions

Enter your response after each situation.

1. During your first job performance review, you were criticized for the way you answered the telephone. You had been asking the caller to state the

purpose of the call before you said whether your manager was in the office. After you found out who the caller was and the purpose of the call, you sometimes said, "Mrs. Burke is not in her office," or "Mrs. Burke is in a meeting." It was true that Mrs. Burke was not in her office when you said this, but apparently the callers were not convinced. What can you do to improve rapport with the callers?

2. You know that your manager, Mr. Perkins, is expecting an important long-distance call. He called Mike Williams at 9:30 a.m., and he is expecting Mr. Williams to return his call. At 4:30 p.m. Mr. Perkins was called to the president's office. A few minutes after Mr. Perkins left his office, Mr. Williams called. You feel you should not interrupt Mr. Perkins. You do not know whether Mr. Perkins will return to his desk before 5 p.m. What should you do? List several alternatives and then select the best one.

3. Robert started working in your department one week ago. His job includes answering the telephone at his workstation. As you are the assistant to the department manager and the person responsible for telephone training, you have noticed that Robert has made the following comments: "Who is this?", "Call back later," "She is still at lunch," and "Hold on." What should you do? What suggestions should you make? What additional training do you think is needed?

4. You have noticed that Lauren spends a great deal of time on the telephone for personal calls. She leaves her desk frequently and transfers her calls to your workstation. You really do not mind taking her calls, but a majority of her incoming calls have been personal ones. What should you do? List several alternatives and then select the best one.

Projects and Activities

1. Use the yellow pages of your local telephone directory to determine how the following are classified: educational services (public schools, private schools, colleges and universities), food catering services, medical doctors (general practitioners), furniture for an office, office stationery, office computers, and airlines. Prepare a list in memo form and submit it to your instructor.

2. Obtain the international telephone codes for three Eastern European countries and two Mexican states.

3. Visit a retail outlet or company that sells telephone equipment. Learn about a specific type of telephone system and briefly describe its features, such as conference calling and caller identification. Summarize your findings in memo form and be prepared to share your findings with the class.

4. Interview an office professional who handles international calls. Ask the person to share tips to help you effectively handle international calls that involve people who are not fluent in the English language. Report your findings in memo form to your instructor. Be prepared to share your findings with the class.

Surfing the Internet

1. Your manager has asked you to locate fax and telephone directories listing names and telephone numbers of businesses in Mexico. You know that there are a number of resources on the Internet. Complete your search by following these steps:

   a. Connect to the Internet and access a search tool such as Yahoo! or Lycos.

   b. Locate resources by entering the following search words: *business, fax, telephone directory, Mexico.*

   c. List at least three directories and summarize your findings.

   d. Be prepared to share your findings with your class.

2. Your manager has asked you to research the topic of voice recognition and send the information to her as an e-mail.

   a. Connect to the Internet and access a search tool such as Yahoo! or Lycos.

   b. Locate resources by entering the following search words: *voice recognition.*

   c. Summarize your findings and include a definition of voice recognition, how it is being used, and a brief description of at least two different software programs.

   d. Present your findings in memo form to your instructor and be prepared to share this information with your class.

3. An office professional on your team has asked you for tips on using the Internet.

   a. Connect to the Internet and access a search tool such as Google, Yahoo!, or Lycos.

   b. Locate guides and tutorials for Internet or Web use by entering http://www.microsoft.com/inside/internet.

   c. Summarize your findings and include references.

   d. Present your findings in memo form to your instructor and be prepared to share this information with your class.

Using MS Office 2002

Use the Contacts Detail Tab

 Let Microsoft Outlook contact cards contain all the information you want for the person or company. Use your Contacts file rather than your Rolodex.

1. Open Microsoft Outlook and then click on Contacts in the Folder List.
2. Open an existing card or create a new card by clicking on New Contact from the Standard toolbar.
3. Fill in the information on the General tab.

4. Click on the Details tab.

5. Fill in as much information as you can.

6. Click on Save and Close.

Using the Contact Card When Placing a Call

1. Have the contact card open when you call that person.

   a. Click on the Details tab to display a contact card.

   b. If the person you normally talk with isn't available, you can quickly ask for another person or ask for the supervisor.

   c. If another person can provide help, then update the contact card with this additional information.

2. Click on Save and Close.

APPLICATION PROBLEMS

APPLICATION 12-A

Receiving Telephone Calls

Supplies needed: Forms 12-A-1 through 12-A-4, Telephone Message Forms.

When your managers are in their offices, they answer their own telephones. However, today—August 11—Mrs. Quevedo, Mr. Rush, and Mr. Levine are not in their offices. Using the telephone message forms, record messages for the following telephone calls:

9:15 a.m. for Mr. Rush from Archie Sellars, 683-4750. He wants to know if parts are available for an electric range, Model 1621. Please return his call.

10:30 a.m. for Mr. Levine from A. L. Wilcox, 442-8761, about a printing order Mr. Levine placed with him. Urgent. Please call.

11 a.m. for Mrs. Quevedo from Mr. Arnett, 366-8184, a speaker for the November Sales Seminar. He has a business conflict and cannot attend the seminar on Wednesday. Please call.

11:15 a.m. for Mrs. Quevedo from Human Resources, Extension 5738, asking, "When can Mrs. Quevedo see an applicant?" Please call.

APPLICATION 12-B

Placing Telephone Calls

Supplies needed: Forms 12-B-1 and 12-B-2, pages for Notes.

Mrs. Quevedo asked you to place some telephone calls. Here is Mrs. Quevedo's conversation with you:

"Mr. Arnett, 366-8184, who was scheduled to speak at the November Sales Seminar on Wednesday, November 12, at 10 a.m., cannot attend on

Wednesday. He is handling his manager's work as his manager has had a heart attack and will not return to work for at least six months. Mr. Arnett must be in the office on November 12. He can, however, attend the seminar on Monday and Tuesday."

"Find a speaker who can trade times with Mr. Arnett. Call James Yates, 674-8609, who is scheduled to talk at 2 p.m. on Monday. If he can't do it, ask Ruth Agway, 608-547-3232, who is scheduled to speak at 11 a.m. on Monday. Another possibility is Ray Morris, 638-1456, who is on a panel on Tuesday afternoon."

"Be sure to call Mr. Arnett and tell him what arrangements you have made."

"Be sure to make the proper notations in the official copy of the program. It would be a good idea to write a confirmation letter to the person whose time is changed."

Note: When you called Mr. Yates, he said he could not attend the seminar on Wednesday.

Before you place any calls, make notes on what you need to say. Record all essential information, such as names, telephone numbers, dates, and time of day. Also write down reminders about what you need to do after you have found someone who can fill in for Mr. Arnett.

APPLICATION 12-C

Telephone Services

Supplies needed: Form 12-C, Telephone Services; a local telephone directory or online telephone directory.

Directions: Use a local telephone directory to complete the questions on Form 12-C.

Your Action Plan

Refer to the guidelines in Chapter 1. Set one goal using the information in Chapter 12.

Your Portfolio

With the help of your instructor, select the best papers representative of your work from Chapter 12. Follow your instructor's directions about formatting, assembling, and turning in the portfolio.

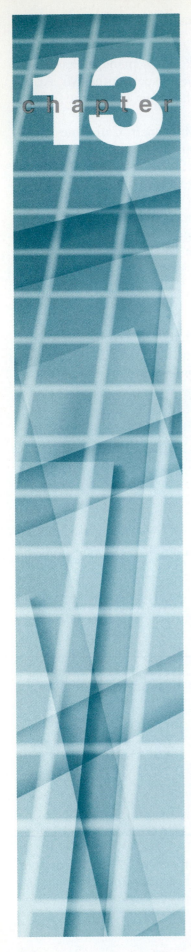

chapter 13

Working in a Medical Office

OUTLINE

The Medical Office
    Types of Medical Offices
    Medical Careers and Skills Needed
    Basic Clerical or Office Skills and Competencies
    Basic Clinical Competencies

Basic Medical Office Positions
    Front Office Staff Personnel
    Clinical Staff Employees
    X-Ray Technician Staff
    Billing Staff Employees

LEARNING OUTCOMES

When you have completed this chapter, you should be able to:

✔ Describe the types of medical offices that employ medical workers.

✔ Discuss the qualifications needed for various medical careers and positions.

✔ Discuss basic office and clinical skills that are needed to work in the four major departments usually found in medical offices.

✔ Explain at least five skills required in the four major divisions in medical offices.

✔ Explain the basic requirements of HIPAA that applies to medical offices.

✔ Define and explain basic medical terminology applicable to most medical offices.

THE MEDICAL OFFICE

You have already learned many procedures and developed the skills necessary to perform tasks in various types of offices. Most offices have certain basic tasks that are performed by their workforce every day. Some tasks are specialized according to the size of the office, the type of work done in the office, or the number of employees. Being expert at basic skills will give you a competitive edge when you seek employment at almost any type of office. Let's now relate all of these skills to working in a medical office: What general basic skills are needed, how can you perfect them, and what do you need in the way of additional, more complex competencies? Isn't that an exciting prospective job?

Types of Medical Offices

Have you been to a doctor lately? Most of us have regular medical checkups and occasionally visit a doctor for an illness or accident or maybe even accompany someone to the doctor's office. The doctor could work as a sole proprietor (in business for himself or herself), or as a partner in a large or small practice (partners own a piece of the business and share in the profits or losses in some way such as a percentage). The doctor may also work as a general member of a corporation (a business that is incorporated under the laws of incorporation of a particular state). A doctor may also be on staff at a hospital, at a clinic, or in a school in the local community or a larger city or town. The word **practice** refers to the professional business of the doctor. Usually the medical office is where the doctor practices, or works.

Medical practices come in a variety of types. You may need to see your primary care or family doctor, a specialist such as an orthopedic (treats joints, bones, and spine) doctor, a nephrologist (a kidney and renal doctor), a chiropractor (a practitioner who performs manual manipulation of joints in the body), an internal medicine doctor, a dermatologist (skin) specialist, a pediatric (infants and children) doctor, and the like to name a few types of practices in which doctors specialize or practice. These are only a minimum of the types of doctors in the medical profession. If you are interested in learning about other types of doctors, a great place to do that is in the yellow pages of the telephone directory, under "physicians."

All doctors have graduated not only from college but also from medical school and even from additional types of programs of specialization, such as urology, oncology, endocrinology, or other types of specialization. Most doctors have completed an internship for a number of years at a hospital or institution in preparation for going into practice.

Because they are so highly trained and because doctors must deal with life-and-death situations in which mistakes may kill, they want a staff that is also highly trained. That is where you come in. Let's go back to the question asked of you earlier: Have you gone to a doctor lately?

Medical Careers and Skills Needed

So, you have been to a doctor's office. What exactly have you seen going on in the doctor's office? What careers have been common and what tasks have the people in these careers been performing? Let's take a moment and reflect on several advertisements for skilled medical workers that have appeared in newspapers lately.

Medical Assistant—Pediatrics
Full-time position responsible for assisting physicians in all clinical areas of the office with some clerical duties. Qualifications include high school diploma, knowledge of medical terminology and procedures. A graduate of an accredited medical assisting program and medical computer experience are preferred. Experience should include 1–3 years physician office experience.

Medical Transcriptionist
Accurate and timely transcription of medical research and correspondence for physicians and nurses from recorded dictation or written documentation. Candidates must be proficient in Microsoft Word. Experience in an orthopedic surgical practice desirable.

Secretary for Medical Practice
Busy medical practice needs a secretary with expertise in Microsoft Office and maintenance of supplies. Confidentiality is imperative.

Transcription/Dictation Coordinator
Busy medical practice specializing in foot and ankle disorders needs a coordinator to interact with outside transcription companies, review all transcription, correct formatting and spelling errors, research missing dictation, print finalized notes and letters, and file dictation in charts. Must be familiar with medical terminology, MS Word, and have good organizational skills and dependability.

Basic Clerical or Office Skills and Competencies

As you review these positions, think about the skills required such as medical terminology, clerical and clinical procedures, organizational ability, and dependability. Let's identify other skills and competencies that may be found under the group called clerical or office procedures. Here are the basic clerical or office skills and competencies needed:

1. **Keyboarding.** Regardless of the position, everyone should know how to keyboard.
2. **Telephone etiquette.** This entails the ability to be friendly, listen to people's problems and communicate correctly what is needed. For example, patients may speak with an accent, and it is sometimes difficult to un-

derstand what they need or what they want from the medical office. Patience and kindness are necessary.

3. **Filing.** Although everyone thinks that knowing the alphabet is an easy task, it is amazing to see files in the wrong place. Finding charts can be time consuming and very problematic if a system is not devised to track down a missing chart in the master filing storage area.

4. **Basic medical terminology.** Although every medical office has its own special vocabulary used by individual doctors, a basic knowledge of some terms is helpful.

5. **Health Insurance Portability and Accountability Act (HIPAA)** forms and regulations. Knowing how to complete a HIPAA form and to explain it correctly is important for those working in the front office such as a receptionist or intake person.

6. **Medical software program.** Knowing how to use medical software to assist a patient in getting an appointment to see a doctor, physician's assistant, or registered nurse practitioner is a needed skill for many workers in a medical office. Knowing how to complete an appointment card for a patient to take as a reminder is also important.

7. **Compose and type notes or letters.** Often a note or letter is needed regarding a particular patient after a visit to the medical office to the referring doctor. The doctor may handwrite this or dictate a letter, and it is the office's responsibility to key it and have it ready for the doctor's signature if necessary.

8. **Billing.** Understanding how important the billing department is to the entire medical office is essential. Without the billing department being successful in collecting moneys from the insurance companies and the patients, the medical practice will not stay in business very long.

9. **Good verbal communication skills.** You must be able to communicate with people with empathy and with understanding.

10. **Good personal grooming.** If the employee wears a uniform, it should be cleaned and pressed to make a good impression on the patient.

11. **A second language.** Being bilingual is now a basic skill that is valued in most areas of the country because the population is so diverse. It would be an added bonus in any office. In a medical practice, people from many ethnic backgrounds converge, and it is very helpful if someone can help a person in pain communicate correctly to a doctor.

Basic Clinical Competencies

You probably have learned most of these skills already from the many business and office courses you have taken. Review these skills and competencies again to assess how you rank in your knowledge of each of them. Then, let's review a few clinical procedures and competencies you will need.

1. **Hazardous waste materials.** Most medical offices give patients injections. Knowing how to dispose of syringes correctly as well as how to use and dispose of medical gloves is important. Medical offices also have other procedures that may produce biological or other hazardous wastes or liquids. Knowing how to dispose of these is critically important for health reasons as well.

2. **Medications.** Knowing the basic types of medications that patients in your practice use will be valuable information. Having a basic knowledge of pharmacology will help you in understanding how to relate the medicines to the patients. They usually ask questions about the medication being prescribed by the doctor. For example, they may ask what the side affects are to taking a certain medication. Knowing what the state pharmacy law allows you to discuss about medication is important.

3. **Equipment procedures.** Knowing how to sterilize instruments is useful information for employees on the clinical side of any medical office.

4. **Sterilization.** Knowing the basics of equipment sterilization is important as noted in number 3, but also knowing how to sterilize a room, beds, and the like is important.

5. **Legal procedures.** Knowing what you can or cannot do or say legally in your position as a medical professional is very important. Your actions are dependent not only on your position, your education, or your certifications but also upon the state requirements in which the practice is located.

BASIC MEDICAL OFFICE POSITIONS

There are basically four areas of positions available in a medical office. First, there are positions that provide opportunities for employees working up front with the patients, getting information from them before and after they see the doctor. These positions may be known as the receptionist, intake personnel, or front office staff.

Second, there is the clinical staff made of medical assistants or medical techs, **nurse practitioners** or **physician's assistants.** Third, there are the x-ray technicians; and last, there are the billing and accounts receivable personnel.

Let's take each of these positions and discuss them according to general and specific responsibilities and then according to the specific skills needed for that position.

A medical office where patients and visitors are greeted.

Front Office Staff Personnel

This could be a staff of two or more persons depending on how busy the office is. For example, if the office sees 200 or more patients per day, more front office personnel would be required in an office where there are many doctors and many physician assistants than in an office that has only one doctor, one nurse or nurse practitioner, and a few medical assistants who see about 55 patients per day.

In a larger office, tasks are quite specialized. This means there may be a switchboard operator and two receptionists or intake persons checking in patients. In addition, there may be two or three other employees (outtake persons) checking patients out of the office.

Receptionists or intake persons who check in patients have them sign a log-in sheet (see Figure 13-1), have them fill out legal forms, ask for their

■ **Figure 13-1**
Patient log-in sheet.

Patient's name: last, first	Arrival time	Have you rec'd a notice of privacy practices?	Ins. carrier	Is there a change in:	Address	Insurance
Brom, Mazie	8:15	✓	United	—	—	yes
Thoms, Terry	8:20	no	Aetna	—	—	yes
Jones, Tommy	8:35	✓	NY Life	—	—	yes
Hanks, Aaron	9:00	✓	United	—	—	yes

insurance card or cards, and collect insurance **co-payments** (charges assigned by the insurance company) or any balance due on their account.

Most health insurance falls into two basic categories: either they are HMOs or PPOs. **Health maintenance organization (HMO)** patients are easiest to handle for the front office staff. The patient just pays the amount printed on his or her insurance card. If the doctor seen is a specialist, the patient needs to obtain a referral from his or her **primary care physician** prior to the office visit. If the patient has a **preferred provider organization (PPO)** insurance policy, more than likely the patient has a **deductible** to be met annually in addition to a copay amount printed on the front of the insurance card. Many times, the patient with a PPO insurance plan also has to pay a copay for x-rays or injections. Here is where the front office staff needs to contact the patient's insurance company prior to the new patient's visit to the practice to find out the amount of the deductible, what has already been paid toward that amount, and any other copays the patient has with the policy written by that particular insurance company. To add to the confusion, insurance companies change policies quite often.

If the patient cannot pay the account in full, the patient is encouraged to sign papers stating that he or she will pay within a certain number of days.

The employees who check out patients hand them their prescriptions, sample medications, schedule tests or physical therapy for them as well as schedule the patients for their next visit when the doctor says they should return. Most patients like to receive an **appointment card** with the next appointment written on it as a reminder (see Figure 13-2). These outtake persons also collect any additional charges that may have occurred while the doctor was with them. For example, if there was an injection or x-ray, many insurance companies require patients to pay a copay for these services.

Likewise, there may be employees (called schedulers or appointment makers) who collect charts of patients coming in the next day and contact them regarding their appointments. These employees review every chart to make certain that the notes and reports are in chronological order, and any outstanding balance is conveyed to the patient at the time of the call so he or she can pay at the appointment the next day. In a specialist's office, these appointment people also make certain that the patient has a valid referral to see the specialist depending on the type of insurance the patient has. A **referral** contains information such as that shown in Figure 13-3.

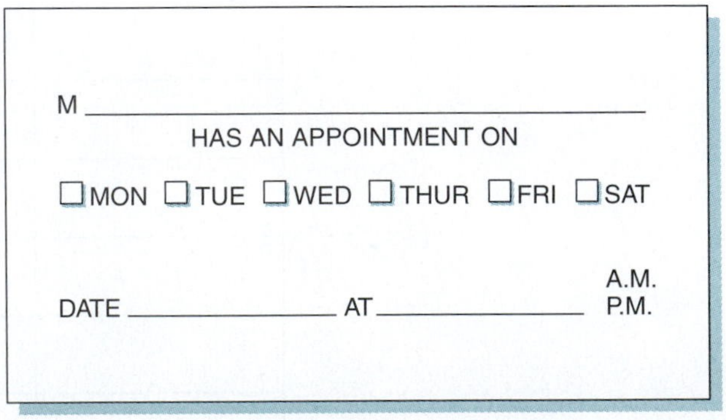

■ **Figure 13-2**
Appointment card.

M _____

HAS AN APPOINTMENT ON

☐MON ☐TUE ☐WED ☐THUR ☐FRI ☐SAT

DATE _____ AT _____   A.M.
                                             P.M.

In larger offices, some employees file charts most of the day when they are not busy with other tasks such as answering the phone, writing thank-you letters to doctors, and sending questionnaires to new patients. Other offices may have a full-time employee who handles legal depositions and second-opinion cases in which the doctor is paid to give a legal opinion of someone's medical condition. A second-opinion interview is called an **independent medical examination (IME)**. These **IMEs** are usually done right at the office and the attorneys bring a court reporter with them to validate what the doctor says.

In small offices, you will not see as many employees as noted in the larger offices just discussed. In a small office, one or two employees may handle all the tasks identified. You can readily see how busy a medical office can be, regardless of whether it is a large or small office.

■ **Figure 13-3**
Referral.

INS – **AUTOMATED RESPONSE**

INS REFERRAL

PAYER INFORMATION
UTILIZATION MANAGEMENT: INS HEALTHCARE
PAYER ID: 100000000

REQUESTER INFORMATION
PROVIDER: SENSE, TEDDY V
ETIN: 5555555

SUBSCRIBER INFORMATION
INSURED OR SUBSCRIBER: PATIENT, TOM P
MEMBER ID: AAAAAABB
DATE OF BIRTH: 09/10/1943
DIAGNOSIS CODE: 7242

SERVICE PROVIDER INFORMATION
MESSAGE: DISK DISEASE
SERVICE PROVIDER: ZAPP, ANNA A
ETIN: 4444444

SERVICE INFORMATION
REQUEST CATEGORY: SPECIALTY CARE REVIEW
CERTIFICATION TYPE: INITIAL
PLACE OF SERVICE: OFFICE
CERTIFICATION ACTION: CERTIFIED IN TOTAL
CERTIFICATION NUMBER: Z00000000
ISSUE DATE: 05/04/2xxx
EXPIRATION DATE: 08/01/2xxx
HCPCS PROCEDURE CODE: 99214
HCPCS PROCEDURE CODE: 99245
HCPCS PRODECURE CODE: 99499
SERVICES DELIVERY: 5 VISITS
MESSAGE: HMO MULTIPLE VISIT REFERRAL - THE FIRST
                             VISIT MUST OCCUR WITHIN 90 DAYS, BALANCE
                             WITHIN 1 YEAR OF EFFECTIVE DATE

THE PROVIDER UNDERSTANDS THAT RECEIPT OR USE OF THIS REFERRAL
INFORMATION DOES NOT GUARANTEE PAYMENT OF ANY HEALTHCARE CLAIM BY
INS AND SUCH INFORMATION IS SUBJECT TO CHANGE, EVEN RETROACTIVELY,
AT ANY TIME.

TRANS REF #:   X00000000

Front office staff skills needed in a small office include:

a. Every employee, regardless of job duty, needs to know how to keyboard accurately.

b. Every employee needs to know how to maneuver around a medical software package to make appointments, reschedule, and cancel appointments.

c. Every employee needs to have a pleasant speaking voice that is courteous and cheerful whether the patient is in front of him or her at the office or being spoken with over the phone.

d. Every employee needs to have good handwriting so that employees in the other departments, or the doctors themselves, can read and understand their notes or questions.

e. Every employee needs good listening skills to hear and understand what the patient is saying, or what the doctor is saying, or what is being said over the phone line.

f. In a small office, several people need to know how to operate the switchboard. In a large office, several people need to rotate their job positions to include time at the switchboard. For example: breaks during the day, for vacations or time off. In this age of technology, some offices have only an answering machine that records the information from each patient who calls. The directions on the answering machine instruct the caller about what information to leave and to expect a return call in answer to any requests or other needs at a particular time.

g. All personnel must maintain a professional decorum and avoid discussing patients' names and medical problems in front of other patients. This is in compliance with HIPAA rules. Other rules and regulations will be discussed later in the chapter.

h. Several people need to know how to handle money when the patient pays a copay or coinsurance charge. This is needed for people who check in patients as well as those who check out patients. The **encounter form** (see Figure 13-4) notes if a patient had x-rays taken that day or an injection given. If so, additional money may need to be collected from the patient at the time of checking out.

i. Every employee needs to know how to verify insurance coverage over the Internet or by speaking to a customer service representative of an insurance company. They can also determine deductible amounts to collect as well as a mailing address where each claim should be sent.

j. Every employee needs to treat all patients with dignity and courtesy. Sometimes that is difficult, because some people are in great distress and they may not be very pleasant to deal with.

k. Every employee should ensure that all the information keyed into the medical software such as social security number and insurance subscriber number are correct.

l. Every employee should know how to file charts and find charts as well as know where charts may be if they are not in the main files.

m. Every staff member must wear washed and pressed uniforms to promote an air of professionalism among patients and coworkers. Good grooming is necessary for everyone.

T. R. JONES, M.D.   S. A. JONES, M.D.   L. A. JONES, M.D.

PROCEDURES

CODE	NEW PATIENT VISIT	FEE
99202	New Pat. Vis.-Expanded	
99203	New Pat. Vis.-Detailed	165
99204	New Pat. Vis.-Compreh.	
99205	New Pat. Vis.-Compreh.	
	ESTABLISHED PATIENT VISIT	
99212	Re - Exam-Prob. Focused	
99213	Re - Exam-Expanded	
99214	Re - Exam-Med Compl.	
99215	Re - Exam-High Compl.	
10000	N/C Office Visit	
99024	Post-Op Visit	
	INJECTIONS	
20600	Small	
20605	Intermediate	
20610	Major	
20610-1	Aspiration, Joint	
J7320	Synvic	
J7317	Hyaigan	
20526	Carpal Tunnel	
20550	Tendon Sheath	
J1030	Methylpred 40 mg	
J1040	Methylpred 80 mg	
J1100	Dexsodphos 80 mg	
20552	Trigger Pts. One or Two Muscle Groups	
	CASTING/SPLINTING	
29085	Gauntlet APP	
Q4013	Gauntlet, Plaster-Adult	
Q4014	Gauntlet, Syn-Adult	
Q4015	Gauntlet, Plaster-Peds	
Q4016	Gauntlet, Syn-Peds	
29075	Short Arm Cast, APP	
Q4009	Short Arm Cast, Plaster-Adult	
Q4010	Short Arm Cast, Syn-Adult	
Q4011	Short Arm Cast, Plaster-Peds	
Q4012	Short Arm Cast, Syn-Peds	
29125	Short Arm Splint, APP	
Q4021	Short Arm Splint, Plaster-Adult	
Q4022	Short Arm Splint, Syn-Adult	
Q4023	Short Arm Splint, Plaster-Peds	
Q4024	Short Arm Splint, Syn-Peds	
29065	Long Arm Cast, APP	
Q4005	Long Arm Cast, Plaster-Adult	
Q4006	Long Arm Cast, Syn-Adult	
Q4007	Long Arm Cast, Plaster-Peds	
Q4008	Long Arm Cast, Syn-Peds	
29105	Long Arm Splint APP	

CODE	CASTING/SPLINTING	FEE
Q4017	Long Arm Splint, Plaster-Adult	
Q4018	Long Arm Splint, Syn-Adult	
Q4019	Long Arm Splint, Plaster-Peds	
Q4020	Long Arm Splint, Syn-Peds	
29405	Short Leg Cast, APP	
29425	Short Leg Walking Cast, APP	
Q4037	Short Leg Cast, Plaster-Adult	
Q4038	Short Leg Cast, Syn-Adult	
Q4039	Short Leg Cast, Plaster-Peds	
Q4040	Short Leg Cast, Syn-Peds	
29515	Short Leg Splint, APP	
Q4045	Short Leg Splint, Plaster-Adult	
Q4046	Short Leg Splint, Syn-Adult	
Q4047	Short Leg Splint, Plaster-Peds	
Q4048	Short Leg Splint, Syn-Peds	
29345	Long Leg Cast, APP	
Q4029	Long Leg Cast, Plaster-Adult	
Q4030	Long Leg Cast, Syn-Adult	
Q4031	Long Leg Cast, Plaster-Peds	
Q4032	Long Leg Cast, Syn-Peds	
29365	Long Leg Cylinder Cast, APP	
Q4033	Long Cylinder, Plaster-Adult	
Q4034	Long Cylinder, Syn-Adult	
Q4035	Long Cylinder, Plaster-Peds	
Q4036	Long Cylinder, Syn-Peds	
29435	PTB Cast, APP	
Q4037	PTB Cast, Plaster-Adult	
Q4038	PTB Cast, Syn-Adult	
Q4039	PTB Cast, Plaster-Peds	
Q4040	PTB Cast, Syn-Peds	
29086	Finger Cast	
29405	Jones Dressing	
29705	Cast Removal	
29580	Unna Boot	
29700	Removal	
	X-RAYS	
73050-ZD	Acromo-Clavicular Joints Bil	
73600-ZD	Ankle-AP & Lat	
73610-ZD	Ankle-Complete	
71021-ZD	Chest	
73000-ZD	Clavicle	
72200-ZD	Coccyx	
73070-ZD	Elbow - AP & Lat	
73080-ZD	Elbow-Complete	
73550-ZD	Femur-AP & Lat	
73140-ZD	Finger-2	

CODE	X-RAYS	FEE
73090-ZD	Forearm-AP & Lat	
73620-ZD	Foot-AP & Lat	
73630-ZD	Foot-Complete	
73120-ZD	Hand-2	75
73130-ZD	Hand-3	
73650-ZD	Heel	
73500-ZD	Hip-1	
73510-ZD	Hip-2	
72190-ZD	Hip & Pelvis-3	
73060-ZD	Humerus	
73560-ZD	Knee-AP & Lat	
73562-ZD	Knee-AP, Lat & Oblique	
73564-ZD	Knee-Complete	
73565	Both Knees Standing	
72170-ZD	Pelvis	
71110-ZD	Ribs	
72220-ZD	Sacrum	
73010-ZD	Scapula	
72090-ZD	Scoliosis Series	
73020-ZD	Shoulder-1	
73030-ZD	Shoulder-Complete	
70260-ZD	Skull Series	
70250-ZD	Skull-2	
72202-ZD	SI Joint	
72020-ZD	Spine-1	
72040-ZD	Cervical Spine-AP & Lat	
72052-ZD	Cervical Spine-Complete	
72070-ZD	Thoracic Spine-AP & Lat	
72110-ZD	Lumbar Spine-Complete	
72100-ZD	Lumbar Spine-AP & Lat	
71120-ZD	Sternum	
73590-ZD	Tibia-AP & Lat	
73660-ZD	Toes	
73100-ZD	Wrist-AP & Lat	
73110-ZD	Wrist-3	
99070	X-Ray Copies	
	GLOBAL FEES	
	Global Fee Today	
	FX Care Today	
	CONSULT ONLY	
99242	Minimal Consult	
99243	Low Complex	
99244	Med-High Complex	
99245	Comprehensive	
99455	MMI/PPI-WC/Impairment Rating	
99456	IME-WC	

CODE	CONSULT ONLY	FEE
99241	Brief Consult	
	SOFT GOODS	
L3930	Abduction Finger Splint	25
A4460	Ace Bandage	5
L1845	ACL Brace, Breg	
L4350	Ankle Stirrup, Aircast	
L1906	ASO Ankle Brace	
E0100	Cane	
L3257	Cast Shoe	
L0120	Cervical Collar-Soft	
L3650	Cervical Figure-8 Brace	
L3800	CMC Brace, Soft	
L3800	CMC Orthosis	
E0112	Crutches	
L3730	Elbow ROM, Breg	
L3730	Elbow ROM, Donjoy	
L3480	Heel Pad, Hapad	
L3980	Humeral Fx Brace	
L1815	Knee Hinged Brace L2435 x 2	
L1830	Knee Immobilizer	
L4380	Knee Infrapatella Band	
L1800	Knee "j" Brace	
L1832	Knee ROM Brace	
L1825	Knee Sleeve	
L4396	Nightsplint, AFO	
L3260	Post-op Shoe	
L0515	Sawa Hamstring Brace	
L3962	Sawa Shoulder Brace	
L3660	Sling	
L3670	Sling and Swathe	
A4570	Staxx Finger Splint	
L3700	Tennis Elbow Band	
L3805	Thumb Spica Splint, Soft	
L3908	Wrist Splint, Cock-up	
L3914	Wrist-Forearm Splint	
L3984	Wrist/Hand/Thumb Orthosis	
L4360	Walking Boot, Standard	
L1990	Walking Boot, ROM	
	Non-Reimbursable Goods	
L2999	Bunion Toes Separator, Gel	
L2999	Bunion Toe Separator, Foam	
L3465	Heel Cups	
L2999	Shoe Orthotics, 3/4 Length	
	Shower Cast Bag	
95903	Nerve Conduciton Study	

ACCOUNT NO.	CHG SLIP NO.	TODAY'S DATE	PATIENT'S NAME	NEW	SEX	BIRTHDATE	AGE	TELEPHONE
3126		6/16/xx	BETTY HURTHAND	x	F	9/28/46	56	(830) 555-9639

ADDRESS/CITY/STATE/ZIP	SOCIAL SECURITY NO.
RR Box 10, Boerne, TX 78015	999 99 00000

SUBSCRIBER OR POLICY HOLDER	INSURANCE CARRIER	POLICY NO.	GROUP NO.

■ **Figure 13-4**
Encounter form.

n. It is expected that medical office personnel understand some general medical vocabulary pertaining to their particular area of interest or specialty.

o. Everyone must realize the importance of confidentiality regarding every patient's health problems. This is also a HIPAA rule.

Clinical Staff Employees

Depending on the size of the office staff, clinical people must either do many different things or, as in the case of a larger office, they specialize in their job duties. For example, in a small office there is a medical assistant who weighs the patient, takes his or her blood pressure and temperature, and records the information in the chart for the doctor's exam. The assistant (also known as a technician, or tech, in specialists' offices) then brings the patient to the examination room. This assistant/tech talks with the patient and verifies the medical history, records medications taken, and writes down the reason for the visit so the doctor does not have to ask the patient. (The doctor will usually verify this information with the patient, however, to get a feel for what the patient is experiencing.) The medical assistant/tech also places the patient's chart outside the x-ray room door face down in a bin if the patient needs x-rays. If not, the assistant/tech places the patient's chart in sequential order in the doctor's dictating room. The assistant or technician logs on a sheet which patient is in which exam room to keep the office moving and avoid the wait some patients experience when seeing a doctor. The chart should not be placed outside the patient's room door because that violates HIPAA rules. Then the medical assistant/tech provides a gown for the patient and, depending on individual circumstances, may assist him or her in putting it on. After the doctor has seen the patient, the assistant/tech assists the doctor with getting samples of medication for the patient before leaving the office. Other duties may include getting a brace or cane for a patient, a wheelchair, or even writing a prescription (if allowed by state pharmacy law) for the doctor to sign to give to the patient after making a copy of the prescription for the patient's file. Finally, the assistant/tech cleans the room and gets the next patient into an exam room. When the doctors have seen all the patients on any given day, the assistant or tech cleans the rooms thoroughly and puts all used syringes and other **biohazardous waste materials** (see Figure 13-5) in the proper containers. Gloves must be used when cleaning the room and handling any biohazardous waste. An approved handler of medical waste materials picks up the waste once a week.

In addition, the assistant or technician removes sutures, dresses wounds, and sometimes makes casts for patients of all ages. He or she may draw medication and prepare syringes for the doctor at the beginning of the day, and sterilize all instruments on a daily basis and repackage them into sterilized packages for reuse the following day. The assistant/tech also takes phone messages and asks doctors about medication refills and return calls left by patients. After the doctor consents to allow a patient to refill a prescription, the tech or medical assistant records the date, time, the medication ordered, and the quantity in the patient's chart. (Assistants/techs must know enough about a medication prescribed by the doctor to inform the patient how to take the drug correctly if allowed by state pharmacy law.) The supervisor in charge of all medical assistants or technicians must call in supply requests to make certain the office does not run out of medical supplies on a weekly basis. The supervisor also interviews potential new clinical staff, evaluates staff members, holds meetings, and schedules the workdays of the clinical staff under him or her. Another specialized employee may measure patients' legs, arms, or feet for braces, walking boots, or crutches or other needed supplies. If the office is small, the medical assistant or technician does this as part of his or her job function. Depending on the type of practice, the assistant/tech may perform various other duties that relate to the particular practice and the patients' needs.

Other medical employees who may be part of a medical practice are nurse practitioners and physician's assistants. They hold advanced degrees so they can write and sign prescriptions themselves (depending on the pharmacy practice law in the state they are employed). They can even admit patients into a hospital when necessary. Should they have questions regarding a medical problem, they consult the doctor before discussing anything with their

■ **Figure 13-5**
Biohazardous waste
container in a medical office.

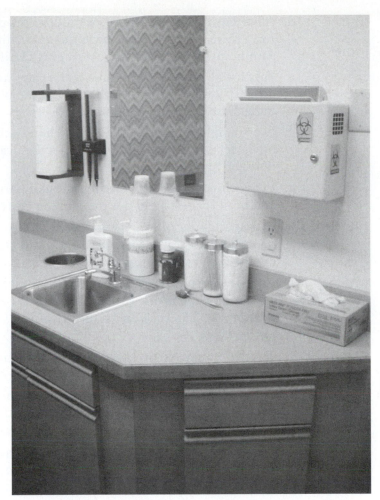

patient as well as review x-rays and **magnetic resonance imaging (MRI)** test results with the doctor present. These specialized employees are dependent upon the supervision of the doctor in charge because the doctor is responsible for all medical treatment of any person in the practice office. Lawsuits can be filed against the doctor, the employees, or the practice itself for violations relating to the way in which patients are treated, any violations of state or federal law, or any violation of pharmacy law.

Clinical staff skills needed are:

a. They must be patient and courteous to every patient. Although the patient might be irritated, the clinical staff cannot show the same feelings. A great sense of humor always helps.

b. They need great listening skills to not only listen to what the patient is telling them, but also listen to what orders the doctor is giving them and to follow through correctly and efficiently. This is a good place for bilingual employees to assist the doctor. They can explain health problems and then tell patients what the doctor's orders are.

c. Employees need to know keyboarding to put notes into the computer about patients who contact the clinical office regarding medication questions, exercises and physical therapy, and even how to clean a wound correctly.

d. All clinical staff must have met all the proper state certification to perform their jobs as well as have the opportunity to attend workshops to gain units of credit toward continuing certification requirements.

e. Polite and pleasant telephone techniques are much in demand when a difficult patient is on the other end of the phone in pain and demanding immediate attention and immediate results.

f. Every employee needs to have good handwriting so that employees in the other departments, as well as the doctors, can read and understand their notes or questions.

g. Every clinical staff member must make photocopies of all prescriptions and refill requests and put them in the correct patient's chart.

h. In a specialist's office, a nurse or tech also fills out paperwork for patients who are going to have surgery and assists the patient in determining the date for the surgery.

i. An employee in the clinical area of a specialist's office must see to it that all signed paperwork is then faxed to the correct hospital or day surgery center. The surgical facility also needs this information for billing purposes.

j. Another employee on the clinical staff then gets authorization from the insurance company for the surgery in a specialist's office.

k. Good verbal communications between the clinical employee and the patient as well as between the doctor and the staff member is an absolute must.

l. Clinical personnel must be made aware of safety requirements necessary around syringes, open wounds, incisions, and so on. They must always wear gloves and sanitize areas where dressings have been changed before the next patient comes into that exam room.

X-Ray Technician Staff

Primary care physicians do not usually have x-ray technicians as part of the staff; however, specialists usually do. How else can they see what the problem is and treat the patient that day without x-rays? If the specialist is still not convinced what the x-rays show, the patient is then sent to get a Magnetic Resonance Imaging (MRI) of the body area in question. An appointment is scheduled for the patient to return a few days after the MRI films and report have been sent to the referring doctor from the facility where the MRI was performed.

These x-ray technicians must not only get the patient from the room and return the patient to the same room after the x-rays are completed, but they must also keep exact filing records on each patient after the visit is over. The x-ray technician must keep a log of every x-ray done and make certain that the x-ray equipment is performing properly. Sometimes, the x-ray technician is asked to mail x-rays back to the original facility where the x-ray was taken. Records must be kept when x-rays are mailed or delivered in person, because x-rays can get lost. Supplies have to be ordered by these technicians and, in some cases, they actually deliver x-rays to the hospitals for upcoming surgeries. In other offices, x-rays are delivered to hospitals by a delivery service.

X-ray technician skills needed are:

a. All x-ray technicians must have met all the proper state certification to perform their jobs as well as have the opportunity to attend workshops to gain units of credit toward continuing certification requirements.

b. The x-ray technicians need to be patient and courteous to every patient. Although the patient might be irritated and in great pain, the technician cannot show the same feelings. A great sense of humor always helps.

c. The x-ray technicians need great listening skills to not only listen to what the patient is telling them, but also to listen to what orders the doctor is giving them and to follow through correctly and efficiently. If the doctor is not satisfied with an x-ray, the technicians must get the exact x-ray the doctor requests.

d. Polite and pleasant telephone techniques are much in demand when a patient is on the other end of the phone demanding to pick up his or her x-rays immediately. That is not always possible, because patients waiting to see the doctor need to be taken care of first.

e. When a patient or patient representative picks up x-rays, the technician must see a driver's license (or other official identification) proving that the patient is the right person picking up the x-rays. If it is a patient representative, the representative must show proper identification as well as a written note that the representative is truly representing the patient. This is part of the HIPAA guidelines now in effect.

f. Good verbal communications between the x-ray employee and the patient as well as between the doctor and the x-ray employee is an absolute must.

g. X-ray technicians must be aware of the safety needs for each patient as well as for themselves and protect themselves from exposure to radiation. All the doors should have lead in them and x-ray technicians should stand behind a leaded protection or cubicle as well. Patients are usually provided with a lead garment to cover parts of the body that are not being x-rayed.

h. X-ray technicians must have full command of the equipment they use so that they immediately know if there is a problem with the machinery.

i. X-ray technicians need time to file all the x-ray films they do on a daily basis, especially if they are doing hundreds of films every day. They also need to know how to file correctly in order to pull films at a later date quickly.

Billing Staff Employees

Without this department collecting the money from insurance companies and, at times from patients, there would be no medical office. The goal of the billing department is to send out claims with no errors and receive payments from insurance companies in a timely manner. That does not always happen because people make mistakes. Front office employees may have keyed incorrect data, and until the claim is denied, it is not discovered and corrected. At times patients do not give the doctor the correct insurance information, either. They may forget to mention that the injury is due to an auto accident or an accident on the job. Many times insurance companies know this ahead of time, and if a medical office attempts to receive payment from the health insurance first instead of from the auto insurer or from workers' compensation, they will always deny payment.

Billing employees need to know **Current Procedural Terminology (CPT)** codes and **International Classification of Diseases (ICD-9)** diagnosis codes. They also need to know how to do both electronic (if the volume justifies the cost) and paper claims. Each insurance company has its own identification numbers, doctor identification number, and peculiarities as to what they will allow on the **HCFA 1500**.

Insurance companies make contracts with doctors as to how much they will allow for each procedure no matter what the doctor charges. Payments that are posted to patient accounts must be adjusted with this in mind, and this is a task of one of the billing employees. Daily denials sent to doctors' offices from insurance companies must be individually reviewed to discover why the claim was denied. Phone calls must be made to insurance companies when claims remain unpaid to determine how to remedy the problem. Sometimes this can be done through the Internet because all insurance companies have Web sites. However, every insurance company has its own policy for allowing members or doctors' offices to obtain classified information about individual medical claims. (This, too, is part of HIPAA rules.) The medical office is usually required to get a password to use their Web site.

Statements are also sent monthly to patients who have a balance left on their account and payment is requested. If a payment is not sent, stronger notices are sent. After a designated period, if the balance has not been paid, notices are sent to the patient that the claim is being sent to a collection agency or an attorney. Many patients ignore these notices, but not paying will affect their credit rating eventually.

Billing staff skills needed are:

a. Every billing employee needs to know how to maneuver around a medical software package to make appointments, reschedule, or cancel appointments.

b. In addition, the billing employee must be able to interpret data and charges recorded to a patient's account to communicate both verbally or in writing the charges, payments, and amount owed by the patient if there is a balance.

c. Each employee needs to know medical terms, medical procedures done in that particular office, as well as the diagnosis codes required for payment by an insurance company. It is vital in communicating with a patient, whether in person or on the phone, to understand what was done for the patient on a particular office visit in question.

d. Each employee needs to document in the medical software package the details of every conversation with a patient or an insurance company representative. The representative's name and phone number should also be recorded for future reviews or contacts.

e. Each employee needs excellent telephone etiquette when attempting to explain to an irate patient why he or she received a statement.

f. There needs to be a spirit of teamwork with each member in the department as well as coworkers from other areas in the practice.

Use MS Word's Thesaurus to Familiarize Yourself with Terms from This Chapter:

1. Open Microsoft Word and click on Tools on the Menu bar.
2. Point to Language, then select Thesaurus.
3. Look up the following words taken from this chapter; use MS Word to list each word and the alternate words you might use.
   - competencies
   - physicians
   - internship
   - terminology
   - bilingual
   - biohazard
   - pharmacy

Note: All you have to do to replace your word is to select the word in the Replace with synonym box.

g. Personal grooming is just as vital to the employees in this department as in any other department of a medical practice, because one can be called upon to see a patient up front almost every working day.

h. Several billing employees need to know how to send claims to insurance companies electronically. Some claims must be done on paper HCFA forms, and every billing employee needs to know how to print them and send out clean claims to insurance companies.

i. Charts are pulled every day from the main filing area, and each billing employee is responsible for returning them to their proper place.

j. As in every other department within a medical practice, confidentiality is of vital importance regarding patient accounts.

Overview

✔ The doctor works as a sole proprietor, a partner in a large or small practice, as a general member of a corporation, or on staff at a hospital, clinic, or in a school in the local community.

✔ The basic clerical or office skills and competencies needed are keyboarding, filing, basic medical terminology, knowledge of HIPAA forms and regulations, medical or word processing software skills, billing experience, and good verbal communication skills. Being bilingual is an added benefit.

✔ The front office staff is comprised of people who enjoy meeting people, working with computers, and dealing with constant interruptions in a calm and efficient manner.

✔ The basic front office staff needs the following skills: keyboarding, knowledge of a medical software program, good handwriting, courteous telephone etiquette, good listening skills, a professional decorum, ability to handle money, knowledge of how to verify insurance coverage over the Internet, ability to treat patients with dignity and courtesy, good filing skills, a general medical vocabulary, and ability to keep information confidential.

✔ The clinical staff has the medical training to make things look easy, even though it might not be, in order to help a patient feel better.

✔ Clinical staff skills needed are patience and courtesy, good listening techniques, keyboarding, state certification, courteous telephone etiquette, good handwriting, knowledge of how to make photocopies, ability to handle paperwork and to get authorization from insurance companies, good verbal communications, and awareness of safety requirements regarding syringes, open wounds, incisions, and so on.

✔ The x-ray staff is also medically trained to perform x-rays requested by the doctor in a courteous, professional manner.

✔ The x-ray staff need the following skills: state certification, patience and courtesy, good listening skills, courteous telephone etiquette, good verbal communications, awareness of safety needs, full command of the equipment, and good filing skills.

✔ The billing staff generates the moneys for the medical practice and solves problems with insurance companies and patients.

✔ The billing staff needs the following skills: knowledge of a medical software program, ability to interpret data and charges recorded to a patient's account, knowledge of medical terminology, courteous telephone etiquette, a spirit of teamwork, excellent grooming, knowledge of how to send claims to insurance companies, good filing skills, and ability to keep information confidential.

Key Terms

Appointment card. The card given to a patient indicating the date and time of the next appointment.

Biohazardous waste materials. All syringes, serums, tubes, dirty dressings or anything associated with injections and blood must be disposed of appropriately. This means that special companies are authorized to do this removal of biohazardous waste labeled containers from all medical offices. A special method is prescribed to remove them from medical offices and incinerate them.

Copayments (copays). This charge is assigned by the insurance company to every subscriber or individual when he or she sees a doctor or dentist. The amount to pay is printed on the insurance card, but not all copays are printed on the card. Sometimes there are special copays for injections and for x-rays. Anyone with an insurance card can call his or her insurance company and get this information.

Current Procedural Terminology (CPT). This book, written and approved by the American Medical Association, gives a numeric five-digit code (ICD-9) for everything a doctor does. For example, it covers office visits, injections, x-rays, and surgeries. This book is used in all fifty states and every insurance company recognizes the codes. The codes are printed on an HCFA form for reimbursement from insurance companies. Whether a claim is printed on paper or sent electronically, every procedure must be coded. If a patient had an x-ray, the procedure code would tell the insurance company what body part was x-rayed. See also *International Classification of Diseases (ICD-9)*.

Deductible. Many people have health insurance policies that allow them to go to any doctor they want to see. They are not limited to certain doctors on a list mailed to them by their insurance carrier. These people usually have a deductible they must meet before their insurance pays the health provider. For example, some people have to pay $500 annually before the insurance company pays. Other people have to pay $1,000 or $2,500 before the insurance company pays anything. Insurance companies will pay a portion, but the subscriber or patient pays most of it until it is met annually.

Encounter form. A sheet from which the doctors write down what they performed for the patient that is billable. For example, did the doctor request x-rays, was a cast put on someone's arm, did the patient get an injection?

Health Care Financing Administration (HCFA) form. Used in all U.S. doctor's, chiropractor's, and surgeon's offices, this form is issued to patients' insurance companies for payment. Other than sending claims to insurance companies electronically, this is the way physicians, dentists, and chiropractors are paid.

Health Insurance Portability and Accountability Act (HIPAA). Guarantees that health insurance coverage is available to workers and their families when they change or lose their jobs. The 1996 law was expanded to include, among other things, the privacy of confidential personal health care information. This part of the law went into effect April 14, 2003.

Here is a sample of the HIPAA Privacy and Security checklist:

1. Medical staff does not discuss confidential patient information among themselves in a public area.
2. Conversations with the patient/family regarding confidential patient information are not held in public areas.
3. Phone conversations and dictation are in areas where confidential patient information cannot be heard.
4. Computer monitors are positioned away from public areas to avoid observation by visitors.
5. Documents with confidential patient information are face down or concealed to avoid observation by patients or visitors.
6. Staff specifically authorized to do so release confidential patient information.
7. Confidential patient information is discarded in a shredder or secure container.
8. Visitors and patients are appropriately escorted to ensure they do not access staff areas, dictating room, chart storage, etc.

Excerpts from *HIPAA Compliance Alert,* October 2002

Health maintenance organization (HMO). Some individuals or groups of employees enroll for insurance with a company in which there is a copay every time the insured sees a doctor within the plan. They also receive prescription benefits. HMOs are usually offered to people of all ages. This means that retirees can be in an HMO as well as people in the workforce. The drawback is that the insured person can see only doctors who take that particular insurance. Insurance companies mail new HMO plan subscribers a list of doctors from whom to choose their care. For subscribers who need to see a specialist, they must first contact their primary care physician and have a referral sent to the specialist's office before they can be seen. Without the referral, the patient pays full price for the visit or is turned away and must reschedule the visit. With the referral, the patient pays just a small copay.

International Classification of Diseases (ICD-9). Every procedure needs a diagnosis code. These diagnosis codes are found in another international classification of diseases book called the *CPT* book. For example, if a doctor saw a patient, there was a reason for the visit. Was the reason that the patient had a cold? If so, the diagnosis could be congestion in the head, sore throat, or fever.

Independent medical examinations (IME). Doctors receive special training to give these examinations. A doctor or surgeon is hired by attorneys to review a medical case and then give sworn testimony of what the medical professional believes should or could be done for the patient.

Magnetic resonance imaging (MRI). This test provides doctors and surgeons with photos of parts of the body so sharp that they can see any abnormalities or injuries readily. Because the photos are much clearer than an x-ray, doctors request MRIs to identify where in the patient's body the health problem is located.

Nurse practitioners. After receiving a registered nurse degree and license, nurse practitioners receive additional medical training that allows them to write prescriptions, admit patients into a hospital, and sometimes assist surgeons during surgery. The nurse practitioner has the equivalent of a master's degree.

Physician's assistants. These professionals have a minimum of a bachelor's degree, but in many cases, also have a master's degree in a field of specialty. For example, there are orthopedic physician's assistants. They can write prescriptions (if allowed by the state pharmacy act) just like nurse practitioners, admit patients to a hospital, and assist surgeons in surgery.

Practice. The term referring to the professional business of the doctor and medical staff work; for example, the medical practice of Dr. Jones.

Preferred provider organization (PPO). Individuals or groups of employees can enroll in a PPO policy. Whereas individuals or groups of people with an HMO policy can see only doctors who take their insurance, people with PPO policies may see any doctor without restriction. Subscribers usually have an annual deductible in addition to copays or coinsurance amounts depending on the medical service provided.

Primary care physician. Sometimes referred to as a PCP, this family or internal medicine doctor recommends patients to specialists where needed. PCPs are often called "gatekeepers." A PCP may have a contract with an insurance company such as Blue Cross HMO, Aetna HMO, Humana HMO, or AvMed HMO to see patients who have enrolled in that particular insurance and any other insurance companies with whom the doctor has a contract. Insurance companies pay the PCP X amount of dollars each month to see X number of patients.

Referral. A form typically issued by the primary care physician to approve a specialty medical service.

For Your Discussion

 Retrieve File C13-DQ.DOC from your student data disk.

Directions

Enter your responses after each question.

1. How do the skills you have already learned—keyboarding, telephoning, proper etiquette, filing, confidentiality, listening, composing correspondence, and similar office skills—relate to the skills you will need in a medical office?

2. Describe three or more types of medical offices or practices and the specialties they may engage in to help patients.

3. Describe at least three medical careers you might be interested in and what your responsibilities would be in each position.

4. List ten basic clerical or office skills you would need to work proficiently in a medical office.

5. List five basic clinical skills you would need to work in a medical office.

6. Name the four basic positions discussed in this chapter that may be available in a medical practice. Discuss briefly the various tasks each job would entail.

7. If you have been in a medical office recently, what changes have you seen since HIPAA has been in effect? For example: Have you had to sign additional forms? Did a medical employee mention HIPAA to you? Did you notice more safety precautions in effect than on your last visit? If you have not been in a medical office recently, what changes would you expect to see (based on the information in the chapter)?

8. Have you ever questioned a doctor about a procedure? Why or why not?

9. Have you ever asked for a second opinion from another doctor? Why or why not?

10. Have you gone to an emergency room recently? What was your opinion of the efficiency of the emergency room staff? Did the emergency room doctor send you or someone you were with to a specialist? Explain. If you have not been in an emergency room, what do you expect to see, based on the chapter information?

11. Do you have friends, relatives, or neighbors in the medical field? Have any of them mentioned HIPAA in passing conversation? If so, how were their jobs changed because of this law? If this question does not apply to you, talk to some of your friends or relatives to get this input on how HIPAA has affected them.

12. Would you enjoy working in a medical office? Why or why not?

BUSINESS MATH WORKSHOP

 Retrieve file C13-WRKS.DOC from your student data disk.

Directions: Compute the deductible, copay, and other fees to determine what payment Pete needs to make prior to surgery and for each visit after surgery.

Scenario #1:   Last weekend while playing touch football in the backyard, Pete felt something rip in his kneecap. He was rushed to the emergency room and x-rays were taken of his knee. The emergency room doctor said he tore his meniscus (fibrocartilage found in certain joints) and that Pete needs to see an orthopedic surgeon.

Pete visits an orthopedic surgeon who confirms his dilemma and schedules him for surgery two days later. Before that surgery takes place, someone in the surgeon's office calls Pete's insurance company. The insurance company tells the employee that Pete has a $1,000 annual deductible that has already been met for the year. His coinsurance responsibility is 20 percent. The policy has a copay charge of $35 per office visit to see a specialist and a charge of $10 every time x-rays are taken. During a postoperative period, charges for an office visit are waived.

The surgeon's charges are estimated to be $1,500. What does Pete have to pay the surgeon's office prior to the surgery?

Scenario #2:   Pete has had the surgery done and he is back at the surgeon's office for a postoperative visit. Every time he comes for a checkup, his knee is x-rayed. What does Pete have to pay each time he sees the surgeon?

On the Job Situations

 Retrieve file C13-OJS.DOC from your student data disk.

Directions

Enter your responses after each situation.

1. Vicki likes to talk more than work, and lately, she discovered she now has health problems. Laurie, who works with Vicki, feels sorry for Vicki and does some of her work. This then puts her under pressure to get her own work done, and Laurie never quite gets caught up. Laurie then feels stressed, but still allows Vicki to put more and more work on her. In fact, other people in the office have noticed this and also dump more work on Laurie.

   What would you suggest Laurie do? What would you tell Vicki? What would you tell their supervisor?

2. Patti and Jeff work in the same office. Over a period of time, their friendship has bloomed into a romance. Although they work in different departments of the medical practice, they are often seen kissing and holding hands or talking to each other on the phone.

Would you consider this professional behavior? What could or should be done? If you were the supervisor, what would you do?

3. Mrs. Jones is a pampered patient. The doctor always sees her because she demands it. Her husband is also a doctor, so she is given preferential treatment. She phoned last week and made an appointment to see the doctor in two weeks. Today she decides she can't wait that long and walks into the waiting room filled with patients, demanding to see the doctor right away. She displays a temper tantrum, and the doctor concedes and sees Mrs. Jones.

    If you were a patient in the waiting room, how would you feel? Would you vent to the person behind the front desk even though it is out of his or her control? If you were the supervisor of the medical office, what would you do?

4. A patient comes to a medical office from the emergency room of a local hospital. The emergency room staff gave this patient an aluminum splint for his finger and told him to follow up with a visit to an orthopedic doctor. After the doctor sees the x-rays, the doctor decides that the aluminum splint is not going to heal the patient's finger properly and puts a Staxx splint on the patient's finger. The patient is enraged and refuses to pay for another splint.

    How would you convince the patient that the second splint is necessary?

Projects and Activities

1. Select one of the four basic medical office positions discussed in this chapter that interests you most. Contact two doctor's, dentist's, or chiropractor's offices and ask if you could observe an employee in that position for twenty to thirty minutes while patients are not around. During your visit, ask questions about performing the job functions, working with computers, and dealing with patients. Then write a one-page, double-spaced report on your visit. Be sure to include the following:
    a. Names and addresses of the medical offices you visited
    b. Names of persons interviewed
    c. Dates of visits
    d. General comments on: the type of medical office, how the office has changed since HIPAA law has taken effect, how each office does specific tasks, and one interesting story shared with you from the office staff
    e. Your comments on whether these visits helped you decide if you want to work in a medical environment

2. Phone your insurance company or go online and find out what are your health insurance benefits. Find the effective date of your policy, and check to see if you have a PPO or HMO policy. (The letters *PPO* or *HMO* are usually printed on the insurance card.) Also find out what your copay is when you visit your family doctor versus visiting a specialist. Check with an insurance company representative (probably by phone) to see if you have an annual deductible and, if so, what the amount is. How much of

your deductible has been met already? What urgency does this request have? When would you need to know this information?

Print all of this information and submit it to your instructor.

3. A deaf patient calls the medical office through a relay service. The deaf person wants to make an appointment, but no one in the office knows how to sign for a deaf patient. What should you do after the appointment is made? Who pays for the charge? Is this an urgent request?

    a. Go online and find the names of agencies that assist deaf persons with medical visits and print the names and addresses of these organizations.

    b. If the Internet is not available, check the yellow pages for deaf services and copy that and submit it to your instructor.

4. A new patient calls your medical office. However, the patient cannot speak or understand English. A relative of the person calls and makes the appointment but tells you that he cannot be there with the patient to interpret for the relative. He asks if anyone in the office speaks Spanish.

    a. What if the answer is no? How could you help this person in need of medical attention?

    b. How urgent is this request?

5. Write a thank-you letter to primary care physician Dr. Ella Jones, 123 Main Street, Anywhere, US 12345–0000. Thank Dr. Jones for referring Dana Perry to your specialty clinic, tell Dr. Jones that the patient, who complained of shoulder pain was indeed diagnosed correctly by her, and that Dana has been advised to have shoulder surgery at her earliest convenience.

6. Type a memo to the staff from Dr. Jones with today's date on it. The subject is: Employee of the Month. The memo should mention that the doctors are instituting this award starting today. Every employee will have a chance to nominate someone during the current month and to list reasons why this employee should be honored on the attached nomination sheet. Mention that the person awarded will have his or her name printed on a brass plaque hung in the waiting room. In addition, the monthly award includes a $50 gift certificate to the restaurant of the winner's choice. The winner will be announced at the beginning of the following month in another memo. Last, state that at the end of the year, a special award will be given to the Employee of the Year selected from the award winners of the previous months. The winner will receive an all-expenses-paid weekend cruise for two.

    Then create a nomination sheet to attach to the memo. Allow enough space for employees to list reasons why this person is worthy of the award, as well as a place for the person to sign his or her name. Request that they hand in their nomination sheets to their supervisor.

7. Telephone the local Jaguar dealer and tell the service adviser that Dr. Smith's Jaguar is stalling and it needs to be serviced. Ask if someone can pick up the car here at the office today. Give the service adviser, Joe Adams, your name, address, and phone number. Also ask him to leave a loaner car for Dr. Smith.

Surfing the Internet

Complete the following exercises. Your instructor may ask that you also complete a Daily Plan Chart (Form 13-A). See C13-DA.DOC on the data disk for these activities.

1. One of the doctors in your office asks you to get special one-day passes to Universal Studios in Orlando, Florida. He wants two passes and two adult tickets for the park. He and his family of four will be arriving there two days from now.

    a. Where will you find this information?

    b. How much will the passes cost the doctor?

    c. Print the prices and any other information required and submit it to your instructor.

2. Another doctor is going to a medical convention in Atlanta, Georgia. She needs room reservations at the Hyatt Regency Atlanta as well as first-class plane reservations (preferably nonstop) arriving late morning. She will be flying next Monday and returning next Thursday morning.

    a. Go online to find out the room rates at the Hyatt Regency as well as two airline flight times and charges. Check to see if they allow AAA discounts.

    b. Print this information as well as any other pertinent information and submit it to your instructor.

3. One of the doctors you work for is making a speech on how his office has changed since the 2003 HIPAA regulations went into effect. Go online and research HIPAA. The doctor needs all the information you can find on this law as well as any updates since it went into effect in April 2003. First, write a summary of HIPAA regulations and pay special attention to any updates in the law. Then write a review on how HIPAA affects a medical practice and submit it to your instructor.

4. You have been asked by your supervisor to plan a surprise event for all the employees in the office. You need to find out the cost of renting a stretch limousine or a bus for a minimum of four hours and also select three caterers in the area who could create box lunches, including beverages and dessert, for thirty-five people.

    a. Check the yellow pages for local limousine or bus services; then surf their Web sites to see what their hourly rates are.

    b. Surf the Web for three local restaurants or caterers and print several menus. If necessary, call the restaurants for this information.

    c. Select a menu from each of the three restaurants or caterers and phone them to find out what their charge would be to provide the lunches.

    d. Assemble this information and key it into a table or chart. Then submit it to your instructor.

Using Excel: Computing Gross Profit/Loss

X You have been asked to set up a chart to show the gross profit for your company for 2004. The chart will show the periods, revenue, expenses, and gross profit/loss for the year as follows:

Periods	Revenue	Expenses	Gross Profit/Loss
1	10,000	8,000	
2	14,900	7,500	
3	18,200	8,500	
4	25,400	9,650	

Set up an Excel chart as follows:

1. Be in Excel and click on a new worksheet.
2. In the first cells across, key Income Statement and press Enter
3. In the first cells below that, key For 2004, press Enter
4. Next, in the next row, set up a cell by labeling it and keying Periods in the first left cell.
5. Tab over and set up a cell across from that by labeling it and keying Revenue.
6. Tab over and set up a cell next by labeling it and keying Expenses.
7. Tab over and set up a cell next by labeling it and keying Gross Profit/Loss, press Enter.
8. Under the Heading Periods enter 1, tab to Revenue, enter the amount, tab to Expenses, enter the amount (get the amounts from the information above); press Enter.
9. Return to left margin under Periods, enter 2, tab to Revenue, enter the amount, tab to Expenses, enter the amount; Enter.
10. Return to left margin under Periods, enter 3, tab to Revenue, enter the amount, tab to Expenses, enter the amount; Enter.
11. Return to left margin under Periods, enter 4, tab to Revenue, enter the amount, tab to Expenses, enter the amount; Enter.
12. Now you are ready to enter the formula to calculate the Gross Profit/Loss. Tab over and go up to the first cell under Gross Profit/Loss. Key in = followed by the cell assigned to Revenue (as B4), then follow the entry with a minus sign and the cell assigned to Expenses (as C4). You should have a formula such as = B4 − C4. The formula should give you the Gross Profit of 2,000 for Period 1. Put the cursor at the corner of the block under 2,000 and click until you get an arrow or + symbol; drag the cursor downward across the next 3 blocks below to bring the formula to give you the Gross Profit for those Periods. Click on any of the Gross Profit cells and the formula shows in the block in the tool bar above.

13. You may center Income Statement and For 2004 over the figure if your teacher directs you to do that. Proofread your work and save it under the name of the exercise as your teacher directs. Print a copy to submit as directed.

Income Statement For 2004

Periods	Revenue	Expenses	Gross Profit/Loss
1	10,000	8,000	2,000
2	14,900	7,500	7,400
3	18,200	8,500	9,700
4	25,400	9,650	15,750

APPLICATION PROBLEMS

APPLICATION 13-A

Setting Priorities

Supplies needed: Form 13-A, Daily Plan Chart.

 Retrieve file C13-DA.DOC.

Directions: Using the notes in Projects and Activities 1 through 7, key the work to be done and assign priorities to the items in Form 13-A, the Daily Plan Chart. Save the file.

APPLICATION 13-B

Evaluating Your Skills

Supplies needed: Form 13-B, Evaluation Form.

 Retrieve C13-EV.DOC from your student data disk.

Directions: Complete Form 13-B.

APPLICATION 13-C

Completing an Appointment Card

Supplies needed: Form 13-C, Appointment Card.

Directions: Complete Form 13-C.

 Retrieve C13-ACARD.DOC from student data disk.

The appointment card is for Ms. Betty Jones for a follow-up appointment on Thursday, current month, next Thursday, at 2 p.m.

Your Action Plan

 Refer to the ACTIONPL.DOC saved on your student data disk, or refer to Chapter 1, FORM 1-B, if necessary.

1. Set one goal using the information you learned in Chapter 13.
2. Follow your instructor's directions for formatting, assembling, and turning in your Action Plan.

Your Portfolio

With the help of your instructor, select the best papers representative of your work from Chapter 13. Follow your instructor's directions for formatting, assembling, and turning in the portfolio.

Working in a Legal Office

OUTLINE

Introduction to the Legal Office

Legal Secretarial or Assistant Careers
Training and Qualifications
Secretarial Openings and Changes in the Work Environment

Frequently Processed Documents
Contracts
Bankruptcy Documents
Wills
Petitions
Affidavits
Powers of Attorney

Document Preparation
Paper Size
Type Font and Size
Number of Copies
Format
Citations
Stapling and Folding
Page Numbers
Dates
Number Treatment
Names and Signatures
Seals
Proofreading
Information for the Documents

LEARNING OUTCOMES

When you have completed this chapter, you should be able to:
✔ Discuss the positions that may be available in a law firm.
✔ Tell how the role of office professionals has changed over the last few years.
✔ Describe the types of certification you may seek.
✔ Forecast employment opportunities in the legal field.
✔ Describe frequently processed documents.

    ✔ Describe the basics of legal document preparation.

    ✔ Discuss how you may increase your proofreading ability.

    ✔ Identify basic legal terms and their meanings.

INTRODUCTION TO THE LEGAL OFFICE

Have you thought about working in a law office? Attorneys (or lawyers as they are often called) hire office professionals in several capacities—from receptionist, to legal secretary, to paralegal (legal assistant), to librarian, to researcher, to transcriber, to financial and records control. Many of these positions provide opportunities for you to use the office skills you already have and to further enhance these skills as well. Do you think the roles of the office professionals in the legal field have changed at all over the years? Let's look at these positions and the roles they play in the legal field.

A receptionist in a law firm has a very responsible position. He or she is often the first contact the public has with the law firm—either by telephone or in person. In addition to greeting the clients, prospective clients, and other visitors, the receptionist may also be assigned other duties such as proofreading, collating materials, and processing the mail.

A legal secretary performs tasks similar to most secretaries in offices. However, in a legal office the secretary performs tasks that demand knowledge of legal document preparation as well as court procedures. We will discuss this in more depth later in the chapter.

A **paralegal** is another name for a legal assistant. A legal assistant works under the supervision of an attorney and provides services such as researching cases, drafting legal documents, conducting initial client interviews, and other duties as prescribed by the supervising attorney.

A librarian is usually found at a large law firm or in a corporate setting where there is a resource center that contains a large volume of legal books, legal software programs, and various multimedia equipment. Skills in filing and finding materials are needed for this position. In addition, the librarian often contributes to research and helps the legal staff with appropriate multimedia solutions for cases.

A legal researcher is more likely to work in a very large law firm or in a corporate research center. Your research skills must be highly developed; you will need to be able to find information and research topics that pertain to various cases quickly and efficiently.

A legal transcriber is tasked to transcribe recorded dictation from an electronic or manual recorder. Knowing the legal format and terminology as well as being proficient in a word processing program is necessary. In addition, excellent grammar, spelling, punctuation, capitalization, and proofreading skills are required to progress in this position.

The financial and records control staff usually are those who process payroll and taxes, and keep other financial records. These positions require good attention to detail, as well as solid accounting and record-keeping skills.

The role of office professional has broadened to include a wider range of new responsibilities than it formerly included. It now may include training, orientation, and supervision of new assistants; doing research; operating and troubleshooting office technologies; and managing the office entirely. Other duties include collecting, processing, storing, retrieving, and interpreting information to distribute to other staff and clients.

Legal employees perform a variety of administrative and clerical duties such as managing information, scheduling meetings and appointments, conducting court research, and providing information via the telephone, U.S. mail, e-mail, fax, and in person. They often prepare correspondence, make travel arrangements, and answer the telephone. In addition, many are asked to log in documents at the courts.

Legal secretaries use various office machines and technologies such as word processors and computer equipment to prepare legal papers such as complaints, notices, motions, responses, subpoenas, and other documents under the supervision of an attorney or paralegal. Think about the law offices in your area. You have probably seen law firms that are owned by one lawyer (a sole proprietorship), those that are owned by two or more lawyers (a partnership), and perhaps you have seen law offices in large corporations or various institutions (such as the military) in your city or town. Each size of office, of course, has varied numbers of employees. Likewise, the duties performed by the staff will vary. In a small office, one or two legal employees handle all the work of the attorney. As the firm's size increases, the jobs and duties become more specialized.

Now, let's focus on legal careers and training. Have you thought about what skills you will need to work in a law office and how much competition for jobs there may be? Read on!

LEGAL SECRETARIAL OR ASSISTANT CAREERS

According to the 2000–2003 *Occupational Outlook Handbook*,[1] there were 279,000 legal secretaries employed in the United States during that period. What type of training and qualifications do you think these legal secretaries needed?

Training and Qualifications

Most legal secretaries have at least a high school diploma, with many having a college education and advanced degrees in business, psychology, or education. Employers look for legal assistants or secretaries who have good interpersonal skills, discretion, good judgment, organizational or managerial ability, initiative, good grooming, a pleasant personality, and the ability to work independently or as a team member. One requirement that most employers stress is confidentiality. You will have access to information about many people and companies. This information is not to be divulged outside the office environment. You may also learn about awards, promotions, or other topics that pertain to the office staff. This is also confidential until you are told differently.

In addition, employers want employees with a high degree of skill in tasks related to the legal office such as keyboarding, use of electronic equipment, Internet research ability, and skills in punctuation, capitalization, proofreading, and editing. Employers in some law firms prefer office

---

[1] Bureau of Labor Statistics, U.S. Department of Labor, *Occupational Outlook Handbook*, 2002–2003 Edition, Secretaries and Administrative Assistants on the Internet at http://www.bls.gov (visited September 03, 2003).

professionals who have certification in some area of secretarial or legal expertise. What certifications are available?

Types of Certification. Legal assistants, secretaries, researchers, and other workers may become certified through the International Association of Administrative Professionals (IAAP) or the National Association of Legal Secretaries (NALS). Certification such as the Certified Professional Secretary (CPS) or the Certified Administrative Professional (CAP) can be attained by meeting the educational requirements and passing the required examination. With one year of legal experience or the completion of an approved training course, a person can acquire the basic designation of Accredited Legal Secretary (ALS) through the testing process offered through NALS. NALS also offers the designation of Professional Legal Secretary (PLS), an advanced certification for legal support professionals. Chapter 16 discusses the various types of professional certification in more detail.

For advanced certification, a person can obtain the Certified Legal Secretary Specialist (CLSS) offered by Legal Secretaries International in civil trial, real estate, probate, and business law after the completion of five years of law-related experience and the successful passing of the examination.

You can earn a paralegal certificate from a number of public and private schools that offer these programs. Usually a paralegal program lasts for six months to a year and consists of various courses in law and other subjects. The courses you are taking now should help prepare you for initial job entry as a receptionist or legal secretary; completing a paralegal certificate program will also give you a competitive edge.

Certification Resources. For additional information on the Certified Professional Secretary or the Certified Administrative Professional designations contact:

International Association of Administrative Professionals
10502 N.W. Ambassador Drive
PO Box 20404
Kansas City, MO 64195–0404
http://www.iaap-hq.org

Information on the Certified Legal Secretary Specialist designation can be found by contacting:

Legal Secretaries International Inc.
8902 Sunnywood Drive
Houston, TX 77088–3729
http://www.legalsecretaries.org

Information on the Accredited Legal Secretary (ALS) and the Professional Legal Secretary (PLS) certification can be obtained by contacting:

NALS, Inc.
314 East 3rd St., Suite 210
Tulsa, OK 74120
http://www.nals.org

As you think about increasing your qualifications through advanced education and training, take a moment to reflect on the employment picture in the legal field.

Secretarial Openings and Changes in the Work Environment

Legal secretarial openings are expected to increase slightly over the next few years, although many lawyers are performing their own administrative services that were formerly the domain of the legal secretary. In addition, many law firms now employ one or more paralegals who are assuming more of the duties formerly relegated to secretaries. However, you will find that employment opportunities are available in most towns and cities in both large and small firms. Review these advertisements that were featured recently in the classified ad section of a local newspaper. All of these ads are taken from one daily paper. So, you see, jobs are available for those who have the skills and competencies required!

Legal Assistant/Secretary
Small law office seeks self-starter. Must be computer literate. Bankruptcy experience a plus. Must be organized and responsible.

Legal Secretary
In-house legal department seeks legal secretary. Responsibilities include typing of pleadings, motions, briefs, memoranda, correspondence; scheduling and other general duties. Knowledge of WordPerfect required. Fast typing and accuracy necessary.

Legal Secretary
Law firm has an opening for a secretary. Excellent typing, organization, communication and bookkeeping skills required. Applicants must have excellent word processing ability, familiarity with personal computers, skilled in Excel and Word, dictating equipment and telephone skills.

Paralegal
Full-time person with experience in civil litigation and workers' compensation knowledge. Experience in handling complex cases, knowledge of filing procedures, and strong organizational and interpersonal skills. Microsoft Word XP a plus.

> **Legal Secretary**
> Large downtown law firm seeks full-time legal secretary. Excellent word processing, spelling, grammar, communication and organizational skills required. Professional work environment.

As you reviewed the advertisements for legal positions, what did you think about the duties specified in the ads? You probably noticed that a variety of tasks were listed along with the requirements for computer literacy and use of word processing programs such as WordPerfect, Excel, and Word. You can expect that these requirements will be standard for most legal positions. In addition, you probably noticed a variety of tasks relating to the type of practice: civil litigation, workers' compensation, and bankruptcy. The duties you assume will also be relative to the size of the practice as well as to the specialization of the workforce in the legal practice. Note that lawyers, like doctors, have a law *practice*. **Practice** is a term used to designate the professional business, or law firm. An attorney (lawyer) practices law or owns a law practice.

Technology will likely play a large role in the work that you do. Attorney Michael Sullivan of Bricker & Eckler LLP in Columbus, Ohio, points out that the biggest changes in the law profession today are in the technology used and how employees spend their time. Now, instead of spending time in libraries, law professionals (attorneys or assistants) can search the Internet for information. According to Sullivan, paralegals now handle much of the research for the attorneys, and librarians are a major source of research as well.[2]

Loyola Law School in Los Angeles is emphasizing the use of technology in the classroom so that students learn to use high-tech equipment even before they open or become part of a law practice. Audio, video, remote control cameras, and other sophisticated equipment are being used to prepare students for the future of litigation.[3]

You probably noticed that the ads discussed earlier frequently mentioned the need for experience with technology and various equipment usage. Knowing how to use various computer software is a must. Dictation equipment is frequently used, so you should be familiar with using a dictation system as well. Being able to place and receive calls on the newest telephone systems will also be a plus.

FREQUENTLY PROCESSED DOCUMENTS

The legal employee will almost always come into contact with some types of legal documents. Because business transactions often involve participants from other areas of the country, you will likely be responsible for processing documents according to the laws of different states as well as the federal government. You must be familiar with a number of uniform statutes (laws), one of which is the *Uniform Commercial Code (UCC)*. Most business documents

---

[2] Ed Lentz, *Business First*, "A Look Back at Almost Four Decades as Capital City Lawyer," August 22, 2003, p. B9.
[3] Karl Manheim, Case Studies, "Technology Is Nine Points of the Law," Loyola Law School, *Syllabus*, September 2003, Vol. 17, No. 2, p. 32.

will conform to the *UCC*. Let's discuss briefly a few of the documents that you may be required to key and process. Your duties in the initial development of these instruments with clients will depend on your expertise and the degree of freedom that the attorney affords you. Naturally, the more experience you have, the more involvement you may have in the preparation of the document contents.

Contracts

A **contract** is a binding agreement made by mutual ascent by parties capable to perform, having consideration, for a lawful object in the form required by law.[4] Some contracts must be in writing, such as those for

- The purchase of real estate
- Time periods that are more than a year
- Marriage being the consideration
- Promise to leave something to someone in a will
- With four exceptions, contracts for the sale of goods of $500 or more

As the legal employee responsible for keying the contract, you will check to be sure it has the following information:

1. Date and place of the agreement
2. Names of the parties
3. Duties of the parties
4. Statement of the consideration (money, services, goods) in payment for the contract
5. Time involved
6. Signatures of the parties

Your responsibility in keying the document is to make sure that you have keyed all the necessary elements correctly to facilitate its legality. To be valid and enforceable, contracts must be within the law. Illegal contracts are not enforceable and have no legal effect. In some instances, a minor error, or typographical omission, may make the document null and void. You must be extra careful to avoid typos or minor errors. They may not be minor in the legal world!

Contract forms can be purchased at an office supply store (see Figure 14-1), but often contracts need to be customized for the particular parties and the situation involved. As a member of the law firm staff, you may also become a party to contracts such as when you ask for a repair order, complete a purchase order, outsource work to agencies, or make a purchase or other agreement as part of the law firm's needs. You should be cautious when you make any of these agreements for the law firm to execute because these agreements can become binding once signed by an executive or representative of the firm.

---

[4] Gordon W. Brown, *Legal Terminology*, 4th Edition, Pearson Prentice Hall, Upper Saddle River, NJ, 2004.

CONTRACT

Agreement made this _____ day of _____ , _____(year), between _____ , hereinafter _____ , and _____ , hereinafter.

The parties to this agreement, in consideration of the mutual covenants and stipulations set out, agree as follows:

SECTION I
INSTRUMENT AS ENTIRE AGREEMENT

This instrument contains the entire agreement between the parties, and no statements, promises, or inducements made by either party or agent of either party that are not contained in this contact shall be valid or binding: this contract may not be enlarged, modified, or altered except in writing signed by both parties and endorsed on this agreement.

SECTION II
EFFECT OF AGREEMENT

This agreement shall inure to the benefit of and be binding on the heirs, executors, assignees, and successors of the respective parties.

IN WITNESS WHEREOF, the parties have executed this agreement on the day and year first above written.

_____   _____
Signature of First Party   Signature of Second Party

_____   _____
Print Name of First Party   Print Name of Second Party

_____   _____
Address of First Party   Address of Second Party

■ **Figure 14-1**
Contract.

Bankruptcy Documents

Bankruptcy is a legal process that allows a **debtor** (one who owes a debt) to have assets converted into cash to be distributed among **creditors** (persons or companies owed), after which the debtor is given a discharge from all debts that have unpaid balances. Bankruptcy proceedings can be initiated by the debtor (voluntary bankruptcy) or by the creditors filing a petition (involuntary bankruptcy). Only a federal court can handle bankruptcy proceedings. A trustee in bankruptcy is appointed by the court to hold the debtor's assets in trust for the benefit of the creditors. An individual or a business can be bankrupt. You are more likely to hear about a business being bankrupt because this often affects the community in terms of employment and taxation.

The Federal Bankruptcy Code provides for five types of bankruptcy proceedings, such as

- Chapter 7—liquidation
- Chapter 9—municipalities
- Chapter 11—business organization
- Chapter 12—family farmers
- Chapter 13—adjustment of debts of individuals

You and your firm may be involved in any of the proceedings, depending on the cases accepted by the firm. Your responsibilities will be dictated by the attorneys for whom you work and how much participation they want from the staff. You will likely key some of the documents, and you must be sure that names, addresses, dates, and dollar amounts are absolutely correct.

Wills

You may have clients who hire your law firm to provide services relating to their estate plan. One such service would be that of drawing up a last will and testament. A **will** is an instrument that a person uses to dispose of property upon death. The person who makes the will is called **testator** (if a man) or **testatrix** (if a woman). A person who benefits from the will or receives a gift under the will is a **beneficiary. Testate** is a term that refers to the state of a person who has made a will. **Intestate** means the person died without a will.

After you have keyed the will for the client and the attorney has verified its accuracy, the client is asked to sign the will in the presence of witnesses who attest to the testator's or testatrix's signature. The witnesses **subscribe** or write below or beneath the testator's signature. All but three states in the United States require two witnesses to a will. Louisiana requires two plus a notary public; Vermont requires three. Pennsylvania has no witness requirement unless the testator signed by mark.

You may be responsible for knowing the requirements for witnesses in your state and for securing the correct information once the will is ready to be signed. You may also be involved in working with a **living will**—a document used to allow a person to die a natural death without heroic or artificial means used to keep the person alive.[5]

Another instrument you may be asked to prepare is the **durable power of attorney** which authorizes another person to act on someone's behalf usually if he or she becomes incapacitated.

A **codicil** changes a will in some way (usually minor ways, as opposed to writing a new will) and must be signed and witnessed just as the original will. Any of these instruments should be placed for the witnesses to sign with only the signature area of the will visible to thwart the chance reading of the contents of the will by the witnesses. They are only attesting to the signature and to the sound mind of the testator (testatrix) and not to the contents of the will.

---

[5] Ibid.

Petitions

A **petition** is a document or instrument that contains a formal request for some action or request for something to be done or not done. If you are responsible for drafting petitions, ensure that they are drafted in a respectful tone and with clear, concise language. The names of the persons who are making the request are stated, along with the explanations of why the request is being made. The reasons are usually stated in the petition in their order of importance. In California, for example, a written application for a court order that begins the process for divorce is called a petition.

Affidavits

An **affidavit** is a written statement sworn to under oath that the facts are true according to the person's belief, information, and knowledge. The person making this statement is known as the **affiant** and makes this statement under oath to a judge, notary public, or other public officer.[6]

You will likely be asked to draft affidavits for most legal documents that you prepare. Your responsibility will be to check the accuracy of the document to be sure that the information included is correct. See Figure 14-2.

Powers of Attorney

A **power of attorney** is a document that authorizes someone to act for another—the **principal** (one in control). The employer may give the legal assistant or secretary a power of attorney to sign checks, to make certain purchases, or perform other acts deemed appropriate. The power of attorney may be made for a certain period, for an indefinite period, or for a special purpose. Only those who have proven their trustworthiness are given these special privileges granted by a power of attorney. Sometimes a client may need to revoke (rescind or call back) a power of attorney. A revocation is used for this purpose.

DOCUMENT PREPARATION

Some of the responsibilities you will assume as you prepare these documents or participate in their preparation have already been discussed. Should you work in a small office, you will likely also key the documents as well as do other tasks involving the legal formatting of these instruments. These tasks will include, but are not limited to, considering the paper size, type font and size, number of copies, format (margins, headings, spacing), citations, stapling and folding, page numbering, dates, and number treatment (including dollar amounts). You will also be responsible for any names and signature areas being properly placed, any seals that should be affixed, and, believe it or not, the final proofing of the document. We will discuss each of these briefly.

Paper Size

Legal documents can be purchased from an office supply store, as mentioned earlier, or keyed on a computer and printed at the law office. The paper used is white, (see the will in Figure 14-3) either 8½ × 11 inches or 8½ × 13 or

---

[6] Ibid.

AFFIDAVIT

BE IT ACKNOWLEDGED, that _____ of _____ the undersigned deponent, being of legal age, does hereby depose and say under oath as follows:

And I affirm that the foregoing is true except as to statements made upon information and belief, and as to those I believe them to be true.

Witness my hand under the penalties of perjury this _____ day of _____ , _____ (year).

_____
Signature of Witness

_____
Name of Witness

_____
Address of Witness

_____
Signature of Deponent

_____
Name of Deponent

_____
Address of Deponent

STATE OF   }
COUNTY OF   }
On _____ before me, _____ , personally appeared _____ , personally known to me (or proved to me on the basis of satisfactory evidence) to be the person(s) whose name(s) is/are subscribed to the within instrument and acknowledged to me that he/she/they executed the same in his/her/their authorized capacity(ies), and that by his/her/their signature(s) on the instrument the person(s), or the entity upon behalf of which the person(s) acted, executed the instrument.

WITNESS my hand and official seal.

Signature _____   Affiant _____ Known _____ Unknown

ID Produced _____

(Seal)

■ **Figure 14-2**
Affidavit.

14 inches. Although **legal cap** (paper with pre-printed ruled margins) is still used occasionally, courts do not require it and regular white bond paper is usually used. As the person responsible for keying documents, you should determine the requirements of the court in which the documents will be filed.

Type Font and Size

In most cases, a good font is used such as Times Roman 12 point or another readable type font and size. Consult with your office staff or attorney to

LAST WILL AND TESTAMENT

STATE OF GEORGIA
COUNTY OF DEKALB

I, JIM RAY THOMAS, JR., a legal resident of said State and County, do make and publish this my Last Will and Testament, hereby revoking any prior testamentary dispositions by me, as follows:

ITEM I

(a) I wish my body buried in a suitable manner and a suitable memorial erected and the cost thereof paid out of my estate.

(b) All of my just debts and any unpaid charitable pledges, whether such pledges are legally enforceable or not, shall be paid out of my estate as soon as practicable.

ITEM II

I give, devise, and bequeath all of the property that I may own or in which I may have an interest, real, personal, tangible, intangible, or mixed, and wherever situated, to my wife, SANDIE SUE THOMAS.

ITEM III

I constitute and appoint my attorney, JOHN L. BAILY, 340 North Building, Atlanta, Georgia 30304 as Executor of this Will and should he

1

■ **Figure 14-3**
Last will and testament on page 1.

determine what type font and size are appropriate for the documents you prepare. In most instances you will *not* use italic or script except for special wording.

Number of Copies

Today, copies are easily made with the computer and printer or the photocopier. Multiple copies are usually required so that every party gets a copy and the attorneys also get a copy. A file copy is made so that it can be kept in your law firm's files. Your task likely would be to ensure that all copies are properly signed and all procedures for witnesses, filing of the document, or distribution of copies have been followed.

Format

If using ruled paper, the margins are designed for you on the paper. Usually the left margin is approximately 1½ inches with at least a ½-inch right margin. The top margin is usually 2 inches on the first page and 1½ inches on the succeeding pages. The bottom margin is normally about 1 inch. Most legal documents are double-spaced. You should check with the attorney for whom you work to determine any variations in the format for the documents you key.

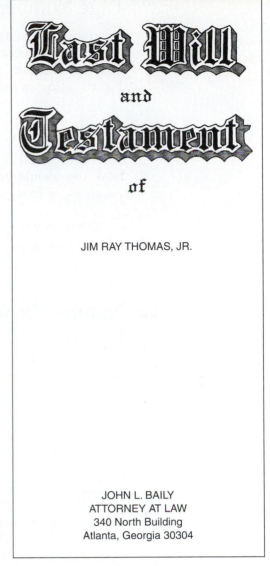

Last Will

and

Testament

of

JIM RAY THOMAS, JR.

JOHN L. BAILY
ATTORNEY AT LAW
340 North Building
Atlanta, Georgia 30304

■ **Figure 14-4**
Legal document in
a legal back.

Citations

Courts often specify the manner in which court cases are to be referenced or cited in legal documents. Ask your attorney or another legal professional to help you with any citations that you are not sure of or find confusing.

Stapling and Folding

Legal papers are usually protected by a **legal back,** within which the document is stapled (usually at the top). Legal backs are often blue or brown paper. If no back is required, you should staple the document as if it were in a back. Avoid removing a document from a legal back after it has been stapled because this could void or make the document invalid. Documents are often folded in thirds or fourths to fit the backing so that the wording on the backing is visible on the outside fold as shown in Figure 14-4. Verify with the attorney what information should be keyed on the legal back.

Page Numbers

Drafts should be numbered and labeled as requested or required by your attorney. Many attorneys require that drafts be labeled such as "First draft" and then the date. Always number the first and last page of documents unless the attorney gives you other directions.

Dates

Date every legal document. Verify with the attorney or office staff exactly how you should key dates, whether they should be keyed in all words or numbers, or in some other way. Examples of styles are as follows:

the sixth day of December, two thousand four

the 16th day of December 2004

16 December 2004

Number Treatment

Documents that have numbers with any legal significance such as money or time periods are usually written both in words and numbers. Again, verify how your office keys these numbers such as

Five Thousand (5,000) Dollars, $5,000, or Five Thousand Dollars ($5,000)

Five Thousand Two Hundred and 50/100 Dollars ($5,200.50)

Thirty (30) days

Names and Signatures

If you know the names of the individuals to sign the document, go ahead and key them the way they usually use their names. If you don't know, then use their legal names. Again, verify with the attorney how the names should be keyed. Some people use nicknames, abbreviations, or aliases. Also, some people are acting in trust or as agents for others. In stating names, you need to be very precise and use the name the client chooses to use.

Seals

Some documents have seals placed on them and some require only the initials *L. S.* for locus sigilli, meaning "in place of the seal." This is usually placed at the end of the line where the parties sign their names to the document.

Proofreading

Proofreading is always your responsibility! If you are weak in grammar, spelling, punctuation, or capitalization skills, take the initiative to upgrade your skills. You may do this independently by obtaining a few business English textbooks or an office reference manual. Another way to upgrade your skills is to take a grammar course at a local college. Proofreading is a necessary skill. You should be able to identify any errors that you have made by carefully checking the copy against the original or by reading over the document line by line, concentrating on each word. If you find that you still have problems finding your errors, have someone partner with you. One person will read the original while the other reads the revision. If the document is new, then have the partner proof the document for you. What should you be checking as you proof?

Verify the accuracy of all names, dates, places, dollars, specifications (like land measurements), or other information that appears in the document and is significant to the legality of the document. Although your computer spell checker may find some errors, do not depend on it. Spell check may find spelling errors but it will not usually locate word choice errors such as *too* for *two* or *affect* for *effect*. Do not let something go by because you are hurried. Making an error in a document could cost your firm the case for your client or cause a client to bring a lawsuit for malpractice against the firm. The best advice is: Ask if you don't understand something!

Information for the Documents

How do you think you will receive the instructions to prepare these documents? You may receive the information in a number of ways, again depending on your experience. If you are new to the workforce, the attorney may assign you to a seasoned assistant to **mentor** you (to partner with you as you learn). That mentor may get the information from the attorney and then assign all of it or parts of it for you to complete under his or her supervision. You will follow your mentor's lead in getting the material ready for signature or for the attorney to approve. In Chapters 15 and 16, you will learn more about mentoring.

Another way you may receive the information is for the attorney to give you the documents with the information handwritten for you to complete. This is often the way forms are handled. The attorney may also dictate the information to you as you key, or ask you to write the information as he or she dictates it to you.

In many offices, the information is dictated on dictation equipment for you to listen to and key. You will probably learn to use dictation equipment in one of your office procedures classes while you are in school. This equipment is not difficult to learn to use. It saves time because the attorney dictates and then sends the material to you on a cassette or electronically for you to key.

Another way you may receive the dictation is through the use of voice-recognition technology. The attorney may use voice-recognition (speech-recognition) software, dictate the legal documents, and then ask you to make any corrections or changes needed to the already keyed document. The use of voice-recognition software is becoming a trend in many professions, including the legal and medical.

Once you have achieved a bit of experience, the attorney may just tell you to prepare a particular document for certain clients and you will know exactly what to do. When that time comes, you will certainly feel proud to be a legal assistant or secretary. Good luck as you continue to get ready for your legal career by completing the exercises that follow.

Use MS Word's Thesaurus to Familiarize Yourself with Terms from This Chapter:

1. Open Microsoft Word and click on Tools on the Menu bar.
2. Point to Language, then select Thesaurus.
3. Look up the following words taken from this chapter; use MS Word to list each word and the alternate words you might use.
   - administrative
   - paralegal
   - litigation
   - ascent
   - liquidation
   - municipalities

Note: All you have to do to replace your word is to select the word in the Replace with synonym box.

Overview

✔ A legal office can provide a variety of employment opportunities for beginners and those seeking a career in a legal field. You may start as a receptionist or legal secretary and look for advanced training. You may decide to train as a paralegal, librarian, or legal researcher. If you like to work with records and money, a position in the financial office of a law firm may be just the thing for you.

✔ The role of office professionals has broadened to include a wider range of new responsibilities than it formerly included. Many office professionals now provide training, orientation, and supervision for new assistants; do research; operate and troubleshoot office technologies; and manage the office entirely.

✔ Most legal secretaries have at least a high school diploma, with many having a college education and advanced degrees in business, psychology, or education.

✔ Types of certifications include Certified Professional Secretary (CPS), Certified Administrative Professional (CAP), Accredited Legal Secretary (ALS), and Certified Legal Secretary Specialist (CLSS).

✔ Preparing legal documents is an exciting way to help clients achieve a legal goal. Knowing the requirements to prepare legal documents is a necessary part of working in a legal office. Frequently processed documents include contracts, forms related to a bankruptcy, wills, petitions, affidavits, and powers of attorney.

✔ Preparing documents requires an office professional to consider the paper size needed, type font and size, number of copies, format, citations, stapling and folding, page numbering, dates, number usage, names and signatures, seals, and proofreading.

✔ Obtaining these documents may mean that an attorney assigns you to a seasoned assistant or mentor; an attorney may give you the documents with the information handwritten for you to complete. Some information may be given to you in dictated form or cassette. You may receive documents that have been recorded using voice-recognition software that requires you to proofread and edit.

Key Terms

Affiant. Person making the statement in an affidavit.

Affidavit. A written statement sworn to under oath that the facts are true according to a person's belief, information, and knowledge.

Bankruptcy. A legal process that allows a debtor to have assets converted into cash to be distributed among creditors, after which the debtor is given a discharge from all debts that have unpaid balances.

Beneficiary. Person who benefits from the will or receives a gift under the will.

Codicil. A document that changes a will in some way.

Contract. A binding agreement made for some lawful object in the form required by law.

Creditors. Persons or companies owed.

Debtor. One who owes a debt.

Durable power of attorney. Instrument that authorizes a person to act on one's behalf, usually if one becomes incapacitated.

Intestate. The person died without a will.

Legal back. Cover in which legal documents are stapled for protection. Usually a color such as blue or brown.

Legal cap. Traditional white, ruled paper used for legal documents.

Living will. A document to allow a person to die a natural death without heroic or artificial means used to keep him or her alive.

Mentor. A seasoned assistant or partner to work with you as you learn.

Paralegal. Another name for a legal assistant.

Petition. A document that contains a formal request for some action or request for something to be done or not done.

Power of attorney. Document authorizing someone to act for another.

Practice. Term referring to the professional business, or law firm.

Principal. The person in control, who needs another person to act for him or her in drawing up a power of attorney.

Subscribe. Writes below or beneath the testator's signature.

Testate. Refers to the state of a person who has made a will.

Testator. A man who makes a will.

Testatrix. A woman who makes a will.

Uniform Commercial Code (UCC). One of the uniform statutes (laws) that most business documents adhere to.

Will. A document or instrument that a person uses to dispose of property upon death.

For Your Discussion

 Retrieve File C14-DQ.DOC legal from your student data disk.

Directions

Enter your responses after each question.

1. How have the roles of legal professionals changed over the years? Cite two examples where their duties have been expanded.

2. What is the meaning of the office title paralegal?

3. What skills do employers look for in legal secretaries?

4. What is the purpose of a contract?

5. When a person completes a codicil to his or her will, does this mean an entirely new will has to be drawn up?

6. Why would a person need to sign an affidavit?

7. If you wish to advance in a legal career, what are some steps you could take?

8. When you work for an attorney, how is work assigned to you?

9. Explain the duties you may perform as a legal secretary. Would these be interesting to you?

10. If you wanted to become a paralegal, what steps would you take to get that certification?

11. What does the word *practice* mean in relation to a law firm?

12. Do you think you would like to work for an attorney? Why or why not?

LEGAL TERMINOLOGY WORKSHOP

 Retrieve file C14-WRKS.DOC from your student data disk.

Directions

Correct any incorrect terminology in the following sentences.

1. The judge asked John Adams, the testatrix, if he had signed his will in the presence of two witnesses.

2. Ms. Jones wants to build a house according to certain specifications from a builder. She asks the attorney to draw up a codicil for her to sign.

3. The ABC Company can no longer pay its debts. As the creditor, it wants to declare voluntary bankruptcy in federal court.

4. Tom Henry signed a power of attorney giving his brother the right to pick up his son after school. In order to take back this power, he wants to have his attorney draw up a will.

5. Ms. Lippencott does not want her life prolonged should she become unable to function on her own. She asks her attorney to provide her with a power of attorney to guarantee that no heroic or artificial means will be used to prolong her life.

On the Job Situations

 Retrieve file C14-OJS.DOC from your student data disk.

Directions

Enter your responses after each situation.

1. You and the legal secretary who supervises your work have met for lunch in a café that is frequented by several of your clients. She asks you if you have heard the rumor that one of the clients who has been in the office is being arrested for fraud. You are sitting near several tables of people, and she has asked this in a rather loud voice. What will you do? Will you answer the question and discuss this situation?

2. Your law firm is handling a rather messy divorce proceeding for one of the leading politicians in a race for mayor of the town in which you live. A reporter comes into the office and asks you on the sly to give him details of the divorce. He tells you that you will not be mentioned in the newspaper report he is preparing. What will you do?

3. Your firm awards a member of the staff every six months with an award and a check for $100 to spend at a local store in the mall. The award is highly confidential until it is announced at a staff meeting. You know who will get the award because you have processed the paperwork for the check. One of the employees comes to you and asks if she is getting the award so that she can be sure to be at the staff meeting being held next week. What will you tell her? (She is the one getting the award.)

4. John, one of the transcribers, constantly makes errors in the reports that he is transcribing and you have to proofread them for him. He has very weak grammar skills. How should you handle this situation which takes up so much of your time? You are his supervisor.

5. You have been a receptionist for almost a year and would like to apply for the legal secretary position that will be available next month. Should you apply? How should you prepare for the interview with the attorney to whom this position reports?

Projects and Activities

1. One of the attorneys in your firm has a meeting in Chicago in two weeks. The meeting starts on Tuesday and is over on Friday. He usually flies first class and needs reservations to arrive in Chicago on Monday before the meeting and leave on Saturday morning. How would you locate this information? Provide several flight options for him to select, with type of plane, fares, and any other information he would need, like connections, stops, and so on. He already has reservations for the convention hotel. Is this an urgent request? After you have researched the information, prepare it in a usable format for the attorney and submit it to your instructor.

2. Your law firm has been asked to lead a discussion at the next Boise Legal Association meeting (the third Tuesday of next month) at the Best Western Hotel. The privacy act that relates to the use of facsimile is the topic that is being requested. One of the attorneys has asked you to research information relating to any privacy laws regarding sending of facsimiles (faxes) and to document them accordingly so that she can develop her speech based on that information. Where will you look and how will you research this information? In what format will you key it so that the attorney can use it for the speech? Is this an urgent request? Present this information in the correct format to your instructor for feedback.

3. Betty, one of the new paralegals, comes to your desk and asks for the phone number and address of one of the clients. She needs to contact the person to come in this afternoon for a meeting, and she needs to have a paper delivered to her home before the client comes to the office. She asks you to also locate the telephone number of a courier to deliver the paper. What should you do with these requests? Are they urgent? Decide how you would handle this situation and write a brief paragraph to submit to your instructor for feedback.

4. Make an appointment with a law office in your area to interview the legal secretaries who work there. Indicate that your instructor has mentioned that this particular law firm (the instructor gives you the firm's

name) would like to talk with students who are interested in the legal profession. During your visit, ask questions about the job functions of the legal secretaries, the training they have received, the type of equipment and technologies they use, and how they see a career as a legal secretary changing. Report your findings in a two-page, double-spaced report. In the report mention the following:

a. The name of the firm and its address

b. Names of persons you interviewed and their official titles

c. General comments on the appearance of the office, the parking, the landscaping, the lighting, the work space for each person, the library (or other source of legal books), and at least one interesting story the interviewees may have shared with you.

d. Comments on whether you have decided on a legal career for your future

Your instructor has assigned this research report to be submitted three weeks from today.

5. Ms. Brown, your attorney in a small office, dictates a letter to you to send out under her signature to a client who has not returned the documents she was to review. The deadline for filing the document with the court is fast approaching—in fact, it is next Friday. Write the letter. What should the letter contain? How will you send the letter? What information will you need to include in the letter? Where will you locate the needed information? Write step-by-step instructions on how you will handle this situation and submit it to your instructor.

6. The lead attorney in the office asks you to key a memo to all the staff reminding them of the fire drill that will take place unannounced sometime next week. It will be monitored by the local fire department personnel. The law firm was notified of the drill but was not told the date or time. The fire department wants to be sure that the building can be evacuated in case of an emergency. Draft the memo for your attorney to approve. What should you include in the memo? Provide a copy of the memo for your instructor.

7. Thomas Haskells, an attorney, calls you into his office and dictates a letter to Ms. Betty Appleton reminding her of her court date next Monday. Today is Wednesday. How would you send the letter, noting the urgency and the impending deadline? Where would you get her address? Mr. Haskells wants proof of delivery from Ms. Appleton. Transcribe the letter and decide in a memo to your instructor how you would resolve the address issue and how you would send the correspondence.

Surfing the Internet

1. One of the paralegals in your office is interested in joining the local paralegal association if there is one in your city or town. She asks you to research this information on the Internet and locate the nearest chapter and any requirements for membership, including cost of joining. Submit the information to your instructor.

2. Mr. Johnson, the founding partner of your law firm, has a friend in another city that he has lost touch with but wants to locate. He knows his name and he thinks he knows the hometown of the lawyer friend. He asks you to locate the information for him. How would you do this?

3. You and the other legal employees in the firm believe that there are newer versions of the voice-recognition software available from at least one of the leading makers of voice-recognition software. Surf the Internet and find out which makers have updated versions and the specifications of each version you find. Report the information in an Excel spreadsheet or in a table that compares the specifications of each version. Be sure to identify the name of the product, its cost, its manufacturer, and how it can be obtained. Submit the report to your instructor.

4. You are so excited about the law profession that you would like to take the Law School Admissions Test (LSAT) and attend law school. Surf the Internet to learn about this exam, how much it costs, where you can take it, and any other information that you can find out. Submit the information in a one-page report to your instructor.

Using Excel 2002

Track Client Trends

 You have been asked to develop a chart/table to show the client trends for the last three years. The information you have researched for the chart/table follows:

Sources	2002	2003	2004
Referrals	301	408	609
Advertisements	106	309	25
Repeats	360	518	712

Set up an Excel chart as follows:

1. Be in Excel and click on a new worksheet.
2. In the first cells across, key Client Trends; press Enter.
3. In the first cells below that, key Sources then years 2002, 2003, and 2004 as follows:
4. Set up a cell by labeling and keying Sources at the left.
5. Set up a cell next by labeling and keying 2002.
6. Set up a cell next by labeling and keying 2003.
7. Set up a cell next by labeling and keying 2004; Enter.
8. At the left margin below Sources, key Referrals; Enter.
9. Next key Ads; Enter.
10. Next key Repeats; Enter.
11. Next key Totals; Enter.
12. Now, you are ready to enter your data under the years for each of the items listed under Sources.

13. On the cell wherein you have Referrals, tab across to each year and enter the amounts from above: 301 408 609; Enter.

14. On the cell wherein you have Ads, tab across to each year and enter the amounts from above: 106 309 25; Enter.

15. On the cell wherein you have Repeats, tab across to each year and enter the amounts from above: 360 518 712: Enter.

16. Tab to Totals; you are ready to enter the formula; so tab over under the column where you see 360.

17. Set up your formula: Key=SUM(B3:B5) for example to identify where you have the data entered; you should get a total for the first column of 767; then put the cursor at the end of the cell with 767 and click until you get an arrow or plus symbol; drag across to fix the formula for the next two totals for the years 2003 and 2004.

18. Tab up to Sources 2002 2003 2004; click on each and click on **B** in the tool bar above to highlight the headings in bold type.

19. Save the file after you have proofread it; print it for submission if so directed by your instructor. You may be asked to center the headings over the chart if your teacher wishes you to do that.

Client Trends			
Sources	**2002**	**2003**	**2004**
Referrals	301	408	609
Ads	106	309	25
Repeats	360	518	712
Totals	767	1235	1346

APPLICATION PROBLEMS

APPLICATION 14–A

Setting Priorities

Supplies needed: Form 14-A, Daily Plan Chart.

 Retrieve file C14-DA.DOC from your student data disk.

Directions: Using the notes in Projects and Activities 1 through 7, key the work to be done and assign priorities to the items in Form 14-A, the Daily Plan Chart. Save the file.

APPLICATION 14–B

Evaluating Your Skills

Supplies needed: Form 14-B, Evaluation Form.

 Retrieve file C14-EV.DOC from your student data disk.

Directions: Complete Form 14-B.

APPLICATION 14–C

Completing a Power of Attorney Revocation

Supplies needed: Form 14-C, Power of Attorney Revocation.

 Retrieve file C14-POW.DOC from your student data disk.

Directions: Complete the power of attorney for Annabelle Lee (grantor) who is rescinding the power of attorney previously given to Frederick Lee dated February 10 of last year. Indicate your state and county and use your name as the person to whom the person is appearing to sign the document. The affiant is unknown to you. Select a method in which you would check the identity of the person before you sign as witness. Use the current date. Make two copies of the document to submit to your instructor.

Your Action Plan

Refer to the ACTIONPL.DOC file saved on your student data disk, if necessary, or refer to Chapter 1, Form 1-B.

1. Set one goal using the information you learned in Chapter 14.
2. Follow your instructor's directions for formatting, assembling, and turning in your Action Plan.

Your Portfolio

With the help of your instructor, select the best papers representative of your work from Chapter 14. Follow your instructor's directions for formatting, assembling, and turning in the portfolio.

chapter **15**

Preparing for Your Job Search

OUTLINE

Locating Job Prospects
Networks
College Career Development Centers
Business News Items
Direct Application
Staffing Services
Federal Government Employment
Newspaper Advertisements
Prospects in Another Geographic Area

Applying for Jobs
Resumes
Application Letters
Application Forms
Portfolios

Interviewing for Jobs
Before the Interview
During the Interview
After the Interview
The Campus Interview
Follow-Up Letters

Conducting an Electronic Job Search
The Internet
Electronically Scanned Resumes

Considering International Employment Opportunities

LEARNING OUTCOMES

When you have completed this chapter, you should be able to:
✔ Suggest methods for locating employment opportunities.
✔ Inventory job qualifications.
✔ Conduct a thorough and effective job campaign.
✔ Prepare a resume.
✔ Prepare an effective letter of application.
✔ Develop a portfolio that illustrates accomplishments and skills.
✔ Complete an employment application form.

✔ Prepare for a job interview.

✔ Answer behavioral descriptive interview questions.

✔ Prepare employment follow-up communication such as thank-you letters, reminders, inquiries, and acceptance and refusal letters.

✔ Use the Internet as a valuable job search and recruitment tool.

✔ Prepare a resume for electronic scanning.

Very few office professionals' assistants' positions are protected from corporate restructuring and job layoffs. Therefore, it is important to plan an effective job campaign.

Search for a job that matches your qualifications, personality, and interests. Your administrative career should be rewarding not only monetarily but also in terms of job satisfaction and opportunities for promotion.

The first part of your job search should be your decision about where you want to work—the geographic area and the type of business. Unless you have specialized in the legal or medical field, do not limit yourself to seeking a job in a specific department, such as human resources, accounting, or sales. Remain open to opportunities; often, getting your foot in the door is the first step to gaining experience and eventually getting the position you really want.

Your office technology skills are transferable. Often the same basic skills are required in different departments; therefore, never limit your opportunities by expressing interest in working only for one department—instead, express interest in working for the organization. Let the interviewer know you are flexible and willing to adjust to the needs of the department. The interviewer will strive to match you to a position that will maximize your talents.

Start your job campaign several months before graduation or keep alert to any reorganization plans in your company. As soon as you decide where you want to work, make a job prospect list, using the sources listed in this chapter. Next, prepare your self-appraisal inventory and your resume, write your application letter, and make a list of the qualifications you plan to emphasize during job interviews. After you launch your job campaign, keep searching until you find the right job for you.

LOCATING JOB PROSPECTS

Some of the sources for job prospects are the Internet, the college placement office, the yellow pages, private and public employment agencies, government service announcements, chambers of commerce, the newspapers, and your network of friends and associates.

Use all of these sources, not just one, to locate job leads. Once you begin your job campaign, keep it going. Be persistent in checking up and following through on what is available for someone with your qualifications and interests.

Networks

In planning an approach to meeting and connecting with others for mutual benefit, consider networking. Put in simple terms, **networking** means exchanging information. Information is the most powerful asset a business professional can have. If you have information and are willing to share it, you will be viewed as a valuable person to have on staff.

During the job hunt networking is an essential step toward gaining successful employment. Sharing employment information with a network of people is probably one of the most effective methods of obtaining employment. You can begin to build your network by discussing your employment goal with your instructors and with business friends of the family. Keep in touch with these people as you move through your course work; they may provide employment opportunities. Attend functions such as career fairs, where prospective employers will be available to meet students. Attend and participate in seminars and other functions where office administrators and assistants will be present. By expressing your keen desire for employment and by leaving a positive impression, you will be increasing your opportunity to learn about possible employment opportunities.

When your contacts give you job leads, follow through on them. Then let the person who told you about the lead know the results. This is a simple courtesy and a way of thanking the person for his or her assistance.

Remember that networking is an *exchange* of information, not a one-way effort. The more information you give, the more information you usually get back.

To be a good networker, you must be a good listener. By applying your best listening skills you will collect accurate information. This, in the long run, may save you time and effort in your job search. By listening to the needs of other networkers, you will be able to offer them greater assistance. In this way, you will be viewed as a valuable network partner. As previously stated, the more information you provide others, the more people will reciprocate.

Networking is a developed skill that will help you enhance your life and your career. It will increase your ability to be employed and to advance.

The following are suggestions for improving your networking skills.

1. If you are employed or have recently been employed, choose a corporate mentor. A corporate **mentor** usually holds a position at a higher level than yours. This person can offer you information and advice about the organization and give you career direction.

2. Never limit your contacts by missing an opportunity to meet new people. Your network may include business associates, friends, neighbors, past graduates from your college, relatives, and many other groups of people. A network should become a vast chain of information. The more effort you put into networking, the more the network will expand, and the greater your chances of career success will be.

3. Make yourself visible. Becoming a leader of a professional organization or volunteering to serve on a committee will open networking doors.

4. Increase your reading of business materials. Remember that information is power and reading will build your information base.

College Career Development Centers

Most colleges maintain a career development office to provide their graduates assistance in making contacts for jobs. At the beginning of your job campaign, register with the career office. Complete the information required, placing your name on the active file with the career development.

The career center directors and counselors keep up-to-date on employment opportunities. Often the career center director arranges for company representatives to conduct interviews on campus. The career center director maintains a list of job openings prepared from the requests of human resources representatives, who call the career center in search of prospective employees.

Watch for the announcement of forthcoming campus interviews at your school and call the career centers to schedule interviews. Be sure to prepare for the interview and to keep the appointment. The campus interview is discussed later in this chapter.

Business News Items

Read the business news appearing in the newspaper in the area where you plan to seek employment for at least a month before you actually apply for a job. Search for news about established organizations that are relocating their offices to your area or opening a branch; established businesses that are moving their offices to new buildings or expanding at their present sites; newly formed organizations; and companies that are merging. Any changes within organizations may indicate career opportunities.

When you find a news item of interest to you, clip it and save it. It should provide you with the complete name, the type of operation, the location, and possibly the opening date of a new office.

The number of office professionals who move to another city when an organization relocates is small compared to the number of executives who transfer to the new location. Therefore, you can expect that any organization that has relocated its offices to another city will be hiring office staff.

A local organization often adds new personnel at the time it moves its offices to a new location. Such a move often happens because the organization needs more space to conduct its current operations and cannot add personnel until it can provide space for them. An organization that is expanding its operations often needs additional office personnel.

A new organization will need someone in the office as soon as it opens and will add personnel to keep pace with the organization's growth.

Direct Application

Often, the best jobs are not advertised. Many organizations prefer to select their employees from applicants who take the initiative to come to them seeking employment. Do not wait for a job to come to you; it probably will not. Take the initiative to search for a job. Decide where you want to work, and apply. Telephone the organization and arrange for an appointment with the person in charge of hiring office staff.

Be optimistic. Some of the organizations on your prospective list may not be seeking office professionals at this time, but an impressive application and interview may put you in line for a future opportunity. If an opening for the job you are seeking does not exist, ask the human resources representative to place your application on file.

If you decide to work in a particular business but do not have a specific company in mind, refer to the yellow pages, which provides a list of local businesses. For example, if you are interested in working for an advertising company, look up *Advertising;* there you will find the names and addresses of the local advertising companies.

Staffing Services

Openings for jobs as office workers are listed with both public and private employment agencies. The state-supported employment offices and the United States Employment Service list openings for all kinds of work—industrial, commercial, and professional. The services are free to the job seeker and the employer. However, the number of jobs listed with a public employment office sometimes is not representative of the openings in the community.

State employment offices generally give a proficiency test in keyboarding and frequently a spelling and vocabulary test to office support applicants. To register with a state employment office, go to the office and fill out an application form. It is more than likely that you will be able to take the tests and be interviewed during your initial trip to the office. If an opening is listed for someone with your skills and work experience, you will be sent to the prospective employer for an interview. After you have registered with a state employment office, check regularly to find out about job openings.

Many private staffing agencies do not charge the applicant a fee for their service. In a number of circumstances, however, the prospective employer pays these fees. You can ask private staffing agencies, such as OfficeTeam and Robert Half, about the services that they offer without being obligated to sign a contract. If you do register with a private staffing agency, study the contract thoroughly and ask questions before you sign it.

Most private staffing agencies give excellent service. They administer tests, advise applicants on their appearance, conduct thorough interviews, and carry out a complete job hunt for each applicant. A staffing agency charges a company a placement fee only if the applicant accepts a job obtained through the agency's effort. Therefore, private staffing agencies make a real effort to refer applicants to jobs for which they are qualified and which they are likely to accept.

Federal Government Employment

If you are interested in securing employment with the federal government, or in transferring from one federal job to another, you will find many, many opportunities.

Visit or call the Federal Employment Information Center (FEIC) in the area you are seeking employment. Also contact the Web site at http://www.usajobs.opm.gov for updated job vacancy listings. Request the following information:

- Announcements of specific types of jobs
- A list of local government agencies
- Application forms

In contacting regional and local agency personnel offices, take the following steps:

- Request agency career opportunities brochures.
- Talk with the agency human resources office and request job announcements and information on special hiring programs.
- Obtain local government field office phone numbers from your telephone directory. Look under "U.S. Government" in the blue pages, generally.

Visit your local library and review these publications:

- The *United States Government Manual*. This book provides agency descriptions, addresses, contacts, and basic employment information.
- The *Federal Career Directory*. If your library doesn't have this publication, check with a local college placement office. This directory provides an agency description and lists typical entry-level positions, agency contacts, student employment programs, and so on.
- The *Occupational Outlook Quarterly Occupational Handbook*. This book, published by the U.S. Department of Labor, Bureau of Labor Statistics, is a highly informational quarterly publication that highlights employment trends and features interesting career articles.

Tests are required for specific groups, including office professional workers and air traffic control personnel, and for certain entry-level jobs. The majority, approximately 80 percent, of government jobs are filled through a competitive examination of your background, work experience, and education, not through a written test.

Newspaper Advertisements

The career sections and help-wanted columns of newspapers are valuable sources for job openings. The jobs will be listed under a variety of headings, such as administrative assistant, office assistant, administrative secretary, executive assistant, and information specialist.

By studying career sections and help-wanted ads, you will gain valuable information concerning trends in employment opportunities, salary ranges, and qualifications required. Study the ads in newspapers early in your job campaign.

When you answer a help-wanted ad, be prompt. Reply the same day, if possible, or at least by the next day. Remember that newspapers are widely read and that looking in them for available jobs requires less effort than other search techniques. It follows that the competition will be very high for jobs posted in newspapers.

Follow instructions. If a telephone number is given, call for an appointment. If a post office box number is given, submit your resume. Many advertisements request that applicants submit resumes by mail, by fax, or by e-mail, and clearly state that they do not want applicants to call. If this is the case, follow the instructions. You risk irritating the employer if you ignore the request for no telephone calls. Of course, it's always more proactive and shows a sense of initiative to telephone the employer and to drop off your resume in person. These techniques should be part of your strategy unless the employer has requested otherwise.

Always study the advertisement carefully to determine all the stated qualifications and then submit an application letter and resume showing that you meet all the qualifications for the job. Follow the suggestions for writing a solicited application letter discussed in the section "Application Letters" later in this chapter. See Figure 15-1 for sample newspaper ads.

Blind Advertisements. Newspaper recruitment advertisements either give the name and address of a company or person to contact, or are **blind advertisements** giving a post office box number or a telephone number. When blind

Office/Clerical Help Wanted

EXECUTIVE ASSISTANT TO THE CITY ENGINEER

Engineering is one of the city's major departments. As Department Head, the City Engineer requires an administrative assistant who has excellent communication and critical thinking skills, is a team player, and who can give support by performing technical and administrative tasks quickly and accurately. The successful candidate will have been trained in ISO 9001 and will have demonstrated commitment to its philosophy.

Duties include preparing for and arranging meetings, taking minutes, composing correspondence, and assisting the City Engineer with administrative tasks. The ability to train junior office workers and to be an office team leader are desirable. There is frequent contact with private executives, professionals, and senior government officials. The diverse duties and responsibilities of this position allow considerable latitude for personal initiative and growth.

The successful applicant will have achieved a postsecondary diploma in office administration and will have superior word processing, database management, spreadsheet, and desktop publishing sills. A university degree would be an asset.

Salary will be commensurate with training and experience. A full benefit package is offered.

Please call (506) 363-1893 for an appointment.

RECEPTIONIST/ BOOKKEEPER

We need an enthusiastic, energetic, and organized assistant to perform general office duties. Experience and training in electronic bookkeeping is required. Bring your resume to 1609 Northfield Rd.

C.A. FIRM

Small C.A. firm requires an enthusiastic graduate of an office administration program to key correspondence and financial statements on word processing and spreadsheeting software. Candidate must be able to assume general office duties, and work well on a team. Salary negotiable. To apply please call Mrs. L. Rossin at (952) 869-0020.

OFFICE ASSISTANT

Required by small sales office. Responsibilities include bookkeeping, payroll, and keying. Applicants must have Microsoft skills (Word, Excel), good organizational skills, and the ability to work with minimum supervision. Reply to Box AM654.

WORD PROCESSING

Trained and experienced people needed for temp. and perm. positions. Please contact J. Johnson, (315) 598-2306.

■ **Figure 15-1**
Sample newspaper ads.

ads are used in a legitimate fashion, it is generally because the organization wishes to avoid having to interview a large number of unqualified applicants. For example, say the local National Hockey League team requires an office professional. If the team advertises its name in the newspaper, it will receive a flood of applicants, many of whom are unqualified but apply because of their desire to work for celebrities. A simple advertisement that lists the responsibilities of the position, the desired qualifications, and a post office box number is more likely to attract those who are legitimately interested in performing the advertised responsibilities.

Scrutinize blind advertisements carefully. Sometimes they are used for purposes other than recruitment for employment, such as preparing a mailing list of prospective purchasers. If you receive a telephone call in response to a reply to a blind advertisement, ask for the name of the company and ask some questions about the job during the telephone conversation to be sure the job advertised is legitimate.

Prospects in Another Geographic Area

To begin your search for job opportunities in another geographic area, do the following:

1. Conduct research on the Internet by city name or by company name.
2. Ask the career counselor in your school to help you. The career counselor will have lots of useful information and tips on how to secure employment and where to look for it.
3. Inquire at the local public library for the telephone directory and the newspapers for the city in which you are seeking employment.
4. Write, e-mail, or fax the chamber of commerce in the desired geographic area.

Your career counselor will have the most recent information and valuable information regarding your career search, industry profiles, and a directory of employers interested in hiring college graduates.

The telephone directory for the city where you want to relocate will be an excellent source of information. Many telephone directories can be found online; however, you often have to subscribe to them. Your public library will have telephone directories for a number of cities, and large public libraries have telephone directories from all the major cities in the United States. The public libraries will have the directories either in paper version or online. Public libraries also subscribe to many newspapers from other cities.

To find out what your public library has on file that will be helpful to you, call the library and ask for Information Service. The librarian will answer your specific questions concerning what telephone directories and newspapers are available. You can also obtain the addresses of a few companies from the librarian by telephone.

When you write to a chamber of commerce, state your employment goal and ask about opportunities in your field in the geographic area. *If* the chamber of commerce sends you a list of prospective employers, realize that the list is limited to chamber of commerce members.

APPLYING FOR JOBS

The resume, the application letter, and the job interview are the applicant's direct contacts with prospective employers. The following discussion will provide you with methods of making all three more persuasive and effective.

Resumes

A **resume**, sometimes called a *vitae, curriculum vitae,* or *CV,* is a summary of an applicant's qualifications for the job being sought. Your resume should answer questions concerning

1. who you are
2. the type of job you are seeking

Jennifer McIntyre
61 Dorset Drive
Fairport, NY 14450
(518) 586-3372

Efficient office assistant with five years' experience. Proven ability to demonstrate organizational skills. Accomplished as a problem solver with interpersonal skills.

Experience

January 1992 - present   Office Assistant
Williams Construction Corporation
Pittsford, NY

Keyboarded all correspondence using word processing, answered telephone system with 8 lines, processed mail, and filed. Evaluated word processing software for office computers.

December 1987 - December 1991   Office Assistant
Robbins-Smith Engineering Company
Rochester, NY

Billed customers, made bank deposits, ordered office supplies, keyboarded correspondence using word processing, answered telephone, and filed.

Education

Associate in Applied Science degree, major in office technology, Monroe Community College.

Special Skills and Knowledge

Keyboarding speed: 75 words per minute.
One semester's experience with Microsoft Word/Office.
One semester's experience with WordPerfect.
Two semesters of machine transcription.
Introductory level of Lotus 1-2-3, dBase, and Harvard Graphics.

Related courses: Accounting Principles, Business Communication, Introduction to Psychology, Business Organization and Management.

References

Furnished upon request.

■ **Figure 15-2**
Chronological resume.

3. the qualifications you have to offer
4. the experience you have to offer

Resume Styles. All resumes should be personalized; however, there are a few formats that offer an attractive and easy-to-read document to the potential employer. The style and benefits of these resumes are listed below. Because the chronological resume is usually the style preferred by employers, we feature it in Figure 15-2.

Chronological Resume. The **chronological resume** format arranges your work experience and education so that the most recent information is first.

Annette M. Jacobson
1565 Ponderosa Street
Dallas, TX 75244 (214) 620-7238

Administrative assistant with seven years' experience. Supervised office functions and directed clerical staff.

Skills

Keyboarding speed:	80 words per minute.
Word processing:	Both on-the-job and classroom experience in using MS Word and WordPerfect software; designing newsletters using WordPerfect's desktop publishing features.
Transcription:	Experienced in machine transcription.
Communications:	Three years' experience in customer service via telephone; ability to compose letters, organize reports, take meeting minutes in shorthand, and transcribe notes.
Organizational ability:	Organized eight seminars for in-house training within a two-year period; set up a new records management system.
Supervision:	Supervised clerical staff for three years.
Other:	Introductory level with Access, Excel, and PowerPoint software.

Work Experience

April 1990 - present	Administrative Assistant, Wilson Products, Dallas, TX.
January 1986 - February 1990	Executive Secretary, Fairfield Oil Company, Dallas, TX.

Education

Bachelor of Science degree, Administrative Management, University of Oklahoma.

■ **Figure 15-3**
Functional resume.

The chronological resume has many advantages: it is the preferred resume for employers because it is easy to follow and shows exactly what the applicant has done, not what the applicant thinks he or she can do. This is certainly the resume format of choice, especially when the applicant has an impressive work or educational history. This format works well for recent graduates because it emphasizes their education and also identifies previous work experience responsibilities that relate to the job being sought.

Functional Resume. The **functional resume** is designed to point to the applicant's skills, abilities, and accomplishments. Refer to Figure 15-3. If you have never been employed, the functional resume will work well. A functional resume will give you an opportunity to point out leadership and organizational experience indicating that you will be a productive employee. A person who has not been employed but has acquired comparable work experience through volunteering and day-to-day living can also prepare a functional resume. In this style of resume, the experience section is organized by functions, without reference to the time of the performance or to an organization.

Targeted Resume. The **targeted resume** format focuses on the applicant's achievements and abilities that relate only to a specific job. The disadvantage of this style is that applicants need new resumes for every job application.

Purpose of the Resume. The purpose of a resume is to obtain an interview. It should be mailed, e-mailed, faxed, or personally delivered with a one-page application letter. As soon as your resume opens the door for a job interview, it has served its purpose. Whether you are offered the job will depend on your qualifications and how well you project your knowledge, abilities, and personality during the interview.

Office professionals (including administrative assistants, executive assistants, and executive secretaries) with excellent skills in communication; software applications such as word processing, spreadsheets, and database management; and customer service are in demand in many areas of the United States. According to many employers of office staff, the most highly desired attribute is excellent communication skills; this includes verbal, written, and computer communications. An attractive, informative, and accurate resume that accents these skills will be partially responsible for getting you the employment you desire.

You will deliver a resume to the place of employment when you respond to the job posting. However, take additional resumes with you to the job interview. Hand one to the interviewer at the beginning of the interview so that it may be referred to during the interview. By bringing along extra copies of your resume, you indicate to the interviewer that you are organized and prepared.

Self-Appraisal Inventory. As a preliminary step to preparing a resume, decide exactly what your qualifications are. Prepare a detailed **self-appraisal inventory** of your educational background, work experience, and personal qualities and interests so that you will know exactly what assets you have to offer an employer.

To prepare your inventory chart, record all the data you think might help you in your job search. Use separate sheets of paper to list your *education, work history, personal qualities,* and *interests.* Include everything as you make your list; record items in any order and rearrange them later, deleting any items that may not be relevant to the job you seek.

Under "Education," list the following:

1. the highest degree, license, or certificate (list first)
2. any special courses that may support your employment hunt
3. your skills, including computer and software training, and the ability to operate any additional equipment
4. school activities that suggest organizational, team, and leadership skills

Under "Work History," list all your jobs, including part-time, summer, and volunteer work. Be sure to include work experience that was unrelated to office work. For each job, give the name and address of the organization, your job title, the details of your duties, and the dates of your employment.

Under "Personal Qualities," list your strengths, such as initiative, leadership, ability to organize, willingness to learn, and participate in a team. Discuss these when you write your application letter.

Under "Interests," list your hobbies and special talents and the ways you spend your leisure time.

Points of Emphasis. Organize your resume so that the interviewer will grasp your most important qualifications if he or she reads only the first line of each section of your resume. Prepare a one-page resume, or put the most essential data on the first page.

Many authorities on resumes emphasize preparing a brief resume. Although some advocate a one-page resume, this is rarely enough space to include the critical facts. As your experience and education expand, so must your resume. Most applicants for office administrative work should have resumes no longer than two pages.

Indicate the type of position you are seeking in the "Objective" section.

Decide whether your work experience or your education will be most persuasive, and then place that section immediately after the "Objective" section.

To highlight your education, list your most recent experience first. It is often helpful to display key courses that relate to the employment opportunity. For the office professional, this often means software or skills-oriented courses.

Be consistent; just as you listed your education, arrange your work experience by listing the most recent employment first, followed by other employment.

Suggested Outline for a Chronological Resume. The resumes of two applicants should not be identical, but effective resumes tend to follow a recognizable pattern. Plan your resume so that it presents all your qualifications and highlights your strongest points.

A resume is a list; it is not necessary to write complete sentences. Use lists to describe duties or skills, and remember to be consistent. A common error in resumes is the use of inconsistent verbs. For example:

Inconsistent Responsibilities List

- Keying documents
- Manage electronic databases
- Plan meetings and conferences

Consistent Responsibilities List

- Keying documents
- Managing electronic databases
- Planning meetings and conferences

Avoid using "I." A resume contains facts only. Statements that reveal philosophy or opinion may be used in the application letter but not in the resume.

Heading. In the heading, include your name, address, telephone number, fax number, and e-mail address. If you have a temporary address, provide a permanent mailing address to ensure that you receive any documentation sent to you. Use a telephone number that has an answering system so you will not miss any important calls from potential employers.

Job Objective. In the "Objective" section, state the type of position you are seeing and the name of the organization with which you are seeking employment. Write the full name of the organization. Using the name of the company in the resume shows that the resume was specially prepared. Here is an example of an effective objective:

To work as an office professional with Cabott Industries.

Some authorities agree that the strongest points may be summarized under a category called "Skills Summary." For example,

Efficient administrative assistant with four years' experience. Proven ability to train and direct people. Successful record in management of three six-month projects, development of training programs, and installation of records management program. Problem solver with interpersonal skills.

Education. Keep in mind the following tips when listing your educational credentials:

1. a. In one entry indicate your degree (certificate or license), your major, and the name of the college conferring your latest degree. The date the degree will be (or was) conferred is not required. If you are still attending school, write "Expected Graduation Date: May 15, 200X."

    b. List any other degree, certificate, or license granted and the name of the institution. If you took courses but did not complete the requirements for a degree or certificate, list the name of the institution and a summary of the courses taken.

2. List your skills. If you are bilingual, indicate "Proficient in Spanish." Indicate your keyboarding speed only if it is applicable and impressive.

3. List the different types of software that you have experience in using.

4. List courses you took that you believe will be helpful to you on the job. List them by name, not number.

5. Add school activities that reflect your organizational, supervisory, and team skills.

Experience. Beginning with your most recent position, list your employment experience. If your work experience has been limited, include part-time, summer, and volunteer work, even when the work was unrelated to office work. Employers place value on experience that is common to all jobs, such as carrying out instructions, being prompt and dependable, working cooperatively with others, and accepting responsibility.

Use a separate entry for each job, and list your current or most recent position first. Give the beginning and ending dates (months and years), the name of the employer, the city in which the organization is located, the position held, and the specific duties performed. If the job was part time or voluntary, place this information under the date. To indicate that you are currently working, leave the date blank following the hyphen after the beginning date.

Interests and Activities. Because the human rights codes relating to equal opportunity employment make it illegal for an employer to discriminate on the basis of age, gender, race, marital status, religion, national origin, or creed, you are not required to include personal data. However, where you believe that certain personal data may be to your benefit, you should include them.

In this section, you may add whatever you believe will support your application, such as honors received, extracurricular activities, and professional associations you belong to.

References. The question of whether to include references is often raised, because employers know that applicants list as references those persons who will give the applicant favorable recommendations. Many employers check with the persons who are listed as references; some do not.

Some resumes say "References available upon request." To keep your resume to one page, provide a separate list of your references. List three or more former employers and teachers who can provide a specific evaluation of your competence, work habits, and attitude toward work. If you include a character reference, do not give the name of a relative. Ask permission of each person before including his or her name as a reference. For each reference, give the full name, position held, telephone number, and complete address, including the ZIP Code. Use a courtesy title before each name. The position held is significant because it will indicate the person's association with you.

Appearance of the Resume. Remember that the resume is a specimen of your work. If you use the appropriate word processing or desktop publishing software features, your resume will be a higher quality document.

1. Create your resume with careful thought and attention to detail. Your resume may not get a second chance; you must get it right the first time.
2. A resume is a list. Do not write complete sentences. Avoid using "I." For instance, instead of saying "I supervised the employees in bookkeeping and the reception area," rephrase the statement to read: "Supervised bookkeeping and office reception area." A resume contains facts only; statements that reveal philosophy or opinion may be used in the application letter but not in the resume.
3. Do not use abbreviations or acronyms. It is, however, appropriate to abbreviate "B.S." for Bachelor of Science. You and others within your industry may be familiar with acronyms and abbreviations, but they can confuse those outside your industry.

Print the resume with a laser printer on bond paper, measuring 8½ × 11 inches. Some authorities suggest soft gray or ecru colors.

Give the resume plenty of white space, using 1-inch margins. The side of the margins will actually depend on the setup and on the usual requirement to fit the resume on two pages. To avoid a crowded look, use ample white space before and after headings and between entries. Too much white space, however, will suggest inefficient planning.

Print the main heading at the top of the first page. It should be centered, and highlighted in such a way that it is eye-catching and easy to read.

Suggestions would be to use bold, enlarged, or italic print. Boxes or lines used in this area will enhance the appearance. Apply the "be conservative" rule. Using too many enhancements will detract from the qualifications your resume is trying to present.

Side headings should be emphasized but should not detract from the main titles. To this end, use a combination of capital letters, underlining, and bold or italic print. However, be moderate; you do not want to reduce the importance of the main heading.

The second page will require a heading. It should consist of your name and the page number.

You must get your resume noticed in the pile that will be received by the human resources (HR) representative or recruiter. An HR staff member sorts the resumes that do not meet the job requirements or that appear unsuitable. These unsuitable resumes will never reach the desk of the recruiter or department head. To ensure your resume is not filtered out, follow these simple rules:

1. Clearly state your skills that meet the key requirements of the job.
2. Carefully follow the instructions. Give precisely what is requested. If the ad states that the company wishes to have resumes dropped off in person, or if it asks for a handwritten application letter, do exactly that. Not following instructions demonstrates poor judgment and can be frustrating for the HR staff.
3. Concentrate on every detail. A good office professional will catch the smallest error when scrutinizing the resumes. Any typographical or spelling error will mean immediate rejection. No employer will want to interview an applicant for an office professional's position who allows errors in a document as important as a resume. For that reason, don't rely only on spell checking your document with your word processing software—manually proofread the document as well.
4. Many ads request that applicants not telephone the company. This request must be respected. If you telephone the employer, you leave the impression that you don't follow instructions, and you may annoy the receptionist or the HR staff.

Put yourself in the position of the person who must sort through and filter out the resumes, and then in the position of the department head. Make their jobs easier by making your resume attractive, applicable, easy to understand, and flawless. If you follow these suggestions, your chances of receiving an interview will be better.

Faxing Your Resume. If you have spent hours printing your resume on bond paper of perfect quality and color, and perhaps have even used colored ink for just the right amount of accent, then faxing your resume will seem like wasted effort. However, it does have the advantage of expediency. Employers will often request that resumes be faxed to save time. Consider the following if you are requested to fax your resume or if you simply determine yourself that faxing is appropriate:

■ A faxed resume will probably not be confidential. In fact, several people may see it before the designated receiver. You may be able to avoid this disclosure by telephoning the recipient just prior to sending the fax and asking him or her to collect the faxed document.

- A faxed resume should always include an application letter, just like the resume you mail or deliver.
- If your resume is attractive enough to earn you points, mail an original in addition to sending the fax.

E-Mailing Your Resume. E-mailing your resume and application letter might be preferable to faxing it. E-mailing has the advantage over faxing of keeping the document relatively confidential. However, it does not guarantee that the document will look more attractive. Although the document may look perfect on your screen, it may not have exactly the same format on the recipient's screen or printer. If you e-mail your resume, also send a backup copy in the postal mail.

Resume Software. Resume software companies advertise their products in magazines, computer stores, and on the Internet. If you access the Internet and enter key search words such as *resume software,* you will find several resume products. The software offers the following:

- Takes the hassle out of creating a resume from scratch by walking you through the entire process from beginning to end, providing tips, examples, and action words.
- Formats your information into the professional resume style of your choice.
- Helps you to write application, thank-you, and follow-up letters.
- Submits your resume to major career Web sites in a clear and readable format, rather than garbled or in an e-mail attachment that can't be opened.

Resume Reminders. Before submitting your resume, use the following checklist to ensure that your document will work for you. Remember that any poor work may cause an employer to send your resume to File 13 (trash)!

Application Letters

Write an application letter as a cover letter for your resume. The main purpose of an application letter is to introduce your resume in the hope of obtaining an interview.

Application letters are either prospecting or solicited. A **prospecting application letter** is written by an applicant who does not know that a job opening exists. It is written to express the applicant's interest in working for a particular organization, to call attention to the applicant's qualifications, and to inquire about the possibility of a job opening. A **solicited application letter** is written in response to an announcement that a job opening exists. The announcement might be made through an ad in the newspaper, placed with a private employment agency, sent to the career center of a school, or disseminated through other sources. As a college graduate, write prospecting application letters; do not wait until you know that a specific job opening exists.

The Prospecting Application Letter. An application letter is a sales letter, and the product is *you.* It represents your initial effort at locating an employer

Resume Checklist

APPEARANCE

✔ The spacing is attractive.

✔ You have plenty of white space.

✔ You have used quality paper that is white or of a conservative color.

✔ You have avoided excessive enhancements.

✔ Your format is consistent.

✔ Your headings are emphasized.

✔ Your information is in bullet form.

✔ You have followed the format described in this textbook.

CONTENT

✔ Resume headings shown in this textbook have been used.

✔ Your resume emphasizes skills and mastery of software.

✔ Your resume shows your most recent education first.

✔ Your resume shows your most recent experience first.

ACCURACY

✔ There are absolutely no errors in your resume. It has been proofread repeatedly by you and by someone else who gave you constructive feedback.

✔ You have used the spell check function to ensure your resume is free of spelling errors.

✔ You have checked your resume for spelling errors that the spell check function would not detect.

✔ Your lists are consistent in wording as well as in format.

OTHER

✔ Your resume has been delivered in an appropriate way.

seeking the qualifications you have to offer and at convincing the employer to consider your qualifications. You increase your application letter's chances of gaining attention when you submit a resume along with it. Let the reader know what qualifications you possess so that he or she can compare them with the requirements of the positions available within the organization.

Organize your application letter around the steps of a sales presentation:

1. Use an opening that gets the reader's attention and arouses interest in knowing more about your qualifications.

2. Focus on facts that convince the prospective employer that you possess qualifications that match the requirements of a position he or she is trying to fill.

3. Make a brief reference to the resume you are enclosing.

4. Use a closing that requests action, which in most application letters is a request for an interview. These points are illustrated in the application letter in Figure 15-4.

The Solicited Application Letter. When you hear or read about a job opening, write a solicited (invited) letter. A solicited application letter can be more specific than a prospecting letter because the applicant knows that a job opening exists.

Use the first paragraph to refer to the job and to reveal how you found out about it. Include a reference to the source. Request in the opening paragraph that you be considered for the job; for example:

> Please consider this resume as an application for the position of Administrative Assistant as advertised in the April 16 issue of *South Bend Tribune*. I recently earned an honors certificate for Office Technology. Through my studies I mastered numerous office skills, including the use

---

2410 Anderson Trail Drive
Dallas, TX 75245
April 5, 200X

Ms. Gloria Redmond
Human Resources Manager
Moore Electronics, Inc.
21 Metro Park
Dallas, TX 75234

Dear Ms. Redmond:

Recently I moved to Dallas, and I am seeking employment as an administrative assistant. From the research that I have done on companies in Dallas, I learned that Moore Electronics, Inc. is a young company that is growing rapidly. My twelve years of experience in offices and my recent studies in office technology and business would enable me to contribute to your growth.

Because of the skills that I possess, as listed on the enclosed resume, I can perform a variety of office duties with ease. I enjoy contacts with people, and I adapt readily to change. I plan to continue my education by attending evening classes.

I have a keen interest in working for Moore Electronics, Inc. I am available for an interview any afternoon after 1 p.m. My home telephone number is 972-555-7238.

Sincerely,

Susan Chung

Enclosure

■ **Figure 15-4**
Prospecting application
letter.

of word processing, desktop publishing, and database management software programs. Because I am an energetic graduate who is willing to learn, I am confident I could contribute to your team.

Write a persuasive letter in such a way that you discuss every requirement mentioned in the announcement and show how you meet these qualifications. It will differ from a prospecting letter in that you will include only the key qualifications that you choose to emphasize.

Enclose a resume and refer to it in the letter. In the resume highlight all the qualifications and key words mentioned in the announcement, and include others that may contribute to your getting the job.

Close the letter by requesting action, which usually is a request for an interview in which to discuss your qualifications for the job.

Appearance of the Application Letter. Key your application letter on good bond paper 8½ × 11 inches. Use plain paper that matches the quality and shade of the paper used for your resume. Include your personalized information above the date. Because your application could get separated from your resume, put your complete mailing address on both the letter and the resume.

Address the letter to a specific person, if possible. Make an effort to find out the name of the employer to whom the letter should be addressed. This information can be obtained with a single telephone call to the company.

Limit your letter to one page. Because you have organized all your facts in the accompanying resume, you can limit your application letter to three or four well-written paragraphs. Most letter styles are acceptable. The key factors in appearance are

- keep the font and format conservative
- keep the appearance professional
- keep the information balanced on the page

Time the arrival of your letter for the most attention. If your letter arrives on Monday, it arrives with the weekend delivery. If your letter arrives on Friday, it may get ignored among the week's backlog. Some authorities agree that your letter should arrive on a Tuesday, Wednesday, or Thursday.

Application Letter Reminders. An application letter is the window to your resume, so it's critical that your letter gives the best view of your skills. Consider your application letter as one of your marketing tools. Refer to the following checklist to help you create an application letter that works for you.

Application Forms

During your job campaign you will be asked to complete application forms. When a company requests that you complete an application form, do so. Your resume does not substitute for a completed application form. If you wish, you may attach your resume to the completed application form, but be sure to complete each section of the application. If a question on the application form does not apply to you, write "Not Applicable" or "Does Not Apply" in the blank. If a question calls for salary expected and you do not want to state a figure, write "Open to Negotiation," which means you would prefer to discuss salary once an offer of employment is made. If you leave the answer blank, the employer may assume (1) you were careless and missed the question or (2) you did not understand the question. Either of these assumptions will eliminate you from the potential candidates.

Application Letter Checklist

APPEARANCE

✔ You have used high-quality bond paper.

✔ Your paper and font match those of the resume.

✔ Your cover letter is stapled to the top of your resume.

✔ The documents have been placed in an envelope large enough that they may lie flat without folding.

CONTENT

✔ You have opened with an attention-getting statement.

✔ You have demonstrated knowledge of the company.

✔ You have included key words that were used in the job posting.

✔ You have clearly stated how you would be valuable to the company.

✔ You have summarized your background.

✔ You have closed with a call to action.

✔ The letter is short and simple.

ACCURACY

✔ You have proofread the letter several times for typos, grammar, spelling, punctuation, and content.

✔ Another person has proofread it and given you feedback on it.

✔ The letter contains the correct information (full address, telephone and fax numbers, and e-mail address).

How to Manage Your Job Campaign

✔ Keep a list of the application letters and resumes you sent, when you sent them, and to whom.

✔ Mark your calendar to call each individual within one week of the date your letter and resume should have arrived to confirm they were received.

✔ Make yourself known in a professional manner.

Each organization designs its own form for employee recruitment in order to include the specific questions it wants applicants to answer. Nevertheless, most application forms are similar.

Supplying information on the application forms you are requested to complete is a significant part of your job campaign. Follow the instructions carefully and supply the information exactly as it is called for. If the instruction reads "Please print," do so. Your printing and handwriting must be legible. After all, you want the application form to stand out in the pile.

Prepare your answers before you write on or key the application form. When you do this, your form will appear neat and organized. A completed application form becomes part of the permanent record of the applicant who is hired.

Many organizations follow the procedure of handing the applicant an application form as the first step of an interview taking place on the organization's premises. (For campus interviews, the interviewer will use the application form that you gave the career center director.)

Be prepared to complete the application. Do you

- Have a pen, preferably black ink?
- Know the current date?
- Have the names, titles, addresses, telephone and fax numbers, and e-mail addresses for your references?
- Have the dates of previous employment?
- Have a list of your volunteer activities and the associations to which you belong?
- Have the dates you attended high school and college?
- Know your social security number?
- Know the exact title of the job you are applying for?

Complete the form as requested even if you have your resume with you. It is acceptable to staple a copy of your resume to the back of the application form.

Portfolios

A portfolio is one of the best marketing tools you can have on a job interview. A **portfolio** is a collection of samples of your best work and should include only perfect work; nothing less than perfect is acceptable. No smudges or writing of any kind should appear on the documents.

The portfolio should consist of samples of your work organized into sections such as

- correspondence
- spreadsheets
- tables
- graphics
- meeting notes
- reports
- newsletters or advertisements

It should also contain (1) your transcripts (but only if it is impressive); (2) letter(s) of reference; and (3) certificates, certifications, degrees earned.

A table of contents and title page are necessary to give the portfolio an organized appearance. Plastic sheets should protect all documents. This work should be packaged into an attractive case with rings to hold the pages. Do not use a binder; a binder doesn't have the professional appearance you need.

During the interview find an appropriate opportunity to introduce the portfolio and discuss your work with the interviewer. Remember that the portfolio is not intended to be an information tool. It is a sales tool, and the product it is promoting is you!

INTERVIEWING FOR JOBS

A job interview gives you an opportunity to convince a prospective employer that you can make a real contribution to the organization. An interviewer can judge your basic qualifications by studying your transcript, application letter, resume, test results, and completed application form. During the interview, the interviewer will evaluate your personality, attitudes, professional appearance, and ability to communicate. See Figure 15-5. An impressive school record and evidence that you possess the necessary office technology skills are pluses, but your success in landing the job you want will hinge on the way you project yourself during the interview.

The purpose of the job interview is twofold:

1. To give the interviewer an opportunity to evaluate the applicant in terms of the needs of the organization.
2. To give the applicant a chance to appraise the job and organization.

Sometimes getting an interview is extremely difficult. If getting an interview seems impossible, don't get discouraged: this difficulty may reflect the competition for jobs in your area.

■ **Figure 15-5**
The interviewer will review your resume and ask questions to determine whether you are qualified for the position.

Attempt to schedule several interviews with organizations that you believe will offer the type of work you are seeking. Don't set your expectations on one particular job. Becoming overly anxious about getting a particular job can create unnecessary tension. Nevertheless, you should enter each interview with the attitude that the job you are applying for is precisely the one you want. As you learn more about the job, it may *become* the job you want.

Before the Interview

Prepare thoroughly for each interview. Your preparation should include

- researching the organization with which you have scheduled the interview
- taking a practice run to the location of the interview
- learning what the current salaries are for office professionals (including administrative assistants, executive assistants, information specialists) in the community
- summarizing your own qualifications
- deciding which qualifications to emphasize
- anticipating the interviewer's questions
- formulating your answers to the interviewer's questions
- choosing clothes appropriate for the interview
- scheduling ample time for getting ready and arriving for the interview

Do Research. Researching the organization is crucial. The following are effective research methods:

- using the Internet to study the organization
- exploring the organization in the reference section of the library
- reading the organization's most recent annual report
- phoning the organization's receptionist and requesting information

  Learn all you can about the organization. Research

- the organization's products or services
- how profitable the organization is
- the number of employees the organization has
- how long the organization has been operating
- the extent of the company's operations
- any recent expansion the company may have experienced
- any mergers or name changes the company has undergone
- the company's competitive standing in the industry
- the organization's hiring practices

Many applicants fall short during an interview because they lack knowledge about the organization to which they are applying. The interviewer will tell you about the organization and its employment opportunities, but you will be able to converse with more ease and ask pertinent questions if you have researched the organization. Lack of knowledge could be viewed as lack of interest in the organization. Prepare thoroughly; show your interest in the organization through your knowledge about it.

Before the interview, research the current salary ranges in your geographic area for the job you are seeking. The best way to do this is by reading the want ads for office jobs in the local paper. You might ask your career center director or local librarian to help you locate a summary of wage rates for all categories of occupations.

Anticipate Questions. Think about what you have to offer and the qualifications you want to emphasize. Review your resume before you go to the interview. The interviewer will expect you to discuss your job objective and why you feel qualified for it. You should be prepared to talk about yourself in an organized way without hesitation.

Anticipate questions the interviewer will ask and know what your answers will be. Realize, too, that you cannot anticipate all the questions the interviewer will ask, but you can expect questions such as the following concerning the job:

1. What do you know about this company?
2. What do you know about the position you are applying for?
3. We are looking for someone with extensive experience. Your resume indicates limited experience as an office professional. How do you expect to compensate for your lack of experience?
4. Why do you think you might like to work for this organization?
5. What do you expect to be doing three years from now? Five years from now?
6. Why did you choose a career as an office professional (or administrative assistant, etc.)?
7. Relating to the responsibilities described in the advertisement for this position, what strengths will you bring to our office?
8. Relating to the responsibilities described in the advertisement for this position, what responsibilities do you believe will be your greatest challenges?
9. Tell me about yourself.
10. How do you rate the education you have received?
11. Throughout your training to be an office professional, what courses did you enjoy the most? The least? Why?
12. Describe the qualities of a good leader. Have you encountered a person like this? Where and when?
13. Describe the characteristics of a poor leader. Have you encountered a person like this? Where and when?
14. Do you plan to continue your education? How? In what field? Why is this important to you?
15. If you were a team leader, what type of team members would you pick? If your team members did not meet your qualifications, what action would you take?
16. What are your feelings about working overtime?

At the outset of the interview you may be asked some general questions relating to your personal interests; or you may be asked to give your opinion about the latest current events. Some interviewers begin with questions that they think will put the applicant at ease. Answer all questions thoroughly but without rambling. Consider your answers to all questions seriously; the interviewer is searching for qualified employees who will stay with the organization if they are hired.

To gain insight into your personality and to check on your attitude, the interviewer may ask questions such as these:

1. Give an example of how you have displayed initiative.
2. Do you prefer working within a team or by yourself?
3. How do you spend your leisure time?
4. What personality characteristics do you think are essential for the job you are seeking?
5. How do you accept criticism?
6. Provide an example of a time when you were criticized. Describe the best/worst employer/teacher you have ever had.
7. Explain a stressful situation you encountered and describe how you handled it.

Behavioral Descriptive Questions. An applicant can prepare thoroughly for an interview; however, it is impossible to anticipate all possible interview scenarios. Behavioral descriptive questions are commonly used by interviewers to sort facts from exaggerations. These interviews use a "demo" questioning technique, in which each question leads to the next and probes deeper into an experience or scenario described by the applicant. A typical set of behavioral interview questions is:

1. Describe a situation where you were a team member and conflict arose within the team.
2. What did you do to resolve this conflict?
3. What did you learn from this experience?
4. Since the conflict, how have you applied what you learned?
5. Who has benefited from your ability to resolve conflict?

Some applicants feel intimidated by the probing nature of these questions. However, these questions, if presented in a diplomatic manner, are highly successful in determining the best candidate. Because many people embellish their resumes and then perform well at exaggerating their talents during the interview, the best candidate is not always selected for the job.

Behavioral descriptive questions are not difficult to answer if the candidate has the experience the recruiter is seeking. If you are asked a behavioral descriptive question and simply don't have the experience necessary to answer the question, be honest. The best policy is to tell the interviewer that you have no experience in this particular area. If you have related experience, ask the interviewer if you might refer to a similar situation in a different type of environment.

Unethical Questions. If interviewers ask personal questions, they must phrase them very carefully. Many questions relating to topics, such as marital status, age, smoking habits, or race, are unethical. Basing employment decisions on these factors is illegal. For example, an interviewer cannot ask an older person if he or she would be considering retirement in the next few years. If the interviewee's response was "yes," the interviewer couldn't base his or her employment decision based on this response.

No questions should be asked about national origin. The interviewer can ask what languages you speak and write fluently but should not ask what your native tongue is. You should not be asked questions about your ethnic background or race.

The interviewer can ask if you have a valid driver's license and if you have ever been convicted of a crime, but he or she cannot ask if you have ever been arrested.

To avoid potential unethical questions being asked during interviews, employers are advised how to conduct job interviews without violating the law.

Compose Some Intelligent Questions. An interviewer will expect you to ask questions, too. Some interviews lend themselves to the applicant asking questions periodically throughout the interview, whereas other interviews give the applicant an opportunity at the end of the interview to ask questions. Your research prior to the interview should help you generate a list of appropriate questions. Mention that you have researched the company Web site and that you prepared a few questions. Choose a selection of questions, take the sheet to the interview, and refer to it. The following is a list of good questions to ask for an interview.

- To whom would I report? To how many people would I report?
- What personal qualities improve the likelihood for success in this position?
- How would you describe the corporate culture of this organization?

Make a Statement with Your Appearance. Although first impressions rarely win jobs, your appearance—your clothes, hair, shoes, cosmetics, and jewelry—can certainly cost you the job before you ever open your mouth. Your goal is to look the part of a business professional. Your appearance should make the statement that you are a professional and that you want to be taken seriously. This is true even in companies that have a casual dress policy. Companies that encourage their employees to dress casually still expect applicants to dress and act professionally in the interview. Once they are successful and join the staff, they may adopt the dress code of the company.

Spend the extra time it takes to look well groomed. Dress conservatively because you want the interviewer to focus on your answers without being distracted by your appearance. By applying the following checklist to your interview preparation, you may be able to convey the proper message.

Whatever you decide will be your image for an interview, consider the strong nonverbal message that your image will send.

Be Punctual. Be sure you know the exact location of the interview. Plan to arrive ten to fifteen minutes early. Avoid rushing before the interview. You can undermine yourself before the interview by becoming stressed because

Interview Preparation Checklist

✔ Your hair should be neat and away from your face.

✔ Your cosmetics should be used sparingly.

✔ Your nails should be well manicured and clean.

✔ Your jewelry should be simple, minimal, and yet complimentary.

✔ Your professional attire should include a suit jacket.

✔ Your clothing should not be revealing; skirts should be a comfortable length and blouses should never reveal cleavage or camisole.

✔ Shoes should be clean, polished, and conventional.

✔ Cologne or perfume and hand lotion should be avoided. A fragrance that is attractive to you could be offensive to another person.

✔ For men, the most appropriate choice of color is a variation of black, navy, brown, or gray. Acceptable business clothing for women tends to be more colorful than that of their male counterparts, although it still must be conservative.

you did not allow yourself enough time. A few days before the interview, travel to the office and note the time it takes to arrive. On the actual day of the interview, allow more time than is needed to get to there.

Never schedule two interviews in the same morning or afternoon. You have no control over the length of an interview, and you will not feel at ease if you are concerned about time.

Know What to Take to the Interview. For the interview, you will want to have important materials on hand, but you will not want to be encumbered with items you do not need.

You should avoid bringing the following items to an interview. (Although it seems like common sense not to bring them, many employers report that applicants often do.)

- Never bring packages. Avoid shopping immediately before an interview, unless you can leave all the packages in your car.

- Women should never carry a large purse. A small handbag with only necessary items will not distract from a professional appearance.

- Men and women should never carry a briefcase that is oversized or resembles a schoolbag. Keep everything neat and simple and nondistracting.

- Most important of all, never bring another person. Naturally you wouldn't bring another person into the interview, but a number of applicants make plans to meet friends or relatives immediately after the interview.

The applicant needs to concentrate on the interview, not on the friends or relatives waiting in the lobby or reception area. In particular, don't bring children because their behavior may cause you to worry. Demonstrate that you are an independent person; arrive alone and leave alone.

Here's what you *should* take to the interview.

- Your portfolio, if prepared to a professional standard, will be one of the best sales tools you have. Bring it to the interview and look for the perfect opportunity to walk through it with the interviewer.

- Always bring along a pen and paper to write down important facts you learn during the interview. Your pen should be attractive and in good condition. One that has been chewed or runs out of ink will not leave the interviewer with the best impression.

- Bring along extra copies of your resume. Offer copies to the interviewer just as the interview is ready to begin. This demonstrates your preparation. You will also need a copy for yourself to refer to throughout the interview.

- Bring a list of three or more references that includes names, titles, company names, company addresses, company telephone and fax numbers, and e-mail addresses. This should be attractively keyed on a single sheet. Be prepared to leave this sheet with the interviewer.

- Bring along a version of the job advertisement if one was posted or appeared in the newspaper. Highlight the key responsibilities listed. Don't be afraid to bring out the ad and refer to it during the interview. This shows that you know exactly what type of job you are applying for and that you are prepared for the interview.

- Bring along your list of questions; you can list the responsibilities of the job and for each one cite specific examples of how you have demonstrated competence. Don't be afraid to refer to this sheet during the interview. The sheet should appear neat and organized and, of course, should be keyed.

- With desktop publishing, you can prepare personal business cards that are professional looking by printing them on cardstock. Or, for a nominal charge, you can have a professional printer produce a small number of business cards. The applicant who leaves a business card leaves a professional image.

During the Interview

Be courteous, confident, and composed. As you approach the interviewer, smile, greet the interviewer by name, and introduce yourself. If the interviewer extends a hand, give a firm handshake. This will express your confidence. Try to relax. You will probably feel a little nervous because the interview is important to you. If you feel nervous, don't call attention to your nervousness by twisting your hair, tapping your foot, thumping on the table, sitting on the edge of the chair, talking too rapidly, or showing other outward nervous signs.

There may be one interviewer or a panel of interviewers. The interviewers have a job to perform; they must match an applicant to the requirements of the job to be filled.

The initial interview probably will last about thirty minutes. A good interviewer will allow the applicant to talk throughout most of the interview.

Some interviewers, but not all, break the interview into the following segments:

1. getting acquainted
2. presenting the organization's opportunities

3. evaluating the applicant

4. answering the applicant's questions

Others begin the interview with one or more broad, open-ended questions, such as "Tell me about yourself," turning the discussion over to the interviewee at once. The interviewer controls the interview by telling the interviewee to discuss what he or she wants to hear about. When this interviewing technique is used, the conversation seems spontaneous rather than structured.

While the interviewer is talking, listen intently. Give the interviewer an opportunity to talk; show that you are an active listener.

When you are asked a question, give a full answer, not simply a "yes" or "no." The interviewer will ask a question or a comment to introduce a subject that you are expected to discuss. Look the interviewer in the eye and answer all questions frankly. Be deliberate; do not start talking before the interviewer completes the question. Avoid talking too much; keep to the point. Do not attempt to answer a question you do not understand. Either restate the question as you understand it or ask the interviewer to clarify it.

While you are talking, keep your goal in mind, which is to promote yourself. Use every opportunity to emphasize your good points and to relate them to what you can do for the organization. To sound sincere, present facts, not your opinion, about yourself. Don't criticize yourself and never make derogatory remarks about an instructor or a former employer.

As you are talking, the interviewer will evaluate your mental and physical alertness, your ability to communicate, your attitude toward life and toward the organization, and your enthusiasm for work. Some interviewers will give tests in order to evaluate your skill level.

As discussed in the section "Before the Interview," you should prepare questions to ask at the interview. Every interviewer likes to be asked intelligent questions. The questions you prepare must be relevant to the organization or to the job opportunity. If all your prepared questions have been discussed during the interview and you are left without questions to ask, ask the interviewer to elaborate further on a statement or on details given earlier in the interview.

Be Prepared to Discuss Salary. At the initial interview, your questions should not concern salary or benefits. Reserve these questions until you are offered the job. However, if the interviewer asks you about your expected salary, be prepared to state a range. Remember that the figure the interviewer is likely to remember and focus on is the low end of your range.

If you have prepared a personal budget and have researched office salaries in your location, you will know what is an appropriate starting salary for this employment opportunity.

The best time to negotiate salary is after the job offer has been made. However, the interviewer is in control of the interview; if the interviewer asks you a salary question during the interview, you must answer it.

Remember that although salary is often a negotiable item, these negotiations must be handled with diplomacy. Although job satisfaction will be achieved mostly through obtaining a challenging and responsible position, don't sell yourself short when salary is discussed. If you have earned a post-secondary certificate and degree, you have gained bargaining power.

Close the Interview Confidently. Watch for cues that the interview is coming to an end. The interviewer may thank you for coming, suggest that you schedule a time to take employment tests, invite you to arrange for a second interview, stand up, tell you that you will hear by a certain date if the organization is interested in your application, or offer you the job.

A good closure to an interview would include the following actions:

- Firmly shaking hands.
- Restating your interest in the position. For example, "I hope you will consider me for the job. I feel confident I would make a positive contribution to your organization."
- Checking the follow-up procedure that will be employed by the organization. Example: "When might I expect to hear from you? If I don't hear from you by that date, may I call you?"
- Leaving a business card.

If you are offered the position, you are not expected to accept it on the spot. You are making a long-term commitment, and you should be sure that it is the job you want. The interviewer would prefer that you give it enough thought to be absolutely certain. You may accept at once if you have no doubt about it. Otherwise, tactfully say that you would like time to consider it. Ask if you can let the interviewer know in a day or two or at some definite time that you can agree upon.

You cannot always accurately judge how you are being rated. Interviewers who rely on the second interview for making a decision are noncommittal during the initial interview. Appear interested and confident as the interview draws to a close. Express appreciation to the interviewer before leaving.

After the Interview

Make each interview a learning experience. Ask yourself the following questions to improve your self-promotion techniques:

1. What points did I make that seemed to interest the interviewer?
2. Did I present my qualifications well?
3. Did I overlook any qualifications that are pertinent to the job?
4. Did I learn all I need to know about the job, or did I forget or hesitate to ask about factors that are important to me?
5. Did I talk too much? Too little?
6. Did I interview the employer rather than permit the employer to interview me?
7. Was I too tense?
8. Was I too aggressive? Not assertive enough?
9. How can I improve my next interview?

The Campus Interview

Many organizations actively recruit postsecondary graduates. Your career center will set up appointments for students nearing graduation to be interviewed by representatives from these companies. These interviews often occur right on the campus.

Stress your strong points; listen attentively; in response to the interviewer's questions, relate how you meet the qualifications for the job; project your personality; and ask relevant questions.

Don't expect that because the interview is held on campus you should dress casually. Give the interviewer a chance to see how you would look on the job if the interviewer hired you. You will look capable of accepting responsibility if you dress accordingly. The interviewer will be comparing your appearance with that of office professionals that already work for the organization, not with the appearance of other college students.

If, as a result of the campus interview, you are invited for a second interview or to take tests, be sure to get the exact address. Write down the date, time, address, and name of the person who will meet with you.

Testing for a Job. The career center director or coordinator and your instructors may know which organizations in your area give tests. If you apply for a job with an organization that administers tests, be prepared to take a word processing production test, a basic math test, a keyboarding test, and a spelling test. The organization could test your skill on any software application or test your ability to compose correspondence.

If you apply for a position at a staffing agency, you will probably be asked to take tests at its location. Be prepared for similar tests, such as basic math, keyboarding, and spelling tests. In addition, you will probably be asked to take computerized tests in word processing, spreadsheets, and databases. The computerized tests generally direct you to perform a function using the specific software. Your score probably will be based on your responses to using the software menus, icons, and keystrokes.

Many tests have time limits. Listen carefully to the instructions you receive. If you do not clearly understand what you are expected to do, ask questions. You will be expected to perform at speed levels determined by the organization administering the tests. Test papers are usually evaluated by degree of accuracy.

Personality tests and mental ability tests are popular. It is not possible to prepare for these tests. The goal of these examinations is to determine which applicants will work well with existing staff members, which applicants will most likely share the company's goals, and which applicants have potential leadership skills.

Follow-Up Letters

The letters essential for continuing and finalizing a job search fall into five categories:

1. Thank-you
2. Reminders
3. Inquiries
4. Job acceptance
5. Job refusal

Key follow-up letters on the same quality paper you used for the resume; be sure to include your return address, telephone and fax numbers, and e-mail address. Check them carefully for accuracy. Be sure that the company's name and the interviewer's name are spelled correctly.

Thank-You Letters.   Writing a thank-you letter following a job interview is not a requirement but a courtesy. Always write a thank-you letter and send it immediately after the interview. If you want the job for which you were interviewed, you can use a thank-you letter to do far more than express appreciation to the interviewer. Not everyone writes thank-you letters; consequently, when your thank-you letter arrives at the interviewer's desk, it will single you out from other applicants and call attention once more to your application.

Say that you definitely are interested in the job and that you want to be considered seriously for it. When interviewers are considering several applicants with apparently equal qualifications, one of the questions they are trying to answer is, "Which applicant has the keenest interest in working for our organization?"

Your letter can be short. In the opening paragraph, thank the interviewer, mentioning either the day or the date of the interview and the specific job discussed. Use the remainder of the letter to refer to something specific about the interview and to express interest in the job. Close with a statement to let the interviewer know you are waiting for a reply. Here is an example of how one applicant expressed interest:

> Talking with you last Wednesday afternoon about the duties of an office assistant with Midwestern Products convinced me that this is exactly the position I am seeking.
>
> I certainly appreciate the time you spent with me, discussing employment opportunities with your company and describing the job requirements for an office assistant's position. I feel confident I can meet these requirements, and I am waiting to hear that you also feel I can.

Reminders.   When you do not receive a response to an application or are told that your application has been placed on file, write another letter after a few weeks have elapsed to remind the interviewer that you still are interested. You will find reminder letters especially helpful when you plan to move from one geographic section of the United States to another and make inquiries about jobs months in advance of your availability for employment.

Do not assume that your resume has been kept on file. Send another copy of your resume with your reminder letter. In the opening paragraph, mention the job you applied for and when. In the body of the letter, briefly state your interest in working for that particular organization, express confidence about what you can do for the organization, and ask if an opening for the type of job you are seeking exists. You may be successful with composing a letter similar to the one shown below:

> In January, I inquired about employment opportunities for office assistants with your company and sent you a resume detailing my qualifications.
>
> Modern Plastics is a company that has enjoyed rapid growth, and I would like to be a member of its dynamic team.
>
> Next week I am moving to Denver. May I please schedule an appointment during the week of May 25 to discuss my qualifications for employment as an assistant with Modern Plastics? Please reply to my Denver mailing address.
>
> For your convenience, I am enclosing a copy of the application letter and resume that I sent to you in January.
>
> I look forward to receiving a positive response. Thank you for your assistance.

Inquiries. Following a job interview, you can write a letter of inquiry or make a telephone call if you have not heard anything by the time the interviewer said you would receive a reply. Be patient. Wait a day or two beyond the time you are expecting a reply and, if you do not hear, telephone or write to inquire. If you are told that the position has not been filled, indicate that you definitely are interested.

Job Acceptance Letters. Follow up with a letter even when you accept a job offer during an interview or over the telephone. You may receive a letter offering you a job and suggesting that you call to accept. Respond by telephone, but also send a letter to leave no doubt about your acceptance.

In the opening, accept the job enthusiastically. Mention the specific position being accepted. If you have received a form for supplying additional information, complete it, enclose it, and refer to it in your letter. Repeat the report-to-work instructions, giving the date, time, and place. In either the opening or the closing, express appreciation. Keep a copy of the letter of offer and your reply. Here is an example of an acceptance response.

> As I expressed over the telephone, I am delighted to accept the position of office assistant in the International Markets Division of Midwestern Products.
>
> Enclosed are the forms you requested I complete after our conference last week.
>
> I appreciate the opportunity to join your team and am eager to report to work on Monday, June 16, at 8 a.m. Thank you for selecting me for the position.

Job Refusal Letters. If you conduct a thorough job campaign, you may be offered more than one job and will have the problem of having to refuse all but one of them. Be as prompt in refusing as possible. If you have already accepted a position, refuse the second offer at once. This is a courtesy you owe the person who must search elsewhere to fill the job offered you.

Because your letter will be disappointing to the reader, you should organize it in the same way that you organize other letters of disappointment. Begin by making a favorable statement concerning your contact with the interviewer or about the organization. Express appreciation for the job offer at either the beginning or the end of the letter. Include at least one reason for refusing the job offer. State the refusal tactfully, but make it clear that you are refusing. By making a definite statement about already having accepted a position or about your continuing to search for a particular job, you will be refusing the offer without making a negative statement. Close with a pleasant comment.

Don't burn your bridges—you may want to work for the organization at some point in the future. Check your letter to make sure that the attitude reflected by your statements does not close the door for you. In the following example, the writer shows appreciation and says that she would be interested in a more senior position.

> Thank you for the job offer to become an information specialist in the Research Department of Renfro Corporation. However, as I mentioned at the time of the interview, I am seeking a position as an executive assistant. Another company in the city has offered me a position at this level of employment, and I have accepted it.

Mrs. Davis, I appreciate the offer to work for your company and the interest you have shown me. In the future, if a more senior position becomes available, I would be very interested in working for Renfro Corporation.

CONDUCTING AN ELECTRONIC JOB SEARCH

Computers and telecommunications have changed almost every facet of the way we work. In fact, they now play a part in how we *search* for work. The Internet has become a popular tool for searching for available employment and for posting resumes for potential employers to view. Yet another innovation is the computer-scanned resume; with this technology, specially prepared resumes get the attention of a computer before they attract the attention of an employer.

The Internet

The computer is a valuable job-searching tool. Searching the Internet for job opportunities will not eliminate the need to practice traditional job-hunting techniques, but it will add another dimension to your job search.

Job announcement databases are available for browsing. By browsing through Web sites, you will reach many online job-search facilities. Here are two Web locations:

- http://www.monster.com
- http://www.occ.com/occ

In the highly competitive search for work, the Internet has become a new job market. The Internet may be used for job searching, but it is also useful for sending your resume to one of the online career services. The online career service will ask you to either complete the online resume builder form, or send a copy of your resume.

Your resume information now becomes part of a database that is accessible to employers looking for employees with the required skills. Any reputable online career service keeps confidential the personal portion of your resume (name, addresses, and contact numbers). When an employer believes that your credentials match a job opportunity available, the employer will offer to purchase your name and contact numbers. With your permission, the online career service will release the header to the paying customer—the potential customer.

Electronically Scanned Resumes

A growing number of companies are using electronic scanning systems to digitally scan, store, and track resumes and application letters. In fact, hundreds of resumes can be scanned in only a few minutes. A **scannable resume** has a plain format that allows companies to scan it as pure text. When recruiters wish to retrieve a group of candidates, they supply key words that are essential for the right applicant. These key words will identify expertise, experience, and education. For example, they might include such words as *bilingual, desktop publishing, database management, teams,* and so on. The computer software scans the database, and within minutes a list of applicants whose resumes match the stated criteria is brought to the screen.

Refer to Figure 15-6 for an example of a partial resume that has been prepared for electronic scanning.

Ms. Kimberly Wong
10507 53rd Avenue NW
Portland, OR 97204-0066
Tel (503) 478-1320
Tel (503) 478-2398
E-mail: kimwong@aol.com

OBJECTIVE
To earn the position of administrative assistant with a company that has a progressive team spirit.

EDUCATION
September 1996–April 1998
Portland Community College
Office Administration Program
Portland
Honours Diploma
Keying 70 words per minute
Microsoft Word
PowerPoint
Excel
President Office Administration Society
Team Leader Graduation Planning Committee
Leader Charity Fundraising

EXPERIENCE
May 1999–Current
Administrative Assistant
Coron Industries
Portland
Supervisor of junior staff
Coordinator of budget
Coordinator of conferences and seminars
Designer of brochures and newsletters
Coordinator ISO 9001

May 1998–May 1999
Administrative Assistant
Image Publishers
Portland
Supervisor of reception desk
Coordinator of media

■ **Figure 15-6**
Example of a partial resume that has been prepared for electronic scanning.

Electronically scanned resumes save the recruiter a large amount of time. However, even a resume with extensive credentials may go unnoticed if the scanner cannot identify them. Scanning can dramatically change the appearance of your resume. Many scanning programs make mistakes when reading words or special characters. To be sure that all the information on your resume is collected by the electronic system, follow these tips to be sure your resume is scanner friendly.

1. Do not use italics. Instead, use a standard typeface.
2. Do not use bullets. Instead, use asterisks and hyphens.
3. Do not bold any text.
4. Do not underline or use graphic lines.
5. Do not use indents or centering.
6. Describe your personal traits in nouns, not verbs.

7. Use the key words found in the job ad.

8. Use straightforward words to describe your experience. Embellished terms will not be on the list of skills for which the recruiter is searching.

9. Use multiple pages if necessary. Unlike humans, computers do not tire of reading.

10. Do not print your resume on colored paper.

11. Increase your lists of key words. Include specific software names such as *Microsoft Word*.

12. Use common resume headings such as "Objective," "Education," "Experience," and "Interests."

One advantage of an electronic scanning system is that electronic storage takes so much less space than paper storage. This means that resumes may be kept on file for an extended period.

If applicants are not aware of the electronic scanning process and submit attractive yet traditionally formatted resumes, they may not be identified by the computer, no matter how outstanding. The best approach when you do not know whether electronic or human screening will be used is to submit two resumes. The resume intended for human scrutiny should be printed on attractive paper, using highlighting features, graphic lines, and so on. Place a removable note on the nicely formatted resume that states "Visual Resume." Place another removable note on the resume destined for electronic scanning that says "Scannable Resume." The reason you have included two resumes should be briefly explained in your application letter.

CONSIDERING INTERNATIONAL EMPLOYMENT OPPORTUNITIES

Working overseas can be an exciting option and is one that is being increasingly pursued by Americans. The potential benefits to working abroad are many, including lucrative salaries, tax exemptions, overseas service premiums, free housing, contract completion bonuses, forty days or more of annual vacation time, international travel, and education allowances for dependents.

The range of international employment opportunities available is broader than most Americans expect. The overseas job market is as diverse as the domestic U.S. market.

Individuals with backgrounds in private business, nonprofit organizations, government work, international agencies, teaching, construction, telecommunications, computer specialties, and management information systems can find opportunities that will satisfy their interests and pay them better than comparative positions in the United States.

The **curriculum vitae (CV)** or international-style resume is used in overseas job hunting. The standard CV is between four and eight pages long and may contain a personal information section, references, detailed information on all former positions held, a list of memberships in professional organizations, overseas living and working experience, publication credits, and detailed education information, and should include a recent color picture. Also, when forwarding a CV to a potential employer, include copies of all diplomas, certificates, transcripts, and passport.

You should be aware that companies and organizations outside the United States are under no legal constraints as to what information they may require from a potential job candidate.

quicktips

Preliminary Work Before Submitting a Resume:

- Take advantage of the Internet.
  - Visit the company's Web site.
  - Learn as much as possible about the company.
- Remember, a good resume doesn't always mean it will fit job openings with *all* companies.
  - Tailor your resume to focus on the company's specific job opening.
  - Editing your resume can be a *minor* task for you, but can make a *major* impact on the person reading it!

Overview

✔ Job prospects can be located through networks, college placement offices, business sections of newspapers, direct application, staffing agencies, the federal government, and newspaper advertisements.

✔ Applying for jobs includes preparing a resume, writing an application letter, and completing an application form.

✔ A resume is a marketing tool and must be prepared in a format that is easy to read and emphasizes your employment history, educational background, and special skills and abilities.

✔ A self-appraisal inventory helps you organize information about your educational background, work experience, and personal qualities.

✔ A chronological resume lists your employment history with your most recent position first and identifies specific employers and positions.

✔ A functional resume itemizes your duties and skills, rather than specific employers and positions. Using a functional resume allows you to focus on experiences that are more applicable to the target position.

✔ The primary purpose of the application letter is to obtain an interview. Write an application letter when the job you are seeking is located in another city, when you are answering an ad, and when you mail or fax a resume.

✔ An applicant who does not know that a job opening exists writes a prospecting application letter.

✔ A solicited application letter is written in response to an announcement that a job opening exists.

✔ To manage your job campaign, keep a list of the application letters and resumes you sent, when you sent them, and to whom; mark your calendar to call each individual within one week of the date your letter and resume should have arrived to confirm they were received.

✔ The application form may be the first impression a company has of you. It is extremely important that you follow the instructions carefully and supply the information exactly as it is called for.

✔ Prepare a portfolio of your best work and organized the samples into sections, such as correspondence, meeting notes, and reports.

✔ The purpose of the job interview is twofold: to give the interviewer an opportunity to evaluate the applicant in terms of the needs of the organization; and to give the applicant a change to appraise the job and the organization.

✔ Before the interview, prepare thoroughly by researching the organization, anticipating questions, planning your appearance, and organizing the important materials to take to the interview.

✔ During the interview, remain courteous, confident, and composed. Listen intently and answer the interviewer's questions by giving a full answer. Remember, discussion about salary is appropriate only after the job offer has been made—unless the interviewer brings up the subject.

✔ Watch for cues that the interview is closing. Remember to firmly shake hands, restate your interest in the position, and check the follow-up procedure that will be used by the organization.

✔ Make each interview a learning experience. Ask yourself questions to improve your self-promotion.

✔ Campus interviews will provide additional experience with interviewing. During the campus interviews, stress your strong points; listen attentively; in response to the interviewer's questions, relate how you meet the qualifications for the job; project your personality; and ask relevant questions. Dress appropriately for the campus interview.

✔ The letters essential for continuing and finalizing a job campaign fall into five categories: thank-you, reminder, inquiry, job acceptance, and job refusal.

✔ Use the Internet as a job-searching tool; it will add another dimension to your job search.

✔ To electronically scan your resume, you must be knowledgeable about the scanning process to submit an attractive resume that will be readable by the interviewer.

Key Terms

Blind advertisements. Give a post office box number or a telephone number but not a company name and are used to eliminate interviewing a large number of unqualified applicants.

Chronological resume. Lists your employment history with your most recent position first.

Curriculum vitae (CV). An international-style resume; it's between four and eight pages long and may contain a personal information section, references, detailed information on all former positions held, a list of memberships in professional organizations, overseas living and working experience, publication credits, and detailed education information.

Functional resume. Itemizes your duties and skills, rather than specific employers and positions.

Mentor. A person who can offer you information and advice about the organization and give you career direction.

Networking. An exchange of information.

Portfolio. A collection of samples of your best work; it serves as one of the best marketing tools you can have on a job interview.

Prospecting application letter. Expresses the applicant's interest in working for a particular organization, calls attention to the applicant's qualifications, and inquires about the possibility of a job opening.

Resume. A summary of an applicant's employment history and educational background.

Scannable resume. A resume that is plain in its format so that companies can scan it as pure text into their resume management systems.

Self-appraisal inventory. A detailed explanation of your educational background, work experience, and personal qualities and interests.

Solicited application letter. A letter written in response to an announcement that a job opening exists.

Targeted resume. The format focuses on the applicant's achievements and abilities that relate only to a specific job.

For Your Discussion

 Retrieve file C15-DQ.DOC from your student data disk.

Directions

Enter your response after each question.

1. Explain how business news items can prove to be a valuable source of job prospects.
2. What is the advantage of searching for job openings that are not advertised?
3. How does answering a newspaper advertisement for a job differ from using other sources for employment?
4. What is the main purpose of the resume? In what other way can it be used?
5. Why should every job applicant prepare a self-appraisal inventory?
6. Suggest why a prospective employer would be interested in information about an applicant's work experience unrelated to office work.
7. What is the purpose of the application letter?
8. How does the purpose of the solicited application letter differ from the purpose of the prospecting application letter?
9. What guidelines should be followed to organize an effective application letter?
10. Why would an organization request that an applicant fill out its application form when the applicant has already submitted a resume?

GRAMMAR WORKSHOP

The office worker who knows correct grammar can communicate effectively with his or her manager, fellow employees, customers, and clients. If you use correct grammar, you are a valuable asset to your manager and company, for you can communicate clearly with others.

For Review

Appendix A: Rule 18: Subject and Verb Agreement
                    Rule 19: Noun and Pronoun Agreement
                    Rule 20: Parallel Construction

 Retrieve C15-WRKS.DOC from your student data disk.

Directions

Write C to the left of the sentence if the grammar is correct. Otherwise, make the necessary corrections.

Rule 18: Subject and Verb Agreement

1. Do the two children has separate insurance policies?

2. A set of specifications for the job are enclosed.

3. Several different opinions about the completion of the project were voiced at the staff meeting yesterday.

4. The president of the Dallas-based banks was at the meeting.

5. The ventures of Murray Investments Inc. was under investigation.

Rule 19: Noun and Pronoun Agreement

1. Each of our field supervisors sends in their daily report for review.

2. The computer, as well as the software and diskettes, has been ordered and they will be shipped next week.

3. When these types of things happen, we should prevent it from reoccurring.

4. Each computer must display their serial number.

5. Everything will be fine if it operates well.

Rule 20: Parallel Construction

1. The customer service representative is determined to help the dissatisfied customer and is open to all suggestions.

2. The disgruntled employees filled the lunchroom and continued with their discussions.

3. She said that she had studied the report and refers it to the central office.

4. We have three stated goals: to increase production to expand our market, and recruiting qualified workers.

5. He smelled the gaseous odor when he opened the door.

On the Job Situations

 Retrieve file C15-OJS.DOC from your student data disk.

Directions

Enter your request after each situation.

1. A job announcement posted on the office technology bulletin board appeals to you. A variety of responsibilities are listed. You believe you have the qualifications required for the position. The salary is excellent. The address of the company is local, but you have never heard of the company. You would like to know more about the company before you apply. When you go to the library to find out about the company, neither you nor the librarian who helps you can find any information. What can you do next to become informed about the company?

2. You have received two job offers. One is from a small metal-building manufacturer who employs a total of 100 employees with only one fabrication facility. The second offer is from a national insurance company with thousands of employees and regional offices covering the United States. The smaller of the two companies offers a starting salary that is $1,000 per year more than the national insurance company, but it has no retirement or profit-sharing plan. The larger company offers $1,000 less in direct compensation but provides a liberal benefits package that includes sick leave, profit sharing, and retirement plans. As you consider these two options, consider the following questions:

   a. Which company offers the greatest potential opportunities for growth both personal and professional, the greatest monetary gain, and the best benefits package?

   b. Are you looking for immediate financial gain with limited career growth?

   c. Are you looking for possible long-term financial gain with possible long-term security?

3. You have been an administrative assistant for three years. Because the company is rapidly growing, three new office support positions have been created in your department. Your manager asked you to review the resumes that applicants have sent. After reviewing the resumes, you find that only three of forty-five resumes look acceptable. List items or features that would not be acceptable in a resume.

4. Your friend asked you to read and comment on an application letter she is sending to the interviewer at your company. Based on what you have learned from this chapter and your experience, you believe that the letter is not effective. Describe how you will help your friend to rewrite her letter to make it more effective.

Projects and Activities

1. Research the classified ads for jobs for which you qualify or for which you would like to qualify eventually. Make a list of your top three job choices. Include the position titles, duties, and the types of industries in which these jobs are found—for example, medical, legal, or insurance. Describe why you would like to obtain these jobs. Report your summary in memo form to your instructor.

2. Visit a private staffing service or public office employment agency in your area to determine how the agency places its clients in office support positions. During your visit, gather information about its testing program. For instance, ask the agency to share with you the kinds of employment test it gives for at least three different office support positions. Report your findings in memo form to your instructor.

3. Visit your college career development center to gather the following information: specific career information about your chosen occupation, employment opportunities in your local area, and interest surveys or assessments that will help direct you in your chosen occupation.

4. In a group, develop items for a Do/Don't checklist, not to exceed a total of ten items. The items represent qualities that make a resume acceptable or unacceptable. Include a rating scale with a range from 1 to 5, with 1 representing unacceptable (U) and 5 being acceptable (A). When your resume is complete, check off items on the form, as you believe they have been accomplished, satisfactorily or unsatisfactorily. Here is an example of a Do/Don't checklist:

Do List	Unacceptable	Acceptable
Self-inventory	1 2	3 4 5
Don't List	**Unacceptable**	**Acceptable**
Misspellings	1 2	3 4 5

Surfing the Internet

A. You have heard about an interview guide placed on the Internet by Allegheny College Administrative/Career Services. Locate the guide.

1. Connect to the Internet and access a search tool such as Yahoo! or Lycos.

2. Enter the following key search words: *business, job interview*.

3. Locate the interview guide placed on the Internet by Allegheny College in Pennsylvania.

4. Print the guide.

5. Check out the "Most Commonly Asked Questions."

6. Write a summary in memo form of the information in the guide and of the most common questions asked.

B. As an office professional in a career consultant's office, you have been asked to locate information on companies that are recruiting and on career counseling.

1. Connect to the Internet and access a search tool such as Yahoo! or Lycos.

2. Locate employment information on the following companies: MCI, Sony, Microsoft, and Hewlett-Packard. Use the following addresses:

http://www.mci.com

http://www.sony.com

http://www.microsoft.com

http://www.hp.com

3. Summarize the employment information available for each company.

4. From the Online Career Center, gather information about administrative assistant (or legal or medical secretary) positions in your city and state.

To access the center, enter the following address: http://www.occ.com/occ.

5. Summarize at least three positions that are advertised online.

6. Combine the employment information in memo form and submit it to your instructor.

Using MS Office 2002

Create a Resume Using Resume Wizard

1. Open Microsoft Word and make sure a blank document screen displays.

2. Click on the File menu and select New.

3. On the New Document task pane at the right of the screen, click on Resume Wizard under New from template.

4. Click on the Next button.

5. Select the style you want: Professional, Contemporary, or Elegant. Then click on Next.

6. Click on the type of resume you want to create: Entry level, Chronological, Functional, or Professional. Then click on Next.

7. Enter your personal data. Then click on Next.

8. Accept or add standard headings for the resume style. Then click on Next.

9. Accept or add optional headings for the resume style. Then click on Next.

10. Accept or change the order for the resume headings. Then click on Next.

11. Click on Finish to view your resume.
12. Click the mouse in each bracketed area [ ] and type the requested information.
13. Proofread your data, save, and print.

APPLICATION PROBLEMS

APPLICATION 15-A

Preparing for an Interview

Supplies needed: Form 15-A, Self-Appraisal Inventory; employment ad from newspaper.

 Retrieve file C15-SELF.DOC from your student data disk.

Find an employment ad in a newspaper that you are interested in answering.

A. Prepare the following:
1. Self-appraisal inventory
2. Resume (from your portfolio—Chapter 15)
3. Application letter (from your portfolio—Chapter 15)
4. Questions that might be asked of you and your responses
5. Questions you might like to ask the interviewer

B. Schedule an appointment with an interviewer. (You may ask someone to interview you or your instructor may set up an appointment for you.) Your instructor may arrange for a video to be made of your interview so that you can review it. From the video review, your instructor or the interviewer may make suggestions to improve your interviewing skills if necessary.

APPLICATION 15-B

Writing a Thank-You Letter

Supplies needed: Plain bond paper.

Write a thank-you letter to the interviewer.

APPLICATION 15-C

Writing a Job Acceptance Letter

Supplies needed: Plain bond paper.

Assume that you have accepted the job from the interview conducted in Application 15-A. Write a job acceptance letter.

APPLICATION 15–D

Completing an Application Form

Supplies needed: Form 15-B, Application for Employment.

 Retrieve file C15-APP.DOC from your student data disk.

Follow your instructor's directions and complete the application form.

APPLICATION 15–E

Writing a Job Refusal Letter

Supplies needed: Plain bond paper.

Assume that you have refused the job from the interview conducted in Application 15-A. Write a job refusal letter.

APPLICATION 15–F

Completing a Job Search Checklist

Supplies needed: Form 15-C, Checklist for Your Job Campaign; a notebook with multiple pockets in which to keep your job-campaign materials.

 Retrieve file C15-CHCK.DOC from your student data disk.

All activities listed in Form 15-C provide guidelines for conducting your own job search. Complete the activities on the checklist, filling in due dates and completion dates.

Your Action Plan

To complete your Action Plan, follow the guidelines outlined in Chapter 1. Set one goal using the information you learned in Chapter 15.

Your Portfolio

With the help of your instructor, select the best papers representative of your work from Chapter 15. Follow your instructor's directions about formatting, assembling, and turning in the portfolio.

Preparing to Meet the Challenges

OUTLINE

Eliminate Stereotypes
Project a Professional Image

Prepare for Advancement
Learn from Your Performance Appraisal
Set Goals
Adapt to Change
Gain More Responsibility
Increase Your Effectiveness
Learn from a Mentor
Advance by Education
Join a Professional Association
Increase Technical Certification
Cross Train

Continue to Develop Professionally
Meet the Requirements of a New Millennium Office Professional
Prepare Yourself for the Role

LEARNING OUTCOMES

When you have completed this chapter, you should be able to:

✔ Describe the professional image of office workers that challenges old stereotypes.

✔ Learn from a mentor.

✔ Research the educational programs and certification offered by professional associations.

✔ Describe the benefits of cross training to both the organization and the employee.

✔ Describe the expectations placed on office professionals in this millennium.

✔ Develop a strategy for professional development.

What does the future hold for you? With the development and application of technology in the office, there is a greater need for professionally trained office professionals such as managers, administrative assistants, information specialists, receptionists, record technicians, and mailroom assistants.

The computer, with the development of new software programs, provides the tool that allows today's office professionals to broaden the scope of their jobs. Today's office professionals must be able to implement the systems needed to process information, for no organization can compete in today's global market without having the information it needs when it needs it. Office professionals will be expected to use technology effectively as well as possess communication and interpersonal skills necessary to be productive members of the team.

Based on employers' employment needs, office professionals should have the following competencies:

- Application software skills
- Communication skills
- Interpersonal skills
- Organization skills
- Decision-making skills
- Records management skills
- Thinking skills
- Creative problem-solving skills

Well-qualified office professionals, competent in these skills, will be in great demand and should find many job opportunities.

An office professional often can take paths that lead to other types of careers, including ones that involve supervision and management. Women and men who initially select a career as an administrative assistant, for example, should mentally prepare themselves for advancement, and for greater challenges and responsibilities.

Office support roles have become broader and more diversified, demanding thorough knowledge of computers and software, as well as strong problem-solving and critical thinking skills. Because this career requires people who have technical expertise as well as excellent human relations skills, it attracts competent people from both genders, various age groups, and diverse backgrounds.

ELIMINATE STEREOTYPES

The attitude that someone is "just a secretary" has no place in the contemporary office. This stereotype developed at a time when women were encouraged to "just get a job." It was perceived that serious positions in the workforce should be held by men because men were to be providers for the family.

This scenario is, of course, no longer accurate or valid. The stereotype of an office worker who typed, filed, took shorthand, did only routine tasks, and was too emotional has been replaced by a new professional image.

Project a Professional Image

A professional image reflects:

- An educated and skilled employee
- A team player who is expected to contribute valuable ideas

- A polished individual whose appearance and communication style are "professional"
- A person who can solve problems and integrate ideas
- A person who takes pride in each piece of work he or she produces
- An employee who works for the betterment of the organization and is not self-serving
- A person who takes pride in his or her career and who has aspirations for the future
- An employee who manages assignments by applying quality standards
- An employee who is willing to work hard and accept new and more challenging responsibilities

The best way to eliminate the stereotypical view is for men and women in this profession to initiate the change themselves. By living up to the new professional image, office workers will replace the old stereotype.

The best way to develop a professional image is to:

1. Set short- and long-term goals that are obtainable
2. Develop desired strategies for achieving these goals
3. Set time lines for each step in the strategies
4. Begin to carry out the steps immediately

PREPARE FOR ADVANCEMENT

Learn from Your Job Performance Appraisal

As soon as you are employed, your goal will shift from getting a job to holding it. The organization that hired you expects you to be a productive worker and to improve as you gain experience on the job.

Organizations have definite policies about evaluating employees' job performance, but the way in which employees are evaluated varies from organization to organization. The procedure for evaluating employees' job performance is called **job performance appraisal.** You can anticipate a job performance appraisal within the first three to six months and at least once a year after that. You may be asked to complete a rating sheet on yourself. Your manager will complete a rating sheet and then discuss it with you.

During the meeting about your performance, you are entitled to ask questions and to discuss your contributions to the organization. At some point during the meeting, your manager may make suggestions for improvement of your job performance. Listen carefully, for you are being given guidelines concerning what is expected of you. You should be aware that in addition to telling you how you are doing, what is expected of you, and ways to improve your job performance, your manager is trying to build mutual confidence and trust.

From the first day on the job, keep notes on your performance, noting particularly how your production has increased and ways in which you are accepting more responsibility. Let your manager know that you have a professional development plan and that you are seeking ways in which to grow. Maintain an impeccable performance record and refer to your notes when you are evaluating your own performance.

When you are comfortably settled in your first job, your initial reaction may be to take it easy. Don't coast. Many opportunities for advancement are available in business, but advancement comes only to those who are prepared to accept additional responsibilities.

Set Goals

If you haven't already set a professional goal for yourself, do so. Do you want to become an executive assistant, a supervisor of office staff, or a manager of office administrative staff for a company? Once you have decided on your goal, study to provide yourself with the background necessary to achieve that goal. Once you achieve that goal, set another one.

To accomplish these goals, you may need support and resources from management. If so, select a person in management on whom you can rely for assistance and with whom you can develop a mentor relationship. To set your goals, keep these steps in mind:

- Write down your goals and look at them frequently.
- List your goals in action terms. Answer the question: What do I need to do?
- Identify your goals in measurable terms. Ask yourself: How will I know that I met this goal?

Adapt to Change

Accept the challenge of change as an opportunity to grow. Identify negative feelings and learn to deal with them by rearranging your priorities and working positively to make adjustments. Keep a positive attitude because it helps you to channel your energies into improving your situation.

Unexpected situations can occur that influence your goals and their achievement. Sometimes situations occur that interfere with your achieving your goals, such as a reorganization of your department. When forces beyond your control interfere with achievement of your goals, make time to reevaluate your plan. Ask yourself: Are your goals realistic? Are your goals appropriate for you? Do your goals need to be changed or even postponed? To handle unexpected situations, you must remain positive and flexible.

Creativity and flexibility are needed in organizations today. Today's organizations require their staffs to "do more with less." This means that effective managers realize that problems often cannot be solved by using the "same old" methods. Today's office workers must have an attitude that allows for recognition and acceptance of new ideas and new ways of solving problems and getting results.

It is a fact that people resist change if they perceive the change, such as new procedures, updated equipment, or a different work schedule, as a threat. Often office workers resist change because management did not effectively communicate the change. Keep in mind that effective communication is the key to introducing change. See Figure 16-1.

When you encounter resistance to change, remember that keeping a positive attitude allows you to be more open to taking steps to improve the situation. Look for opportunities that can come your way as a result of the change.

■ **Figure 16-1**
Effective communication
is the key to introducing
change.

Gain More Responsibility

To be an effective office professional (whatever your job title), you must be clear on what you want out of your position and be willing to make it happen. If you have determined your professional goals, then you are working to make them happen. It is a fact, though, that people need responsibility to be motivated on their jobs. To keep up your enthusiasm, you can be of tremendous help to your manager by taking the initiative to ask for responsibilities that he or she might otherwise have to handle. When asking for additional responsibility, remind your manager of your success in handling a particular project in the past with little or no instruction.

Increase Your Effectiveness

Make your supervisor look good. This means meeting deadlines; being willing to do "extras"; making your work look more professional and polished; and being informed so that your supervisor is never caught off-guard.

- Ask questions to learn the "why" behind what goes on in the daily office routine.

- Ask for frequent feedback on your work; mention special contributions you have made to the team; inform your manager about any courses you are taking or additional training you would like to have.

- Understand, accept, and respect the chain of command in your organization.

- Remain loyal to your own values, your manager, and the organization. It helps your professional image if you do not make negative remarks about either your manager or the organization—its employees, policies, products, or services.

Learn from a Mentor

As you learned in Chapter 15, mentors are people in your profession who are more senior than you. They understand the organization's policies, procedures, politics, and history, and they are willing to share useful advice with more junior members. They help people who are new to the organization or the profession become successful. The mentor relationship often involves a new employee and an office veteran. The new employee may have strong state-of-the-art technical skills, but the veteran knows the organization's culture.

Meetings with mentors and the information they share is confidential because a mentor's advice is intended to show a junior member a shortcut to success. They welcome the questions of a junior staff member and see it is as their responsibility to nurture younger people with potential for success.

People often consider their mentor as the most important person in their professional career. A mentor has to be a person with whom you feel comfortable and who is pleased to answer your questions. The mentor has to consider the advice he or she gives you as confidential. As well, the mentor has to be someone who has the answers to your questions about:

- How the organization works
- How information flows in the office
- With whom to associate
- Whom to avoid in the office
- How to avoid conflict
- How the organization selects people for promotion
- Who holds the power to make decisions
- How to get your ideas noticed and accepted

Advance by Education

A college degree is very useful in advancing to a higher level office position. In fact, any additional education will prove helpful. When you have an efficient and effective performance record, additional education may provide the competitive edge you need to get ahead.

Many organizations offer in-house training. The courses usually are of short duration and do not offer college or university credit. Talk with your supervisor to find out what is available. Express an interest in taking courses that will help you perform your job or advance in your career. When you successfully complete enough courses, they will become an impressive part of your employment record and will support your efforts toward promotion.

Most large organizations have educational benefits. Some organizations will pay all or part of the tuition for job-related courses that are successfully completed. Ask your supervisor about the educational benefits; express your interest in taking job-related courses. Consider courses in these areas:

- Project management
- Team building
- Communication
- Time management

- Business administration
- Software applications
- Organizational behavior
- Office supervision or management

The emphasis in education today is on continuing education. By committing yourself to lifelong learning, you will be increasing your opportunities for promotion and enriching your personal life. Employees who believe and practice continuous education are more likely to survive during periods of company right-sizing and recession. **Right-sizing** is the process of optimizing company resources to achieve efficiency.

As an office assistant, you choose either to have a job or to have a professional career. If you have a strong desire to advance and to earn a reputation for being a professional who contributes to the organization, you will seek ways to achieve professional recognition.

Join a Professional Association

Becoming a member of a professional association is an excellent way of gaining educational skills and new credentials in your field. A number of associations that promote office professionalism are available. The following discussion will identify three associations that offer credentials to office professionals willing to study and take the challenge.

If you are interested in joining or establishing a branch of one of these professional associations in your community, write or call the head office for information.

International Association of Administrative Professionals (IAAP). The **International Association of Administrative Professionals (IAAP)** is an association committed to advancing office professionals by promoting high standards and enhancing the image of the profession. This association provides resources and information to help its members enhance their skills so they may contribute to their organizations in an even more effective manner. Not only does it work to improve the professional skills of its members but it also works to educate the public about the value of the office professional.

The education program of IAAP includes workshops, seminars, and study courses on administrative topics. This proactive organization holds an international conference each year and publishes a popular magazine called *OfficePRO*.

IAAP has a professional certification program where successful candidates earn their **Certified Professional Secretary (CPS)** or their more advanced **Certified Administrative Professional (CAP)** rating.

The CPS rating requires successful completion of a one-day exam covering the following areas:

- Finance and business law
- Office systems and administration
- Management

The CAP rating is achieved after successful completion of the CPS exams plus an additional exam in

■ Organization planning

For more information about the IAAP and the CPS and CAP certifications, visit the Web site at http://www.iaap.hq.org.

National Association of Legal Secretaries (NALS). The **National Association of Legal Secretaries (NALS)** is a professional association that provides a testing program and professional certification for administrative assistants. Part of its mandate is to offer continuing legal-education training programs and networking for its members. Office professionals who wish to demonstrate their commitment and aptitude for the legal secretarial profession are encouraged to take the examination leading to the **Accredited Legal Secretary (ALS)** or **Professional Legal Secretary (PLS)** certificates.

Those who attain the ALS are awarded certification. Testing for the ALS certification covers the following topics:

■ Written communication
■ Office procedures and legal knowledge
■ Ethics, human relations, and judgment

NALS also offers an advanced certification for legal professionals. This certification is called the Professional Legal Secretary. The PLS is a designation for lawyers' assistants who want to be identified as exceptional. This one-day, four-part exam includes questions on:

■ Written communication
■ Office procedures and technology
■ Ethics and judgment
■ Legal knowledge and skills

Those applicants who are successful in the examination will earn the PLS certification.

If you require more information, contact NALS through its Web site at http://www.nals.org.

Increase Technical Certification

Technical skills are some of the most highly valued skills of office professionals. By continuing to upgrade technical skills, office professionals can improve their resumes and increase their opportunities for employment and advancement. To validate technical skills, office professionals should earn certification from recognized programs. One of the most recognized technical certifications is the **Microsoft Office Specialist (MOS)** program.

The MOS certification is available at three levels: Core, Expert, and Master. Candidates begin by selecting the Microsoft Office product for which they want certification and the appropriate level of expertise. If they require training before taking an exam, candidates can find training providers, including Microsoft Office Specialist Approved courseware at http://www.microsoft.com/mous.

Cross Train

Cross training involves learning and performing the responsibilities of your coworkers. It is very valuable to the organization. When one employee is absent from work, other employees can simply fill in. However, it has even greater benefits to the person who has the initiative to learn how to perform other people's jobs. The more you know and the more you can do, the more valuable to the organization you will be.

The office assistant who is preparing for advancement, or who just wants to protect the security of his or her current job, should learn as many skills and gather as much information as possible.

Cross training gives the office professional the opportunity to:

- Take on new technical and communication challenges
- Learn more about the organization and the flow of work
- Get more exposure by working with new people
- Get acknowledgment from management

Cross-trained employees are more challenged, more knowledgeable, more interesting, and generally are happier.

CONTINUE TO DEVELOP PROFESSION- ALLY

As you read this chapter, you may conclude that preparation for a successful career is endless. Your conclusion is right.

Continue to increase both your general knowledge of office procedures and your special skills. The ability to relate well to customers, clients, and coworkers is essential. See Figure 16-2. A working knowledge of computer

■ **Figure 16-2**
The ability to relate to clients and coworkers is essential for professional growth.

software—for word processing, spreadsheets, project management, graphics, desktop publishing, electronic messaging and calendaring, database management, and so on—is essential. Computer technology and software are changing at a rapid pace. Develop an affinity for new equipment and learn the new applications.

To advance in your career, you need a broad, general education. An understanding of how to deal with all types of people and business and management concepts is a valuable asset. Organizations are looking for employees who are critical thinkers and problem solvers.

If you wish to advance professionally, make decisions and carry them out. Then take responsibility for both your successes and your failures. Procrastination and the inability to make decisions will be viewed as weaknesses and will prevent opportunities for promotion.

Meet the Requirements of a New Millennium Office Professional

To plan for your future professional development, you should understand what the new millennium office requires. Professionals in the office of the new millennium will:

- Supervise people in nontraditional work styles that include flexible working hours in flexible locations
- Use the most current office technology and high-tech communication
- Rely almost exclusively on the office network and the Internet to access and manage information
- Make greater productivity their primary focus
- Work effectively with people from diverse age groups and cultural and religious backgrounds

Involvement in professional organizations and lifelong education are the keys to keeping current and continuing to develop professionally.

Prepare Yourself for the Role

To begin your path of professional development, you should:

- Subscribe to and read professional magazines
- Listen to motivational or informational tapes while you drive to work
- Read office bulletins and newsletters to remain up-to-date on corporate affairs
- Attend seminars, conventions, conferences, and workshops to keep abreast of new technology and procedures
- Volunteer to be a committee member or chairperson for special events
- Apply or offer to work on special task forces
- Request that you be placed on the office circulation list for all information and professional materials
- Make a point of meeting new people and listening to their ideas

quicktips

Why is There an Administrative Professionals Week? Should There Be One? Here Are Some Facts That Will Help You Answer These Questions

- Administrative Professionals Week is observed internationally every year in April.
- The International Association of Administrative Professionals (IAAP) is the sole official sponsor of Administrative Professionals Week.
- The observance of this week is designed to educate the public, especially business leaders, about the critical contribution made by office administrators and the need for continuous upgrading and education in this profession.
- Common forms of recognition during this week are gifts, time off, flowers, and complimentary lunches.
- Many administrative professionals report that being sponsored for a professional seminar or course or receiving a subscription to a professional magazine is the recognition they most prefer.

- Read the newspaper to follow local and international events
- Travel to as many locations as possible
- Visit libraries and make note of the many resources available to you
- Make appoints with the corporate competition to learn more about other companies
- Become aware of your company's policies
- Make a point of watching documentaries on television and reading or studying new topics
- Make learning a lifelong commitment

Professional growth is stimulating. It has a motivating effect, and your reward will be a successful and enjoyable career.

Overview

✔ Employers are seeking the following important competencies: application software skills, such as word processing and spreadsheet; oral and written communication skills; interpersonal skills; organization skills; decision-making skills; records management skills; thinking skills; and creative problem-solving skills.

✔ The stereotype of an office worker who typed, filed, took shorthand, did only routine tasks, and was too emotional has been replaced by a new professional image.

✔ Preparing for advancement includes learning from your performance appraisal, setting goals, adapting to change, gaining more responsibility, increasing your effectiveness, learning from a mentor, advancing by education, joining a professional association, increasing technical certification, and cross training.

✔ Continue to develop professionally by preparing for the millennium office and developing a career path.

Key Terms

Accredited Legal Secretary (ALS). Professional certification rating achieved by successfully completing tests on written communication; office procedures and legal knowledge; and ethics, human relations, and judgment.

Certified Administrative Professional (CAP). Professional certification rating achieved after successful completion of CPS exams plus an exam in organization planning.

Certified Professional Secretary (CPS). Professional certification rating achieved by completing a one-day exam covering finance and business law, office systems and administration, and management.

Cross training. Involves learning and performing the responsibilities of coworkers.

International Association of Administrative Professionals (IAAP). An association committed to advancing office professionals by promoting high standards and enhancing the image of the profession.

Job performance appraisal. The process for evaluating employees' job performance.

Microsoft Office Specialist (MOS). Earning this technical certification documents that an employee knows how to use Microsoft Office applications efficiently and productively. The employee must pass one or more certification exams, available at three levels: Core, Expert, and Master.

National Association of Legal Secretaries (NALS). A professional association that provides a testing program and professional certification for administrative assistants.

Professional Legal Secretary (PLS). Advanced certification earned by successfully completing a one-day, four-part exam on written communication; office procedures and technology; ethics and judgment; and legal knowledge and skills.

For Your Discussion

 Retrieve file C16-DQ.DOC from your student data disk.

Directions

Enter your response after each question.

1. Identify six qualities that help to make a professional image.
2. List steps to follow when setting goals.

3. Discuss the steps to take when handling change.

4. Explain the purpose of having a mentor.

5. Name two associations that provide professional certification for administrative assistants. What are the certifications they award?

6. What is required for an office professional to gain Microsoft certification? How can this certification be useful to the office professional?

7. Explain the meaning of *cross training*.

8. Describe the advantages to the employee of cross training. Describe the advantages to the organization.

9. Identify the expectations that have already and will continue to be placed on the office professional in this new millennium.

10. Suggest ten ways to grow professionally once you are already employed.

GRAMMAR WORKSHOP

Taking time to review grammar principles or rules will help you gain confidence in communicating clearly. The ability to use correct grammar is essential for an office assistant's success.

For Review

Appendix A: Rule 21: Make Modifiers Clear

Rule 22: Use Adjectives and Adverbs Correctly

 Retrieve file C16-WRKS.DOC from your student data disk.

Directions

Write C to the left of the sentences if the grammar is correct. Otherwise, make the necessary corrections.

Rule 21: Make Modifiers Clear

1. Jason drew a design for his supervisor on the board.
2. Working hard last weekend, the computer program was completed.
3. Being busy, I helped Grady to finish the project.
4. Mary found Jane in the drawer with all of her files.
5. Since his logic is faulty, Ted helped Gordon find the solutions.

Select the correct word in parentheses by underlining it.

Rule 22: Use Adjectives and Adverbs Correctly

1. She played the piano (beautiful, beautifully).
2. They did such a terrific job on the proposal that they were commended for doing (good, well).
3. They were told to move very (quick, quickly) when the portable walls were moved.
4. His supervisor felt (bad, badly) that there were no merit increases.
5. You will need a (considerable, considerably) larger supply of ribbons and diskettes.

On the Job Situations

 Retrieve file C16-OJS.DOC from your student data disk.

Directions

Enter your response after each situation.

1. You have just been promoted to a supervisory position in the purchasing department. For the past three years, you have been employed in that department as an administrative secretary, and you have realized that several of the office procedures need to be changed. In preparation for making a major change in an office procedure that will affect others in your department, determine at least five questions that you should answer that will help you implement change effectively.

2. You are sitting at break time with two of your peers, Shannon, personnel assistant from Human Resources, and Phoung from Accounting, discussing obstacles and opportunities in different career options. Shannon and Phoung have just graduated from the local community college with associate degrees. You ask Shannon and Phoung to respond to the following question: "As a secretary, how important is it for me to have a college degree?" If you were asked this question, how would you respond?

3. On a number of occasions, Kim has complimented you on your successful startup with the company because you have been very thorough, positive, and professional in your area of responsibility. Kim feels that she is not "going anywhere" in her current position in data entry. She feels that she doesn't have any direction; she appears very dissatisfied with her job, but she would like to continue in the computer field. She has asked you, "How do you meet the challenge of the position?" In other words, how do you do it? What do you tell her?

4. For several years your company has used a particular word processing software package, and you have been the support person and trainer for the company employees. Now your department has shared with you that the company will be changing to another word processing software package in eight to ten months. Your company expects everyone to switch to this new software and become effective users in it as soon as possible. Most all employees are grumbling about having to learn another software package. You were told that your number one goal is to become an expert in the software and be able to provide training and support during and after this changeover. List some training methods that you feel will help you learn this new software. List ways your training and support can project a positive attitude toward this new software.

Projects and Activities

1. Interview two office assistants, word processing specialists, or other office professionals, each from a different organization. Consider the following questions:
   a. Do they wish to be promoted in the organization? If so, ask them into what position?
   b. Does the position require any additional training, experience, or college courses? If so, identify the requirements.

    c. Be prepared to share your findings with the class.

    d. Prepare your notes to turn in to your instructor.

2. Identify one goal that you want to reach one year from now.

    a. List the steps to be taken within three months, six months, nine months, and twelve months to accomplish this goal.

    b. Turn in your plan to your instructor.

3. Describe an example of a major change in your professional or personal life. Answer the following questions.

    a. Who initiated the change?

    b. How was the change communicated to you?

    c. How did you feel about the change?

    d. How do you feel about the change now?

    e. How did the change affect you?

    f. What opportunities did you seize as a result of the change? If there were none, why do you think you did not take advantage of the change itself or the results of the change?

4. Determine the position titles, responsibilities, and skills that are specific in the legal or medical career paths. Be prepared to share your findings with the class; turn in your written results to your instructor.

Surfing the Internet

One of the office assistants in your office has asked you to help her locate information on the following topics:

- Cross training
- Qualities of a great mentor.

You know information about these topics is available on the Internet.

1. Connect to the Internet and access a search tool such as Yahoo! or Lycos.
2. Enter the following key search words: *cross-training techniques* (or *tips*) and *mentoring techniques* (or *tips*).
3. Write a summary of the information in memo form of the information regarding these two topics. Be prepared to share the results with other class members and your instructor.

Using MS Office 2002

Learn How to Get Microsoft Office Specialist Certified

   You can get certified in any or all of Microsoft products: Access, Excel, Outlook, PowerPoint and Word. Visit the Web site http://www.microsoft.com.

1. Select the MS Office application you want information on.
2. View and print the topic information covered in the test.

3. While at the Web site, search for certified testing centers located in your area.

4. While at the Web site, view information on ordering learning materials. Microsoft sells a CD that gives hands-on experience and results similar to the test.

5. Once you learn the topics that will be covered on the test or you order training materials, practice, practice, practice, and practice some more!

6. When ready for the exam, call the certified training site and schedule a test. These tests are timed, usually 45 minutes.

7. Immediate feedback is provided after the test, indicating if you passed or failed. Regardless of whether you pass or fail, you will get a printout showing how you scored in each area. If you passed, Microsoft will mail a certificate to you.

You decide the level of certification:

- MOS Master Certificate (requires all five applications)
    - ✔ Word Expert
    - ✔ Excel Expert
    - ✔ PowerPoint
    - ✔ Outlook
    - ✔ Access
- MOUS Core Certificate (requires core level only)
    - ✔ Word Core
    - ✔ Excel Core
- Application Certificate (you choose which level for the application)
    - ✔ Any one application

APPLICATION PROBLEMS

APPLICATION 16-A

Earning MOS Certification

Supplies needed: Access to the Internet; plain bond paper.

You have been asked to research the Word and Excel MOS certification program offered by Microsoft Corporation. The results of your research regarding the certification program should include benefits, requirements, and exam preparation. Prepare your information in memo format; be prepared to share the information with other class members and your instructor.

APPLICATION 16-B

Developing a Strategy for Your Professional Development

Supplies needed: Plain bond paper.

Develop a strategy for your own professional development. To do so, design an electronic spreadsheet or use word processing that will capture the following information:

- State your immediate career goal.
- State your career goal for the end of a five-year period.
- Identify the gap between the two goals in terms of the experience, training, certification, human relations skills, and supervision/management skills needed.
- For each of the factors in the gap, describe your plan of how you will achieve the necessary skills to close the gap.

Action Plan

Complete your Action Plan; if necessary, refer to the guidelines in Chapter 1.

1. Set one goal using the information you learned in Chapter 16.
2. Follow your instructor's directions for formatting, assembling, and turning in your Action Plan.

Your Portfolio

With the help of your instructor, select the best papers representative of your work from Chapter 16. Follow your instructor's directions about formatting, assembling, and turning in the portfolio.

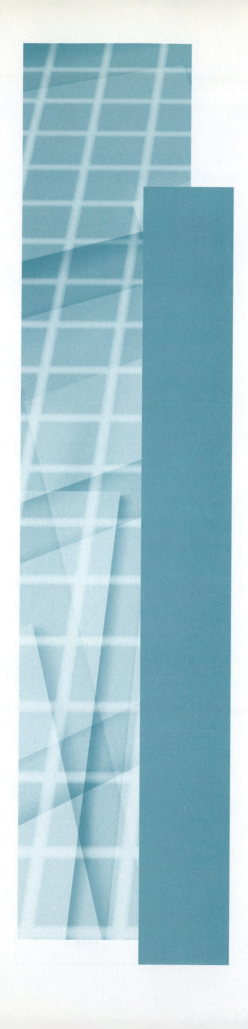

Working Papers

SKILLS EVALUATION CHECKLIST

Directions

In order to be successful, you must have a good understanding of your skills. Rate yourself using the following self-evaluation checklist. Place a check mark in the appropriate box using the following rating system:

	Ready	Need Some Review	Need Complete Update
TECHNICAL SKILLS	3	2	1
1. Organizational skills	_____	_____	_____
2. Time management skills	_____	_____	_____
3. Work attitude	_____	_____	_____
4. Setting priorities	_____	_____	_____
5. Word processing software	_____	_____	_____
6. Spreadsheet software	_____	_____	_____
7. Database software	_____	_____	_____
8. Presentation software	_____	_____	_____
9. Sending/receiving e-mail	_____	_____	_____
10. Electronic calendar	_____	_____	_____
11. Desktop publishing	_____	_____	_____
12. Voice mail procedures	_____	_____	_____
13. Web page design	_____	_____	_____
14. Telephone skills	_____	_____	_____
INTERPERSONAL SKILLS	3	2	1
15. Customer services	_____	_____	_____
16. Dealing with difficult people	_____	_____	_____
17. Dealing with stress	_____	_____	_____
18. Accepting positive criticism	_____	_____	_____
19. Patience	_____	_____	_____
20. Listening	_____	_____	_____
21. Loyalty	_____	_____	_____
22. Ethics	_____	_____	_____
23. Honesty	_____	_____	_____
24. Trustworthiness	_____	_____	_____
25. Other:	_____	_____	_____
_____	_____	_____	_____
_____	_____	_____	_____
_____	_____	_____	_____

Name _____   Date _____

FORM 1-A

ACTION PLAN

Chapter: _____   Name: _____

Specific Goal: (Stated below)

"When I go to work today, I am going to locate a copy of our organizational chart, determine if it is a line or a line-and-staff type chart by following the chapter information, and make a copy of it to give to my instructor. I will do this before I leave by 5 p.m., Friday, October 30, to give to my instructor on Monday, November 1."

Measurable: I can measure each item by trial or observation.

Results at end of time limit:

Organizational chart:	I located one copy of the chart.
Line organization:	I compared the chart with the text information—no, we do not have a line organization where authority flows up and down only through the organization.
Line-and-staff organization:	Yes, we have a line-and-staff organization. The Assistant Director reports only to the Director. The Assistant Director has no one reporting to him.

Attainable: With only two items to check, the goal should be easily attainable by November 1.

Results at end of time limit:

With only two items to check, the goal was easily attainable by November 1.

Time-limited: The entire evaluation process should take no more than 30 minutes of my time.

Results at end of time limit:

I completed my evaluation and copying within 20 minutes. I turned in the copy to my instructor on November 1.

How did I or will I benefit from this experience?

Results at end of time limit:

I feel I am more knowledgeable about my company. I have a chart, which I can refer to if needed. Because no names were given, I have written in each person's name beside the title and will keep it current for my reference.

FORM 1-B

ACTION PLAN

Chapter:		Name:	

Specific Goal: (Stated below)

Measurable:

Results at end of time limit:	

Attainable:

Results at end of time limit:

Time-limited:

Results at end of time limit:

How did I or will I benefit from this experience?

Results at end of time limit:

DIVERSITY SELF-ASSESSMENT

Are you knowledgeable and understanding of diversity in your workplace? The following assessment will help you determine your strengths, as well as areas where you need improvement, as we begin our Diversity in the Workplace Workshop.

Directions
Place a check mark in the blank that best describes how you agree or disagree. Save the file.

	Agree	Somewhat Agree	Do Not Agree
1. I believe I understand cultural diversity.	_____	_____	_____
2. I communicate effectively with friends and coworkers from different backgrounds.	_____	_____	_____
3. I work well or think I would work well in diverse teams.	_____	_____	_____
4. I am familiar with other cultures' backgrounds and traditions.	_____	_____	_____
5. I avoid stereotyping other people.	_____	_____	_____
6. I can list all the areas of diversity in the workplace.	_____	_____	_____
7. I understand the role of gender in the workplace.	_____	_____	_____
8. I avoid all references in my language that could be interpreted as offensive to others.	_____	_____	_____

Name _____ Date _____

FORM 2-A

SELF-ASSESSMENT INVENTORY

Directions

Enter an **S** (strong), an **A** (average), or an **I** (needs improvement) in the Assessment column.

Skill	Assessment
1. I am creative in solving problems.	_____
2. I am able to communicate effectively.	_____
3. I know how to use computer software applications.	_____
4. I work as a team member.	_____
5. I am willing to accept change.	_____
6. I take responsibility for my business and personal life.	_____
7. I am committed to quality and excellence.	_____
8. I have a desire for continued learning and growth.	_____
9. I don't mind taking the initiative to get something done.	_____
10. I am able to manage time and other resources effectively.	_____

Name _____   Date _____

FORM 2-B

DAILY PLAN CHART

Date _____

Rank	Calls to	Phone No.	Notes	Rank	Reminders

Rank	Letters and Memos to	Notes	Rank	Other Tasks

Priority Rank: 1, urgent; 2, today; 3, as soon as time allows

FORM 3-A

Evaluation Form

Directions

Use the following evaluation to rate your work and time management by marking

A (always)　　*S* (sometimes)　　*N* (never)

following each question. Save the file.

1. Do I complete tasks as efficiently as possible?

2. Do I divide large projects into manageable segments of work?

3. Do I group related tasks to reduce the time consumed in changing from one unrelated task to another?

4. Do I match the work to the time frames in which it must be performed?

5. Do I get organized before I begin an assignment?

6. Do I control my attitudes and emotions that have a tendency to steal time?

7. Do I prioritize my work into categories?

8. Do I know how much time it takes to complete a task?

9. Do I know if the task to be completed is a priority of my immediate supervisor?

10. Do I maintain a to-do list?

Give yourself the following points for your responses:

    2 points = Always
    1 point = Sometimes
    0 point = Never

If you scored 20 points, you are a star manager of your work and time! If you scored 18 points or higher, you are above average in managing your work and time. If you scored 15 points or less, you need to improve in your management skills. If you scored 10 points or higher, you will not be recognized as being either effective or efficient.

Name _____　Date _____

FORM 3-B

STRESS ASSESSMENT QUESTIONNAIRE

Directions
Following the instructions given in the memo shown in Application 3-C, read and then rate the items below. Save the file.

Stress is a necessary part of living. When you get up in the morning, there may be a lack of time to do all the things you want to do. As you travel to work, you may experience additional stress. As you cope with a wide range of demands in your work environment, you experience additional stress. At times it seems that virtually everything causes stress!

Stress is not entirely bad; it can provide stimulation. Think about those stressful events that can be relaxing and exhilarating, such as taking a vacation or getting a new job. However, prolonged emotional and "wear-and-tear" experiences can lead to distress or anxiety. People must have opportunities to restore the emotional and physical resources that it takes to cope with stressful situations.

An accumulation of a variety of stresses can lead to nervousness, irritability, and fatigue, which, in turn, can affect your work, home, and personal life. The accumulation of stress on the job decreases worker motivation, quality of relationships, concentration and attention span, participation, general attitude, and enthusiasm. How intense is the stress in your life?

In Parts A and B, rate the following items from 1 (representing no discomfort) to 5 (representing extreme discomfort).

Part A: Primary Concerns

1. Financial problems	_____	6. Fear of failing	_____
2. Lack of time	_____	7. Dull, boring life	_____
3. Deadlines	_____	8. Social obligations	_____
4. Your health	_____	9. Coping with family relationships	_____
5. Imbalance in major areas of your personal life (career, spiritual)	_____	10. Other	_____

Part B: Symptoms

1. Need for more sleep	_____	6. Mood swings	_____
2. Headache	_____	7. Always rushed	_____
3. Feeling of exhaustion	_____	8. Shaky feeling	_____
4. Forgetfulness	_____	9. Digestive distress	_____
5. Impatience	_____	10. Other	_____

Part C: Summary

1. List the three concerns that cause you the most discomfort.
   a. _____
   b. _____
   c. _____

2. List the three symptoms that cause you the highest discomfort.
   a. _____
   b. _____
   c. _____

3. List three things you intend to do to relieve the stress.
   a. _____
   b. _____
   c. _____

Name _____   Date _____

FORM 3-C

TO DO LIST

TO DO LIST

FORM 3-D

SUPERVISION ← *Bold*

As a supervisor, you must rely on others to accomplish your goals. To perform the human relations aspects of a supervisory job smoothly, *you should* develop an awareness of basic principles of supervision and become skilled in applying them.

Recruiting Employees

You should share with your ~~boss~~ *manager* and the ~~personnel~~ *human resources* department in the selection of a new employee whom you will supervise. However, your responsibilities may range from very little responsibility to a major role.

When you are recruit*i*ng an employee, begin with an up-to-date description of the ~~job~~ *position* to be filled. List the duties to be performed and the qualifications *needed to perform the job*. Rank the qualifications in the order of importance ~~for the job.~~ Consider the applicant's potential for promotion within the organization, for an objective of every organization is promotion from within.

Use the list during the interview. Learn how to conduct job interviews. Consult references on personnel management for techniques to apply. ~~Interview more than one application for each job.~~

stet In making the final selection, use all the criteria available concerning each applicant. After you have narrowed the selection to ~~two or~~ three prospects, discuss them with your ~~boss. Solicit~~ *manager. Ask for* his or her questions and comments.

Spend ample time in making the selection. By making the right selection, you can add to the organization's ~~payroll~~ a productive worker who enjoys his or her job. The wrong selection can result in work problems or personnel problems or both and may eventually lead to ~~firing the employee.~~ *termination*

Orientating the Employee

How an employee is treated is an important factor in morale building in any office. Allow time on your schedule for helping the new employee *to* adjust to his or her job.

FORM 4-A

Greet the new employee in a friendly way and introduce him or her to the *other* employees

in the office.

Tour the office building, pointing out the restroom or lounge, break area, cafeteria, and

building entrances. If the new employee drives a car and parking facilities are provided,

show the location where arrangements *are made* for parking.

Even though the ~~personnel~~ *human resources* department explained ~~his or her~~ *the employee's* working hours, discuss

what time to report to work, the length of the breaks, and the time and length of lunch.

Arrange for the new employee to go to lunch with others for the first few days. If your

organization does not have a ~~personnel department~~ *human resources department*, brief the new employee on all the

personnel policies yourself.

Give an overview of the ~~job~~ *position* and assure the new employee that he or she will work into

the job gradually. *Explain the probationary period, its length, and what will occur after the period is over.*

Explain how to use the organization's telephone directory, pointing out names the new

employee will need to know. Usually the names of executives *or* managers and ~~of~~ *their* departments

are located in one section of the organization's directory.

As you talk, allow time for the new employee to ask questions and to make comments.

For the first day, choose work at which the new employee can be successful and keep busy.

Be considerate and convey the impression that you are considerate.

Training

One of ~~the~~ *your* main functions will be training the new employee to perform the job with a

minimum of supervision. Start with a part of the job which will be fairly easy for the new

employee to perform and then gradually guide him or her into the total job. ~~Find out~~ *Determine* what

the new employee ~~she~~ already knows about the type of work ~~she will~~ *to be* perform*ed*.

Put the employee on his or her own as soon as you can. Check frequently, but do not

oversupervise. Let the new employee know you are willing to answer questions.

Assigning Workloads

You can pave the way for an employee to experience a feeling of accomplishment by dividing work into batches and giving the employee one batch at a time, perhaps an assignment ~~which~~ *that* can be finished in two hours. Setting ~~subgoals~~ *short goals* for the *new* employees you supervise will be an important part of your work.

Check the finished work at the time it is submitted to you to assure the employee that it is satisfactory and to spot errors which must be corrected.

Give a new employee some repetitive tasks so he or she can work successfully for a period of time without asking for help. However, rotate the work to provide enough variety to keep the employee from becoming bored or experiencing unnecessary fatigue.

Workers experience the greatest job satisfaction from performing ~~the~~ *a* complete ~~job.~~ *assignment.* Therefore, look for ways to change a new employee's assignment from performing a segment of a ~~job~~ *project* to that of beginning a project and following it through to completion.

Gaining Cooperation and Respect

One way to gain the cooperation of employees is to be cooperative yourself. Cooperation and respect ~~are~~ *must be* earned. To be successful as a supervisor, you must earn the respect of those whom you supervise.

Two major factors in gaining cooperation and respect are how the supervisor plans, organizes, and schedules work and the supervisor's attitude toward the employees. Some supervisors create problems that need not exist because their performance as a supervisor is inadequate.

A supervisor's attitude toward the employees should reflect respect for them, a recognition of their needs, and a sincere appreciation of their contribution to the objectives of the organization. A successful supervisor will request that work be done. There is no need to destroy morale by demanding or controlling with fear. However, a successful supervisor must be impartial, and this requires being firm and consistent. Rules and regulations must be followed by everyone.

FORM 4-A

Handling Personnel ~~Problems~~ *Situations*

Personnel problems will arise, and each one must be studied carefully and handled as a specific case. Be careful not to show favoritism. You can keep down resentment by being absolutely impartial.

Before you take action on any ~~problem,~~ *situation,* get the facts and look for the ~~problem~~ *source* behind the immediate problem; for instance, an employee's absenteeism may be due to lack of interest in the job.

A new supervisor can take problems too seriously. Do not be overly concerned about problems. Do not spend your time on a ~~problem~~ *situation* that will correct itself, yet face up to the problems you must handle. A subtle approach may be the best means of tackling certain problems; for example, you can set short-range goals for a worker who lacks perseverance rather than discussing the problem.

<u>Advising on Personnel Problems</u>

Employees who respect you and look to you for leadership on the job may seek your advice concerning personal problems. Do not encourage employees to bring their personal problems to you, but when someone does, listen. Serious personal problems do ~~e~~*a*ffect a person's job performance. Knowing an employee's ~~problem~~ *situation* will enable you to be sympathetic and understanding.

Do not give advice on personal problems. Listen while an employee talks ~~out~~ *about* his or her problem and help the employee to see what his or her choices are and the consequences related to each choice.

Be extremely cautious in dealing with personal problems. Proceed so cautiously that an employee who makes the wrong decision cannot and would not blame you for poor advice. A person who has serious difficulties frequently tries to place blame.

FORM 4-A

532

Making Blind-Copy Notations

When you send a copy of a letter or memorandum to one or more persons without the knowledge of the addressee, make a notation on the copy but not on the original. This is known as a _blind copy_ _(bc)_. You need a notation on the file copy concerning who received copies. A recipient should be aware that he or she has received a blind copy.

To type the notation, use _bc_ (blind copy) followed by the names of the recipients of the blind copies, thus:

bc: Agnes Wheeler
    John Bledsoe

Here is a common method for placing the _bc_ notation on the page:

1. Key the _bc_ notation on the second line below the last item in the document (whether reference initials, an enclosure notation, or a copy notation).

2. The form of the _bc_ notation should follow that of the copy notation. If you have used _c_ or _cc_, then use _bc_ or _bcc_ accordingly.

3. Remember to add the _bc_ notation to your file copy so that you will have a record of the notation and the name of the recipient(s) receiving the correspondence with the _bc_ notation.

FORM 5-A

SA Supreme Appliances, Inc.

TO: Amanda Quevedo   DATE: October 10, 20–

FROM: (Your name)
        Resevrations for Seminar

SUBJECT:

Reservations have been con firmed at the Splendid Hotel for a meeting room and a luncheon for Friday Nov. 16, from nine until five o'clock. for the seminar on "Supervising Employees".

The meeting room, called the Rose Garden, will seat 125 people. The room is well lighted, beautifully Decorated, and faces the rose garden. The chairs are comforable.

While I was at the splendid hotel, I asked about parking space and i talked with the banquet mgr. about a luncheon menu. Parking space isadequate. Mr. Lawrence, the banquet manager, gave me a choice of menus. the ist of choices available is atttached. Do you have a preference? We must give a firm com mitment on the number who will attend the luncheom by ten oclock the day of the luncheon.

14 Shady Lane, Rochester, NY 14623

FORM 5-B

LETTER COPY

1. Mr. Raymond Jones, Plant Manager, Southwestern Manufacturing Plant, Supreme Appliances, Inc., 2600 W. Vickery Boulevard, Fort Worth, TX 76102-7105. Dear Raymond: The demand for freezers is so great this season that we are offering the 20-cubic-foot freezer for only $50 more than the 16-cubic-foot freezer. (P)* As you are aware, our supply of 16-cubic-foot freezers is almost exhausted. Many more have been sold since our conversation yesterday. The demand for the 20-cubic-foot freezer will increase rapidly. (P) This letter is your authorization to ship thirty 20-cubic-foot freezers to each of our four regional sales offices immediately. Sincerely yours, Amanda Quevedo, Vice President, Marketing cc Mr. John Reddin (Mr. Reddin's address is Mr. John Reddin, Manager, Sales Office, Southwestern Region, 1508 Commerce Street, Dallas, TX 75201-4904.)

2. Mr. Kyle Rhodes, Manager, Sales Office, Supreme Appliances, Inc., 1400 Lincoln Street, Denver, CO 80203-1523. Dear Mr. Rhodes: At Thursday's meeting of the Executive Committee of the National Sales Association, we selected the speakers we hope will accept our invitation to participate in our annual sales conference from March 16 to March 20 in Chicago. (P) Several of the council members said that they heard you speak last year at the Western Division of Administrative Managers and recommended that you be invited to give the keynote address at the spring conference of the National Sales Association on Tuesday, March 16, at 10:30 a.m. in the Luxury Hotel, Chicago. Your expenses will be paid, and you will receive an honorarium. (P) Will you accept our invitation to be the keynote speaker? Sincerely, Amanda Quevedo, Program Chairperson.

3. To: Michael Carter From: Amanda Quevedo Subject: National Sales Association Meeting, March 16–20. Plans for the March conference of the National Sales Association are complete, and we can look forward to a motivating and challenging conference. (P) Thank you for meeting as a group and evaluating the ideas for the conference. You contributed many ideas that were incorporated into the program. (P) I am looking forward to the week of March 16–20 in Chicago. I will see you there. Send copies to: J. R. Rush, Thomas Strickland, Sid Levine, and Karen Baxter. (Refer to Application Problems, Chapter 1, for addresses.)

*(P) means make a new paragraph.

FORM 5-C-1

SA Supreme Appliances, Inc.

14 Shady Lane, Rochester, NY 14623

SA Supreme Appliances, Inc.

14 Shady Lane, Rochester, NY 14623

FORM 5-C-3

SA Supreme Appliances, Inc.

14 Shady Lane, Rochester, NY 14623

FORM 5-C-4

538

Notes on Incoming Mail for Monday, July 14

1. The August issue of *Sales and Marketing Management*.

2. A personal letter for Karen Baxter.

3. A complaint from a customer in the Southwestern Region. The copper tone of the new dishwasher she had installed does not match her other copper-tone appliances.

4. A letter to A. Quevedo asking her to speak at the International Conference of the Society of Administrative Management.

5. A letter from Microwave Ovens, Inc. saying that the catalog A. Quevedo has requested is out of print and will be mailed as soon as it is off the press.

6. The July issue of *Internet World*.

7. A memorandum from the Human Resources Department on new personnel policies for Supreme Appliances, Inc.

8. A letter from the Sales office in Portland, Oregon, saying that the demand for appliances in harvest gold is twice as great as that for appliances in other colors. What can be done to increase the shipments of harvest gold appliances?

9. The August issue of *Administrative Management*.

10. A letter from a customer in Denver complaining that the surface on the hood installed with her new electric range is peeling. Will Supreme Appliances replace the hood?

11. A sales letter from Microwave Ovens, Inc. on the new features of its latest microwave oven.

12. A letter from the manager of the Western Manufacturing Plant offering suggestions for speeding up delivery of appliances after they are manufactured.

13. A letter from the sales office in Boston saying that the demand for appliances in harvest gold is twice as great as that for appliances in other colors. Send more harvest gold appliances.

14. A letter from the Southwestern Manufacturing Plant saying that the parts ordered are not available and will have to be manufactured.

15. A letter from Maybelle Anderson giving the title of her talk for the November Sales Seminar.

16. A complaint from a customer in the Eastern Region. She is dissatisfied with her electric range, which is only two years old, because the element in the oven burned out. Will Supreme Appliances replace the element?

17. A request from the executive vice president asking for a comparative sales report for the past five years.

18. An expiration notice for Administrative Management.

19. A letter from the local chamber of commerce asking A. Quevedo to serve as chairperson of the Community Development Committee.

20. A letter from Jack Winfield canceling the appointment he has with A. Quevedo on Friday, August 22.

FORM 6-A-1

DAILY MAIL RECORD

Date	Description	To Whom Sent	Action to Be Taken	Follow-up

Name _____ Date _____

FORM 6-A-2

540

TO-DO LIST

TO-DO LIST

Name _____   Date _____

ROUTING FORMS

Date _____			
Routing Sequence	**Person**	**Date**	**Initial**
	K. Baxter		
	S. Levine		
	J. Ross		
	T. Strickland		
	Return to A. Quevedo		

FORM 6-A-4

Date _____			
Routing Sequence	**Person**	**Date**	**Initial**
	K. Baxter		
	S. Levine		
	J. Ross		
	T. Strickland		
	Return to A. Quevedo		

FORM 6-A-5

Date _____			
Routing Sequence	**Person**	**Date**	**Initial**
	K. Baxter		
	S. Levine		
	J. Ross		
	T. Strickland		
	Return to A. Quevedo		

FORM 6-A-6

Date _____			
Routing Sequence	**Person**	**Date**	**Initial**
	K. Baxter		
	S. Levine		
	J. Ross		
	T. Strickland		
	Return to A. Quevedo		

FORM 6-A-7

Name _____ **Date** _____

LIST OF OUTGOING MAIL

Item	Class of Mail
1. Typewritten checks	_____
2. Handwritten letter	_____
3. Keys	_____
4. Package weighing 3 pounds	_____
5. Business reply cards	_____
6. Photocopy of a letter	_____
7. Bills and statements	_____
8. Plants	_____
9. Photocopy of a letter	_____
10. Regularly issued periodicals	_____
11. Catalog with twenty-six bound pages	_____
12. A film sent to a school	_____
13. Typewritten letter	_____
14. Magazines sent at transient rate	_____
15. Material sealed against postal inspection	_____

FORM 6-B

MAIL OPERATIONS—Field Trip Activity

Location _____

Date _____

Contact Person _____

Title _____

Incoming Mail:

1. Where does the mail enter the building?
2. What happens to it then?
3. How is it distributed through your offices and how often?
4. Which personnel handle the mail?
5. From the time the mail arrives at your receiving door, how long does it take to distribute it?
6. How do you report errors made using the postage meter?
7. Do you log any information in a record book when you use the postage meter, or do you receive a printout?
8. What kind of information does the postage meter provide you?

Outgoing Mail:

1. How is the outgoing mail consolidated?
2. How is it prepared—wrapped, labeled, stamped, etc.?
3. How is it divided into classes of mail?
4. How often is it taken to the post office?
5. Is it scheduled to meet outbound postal schedules?

General Procedures:

1. How do you obtain a postage meter?
2. What steps should everyone take to eliminate expensive mailing costs?
3. Because your organization is using e-mail and faxes, have you noticed a decrease in the amount of mail being distributed among departments or outgoing?
4. How much mail makes a postage meter practical?
5. How do you think your employees can improve their preparation of mailings?
6. What special equipment is needed to have in a small company to prepare the mailings?
7. What are the most important reference manuals that you use in your mailroom?
8. Do you create any type of mailing usage report for your organization?
9. What will be trends affecting mail operations?

Your Name _____

Date _____

FORM 6-C

544

ANSWER SHEET FOR 7-A

A	B	C	D	E	F	G	H	I	J	K	L	M	N	O	P	Q	R	S	T	U	V

Name _____ Date _____

ANSWER SHEET FOR 7-B

A	B	C	D	E	F	G	H	I	J	K	L	M	N	O	P	Q	R	S	T	U	V

Name _____ Date _____

FORM 7-B

ANSWER SHEET FOR 7-C

A	B	C	D	E	F	G	H	I	J	K	L	M	N	O	P	Q	R	S	T	U	V

Name _____ Date _____

PETTY CASH ENVELOPE

Petty Cash Fund		Date	No.	Explanation	Distribution of Payments					
Received	Paid Out									

FORM 8-A-1

Amount _____ No. _____

PETTY CASH VOUCHER

For _____

Paid to _____

Charge to _____

Date _____

Approved by _____

FORM 8-A-2

Amount _____ No. _____

PETTY CASH VOUCHER

For _____

Paid to _____

Charge to _____

Date _____

Approved by _____

FORM 8-A-3

Amount _____ No. _____

PETTY CASH VOUCHER

For _____

Paid to _____

Charge to _____

Date _____

Approved by _____

FORM 8-A-4

Amount _____ No. _____

PETTY CASH VOUCHER

For _____

Paid to _____

Charge to _____

Date _____

Approved by _____

FORM 8-A-5

Amount _____ No. _____

PETTY CASH VOUCHER

For _____

Paid to _____

Charge to _____

Date _____

Approved by _____

FORM 8-A-6

Amount _____ No. _____

PETTY CASH VOUCHER

For _____

Paid to _____

Charge to _____

Date _____

Approved by _____

FORM 8-A-7

Amount _____ No. _____

PETTY CASH VOUCHER

For _____

Paid to _____

Charge to _____

Date _____

Approved by _____

FORM 8-A-8

Amount _____ No. _____

PETTY CASH VOUCHER

For _____

Paid to _____

Charge to _____

Date _____

Approved by _____

FORM 8-A-9

Amount _____ No. _____

PETTY CASH VOUCHER

For _____

Paid to _____

Charge to _____

Date _____

Approved by _____

FORM 8-A-10

Amount _____ No. _____

PETTY CASH VOUCHER

For _____

Paid to _____

Charge to _____

Date _____

Approved by _____

FORM 8-A-11

Amount _____ No. _____

PETTY CASH VOUCHER

For _____

Paid to _____

Charge to _____

Date _____

Approved by _____

FORM 8-A-12

Amount _____ No. _____

PETTY CASH VOUCHER

For _____

Paid to _____

Charge to _____

Date _____

Approved by _____

FORM 8-A-13

BANK RECONCILIATION FORM

1. **Compare your checking or savings register with your statement.** Put a check mark (✔) in your register beside each check, deposit, or bank card transaction that appears on your statement. Be sure all amounts in your register match those on your statement. Assume for this problem this has been done and is correct.

2. **Identify outstanding checks or withdrawals.** List any checks or withdrawals you've written that have not yet appeared on your statement, and total the list in the column provided.

Check Number	Dollars	
Total	$	

3. **Identify deposits made after your statement date.**

Deposit Date	Dollars	
Total	$	

4.	Balance in checkbook	
5.	Subtract service charge	
	Minus amount of service charge	
	Adjusted checkbook balance	
6.	Balance in bank account	
	a. Ending balance shown on bank statement	
	b. Plus deposits made after statement date (from step 3)	
	c. A plus B	
	d. Minus total of outstanding checks (from step 2)	
	e. C minus D (Total should match register balance)	

Name _____ Date _____

FORM 8-B-1

WEEKLY PAYROLL REGISTER

For Week Ending: July 19, 200X

Name	Marital Status	Withholding Allowance	Hourly Rate	Reg Hrs	Overtime Hrs	Regular Earnings	Overtime Earnings	Gross Earnings	OASDI	HI	Federal Income Tax	Group Med Ins	Group Dental Ins	Total Deductions	Net Pay
Brown, J. K.	M	3	13.00	40	8						38.00	22.00	13.00		
Caton, L. M.	M	1	10.80	40	5						31.00	38.00	8.00		
Rodriguez, J. L.	M	1	11.00	40	9						42.00	41.00	11.00		
Thai, J. T.	M	1	12.25	40	12						61.00	22.00	5.00		
Ussery, D. A.	M	3	14.00	40	3						30.00	12.00	8.00		
Venzor, L. T.	M	2	10.00	40	2						16.00	41.00	10.00		
Williams, O. M.	M	2	9.00	40	4						14.00	38.00	11.00		
Yancy, K. K.	M	0	13.00	40	5						55.00	22.00	8.00		
Yeamon, B. E.	M	0	11.00	40	9						51.00	38.00	13.00		
Yeoman, E. A.	M	4	12.50	40	12						36.00	38.00	10.00		
Totals															

Name _____

Date _____

FORM 8-C-1

APPOINTMENT CALENDAR

Amanda Quevedo

DATE _____

TIME	APPOINTMENTS
8:00	
8:20	
8:40	
9:00	
9:20	
9:40	
10:00	
10:20	
10:40	
11:00	
11:20	
11:40	
12:00	
1:00	
1:20	
1:40	
2:00	
2:20	
2:40	
3:00	
3:20	
3:40	
4:00	
4:20	
4:40	

REMINDERS

Name _____ Date _____

FORM 9-A-1

APPOINTMENT CALENDAR

(Student Name)

DATE _____

TIME	APPOINTMENTS
8:00	
8:20	
8:40	
9:00	
9:20	
9:40	
10:00	
10:20	
10:40	
11:00	
11:20	
11:40	
12:00	
1:00	
1:20	
1:40	
2:00	
2:20	
2:40	
3:00	
3:20	
3:40	
4:00	
4:20	
4:40	

REMINDERS

Name _____ Date _____

FORM 9-A-2

554

Notes on Mrs. Quevedo's Trip to the Southwestern Region

Appointments

Tuesday, September 2

    9 a.m.–11 a.m. Art Jacobs, manager of small appliance sales, Southwestern Region.

    2 p.m. James Taylor, manager of refrigerator sales, Southwestern Region.

Wednesday, September 3

    Visit the manufacturing plant of Supreme Appliances, Inc. in Fort Worth. Contact is A. C. Matlock, vice president, manufacturing.

Thursday, September 4

    10 a.m. L. C. Appleton, speaker at the November sales seminar. Meeting will take place at the University of Houston, Management Building, Room 326.

    8 p.m. Speak to the Sales Management Club, University of Houston.

Lunch and dinner appointments

Monday, September 1

    8 p.m. Take Mr. and Mrs. Reddin to dinner at Sweeney's Restaurant.

Tuesday, September 2

    12:00 Lunch with Mr. Reddin and Mr. Jacobs.

    7:30 p.m. Dinner at Sweeney's. Mrs. Quevedo's guests: Mr. and Mrs. James Taylor, Mr. and Mrs. John Smith, and Mr. and Mrs. Art Jacobs.

Wednesday, September 3

    Lunch with Mr. Matlock.

Thursday, September 4

    Lunch with Mr. Appleton.

Hotel reservations

    Americana Inn of the Six Flags for September 1 and 2; at the Americana Hotel in Houston for September 3 and 4. (Hotel confirmations are in envelope with airline tickets.)

Travel plans

Monday, September 1

    2:15 p.m. Leave Rochester Airport on AA Flight 613 to Chicago.

    (One-hour wait in Chicago.) AA Flight 272 from Chicago to DFW.

    Mr. John Reddin, manager, Southwestern Region, will meet Mrs. Quevedo at DFW.

Wednesday, September 3

    Drive to Fort Worth. Car reserved with Hertz. Car is to be delivered to Inn of the Six Flags at 8 a.m. Wednesday.

    At 3 p.m. drive to DFW. Take AA Flight 314 to Houston. (Mrs. Agnes Wiggins, professor of marketing, University of Houston, will meet Mrs. Quevedo at the Houston Airport. Mrs. Wiggins will also pick Mrs. Quevedo up at 6:15 p.m. on Thursday at the Americana Hotel to drive to the University of Houston in time for the Sales Management Club banquet at 7:00 p.m.)

Friday, September 5

    Take AA Flight 312 to Chicago at 9:15 a.m. (Take courtesy van from Americana Hotel to airport.) Arrive in Chicago at 12:09 p.m.

    1:17 p.m. Leave Chicago on AA Flight 416 for Rochester.

Additional information

Thursday afternoon

    Mrs. Quevedo goes back to the Americana to put finishing touches on her speech for the Sales Management Club.

FORM 10-A

Expense Reimbursement Voucher

DRAFT

Name: _Sheryl Robinson_ Department: _Sales_

For Period Beginning _5-4--_ Ending _5-9--_

Purpose of Business Trip: Sales Exposition - Southwest Region

		5–4	5–5	5–6	5–7	5–8	5–9	Total
Date								
Destination From		Dallas		New Orl	Dallas	Dallas		
To		New Orl		Dallas	Ft Worth	Dallas		
Transportation — Car Travel	Mileage				58 mi	35 mi		120
	Rate × Miles				23 38	9 63		33 01
	Car Rentals	24 00		37 48				61 48
	Parking	7 00	7 00	7 00	4 00			25 00
	Tolls				1 00	1 00		2 00
	Air Fare (RT)	243 76						243 76
	Rail Fare							
	Carfare & Bus							
	Limousine/Taxi	10 00		10 00				20 00
	Tips	2 00		2 00				4 00
Hotel	Room Charge	78 97	78 97					157 94
	Hotel Tips	2 00		2 00				4 00
Misc.	Postage					1 95		1 95
	Telephone/Telegrams	1 50	4 95	3 80	50	75		11 50
	Laundry			9 40				9 40
	Other, Attach Statement							
	Subtotal							
Meals and Entertainment	Meals on travel status	15 75	36 80					52 55
	Meals w/bus. discussion*			39 00	14 00			53 00
	Other bus. entertainment*	8 00	14 00			5 50		27 50
	Subtotal							
	Meals w/ no bus. discussion							
Total		392 98	141 72	110 68	42 88	18 83		707 09

I certify these travel expenses were incurred by me in the transaction of authorized company business

	Less Amount Advanced	500 00
Signature _Sheryl Robinson_	Balance Due	214 84

*(explain on reverse side)

FORM 10-B

Expense Reimbursement Voucher

Name: Sheryl Robinson   Department: Sales

For Period Beginning 5-4- - -   Ending 5-9- - -

Purpose of Business Trip: Sales Exposition - Southwest Region

		5-4	5-5	5-6	5-7	5-8	5-9	Total	
Date									
Destination From		Dallas		New Orl	Dallas	Dallas			C/1
To		New Orl		Dallas	Ft Worth	Dallas			
Transportation									
Car Travel	Mileage				58 mi	35 mi		120	1. ——
	Rate × Miles				23 38	9 63		33 01	2. ——
	Car Rentals	24 00		37 48				61 48	3. ——
	Parking	7 00	7 00	7 00	4 00			25 00	4. ——
	Tolls				1 00	1 00		2 00	5. ——
Air Fare (RT)		243 76						243 76	6. ——
Rail Fare									
Carfare & Bus									
Hotel									
Limousine/Taxi		10 00		10 00				20 00	7. ——
Tips		2 00		2 00				4 00	8. ——
Room Charge		78 97	78 97					157 94	9. ——
Hotel Tips		2 00		2 00				4 00	10. ——
Misc.									
Postage						1 95		1 95	11. ——
Telephone/Telegrams		1 50	4 95	3 80	50	75		11 50	12. ——
Laundry				9 40				9 40	13. ——
Other, Attach Statement									
Subtotal									
Meals and Entertainment									
Meals on travel status		15 75	36 80					52 55	14. ——
Meals w/bus. discussion*				39 00	14 00			53 00	15. ——
Other bus. entertainment*		8 00	14 00			5 50		27 50	16. ——
Subtotal									
Meals w/ no bus. discussion									
Total		392 98	141 72	110 68	42 88	18 83		707 09	17. ——

Less Amount Advanced	500 00	
Balance Due	214 84	18. ——

I certify these travel expenses were incurred by me in the transaction of authorized company business

Signature _____

* (explain on reverse side)

Meeting of Executive Committee for November Sales Seminar
Wednesday, Sept. 10, 5 p.m.
Mrs. Quevedo's office
All members present.

Announcement: Sid Levine has agreed to help with the Nov. Sales Seminar. He will be responsible for registration.

The minutes of the August meeting of the Executive Committee were distributed. One correction was called for. Honorariums will be paid to the keynote speaker and the banquet speaker but not to the luncheon speakers. The minutes were approved as corrected.

James Bradford proposed that the keynote speaker and the banquet speaker each be paid an honorarium of $500. Committee members agreed.

Lisa Rogers reported that James Atwell, who is in charge of working with the hotel on setting up audiovisual equipment, is ill and has asked to be relieved of this responsibility. Whom shall we ask to do this? After some discussion, Mr. Bradford volunteered for the job.

FORM 11-A-1

Louise Witherspoon reported that increased attendance at the seminar (over attendance of previous years) is anticipated. Therefore, some of the meeting rooms that have been assigned to the sectional meeting of the Nov. Sales Seminar may be too small. She raised the question: Should we ask for larger rooms? The Executive Committee instructed her to check with the hotel to see if larger rooms are available and, if so, to make arrangements to shift the large sectional meetings to larger rooms. Be sure to give the information on room changes to A. C. Rothbaum, who is responsible for having the program printed. He needs the room changes by Sept. 20.

Meeting adjourned, 6:30 p.m.

A. Quevedo

FORM 11-A-2

MEETING CHECKLIST

BEFORE THE MEETING		
General	Target Date	Completion Date
Secure names/addresses		
Reserve meeting room(s)		
Make calendar notations		
Prepare meeting notice		
Prepare agenda		
Send notice/agenda		
Prepare list of materials, supplies, equipment needed		
Order refreshments (or meal)		
Prepare meeting evaluation forms		
Prepare handouts		
Make hotel reservation(s)		
Confirm meeting room(s)		
Meeting Room(s)		
Location of electrical outlets		
Extension cords		
Audiovisual equipment		
Audiovisual supplies		
Name tags/name cards		
Seating arrangements		
Arrange for water pitcher/glasses		
Arrange for pads/pens		
THE MEETING DAY		
Final check on meeting room(s)		
Final check on food		
Final check on equipment		
AFTER THE MEETING		
Prepare/distribute notes/minutes		
Prepare follow-up correspondence		
Summarize evaluation forms		

Name _____ Date _____

FORM 11-B

TELEPHONE MESSAGE FORMS

FORM 12-A-1

Message For: _____ Urgent ❑

For _____

Date _____ Time _____

Message From:

M _____

Of _____

Phone _____

AREA CODE   NUMBER   EXTENSION

Called while you were out ❑	Please call ❑
Stopped to see you ❑	Will call you back ❑
Returned your call ❑	Wishes to see you ❑

Message _____
_____
_____
_____
_____
_____
_____

Signed _____

FORM 12-A-2

Message For: _____ Urgent ❑

For _____

Date _____ Time _____

Message From:

M _____

Of _____

Phone _____

AREA CODE   NUMBER   EXTENSION

Called while you were out ❑	Please call ❑
Stopped to see you ❑	Will call you back ❑
Returned your call ❑	Wishes to see you ❑

Message _____
_____
_____
_____
_____
_____
_____

Signed _____

FORM 12-A-3

Message For: _____ Urgent ❑

For _____

Date _____ Time _____

Message From:

M _____

Of _____

Phone _____

AREA CODE   NUMBER   EXTENSION

Called while you were out ❑	Please call ❑
Stopped to see you ❑	Will call you back ❑
Returned your call ❑	Wishes to see you ❑

Message _____
_____
_____
_____
_____
_____
_____

Signed _____

FORM 12-A-4

Message For: _____ Urgent ❑

For _____

Date _____ Time _____

Message From:

M _____

Of _____

Phone _____

AREA CODE   NUMBER   EXTENSION

Called while you were out ❑	Please call ❑
Stopped to see you ❑	Will call you back ❑
Returned your call ❑	Wishes to see you ❑

Message _____
_____
_____
_____
_____
_____
_____

Signed _____

NOTES

NOTES

TELEPHONE SERVICES

Directions

Answer the following questions. Research for all answers should be gathered from either your local telephone directory or an online telephone directory.

1. List the following emergency numbers.
   a. Fire
   b. Police
   c. Your doctor
   d. Relative/Neighbor/Friend

2. List the following general information numbers.
   a. Gas trouble
   b. Power trouble
   c. Water trouble
   d. Time

3. List the area codes for the following locations.
   a. Your town or city
   b. Three major cities in your state

4. In what part of the telephone directory or online do you find local government listings?

5. If you want to inquire about obtaining or renewing a driver's license, what number would you call?

6. List the names and telephone numbers for two travel agencies in your town or city.

7. List the name, address, and telephone number for a professional moving and storage company located in your town or city.

8. If you place a call when your local time is 6 p.m. (1800), what time is it in the offices located in the following cities?
   a. Dallas
   b. San Francisco
   c. Chicago
   d. Calgary
   e. Miami
   f. Boston

9. If all the offices referred to in question 8 kept office hours of 9 a.m. to 5:30 p.m. (0900 to 1730), which offices would be open when you placed your call at 6 p.m. (1800) your local time?

10. List the names and telephone numbers for two local pharmacies in your town or city.

FORM 12-C

DAILY PLAN CHART

Date _____

Rank	Calls to	Phone No.	Notes	Rank	Reminders

Rank	Letters and Memos to	Notes	Rank	Other Tasks

Priority Rank: 1, urgent; 2, today; 3, as soon as time allows

FORM 13-A

Evaluation Form

Directions

Use the following evaluation to rate your work and time management by marking

A (always)   *S* (sometimes)   *N* (never)

following each question. Save the file.

1. Do I complete tasks as efficiently as possible?

2. Do I divide large projects into manageable segments of work?

3. Do I group related tasks to reduce the time consumed in changing from one unrelated task to another?

4. Do I match the work to the time frames in which it must be performed?

5. Do I get organized before I begin an assignment?

6. Do I control my attitudes and emotions that have a tendency to steal time?

7. Do I prioritize my work into categories?

8. Do I know how much time it takes to complete a task?

9. Do I know if the task to be completed is a priority of my immediate supervisor?

10. Do I maintain a To-Do list?

Give yourself the following points for your responses:

    2 points = Always
    1 point = Sometimes
    0 point = Never

If you scored 20 points, you are a star manager of your work and time! If you scored 15 points or higher, you are above average in managing your work and time. If you scored 10 points or less, you need to improve in your management skills. If you scored 9 points or higher, you will not be recognized as being either effective or efficient.

Name _____ Date _____

M _____

HAS AN APPOINTMENT ON

MON.   TUES.   WED.   THURS.   FRI.   SAT.

A.M.

DATE _____ AT _____ P.M.

FORM 13-C

DAILY PLAN CHART

Date _____

Rank	Calls to	Phone No.	Notes	Rank	Reminders

Rank	Letters and Memos to	Notes	Rank	Other Tasks

Priority Rank: 1, urgent; 2, today; 3, as soon as time allows

FORM 14-A

568

Evaluation Form

Directions

Use the following evaluation to rate your work and time management by marking

A (always)   *S* (sometimes)   *N* (never)

following each question. Save the file.

1. Do I complete tasks as efficiently as possible?

2. Do I divide large projects into manageable segments of work?

3. Do I group related tasks to reduce the time consumed in changing from one unrelated task to another?

4. Do I match the work to the time frames in which it must be performed?

5. Do I get organized before I begin an assignment?

6. Do I control my attitudes and emotions that have a tendency to steal time?

7. Do I prioritize my work into categories?

8. Do I know how much time it takes to complete a task?

9. Do I know if the task to be completed is a priority of my immediate supervisor?

10. Do I maintain a To-Do list?

Give yourself the following points for your responses:

    2 points = Always
    1 point = Sometimes
    0 point = Never

If you scored 20 points, you are a star manager of your work and time! If you scored 15 points or higher, you are above average in managing your work and time. If you scored 10 points or less, you need to improve in your management skills. If you scored 9 points or higher, you will not be recognized as being either effective or efficient.

Name _____   Date _____

FORM 14-B

POWER OF ATTORNEY REVOCATION

Reference is made to certain power of attorney granted by _____ (Grantor)

to _____ (Attorney-in-Fact), and dated _____ , _____ (year).

This document acknowledges and constitutes notice that the Grantor hereby revokes, rescinds and terminates said power-of-attorney and all authority, rights and power thereto effective this date.

Signed under seal this _____ day of _____ , _____ (year).

_____
Grantor

Acknowledged by Attorney-in-Fact:

_____

STATE OF _____ }
COUNTY OF _____ }

On _____ before me, _____ , personally appeared _____ personally known to me (or proved to me on the basis of satisfactory evidence) to be the person(s) whose name(s) is/are subscribed to the within instrument and acknowledged to me that he/she/they executed the same in his/her/their authorized capacity(ies), and that by his/her/their signature(s) on the instrument the person(s), or the entity upon behalf of which the person(s) acted, executed the instrument.

WITNESS my hand and official seal.

Signature _____

Affiant _____ Known _____ Unknown

ID Produced _____

(Seal)

FORM 14-C

SELF-APPRAISAL INVENTORY

Answer the following questions in preparation for developing your resume.

PART I: PERSONAL INFORMATION

Name	
Address	
Telephone	
Fax	
E-Mail	

PART II: EMPLOYMENT BACKGROUND

Use action verbs to write sentences that list your work-related accomplishments.
Begin your sentences with some of the following verbs.

Earned	Developed	Supervised	Organized
Designed	Improved	Analyzed	Trained
Established	Managed	Prepared	Researched

1.
2.
3.
4.
5.
6.

Think of all the employment you have had, both career related and other.
Use reverse chronological order (most recent first) to record your answers.

Working Title	
Company Name	
City Where Company Is Located	
Date Commenced and Ended	
Key Responsibilities	
Working Title	
Company Name	
City Where Company Is Located	
Date Commenced and Ended	
Key Responsibilities	

FORM 15-A-1

Continue to record information about your employment.

Working Title	
Company Name	
City Where Company Is Located	
Date Commenced and Ended	
Key Responsibilities	

PART III: EDUCATION AND TRAINING

Use reverse chronological order to record the following information.
Use this area to record postsecondary education (full-time, extension, adult education, etc.).

Degree/Diploma/Certificate Earned	
Name of Institute	
City Where School Is Located	
Date Commenced and Ended	
Grade Point Average	
Key Courses Completed	

Use this area to record information about your high school education.

Diploma/Certificate Earned	
Name of School	
City Where School Is Located	
Date Commenced and Ended	
Grade Point Average	

PART IV: INTERESTS AND ACTIVITIES

List professional organizations that you have held or currently hold membership in.	1. 2. 3.
List volunteer positions you have held or currently hold in your community.	1. 2. 3.
List sports or hobbies you participate in.	1. 2. 3.

FORM 15-A-2

APPLICATION FOR EMPLOYMENT

PERSONAL INFORMATION

Social Security No. _____

	Last	First	Middle

NAME: _____

	Street	City	State	Zip Code

ADDRESS: _____

PHONE: _____ FAX: _____ E-MAIL: _____

REFERRED BY: _____

If related to anyone in our employ, state name and department: _____

TYPE OF EMPLOYMENT DESIRED

POSITION: _____ When can you start? _____ Salary desired _____

Are you employed now? _____ May we contact your present employer? _____

EDUCATION	Name and Location of School	Years Attended	Date Graduated	Major Subjects
UNIVERSITY				
COLLEGE				
HIGH SCHOOL				
OTHER				

List specialized courses _____

_____

What foreign languages do you speak fluently? _____ Read? _____ Write? _____

FORMER EMPLOYMENT (List employers, starting with last one first.)

Date Month and Year	Company Name and City	Salary	Position	Reason for Leaving
From				
To				
From				
To				
From				
To				

VOLUNTEER ACTIVITIES (List any community service or volunteer work you have done.)

Position	Name or Organization	Date Commenced and Ended
1.		
2.		

MEMBERSHIP (List any professional organization you hold membership in.)

Name or Organization	Position Held
1.	
2.	

REFERENCES (Give the names of three persons not related to you.)

Name and Title	Address	Telephone	E-Mail	Years Acquainted
1.				
2.				
3.				

I understand that misrepresentations or omission of facts called for in this application is cause for dismissal.

Date _____ Signature _____

FORM 15-B-2

CHECKLIST FOR YOUR JOB CAMPAIGN

Activity	Date Due	Date Submitted
1. Prepare a self-appraisal inventory (Form 15-A-1).		
2. Use a financial manual or directory, available in either the school or public library, or on the Internet, to prepare a concise report on a local company.		
3. From the placement office, obtain literature that may be helpful to you in your job campaign.		
4. Join a committee to study employment opportunities for administrative assistants in your community. Obtain literature and share your findings with committee members.		
5. Prepare a list of qualifications you plan to emphasize during job interviews. Prepare a list of questions you expect to be asked and their answers. Prepare a list of questions you want to ask the interviewer.		
6. Prepare a resume.		
7. As directed, write either a prospecting job application letter or a solicited job application letter.		
8. Edit your resume after your instructor has reviewed it.		
9. Prepare a portfolio displaying samples of your work.		
10. Study job advertisements. Analyze the advertisements for administrative assistants.		
11. Write an evaluation of your performance during an early job interview.		
12. Complete the job application form (Form 15-B-1).		
13. Prepare a job acceptance letter and a job refusal letter.		

Name _____ Date _____

FORM 15-C

Appendix A

Punctuation

Perhaps the most misunderstood punctuation mark is the comma. A comma alerts the reader to a rest or a pause between two ideas. An omitted or misplaced comma in documents can lead to significant misunderstandings and embarrassing situations.

Rule 1: Commas Used with Conjunctions (Chapter 1)

Commas are always placed before coordinating conjunctions when they separate two independent clauses in a compound sentence. Examples of coordinating conjunctions are *nor, for, yet, neither, or, and,* and *but.*

> Dave is a good programmer, and he has been given the lead programmer's job for a month's trial.
>
> If clauses are short and related, you may omit the comma before *and.*

TIP: Therefore, however, and *accordingly* are not considered true coordinating conjunctions. Use a semicolon before these words, not a comma.

Rule 2: Commas Used with Nonrestrictive Words, Phrases, and Clauses (Chapter 1)

A word, phrase, or clause that is not absolutely essential to a sentence may be set off in commas. Restrictive words, phrases, and clauses are essential to the meaning of the sentence and are not set off by commas.

Word:	The meeting, *however,* ran well into the evening.
Phrase:	Mrs. Gonzales, *the data processing coordinator* [nonrestrictive], retired after 25 years with the company.
	Data specialist: [restrictive] Ernest Johnson will be giving a seminar next week.
Clause:	Talk to your manager about it tomorrow, *when she returns to the office* [unrestrictive].
	Write down the message *as soon as you hang up* [restrictive].

Rule 3: Commas Used with a Series (Chapter 2)

When you have a series of words, phrases, or clauses, set them off with commas.

> The will of the Slaton estate was to include Shannon, Joe, and Mark.

It is critical to retain the comma between the last two items in this example to prevent any possible misunderstanding of your meaning. Should this example read: ". . . to include Shannon, Joe and Mark" would make a tremendous difference in sharing a portion of the estate.

Rule 4: Commas Used Between Adjectives (Chapter 2)

When a series of adjectives have the same worth and refer to the same noun, they should be separated with commas. If the word *and* can be substituted and be grammatically correct, a comma is required.

> They are bright, young, attractive lawyers. (*Bright, young,* and *attractive* are adjectives of equal value.)

Compare this example to the next one.

> The red modern building is the second to be recognized for its structure. (*Red* and *modern* are not of equal value.)

Rule 5: Commas Used with Introductory and Parenthetic Phrases (Chapter 2)

Place commas after introductory words, phrases, and clauses. Commas are almost always placed after long introductory elements and those containing verb forms.

> As the earthquake intensified, the employees gathered around the radio.

Parenthetical and defining words and phrases are set off in commas unless they have a close relation to the rest of the sentence.

> They can, *I believe,* meet the deadlines.
> They were *definitely* the best presenters for the new products.

Capitalization

Because capitalization will vary according to the situation, a number of rules must be followed. The main rule to remember is to be consistent when capitalizing. Here are the main rules and examples of capitalization.

Rule 6: Personal Titles (Chapter 3)

Capitalize all titles (academic, business, religious, military, as well as titles of respect or honor) in these situations:

a. When they immediately precede a name.

> Professor Rochelle, Dr. Todd, Chairperson Stone, President Clinton, Lieutenant Gibbs, Queen Elizabeth, Vice President Louise White, Ambassador Saxton

b. When they are used in mailing, such as titles following the names.

> Mrs. Gwen Hilton, President
> Hilton International Services, Inc.
> 1231-A International Boulevard
> Dallas, TX 75244

Do not capitalize the following titles under these circumstances:

a. When following a name or used alone.

Mr. Carlos, the president of Datalife; the secretary of state; the district attorney

b. When a title precedes a name, but separates a name.

The chairperson, Nick Nelson, arrived yesterday.

Rule 7: Organizations, Institutions, and Education (Chapter 3)

Capitalize official names of organizations.

Rotary Club, Young Men's Christian Association, United Methodist Women, Phi Beta Kappa, Girl Scouts of America

Capitalize names of schools or colleges and their departments.

Van High School, Music Department

Capitalize names of classes of a high school, college, or university; official names of courses; and course subjects when they are derived from proper names.

Senior Class, Computer Science I, Latin, English

Capitalize academic degrees, whether abbreviated or written in full, if the person's full name is given.

John Rochelle, M.S. (or Master of Science)

Do not capitalize general terms referring to organizations or institutions.

the chamber of commerce, the parent-teacher association

Do not capitalize course subjects not derived from proper nouns.

We are studying economics this quarter.

Rule 8: Enumerations (Chapter 4)

Capitalize the first word in each section of an enumeration if the enumerations are in a complete sentence.

The assistant uses the outguide in the following cases: (1) Someone outside the agency wants the material. (2) The manager takes the material out of the office.

Capitalize itemized listings.

The technical skills required for the position are

1. Windows
2. WordPerfect, Microsoft Word
3. Lotus 1-2-3 or Excel
4. Access, Paradox

Lowercase an enumerated item not preceded by a colon.

She listed the technical skills as (1) keyboarding and (2) applications, such as Word, Excel, and Access.

Rule 9: Nouns and Adjectives (Chapter 4)

Capitalize nouns or abbreviations used with numbers or letters in a title.

Division IV, Precinct 4, Act 11

Capitalize *Room, Suite,* etc. when used in addresses.

> Odenwald International Connections, Inc.
> Jefferson Building, Suite 111
> 130266 Forest Lane
> Dallas, TX 75234

Do not capitalize *section, grade,* or *article* when used with letters or numbers.

> grade 6, section A

Rule 10: Money (Chapter 5)

a. In legal documents.

> Nine Hundred Twenty-Five Dollars ($925.00)

b. In writing checks.

> Three Hundred and No/100

Do not capitalize amounts of money in general writing.

> They made over two hundred dollars.

Rule 11: Geographical Terms (Chapter 5)

Capitalize the following:

a. Points of the compass when they refer to a specific section of the United States.

> the South, the Midwest, the East

b. Popular names of specific localities.

> the Bible Belt, the Cotton Belt, the Corn Belt

c. *Coast* when it refers to a specific locality or stands alone.

> East Coast, Gulf Coast

Do not capitalize the following:

a. Points of the compass when they denote simple directions or specific compass points.

> moving west, south two blocks, east shore

b. Regional terms that merely localize adjectives.

> northern Italy, western Texas

c. *Coast* when used with geographic names.

> Texas coast, Florida coast

d. Adjectives derived from political divisions and major parts of the world.

> southern United States, tropical Africa

Rule 12: Government and Political Terms (Chapter 5)

Capitalize the following:

a. *Government* and *administration* when part of a title.

United States Government
The Reagan Administration

b. *Federal* when part of a title.

Federal Register, Federal Reserve System, Federal Reserve Board Regulation W

c. *National* when part of a title.

The National Science Foundation, the National Guard

d. *State* when part of a title.

New York State, Washington State, State of the Union Message

e. *County* when part of a name.

Dallas County

f. *District* when part of a name.

Alexandria School District, District of Columbia

g. *Ward, Precinct,* when part of a name.

First Precinct

h. *Legislature* when part of a name of a specific group.

Texas Legislature

i. *Conference* and *Congress* when part of a name.

Judicial Conference of the United States, Tenth Annual Conference of the United Office Workers, Congress of Parents and Teachers

j. Full titles of government departments, commissions, bureaus, boards, and committees.

Houston Police Department, Yale University Department of Economics, Commission on Fine Arts

Number Usage

Office workers encounter general and specific numbers in documents.

a. References to general numbers are expressed in words.

Approximately two hundred executives attended today's workshop.

b. References to specific numbers are expressed in figures.

There were 197 executives attending today's workshop.

TIP: Remember to be consistent in your number style. Here are some guidelines to follow when working with numbers.

Rule 13: Numbers One Through Ten (Chapter 6)

Use words for:

a. Numbers under ten.

They ordered five SVGA computer monitors.

b. Street names under ten.

4012 Seventh Avenue

c. Units of time.

Her manager stayed in Europe for six months.

d. Numbers appearing consecutively that can be written with fewer letters.

Everyone recommends drinking at least six 8-ounce glasses of water daily.
We must approve the fire code in 18 ten-unit buildings today.

Use figures for:

a. References to numbers below and above ten when used together.

We ordered 6 computer mice, 11 enhanced keyboards, and 20 scanners.

b. References to numbers above ten.

She is 36 years old.

Rule 14: Dates (Chapter 6)

Use words for:

a. Formal usage.

The opening invitation read: September ninth, two thousand four

Use figures for:

a. Dates in business documents.

November 10, 2004
10 November 2004 (military, foreign, and some government correspondence)

b. A date when it follows the name of the month (never use *th, d, st, rd,* or *nd* when a date follows the name of the month).

The report will be presented at the staff meeting on June 7 (not June 7th).

c. A date including the word *of*. In this case, use *th, nd, rd,* or *st* after the figure, or else spell out the number.

The report will be presented at the staff meeting on the 7th of June.
The report will be presented at the staff meeting on the seventh of June.

Rule 15: Percentages (Chapter 6)

Use the figure:

a. Plus the word *percent*.

The report showed 25 percent of the respondents . . .

b. In tabulations with the % symbol.

Diskettes   89%
CD-ROMs   11%

Rule 16: Time (Chapter 7)

Use words for:

a. Clock time if the word *o'clock* is used or understood.

They arrived at six o'clock.

Use figures for:

a. Clock time if the expression is followed by *a.m.* or *p.m.*

They arrived at 8 a.m.

(Note that the colon and zeroes are not used for "on the hour" time. However, use the colon and zeroes in a listing of times to provide consistency.)

b. Exact units of time.

Their observations took 1 year and 3 months.

Rule 17: Serial and Similar Numbers (Chapter 7)

Use figures for:

a. Measures and measurements.

The cyclists finished the last 30 miles of their trip. The length of the desk measured 6 feet 3 inches.

b. Serial, model, policy, invoice, and number (No.) references; capitalize *serial, model, policy,* and so on when used.

The computer system was listed as Serial WX-01-128-6399 and Model 486DX.
His Policy No. 32-00789-1 was being reevaluated.

Office Reading Skills (Chapters 9 and 10)

The ability to read is one of the most important skills you can have. With the fast information flow in today's office, reading is becoming more important every day. No matter what kind of work you do, you will encounter reading in every part of your job. You must be able to read to do your job competently.

Why are competent reading skills important?

Competent reading skills will make your job easier. When you can apply competent reading skills, you will be able to find answers to on-the-job questions. For instance, you may be required to read a medical claim insurance form to pinpoint facts or spot specific information. Or, you may need to read a section in a printer manual to solve a printing problem.

What are your goals in reading?

At times, you will read materials to understand as many details as you can in order to learn or master the information so that you can recall and use the information in the future to perform a job task. Your goal is reading to apply what you have read. At other times, you will read materials to find an answer to a question. Your goal is reading to do something that may not require you to memorize or understand the answer.

Reading includes a number of skills, such as comprehending and verifying. Comprehending involves reading material to understand, then deciding if statements about the information are accurate. Verifying means comparing information that has been transferred from one place to another to be certain that it has been transferred accurately. To comprehend and verify information successfully, you must use a number of skills, such as following directions, locating facts or specifics, and recognizing errors.

Here are some tips to use when reading materials.

1. Use a ruler or colored index card to pull your eyes to each word, date, proper name, and figure.
2. Check the final copy with an original, a draft, or rough notes.
3. Read the information two or three times if necessary.

Business Math (Chapters 8, 11, 12, and 13)

Understanding the basic part, rate, base formula can be reviewed from a visual approach using a triangle. Business applications with percents consist of three components of information: the part, rate, and base. You must be able to identify each component to perform the calculation.

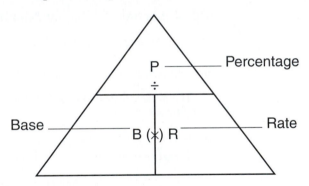

Because the formula has three variables, if you know any two of them, you can find the remaining one. The triangle may help you solve the formula more easily. The basic formula is $P = B \times R$; P is always the top half of the triangle. To find P, B, or R, simply cover up the component you are trying to determine. The remaining components will provide the formula. For example, to determine the formula for part, cover up the P. If the remaining components are horizontal, multiply them; if they are vertical, divide them.

a. Given B and R, find P by multiplying B and R.

Part = Base × Rate

b. Given P and B, find R by dividing P by B.

Rate = Part/Base

c. Given P and R, find B by dividing P by R.

Base = Part/Rate

The following application gives examples of part, rate, and base.

Cathy Chu made $1,025 per pay period. She received a raise of 4.8%. How much does Cathy's salary increase per pay period? Given the *base* ($1,025) and the *rate* (4.8%), find the part by:

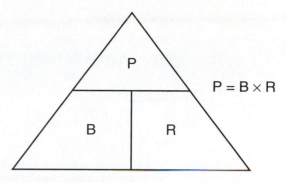

Base = $1,025 (original amount or whole)

Rate = 4.8% (Often rate is a percent; it can also be a decimal or fraction.)

Percentage = $49.20 (or a part of the whole)

Finding the Part

Here is a sample business application in which determining the part is necessary.

A recent audit report of The Marketing Associates showed that 10% of 120 employees earned more than $30,000 each year. How many employees earn more than $30,000?

Given the *rate* (10%) and the *base* (120), find the part by:

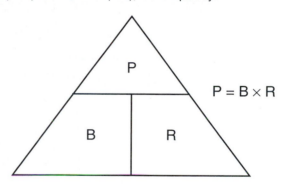

Part = Base × Rate

Part = 120 × 10% (.10)

Part = 12 (Of the 120 employees, 12 earn more than $30,000.)

Finding the Rate

Here is a sample business application in which finding the rate is necessary.

Sylvia Compton earned $22,790 last year. This year she received a raise of $1,139.50. What is the percent of Sylvia's raise?

Given the *part* ($1,139.50) and the *base* ($22,790), find the rate by:

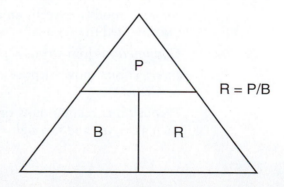

Rate = Part/Base

Rate = $1,139.50/$22,790

Rate = .05 or 5% ($1,139.50 is 5% of $22,790.)

Finding the Base

Here is a sample business application in which determining the base is necessary.

Robert Hughes received a raise of 4.8%. He is now making $55.20 more per pay period. How much did Robert make before his raise?

Given the *part* ($55.20) and the *rate* (4.8%), find the base by:

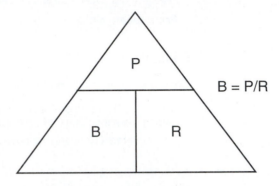

$B = P/R$

Base = Percentage/Rate

Base = $55.20/.048 (or 4.8%)

Base = $1,150 (4.8% of $1,150 is $55.20.)

Grammar

Grammar is a system of principles or rules that tells us how to use the parts of speech correctly. Once you know the basic rules, it is easier to communicate. Before you study the following rules and then complete the exercises, review the parts of speech and how they are used.

Nouns name people, animals, places, ideas, concepts, activities, qualities, and things.

Pronouns are words that replace nouns, such as *his, her, them.*

Adjectives modify or describe a noun or pronoun, such as "He is a *fast* transcriber."

Verbs show action or link a noun with words that describe the noun, such as "The president *called a* meeting."

Adverbs modify a verb, an adjective, or another adverb, such as "She *quickly* filed the report."

Conjunctions join words together, such as *and, or,* and *but.*

Interjections show surprise or other strong emotion, such as *My!, Oh!,* or *Great!*

Prepositions relate nouns or pronouns to other words in the sentence, such as *in, at,* and *through.*

Rule 18: Subject and Verb Agreement (Chapter 15)

a. The subject and verb must always agree in person and number. A singular person must have a singular verb.

Subject	Verb
Each [singular] of the workers	*fills* [singular] in the report.
All [plural] of the workers	*fill* [plural] in the report.
The *president* [singular], as well as the other officers,	*has* [singular] arrived.

b. Use a plural verb if two or more singular nouns are linked by *and*.

Helen and Pam [plural] *work* [plural] in the afternoon.

c. Use a singular verb if two or more singular nouns are linked by *nor* or *or*.

Neither Helen *nor* [singular] Pam works [singular] in the afternoons.

Rule 19: Noun and Pronoun Agreement (Chapter 15)

A noun and its pronoun must agree in person and number.

Every *one* of the branch offices had *its* own Christmas party.

Note: The pronouns anyone, each, everyone, everything, someone, either, neither, nobody, and another are always singular; therefore, a singular verb should be used.

Rule 20: Parallel Construction (Chapter 15)

Parts of a sentence that are parallel in function should be parallel in form.

Correct: The president *approved* the last three policies, and then the board of directors *rejected* them.

Incorrect: Stephanie enjoys *swimming, hiking,* and *played* basketball.

Rule 21: Make Modifiers Clear (Chapter 16)

Modifiers (words, phrases, and clauses) describe, limit, detail, or in some way change the meaning of the subject. Place the modifier close to the word it is supposed to modify.

Incorrect: *Having been trained on word processing software,* the *manager* asked *Yun-Sung* to demonstrate it. (Who had been trained on the software?)

Correct: The manager asked *Yun-Sung,* who had been *trained on the word processing software,* to demonstrate it.

Rule 22: Use Adjectives and Adverbs Correctly (Chapter 16)

Use adjectives to modify nouns and pronouns and adverbs to modify verbs, adjectives, or other adverbs.

Incorrect: She works careless (adjective).

Correct: She works carelessly (adverb).

Incorrect: Mary proofs considerable (adjective) faster than Jenneth.

Correct: Mary proofs considerably (adverb) faster than Jenneth.

Commonly misused words: *good* and *well,* and *real* and *really.* *Good* (adjective) must modify a noun; *well* is used as an adverb or an adjective.

Incorrect: He did good.

She doesn't feel good.

Correct: He did a *good* [adjective] job.

He did well.

She doesn't feel well.

Real is an adjective; *really* is an adverb.

Incorrect: They are *real* effective presenters.

Correct: They are *really* [adverb] effective presenters.

She is wearing a *real* [adjective] leather jacket.

Index

Photo Credits

pp. 5, 29, 30: Business/ Finance Goodshots; **p. 389:** Business/ Communication Goodshots; **pp. 33, 284:** Faces of Business; **p.89:** Gateway, Inc.; **p. 9:** Wacom Technology Corporation; **p. 9:** Caere Corporation; **pp. 92, 156:** Ricoh; **pp. 95, 96, 210:** Getty Images, Inc.; **p.99:** Ford Motor Company; **p. 137:** Xerox Corporation; **p. 157:** Hewlett-Packard; **p. 175:** Pitney-Bowes, Inc.; **p. 476:** Stock Boston; photo by Bob Daemmrish; **p. 205:** National Institute on Aging; **p. 206:** Dorling Kindersley Media Library; photo by Gary Ombler; **p. 207:** Dorling Kindersley Media; **p. 387:** Panasonic Communications.

Proofreading Symbols

Proofreader's Mark	What it Means	How to Use it	Corrected Version
ℒ	Delete or omit	beginℒ	begin
⋀	Insert	occurₑences	occurrences
⌒	Transpose	revelent, decied	relevant, decide
STET...	Retain crossed-out characters with a dot underneath	if you Harry, and I go	if you and I go
#	Insert space	fountain⋀pen	fountain pen
⌒	Close up space	stock holder	stockholder
ℙ	Start a new paragraph	days. We are ready	days. We are ready
⌐	Move left	⌐ Dear Ms. Adams:	Dear Ms. Adams:
⌐¬	Move right	Sincerely, ⎯⎯⎯¬	Sincerely,
/	Change capital letter to lower case	the Advertsiing Budget	the advertising budget
≡	Change lower case letter to capital	new year's eve	New Year's Eve
SP	Spell out	5 days in NYC	five days in New York City
SS	Single space	This plan is under SS consideration now.	This plan is under consideration now.
DS	Double space	This plan is under DS consideration now.	This plan is under consideration now.
⊃	Run in; no new line	four years. We'll be	four years. We'll be